GW00686419

REFLECTIONS

on an Ageless Wisdom

REFLECTIONS
on an Ageless Wisdom

A COMMENTARY ON
THE MAHATMA LETTERS TO A. P. SINNETT

JOY MILLS

Theosophical Publishing House
Wheaton, Illinois • Chennai, India

Quest Books
Theosophical Publishing House
P. O. Box 270
Wheaton, Illinois 60187-0270

www.questbooks.net

Front cover image: *Burning of Darkness* by Nicholas Roerich from "His Country" series, 1924, courtesy The Nicholas Roerich Museum, New York, NY.
Cover design by Margarita Reyfman

Library of Congress Cataloging-in-Publication Data

Mills, Joy.
Reflections on an ageless wisdom: a commentary on the Mahatma letters to A. P. Sinnett / Joy Mills.—1st Quest ed.
    p.   cm.
Includes bibliographical references and index.
ISBN 978-0-8356-0885-5
1. Theosophy.   2. Blavatsky, H. P. (Helena Petrovna), 1831–1891—Correspondence.   3. Sinnett, A. P. (Alfred Percy), 1840–1921—Correspondence.   I. Title.
BP585.B6A4 2010
299'.934—dc22   2009052024

Printed in the United States of America

Contents

FOREWORD

Ever since *The Mahatma Letters to A. P. Sinnett* was first published in 1923, the book has stirred an enormous amount of curiosity. Who are the Mahatmas, and what do they do? How can they be Mahatmas when they can be so blunt and say things that the stereotypical saint would never say?

In her introduction to *Reflections on an Ageless Wisdom*, Joy Mills clearly and succinctly sets the letters and their authors in their proper light. She first makes it clear that the letters are not a textbook; rather, they are in answer to specific questions posed by A. P. Sinnett. Then, quoting H. P. Blavatsky, she points out that the Mahatmas "are living men, not spirits."

Many have read the letters, but because they are just that—letters—much contained in them pertains to events and people at the time they were written. Even a serious student will have some difficulty sorting through what is now irrelevant and what is timeless wisdom. Joy goes through each letter and highlights what is relevant today. In addition, she consistently asks readers to consider their own attitudes and behavior. "What would we do?" is a question often asked. In this way Joy makes the letters come alive. She makes us think about our own way of life and how it might affect others. She gives us an opportunity to consider the Mahatmas' advice as if they were speaking directly to us.

Readers of the letters know that one often goes through pages of comments that were important at the time but have no relevance to us now. By quoting and commenting on only what might help us to better understand ourselves and the contemporary world, Joy has dug out the pearls and spared us the tedious work of finding them for ourselves. In the spirit of a true Theosophist, Joy does not attempt to give us final answers. She asks questions of herself and suggests that we might ask ourselves the same questions.

Reflections on an Ageless Wisdom will be treasured by all students of the Mahatma Letters, those familiar with them as well as those who have never read them. Readers who ponder the statements quoted and the questions asked will find something that is likely to have a transformative effect on their lives. That, of course, has always been a principal aim of the Mahatmas, and it is clearly the central theme of *Reflections on an Ageless Wisdom.*

—Edward Abdill
New York, December 2009

ACKNOWLEDGMENTS

So many people have aided me in this project that it is not possible to name them all. Through the many years of studying the letters, I have had the good fortune of discussing their contents with numerous senior students far wiser than I in Theosophical understandings. Fellow students in classes at the Krotona School of Theosophy, the School of the Wisdom at Adyar, and the European School of Theosophy have contributed to my own ever-growing understanding, and I owe a debt of gratitude to them all. The idea for this commentary grew out of the insistence of Dr. Nelda Samarel, past director of the Krotona School of Theosophy, that I should organize my extensive notes into a form useful to future students of the letters; I am grateful for her support and assistance as the project proceeded.

I extend special thanks to Nicholas Weeks for his invaluable help in identifying a number of references, particularly information about the Nepalese Svabhavikas (mentioned in Letter 90). Appreciation also goes to Dara Eklund, whose familiarity with HPB's *Collected Writings* aided me in locating several important references in those volumes.

To Shirley Nicholson, resident head of the Krotona Institute of Theosophy, and to the members of the Institute's Board of Trustees, I extend my gratitude for their support and encouragement, and to Shirley especially for making available office space where the work could go forward as various assistants, particularly Brenda Knight, transcribed many of my classes on the letters. Special appreciation is offered to the Sellon Charitable Trust for their generous grant to support the project with the necessary equipment for the transcription work and furnishing an office, alongside their interest in my efforts to bring about a useful compendium.

My grateful appreciation is owed to Sharron Dorr, production manager of Quest Books at the Theosophical Publishing House, Wheaton, not only for her willingness to undertake the publication of the book but also for her intuitive wisdom in linking me with such a superb editor as Carolyn Bond. I express my deepest appreciation and thanks to Carolyn for her perceptive understanding of my often entangled sentences; she seemed to know just when to prune, when to query meaning, and when to suggest alternative wordings. Fortunate indeed is the author who has such a professional and remarkably sensitive editor!

Beyond all others, one person especially deserves my profound gratitude—my late colleague Virginia Hanson. She left me her extensive notes on the letters, many of which were used by Vicente Haó Chin Jr. in his chronological edition of the letters. Through our years of study together, exploring and discussing the letters and sharing ideas, Virginia and I often found it impossible to distinguish whether an idea was mine or hers. Consequently, even as I have drawn upon her unpublished notes in constructing this commentary, I am still not certain whether what I express about a particular letter reflects her understanding or my own. Our shared enthusiasm for the study as well as for the work of the Society cemented a friendship that was, and in a profound way still is, truly a blessing on my life and that will, I am sure, continue through all lives to come.

INTRODUCTION

In the catechisms and texts of many spiritual traditions through the centuries, sacred knowledge has been transmitted through the art of questioning. The Upanishads of ancient India and the Dialogues of Plato are just two of the more famous examples. The twentieth-century philosopher-teacher J. Krishnamurti frequently began his talks with a question, either explicit or implied. Questions still lead inquirers on journeys to probe the mysteries of the universe, the origins of life, the nature of consciousness, or the meaning and purpose of existence. Sometimes the simplest question opens a door to the most complex and strange reply.

The spirit of inquiry has characterized the Theosophical Society since its inception. In his 1875 Inaugural Address, President-Founder Henry S. Olcott described the members of the new Society as "simply investigators, of earnest purpose and unbiased mind," adding, "We seek, inquire, reject nothing without cause, accept nothing without proof; we are students, not teachers." Through the ensuing years, the Society's leaders have frequently echoed Olcott's words, referring to the organization as a body of inquirers whose freedom of thought is guaranteed in official resolutions.

In the Society's early years in India, following its move from New York, the name of one questioner stood foremost: the brilliant and well-educated English journalist Alfred Percy Sinnett. Meeting co-founder Helena P. Blavatsky (HPB) and Olcott soon after their arrival in Bombay (today Mumbai) in early 1879, Sinnett was intrigued by HPB's explanations of the phenomena she could produce, and even more intrigued by her insistence that her abilities were the result of her training under her own Teacher, the Mahatma known as Morya.

Had Sinnett been content simply to witness HPB's phenomenal productions and ask her a few questions about the occult, the history of the Society might have been quite different. But such was his desire to inquire into the mysteries of occultism that he could not rest until he had at least tried, through her, to contact those Teachers for himself. So it was that asking one simple question—would she, could she, put him into contact with the Mahatmas?—launched Sinnett into a correspondence that today stands as essential foundational literature of the Theosophical movement. Allan Octavian Hume, a friend of Sinnett's who was in the Indian Civil Service and to whom Sinnett had introduced HPB, joined him as a correspondent.

Who was A. P. Sinnett? And who was A. O. Hume? Excellent brief biographies of these two men are available as appendices in the valuable work *A Readers' Guide to the Mahatma Letters* by George E. Linton and Virginia Hanson. And who were the Mahatmas, sometimes called "Masters," or "Adepts," with whom Sinnett and Hume carried on a correspondence from 1880 to 1885? Sometimes signing themselves only by their initials, KH and M, they were known as Koot Hoomi and Morya. HPB comments in a letter of July 1890 (published in *The Theosophist*, September 1951): "The Mahatmas are living men, not 'spirits.' Their knowledge and learning are immense, and their personal holiness of life is still greater—still they are mortal men and none of them 1,000 years old, as imagined by some." She clarified further a few years earlier:

> A Mahatma is a personage who, by special training and education, has evolved those higher faculties and has attained that spiritual knowledge which ordinary humanity will acquire after passing

through numberless series of incarnations during the process of cosmic evolution, provided, of course, they do not go, in the meanwhile, against the purposes of Nature. . . . This process of the self-evolution of the Mahatma extends over a number of "incarnations," although, comparatively speaking, they are very few. . . . The real Mahatma is . . . not his physical body but that higher *Manas* which is inseparably linked to the *Atma* and its vehicle (The 6th principle). ("Mahatmas and Chelas," *The Theosophist*, July 1884)

The two Mahatmas' correspondence with Sinnett and Hume has intrigued, excited, challenged, and instructed students since it was first published and thus made broadly available in 1923. A few have ridiculed it, labeling it a mass of forgeries. Others have found inspiration, spiritual guidance, and enlightenment in its pages. Some have questioned what appear to be inconsistencies, either between letters or with later Theosophical literature, while still others have imputed to the work the status of absolute and final authority. Many have become confused by references to names and events long since forgotten. A few have even been discouraged from studying the book because of statements they feel are "un-Mahatma-like" in tone or expression.

Whatever the source of the Mahatma Letters, whether penned by *chelas* (pupils of the Mahatmas) or the Mahatmas themselves, and whether transmitted through the agency of HPB or, as has been amply proven, without that agency or "precipitated" by occult means, the letters stand on their own merits, a remarkable and so far unrepeated correspondence among *living* men. The letters have altered attitudes, stormed the bastions of racial and religious prejudice, affected the history of the Theosophical Society, and continue today to influence Theosophical students throughout the world. They are still quoted, sometimes misquoted; they continue to puzzle, inspire, and tantalize the minds and hearts of countless individuals.

The dramatis personae who move through the pages of the Mahatma Letters are as interesting, strange, and sometimes bizarre a collection of human beings as one finds in any novel. They include high-caste Brahmins; educated and intelligent Englishmen; several Americans, including Olcott and HPB (who, although of Russian birth, had become an American citizen); clairvoyants, mediums, and chelas, Spiritualists and atheists; frauds and scoundrels, saints and sinners—in short, a small cross section of humanity.

The book itself is often considered one of the more difficult texts in Theosophical literature. For one thing, many of the events it touches upon are no longer of much importance—although some seriously affected the course of the Society's history. For another, the profound ideas presented are made more abstruse by the fact that, at the time, no definite nomenclature had been developed for communicating the occult philosophy in English. The book is at once a work of philosophy and revelation, a drama of human aspiration, success, and failure, and a narrative in time with a timeless message.

Toward the end of his life, Sinnett published his own recollection of the Mahatmas' occult instruction in a two-part article, "The Masters and Their Methods of Instruction," which appeared in the American Section journal, *The Messenger*, in November 1918 and January 1919. Commenting that "the Masters Themselves wish to be better understood in the Society they originated than was generally possible at first," he states that he wrote the articles "to show how intimately the activities of the Occult Brotherhood are blended with the affairs of the world, how the Masters are much more numerous than was at first supposed, and how They specialize in dealing with the various departments of life, while working together in absolute harmony of purpose, how Their divine aspect—as we regard Them from our point of view—is blended with an intensely human aspect as They deal with us individually, and how They in turn are guided in Their action by the still loftier Will above."

Regarding how the Mahatmas presented their teachings in the time-honored way of responding to students' questions, Sinnett writes: "If the only purpose that the Masters had in view when beginning to give some of us 'instruction' in certain occult mysteries, had been instruction in the literal sense of the word, their method would undeniably have been open to criticism. They set us no lessons to learn; they merely indicated a willingness to answer questions if these did not seek information of a kind They were forbidden to disclose."

Referring to some of the questions asked, Sinnett continues: "We felt that we were in close touch with almost infinite wisdom and knowledge and we plunged into some of the most enormous problems of human evolution. 'How did humanity originate?' (We got a clue to the existence of worlds besides this.) 'What other worlds?' (We got a clue to the planetary chain.) We asked innumerable questions about it. We wanted to know how to become a Master. Got very little satisfaction along that line of inquiry."

Responding to his own rhetorical question as to why the teachings were given as they were, in a nonsequential manner, Sinnett comments:

> There seems to be a settled habit in the occult world defining teaching as a response to enquiry. Our method is so different because for the most part instruction has to be rammed into unwilling pupils. There are no unwilling pupils in the occult world, and knowledge is most firmly implanted when it comes in response to a definite desire for knowledge. . . . The purpose of the Masters in making the great theosophical experiment was not to put the world into possession of occult knowledge but to train those who proved qualified by developing appropriate aspiration to become like the Masters morally as far as possible so that they might ascend the path of spiritual progress.

A study of the Mahatma Letters reveals not only knowledge concerning "the magnificent Occult Science" but, more significantly, the ethical and moral values that are essential if a person wants to be of service to the world. Knowledge must lead to wisdom, and wisdom combined with compassion gives birth to the understanding heart. Action that flows from an understanding heart becomes a benediction of peace and healing to suffering humanity. The Mahatmas emphasize again and again throughout the correspondence that ascent of the spiritual path is not for selfish purposes, for gaining psychic powers or attaining some lofty occult status. "The only object to be striven for," as the Mahatma KH says, "is the amelioration of the condition of man" (Letter 120). Any study that leads to such a goal is surely of supreme importance. This, for countless individuals, has been and continues to be the object in exploring the Mahatmas' letters.

The letters have appeared in published form in multiple editions over time. The first edition, *The Mahatma Letters to A. P. Sinnett from the Mahatmas M. and K.H.*, was transcribed from the handwritten originals and compiled, with an introduction (London: Rider and Company, 1923) by A. Trevor Barker, who was entrusted with the task of publication by Miss Maud Hoffman, executor of Sinnett's estate. The second edition, published in 1926, had the same title, editor, and publisher but was significantly revised. The third edition, also revised, had the same title but was edited by Christmas Humphreys and Elsie Savage (Adyar: Theosophical Publishing House, 1962).

Two principal methods for studying the published letters have been suggested by various students. The first is to read the book straight through as one would any text. However, with the three initial editions of the Mahatma Letters, which all followed the pattern established by Barker in the first edition, this posed certain difficulties. Since the letters came into Barker's care not in any particular order, he decided to arrange them by subject matter. However, because the letters were not chronologically arranged, events and individuals referred to in one letter were sometimes explained in letters found much earlier or much later in the book. Moreover, since comments on a particular topic are often scattered throughout the letters, it was difficult to categorize the correspondence accurately. Reading straight through one of those three editions often led to confusion, and many would-be students abandoned the study altogether.

A second approach, often more fruitful, has been to use the index to any of the editions to find all references to a particular topic (e.g., planetary chains, karma, nirvana, devachan). The student could then correlate what the letters say on a given subject with information found elsewhere in the Theosophical literature, especially *The Secret Doctrine* and other writings of HPB. This method made the letters an invaluable reference tool, one to be consulted again and again, not as "authority" but as a guide to many aspects of the occult philosophy and the steps to attainment of spiritual wisdom.

Through the years, various students have attempted to develop a chronology for the Mahatma Letters. Two such chronologies were published, one by Mary K. Neff (*The Mahatma Letters to A. P. Sinnett, Their Chronological Order* [Wheaton: Theosophical Press, 1940]) and the other by Margaret Conger (*Combined Chronology for Use with The Mahatma Letters to A. P. Sinnett and The Letters of H. P. Blavatsky to A. P. Sinnett* [Pasadena: Theosophical University Press, 1973]), but a number of inaccuracies were found in both of those works. Consulting both the Neff and Conger chronologies as well as some unpublished ones and engaging in further extensive research, Virginia Hanson developed a chronology that, most students agree, is as accurate as possible.

Using Virginia Hanson's chronology alongside the third edition of the Mahatma Letters, Vicente Haó Chin Jr. arranged and edited what is in effect a fourth edition of the letters, in chronological sequence. This was published as *The Mahatma Letters to A. P. Sinnett, transcribed and compiled by A. T. Barker, in Chronological Sequence* (Adyar: Theosophical Publishing House, 1998). This chronological edition made it possible to study the letters following the thread of exposition as it unfolded for the original recipients. Each letter is introduced by historical information drawn from Virginia Hanson's invaluable notes. The present commentary is based on this chronological edition, including the references to specific letter numbers and page numbers.

It is not my intention in this commentary to answer all the questions that may arise in the minds of students, nor do I seek to defend the authors or the teachings they presented. A number of existing published works answer those needs. Every student should be familiar with Sinnett's own record of how the correspondence began, which is included in his book *The Occult World*. A general acquaintance with his second book, *Esoteric Buddhism*, gives insights into how Sinnett understood the teachings he was receiving and how he so capably synthesized them, producing what is considered the first textbook of Theosophy. The full story of the letters, including identification of the various individuals and events mentioned, is wonderfully told in fictionalized form, though with complete historical accuracy, by Virginia Hanson in her book *Masters and Men*. Geoffrey A. Barborka provides a detailed analysis of some of the letters, together with helpful comments, in his work *The Masters and Their Letters*. I have already mentioned the invaluable resource *A Readers' Guide to the Mahatma Letters* by George Linton and Virginia Hanson.

In addition to the texts just noted, I cite a number of other works in the course of the commentary. Particularly relevant are the writings of HPB, especially *The Secret Doctrine*, in which she elaborates on many of the concepts the Mahatmas present. I refer the student as well to compilations of other letters from the Mahatmas, particularly the two-volume *Letters from the Masters of the Wisdom* by C. Jinarajadasa, First and Second Series, as well as *The "K. H." Letters to C. W. Leadbeater*, which includes a commentary by C. Jinarajadasa. These various compilations indicate that at least twenty other individuals, most of them members of the Theosophical Society, received communications from M and KH, as well as from a few other Mahatmas.

While I draw on all of the works directly concerned with the letters, my principal aim is to share with fellow students such insights and understandings as I have gained from nearly a lifetime of Theosophical study and teaching. As one for whom the letters come alive every time the book is opened, I hope my comments convey something of my own excitement in discovering ever-deeper insights into the ageless truths of the occult philosophy, my delight in coming upon new glimpses into that "real" world that lies just beyond our normal vision, and, above all, my profound gratitude to those who call themselves "Brothers" for the inestimable gift of their wisdom and compassion. If these reflections help others to discover that these letters are as living and meaningful today as they were when written over a hundred years ago, I shall feel my aim has been accomplished.

ABBREVIATIONS

CW	*Collected Writings of H. P. Blavatsky*
HPB	Helena Petrovna Blavatsky
Isis	*Isis Unveiled* by H. P. Blavatsky
KH	Mahatma Koot Hoomi
LBS	*Letters of H. P. Blavatsky to A. P. Sinnett,* transcribed and compiled by A. T. Barker
LMW	*Letters from the Masters of the Wisdom,* First and Second Series, edited by C. Jinarajadasa
M	Mahatma Morya
ODL	*Old Diary Leaves* by H. S. Olcott
SD	*The Secret Doctrine* by H. P. Blavatsky

COMMENTARY ON *THE LETTERS*

LETTER 1

"Esteemed Brother and Friend"—so runs the salutation that initiates a remarkable correspondence. We may pass over those words all too quickly, as Sinnett himself might have done, in our eagerness to get on with the letter itself. Yet significantly, at the very outset of responding to Sinnett's initial inquiry—which Sinnett had addressed "to the Unknown Brother"—one of the "Brothers," as HPB told Sinnett they call themselves, establishes a beautiful relationship with Sinnett: brother and friend. It implies a relationship deeper than that of the ordinary teacher and pupil, for it suggests warmth of understanding and affectionate kinship. The Mahatma is writing, not from some superior position—although he is, of course, superior in his occult status, knowledge, and wisdom—but as a good friend might write to one whom he would lovingly guide along the way. It is as though KH (who signs this and several subsequent letters with his full mystic name, Koot Hoomi Lal Singh) has read not simply the words in Sinnett's first letter, nor even just between the lines, but has seen into Sinnett's heart, recognizing there a longing of which Sinnett was not even aware.

Throughout the correspondence, KH often addresses Sinnett in this manner. Sinnett, on his part, comes to address the Mahatma as

"Dear Guardian." Quite a different relationship was established with the other major recipient of the Mahatma letters, A. O. Hume, who KH addresses as "Dear Sir" in the first letter responding to Hume's inquiries. We may also note the various salutations the Mahatma M uses when writing to Sinnett: "Very kind Sinnett Sahib" in his first letter, "My dear young friend" a little later, and later still, "My impatient friend." Of course, many of the letters carry no opening salutation at all.

We can reflect on the meaning of an initial greeting in our own lives. When answering—even by e-mail—a letter from someone we do not know, the salutation can establish at the outset whether the relationship will be quite formal or warm and friendly. How do we address, even in conversation, those who come to us with questions? Do we treat each questioner as friend and brother (or sister), or as someone to be readily dismissed?

Note, then, the patience of KH's response. Not taking up more than four pages in the published book, the original letter consists of six sheets handwritten on both sides of the paper. We will have occasion throughout our study of these letters to note KH's patience in explaining matters to Sinnett, a virtue not always easy for many of us to emulate. Here, at the very outset of what came to nearly 150 letters, the Mahatma recognized not only Sinnett's sincerity and his longing for spiritual understanding but, even more, Sinnett's possible usefulness in advancing the cause of truth.

Evidence for that possibility is patent in the penultimate paragraph of the first letter, where the Mahatma urges Sinnett to "notify the public" of the various phenomena that have already occurred. As a journalist and editor of an influential newspaper in India, Sinnett was in the unique position of serving as a "truthful and intelligent witness" to those phenomena, taking the onus of this responsibility from HPB's shoulders. Sinnett, in fact, is told that not only does he have a right to assert the validity of his own testimony but, more important, he has a "sacred duty to instruct the public and prepare them for future possibilities by gradually opening their eyes to the truth."

Perhaps there is a lesson for us in these words. Are we willing to stand by what we know? Is it our "sacred duty" to aid in the dissemination of a philosophy that has meant so much in our own lives?

Having considered the salutation with which the letter opens, we can move on to the letter itself. What does the letter tell Sinnett, and what is it telling us today? First, of course, that the Mahatmas "work by natural not supernatural means and laws," which means that a lawfulness underlies all things, all phenomena, all nature. Further, KH may be giving a clue to the "natural . . . means and laws" by which all things work when, a little later in the letter, he tells Sinnett that to understand the production of phenomena (and we may remember that the entire manifested system is a phenomenon in the true sense of the term) requires a "thorough knowledge of Akas, its combinations and properties."

Sinnett would have been familiar with the term *akasha* from his reading of *Isis Unveiled*. In that work, HPB refers to akasha as "designat[ing] the imponderable and intangible life principle. . . . It enters into all the magical operations of nature, and produces mesmeric, magnetic, and spiritual phenomena" (*Isis*, 1:139–40n). In a fuller explication of the term, HPB states: "The language of the Vedas shows that the Hindus of fifty centuries ago ascribed to it the same properties as do the Thibetan [*sic*] lamas of the present day; that they regarded it as the source of life, the reservoir of all energy, and the propeller of every change of matter. . . . Akasa is the indispensable agent of every Kritya (magical performance) either religious or profane" (*Isis*, 1: xxvii). Particularly relevant and certainly very helpful is a contemporary reference in *Science and the Akashic Field* by Ervin Laszlo, a professor of philosophy, systems theory, and futures studies. He proposes that the idea of an akashic field, in addition to solving contemporary puzzles in the fields of cosmology, quantum physics, biology, and consciousness research, provides "an integral theory of everything."

Even a limited grasp of the concept of akasha gives us a key to understanding both the interconnectedness and the coherence of all universal processes, and therefore the production of such phenomena as those exhibited by HPB and even of these letters. In quite simplistic terms, not only is the akashic field, as Dr. Laszlo proposes, the, or at least one of the, fundamental fields of the universe, a holographic information field, but it is also analogous to light (which is one of its basic characteristics, the other being sound) in that it is both matter and energy. We will have occasion to refer to this concept again when we consider Letter 88, the famous "Notes" given to A. O. Hume for a chapter he was writing on God.

As we know from Sinnett's account of the beginning of his correspondence with the Mahatmas, the journalist was eager not only to prove that scientifically inexplicable phenomena could be produced by such individuals as HPB as well as her Teachers, but even more, to prove that such Teachers as the Mahatmas do actually exist. That eagerness, evidenced by his proposal for what he felt was a "fool-proof" test (see *Occult World*, 82), led the Mahatma, in refusing the test, to emphasize two significant and related points. The first, and perhaps the simpler to consider, concerns the nature of proof and the role of the skeptic. Just what constitutes proof of anything? We may say that we were an eyewitness to a certain event, only to be contradicted by another claimant to that designation. There are those today who say that the existence of the letters is no proof that they were written by Mahatmas or even by advanced pupils (chelas) of such wise individuals. So KH asks Sinnett, "Would the lifetime of a man suffice to satisfy the whole world of skeptics?" As every student knows when attempting to explain some Theosophical doctrine to a skeptical friend, skepticism is not easily conquered!

Doubt and skepticism nevertheless have their uses. As KH notes: "The only salvation of the genuine proficients in occult sciences lies in the skepticism of the public." In a later letter (Letter 29, page 93), the Mahatma M addresses both Sinnett and Hume in the same vein: "Please realize the fact that so long as men doubt there will be curiosity and enquiry, and that enquiry stimulates reflection which begets effort." KH continues in the first letter, "The charlatans and the jugglers are the natural shields of the 'adepts.' The public safety is only ensured by our keeping secret the terrible weapons which might otherwise be used against it, and which, as you have been told, became deadly in the hands of the wicked and selfish." This is further emphasized by M in Letter 29 (page 93): "Let our secret be once thoroughly vulgarized and not only will sceptical [*sic*] society derive no great good but our privacy would be constantly endangered and have to be continually guarded at an unreasonable cost of power."

The second, closely related fact that KH points to concerns the possible consequences of producing the phenomena requested. There is, as KH puts it, an "inexorable shadow which follows all human innovations," or, we might say, the law of karma decrees that every action has its inevitable reaction on the individual or individuals who initiated the action. How often do we consider the possible consequences of our undertakings? The question of motive is addressed in Letter 2. But here in the first letter Sinnett is called on to recognize the need for a "thorough knowledge of the people around you," and what might well occur were the Master to accede to Sinnett's desire.

Even today, when Theosophical ideas are more widely known and a considerable literature exists expounding those ideas, how many are genuinely interested in what KH calls "these abstruse problems . . . the deific powers in man and the possibilities contained in nature"? These, we may note, are the "problems" addressed in the Third Object of our Society. All too often it is assumed that the "powers latent" within us are the psychic ones, but what, it may be asked, are the "deific powers"? And if we are to explore the "hidden laws in nature," what are nature's infinite possibilities?

Defining what he calls the "characteristics of your age," KH states unequivocally: "As for human nature in general, it is the same now as it was a million of years ago: Prejudice based upon selfishness; a general unwillingness to give up an established order of things for new modes of life and thought . . . pride and stubborn resistance to Truth." And he adds: "We know something of human nature, for the experience of long centuries—aye, ages—has taught us. And we know, that so long as science has anything to learn, and a shadow of religious dogmatism lingers in the hearts of the multitudes, the world's prejudices have to be conquered step by step, not at a rush."

However much we may feel humanity has advanced in the century and more since Sinnett read those words—with all that science has discovered about our universe and all that is within it, and with parliaments and alliances that promote interfaith and interreligious understandings—has human nature changed? Because the Mahatmas did open the door to their world of wisdom, and because Sinnett and HPB and those who followed in their footsteps wrote and spoke and lived in the light of that world, surely some small progress has been achieved. But the fact remains: our work is not yet done, and reading this letter should stir us to a renewal of purpose and a new clarity of vision for the path that lies ahead.

Before leaving Letter 1, I would like to call attention to another letter from KH, one written to W. T. Brown in 1883 and published in *Letters from the Masters of the Wisdom*, First Series. Brown, a Scottish-born lawyer, joined the Society in London and went to India in 1883, where he joined Colonel H. S. Olcott and Damodar K. Mavalankar on a tour in North India. Later, while visiting the United States, Brown wrote a series of articles about his experiences, "Scenes in My Life," which were published in *The Post Express* of Rochester, New York.

During the course of their tour in North India, when in Lahore, Brown, Olcott, and Mavalankar were visited by the Mahatma KH in person. Later, it appears that Brown must have requested the Mahatma to perform some phenomenon that would, to quote KH's letter, "leave no room in the minds of your countrymen for doubt." Like Sinnett, Brown evidently wanted further proof, to which KH responded: "Pray, can you propose any test which will be a thorough and perfect proof for all?" Then the Mahatma continues:

> Do you know what results would follow from your being permitted to see me here in the manner suggested by you and your reporting that event to the English Press? Believe me they would be disastrous

for yourself. All the evil effects and bad feelings which this step would cause would recoil upon you and throw back your own progress for a considerable time and no good will ensure. . . . If you are earnest in your aspirations, if you have the least spark of intuition in you, if your education of a lawyer is complete enough to enable you to put facts in their proper sequence and to present your case as strongly as you in your innermost heart believe it to be, then you have material enough to appeal to any intellect capable of perceiving the continuous thread underneath the series of your facts. For the benefit of such people only you have to write, not for those who are unwilling to part with their prejudices and preconceptions for the attainment of truth from whatever source it may come. It is not our desire to convince the latter. . . . Moreover, our existence would become extremely intolerable, if not impossible, were all persons indiscriminately convinced.

So, it may be suggested, there is still a need for us today to consider to whom we are speaking when we talk of the existence of Mahatmas or Adepts, as well as where and when we voice our own inner convictions. In a world where so many claim exalted spiritual status, how should we convey what seems to us to be the truth?

Letter 1 concludes with the word that we find the Mahatmas using again and again to encourage those who would seek to unlock the treasure box of wisdom: TRY!

LETTER 2

As we know from Sinnett's own account (see *Occult World*), such was his eagerness to prove the existence of the "Brothers," as well as to show that he knew the Western mind far better than his illustrious correspondent, that he wrote again, even more urgently pressing his case for what he considered indisputable proof. Almost immediately KH responded at some length, setting forth two important considerations, as valid today as when they were written in October of 1880: the methodology for studying the "occult sciences" and the motive for undertaking such study.

The term "occult science"—as also "occult" and "occultism"—was often used in early Theosophical literature as both a synonym for Theosophy and to refer to what might more properly be called the occult arts or practices, such as the production of phenomena, clairvoyance, clairaudience, astral travel, various forms of divination, and the whole range of psychic abilities. To understand such arts, the Mahatma tells Sinnett, the student needs to "penetrate behind the veil of matter into the world of primal causes," which means to study first the universal principles underlying the phenomenalistic world, which are the main subject matter of Theosophy.

Throughout this letter KH emphasizes the distinction between the methodology of "occult science" and that of Western science, with which Sinnett was so familiar. To quote: "Occult science has its own methods of research as fixed and arbitrary as the methods of its antithesis physical science are in their way." The methodology for studying occult science involves two significant factors: first, a genuine spirit of inquiry free of preconceived notions, and second, an appropriate way of life. Concerning the first factor, KH writes: "The adept is the rare efflorescence of a generation of enquirers; and to become one, he must obey the inward impulse of his soul irrespective of the prudential considerations of worldly science or sagacity."

As HPB points out in a letter published in the journal *Spiritual Scientist* in September 1875 (*CW*, 1:128), the aspirant in the occult or hermetic sciences must "part, once for all, with every remembrance of his earlier ideas, on all and on everything. If he wants to succeed he must learn a new alphabet on the lap of Mother Nature, every letter of which will afford a new insight to him, every syllable and word an unexpected revelation." Later, in her Preliminary Memorandum establishing the Esoteric Section of the Theosophical Society, HPB describes the spirit of inquiry in these words:

The attitude of mind in which the teachings given are to be received is that which shall tend to develop the faculty of intuition. . . . Practical esoteric science is altogether *sui generis*. It requires all the mental and psychic powers of the student to be used in examining what is given, to the end that the real meaning of the Teacher may be discovered, as far as the student can understand it. He must endeavor as much as possible to free his mind, while studying or trying to carry out that which is given him, from all the ideas which he may have derived by heredity, from education, from surroundings, or from other teachers. His mind should be made perfectly free from all other thoughts. . . . Otherwise, there is constant risk of his ideas becoming . . . colored with preconceived notions. (*CW*, 12:492)

Such true inquiry is as necessary for us today as it was for Sinnett. Can we learn to "obey the inward impulse of the soul" free of all contamination that may have "infected" us because of the circumstances in which we live? What is it to inquire from a completely free mind?

Another aspect of the spirit of inquiry concerns understanding the method of investigation utilized in studying the occult sciences, or Theosophy. Much later in the correspondence (see Letter 44), the Mahatma M informs both Sinnett and Hume that "in our doctrine you will find necessary the synthetic method; you will have to embrace the whole—that is to say to blend the macrocosm and microcosm together—before you are enabled to study the parts separately or analyze them with profit to your understanding."

In an article in *The Theosophist* of July 1883 ("Footnotes to 'The Swami of Almora,'" *CW*, 4:569), HPB states: "The occult philosophy we study uses precisely that method of investigation which is termed by Spinoza the 'scientific method.' It starts from, and proceeds only on 'principles clearly defined and accurately known,' and is therefore 'the only one' which can lead to true knowledge." In essence, we must begin, as does *The Secret Doctrine*, with universal principles and so proceed to their outworking in the realm of the phenomenal. As HPB writes in a "fragment" published posthumously: "Theirs is a synthetic method of teaching: the most general outlines are given first, then an insight into the method of working, next the broad principles and notions are brought into view, and lastly begins the revelation of the minuter points" (*CW*, 13:285).

The way of life that this pursuit calls for, KH says, is one that not only proves to be an example to others but differs totally from our ordinary existence. As he tells Sinnett, "He [the one aspiring for occult knowledge] must be the first to change his modes of life." KH adds later: "We invariably welcome the new comer; only, instead of going over to him he has to come to us." Then he questions, "Is any of you so eager for knowledge and the beneficent powers it confers as to be ready to leave your world and come into ours?"

It is probably not possible for us to understand fully the nature of their "world," although surely it is not simply a physical or geographical locality. Nor is the kind of life to be lived only a matter of external conditions. It lies, rather, in a total reformation of the personal nature—body, emotions, mind—in accordance with such guidelines as have been given to all spiritual aspirants in every sacred text. Within the Theosophical tradition, we may look to such sources as *At the Feet of the Master, Light on the Path, The Voice of the Silence,* and HPB's beautiful "Golden Stairs" (*CW*, 12:591). All of these point clearly to the work that is to be done on the personality to become a proper instrument for the true Self.

KH states that the individual who seeks occult knowledge must have "reached that point in the path of occultism from which return is impossible, by his having irrevocably pledged himself to our association," implying that there are stages on that path, steps to be taken, and pledges to be made. The entire question of the nature of the pledge needs careful examination, as it involves what KH calls "the seal of the mysteries" that "has locked his lips even against the chances of his own weakness or indiscretion." As HPB points out in some of her later writings, the true pledge is not taken to an external guru or teacher but always to one's own interior Self.

The second important consideration that KH analyzes in this letter is the motive for undertaking the study of occultism. Here it is very interesting to note how KH distinguishes between the "motives and aspirations" that have impelled Sinnett's inquiry and those that have compelled his colleague, A. O. Hume, which KH says are "of diametrically opposite character." We will consider that distinction more closely when we look at KH's first response to Hume, as it may help us to understand our own motives and aspirations more clearly.

Certainly it must be as true today as when KH wrote to Sinnett: "The first and chief consideration in determining us to accept or reject your offer lies in the inner-motive which propels you to seek our instruction, and in a certain sense—our guidance." While Sinnett's "offer" may differ from ours in its particulars, if we have offered ourselves to be of service to the Adepts in their work for the world, ours and his are essentially the same. KH's thorough analysis of Sinnett's motives may aid us in looking more closely at our own.

The first motive KH points out is "the desire to receive positive and unimpeachable proofs that, there really are forces in nature of which science knows nothing." This may not seem to be our motive today, particularly as some current thinkers on the frontiers of science are now arguing that such "forces" do underlie the universe. (See, for instance, the excellent work by Lynne McTaggart, *The Field: The Quest for the Secret Force of the Universe.*) But as we consider the second motive to which KH refers, we may see to what extent "the hope to appropriate them [the forces in nature] some day" is present in us. That is, how eager are we to gain control over the "forces in nature"? And for what purpose? KH analyzes Sinnett's motives further: to "appropriate" such forces in order "to demonstrate their existence . . . ; to contemplate future life as an objective reality . . . ; to learn . . . the whole truth about our Lodges and ourselves." These may seem to be worthy motives. Yet as KH goes on to say: "To our minds then, these motives, sincere and worthy of every serious consideration from the worldly standpoint, appear—selfish." And why? "Because the chief object of the T.S. [Theosophical Society] is not so much to gratify individual aspirations as to serve our fellow men."

Of greatest significance for us, as we seek to apply KH's statements to our own situation, is his emphasis on the meaning of the term "selfish." He states, "In our view the highest aspirations for the welfare of humanity become tainted with selfishness if, in the mind of the philanthropist, there lurks the shadow of desire for self benefit or a tendency to do injustice, even when these exist unconsciously to himself"—a remarkable statement that surely causes us to pause and look ever more deeply into our own desires, motives, aspirations, and hopes. It also gives us a glimpse into "their world," a consciousness totally without the shadow of personal desire or "taint of selfishness."

Can we ever know all that "lurks" within us, including at the unconscious level? How can we bring what exists unconsciously into the light? Is this not the reason why we have been given so many wonderful guidebooks on the spiritual path?

KH concludes his second letter to Sinnett with the assurance of a friendship that is both understanding and compassionate.

LETTERS 3A, 3B, 3C, AND 4

Since the fascinating story behind the four brief Letters 3A, 3B, 3C, and 4 is well summarized in the prefatory comments to these letters in the chronological edition of the letters, there is little reason for us to consider them here in detail. Just one sentence in Letter 3A may be of significance for its comment about dreams: "In dreams and visions at least, when rightly interpreted there can hardly be an 'element of doubt.'" We should note especially the words "when rightly interpreted," for there are certainly occasions when we read more into a dream than is actually there, as well as times when we fail to appreciate the inner meaning a dream or vision may be conveying to us. HPB's comment in the first of her Esoteric Section (E.S.) Instructions may be relevant here:

Remember that with our physical senses alone at our command, none of us can hope to reach beyond gross matter. We can do so only through one or another of our seven spiritual senses, either by training, or if one is a born seer. Yet even a clairvoyant possessed of such faculties, if not an Adept, no matter how honest and sincere he may be, will, through his ignorance of the truths of Occult Science, be led by the visions he sees in the Astral Light only to mistake for God or Angels the denizens of those spheres of which he may occasionally catch a glimpse. (*CW*, 12:528)

And in the "fragment" from HPB's pen, referred to in the commentary on Letter 2, she tells us: "Knowledge comes in visions, first in dreams and then in pictures presented to the inner eye during meditation." And she adds: "Thus have I been taught the whole system of evolution, the laws of being and all else that I know—the mysteries of life and death, the workings of karma. Knowledge so obtained is so clear, so convincing, so indelible in the impression it makes upon the mind, that all other sources of information, all other methods of teaching with which we are familiar dwindle into insignificance in comparison with this" (*CW*, 13:285).

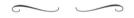

LETTERS 5 AND 6

The prefatory notes to Letters 5 and 6 summarize the circumstances surrounding Letter 5 and indicate that Letter 6 is actually a postscript to 5. Though a bit complicated, the entire episode provides one of the most convincing pieces of evidence anywhere in our literature as to the existence of the Mahatma and his powers. (A detailed analysis of all that occurred, as well as a photographic reproduction of the telegram referred to in the letter, may be found in chapter 11 of Geoffrey Barborka's *The Mahatmas and Their Letters*.

Sinnett also refers to the incident, although briefly, in "Recent Occult Phenomena" in *Occult World*.)

Letter 5 contains much that deserves consideration. The statement near the beginning that "it is men not ceremony-masters, we seek, devotion, not mere observances" helps us understand the attitude required in one who would approach the Mahatmas. Statements elsewhere in the letters also make clear that the Mahatmas seek individuals who are self-reliant, devoted to the cause of humanity's welfare, and selfless in service to the ideal of true brotherhood. KH's words "We have weightier matters than small societies to think about" reveals that their concern encompasses a larger field of world affairs than many of us realize. At the same time, the additional comment "yet, the T.S. must not be neglected" shows the importance they gave to the Theosophical Society as an instrument to bring about a change in human consciousness.

KH's beautiful tribute to Colonel Olcott is surely a wonderful reminder of all that we owe to the president–founder of the Society. His trustworthiness, his loyalty to the cause, his devoted service whatever the cost to personal comfort, his willingness to admit to error, and his far-sighted vision in establishing the initial Rules of the "Parent Society"—all these and more deserve our lasting gratitude. It was Olcott who established the principle of Lodge (or Branch) autonomy within the general framework of the Society's Rules, a principle based on his American experience of states' rights within a federal union. It was Olcott who established the ideals later formalized in Resolutions of the Society's governing body, the General Council, as "Freedom of the Society" (referring to the principle of the Society's neutrality) and as "Freedom of Thought" (referring to the lack of dogma or creed in the Society). We will see these ideals referred to again in Letter 120, addressed to the members of the London Lodge.

An interesting aspect of the letter is KH's recognition of Sinnett's attitude of disdain toward Olcott for what Sinnett felt was the American's lack of proper breeding. KH reminds his correspondent that his likely prejudice toward Indians would probably come into play were he to see KH in person, should one among the "Aryan Punjabees . . . natural mystics" consent to become "an agent between yourself and us."

We may think we are freer today of such "national prejudices," but much that KH says on this matter is worth our consideration. Just how often do we judge others on the basis of outer appearance—their speech, their dress, their behavior? Do we assume that someone who appears "very dirty and slovenly" could not possibly be wise enough to teach us? To what extent do we carry a bias against individuals of another ethnic background or culture? How do we react when an individual whose outer appearance is unsavory or whose speech is so ungrammatical as to seem illiterate appears at our Lodge or study group's door? These are not idle questions but bear directly on the full meaning of brotherhood that is given such emphasis in the final paragraph of Letter 5.

Before considering that beautiful concluding paragraph, we need to comment on the significance of KH's calling himself a "Cis and Trans-Himalayan 'cave-dweller.'" In two other letters (Letters 47 and 55) KH refers to himself as "your trans-Himalayan correspondent" and "your trans-Himalayan friend." One could easily assume that the reference is to a geographical location, the Mahatmas' Himalayan residence. However, further study suggests that KH is really indicating the doctrine in which both he and Morya were trained and which was being conveyed to the world by HPB. Throughout her writings, HPB used a variety of terms to denote the philosophical system in which her Teachers, the Mahatmas, had instructed her. So we find such phrases or words as the "Tibetan esoteric doctrine," the "trans-Himalayan School," the "Universal Wisdom-Religion," "Theosophy," the "occult doctrine," and so on.

In her editorial notes to an article by T. Subba Row ("The Aryan-Arhat Esoteric Tenets on the Sevenfold Principle in Man"), HPB states that the Cis-Himalayan is a variety of rationalistic Vedantism, while the Trans-Himalayan is Transcendental Buddhism (see *CW*, 3:422; see also *Esoteric Writings* by T. Subba Row and HPB's article, "Re-Classification of Principles," in *CW*, 7:345–51). Therefore KH's reference as a "Cis Trans-Himalayan" correspondent is to the system that the Mahatmas sought to convey through their letters to both Sinnett and Hume.

The final paragraph of Letter 5 contains one of the most beautiful statements in all the letters concerning the Mahatmas' central aim in sharing their knowledge with the world: the ideal of "Universal Brotherhood." This is no "idle phrase," as KH points out, and if it is a "dream," he says, at least it is the "aspiration of the true adept." As one reads the letters, it becomes obvious that the concept of brotherhood has a deeper meaning with the Mahatmas than we usually give to it. As the "foundation for universal morality," brotherhood must be the purest of relationships arising out of our spiritual roots in the One Existence. If indeed "humanity in the mass" has a "paramount claim" upon the Adept, it is also true that the Adepts lend their strength and support to our efforts only when our motive is without any trace of self-interest (as KH tells Sinnett in Letter 2). It is the whole of humanity, not simply any of its parts, that must benefit, and the attention the Mahatmas give to individuals (whether to their chelas or, in this case, to Sinnett and Hume) is solely for enabling those individuals to act for the common good.

LETTER 7

Letter 7 needs no comment. In brief, it concerns KH's reason for deferring his reply to Sinnett's questions and the assurance that those questions will be answered as soon as the Mahatma's time permits.

FIRST LETTER FROM KH TO A. O. HUME

Since Letters 8 and 9 are part of the correspondence with A. O. Hume, it is appropriate at this point to turn to KH's first letter to that gentleman. In Letter 2, KH refers to the fact that Hume has written to him, while early in Letter 5 there is a reference to "Mr. Hume's important offer," about which KH approached one whom he calls his "chief." For whatever reason, KH's first response to Hume was not included in any of the previous editions of *The Mahatma Letters*. However, we do know that Sinnett's wife, Patience, copied out the letter and Sinnett himself referred to it, writing in *Occult World*, "I am here enabled to insert the greater part of a letter addressed by Koot Hoomi to [my] friend [Hume]." The letter in its entirety, checked against Mrs. Sinnett's handwritten copy in the British Museum, appeared in the little work *Combined Chronology* by Margaret Conger. Geoffrey A. Barborka provides a detailed analysis of the letter in *The Mahatmas and Their Letters*. It is now available as appendix 1 (page 469) in the chronological edition of the letters, on which this commentary is based.

Perhaps the first thing one notices in KH's first letter to Hume is the formality of the salutation. In contrast to his greeting to Sinnett as "Brother and Friend," the Mahatma addresses Hume simply as "Dear Sir." Then follows a letter nearly twice as long as the first letter to Sinnett in which KH responds to Hume's proposition, which must have concerned an "offer" to become the recipient of occult knowledge in order to convey it to others according to a method Hume himself thought best. The letter details why "the idea entertained by Mr. Sinnett and yourself is impracticable." KH states unequivocally: "What we do refuse is to take any other responsibility upon ourselves than this periodical correspondence and assistance with our advice."

The Mahatma's remark that "a man can only think in his worn grooves" may remind the student of Robert Bowen's comment in his Notes on the study of *The Secret Doctrine*, which are based on classes with HPB. Evidently paraphrasing HPB, Bowen says: "Ordinary intellectual activity moves on well beaten paths in the brain. But this new kind of mental effort [the study of *The Secret Doctrine* and presumably the occult sciences or Theosophy in general] calls for something very different—the carving out of 'new brain paths,' the ranking in different order of the little brain lives. . . . This mode of thinking she (i.e., HPB) says is what the Indians call Jnana Yoga" (see

Hoskins, *Foundations of Esoteric Philosophy*, 66). A full study of the "Bowen Notes," published in several places and as a small booklet, *Madame Blavatsky on How to Study Theosophy*, may be a helpful supplement to KH's statements to Hume.

Just as he does in his letters to Sinnett, KH devotes a great deal of this letter to the contrast between the methods of "exact modern science" and occult science. He tells Hume: "You do not seem to realize the tremendous difficulties in the way of imparting even the rudiments of our Science to those who have been trained in the familiar methods of yours." Pointing up "the difference between the modes of—physical called exact— . . . and metaphysical sciences," he comments that "no fact of either of these sciences is interesting except in the degree of its potentiality of moral results, and in the ratio of its usefulness to mankind." Moreover, as he states later in the letter, "Exact experimental Science has nothing to do with morality, virtue, philanthropy, therefore can make no claim upon our help, until it blends itself with the metaphysics." This emphasis on a way of life, as well as a mode of knowing, directed always toward the welfare of humanity and the ideal of a genuine brotherhood occurs again and again throughout the correspondence with both Sinnett and Hume.

The discussion on energy in this letter may be a response to what KH called in his first letter to Sinnett the need for "a thorough knowledge of Akasa, its combinations and properties" (see page 3). Especially significant for us today are KH's comments on the use of energy by individuals whose intent and purpose are not propelled by concern for humanity and brotherhood. "And why? Because every thought of man upon being evolved passes into the inner world and becomes an active entity by associating itself—coalescing, we might term it—with an elemental . . . one of the semi-intelligent forces of the kingdoms. It survives as an active intelligence, a creature of the mind's begetting, for a longer or shorter period proportionate with the original intensity of the cerebral action which generated it."

Could we but consciously realize that we are "continually peopling [our] current in space with a world of [our] own, crowded with the offspring of [our] fancies, desires, impulses, and passions," what care we would take of our thoughts and emotions! Further, realizing that our "current in space"—peopled with our thoughts and feelings— "reacts upon any sensitive or and [*sic*] nervous organisation which comes in contact with it in proportion to its dynamic intensity," we would recognize our responsibility toward all life. In every way, we are one with all that lives. We may well ask ourselves whether, by failing to recognize our responsibility to use the power of thought for the benefit of all humanity, we—like Hume—may be "caus[ing] a waste of cosmic energy by tons"!

KH's response to Hume's question regarding "the presumed failure" of the Adept "Fraternity" in influencing historical events leaves us much to contemplate. It is true that any study of the history of the world would turn up many instances in which a "special providence" seems to have intervened. So, as KH informs Hume, "There never was a time within or before the so-called historical period when our predecessors were not moulding events and 'making history,' the facts of which were subsequently and invariably distorted by 'historians' to suit contemporary prejudices." At the same time, nothing happens outside the fundamental lawfulness of the universe, for as KH puts it, the Mahatmas too have "to deal with an immutable Law, being ourselves its creatures," so "the cycles must run their rounds. Periods of mental and moral light and darkness succeed each other. The major and minor yugas must be accomplished according to the established order of things." It appears that the Mahatmas do what they can and then "rest thankful." Yet surely no effort is ever lost, and if indeed the "Earth is the battle ground of moral no less than of physical forces," it is for us also to do what we can in aiding the Brotherhood in its ceaseless endeavors. As it says in *Light on the Path*: "Try to lift a little of the heavy karma of the world; give your aid to the few strong hands that hold back the powers of darkness from obtaining complete victory."

One of KH's statements invites us to consider deeply the nature of "cycles" as they affect humanity. He writes: "Our numbers are just now diminishing . . . because we are of the human race, subject to its cyclic impulse and powerless to turn that back upon itself." We can only speculate on all that this statement, written of course toward the end of the nineteenth century, means. Have the Masters moved on in their evolutionary journey and more earnest aspirants are needed to enter upon the path toward adeptship? The Mahatma says later, "This is the moment to guide the recurrent impulse which must soon come." What then, we may ask, is the role of the Theosophical Society in helping to guide that impulse? What, indeed, is the work of each member who has had the privilege of being exposed to the Theosophical truths? How can we really work in cooperation with those who, still of our human race, are yet our elders—"a little wiser" as KH says, "as a result of special study"? To what extent are we really willing to step "out of this world into theirs," as seems to be the requirement if we would join them in aiding humanity?

There is much more to consider in this first letter to Hume. Many questions will occur to the student while reading it, and many of the subjects treated here are discussed in further depth in later letters, as we shall see. At the same time, this letter sets forth two fundamental principles that underlie all the letters to come: first, that the study of occult science requires a different mode of thinking from that with which both Sinnett and Hume are familiar, and second, that the teaching is not for their personal gratification but for them to use in benefiting others. Both of these factors are reflected in the Mahatma's statement: "Education enthrones skepticism but imprisons spiritualism. You can do immense good by helping to give the Western nations a secure basis upon which to reconstruct their crumbling faith."

KH points out that a change in the educational system is needed not only in the West but in India as well. (Note, by the way, the typographical error near the bottom of page 474: the word "Princess" should be "Princes.") Consider, then, how Theosophists and the Society itself might influence the field of education. To what extent can we aid in the "spiritualizing" of education? What is our responsibility in this area today?

The letter concludes with a heartfelt plea to "help furnish the materials for a needed universal religious philosophy"—a philosophy still so much needed today in the twenty-first century, when "superstitions and skepticism" yet flourish along with a science only occasionally open to "metaphysics." Is not the call as clear today as it was more than a century ago? Reading the entire letter, one feels KH's longing to enroll Hume—and so each one of us—in that "grand and noble work" to which the Mahatmas are devoted. Having begun his letter with the formal "Dear Sir," KH now signs himself "Sincerely your friend."

LETTERS 8 AND 9

The prefatory note to Letter 8 indicates that Letter 8, which is from Hume, and Letter 9, KH's response to Hume's letter, must be considered together. Of note is the fact that Hume's letter was conveyed to the Mahatma via Sinnett, who gave it to HPB for transmittal, and KH's response was written to Sinnett rather than to Hume directly. We know from Sinnett's account in *Occult World* that Hume had written a lengthy reply to the Mahatma's first letter to him, and then wrote an additional letter consisting of his comments on Letter 5, a letter to Sinnett that Sinnett had shared with Hume. Letter 8 is that additional letter, which was obviously returned to Sinnett along with Letter 9. It reveals much about Hume's character and attitude, his general impatience with the manner in which the Mahatmas work, and his sense of his own superiority in knowing how to deal with the "European" or Western mind.

Before we too hastily criticize Hume for his pride, which was undoubtedly wounded by statements KH made in Letter 5 concerning Hume's "proposition," we need to consider how we might have responded in a similar situation. Hume evidently feels that KH does not really understand him, so he endeavors now to state very clearly his views on how best to "ensure the attention of all sincere minds" in presenting the teachings. We might ask: Was Hume aware of his pride? Or did he see himself only, as he writes in Letter 8, as one willing to come forward "to teach gratuitously, manifestly at the sacrifice of his own time, comfort and convenience . . . what he believed to be for the good of mankind to know"? How often do we defend our own position, convinced that we are proposing to do something out of the best of motives and that our method is the best under the circumstances? It is not always so easy to see our own shortcomings, our innate prejudice or pride—the covering, as the Mahatma puts it in Letter 9, of "a thick crust of self sufficiency and egoistical stubbornness."

Many students have been puzzled by Letter 9's satirical tone, which seems far from KH's usual mellifluous style and patient, even kindly, efforts to enlighten the two Englishmen. In fact, the letter seems almost too brusque, as though the Mahatma has, as one student suggested, a "chip on his shoulder." It has even been suggested that one of KH's chelas or even HPB may have written it on behalf of the Mahatma. Another student of the letters has proposed that Letter 9 could have been a test. In Letter 92 (page 294), for example, Sinnett is told: "No one comes in contact with us, no one shows a desire to know more of us, but has to submit to being tested." In Letter 74 (page 227), writing about chelaship, KH mentions the "rule" that every aspirant has to be "tested, tempted and examined by all and every means, so as to have his real nature drawn out." And the postscript to Letter 136 (page 451) says, "The aspirant is now assailed entirely on the psychological side of his nature."

In a letter to Colonel Olcott, written in quite another context, KH makes a comment that may be relevant to the policy of testing: "Those who have been perplexed and *puzzled* over our policy . . . will understand its necessity better when they become better acquainted with the very occult art of drawing out the hidden capacities and propensities of beginners in occult study" (*LMW*, First Series, Letter 18). Perhaps at this early stage of the correspondence with Hume, even while rejecting his "proposition," the Mahatma still hoped that

Hume would prove useful in the work. Certainly both KH and M tried for quite a long time to work with Hume, although in the end the Englishman failed, his pride being so ingrained that he was quite incapable of acknowledging it. Yet Hume was, for all that, intellectually brilliant as well as a real philanthropist. Much later (Letter 75, page 235) M writes of Hume, "'Egotistic philanthropist' is a word which paints his portrait at full length."

One statement in Letter 9, written in response to Hume's accusation that the Brotherhood, in effect, was jesuitical, should be highlighted for consideration. "No men living," writes KH, "are freer than we when we have once passed out of the stage of pupilage. Docile and obedient but never slaves during that time we must be; otherwise, and if we passed our time in arguing we never would learn anything at all." Applying this to ourselves, we may ask: to what extent do we engage in needless argument over obscure points rather than opening our minds to the possibility of new ideas and thus learning more of the teachings set before us?

LETTER 10

At the close of Letter 9, the Mahatma writes: "I mailed a letter for you the other day at Umballa [now spelled Amballa]." Letter 10 is that letter. Although addressed to Sinnett, it in some respects continues KH's very perceptive analysis of Hume, particularly that Englishman's overweening pride. It appears that enclosed with this letter were Hume's response to the Mahatma's letter and KH's reply to Hume (which is Letter 11). While KH says that this reply is "my final epistle," we know, of course, that it was not, as there are several more letters to Hume, including the famous "Notes" for a chapter Hume was writing on the subject of God (Letter 88). The actual break with Hume came some two years later, when he resigned from the presidency of the Simla Eclectic Branch of the Society, and even after that event there are references to Hume.

A number of statements in Letter 10 deserve our attention for their practical bearing on our own spiritual growth. For example, while pointing to Sinnett's strong racial prejudice, which was certainly the prevalent attitude at that time not only in England but in the Western world generally, the Mahatma indicates that in Sinnett "intensity of aspirations makes one disregard all other considerations." Similarly, when such intensity is present in us, at least some of our faults may be overlooked. Later KH tells Sinnett, "I will not tell you to give up this or that, for, unless you exhibit *beyond any doubt* the presence in you of the necessary *germs* it would be useless as it would be cruel." Then he adds the admonition so often found throughout the letters, "*TRY*. Do not despair. . . . *Strong will creates* and sympathy attracts even adepts." What, we may ask, are the "necessary germs" that must be present in the aspirant, and if we feel we hold such "germs" or seeds, how do we nurture them? When we seek to come closer to the Masters, do we have that "intensity of aspirations," that "strong will," that may bring us nearer our goal? Casual indifference, a lackadaisical attitude, and half-heartedness are all identified obstacles to the occult life.

Letter 10 again emphasizes the central aim of bringing about a genuine brotherhood, which KH here defines as: "an association of 'affinities' of strong magnetic yet dissimilar forces and polarities, centred around one dominant idea." Such a definition indicates that there may be differences of view, even strong opinions, within a group, but when an inner, "magnetic" harmony, a deep "affinity" for one another is present, then a true brotherhood exists. As Dr. George Arundale often said during his presidency of the Society, we can work together differently. "Magnetic harmony" does not mean that we all sing the same note, as it were, but rather that we recognize the common bond that unites us in our work.

This letter also contains interesting hints about the organization of the Brotherhood: "There is a distinct group or section in our fraternity who attend to our casual and very rare accessions of another race and blood." This suggests that various members of the Adept Brotherhood are responsible for working with aspirants or pupils from various national backgrounds. It has been said that different members of the Brotherhood overshadow, guide, or are responsible for different countries or different parts of the world. For example, the Prince is concerned chiefly with Europe and the United States.

As to the method KH employs in writing his letters, he says, "These my letters, are not written but impressed or precipitated and then all mistakes corrected." This process is referred to several times throughout the letters as well as in several books, particularly useful being the chapter on this subject in Geoffrey Barborka's *The Masters and Their Letters*. Charles Johnston's account of his first meeting with HPB, in London in 1887 (*CW*, 8:392 *et seq.*) may be of special interest as well. The process of precipitation is actually explained in a later letter (Letter 117) and eventually is "prohibited," as we shall see. The fact that "all mistakes" were not really "corrected," as KH states here, led to some truly unforeseen events I will comment on later.

Toward the end of the letter, Sinnett is advised to correspond with a gentleman known as Lord Lindsay, and this advice is reiterated in Letter 12. Lord Lindsay, referred to in Letter 15 as Lord Crawford and Balcarres because he was the twenty-sixth Earl of Crawford and ninth Earl of Balcarres, was a British astronomer of note at the time; interested in occultism, he became a member of the Society and for a time was one of its counselors. (For a full biography of Lord Lindsay, see *Damodar* by Sven Eek, 635–38.) Perhaps KH hoped that Sinnett, by telling Lord Lindsay of the Simla phenomena (which Sinnett had recorded in *Occult World*) and the current correspondence concerning those phenomena, could gain the attention of a reputable scientist who would then aid in persuading the British Spiritualists to shift from their fascination with phenomena to a recognition of the laws underlying such productions, and so come to a study of Theosophy. There are other indications in the letters that KH was particularly eager to see Theosophical philosophy or genuine occultism gain a foothold in the Western world, attracting individuals who, because of their backgrounds, might be useful in the work.

LETTER 11

In contrast to KH's comments about Hume in letters sent to Sinnett (Letters 9 and 10)—the Mahatma knowing, of course, that Sinnett would share those comments with Hume—Letter 11 is written directly to Hume, in response to Hume's initial reply to KH's first letter to him. While Letter 11 may seem of less concern today, except to note the Englishman's attitude and the relationship between him and the Mahatma at this early stage of the correspondence, in fact it is rich in provocative statements that the serious student should consider carefully. It is all too easy to feel annoyance with Hume for his "haughty and imperative spirit," thinking that we would approach the Mahatma with a more humble attitude. But have we searched our hearts for any traces of selfishness, of egotism, even of prejudice?

As he does in his first letters to Sinnett, KH reminds Hume that the world in which the Mahatmas live and act is "quite a different world" from the Englishmen's and that their "modes of life and thought" are of a different order. It may not be easy to understand fully the nature of their world or all that is meant by the term "Universal Brotherhood." Even today, while "the aspiration for brotherhood between our races" remains the Theosophical Society's chief objective, how far are we from full realization of that aim? The Mahatma's statement "It has been constantly our wish to spread on the Western Continent among the foremost educated classes 'Branches' of the T.S. as the harbingers of a Universal Brotherhood" gives us much to ponder as we survey our fragmented world. To what extent are our Branches (or Lodges) today "of the Universal Brotherhood but in name"? Are we "intensely selfish in [our] aspirations"? Evidently, from the outset the achievement of the goal was not certain, for as KH states, "We are not gods, and even they, our chiefs—they hope."

The Adepts' earnestness, their unfailing patience in explaining again and again why the teachings were being given, and their willingness to continue trying to satisfy the two Englishmen's desire for "instruction" while helping them to understand their purpose in giving that "instruction" should help us realize why our own studies must be for humanity's benefit, not for selfish aims. As he does in Letter 2 to Sinnett, KH now stresses to Hume the importance of motive: "As man is a creature born with a free will and endowed with reason, whence spring all his notions of right and wrong, he does not per se represent any definite moral ideal. The conception of morality in general relates first of all to the object or motive, and only then to the means or modes of action" (page 32).

Later in the letter, KH compares the Brotherhood's view of morality with that of Kant: "We, who have studied a little Kant's moral teachings, analyzed them somewhat carefully, have come to the conclusion that even this great thinker's views on that form of duty (*das Sollen*) which defines the methods of moral action—notwithstanding his one-sided affirmation to the contrary—falls short of a full definition of an unconditional absolute principle of morality—as we understand it" (page 35). Pointing out that it is this "Kantian note" that permeates Hume's letter, KH emphasizes that the moral basis for any "philanthropic feeling . . . having no character of universality" is inadequate, for "it is necessarily unable to warm all mankind with its beneficent rays." And he writes, then, of "an absolute standard of moral activity" as "one productive of efficient action" that must be truly universal in its nature. The absence of such a "character of universality," KH says, is "the secret of the spiritual failure and unconscious egotism of this age."

One of the clearest statements regarding the kind of individuals needed to serve the cause for which the Adepts themselves constantly labor occurs in this letter, couched in KH's beautiful, poetic language:

We neither want men to rush on blind-fold, nor are we prepared to abandon tried friends—who rather pass for fools than reveal what they may have learnt under a solemn pledge of never revealing it unless permitted—even for the chance of getting men of the very highest class,—nor are we especially anxious to have anyone work for us except with entire spontaneity. We want true and unselfish hearts; fearless and confiding souls, and are quite willing to leave the men of the "higher class" and far higher intellects to grope their own way to the light. (page 34)

Unless Hume is willing, which KH realizes may be an impossibility, to accept the mahatmic terms for establishing a Branch of the Theosophical Society for study of the teachings they are prepared to give, the Masters would continue "content to live as we do—unknown and undisturbed by a civilization which rests so exclusively upon intellect. Nor do we feel in any way concerned about the revival of our ancient arts and high civilization, for these are as sure to come back in their time, and in a higher form" (page 35).

The Mahatma adds, "We have the weakness to believe in ever recurrent cycles and hope to quicken the resurrection of what is past and gone. We could not impede it even if we would. The 'new civilization' will be but the child of the old one, and we have but to leave the eternal law to take its own course . . . yet, we are certainly anxious to hasten the welcome event." Here KH refers to the doctrine of the *yugas*, those vast cycles HPB was to write of in *The Secret Doctrine*. This doctrine, well known in Greek philosophy as the *aions*, is a teaching of tremendous optimism that sees the darkest periods of existence followed by periods of renewed light.

KH concludes so beautifully: "Fear not . . . our knowledge will not pass away from the sight of man. It is the 'gift of the gods' and the most precious relic of all. The keepers of the sacred Light did not safely cross so many ages but to find themselves wrecked on the rocks of modern scepticism." He reminds Hume, and us: "We will always find volunteers to replace the tired sentries, and the world, bad as it is in its present state of transitory period, can yet furnish us with a few men now and then."

Well may we ask: what role do we—collectively and individually as heirs to this rich tradition of wisdom—play in this great work, this noble cause of Universal Brotherhood? In answer to that question, KH tells us we have "a sure guide" in our "own inner moral perceptions or—conscience." At the same time, "Conscience may perchance tell us what we must not do; yet it never guides us as to what we ought to perform, nor gives any definite object to our activity. And—nothing can be more easily lulled to sleep and even completely paralyzed, than this same conscience."

KH ends the letter on an interesting note: "Imagination as well as will—creates. Suspicion is the most powerful provocative agent of imagination." And so he warns Hume (a warning we may take to heart): "Beware! . . . Instead of the realization of your purest and highest ideals you may one day evoke a phantom, which, barring every passage of light will leave you in worse darkness than before, and will harrass [sic] you to end of your days." One cannot help but wonder at the possible irony in KH's final words to this remarkable and beautiful letter: "Your most obedient Servant."

LETTER 12

Although relatively brief and undoubtedly written in response to a further inquiry from Sinnett, Letter 12 is significant for a number of reasons. First, the opening paragraph gives further clues as to the method the Mahatma employed in reading Sinnett's (and presumably also Hume's) letters and "precipitating" the responses. KH refers briefly to the process of precipitation in Letter 10, and now in Letter 12 he provides a more detailed explanation. However, as we shall see later, with this particular letter the process may have been entrusted to an inexperienced chela, for the letter had serious repercussions leading to what has come to be called "the Kiddle incident," which was finally resolved by an explanation given in Letter 117.

Leaving aside whatever we are able to comprehend of how the Mahatmas read and wrote their letters, we should note particularly KH's statement, "We but follow and servilely copy nature in her works." Could this point to one of the Adeptic "powers": understanding and working with those "hidden laws of nature" with which we at our stage are not yet truly familiar? Is KH indicating that the Mahatmas work with the unseen or invisible forces (or energies) in nature to produce what seem to be "supernatural" results? We may recall his words in Letter 1: "We work by natural not supernatural means and laws."

A second reason for this letter's significance lies in KH's comments about teaching "isolated individuals," particularly with regard to instructing Sinnett and his wife, Patience, whose "magnetisms are too similar" to receive anything of value. The remark concerning individuals underscores again that the teachings given to Sinnett and even to Hume were never to be for their personal benefit but always to be in some manner disseminated to as wide an audience as possible. Certainly Sinnett fulfilled this purpose in writing his several books, particularly *Esoteric Buddhism*, in which he presents the teachings he received through the letters in sequential form to the Western public. KH's remark pertaining to Mr. and Mrs. Sinnett sitting together for instruction, suggests that the receipt of messages (for which Sinnett was obviously asking) involves the set-up of currents that requires a polarity, as in electricity. In Letter 120, written to the London Lodge, KH refers again to the need for such a polarity, stating that Anna Kingsford and Sinnett were "both useful, both needed . . . just because they are the two poles calculated to keep the whole body in magnetic harmony." Two more different individuals one cannot imagine, yet both were needed in the work of the Lodge. Perhaps it is a question of a necessary polarity when individuals in our groups or Lodges disagree with us or present quite different interpretations of concepts to which we are inclined to attach one (and only one!) meaning!

This letter is also important for its emphasis on the purpose for which the teachings were being given. There could be no clearer statement of that purpose than the following: "The truths and mysteries of occultism constitute, indeed, a body of the highest spiritual importance, at once profound and practical for the world at large. Yet, it is not as a mere addition to the tangled mass of theory or speculation in the world of science that they are being given to you, but for their practical bearing on the interests of mankind" (page 38).

Adding that "this is why our chiefs have determined" to give out so much of the esoteric philosophy, KH then draws a truly heartening picture of the benefits of "a genuine, practical Brotherhood of Humanity where all will become co-workers with nature, will work for the good of mankind with and through the higher planetary Spirits—the only 'Spirits' we believe in." That final phrase is an oblique reference to the "spirits" of the Spiritualists, which the Master says in a later letter (Letter 18) are not spirits in the true sense. To "become co-workers with nature," to work "with and through" the planetary spirits should be our own aim, if we would share in the efforts of the Occult Fraternity and so aid humanity—a truly magnificent task and undoubtedly the only one worth working toward.

Who or what, then, are the "planetary Spirits" with whom we are to work? For we should know something of these forces if we are to cooperate with them wisely and usefully. In *Isis Unveiled* (1:158), HPB writes of "a high Planetary Spirit, one of the class of beings that have never been embodied (though there are many among these hierarchies who have lived on our earth), descends occasionally to our sphere, and purifying the surrounding atmosphere enables the subject to see, and opens in him the springs of true divine prophecy." In the *Theosophical Glossary* (237–38), HPB defines the planetary spirits as "primarily the rulers or governors of the planets" and then says:

As our earth has its hierarchy of terrestrial planetary spirits, from the highest to the lowest plane, so has every other heavenly body. In Occultism, however, the term "Planetary Spirit" is generally applied only to the seven highest hierarchies corresponding to the Christian archangels. These have all passed through a stage of evolution corresponding to the humanity of earth on other worlds, in long past cycles. Our earth, being as yet only in its fourth round, is far too young to have produced high planetary spirits. The highest planetary spirit ruling over any globe is in reality the "Personal God" of that planet and far more truly its "over-ruling providence" than the self-contradictory Infinite Personal Deity of modern Christianity.

In *The Key to Theosophy* (see my *Abridgement*, 62), in response to a question about her statement in *Isis* that "planetary Spirits or Angels . . . will never be men on our planet," HPB says, "Some classes of higher Planetary Spirits . . . will never be men on this planet, because they are liberated Spirits from a previous, earlier world, and as such they cannot rebecome men on this one. Yet all these will live again in the next and far higher Mahamanvantara." There is also much on the subject in *The Secret Doctrine*. In summary we can say that every entity in space is under the guiding influence of spiritual and quasi-spiritual beings, which are likewise in varying stages of evolution. The term "Planetary Spirits" refers to the highest class of such beings, who govern a planet or globe. Yet they too, in long-past cycles of cosmic evolution, would have passed through what we would call the "human stage."

The planetary spirits of our earth are intimately linked with the origin and destiny of humanity, for not only are they our predecessors on the evolutionary path, but certain classes of them are humanity's spiritual guides and instructors. HPB points out in *The Secret Doctrine* that we, in our turn and in ages yet to come, may become planetary spirits on a planetary chain that is the progeny, the child or grandchild, of our present earth chain, and as such we would become guides and guardians of the host of entities evolving during that planetary chain's various rounds.

In the first set of Cosmological Notes, the planetaries are called "the artificers of the world" (page 514). KH gives additional information about the planetary spirits in Letters 18 and 93B, so we will explore this subject further as we take up those letters.

The section of Letter 12 beginning with the words "Plato was right" is the cause of the famous "Kiddle incident." More significantly, it is also in this section of the letter that we learn the tremendous scope of occult study. More than one student has suggested that KH's words provide a clear "program of study" even for us today:

> It is not physical phenomena but . . . universal ideas that we study, as to comprehend the former, we have first to understand the latter. They touch man's true position in the universe, in relation to his previous and future births; his origin and ultimate destiny; the relation of the mortal to the immortal; of the temporary to the eternal; of the finite to the infinite; ideas larger, grander, more comprehensive, recognising the universal reign of Immutable Law. . . . This is what we study and what many have solved. If this is what the Mahatmas "study," then surely we should take up no less an assignment if we wish to comprehend the theosophical doctrine! (page 39)

The letter concludes by setting a choice of two paths before Sinnett, the same choice still set before aspirants, and so we can also ask ourselves which we intend to follow: "the highest philosophy or simple exhibitions of occult powers." "Simple exhibitions" by pseudo-gurus are still available, usually for a price, and there are many "dabblers" in the occult arts to lead the unwary away from the true goal of occult study. But for those who persist sincerely to learn and understand "the highest philosophy," KH sets forth the aim of that study in magnificent language that calls to the very soul of our being: "The Chiefs want a 'Brotherhood of Humanity,' a real Universal Fraternity started; an institution which would make itself known throughout the world and arrest the attention of the highest minds."

Some have asked what KH means by the phrase, "the highest minds." Surely this refers not just to the academically superior—

although there is evidence that the well-educated individual may have a significant role in this work—but to those in whom the mind (*manas*), unencumbered by prejudice or bias, is "highest" in qualities of openness, inquiry, and receptivity to inspiration, compassion, and understanding of the needs of others. In other words, those in whom "the holy lamp of spiritual light [is] burning . . . however dimly."

KH poses the question: "Will you be my co-worker and patiently wait" for whatever signs may be given? How do we today answer this?

LETTER 13

Letter 13 opens with a note of reassurance to Sinnett, who continued to hope for some direct personal contact. Letter 3A refers to Sinnett's experience of a visit by KH during sleep. Evidently, Sinnett's longing to see the Mahatma in the waking state was still strong, and in Letter 13 the Mahatma seems to encourage Sinnett in the possibility of such a visit. But KH also reminds Sinnett that even without such direct contact he can be content with the relationship he has with the Mahatma through this correspondence, "Happy, thrice happy and blessed are they, who have never consented to visit the world beyond their snowcapped mountains; whose physical eyes have never lost sight for one day of the endless ranges of hills, and the long unbroken line of eternal snows! Verily and indeed, do they live in, and have found their Ultima Thule." The phrase "Ultima Thule" figuratively denotes the most distant and highest goal of human aspiration, "Thule" being the name the ancients gave to the most northerly land of Europe. I am reminded of HPB's beautiful words at the conclusion of one of her E.S. Instruction papers:

> Finally, keep ever in mind, the Consciousness that though you see no Master by your bedside, nor hear one audible whisper in the

silence of the still night, yet the Holy Power is about you, the Holy Light is shining into your hour of Spiritual need and aspirations, and it will be no fault of the Masters, or of their humble mouthpiece and servant, if through perversity or moral feebleness some of you cut yourselves off from these higher Potencies. (*CW*, 12:640–41)

Earlier in that same Instruction paper (page 640) HPB writes: "Be not discouraged, but try, ever keep trying, twenty failures are not irremedial if followed by as many undaunted struggles upward." So KH always kindly and gently encouraged Sinnett, assuring him that "it is all but a matter of time" and reminding him that "the world was not evolved between two monsoons, my good friend." He also reminds Sinnett that he was "not asked or expected to revolutionize [his] life habits," although he was "warned not to expect too much" as he was.

This should tell us that we are never asked, certainly never required, to change our habits; any change must come from our own conviction that change is necessary if we are to achieve our goal. No one else dictates what we must do; it is for each of us to determine how we shall live, to be responsible for our own spiritual journey.

Now KH, as Sinnett's mentor, asks Sinnett to see himself clearly as he is, "not as the ideal human image which our emotional fancy always projects for us." This is very useful advice today, for how many of us can bear to see ourselves as we really are, without judgment— which means without either idealizing or condemning ourselves? So, says KH, "Be patient . . . be our helpful co-worker; but in your own sphere, and according to your ripest judgment." Whatever we are at the moment, however we see ourselves, recognizing both our strengths and our weaknesses, we can still do something within our own sphere of action. Only when we act out of our own best judgment, not dependent on the judgment of someone else, can we develop the qualities needed to be of further service in the great work. Hence "the practical value of good motives is best seen when they take the form of deeds."

This letter is relatively brief. Yet it offers Sinnett an optimistic outlook and likewise encourages us in our own efforts, whatever path we decide to take.

LETTERS 14A AND 14B

Letters 14A and 14B are interesting chiefly for their historical value in understanding the early development of the Society's structure, especially after the founders moved to India. Sinnett, we know, was sincerely concerned about the welfare of the Society and undoubtedly expressed that concern to the Mahatma. While not specifically stated, it may be assumed that the Mahatma instructed his chela Damodar to write to Sinnett, giving the point of view of the Indian members. Damodar writes (Letter 14A) that to Indians the Society appeared to be "a religious sect" totally devoted to the study of occultism. We might well compare that comment to the way the general public in the West often considers Theosophy a religion, or at least a sect if not a cult.

Damodar evidently had a clear understanding of the Society's main purpose: that it was to be based "upon the broad Humanitarian principle of Universal Brotherhood." Consequently, he proposes that the study of occultism should be "an entirely secret study." This seems to have been the attitude of many Indian members at that time. Subba Row, for example, felt strongly that the teachings of occultism were too sacred and private to be divulged to the world at large. Damodar echoes this view: "From time immemorial this sacred knowledge has been guarded from the vulgar with great care," and adds that "the world is not yet prepared to hear truth about this subject." It may well have pained Damodar, as it certainly did Subba Row, that so much of "this invaluable treasure," the sacred and hitherto secret knowledge, was being given out through the correspondence with Sinnett and Hume, as well as through HPB's writings.

Damodar is also eager to correct the Indians' misconception that the Society was "under the sole management of the Adepts," emphasizing rather that "the entire executive management is in the hands of the Founders." This misconception had led many of the Indian members to conclude that either the Adepts did not exist or those connected with the Society were of a "very low order" because so many mistakes in management seem to have occurred. On a related note, both Sinnett and Hume, being convinced that Olcott was not a suitable person to give them advice, were eager to see that Olcott, as president of the Society, had no part in the work of the proposed Anglo-Indian or Simla Eclectic Branch of the organization. They both wanted to receive instruction directly from the Mahatmas, as well as to manage their own affairs. Again, all of this is valuable only from a historical point of view, although it may have some parallels with present-day relationships between local Branches and the national or international Societies of which they are a part.

Damodar's discussion of fees may certainly bring a smile to many students, as the issue of whether it is too easy for people to join the Society, or whether the dues are prohibitive for many and admission to the Society should be freely obtainable, still arises occasionally. Damodar's comment that "we need men of principle and serious purpose" echoes his guru's words in Letter 11: "We want true and unselfish hearts; fearless and confiding souls." For Damodar, quality of membership is more important than quantity, a view which many still hold these days. So, concludes Damodar, if the fees seem too high, surely we can admit individuals "who appear especially deserving" but cannot afford the amount by forgiving their dues. Just who is to determine which applicants for membership may be "especially deserving" Damodar does not say. In any event, Letter 14B is the Mahatma's review of Damodar's letter and, "with the exception of fee," approved his chela's views. However, KH subsequently requests Sinnett to "add a paragraph" to Damodar's statement "showing the Society in its true light" and advises him to "Listen to your inner voice."

We may presume from these letters that Damodar, who assisted Olcott and HPB when the Society's Headquarters were in Bombay (now called Mumbai) and accompanied them when the Headquarters were moved to Adyar, where he held the offices of Recording Secretary and Treasurer, was a key player in the development of the Society's administrative structure. Sinnett likewise continued throughout his life to be involved with the Society's administrative affairs, serving for some years as the Society's vice-president and even as acting president for a brief period following Olcott's death and prior to Annie Besant's succession to the presidency.

LETTER 15

One of the longer letters, the original covering both sides of twelve full sheets of paper, Letter 15 is also one of the most interesting early letters. The tone of warm affection reveals the Mahatma's deep respect and concern for Sinnett as well as his eagerness to share as much as possible with his questioning correspondent. Addressing Sinnett in the opening as "My dear friend," as he has from the beginning of the correspondence, KH at the conclusion of this letter calls him his "co-worker," indicating the Mahatma's hope for the work that Sinnett would or could do for the cause. KH is a master of the light touch, with a gentle humor that brings a smile to the reader as it must have done to Sinnett, but the Mahatma can also be extremely serious when writing of the occult tradition and explaining various aspects of esoteric philosophy. The student inevitably feels that KH rather enjoyed writing, perhaps out of a longing to communicate that philosophy as clearly as he could, especially in its bearing on human affairs. This letter also reveals the Adept's remarkable patience in trying to clear away misunderstandings and misapprehensions in the mind of his English correspondent.

The letter opens with encouraging words: "You are certainly on the right path; the path of deeds and actions, not mere words." While applying specifically to Sinnett's efforts as vice-president of the Theosophical Society to either amend the Rules of the organization or ensure that the Rules were followed, the words still carry a strong message for us today. It is easy enough to speak, but do our actions match our expressed intentions? Do we, as the phrase goes, "walk the talk"? The "right path" seems to be one on which what we do is far more important than what we say.

We need to remember that at the time the Mahatma was writing this letter, the Society was just a little over five years old. It was struggling and almost vanishing in the land of its birth; and it was not much stronger in London, where a Branch existed with a few members, mainly Spiritualists, meeting under the leadership of the Hermeticist Anna Kingsford. Now through the work and travel of Olcott and HPB, the Society was slowly gaining a foothold in India. In many ways, though, it seemed truly "the black night of the perishing T.S.," and KH is grateful to Sinnett for the efforts he is making or may be able to make to keep the Theosophical ship afloat.

There is no clue regarding the identity of the "*special delicate task*" with which the Mahatma had been entrusted (presumably by his superior), but in spite of whatever may have occupied his attention, KH seems concerned enough that Sinnett understand a number of matters that he has decided to write "a somewhat lengthy farewell epistle" before the Englishman, with his wife and son, departs from India for a four-to-five-month "home leave" in England. Sinnett must have written the Master that he intended to write a book during his forthcoming long sea journey, and believing that recounting such an experience as evidence for the Mahatmas' existence would add credence to the work, asked again for a direct personal encounter with his teacher. KH agrees that such a "direct communication" might indeed be of "enormous advantage," but Sinnett's request cannot be granted for several reasons stated previously, of which the Mahatma says he will now give a "brief retrospect of principles" involved.

Much of the early part of the letter, then, concerns KH's "refusal" of any "direct communication." He points out that were a personal encounter dependent on himself alone, it might be granted, but obviously KH is subject to a higher authority, in addition to his "enforced compliance with our time honoured *Rules*." Not only does Sinnett's "life-long environment" militate against a face-to-face meeting, says KH, but "the most vital point" in refusing Sinnett's request "concerns as much *your own salvation*" as it does any other factors. This may seem a puzzling statement until we examine it closely. The Mahatma may have been attempting to shield Sinnett from likely ridicule or criticism if his first published book contained an account of meeting a Master face to face.

Studying carefully KH's two examples, first "the case of the Lord Crawford and Balcarres" (Lord Lindsay) and second "the case of Olcott," offers insight into how the Adepts work with different individuals. KH had asked Sinnett to write to Lord Lindsay (see Letters 10 and 12). Presumably Sinnett did initiate a correspondence with the man, since KH refers in Letter 15 to "His Lordship's letter to you" and in the postscript to Letter 15 refers to Lord Lindsay's acquaintance with the disreputable American medium Daniel Home. Whether Sinnett actually met Lord Lindsay during his sojourn in England at this time, or even later when he was permanently resident in London, is not recorded.

A number of points in KH's comments about Lindsay deserve consideration—first, that the man had "an exhaustless source of magnetic fluid which . . . he could call out in torrents." What, we may ask, is meant by "magnetic fluid"? Might this be an aspect of *prana* or even of that mysterious power called *Fohat* in *The Secret Doctrine*? Is it the basis of what is known as magnetic or psychic healing as well as other psychic abilities? A number of books on the subject are helpful in this study; particularly recommended is the little work *The Psychic Sense* by Phoebe Payne and Laurence Bendit.

Here I remind the reader of the end of Letter 12 where KH calls on Sinnett to decide whether he would have "the highest philosophy or simple exhibitions of occult powers." This same choice was before Lord Lindsay, who evidently chose the "whirling, showy, glittering world, full of insatiable ambition," the psychic realm of phenomena. And so KH laments, "How many recruits could we not have . . . if no sacrifice were exacted." There is indeed much we can learn from a study of the Mahatma's comments on "the case of the Lord Crawford and Balcarres."

Before we leave Lord Lindsay, there is one further point the student should consider. KH writes of the "nobler study of MAN as an integral Brahm, the microcosm free and entirely independent of either the help or control of the invisible agencies" that the Spiritualists refer to as "Spirits." We might call such "invisible agencies" elementaries, the denizens of the realms in which human beings function. Perhaps the simplest explanation of the human being as "an integral Brahm" is found in the oft-repeated statement "Man is a god in the becoming," indicating the god-like nature within us, the true Self. In his first letter to Sinnett, KH told the Englishman that it is "the *deific* powers in man" (page 2) that are of paramount concern. It is to that study that KH again calls attention here.

Turning then to the "case of Olcott" and the reason why the president–founder was "permitted to communicate face to face" with the Mahatmas, KH informs Sinnett that, had it not been for such encounters, Olcott might have "shown less zeal and devotion" to the work of the Society. Olcott himself questioned why he was so favored, writing in *Old Diary Leaves*:

> People have often thought it very strange, in fact incomprehensible, that, of all those who have helped in this Theosophical movement, often at the heaviest self-sacrifice, I should have been the only one so favoured with personal experiences of and with the Mahatmas, that the fact of Their existence is a matter of as actual knowledge as the existence of my own relatives or intimate friends. I cannot account for it myself. I know what I know, but not why many of my colleagues do not know as much. As it stands, many people have told

me that they pin their faith in the Mahatmas upon my unchanging and unimpeached personal testimony, which supplements the statements of HPB. Probably I was so blessed because I had to launch the ship "Theosophy" with HPB for HPB's Masters, and to steer it through many maelstroms and cyclones, when nothing short of actual knowledge of the sound basis of our movement would have influenced me to stick to my post. (1:218–19)

One can only wonder what might have been the Society's fate in its early days had Olcott not had this direct personal experience. We may also note in passing that he too must have had "an exhaustless source of magnetic fluid," for we know that the president–founder was quite familiar with the subject of magnetism and used his own magnetic, or mesmeric, powers in performing numerous healings.

KH next informs Sinnett of the three "only possible means" by which a direct communication with the Mahatma could take place. First, the "material impediment" would have to be overcome, since KH and Sinnett in their physical vehicles are in different places. Second is the "spiritual impediment," which prevents the two from meeting "in our astral form." While KH says this is an obstacle for Sinnett, we may recall that earlier the Englishman had a dream in which he saw KH "in astral form" (note Letter 3A).

The third "impediment" concerns the auditory reception by which Sinnett hopes to "hear" the voice of the Mahatma. KH implies that this was the method by which HPB responded to the "call" of the Mahatmas, and Olcott also refers to her ability to hear her Master's voice at the time she was writing *Isis Unveiled* (see *ODL* vol. 1, chs. 8 and 14). KH's analysis of the third possible mode of direct communication between the Mahatma and Sinnett deserves careful study, since in order to "hear" the Master's voice two conditions must be met: first, "one's *spiritual* senses" must be open; second, one "must have ... mastered the great secret ... of ... abolishing all the impediments of space." It is worth noting that KH was writing before the advent of radio, telephone, and other modern means for the transmission of sound. From the occult point of view, a complete understanding of "the occult powers of air (*akas*)" is required for auditory reception, reminding us of KH's statement in his first letter (page 3), that "a thorough knowledge of *Akas*, its combinations and properties" was necessary to understand any of the phenomena that could be produced.

KH goes on to mention a "still more serious inconvenience . . . an almost insurmountable obstacle" that affects even the continued correspondence with Sinnett. This is the question of terminology, of finding words to convey the occult philosophy. So KH laments, "How shall I teach you to read and write or even comprehend a language of which no alphabet *palpable*, or words *audible* to you have yet been invented!" KH recognizes his inability, at this stage of the correspondence, to make the Englishman understand his explanations "of even physical phenomena, let alone the spiritual rationale."

The question of terminology occurs again and again in the correspondence, and we need to remember that in the Society's early years there was still some indefiniteness concerning vocabulary. Elsewhere in the letters, we find the Mahatma M writing to Sinnett: "You ought to come to some agreement as to terms used when discussing cyclic evolutions. Our terms are untranslatable" (Letter 46, page 129). We might well keep this in mind even today as we use Theosophical terms thinking we know precisely what they mean!

Continuing in Letter 15, KH writes that unless "the simple transmission of ideas" is "unencumbered by the conditions of matter" so that a "union of your mind with ours" occurs, it is "impossible either for [the Western mind] to comprehend or for us [the Adepts] to express in their own languages anything of that delicate seemingly ideal machinery of the Occult Kosmos." What an amazing statement this is, one that needs careful pondering to explore its full meaning. No wonder that, throughout the letters, Sinnett is told again and again to awaken his intuition, for it may be the only means by which he, or anyone, can come to a fuller understanding of the esoteric philosophy.

One has to begin at the beginning in the study of the occult philosophy, as KH points out. "Only thus does it [the philosophy], strengthening and refining those mysterious links of sympathy between intelligent men—the temporarily isolated fragments of the universal Soul and the cosmic Soul itself—bring them into full rapport." This point is stressed in a number of the letters: the need for the *chela*, or pupil, to bring his (or her) mind *en rapport* with the mind of the Teacher. When such rapport is established, writes KH, those awakened sympathies connect the individual with "that energetic chain which binds together the material and Immaterial Kosmos, Past, Present, and Future, and quicken his perceptions so as to clearly grasp, not merely all things of matter, but of Spirit also."

What is that "energetic chain"? Could it be related to that primordial dynamism called *Fohat,* the essence of "cosmic electricity," which HPB calls "the dynamic energy of Cosmic Ideation"? (See the numerous references to Fohat throughout *The Secret Doctrine,* especially 1:16.) Is it, more simply, what we call the One Life that "binds together" all things from highest Spirit to lowest matter? And what is meant by the union of past, present, and future? These are questions that serious students need to ponder deeply, for only such pondering will bring insights leading to understanding. Much later in the correspondence (see Letter 44, page 118), Sinnett and Hume are told: "In our doctrine you will find necessary the synthetic method; you will have to embrace the whole—that is to say to blend the *macrocosm* and microcosm together—before you are enabled to study the parts separately." Here in Letter 15, could KH be hinting at this great truth, even as he writes of the "insurmountable difficulties in the way of attaining not only *Absolute* but even primary knowledge of Occult Science"?

Yet another barrier to KH's efforts to communicate with Sinnett is the Englishman's total unfamiliarity with an esoteric language of sound and color. Hence KH poses the question: "How could you make yourself understood—*command* in fact, those semi-intelligent Forces, whose means of communicating with us are not through spoken words but through sounds, and colours, in correlations between the vibrations of the two? For sound, light and colours are the main factors in forming these grades of Intelligences, these beings, of whose very existence you have no conception."

Many clairvoyants, including such well-known Theosophists as Geoffrey Hodson and Dora Kunz, have sought to describe their own observations of those "semi-intelligent Forces." Whether known as elementals, angels, devas, or by other names, they populate a realm just beyond our normal vision of which we can become aware if we are sensitive to their presence. There is today a considerable literature on the subject and certainly a growing recognition that we are surrounded by entities that clothe themselves in sound and color. (An excellent overview of the subject is *Angels and Mortals: Their Co-Creative Power* compiled by Maria Parisen.)

As Letter 15 continues, KH seems eager to help Sinnett in "the noble work you have just begun . . . the task you are so bravely undertaking," which is, of course, the writing of his first book. But the Mahatma cautions him—giving him some *avera pro gratis*, "free advice"—that "those who engage themselves in the occult sciences . . . 'must either reach the goal or *perish*. Once fairly started on the way to the great Knowledge, to doubt is to risk insanity; to come to a dead stop is to fall; to recede is to tumble backward, headlong into an abyss.'"* A truly staggering statement and a warning! It is as relevant today as when the Mahatma penned it, and every sincere seeker needs to take it to heart. KH points out further that Sinnett may be sincere *now*, but "Are you so sure of yourself, as to the *future*?" How many have bravely started out on the spiritual path only to fall by the wayside?

---

* I am indebted to a fellow student, Terry Hunt, for pointing out that the Mahatma here is quoting directly from Eliphas Levi's *Dogme et Ritual de la Haute Magie*, first published in 1855; a later English translation by Arthur Edward Waite appeared as *Transcendental Magic: Its Doctrine and Ritual*. In the French edition of 1948 (1:115), we read: "Dans la voie des hautes sciences, il ne faut pas s'engager temerairement, mais, une fois en marche, il faut arriver ou perir. Douter, c'est devenir fous; s'arreter, c'est tomber, reculer, c'est se precipiter dans un gouffre" (In the pursuit of the superior sciences, one must not proceed timidly. Once started, one must either arrive or perish. To doubt is to become mad, to stop is to fall, to back up is to plunge into an abyss)."

How certain are we that we shall persevere despite all difficulties and obstacles? Only we ourselves, in the profound silence of our deepest meditation, can answer the Mahatma's question.

Incidentally, KH refers, in the paragraph just cited, to his "last letter," and there are two further references to such a letter (on pages 50 and 51). The Mahatma tells Sinnett that he can publish anything he, KH, has written but "*not to use one single word or passage from my last letter to you.*" That letter no longer exists, or at least it is not among the published letters we are studying. Sinnett, it may be noted, was told to "lay it by in a separate and sealed envelope." We can only assume that Sinnett followed the Mahatma's instruction and that later it was lost.

Continuing with Letter 15, on page 48 the Mahatma writes especially beautifully concerning the nature of an Adept. He tells Sinnett that the Mahatmas are not "the heartless, morally dried up mummies" some might suppose from reading Bulwer-Lytton's then popular occult novel, *Zanoni*, in which the hero, Mejnour, is quite an unrealistic figure. He goes on to say that

> Until final emancipation reabsorbs the *Ego*, it *must* be conscious of the purest sympathies called out by the esthetic effects of high art, its tenderest cords respond to the call of the holiest and noblest *human* attachments. . . . The greater the progress towards deliverance, the less this will be the case until, to crown all, human and purely individual personal feelings—blood-ties and friendship, patriotism and race predilection—all will give away, to become blended into one universal feeling, the only true and holy, the only unselfish and Eternal one—Love, an Immense Love for humanity—as a *Whole*! For it is "Humanity" which is the great Orphan, the only disinherited one upon the earth . . . and it is the duty of every man who is capable of an unselfish impulse to do something, however little, for its welfare.

Truly no more magnificent words have been written to describe our ultimate goal and the work to be done as we move along the path to "final emancipation." Just previous to this passage KH has said,

"Answering Addison . . . it *is* 'the business of magic to humanise our natures with compassion' for the whole mankind as all living beings." (Joseph Addison, 1672–1719, a witty and urbane English essayist, had written that it was *not* the business of magic to humanize our natures.) Perhaps, then, our "business" is to become fully human, for only then can we become spiritual.

The passage just quoted includes the oft-quoted metaphor, "humanity the great orphan." While a full explanation of the phrase would involve a review of human development through the rounds and races, as depicted by HPB in *The Secret Doctrine*, in brief, it refers to the idea that the great Beings who were the "parents" of our humanity returned to the superior spheres from which they had descended, thus leaving humanity "orphaned." It is said that these Beings did not leave until they had given infant humanity the seed that, through its own internal dynamic, must grow into the flower of adeptship: the goal set before us. Two works by Geoffrey Barborka are especially helpful in understanding the orphaning of humanity: *The Story of Human Evolution* and *The Peopling of the Earth*.

Reading further in Letter 15, we find the Mahatma making an endearing and heart-warming admission: He is "not exempt from some of the terrestrial attachments," and he is "still attracted towards *some* . . . more than toward others. He comments: "Philanthropy . . . has never killed in me either individual preferences of friendship, love for my next of kin, or the ardent feeling of patriotism." (In his first letter to Hume, KH uses the words, "I, and every other Indian patriot," thus clearly identifying himself as Indian.) To emphasize his answer to humanity's "cry" of pain, KH quotes two lines from Sir Edwin Arnold's *The Light of Asia*, although juxtaposing them, since the first appears almost at the end of Book 4 of that work, while the second line is found at the end of Book 3.

On several occasions through the letters, both M and KH tell Sinnett that he has failed to understand their nature. So here, in Letter 15, as KH is speaking of himself, it may not be amiss to quote HPB concerning his noble human qualities. Although she was not

KH's chela, she knew him personally and acted as his amanuensis for the transmission of many of the letters. In *LBS* (page 110), she speaks of KH's karma when he undertook the correspondence with Sinnett: "If you [Sinnett] have never given a thought to what may be His [KH's] suffering during the *human* intervals of His Mahatmaship—then you have something yet to learn. . . . He says He is glad He is yet no Mejnoor, no dried up plant, and that had He to suffer over and over again—He would still do the same [i.e., correspond with the Englishman] for He knows that real good for humanity has come out from all this suffering." She continues, "He suffers more, perhaps, than any one of us. . . . Even *you* can never love Him as well as He loves you—*that particle of Humanity which did its best to help on and benefit Humanity*—'the great orphan' He speaks of in one of His letters."

In another letter (*LBS*, 23), HPB calls KH "the brightest, best, purest of all" the Adepts. And on yet another occasion (*LBS*, 34), she speaks of him as "the grandest, noblest, purest of men," adding that he is "one who young as he is may have become Chohan and perfect Boddhisatwa [*sic*] long ago, were it not for his really divine pity for the world." KH himself, in a later letter (Letter 70C) speaks of a "*full adept*," adding, "which unhappily I am not." As we progress through the letters, we will find many more statements by both KH and M concerning the nature of adeptship, but none is more beautiful than this one in Letter 15.

Before leaving the paragraph in which KH speaks of his "terrestrial attachments," we should note his statement that there are "enormous differences . . . between 'Hatha' and 'Raj' Yog." Some familiarity with the various schools of Yoga may be helpful in the study of the letters, at minimum the distinction between Hatha and Raja Yoga, and why the emphasis in Theosophical thought has been on Raja Yoga, and Jnana Yoga. Many will recall HPB's well-known statement recorded in the "Bowen Notes" (referred to in the commentary on KH's first letter to Hume): "The true Student of *The Secret Doctrine* is a Jnana Yogi, this Path of Yoga is the True Path for the Western student."

As Letter 15 continues, KH writes (bottom of page 49): "'Precipitation' in your case having become unlawful. . . ." There has been considerable speculation about the reason for this apparently temporary prohibition. Some have suggested that it had to do with Hume's actions and the statement in Letter 85B (page 258) that "we are forbidden to use one particle of our powers in connection with the *Eclectic* [the Branch in Simla of which Hume was president]." Others have proposed that the prohibition arose out of the Mahatma's knowledge of the consequences that would arise from statements in Letter 12—the "Kiddle incident." Or the Mahatma may have been prohibited from using occult powers to produce a precipitation simply because normal means of communication were available (pen and paper, though they were "in short supply").

As KH draws his long letter to a close, he returns to the subject of Sinnett's proposed book, writing that "the idea is an excellent one," and adding, "Theosophy needs such help, and the results will be what you anticipate in England." Sinnett's first book, *The Occult World*, did indeed give great stimulus to the work of the Society; published shortly after his arrival in England in 1881, the book soon went into its second edition. A wealthy American, Sam Ward, who appears in some of the later letters, ordered a ten-cent edition to be printed in New York so that it might be "scattered broadcast throughout America" (Ransom, *A Short History of the Theosophical Society*, 157).

The Mahatma proceeds to suggest to Sinnett just what should be in the book, particularly that he should pay attention to "small circumstances," being sure "not to omit one jot or tittle of collateral evidence" concerning the phenomena he reports. The emphasis KH places on giving attention to "such trifles," which will serve "as the most powerful shield for yourself against ridicule and sneers," recalls the advice HPB gave to a group in London who asked her for instruction. In a letter written in 1887, available to us by means of a copy that the Countess Wachtmeister included in her diary, HPB asked her students: "Why have you never followed those daily records in the life of every one of you—those trifling events of which that life is composed, for no better proof can you ever get of the invisible Presence among yourselves?" Toward the end of the letter she says: "There are no more *meaningless* or trifling circumstances in his [the student's] life, for each is a link purposely placed in the chain of events that have to lead him forward to the 'Golden Gate' or the 'Gates of Gold.' Each step, each person he meets with, every word uttered may be a word purposely placed in the day's sentence with the purpose of giving certain importance to the chapter it belongs to and such or another (Karmic) meaning to the volume of life." (For the complete letter see Michael Gomes's "Extract of a Letter from H.P.B. to a London Group, 1887," *The Theosophist*, July 1988.)

Sinnett certainly followed KH's advice, for as one reads *The Occult World*, with its reports of occult phenomena that took place at Simla, one is aware of the journalist's careful eye for detail. However, Sinnett does not seem to have followed through on the Mahatma's next suggestion for the book, which was "to show that this Theosophy is no new candidate for the world's attention, but only the restatement of principles which have been recognised from the very infancy of mankind." The Mahatma proposes that Sinnett trace the historical sequence of the presentation of Theosophical ideas "through the successive evolutions of philosophical schools . . . illustrated with accounts of the experimental demonstrations of occult power ascribed to various thaumaturgists." What a tall order! Such a work would surely be a life-time undertaking. Even so, many students have written in general about the Eastern and Western roots of the Theosophical tradition. And probably every Theosophical speaker or writer has cited at one time or another towering figures such as Pythagoras, Plato, Sri Shankaracharya, Nagarjuna, and the founders of the major religions to illustrate the presence of Theosophical principles through the history of world thought.

In recent years a number of scholarly works have been written documenting the existence of a "theosophical current" through various historical periods. Two in particular are: *The Theosophical Enlightenment* by Dr. Joscelyn Godwin, professor of music at Colgate University, and *Theosophy, Imagination, Tradition: Studies in Western Esotericism* by Dr. Antoine Faivre, professor of religious studies at the Sorbonne. A number of excellent articles on the historicity of Theosophical ideas have also appeared in the journal *Theosophical History*, edited by Dr. James A. Santucci of the University of California, Fullerton.

Continuing with Letter 15, KH states (page 51) that it was "the tidal-wave of phenomena, with its varied effects upon human thought and feeling" that "made the revival of Theosophical enquiry an indispensable necessity." Can we compare the interest in phenomena that characterized late-nineteenth-century movements such as Spiritualism with the more recent interest in phenomena such as channeling and other psychic occurrences? To what extent is Theosophical "enquiry" still a necessity? What opportunities are before us today when it comes to addressing or responding to such a "tidal-wave"?

KH's words "What I meant by the 'Forlorn Hope'" is the third reference to what must be the unpublished (and presumably lost) letter from which Sinnett was not to quote when writing his book. Notably, in Letter 45 (page 125), the Mahatma M refers to KH's use of those words, "Forlorn Hope," so apparently both Mahatmas were familiar with the contents of that missing letter. Be that as it may, what KH writes concerning those words is significant for us. There may be times when we feel we are battling against overwhelming odds in our efforts to disseminate Theosophical ideas. At those times we need to ask ourselves: Have we seen, as evidently Sinnett had, the "large purpose" for which the Society was established? Do we keep that vision before us in all we do to further its work?

Many still ask why the Mahatmas did not take a direct hand in guiding the Society, and why they do not today give personal direction to its efforts. KH makes clear to Sinnett that the Mahatmas could not control or even intervene in the management of the Society's affairs, "nor was it the plan," and we need to be clear on this matter. Perhaps it is a question of karmic consequences: theirs and ours. We are left free to do what we can, to make our own mistakes and to benefit from our small triumphs. We can supplement KH's statements in this letter with HPB's remarks in her essay published as *The Original Programme of the Theosophical Society*: "The two chief Founders were not told what they had to do, how they had to bring about and quicken the growth of the Society and results desired; nor had they any definite ideas given them concerning the outward organization—all this being left entirely with themselves. . . . But if the two Founders were not told *what they had to do*, they were distinctly instructed about *what they should never do*."

Letter 15 contains not only much of significance but also much that is relevant today in terms of our attitudes, our aspirations, and our work for the Society. The earnest student will find much to explore that has been left without comment here. KH writes toward the close of the letter, "All quick thinkers are hard to impress—in a flash they are out and away in 'full cry'—before half understanding what one wants to have them think." Let us not then be too quick to think we understand all that KH has written in this and other letters, but, giving attention to what seem to be "trifles," probe more deeply into the meaning of his message.

LETTER 16

Although very brief, Letter 16 is interesting for several reasons. First, it was received by Sinnett in Ceylon when he and his family were en route to England; however its transmittal was through Olcott rather than through HPB. The transmittal note accompanying the letter is found in *LBS* (page 363), with Sinnett's own record as to the day and time it was received. That note reads: "Dear O., Forward this immediately to A. P. Sinnett, and do not breathe a word of it to HPB. Let her alone, and do not go near her for a few days. The storm will subside. K.H.L.S."

The cause of the "storm" is found in Olcott's *ODL* (2:293). There the Colonel relates that arrangements had been made for his return visit to Ceylon to begin with "the collection of a National Education Fund to promote the education of Buddhist boys and girls." The "scheme," he writes, had the approval of both the Mahatmas and HPB. However, almost on the eve of his departure, HPB wanted him to cancel the engagement in order to assist her with editing *The Theosophist*. When Olcott refused, "she fell into a white rage" and, as he relates:

> She shut herself up in her room a whole week, refusing to see me, but sending me formal notes of one kind or another, among them one in which she notified me that the Lodge [a reference to the Occult Brotherhood] would have nothing more to do with the Society or myself, and I might go to Timbuctoo if I liked. I simply said that my tour having been fully approved of by the Lodge, I should carry it through, even though I never saw the face of a Master again; and that I did not believe them to be such vacillating and whimsical creatures. . . . Her ill-temper burnt itself out at last.

The opening paragraph of Letter 16 refers to HPB's condition at the time and indicates why the communication is sent via Olcott. KH was apparently eager to communicate with Sinnett during his stopover in Ceylon so he could urge Sinnett to encourage the Buddhist education program for which Olcott himself was also to travel there. KH even tells Sinnett the person he is to contact (via telegraph) in Galle. The identity of "*another* person," whom the Mahatma will have HPB contact, is unclear—perhaps a chela resident in Ceylon or even a Brother known to KH.

The signature of this letter, too, presents a mystery: "KH and ———." Again, perhaps this is the "friend" referred to as "*another* person," or perhaps KH's chela Djual Khul, (also referred to as DK, and with various spellings of "Khul") who was with KH when he was writing his long farewell letter to Sinnett. Or it may have been the chela who transmitted the letter to Olcott for forwarding to Sinnett.

We can identify the "friends in Europe" with whom Sinnett was to consult, as they are mentioned in previous letters. Among them are the members of the Society in London, as well as Lord Lindsay and Dr. Wyld, who had such "original" ideas about the Brothers. As the letter opens with the salutation "My dear Ambassador," KH evidently hopes that Sinnett really will correct erroneous ideas about the Mahatmas and present a true picture of them, particularly in the work he intends to write.

LETTER 17

As stated in the prefatory note to Letter 17, this is probably the only letter Sinnett received while he was in England on home leave. For whatever reason, he preserved the envelope, perhaps because it had a French stamp affixed to it with the indication that the letter was posted in Paris. This fact has prompted speculation regarding its transmission, since the Mahatma records that he is writing from an isolated area of eastern Tibet. The opening sentence paints a beautiful, almost poetic word picture of KH's location, demonstrating again how skillfully KH could use the English language.

Sinnett had evidently written to KH, perhaps before even reaching England, asking once again whether the Mahatma could visit him in "tangible form." KH writes back that this is not possible either astrally or physically, although he will be and often has been with Sinnett in thought. The reason is the atmosphere in London as well as the situation with Sinnett himself, a reminder to Sinnett that the aura of meat eating and alcohol consuming surrounding him is an obstacle to any visit.

The comments on Sinnett's "future book" are interesting from the point of view that the Mahatma could not have physically seen the work but is obviously familiar with its contents. Perhaps he had scanned it mentally, for even while praising it, KH seems dismayed that Sinnett has been "too cautious" rather than writing boldly of what he knows to be the truth. The allusion to "Mr. Wallace's work" seems to refer to some publication by Alfred Russell Wallace, the noted English scientist who, independently of Charles Darwin, developed a theory of evolution. It is known that Wallace was much interested in Spiritualism and had written on that subject in addition to writing scientific papers.

KH now seems in a deeply reflective mood—following his own thoughts, as he says later in the letter, and sharing with Sinnett the nature of all that he, as an Adept, has experienced. His definition of "world," (bottom of page 54) "meaning that of individual existences," is reminiscent of HPB's response when a member of her *Secret Doctrine* class, several years after the writing of this letter, asked her what she meant by the term. According to the "Bowen Notes," HPB responded: "'The World' means Man living in the Personal Nature." These two statements are worth considering in depth, perhaps comparing them with our usual definition of the word.

Next KH gives a remarkable definition of "occult sciences," in effect saying that occultism is "reason elevated to supersensuous Wisdom," which we might translate as *manas* illumined by *buddhi*. KH seems to be speaking from personal experience when he writes: "There comes a moment in the life of an adept when the hardships he has passed through" are well rewarded.

What are those hardships, we might ask? What is the nature of the training for adeptship that yields such a rich reward as to be "accorded an instantaneous, implicit insight into every first truth"? And what is meant by the phrase "every first truth"? This entire section of the letter deserves careful consideration. How is it possible to move from truths perceived by the intellect alone to that state in which "the adept sees and feels and lives in the very source of all fundamental truths— the Universal Spiritual Essence of Nature"? Is this, perhaps, to come to the very essence of Truth itself, to experience the supreme truth of the Oneness of all?

And what does it mean for someone, especially a Mahatma, to labor "for more than a quarter of a century night and day to keep" (page

55) his place within the Brotherhood, all for the service of humanity? This work for humankind, whether recognized or not, is the "duty" of a Mahatma. A much later letter (Letter 126, page 422), includes the wonderful statement: "Duty, let me tell you, is for us stronger than any friendship or even love; as without this abiding principle which is the indestructible cement that has held together for so many milleniums, the scattered custodians of nature's grand secrets—our Brotherhood, nay, our doctrine itself—would have crumbled long ago." And Morya writes so beautifully (Letter 29, page 92): "I am as I was; and, as I was and am, so am I likely always to be—the slave of my duty to the Lodge and mankind." It is worthwhile pondering how and in what respect the Mahatmas perform this "duty" to humanity.

As we consider KH's reflections, evidently stimulated by reading Sinnett's book or at least becoming familiar with its contents, we can begin to understand why the Mahatma felt disappointed that Sinnett had not written with more conviction about the Brotherhood and about his contact with KH particularly. At the same time, KH recognizes that the Englishman's efforts may "teach the world but one single letter from the alphabet of Truth," and for that, of course, Sinnett will have his reward.

KH's question as to Sinnett's view on the "'mystics' of Paris and London" is to some extent answered by the Englishman in later correspondence. Among such "mystics" were Stainton Moses and Anna Kingsford, both of whom figure rather prominently in subsequent letters.

LETTER 18

The lengthy prefatory note to Letter 18 gives fascinating details of the way Sinnett received this letter, a significant one among the entire correspondence, as it plunges us into some of the most profound esoteric teachings. The letter opens on a warm and affectionate note, the Mahatma welcoming Sinnett back to India after his stay in England and greeting him as "brilliant author," Sinnett's first book, *The Occult World*, having been published.

During his stay in London, Sinnett has made some valuable contacts, particularly among the leading Spiritualists of the day—the so-called "Elect" to which the Mahatma makes reference. One may imagine that during that time at home Sinnett and his new friends engaged in many far-ranging discussions about occult philosophy, the production of the phenomena reported in his book, and the role of HPB and her Teachers in the events about which he has written, all leading to further questions. We see a touch of the Mahatma's humor as he writes to Sinnett that now "you will become an incarnate note of interrogation." And certainly many of the succeeding letters contain numerous questions about the philosophy the Mahatmas were seeking to convey through both Sinnett and Hume. But KH cautions Sinnett that it may not be possible to respond to every question, for he feels "a hand on my throat whenever trenching on the limits of forbidden topics"—the hand of his superior, the Mahachohan. Yet he admits that he may trespass beyond what is normally permitted "*pro bono publico*," for the public good, perhaps because he is confident that Sinnett will ultimately write another book sharing the teachings with all who are interested.

As a sidelight on KH's reference to his superior as the "Rock of Ages," I include here some comments on the Mahachohan, to whom HPB refers in a letter to Sinnett (*LBS*, 22): "KH and M and the old Chohan." Mary K. Neff, in her personal copy of *LBS*, inserted a marginal note: "There was now a new one; the holder of the office had changed." While she does not document this statement, it is underscored by Fritz Kunz near the conclusion of his article "The Ray Key," published in *The Theosophist* in 1935:

The Personage who occupied the office of Mahachohan on our globe when the T.S. was first instituted and during its early years has given place to another. The current office holder is not the Chohan beloved of the Master KH, whose directions he digested and which have been published as the first letter in *Letters from the Masters of the Wisdom*, First Series, and to whom he referred as the most beloved of all Hobilgans.* The current office holder, in response to the needs of the time, is in appearance ascetic, incisive, and rapid and final in his decisions. The needs of our time, rapid in movement, have evoked him.

We do know that at the beginning of the correspondence, KH's superior agreed, although with some reluctance, to the exchange of letters between the two Englishmen and the Mahatmas. From the outset it was considered an experiment, a point that is emphasized toward the end of the correspondence (Letter 128, page 428). We know from various statements by both KH and HPB (see reference to *LBS*, 110 in comments on Letter 15) that the Mahatma assumed personal responsibility for what he was doing, but always with the acknowledgement that he had his superior's permission. In letters preceding this one KH speaks of the Mahachohan as "our venerable Khobilgan" (Letter 13, page 40) and again as "the sternest of Khobilgans" (Letter 15, page 43).

Perhaps because he felt he might have overstepped the limits of the permissible with regard to what he has shared with Sinnett, KH compares *The Occult World* to *Le Quart Livre*, the fourth in François Rabelais' series of five works, all satirical in nature, discussing education, politics, and philosophy. For that work, Rabelais received censure from the Sorbonne as well as from Parliament, and for a time

---

* *Hobilgan* is a variant spelling of *Khobilgan*; other variant spellings are *Khubilkhanor* and *Khulbikhan*. A Mongolian term, it is equivalent to the Tibetan terms *(T)Chutuktu* and *Shaberon*, said to refer to "reincarnations, not of Buddha, but of his Buddha-like divine spirit" (*Theosophical Glossary*). Further information may be found in a most interesting article by HPB, "Lamas and Druses," first published in *The Theosophist*, June 1881, now available in *CW* 3:175–89. Detailing the Lamaic hierarchy, HPB lists five "Hubilgans" and states that the Shaberons "are one degree lower."

was in considerable physical danger. Naturally KH is concerned now with the Mahachohan's reception of Sinnett's work, so playing on the name of Rabelais' book, the Mahatma suggests that "the quarter hour" may be striking. The equivalent might be the contemporary expression "the eleventh hour," indicating the approach of some catastrophe. One may speculate that the Mahatma endured some uncomfortable interviews with his chief, perhaps the more severe in proportion to his efforts to bring light into the materialistic Western mind. While some results were excellent, apparently some were not so good, and undoubtedly the Mahachohan held KH responsible.

The opening paragraph of the letter concludes with a warning: "We must all be *blindfolded* before we can pass onward." We need to ask ourselves: to what and how are we "blindfolded" and, above all, why is this necessary? Students familiar with the Masonic tradition will recognize the symbolism in KH's words. It appears that in all the mystery schools the neophyte entered with eyes covered, symbolic of an inner state of darkness. Pondering the Mahatma's words may reveal further meanings.

KH also refers to his own work, which he spoke of in Letter 15 as "*a special delicate task I have been entrusted with,*" concerning which he now comments that it is "one of the unfortunate necessities of life that imperial needs do sometimes force one apparently to ignore the claims of friendship." He must not only fulfill the task assigned to him but also—a necessity that he also considered "imperial"—give attention to Sinnett's "future welfare." KH's karma presumably arises from his obligation to the Fraternity of which he is a part, on the one hand, and from his relationship with Sinnett and all that Sinnett might do in the future, on the other. Having opened the door, as it were, to instructing Sinnett, KH certainly seems eager to continue that instruction, even though he is, as he says in this letter, "a lonely labourer in the field . . . refused higher help."

Then he confides to Sinnett, "We are playing a risky game and the stakes are human souls." We need to give serious thought to this statement. Why was imparting as much of the occult philosophy as could be shared with the Englishman a "risky game"? Perhaps speaking of the esoteric wisdom outside the secret schools and ashrams in which it had been kept from time immemorial posed a risk for the Mahatmas. For knowledge is power, and knowledge misused for selfish purposes can lead to the corruption of power. Could disseminating the wisdom tradition still be considered today a "risky game"? As we consider such questions, we may well ponder our own responsibility in sharing whatever of the philosophy we have absorbed. And what part does our motive play in seeking and then sharing more and more of that philosophy? Yet for the sake of humanity's redemption, KH was willing to take on the karma of working with Sinnett to bring this wisdom to the Western world. We will return to this subject when we examine some of the final passages in this very long letter.

The scope of KH's karmic responsibility for Sinnett's "welfare" may well have included the repercussions this letter was destined to have as a result of Sinnett's indiscretion in making copious extracts from it for the leading Spiritualist William Stainton Moses. Presumably, KH hoped that Sinnett's meeting with Moses during his visit home, particularly with the publication of *The Occult World*, would awaken within Spiritualist circles a deeper and more accurate understanding of the occult philosophy. The attention KH gives to Moses in Letter 18 indicates the regard KH had for him as a possible candidate to aid in bringing about such a change in Western thought.

Sinnett, too, must have recognized the influence that Moses, along with Mrs. Anna Kingsford, a Hermeticist and later president of the London Lodge, could have in forwarding the Theosophical movement. He evidently recounted to the Mahatma a dream ("shall we call it a vision?" asks KH) he had involving himself, Moses, and Mrs. Kingsford. KH reminds Sinnett not to forget the Society as a key part of the "vision." Remembering KH's comment in Letter 3A (page 10) that he planned to be "near" the Englishman one night, one wonders whether the Mahatma might have played some part in the production of that dream, or vision. Whether this conjecture is true or not, the key point is that KH agrees with Sinnett's "vision" that he,

Stainton Moses, and Mrs. Kingsford were "all parts of a large plan for the manifestations of occult philosophy to the world." The Mahatma must have rejoiced at the prospect, which seemed at the time so bright, but such a collaboration was not to be. (A lesson can be learned here. We sometimes place hope for future workers in promising candidates, only to see them drop by the wayside; nevertheless, we must give every aspirant who comes our way the opportunity to aid in the work.)

Since so much of Letter 18 is devoted to Moses—and there is much to learn from KH's comments about that gentleman—more needs to be said about him. "Moses" was said to be a corrupt form of his real name, Moseyn. A leader in the Spiritualist movement, Colonel Olcott described him as "a progressive, truth-seeking, highly educated" person (see *ODL*, 1:300). Often signing himself "M. A. Oxon," Moses had a guide whom he called "Imperator," usually designated in the letters by the symbol + . There is much speculation concerning the identity of this control, intimated at one time as one of the Brothers and at other times as some other entity, perhaps an elemental, or again, perhaps Moses' own higher Self.

Moses' associate in the Spiritualist movement, Charles Carlton Massey, is also mentioned throughout the letters, including here in Letter 18 (page 58), as one who might help Sinnett in the work. Massey was an English lawyer who visited the United States in 1875 to verify for himself Olcott's accounts of the phenomena at the Eddy home in Vermont. One of the first members of the Society at the time of its organization in New York, and later a founder and first president of the Theosophical Society in England, Massey was also a founder of the Society for Psychical Research, of which Moses became one of the vice-presidents. Both Moses and Massey resigned their membership of the Society after the infamous Hodgson Report was issued. KH makes a comment worth considering about Massey (page 58): that he has "every requisite for a *student* of occultism, but none for an *adept*."

About KH's statement concerning Olcott (page 58), that he is "in *exile*—fighting his way back to *salvation*," we may note that the president–founder was sent, presumably by the Mahatmas or at least by his own guru, M, to Ceylon for a time—the unfortunate result of an article he wrote about the phenomena that took place at the Sinnetts' home in Simla. The article, "A Day with Madame Blavatsky," though not intended for publication, was sent to Damodar in Bombay, and was somehow picked up by *The Times of India*, leading to a great deal of controversy and misunderstanding. As KH says, Olcott was "compromised more than you imagine by his Simla indiscretions." Olcott, however, made positive use of his time in Ceylon, establishing an Education Fund for Buddhist schools, and it was at this time that he wrote *The Buddhist Catechism*, which continues to be a major text on Buddhism.

To continue with the story as it unfolds in Letter 18, KH is at pains to help Sinnett understand not only who Moses' "spirit-guide" may be but as much as possible about the man's "weird, rare nature." KH apparently knows a great deal about Moses and has long taken an interest in his development. After various experiences, Moses is now devoted to Jesus, "a once embodied, now disembodied Spirit" who provided Moses with "evidence of his personal identity" and is "a reality" for the man. In *The Short History of the Theosophical Society* Josephine Ransom writes (page 50): "There seems little doubt that the real Imperator was the great Elder Brother, the Master Jesus, for whom Moses had the profoundest devotion, but whose identity as 'Guide' he doubted, because of the likelihood of impersonation, and his own tendency to confuse Imperator with the vision of his own higher Self."

In this connection, HPB, in a letter to Sinnett (*LBS*, 22–23), refers to an article in the British Spiritualist paper *Light*. "Read carefully . . . *Light*," she writes, "and tell me whether the dialogue between + and S.M. is not a mental dialogue between himself and himself—his emotional self and his intellectual reasoning self." She continues: "S.M. declares the statement of + being a Brother" is absolutely false, adding that "the + of his early mediumship is a Brother."

Whatever the case may have been, KH writes: "Whenever under the influence of Imperator he [Stainton Moses] is all alive to the realities of Occultism. . . . When standing face to face with his inner Self . . . he realizes the truth that there is something higher and nobler than the prittle-prattle of pseudo-Spirits" (page 59). Then KH asks: if Imperator were really what Moses believed him to be, would he not have made the man's will wholly subservient to his own by this time?

It is at this point in the letter that KH sharply contrasts how the Adept Brothers proceed against the method used by the "Brothers of the Shadow," those who are working against the forces of evolution and progress. And he makes a most significant statement concerning the mahatmic mode of training: "Alone the adepts, i.e., the embodied spirits—are forbidden by our wise and intransgressible laws to completely subject to themselves another and a weaker will—that of free born man."

Making the same point elsewhere in Letter 48 (page 134), the Mahatma M comments: "We advise—and never order." And in Letter 92 (page 294), KH states: "The fact is, that to the last and supreme initiation every chela . . . is left to his own device and counsel." Theosophical literature contains many statements indicating that every human being is "free born"; we are free to make our own mistakes, though we must ultimately pay the price for that freedom. Occasionally one comes across a passage in which one of the Mahatmas seems to have "ordered" a chela to do some particular thing. An interesting light is shed on this matter by a passage in Sinnett's book, *Incidents in the Life of Madame Blavatsky*:

> A chela—however perfect his occult communications may be through the channel of his own psychic faculties, between himself and his masters—is never allowed to regard himself for an instant as a blind automaton in their hands. He is, on the contrary, a responsible agent who is left to perform his task by the light of his own sagacity, and he will never receive "orders" which seriously conflict with that principle. These will be only of a general character, or, where they refer to details, will be of a kind that do not, in occult phrase, interfere with karma; that is to say, that do not supersede

the agent's moral responsibility. Finally, it should be understood, in regard to "orders" among initiates in occultism, that the order of an occult guru to his chela differs in a very important respect from the order of an officer to his soldier. It is direction that in the nature of things would never be enforced, for the disregard of which there could be no positive or prescribed penalty, and which is only imposed upon the chela by the consideration that if he gets an order and does not obey it, he is unlikely to get any more. It is to be regarded as an order because of the ardour of obedience on the side of the chela, whose aspirations, by the hypothesis, are wholly centered on the Masters. The service thus rendered is especially of the kind which has been described as perfect freedom.

Later in Letter 18 (page 61), KH again refers to the "Brothers of the Shadow," remarking that in September of 1875, Moses "knew nothing" of these entities and calling them "our greatest, most cruel, and—why not confess it—our most potential Enemies." This is followed by a review of a dialogue with HPB and a reference to Bulwer-Lytton's novel, *Zanoni*, in which the "Dweller on the Threshold" appears. While in one sense these entities should not be called "brothers," since they really do not work in mutual concord, they do form a group, a "gang" we might say, that, from one point of view, has a necessary work to perform.

Letter 18 includes the remarkable statement that there are in the world "countless kosmical [*sic*] influences which distort and deflect all efforts to achieve definite purposes" (page 67). This statement calls for deep consideration. Evidently there is a force or energy built into the universe that is resistant to progress, a devolutionary energy resulting in the ongoing battle between good and evil takes place. How else would we gain spiritual strength if there were no struggle against forces that would seek to hold us back from achieving our purpose? KH says further, "If we remember, moreover, the direct hostility of the Brethren of the Shadow always on the watch to perplex and haze the neophyte's brain, I think we shall have no difficulty in understanding how even a definite spiritual advance may to a certain extent lead different individuals to apparently different conclusions and theories."

Just as there are degrees or stages on the mahatmic path to light, so there appear to be stages among those on the devolutionary path. HPB, in Letter 30 (pages 95–96), quotes her Master, M, as speaking about "the unprogressed Planetaries who delight in personating gods and sometimes well known characters who have lived on earth": "There are Dhyan-Chohans and 'Chohans of Darkness,' not what they term devils but imperfect 'Intelligences' who have never been born on this or any other earth sphere, any more than the 'Dhyan Chohans' have, and who will never belong to the 'builders of the Universe,' the pure Planetary Intelligences, who preside at every Manvantara while the Dark Chohans preside at the Pralayas." HPB interjects here, "M. means . . . that they have no right or even power to go against the natural or that work which is prescribed to each class of beings or existing things by the law of nature." The opposition between the work of the "light" and "dark" forces may be related to the law called in Letter 66 (page 175) "the principle of acceleration and retardation." There is always in nature an impulse toward entropy—toward fragmentation and away from organization— alongside the natural impulse toward order and unity.

Continuing in Letter 18 (page 59), KH tells Sinnett of the one exception to the freedom that is enjoyed by all beings, from the lowest to the highest—an "isolated exception," the Mahatma calls it—which is the work of "the highest Planetary Spirits, those who can no longer err." Why, it might be asked, can't they err? Each student needs to ponder this. These entities "appear on Earth but at the origin of every new human kind; at the junction of, and close of the two ends of the great cycle." Their work is to impress on the "plastic minds" of the new "race" the great eternal truths that guide humanity. Therefore, "the mission of the planetary Spirit is but to strike the Key Note of Truth," and once its "vibration" has coursed through all existence, the planetary spirit withdraws. "The vibrations of the Primitive Truth are what your philosophers name 'innate ideas.'" Those "vibrations" become audible and even visible to those who hear and see the underlying harmony and beauty of the entire system.

The entire subject of the planetary spirits deserves careful study, especially as treated in *The Secret Doctrine*, where HPB speaks of them as "a mystery" at the same time connected with the principles in the human constitution (see vol. 2, especially page 29; see also what the Mahatma wrote on the subject in Letter 12, along with the commentary). Here in Letter 18, in response to Sinnett's question as to whether a planetary spirit may "have been humanly incarnated" (page 62), KH says, "There can be no Planetary Spirit that was not once material or what you call human." Students familiar with *The Secret Doctrine* will recall HPB's statements on this point. Writing of the "almost endless series of Hierarchies of sentient Beings," she comments: "Each of these Beings either *was*, or prepares to become, a man, if not in the present, then in a past or a coming cycle (Manvantara). They are *perfected*, when not *incipient*, men. . . . Every so-called "Spirit" is either a *disembodied or a future man*" (1:275). This entire passage in *The Secret Doctrine* is worth studying, particularly HPB's emphasis on the fact that "human consciousness or intelligence" must be acquired "personally and individually." This can only be achieved in the present cycle of manifestation by means of human incarnation.

Continuing on the subject of planetary spirits in Letter 18, KH gives Sinnett a glimpse into what HPB later calls the "mystery of the Buddha" (see *CW*, vol. 14, the section "Mystery of the Buddha" which includes two relevant articles, one on the Buddha and the other on Tsong-ka-pa). KH writes (page 62): "When our great Buddha—the patron of all adepts, the reformer and the codifier of the occult system—reached first Nirvana on earth, he became a Planetary Spirit; i.e., his spirit could at one and the same time rove the interstellar spaces in full consciousness, and continue at will on Earth in his original and individual body. For the divine Self had so completely disfranchised itself from matter that it could create at will an inner substitute for itself. . . . The planetary Spirit of that kind (the Buddha like) can pass at will into other bodies."

This, says KH, "is the highest form of adeptship man can hope for on our planet." It may also be the key to understanding the nature of the Nirmanakaya vehicle, as spoken of in *The Voice of the Silence*, as well as the meaning of KH's comment that those who achieve such full adeptship as the Buddha and Tsong-ka-pa "are able to exercise their *Nirira namastaka* fully, when completely out of the body." KH adds: "There are many other grades and orders, but there is no separate and eternally constituted order of Planetary Spirits"—truly a mystery to be explored and perhaps one day experienced.

Two earlier statements by KH in his effort to help Sinnett understand Stainton Moses' character should not be overlooked. The first concerns the distinction between elementals and elementaries. The Mahatma writes (page 60) that Moses often confused them, and so may many students; therefore it is necessary to distinguish the two terms. HPB, in *The Theosophical Glossary*, gives explicit definitions, and the student will find further explanations in other glossaries such as *Occult Glossary* by G. de Purucker. Briefly, the elementals are the entities evolved in and embodying the elemental kingdoms of earth, water, fire, and air, sometimes referred to as nature spirits of various grades and levels. The elementaries, on the other hand, are the disembodied "souls" of the depraved, inhabiting *kama-rupa*, or the astral realm, after death. Elementaries, or "phantoms," may haunt the séance room and can be a very real danger to psychic health, as they seek to possess the medium. The possibility of such possession is one reason why KH states (page 61) that "mediumship is abnormal."

The second comment that deserves our attention may seem a rather casual one. The Mahatma writes (top of page 61) that a person "rarely becomes an adept without being born a natural Seer." Evidently, being a "Seer" is very different from being a medium, but just what is it? KH refers to Anna Kingsford, for example (Letter 49, page 138), as a "Seeress." Why would seership appear to be necessary for adeptship?

Such questions require our consideration if we would understand the nature of the Adept and the requirements for achieving that state.

With a few concluding remarks about "Imperator," KH turns from a consideration of Stainton Moses to other matters. It is actually a relief to leave Moses and his problems, and one wonders why the Mahatma wrote so many pages about the man. Yet, as we read through those pages, we find much to consider not only about ourselves and our own need to develop true discernment, but also about individuals who may be similar to Moses in their attitudes and convictions.

One wonders why Sinnett took it upon himself to pass on all that KH wrote about Moses to Moses himself, an action that was to bring very unhappy repercussions. Perhaps Sinnett thought he would finally convince Moses that "Imperator" was not a disembodied spirit, but that proved impossible. In a later letter (Letter 21, page 76), KH says, "I advised you to be prudent as to what you allowed S.M. to learn of + and his own mediumship, suggesting that he should be told merely the substance of what I said. When watching you at Allahabad I saw you making instead copious extracts for him from my letter, I again saw the danger but did not interfere." Note, again, the freedom granted to Sinnett; as KH has said, the Adepts never subject the will of individuals to their own wills. HPB, writing to Sinnett some time later (see *LBS*, 23), asked in some desperation: "Oh why did you ever have the unfortunate idea of writing to him [Moses] what KH said! He was a theosophist, lukewarm still open to conviction then and now he is an *inveterate enemy of KH.*"

As Letter 18 continues, KH undertakes not only to answer what must have been a number of questions sent by Sinnett but also to elucidate many points of occult philosophy. First, he mentions a conversation he had with Fechner (page 63), apparently another reference to the Mahatma's university education in Europe, particularly Germany. Gustav Theodor Fechner (1801–1887) was a German philosopher, considered the founder of psychophysics. Several points in the paragraph need to be considered, most particularly the use of the word "soul." In the broadest sense, the term usually designates that "something" existing between body and spirit. As spirit or atman is not an individual principle (according to HPB), soul could be said to constitute the whole of the inner being and sometimes any part of it. Hence KH's sentence, "There is a hierarchy of souls from the lowest forms of matter up to the World Soul." It is essential to bear in mind the wide sense in which the word "soul" is used. Also worth our consideration is KH's statement: "Every diamond, every crystal, every plant and star has its own individual soul, besides man and animal"—essentially emphasizing that consciousness is present in every form, from the simplest to the most complex.

In the same paragraph KH discusses the primary reason why real communication with the deceased is so rare: because it involves different planes or different states of matter as well as different levels of consciousness. The "disembodied spirit," the so-called Ego, does not exist on or in our plane or state of matter; as a consequence, the disembodied "*cannot* even if they would span the abyss that separates their worlds from ours. *They can be visited in Spirit*, their Spirit cannot descend and reach us." The paragraph concludes with a parenthetical statement about HPB's first book, *Isis Unveiled*. Note especially KH's statement that the book was "a tentative effort" to change the view of the Spiritualists, and for that HPB "was made to . . . say what things *are not*, not what they are."

The succeeding paragraphs introduce the vast panorama of the involutionary-evolutionary scheme of cyclic manifestation known as the doctrine of the planetary chains. These paragraphs, beginning with the last paragraph on page 63 through to the penultimate paragraph on page 66, need careful study, as so much of the philosophy is given in a highly concentrated form, idea after idea almost exploding from the pages. As KH admits toward the end of page 65: "It is very difficult to convey my meaning to you at this point . . . I am aware of my failure to bring before you these— to us—axiomatical truths in any other form but that of a simple logical postulate. . . . they being capable of absolute and unequivocal demonstration but to the highest Seers."

The occult lore as presented in these pages is not fully systematized, as it would be later in *The Secret Doctrine,* so the student needs to proceed slowly in order to grasp the essential reason "why," as KH states (page 65), "it is deemed supremely difficult if not utterly impossible for pure *disembodied* Spirits to communicate with men through mediums." Moreover, at the time KH was writing (fairly early in the correspondence with Sinnett) the nomenclature for occult ideas had not yet been developed. The very terms used—"rounds," "strings," "rings," "globes," "chain of worlds"—led Sinnett (and Hume) to accuse the Mahatmas of contradicting themselves, as we will see in some of the later letters. KH and M themselves comment on the difficulty concerning terms later in the correspondence: In Letter 46 (page 129), M states: "You ought to come to some agreement as to the terms used when discussing cyclic evolutions. Our terms are untranslatable; and without a good knowledge of our complete system (which cannot be given but to regular initiates) would suggest nothing definite to your perceptions but only be source of confusion." In Letter 85B (page 258), KH writes of "mistakes arising from occasional confusion of terms that *I had to learn from you*—since it is *you* who are the author of 'rounds'—'rings'—'earthly rings'—etc."

In view of the confusion that may arise with regard to terminology, we need to give particular attention to the Mahatma's description of the "cycle of intelligent existences" (page 63) as he calls cyclic evolution. The word "man" is used here to denote the inner principles, the highest triad of that being which will become the human individual. At the beginning of the cycle, such a being is not "man" or "human" as we think of that condition, because at that level the inner principles are still latent and unconscious. Note also KH's emphasis on the occult teaching that the "Great Cycle the *Macrokosm* . . . is the Prototype of the smaller cycles." This is the beautiful Hermetic axiom: "As it is above, so it is below." Keeping this principle in mind is the key to understanding the very long paragraph on page 64.

The pattern for the entire cycle is stated in two sentences: "Propelled by the irresistible cyclic impulse, the Planetary Spirit has to descend before he can re-ascend. On his way he has to pass through the whole ladder of Evolution, missing no rung, to halt at every star world [globe or planet of the planetary chain] as he would at a station." Clearly, there are no shortcuts. Every rung of the ladder of evolution has to be experienced in its turn. The "planetary spirits" became better known as Dhyani Buddhas, those beings who, we are told, are a mystery. They are connected with the higher triad, the "Monad-Ego" as it is called in *The Secret Doctrine*, whereas the Dhyan Chohans (when that term is not used generically to indicate all spiritual beings) are connected with substance and form, the lower quaternary.

We should note that there is no contradiction between using the term "planetary spirits" (page 64) in connection with the cyclic journey of the monads destined to become human and the reference to planetary spirits (page 59) as "those who cannot err." They are essentially the same, differing only in development. The distinction in terms of evolutionary development may become clearer if the student reads stanza 7, sloka 7, of the Stanzas of Dzyan in *The Secret Doctrine* and HPB's commentary on that sloka (1:265–68). It may also help to understand that we are now at "the lowest point of [our] pilgrimage," with the "Earth's cycle to perform" where "spirit and matter have become pretty much equilibrized." Thus humanity is said to be on Globe D (the densest globe) of the earth's planetary chain, just past the middle of the fourth round, in the fifth root race (better called the fifth developmental stage) of that round. And we are "returning and reincarnating as many times as [we] fail to complete" our appointed work for this cycle.

Much more is said on the subject of the planetary chains, later called the "cycle of necessity," in Letters 44 (page 120) and 67, as well as in various places in *The Secret Doctrine*. A few other references may be helpful here, particularly chapter 7, "The Doctrine of the Spheres," in *The Divine Plan* by Geoffrey Barborka, as well as Adam Warcup's *Cyclic Evolution*. Especially to be recommended is the monograph by E. L. Gardner, *Whence Come the Gods*, in which one section is devoted to "The Planetary Chain Problem."

HPB hints at the difficulty in comprehending the doctrine of the "chain of worlds" in *The Secret Doctrine*, in the section titled "A Few Early Theosophical Misconceptions Concerning Planets, Rounds and Man" (1:152–70). She opens that section with the statement: "Among the eleven Stanzas omitted there is one which gives a full description of the formation of the planetary chains one after another." Later she substantiates KH's statement (Letter 18, page 65) regarding the "dissimilarity of physiological and spiritual conditions" of the several globes in any chain of worlds, quoting from a mahatmic communication: "As Globes, they are in CO-ADUNITION but not in CONSUBSTANTIALITY with our Earth and thus pertain to quite another state of consciousness" (*SD*, 1:166).

Two more points in this section of Letter 18 deserve our special attention. At the bottom of page 64 and top of page 65, KH comments that at the "lowest point" of the cycle "the great Law begins its work of selection." As was said earlier, we have now passed the nadir of the cycle and have begun the ascent, but some may wonder what it might mean that at the "lowest point" the "laggard *Egos* perish by the millions." In fact, these are not individualized, self-conscious units. A statement from *The Secret Doctrine* may help us here: "It would be very misleading to imagine a Monad as a separate Entity trailing its slow way in a distinct path through the lower Kingdoms and after an incalculable series of transformations flowering into a human being" (*SD*, 1:178). The student may wish to read the entire passage by HPB to gain a clearer idea of the true nature of the monad.

At the top of page 65, KH provides another definition of *akasha*: "No adept has ever penetrated beyond the veil of primitive Kosmic [*sic*] matter." Then he adds: "The highest, the most perfect vision is limited to the universe of *Form* and *Matter*." We need to keep this in mind when we consider later on the statement in Letter 88: "We believe in MATTER alone, in matter as visible nature and matter in its invisibility as the invisible omnipresent omnipotent Proteus with its unceasing motion which is its life." So it is that all the "globes" in our "chain of worlds" (the earth planetary chain), whether worlds of causes or worlds of effects (see page 65), are composed of "matter," and that "all movement is, so to say, polar."

The pages of Letter 18 indeed contain an incredible amount of occult philosophy for us to study and digest! The Mahatma recapitulates the teaching in the middle of page 65, adding, in point (*c*), that the "chain of worlds . . . is an *epicycloid*." An epicycle is one circular motion superimposed upon another. The moon's journey around the sun is an example: the moon circles around the earth while the earth circles around the sun, so the moon's orbit around the sun is a circle of loops. Note how the Mahatma applies this principle to our state. This is reminiscent of the verse in *The Voice of the Silence*: "The Self of matter and the Self of Spirit can never meet. One of the twain must disappear; there is no place for both." We need to consider what this means in light of the fact just stated: that manifestation involves both form and matter.

KH next focuses on "still another and far mightier impediment" to communication with the dead, the existence of worlds of causes and worlds of effects—discussed for the first time in this letter but mentioned again in later letters, particularly Letter 44. For now it is enough to note that our world is a "sphere of Causes . . . inter-linked with, and surrounded by, but actually separated from . . . the higher sphere of Causality by an impenetrable atmosphere . . . of effects." This statement should be carefully considered, particularly in light of so many reported communications with entities in the astral realm, as well as near-death experiences in which such interchange seems to have taken place. Could it be that it is only after the Ego passes through kama-loka that communication is no longer possible? The student also needs to be clear about the meaning of "intermediate spheres." More information on many of these concepts is given in later letters, particularly in Letter 68, where the after-death states are described in greater detail.

Moving on toward the letter's conclusion, the Mahatma discusses Sinnett's concern that "the views of the three mystics" are quite dissimilar (page 66). These three (the "three great London Seers") are

Stainton Moses, Anna Kingsford, and Charles Massey, whose spirit "guides" must have given contradictory information. KH then makes a significant statement that we need to keep in mind when besieged by differing accounts of psychic and even spiritual "visions": "Truth is *One*, and cannot admit of diametrically opposite views and pure Spirits who see it *as it is*, with the veil of matter entirely withdrawn from it—cannot err."

When so baldly stated, it may seem obvious that there is but one truth. Yet in considering all that has passed as Truth or Theosophy since these letters were written, perhaps this fact does need emphasis. The facts given us in the letters are the result of direct perception by the Adepts, who are skilled in using the inner powers of nature and on many occasions say, in effect, that they write but what they know. However, it is also true that different investigators may see "different aspects or portions of the Whole," so discrimination and intuition are called for in assessing varying accounts. At this point in the letter, we also get a hint that not all the Mahatmas operate in the same way; within the rules of the Brotherhood, each apparently has freedom to follow his own policies in the development of different individuals.

KH's reference to Sinnett's book, *The Occult World*, as the "*first serious shot*" at the enemy" (page 67) may come as something of a surprise. One might have thought that HPB's first work, *Isis Unveiled*, published before Sinnett's book, would have been counted as the initial "shot" directed against the "enemy" of materialism and religious dogmatism. But we must take cognizance of the general attitude at that time toward women authors, particularly those involved with spiritualistic phenomena. While *Isis* was certainly successful with regard to early sales of the two volumes, HPB's presumed association with the Spiritualist movement militated against its serious acceptance by any but those interested in that movement. The Mahatma also mentions, along with *Isis*, another work by a woman, *Art Magic* by the American Spiritualist Emma Hardinge Britten, a founding member of the Theosophical Society and elected one of its counsellors at the organizing meeting in 1875. Many of the Society's early meetings were held in her home. Britten claimed that her book was written by "an adept of her acquaintance" for whom she was "acting as translator and secretary." She left the Society after a short time, becoming quite hostile toward it and spreading falsehoods about HPB. (For a full biography of Emma Britten, see *CW*, 1:466–67.)

As KH draws his lengthy letter to a close, he writes some of the most beautiful and profoundly moving statements found anywhere in the correspondence—statements that need to be read and reread, pondered over, and meditated upon. Speaking of the world's "absolute unfitness" to receive the esoteric philosophy, "the Knowledge of our Knowledge," the Mahatma indicates that if the world still refuses to receive it, "then will we at the End of this cycle retire into solitude and our kingdom of silence once more."

So, we must ask, what is the state of the world today? Have the wise and compassionate ones withdrawn, or are they still with us? What have we made of the teachings they so magnificently shared in their letters to Sinnett and Hume and through their agent, H. P. Blavatsky? Have we studied and assimilated the gift of their Knowledge so that our lives have been transformed, our minds and hearts made aflame with the love for all humanity that they profess? What a stupendous "offer" KH extends as he informs Sinnett: "We have offered to exhume the primeval strata of man's being, his basic nature, and lay bare the wonderful complications of his inner Self. . . . It is our mission to plunge and bring the pearls of Truth to the surface." And then those words that have inspired generations of Theosophical students and continue to inspire every earnest sincere aspirant who would tread the path that leads to full Self-Realization:

> For countless generations hath the adept building a fane of imperishable rocks, a giant's Tower of Infinite Thought, wherein the Titan dwelt, and will yet, if need be, dwell alone, emerging from it but at the end of every cycle, to invite the elect of mankind to co-operate with him and help in his turn enlighten superstitious man. And we will go on in that periodical work of ours; we will not allow

ourselves to be baffled in our philanthropic attempts until that day when the foundations of a new continent of thought are so firmly built that no amount of opposition and ignorant malice guided by the Brethren of the Shadow will be found to prevail.

It is to that task that we are still called: to aid in building the foundations of a "new continent of thought," to help in our turn bring light and understanding to poor suffering humanity, "to lift a little of the heavy karma of the world," as *Light on the Path* describes the work before us, giving our "aid to the few strong hands that hold back the powers of darkness from obtaining complete victory."

Letter 18 concludes with a quotation from Tennyson. This, as we learn in Letter 20 (page 75), puzzled Sinnett, as the Englishman was something of an authority on Tennyson (some years after this correspondence he wrote a slim work titled *Tennyson the Occultist*) and could not locate this poem in the texts he had before him. Later, however, Sinnett found the lines in an 1830 edition of Tennyson's works under the title *Poems Chiefly Lyrical.* The complete poem, titled "The Mystics" and written when Tennyson was twenty years of age, was not included in any of Tennyson's later works. In Letter 20 (page 75), responding to Sinnett's query, KH writes: "Quotations from Tennyson? Really cannot say. Some stray lines picked up in the astral light or in somebody's brain and remembered. I never forget what I once see or read."

The omissions near the top of page 68 and at the close of the letter on page 69 (referred to in Letter 19) concerned the possibility, even the promise, of a visit by the Mahatma to Sinnett while Sinnett would be asleep. Evidently Sinnett retained no memory of the visit, but KH refers to the event in Letter 20: "'Woke up sad on the morning of the 18th.' Did you? . . . Something *has* occurred, though you have preserved no consciousness of the event."

This very long letter contains some of the most profound doctrines of the esoteric philosophy, teachings that, as we shall see, led to further questions on the part of Sinnett and his colleague Hume. Indeed, as KH prophesied at the beginning of Letter 18, both

Englishmen became "incarnate note[s] of interrogation." Sinnett was to collate all the teachings given to him on the various topics, ultimately producing the book *Esoteric Buddhism*, considered the first "textbook" setting forth the doctrines of Theosophy.

LETTER 19

Letter 19 may be considered a postscript to Letter 18, referring as it does to the "blanks" near the end of that letter (indicated by a series of ellipsis points in the printed version), which must indeed have puzzled Sinnett. Some students have suggested that the erasures and deletions were done by KH's superior, rather than by KH himself. Whoever made them, the erasures show on the original as smudges, almost indicating words being "lifted" out rather than simply erased.

LETTER 20

It would seem from KH's comment at the opening of Letter 20 that Sinnett has indeed become "an incarnate note of interrogation," since the Mahatma refers to the number of questions he now intends to answer, many of which must have been prompted by the teachings in Letter 18. Yet, as KH tells Sinnett, "thirst for knowledge was never regarded as a sin." If we, with so much more material available for studying what KH here calls "the occult philosophical view of creation" still find it difficult to comprehend, we may imagine the extent of Sinnett's "thirst."

Reminding Sinnett that "our correspondence was established for the good of the many," KH encourages him now to "recast the teachings and ideas" in his "future book." Perhaps recognizing that the Englishman would indeed so utilize the teachings—eventually producing his second work, *Esoteric Buddhism*—KH, and later Morya, expand upon the early teachings throughout the course of the correspondence. Happily for us, in due time HPB added her own exploration and elucidation of the teachings in her comprehensive work, *The Secret Doctrine*, as well as her many other writings during the final years of her life. As the Mahatmas emphasize again and again, the teachings were never given to "gratify individual aspirations" or so the Theosophical Society would become "an academy of magic and a hall of occultism." We can ask ourselves, then: To what extent are we using the teachings "for the good of the many"? Can we "recast the teachings and ideas" in our own language, in the language of our times? For surely our present century is, from the spiritual and ethical point of view, not much different from Sinnett's, characterized by KH as a "century of conceit and mental obscuration."

In Letter 20 KH makes references to various individuals, indicating the extent of not only his familiarity with historical figures involved in occultism, but also his acquaintance with current publications, particularly those pertaining to the Spiritualist movement. First, he mentions Eliphas Levi and his book, *Haut Magie* (High Magic). Levi was a renowned French occultist and Kabbalist who the Mahatmas mention in a number of the letters. (An excellent brief biography of Levi by Boris de Zirkoff appears in *CW*, 1:491–95.) HPB published an article by Levi ("Death and Satan") in *The Theosophist* of October 1881, just a few months after Sinnett received Letter 20. Margin comments in KH's handwriting are included in the copy received by Sinnett (see appendix to the chronological edition, page 501).

Next KH refers to the Comte de St. Germain, about whom Isabel Cooper-Oakley wrote a biography, and whose "last exit" Clara Codd refers to in *The Way of the Disciple* (pages 100–102). KH also refers briefly to Isaac Newton, saying that Newton understood the Pythagorean doctrines. Finally he mentions one of the greatest imposters of the day, "the formidable J.K. . . . a dangerous enemy," the initials being those of a certain Julius Kohn, known as a "Jewish Kabbalist," about whom HPB wrote some scathing passages (see *CW*, 3:262 *et seq.*). These several references may not seem of much importance today, yet their relevance is not solely historical. They do help us to understand the Mahatmas' concern with identifying those who were working with them in their efforts to aid humanity as well as those who were working to obstruct the spread of truth. From this we can deduce that we, too, need to be aware of the forces that work through various individuals either to help or to hinder humanity's progress.

KH's comments indicate that Sinnett must have offered to take a "solemn pledge" of secrecy concerning the occult teachings, if only the Mahatma would convey those teachings to him. Here we learn a most valuable lesson as KH reminds his correspondent of two occasions when Sinnett evidently made some unfortunate comments, recorded, we may say, on the "akashic record," which now prevented the kind of communication for which Sinnett longed. In Letter 15 (page 48), KH asked Sinnett whether being sincere at the time guaranteed what he would be in the future. Statements made lightly, sometimes without thinking, may indeed come back to haunt us, or at least produce unforeseen consequences. Now KH tells Sinnett that as a result of his words at an earlier time, "We have to travel . . . at the same slow rate."

At this point KH places before Sinnett, and therefore us, some of the most beautiful and also most profound statements regarding chelaship and the path to adeptship. "The Occult Science," he writes, "is not one in which secrets can be communicated of a sudden, by a written or even verbal communication." How easy it would be if there were a "Hand-book of the art," or if the Mahatmas would simply tell us all that we yearn to know about the way to enlightenment! "The truth is that till the neophyte attains to the condition necessary for that degree of Illumination to which, and for which, he is entitled and fitted, most *if not all* of the Secrets are *incommunicable.*" Is this not what the Mahatma has told Sinnett from the very beginning of the correspondence?

How willing are we to undergo the training necessary for the communication of deeper wisdom? How many have been willing to heed the Mahatmas' instruction to "come out of your world into ours," to change their mode of life and follow the inner pathway to Self-Realization? For the pathway, as always, leads through thickets of self-understanding and mazes of self-discipline, and the "Guru or initiator can but assist" the aspirant as he or she walks toward the final goal. Now, as from time immemorial, "The illumination *must come from within,*" KH tells Sinnett. It may seem to come from without, but in fact the true light is uncovered within as the "animal passions and impulses" submit to the "government" of the inner Self and there is an "utter unselfishness of intention."

We are helped, of course, and the training, KH says, recognizes "the peculiar physical, moral, and intellectual conditions" of each neophyte, and the "instructor" has "to adapt his conditions to those of the pupil." While KH discusses in both earlier and later letters the qualifications necessary for chelaship, here he gives Sinnett an insight into the sacrifice made by the Adept-guru who takes on anyone as disciple: "We have to bring ourselves into a full rapport with the subject under training . . . and the strain is terrible." Yet, writes KH, "Let those who really desire to learn abandon all and come to us."

Once KH has opened the door, as it were, to all that is involved in the communication of esoteric knowledge, he must help Sinnett understand not only the difficulties involved—"How am I to give expression to ideas for which you have as yet no language?"—but also the risks: "To give more knowledge to a man than he is yet fitted to receive is a dangerous experiment." He adds, "The misuse of knowledge by the pupil always reacts upon the initiator," followed by the startling statement, "Nor do I believe you know yet, that in sharing his secrets with another the Adept, by an immutable Law, is delaying his own progress to the Eternal Rest."

Besides the lack of a language for communicating occult philosophy and the risk of giving knowledge the pupil may not be "fitted to receive," there is a point we passed over rather hastily to which we need to return, and that is the fact that "illumination *must come from within.*" Just what does this mean, particularly in the light of the information KH and M are giving Sinnett, as well as Hume, throughout the course of the correspondence? All of this information about the human constitution, the origin of the universe, the work of the many orders of Dhyan Chohans, the after-death conditions, reincarnation, the law of karma, and much else concerning the esoteric philosophy is for us to study and attempt to understand. It is knowledge that Sinnett incorporated in his second book, knowledge further expounded upon by HPB and by subsequent Theosophical writers. But what about that inner illumination that must one day come to each one of us? And how do we prepare ourselves to receive it? These are serious questions that every aspirant must ultimately answer, although perhaps not so much in words. For we may never be able to verbalize the experience, since life thereafter is lived from a new state of consciousness. Only when we become the truth, when we become the light, do we enter into the illumination that is both compassion and wisdom.

KH leads Sinnett as far as he can in understanding what is involved in the training as well as the attitude required for one who would unlock the door to true knowledge. Only a reading and rereading of KH's words can bring about a deep understanding of all that is implied here.

We need to pause also on KH's reminder that "a *Price* must be paid for everything and every truth by *somebody*, and in this case—WE pay it." Yet it is a payment made willingly, for the Mahatmas' concern is always for the welfare of humanity, and here specifically for Sinnett, hoping and expecting that he may assist with the work they have at heart. Why must a "price" be paid for every truth? And what is the nature of that price? These are questions to consider thoughtfully and deeply if we would understand even to some small degree the work of the Occult Brotherhood, particularly of those Brothers who accept the role of teacher and guide.

A most intriguing statement (page 75) concerning one of the adeptic powers, and evidently related to what KH said in Letter 18 about planetary spirits, calls for careful study: "An adept who has, by the power of his knowledge and soul enlightenment, become exempt from the curse of Unconscious transmigration . . . may, at his will and desire, and instead of reincarnating himself only after bodily death, do so, and repeatedly—during his life if he chooses. He holds the power of choosing for himself new bodies—whether on this or any other planet—while in possession of his old form, that he generally preserves for purposes of his own."

Many students feel that here KH is referring to the art of *tulku*, the power of taking over another physical body while retaining one's own. (For a full discussion of this power, as well as commentaries on HPB's possession of it and her often serving as tulku when the Mahatmas used her physical vehicle, see Geoffrey Barborka's *H. P. Blavatsky, Tibet and Tulku*.) In addition to all that is meant by the term *tulku*, there may be other, indeed multiple, meanings to KH's statement, particularly since he says "reincarnating himself." Consider, for instance, that the term "planet" at the time of the correspondence referred to the "globes" or "planes" of the planetary chain; hence KH's reminder about what he wrote on the subject of planetary spirits in Letter 18. Thus this passage may refer to taking over other bodies on other "globes" of our planetary chain—or even one "soul" taking over multiple bodies for the purpose of hastening evolution. We know so little, really, about reincarnation that unless and until we explore all aspects of the subject, we may be limiting ourselves to a single interpretation that may not be wholly accurate. The subject of reincarnation is complex and involves, among other factors, a thorough understanding of the human constitution, the seven-fold principles that comprise the human entity.

In addition to possibly alluding to the mystery of tulku—or the cognate Sanskrit term, *avesha* (entering into or taking possession of a vehicle)—KH also refers to another concept in the sentence quoted above. This is the idea that the Adept is "exempt from the curse of Unconscious transmigration," implying that we, at our stage, are not free from such a "curse." Here I refer the student to an important article by HPB, "Transmigration of the Life-Atoms," which originally appeared in *The Theosophist* of August 1883 (*CW*, 5:109–17). If we would free ourselves from "unconscious transmigration," becoming fully conscious of and therefore responsible for our every action, thought, and feeling, then we need to understand the processes operating in and through our various vehicles.

I have already commented on the quotation from Tennyson with which KH concluded Letter 18, but it is evident from KH's comments in Letter 20 that Sinnett was troubled that he could not find the quotation in the published works of Tennyson that he had at hand. Especially interesting is KH's comment: "I never forget what I once see or read." It was this phenomenal memory that, to some extent, accounted for the unfortunate "Kiddle incident," which we will consider in a later letter.

A final comment before we leave Letter 20 concerns the mention of Ross Scott in the postscript. It remains unclear why KH would say about this young man, "I need him," but because of that statement we should know a bit about him. An Irishman and British civil servant, Scott became acquainted with HPB and Olcott on shipboard when they were sailing from England to Bombay in 1879. Olcott calls him "a noble fellow and an Irishman of the better sort," and relates a phenomenon that HPB produced for Scott's benefit shortly after their arrival in India. Apparently Scott had an injured leg, which the Mahatmas promised HPB they would cure if he passed the six months' probation on which they had placed him.

Scott became a secretary to Hume and was the first secretary of the Simla Eclectic Theosophical Society, even receiving a letter from M in the late fall of 1881 (about the time of Letter 20, in fact), and later was visited by M "in astral shape" (Letter 92). The Mahatmas told HPB to try to find a suitable wife for Scott—certainly one of their stranger requests—and perhaps it was because of HPB's efforts in that direction that Scott married Minnie Hume, A. O. Hume's only daughter. Later, we learn from some of HPB's letters, Minnie returned to her parents' home, and eventually she went blind. It appears that Scott failed his probation, partially because of his wife's attitude toward the Adepts, but he never left the Theosophical Society. On one occasion when he served as chairman for a lecture Olcott gave at Moradabad, Olcott called him (*ODL*, 3:434), "ever our brave colleague who has stood up for us through good report and evil report."

LETTER 21

The opening statements in Letter 21 concern Sinnett's unfortunate sharing of the comments KH made in Letter 18 about Stainton Moses with the English Spiritualist himself. Yet the Mahatma's remark "I believe the time fully come when social and moral safety demands that someone of the Theos. Soc. should speak the truth though the Himalaya fall on him" indicates that KH is increasingly eager for the Spiritualist movement to be penetrated by an understanding of the esoteric philosophy. He obviously has little use for spiritualistic communications, writing, "Truth will stand without inspiration from Gods or Spirits, and better still—will stand in spite of them all," and he is certainly looking to Sinnett to correct the current misunderstandings in that movement regarding communications from the "disembodied."

He acknowledges that while Sinnett "produced incalculable harm" by sending Moses "copious extracts" from his letter, at the same time Sinnett's "motives" were "sincere and good." KH informs Sinnett that henceforth "we will have to limit ourselves entirely to philosophy," suggesting that the Mahatma does not intend to speak any more of individuals—although in later letters, we do find many people discussed in both complimentary and not so complimentary terms.

Probably every thoughtful person has realized that some good comes out of unfortunate incidents, however dire or tragic they seem at the time. Along the same lines, when the Mahatma comments in a later letter (Letter 103B, page 351) on what he calls "sundry noted cases of theosophical failure," he then points out how everyone who has created a problem has also, in some way, proved to be "a useful factor toward producing the net result." And he adds, "In each instance the individual traitor and enemy was given his chance, and but for his moral obliquity might have derived incalculable good from it to his personal karma." Perhaps, in KH's view, Stainton Moses was likewise given a "chance" to derive benefit from knowing what the Mahatma had said about him.

Again in Letter 21, KH gives Sinnett a sharp reminder: "Remember that you are at a hard school, and dealing now with a world entirely distinct from your own." As reiterated so often and in the early letters particularly, the world of the Adept is very different from the one in which we normally live. The "school" of occult training is never easy, but it is we who put ourselves on probation, just as it is we who undertake the journey in quest of light and wisdom. So KH cautions Sinnett to have patience, traveling at what he calls, in Letter 20, "the same slow rate."

Yet he, and we, are the beneficiaries of the wisdom for which the Mahatmas and their predecessors had to labor: "Our predecessors had to learn everything they know by themselves, only the foundation was laid for them." Perhaps that "foundation" was the "keynote" embedded in their very being by the planetary spirit whose mission is so well described in Letter 18. Just as that foundation was laid for the earliest seers and teachers, Mahatmas, and enlightened masters, who "ages ago . . . began to make certain rules, according to which they intended to live," so KH promises that the Mahatmas will now give us such a "foundation" on which to build our own understanding. We today are truly fortunate, for if "All these rules have now become LAW," we may be certain that in their very lawfulness lies their applicability to our own lives.

It is in this letter that we first learn that KH will be leaving for a period of three months and therefore unable to continue the correspondence for that length of time. The reference, of course, is to his "retreat," a time when he undoubtedly underwent further initiation on the path of adeptship.

LETTER 22

With Letter 22, we are introduced to some of the most mysterious aspects of the psychospiritual mechanism of an individual destined to serve as a bridge between the world of the Occult Brotherhood and our ordinary everyday world. The letter seems to start midway in response to some questions Sinnett may have asked, but we know it concerns HPB since Sinnett wrote on it, "KH's confidential Memo about Old Lady," the term he used for HPB. What happened to the beginning of the letter we do not know, but we may assume that Sinnett had been criticizing HPB for what KH now calls her "habitual incoherence." Then the fact that KH uses the words "kind Brothers" indicates that though "confidential," the memo about HPB was to be shared with Hume. That this was done is evidenced by a letter from Hume to HPB, which needs to be considered alongside the explanation of her condition the Mahatma gives here (see *LBS*, 305–7; appendix to the chronological edition, pages 490–94).

The entire question of just who Helena Petrovna Blavatsky was has perplexed students for over a century now, since she first appeared on the public scene. What do we, even if we are students of her incredible corpus of writings, really know about her? How was she viewed by those who worked with her, studied under her, befriended her, and tried to aid her? Is it possible to know fully what KH here calls "the great Mystery," about which he was "empowered," as he puts it—undoubtedly referring to permission given him by his superiors—to allow the two Englishmen "a glimpse behind the veil"? While we have biographies of her and the many statements about her activities she herself made in letters and notes, the full story from the occult point of view may never be known. Perhaps it cannot be told in words but only understood in the silent depths of our own unfolding spiritual comprehension.

The beginning of KH's explanation seems straightforward enough, for he tells us that HPB's state is "intimately connected with her occult training in Tibet." However, this seemingly simple statement has caused a great deal of speculation, even during HPB's lifetime, some critics disputing the idea that she could have spent seven years in that country. She herself wrote rather ambiguously at different times about her Tibetan experiences, her visits to the Mahatmas, and her own psychological makeup. The earnest student can consult a number of references concerning her life that particularly deal with her psychospiritual and occult development. Probably the most complete biography is Sylvia Cranston's *The Extraordinary Life and Influence of Helena Blavatsky*, but many other books and articles refer in whole or in part to her occult training. For example, regarding her time in Tibet, she herself wrote a lengthy letter to the Spiritualist journal *Light*, published in England and edited by Stainton Moses, in which she refuted many statements critical of her own account (see "Mr. A. Lillie's Delusions" in *CW*, 6:269–80). Throughout her letters to Sinnett, and in a number of other places, HPB wrote of her "dual nature" and changes that took place in her at times of crisis, particularly severe illnesses. Colonel Olcott also records some of these crisis periods, as well as occasions when various Mahatmas occupied her body (see especially *ODL*, 1:263). Using HPB's own words, Mary K. Neff in *Personal Memoirs of H. P. Blavatsky* has assembled statements concerning visits to Tibet and what could be called personality changes as a result of occult training.

Other useful resources include the work by Geoffrey Barborka, *H. P. Blavatsky, Tibet and Tulku*, especially chapter 6, and a book by G. de Purucker, *H. P. Blavatsky: The Mystery*. Regarding HPB's strange duality, de Purucker suggests that her case rests upon "foundations laid in some of the most mysterious and, to the Occident, utterly unknown secrets of human spiritual-psychological economy." He then adds: "The Inner Self of her was one of the Great Ones of the ages, an actual, real, self-consciously energic Individuality or Power, which worked through her and used her both psychologically and physically as the fittest instrument for the saving of the souls of men that the Occidental world has seen in many ages."

In Letter 22, we find the amazing statement that nearly a century had been spent searching for an appropriate individual to serve as a "connecting link" between Europe and Tibet. This leads us to consider the uniqueness of HPB's role as messenger of the Brotherhood. It also raises a number of questions, including why she was chosen. Recall that in Letter 9, KH writes to Sinnett in regard to HPB: "Imperfect as may be our visible agent—and often most unsatisfactory and imperfect she is—yet she is the best available at present." There are many other statements throughout the letters concerning the two Mahatmas' view of HPB, including acknowledgment of her "strong defects." The student wishing to understand as fully as possible her role as their "agent" in the transmission of the occult teachings as well as of the letters may wish to compile these. Some statements may seem contradictory, inviting the student to probe ever more deeply into the nature of her relationship to the Teachers.

There has been much speculation concerning the Mahatma's statement that no one "can leave the precincts of *Bod-Lhas* [the abode of the Fraternity] and return back into the world in his integral whole" without leaving "*one* at least of his seven satellites" as the link between their world and ours. The concept of the "crippling" of principles, if we may call it that, is not easy to grasp and needs to be carefully thought through. M's statement, recorded in Hume's letter to HPB (see the first paragraph of this comment), to the effect that it may not be "*one of the seven* particularly but all . . . every one of them [that is, the principles] a 'cripple' and forbidden the exercise of its full powers" only compounds the difficulty in understanding all that is meant. Just how any one "principle" of the human constitution, or even any aspect of all the principles, can be "crippled" remains a puzzle for each student to contemplate.

We do know from the records of those closely associated with HPB that on occasion a "vacancy" was created in her consciousness that was occupied by various Adepts, among whom were M and KH. At other times, it is said, the "vacancy" was occupied by her own Higher Self, and sometimes by a "very high Initiate," vastly higher even than the Mahatmas responsible for the letters. Boris de Zirkoff, one of the ablest students of the literature, writes in regard to the last: "This Initiate is a Slavonian in his latest incarnation, and it is precisely because of his peculiar type of psycho-mentality, due to his racial stock, that the Messenger of the present era had to be chosen, if at all possible, from among the Slavic people. This permitted HPB to be 'attuned' to his vibratory rate, as it were" (see de Zirkoff's journal, *Theosophia*, January-February 1948).

Certainly Letter 22 is a most significant one, touching as it does on a real mystery concerning the relationship between a chela, even an initiate if we presume HPB to have been more than an ordinary chela, and the Occult Fraternity in which the chela is being trained and for which she served as an "agent" to the world. It is certainly true that *their* world is not *our* world, and as Sinnett is told again and again throughout the letters, if we would enter their world, come closer to the Mahatmas, learn more of their "secrets," we must adapt ourselves to their ways, accepting their conditions. There is much to learn if we would understand both HPB and the teachings conveyed through her. Above all, it may be necessary to withhold judgment regarding what appear as contradictions and ambiguities in her life, at the same time appreciating the tremendous sacrifices she made that we might have these teachings.

LETTER 23

It appears from Letter 23 that, in spite of all that KH has written concerning HPB's state and the reasons for her "habitual incoherence" and "strange outbursts," Hume may still be criticizing her, persisting in "following out a line of argument" that would cause future problems.

Much of Letter 23 deals with the fact that KH is about to leave on his retreat, evidently departing on September 27 or between that date and the first of October. A period of three months is needed for the initiatory step he is to take, and since his "chiefs" require him to be at the New Year's festivals, which occur in February, he must, he writes, "avail myself of the three intervening months," meaning October, November, and December, giving himself January to recover from the experience.

We learn that while at the outset of the correspondence, only KH was willing to undertake the task of instructing the two Englishmen in response to their questions, the Mahatma has now persuaded his "beloved but very obstinate Brother M" to take on some of that work. Notably, although M did take on the correspondence during the three-month period (sending some twenty letters to Sinnett and Hume, exclusive of the two sets of Cosmological Notes, about which I comment later), at the time of KH's departure he only promised to "refresh [HPB's] failing memory and to revive all she has learned . . . in as bright a way as could be desired." Presumably, then, it was M's intention to use HPB, who was his chela, as the chief communicator. Yet M also agreed to answer Sinnett's letter "through a third party"— probably Damodar, although it could also have been Djual Khul, who, writes KH, was left "to watch over *all* as much as it lies in his weak powers." From M's subsequent letter we can understand that before his departure, KH had "dictated" a letter to Damodar, who seems to have "bungled up the message," as M says in Letter 25.

So KH leaves on what he terms "my long, *very* long journey." The next letter from him in the chronological series is Letter 47. Was the journey on which he embarked "long" in physical distance or in terms of consciousness? Or both? We may speculate on this when we consider future references to KH's period of outer silence.

LETTERS 24, 25, 26, 27, AND 28

The contact with Morya begins with a series of quite short notes mainly concerned with the letter Damodar wrote on behalf of

KH, which, as already noted, Damodar seems to have "bungled." The prefatory note to Letter 24 gives a lengthy quotation from Sinnett's book *Occult World*, emphasizing the "change" that came over the tone of the communications as M accepted his Brother's request to respond to Sinnett and Hume. Something of that change of tone is evident in M's manner of address to Sinnett, calling him "Very kind Sinnett Sahib," a much more formal beginning than KH ever used.

A few items of special interest may be noted in these brief letters. One is the reference to Sinnett's gift of a pipe to Morya. HPB said— and it may have been she who suggested to Sinnett that he obtain such a gift for the Mahatma—that Morya smoked what is known as a water pipe, or hookah, the bowl of which is "coolated," or placed in water. Somewhere HPB refers to the "soft, burble-burble of M's pipe." Anyone who has seen or, more especially, heard the sound of some one smoking a hookah will agree with HPB's description.

A second item that particularly deserves our attention is M's statement: "The situation is more serious than you may imagine." He is referring, it is believed, to events that were building up within the Society prior to the anniversary celebration scheduled for January of 1882, that year being especially significant as the seventh year of the Society's existence. KH emphasized the importance of Sinnett's presence at that anniversary meeting in a brief letter just before he left on retreat (see "Miscellaneous Letters," in *LBS*, 365). KH writes: "Your presence in Bombay would save *everything*, and yet seeing how reluctant you feel I will not insist." We will return to this topic in Letter 39.

A comment of M's in Letter 25 to which we may give some thought concerns the "state" his Brother KH was now in. M uses the Tibetan term *Tong-pa-ngi*, often translated as the "Void." Although not familiar with Tibetan, I suggest that M's use of that term refers to something more than the English term "void." Certainly it was a state of consciousness, for which the physical body had to be in a state of "lifelessness," as M describes in Letter 29.

What is that state of consciousness? Is it a consciousness stripped of all mental accumulations? A state of non-egoism? J. Krishnamurti often spoke of the need to "empty the mind," or free the mind, so it is not crippled by memory, thought, or fear. On one occasion when he was asked what would happen when the mind was emptied of all content, Krishnamurti responded, "Try it and see." Is that state of consciousness perhaps analogous to an expansion in space referred to by HPB in her Diagram of Meditation, when she directed her students to "Conceive of Unity as Expansion in Space and Infinite in Time"? Is such a state similar to or the same as the Buddhist "emptiness"? For some, the concept of a void may suggest darkness, while for others it may suggest total light. Perhaps the void, or whatever is meant here by the Tibetan term, is Ultimate Reality. Or if KH's retreat was for the purpose of taking a further step on the Bodhisattva path, it may be Boundless Love. Each student should ponder this matter if he or she wants to approach an understanding of the state into which KH entered during those three months.

My final comment concerns the letter (mentioned in Letter 25) that Damodar wrote on behalf of or received as dictation from KH before the Mahatma left on his retreat. The letter itself is missing, and we can only conjecture that in its altered form it was given by Sinnett to Hume, who then did not return it. Damodar "bungled the message" in a way that would have upset Hume (see Letter 27). M erased the offending portion in the letter, substituting another sentence by precipitation (see Letter 28), even though he has told Sinnett that "as for phenomena you will have none." In *The Occult World*, Sinnett states that the Mahatma adhered strictly to this policy throughout the first three months of the correspondence, that is, during KH's entire absence. Later, M did perform a few phenomena "in friendship and kindness," Sinnett says, "long after all idea of confirming my belief in the Brothers was wholly superfluous." I refer the student to Sinnett's *Occult World*, particularly pages 160–167, for comments on the Mahatmas' use of and views on the production of phenomena.

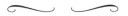

LETTER 29

We come now to M's very long letter—"the longest letter I have ever written in my life," as the Mahatma himself describes it—a letter so full of information, advice, and wisdom that the student must feel nearly overwhelmed with its power and beauty. Addressed to both Sinnett and Hume, the letter opens with M's acknowledgment that in spite of Hume's "superficial disagreeableness," the Englishman's "goodness of motive, his abilities, his potential usefulness" deserve the Mahatma's gratitude.

The background for this expression of gratitude is summarized in the prefatory note to the letter and therefore need not be repeated here. However, we may call attention to M's deep feeling for his "poor old chela," a reference to HPB, since he is now willing to do "for her sake what I might have refused doing even for the Society." We know that, from the beginning of the correspondence, HPB had urged the Mahatmas to give the two Englishmen instruction in the occult sciences, perhaps because she felt that only then would these two proud individuals accept her knowledge as valid and authentic.

At the outset, as we have seen, it was KH who undertook the instruction. Now it is M's turn to take up that work, fulfilling a "sacred . . . debt of gratitude" for Hume's defense of HPB. Whatever we may think of Hume, then—his attitude toward the Mahatmas, his overweening arrogance—we may well be grateful that the Mahatmas see beyond the faults of an individual to the good and useful qualities that may be nurtured.

There is a beautiful lesson for all of us in M's words: "We of the Indo-Tibetan hovels never quarrel," since they—or "those of us who are *dikshita* [initiates]"—are able to "take in a situation at a glance," and "conclusions are never drawn from secondary data." We may be reminded of KH's words in Letter 17: "There comes a moment in the life of an adept when . . . to acquire further knowledge, he has no more to go through a minute and slow process of investigation and comparison . . . but is accorded an instantaneous, implicit insight into every first truth. . . . The adept sees and feels and lives in the very source of all fundamental truths." Now in Letter 29, M comments on the nature of "fact": "That which is regarded by most men as a 'fact' to us may seem but a simple RESULT, an after-thought unworthy of our attention, generally attracted but to primary facts. . . . We fix our gaze upon the producing Cause . . . we concern ourselves but with the main facts."

Well may we ask: just what is meant by a "fact"? Are we often so caught up in our search for details that we overlook or forget the primary principle involved? Do we substitute opinion for fact or our own interpretation for the truth? And how can we know when a "fact" is a "simple result" and when it is the "producing cause"? Though not easy questions to consider, they are important ones for us to contemplate. Later in Letter 29, speaking of Hume, the Mahatma says: "He has also to learn in what particular cases results may in their turn become important and primary causes, when the result becomes a Kyen." We will meet with the word *Kyen* again when we consider the Cosmological Notes (see page 509, also my commentary on the Notes), where the Mahatma indicates its meaning as "cause; itself a result of a previous or some primary cause."

M seems intent on trying to explain how the Mahatmas regard any discussion, pointing out that they are "accustomed to rather follow the thought of our interlocuter [*sic*] or correspondent than the words he clothes it in." Anyone who has attempted to answer questions following a talk knows that it is more important to understand the thought behind the question, the "unasked question," than simply listen to the words spoken!

M quotes his Brother KH in a tone that seems almost born of frustration, reminding us sharply of the difficulties the Mahatmas faced in carrying on this correspondence: "Under the most favorable aspects this correspondence must always be unsatisfactory, even exasperatingly so. . . . It is as though we were hallooing to each other across an impassable ravine. . . . There is nowhere in physical nature a mountain abyss so hopelessly impassable and obstructive to the traveller as that spiritual one, which keeps them [the two Englishmen] back from me [KH]." Besides the problem of terminology, to which reference has already been made, undoubtedly the major difficulty lay in the lack of sympathetic attunement of the minds of Sinnett and Hume with the consciousness of the Adept Teachers. The need for such mental attunement and having a mind free of preconceived ideas, prejudices, likes and dislikes, is emphasized on many occasions through the letters.

As we know, M was averse from the beginning to enter into communication with the Englishmen. It was only after his refusal that HPB applied, as it were, to KH to respond to Sinnett's inquiries. But when KH had to suspend the correspondence because of his commitment to a "journey" that would require his absence from the outer world, he appealed to his Brother to "watch over" his "work . . . [to] see it falls not into ruin." Here, in Letter 29, we have M's beautiful response: "I promised. What is there I would not have promised him at that hour!" It is a response that reveals the depth of affection between the two Adepts, perhaps called forth because M, who was evidently senior to KH, knew from his own experience the nature of the inner journey on which KH had embarked.

The description that M then gives of the site of KH's retreat has given rise to much speculation regarding its exact location in Tibet. An English student of the letters, G. N. Drinkwater, in an article entitled "Master KH's Retreat and the Tower of the Bodhisattvas," (*The Theosophist*, August 1978) speculates:

> The mention of the "chasm" and the "raging torrent" would seem to rule out the oasis of Shamballa. It is also unlikely that it could be situated anywhere in the Indian plains, more especially as a lamasery suggests a Tibetan form of Buddhism. . . . There are lamaseries situated in Ladakh—the eastern portion of Kashmir where it joins the western highlands of Tibet. . . . HPB also speaks of lamaseries

in the Altyn Tag and the Kuen Lun mountains on the southern and western Tibetan borders. On another occasion, Master KH speaks of visiting a lamasery near Darjeeling. . . . Kashmir is noted for its great natural beauty and for the deep gorges cut by its rivers. It may be concluded that a possible locality is between Ladakh and western Kashmir, somewhere on or near the boundary and ill-defined on maps.

More recently, an article titled "Towering Mysteries" in the April 2004 issue of the *Smithsonian* magazine reported the findings of an amateur archaeologist Martine "Frederique" Darragon concerning a number of old stone towers scattered across the Himalayan foothills. Darragon is credited with photographing and measuring nearly two hundred such towers located in the Sichuan Province of western China and in Tibet. Radiocarbon-dating wood samples from thirty-two of these towers showed that they are several hundred years old, although one structure in Kongpo, Tibet, proved much older and was likely built between one thousand and twelve hundred years ago. Darragon was particularly intrigued by the star shape of the towers, some having eight points and others twelve points. There is, quite naturally, a mystery about these towers and considerable speculation about their purpose.

Of greater significance is the question as to the nature of KH's retreat. In a letter, the date of which is not noted, HPB wrote to the American medium Mrs. Hollis-Billings (published in *The Theosophical Forum*, May, 1936):

KH or Koot-Hoomi is now gone to sleep for three months to prepare during this Sumadhi (*sic.*) or continuous trance state for his initiation, the last but one, when he will become one of the highest adepts. . . . Poor KH his body is now lying cold and stiff in a separate square building of stone with no windows or doors in it, the entrance to which is effected through an underground passage from a door in Toong-ting (reliquary, a room situated in every

Thaten [temple] or Lamasery); and his Spirit is quite free. An adept might lie so for years, when his body was carefully prepared for it beforehand by mesmeric passes, etc. It is a beautiful spot where he is now in the square tower. The Himalayas on the right and a lovely lake near the lamasery. His Chohan . . . takes care of his body. M also goes occasionally to visit him. . . . Now Morya lives generally with Koot-Hoomi who has his house in the direction of the Kara Korum Mountains.

In regard to initiations, we may turn to *The Secret Doctrine* (1:206–7) for HPB's description:

There are four grades of initiation mentioned in exoteric works, which are known respectively in Sanskrit as "Srotapanna," "Sakridagamin," "Anagamin," and "Arhat"—the four paths to Nirvana, in this, our Fourth Round, bearing the same appellations. The Arhat, though he can see the Past, the Present, and the Future, is not yet the highest Initiate; for the Adept himself, the initiated candidate, becomes chela (pupil) to a higher Initiate. Three further grades have to be conquered by the Arhat who would reach the apex of the ladder of Arhatship. There are those who have reached it even in this fifth race of ours, but the faculties necessary for the attainment of these higher grades will be fully developed in the average ascetic only at the end of this Root-Race, and in the Sixth and Seventh.

If indeed, KH lay prone, "cold and stiff," in an "old tower, within whose bosom have gestated generations of Bodhisattvas," we may gain some further insight into both the Mahatma's state of consciousness and the nature of the Tower itself from the Buddhist text *The Gandavyuha*. A translation with commentary is provided by Buddhist scholar, D. T. Suzuki in *On Indian Mahayana Buddhism*. Suzuki writes that the Tower is known as *Vairocana-vyuha-alankara-garbha*, or "the tower which holds within itself an array of brilliantly shining ornaments," though these ornaments are not objective in nature. "When the Vairocana Tower is . . . described as the Vihara (abode or retreat) of Maitreya, the attributes enumerated . . . apply . . . to all the Bodhisattvas." Then follows a symbolic description of all that lies within the Tower in terms of bodhisattvic qualities.

The acquisition of those qualities, however, may call for the aspirant to undergo some very challenging experiences. Hence the necessity for KH's "retreat." As HPB speaks of a "ladder of Arhatship" in the passage just quoted from *The Secret Doctrine*, we can only guess at the nature of the step KH is now taking. The late Fritz Kunz, a prominent American student, once suggested in a private conversation that one of the steps, and quite possibly the one KH took on his retreat, involved a passage through the "nether world," confronting the demonic denizens below the earth. To explore this further, one needs to study a subject given only a little space in *The Secret Doctrine* but dealt with by HPB in her esoteric writings. That is the subject of what are known as the *lokas* and *talas*, both words definable as worlds, places, or states. As G. de Purucker explains in his *Occult Glossary*, "Lokas and talas . . . may be considered to be the spiritual and the material aspects or substance-principles of the different worlds which compose and in fact are the kosmic [*sic*] universe." The English Theosophist E. L. Gardner, in his little work, *The Wider View*, writes: "The Lokas are 'up,' just as heaven is said to be 'above,' but the Talas are here at the surface of the earth, and 'down' beneath" (see particularly chapter 26, "After Death States"). In her E.S. Instruction No. 4 (see *CW*, 12:663–72 and diagram 5), HPB states: "The Lokas and Talas represent planes of consciousness on this earth, through some of which all men must pass, and through all of which the Chela must pass on his way to Adeptship." As though reiterating this fact she adds: "These . . . are planes from without within, and states of consciousness through which man can pass and must pass, once he is determined to go through the seven paths and portals of Dhyani. . . . All this is reached on earth in one or many of the incarnations." It seems reasonable to assume, from any study of the lokas and talas, that KH's retreat may have been related with passing through states of consciousness indicated by those terms.

Before continuing with Letter 29, it seems appropriate to call attention to KH's own comment in a later letter regarding his retreat. Writing in Letter 117 about the circumstances that gave rise to the famous "Kiddle incident," he states, "Since the palmy days of the 'impressions' and 'precipitation'—'KH' has been born into a new and higher light, and even that one, in no wise the most dazzling to be acquired on this earth. Verily the Light of Omniscience and infallible Prevision on this earth—that shines only for the highest Chohan alone—is yet far away from me!"

After this lengthy digression concerning KH's "retreat" and M's beautiful and moving description of its site, we can return to the remainder of Letter 29, commenting on a few of the very significant statements we find in it. Much of the letter deals with Hume's reaction and quite false accusation of HPB. To understand the full context of M's remarks, we need to review a few events. First, during Colonel Olcott's stay in Ceylon, he wrote a letter to Hume in which he said: "I do not know whether or not there is any significance in the fact of my Chohan's [M's] visiting me on the night of the 27th but you may. He made me rise, sit at the table, and write from his dictation" (*Hints on Esoteric Theosophy*, no. 1, 2nd ed., 1882, 82–83). Replying to Olcott, Hume mentions that he and Sinnett had written a letter to KH that M and HPB had "so muddled and misunderstood . . . as to lead to our receiving a message wholly inapplicable to the circumstances." There is a final reference, in the next to the last paragraph of Letter 29 (page 94), to Olcott's letter (called here his "*memo*, which produced such disastrous results") and the fact that KH asked M to speak to Olcott. This may seem a bit strange, until we realize that Olcott was a chela of M's and from other references in the letters, it appears there are strict rules regarding contacts with chelas of other Adepts. Yet note again the beautiful bond between the two Mahatmas, as M tells Sinnett, "KH wishes are—law to me."

This, in brief, is the background to M's statements (page 88) in Letter 29, and one can only wonder at the length to which M goes in reviewing all the consequences of Hume's "irritation" with HPB over what he perceived as misstatements. What emerges, of course, is M's deep concern for HPB and his warning to her that unless "she learned to control herself better than she did, I [M] would put a stop to that dak business," meaning her service as a kind of post office for transmitting letters from Hume and Sinnett to the Mahatmas.

Notably, the Mahatma can be sharply critical and generously approving of the Englishman in the same sentence. For example, he calls Hume "the most sincere and outspoken man in India" and adds that he is "unable to tolerate a contradiction and, be that person Dev or mortal, he cannot appreciate or even permit without protest the same qualities of sincerity in any other than himself. Nor can he be brought to confess that anyone in this world can know better than himself anything that HE has studied and formed his opinion thereupon." M quotes Hume as complaining, in his letter to Olcott, that the Masters "will not set about the joint work in what seems to ME the best way" and then comments that this sentence alone gives the key to Hume's whole character. Yet later the Mahatma says, "When the spiritual soul is left to guide him, no purer, no better, nor kinder man can be found. But when his fifth principle [manas] rises in irrepressible pride, he will always confront and challenge it."

The letter also contains some remarkable statements about the principles rather than the personalities involved, and it is these to which we should give particular attention. A statement that may well apply to all of us concerns the need to know ourselves: "He who is desirous to learn how to benefit humanity, and believes himself able to read the characters of other people, must begin first of all, to learn to know himself, to appreciate his own character at its true value." So we may ask ourselves: Just how well do we know ourselves? What are our likely reactions in any particular circumstance or to people we meet?

Then there are the beautiful statements that aid us in understanding the nature of the Mahatmas themselves. "Disabuse your minds," writes M, "and remember that the first requisite in even a simple fakir, is that he should have trained himself to remain as indifferent to moral pain as to physical suffering. Nothing can give us personal pain or pleasure. And what I now say is, rather to bring you to understand us than yourselves which is the most difficult science to learn." And revealing the Mahatma's commitment to the ideal of brotherhood and service: "I am as I was; and, as I was and am, so am I likely always to be—the slave of my duty to the Lodge and mankind; not only taught, but desirous to subordinate every preference for individuals to a love for the human race." To which he adds, "Law is LAW with us, and no power can make us abate one jot or tittle of our duty."

As we know, at the very beginning of the correspondence, Sinnett, followed by Hume, wanted to have phenomena produced that would prove conclusively that the Mahatmas really existed. In this letter M states: "We do not wish Mr. Hume or you to prove conclusively to the public that we really exist. Please realize the fact that so long as men doubt there will be curiosity and enquiry, and that enquiry stimulates reflection which begets effort; but let our secret be once thoroughly vulgarized and not only will sceptical society derive no great good but our privacy would be constantly endangered and have to be continually guarded at an unreasonable cost of power." Surely this statement gives us much to ponder!

As M draws his letter to a close, he reminds Sinnett: "You have been chasing us around your own shadows . . . never coming near enough to escape the gaunt skeleton of suspicion. . . . You have not patience to read the volume to its end. For you are trying to penetrate the things of the spirit with the eyes of the flesh." Do we, too, like Sinnett and Hume, chase our own shadows, desire proof, fail to awaken our spiritual vision, which, as we shall see, is spoken of in Letter 31? So closes a letter pregnant with so much meaning, so much for us to consider and reflect upon and try to understand. It is truly a beautiful letter that introduces us to the greatness, the nobility, the generosity, and the wisdom of the Mahatma M.

LETTER 30

As the prefatory note says, Letter 30 is from HPB, written during her travels in Northern India and incorporating a message dictated to her, as she says, by her Master. We may presume that it follows closely on the letter she sent to Sinnett, quoted just below, as she indicates that she has at last seen M and he has "dictated" a reply to Sinnett's query. We do not know the nature of Sinnett's question, but it evidently concerned certain members in Allahabad who wished to be put in contact with the Mahatmas.

As we know from the letters, the Mahatma M did not like writing, so it appears that on at least two occasions (the one we are considering and the one noted below) he used his chela HPB to communicate to the two Englishmen. We can only surmise that his "longest letter" (Letter 29) must have been quite an exception, and, of course, there are further letters from him, whether written by him or by chelas we do not know. A significant point, one we will return to later, is that when chelas are the transcribers or transmitters of the Mahatmas' letters, some distortion, or even alteration, of the ideas the Mahatmas intend to convey is always possible.

Before considering Letter 30 itself, we should examine a letter HPB wrote to Sinnett about the same time, early November 1881. HPB heads her letter: "Ordered by My Boss to tell Sinnett, Esq., the following," and then she lists seven points (*LBS*, 5–6). While only points 3 and 6 relate to items in Letter 30, the entire letter is quite fascinating, so I quote it here in full, with comments added in square brackets:

1. Not to lose the opportunity to night (*sic*) of acquainting R. S. [Ross Scott] with *every detail* of the situation he can think of, whether relating to the Society or his projected matrimonial ideas. [Ross Scott and Minnie Hume, daughter of A. O. Hume, were married on December 28, 1881.]

2. To insist upon having a true copy of the hitherto written sketches of Cosmogony with the Tibetan words, M's notes etc. HPB is also ordered to have one, as she has to know thoroughly what Mr. Hume has noted and how much he has elaborated of the explanations. Otherwise when the reaction comes and Mr. Hume begins studying once more—neither Mr. Sinnett nor HPB will be *au courant* of his thoughts; and he will begin once more abusing—like the quartette of musicians in Aesop's fable—the *instruments* on which he does not know to play. [This refers to the first set of Cosmological Notes in the appendix, pages 508–18, on which I comment in a prequel to Letter 44.]

3. Mr. Sinnett is advised, once he is in Allahabad, to announce the formation of the Allahabad Society, calling it "The Anglo Indian Investigation (Theosophical) Society" or some such name which would not jar upon the nerves of the unbelieving community. Let it be distinct from the other Branch in Allahabad called the "Prayaga Theos. Society" though the Hindus in it might be very useful to Mr. Sinnett and he will find wonderful *mesmeric* subjects in it, if he but searches. [Sinnett's home was in Allahabad, but he had been at his summer residence in Simla. The Prayag Psychic Theosophical Society was established on November 6, 1881.]

4. Mr. Sinnett is advised by M to make a special duty to prevent his little son being made to eat meat—not even fowls, and to write so to Mrs. Sinnett. Once the Mother has placed the child under KH's protection let her see nothing pollutes his nature. The child may become a powerful engine for good in a near future. Let him be trained as *his own nature* suggests it. [The Sinnetts' son, Denny, was born in 1877 and died from tuberculosis in 1908, after what has been called a "short life of unbroken failure." Certainly he never became "a powerful engine for good" as the Mahatmas had hoped.]

5. Mr. S. is reminded to telegraph O. not to answer one word to M. Hume until he receives a letter from Mr. Sinnett. [This appears to have to do with a pamphlet that Hume had written on Theosophy;

it seems that Hume had made some remarks skeptical of the Mahatmas, to which Olcott was taking exception.]

6. Mr. S. is advised, now that he will be alone, to put himself in communication through Adytyarum B. with some Hindu mystics, not for the sake of philosophy but to find out what mental phenomena can be produced. At the *Mela* [festival] there is a number of such visiting the town. [Prof. Adytyarum Bhattacharya was a noted Sanskritist, referred to in Letter 30, and should not be confused with Benemadhab (or Benee Madhab Bhattacharya) also mentioned in the same letter.]

7. Whenever he feels like writing or needs M advice, Mr. Sinnett is invited to do so without hesitation. M will *always* answer him, not only for KH's sake but his own sake, as Mr. S. has proved that even an Anglo-Indian can have the true S——— Spark in him, which no amount of brandy and soda and other stuff can extinguish and which will occasionally glitter out and very brightly. [It is not known what word the Mahatma had in mind to complete the "true S———" or what word HPB may have thought he had in mind. Students have speculated that it could have been "Sannyasi," meaning a holy person.]

The list is followed by a note in M's handwriting (printed in bold type in the book) which concludes: "All of the above is correct. Yours, M."

Letter 30 itself was destined to become one of the most controversial letters in the correspondence. Called the "Prayag Letter," as it concerns individuals who were or later became members of the Prayag Psychic Theosophical Society (see item 3 in HPB's letter above), its authenticity was called into question some years after HPB's death. (For the full extent of the controversy see the extensive correspondence and published articles brought together as appendix B: "The Prayag Letter" in *The Judge Case* by Ernest Pelletier.) The controversy centered on statements early in the letter that seemed to attack the Brahmanic philosophy and require members to become

Buddhists. Whether HPB, in transmitting her Teacher's words, got herself into the picture, as it were, is a question each student is invited to consider without bias or prejudgment.

However one views Letter 30, it does contain some remarkable statements, even in the early controversial part of the letter, that deserve pondering. What, for instance, is meant by being "prepared to become a thorough theosophist"? Are we to become "Nastikas"? Some years later, HPB would write in *The Secret Doctrine*: "The Secret Doctrine teaches no *Atheism*, except in the Hindu sense of the word *nastika*, or the rejection of idols, including every anthropomorphic god. In this sense every Occultist is a *nastika*" (*SD*, 1:279).

Then there are the comments in Letter 30 regarding the "'Chohans of Darkness' . . . imperfect 'Intelligences'" who, it is said, "preside at the Pralayas." One may smile a little at HPB's interjection "I can't" to M's instruction to her to "Explain this to Mr. Sinnett." Are these the "Brothers of the Shadow" spoken of in Letter 18? Are the dual forces that we term "good" and "evil" always operating throughout the universe? What does it mean that the "Brothers [the Mahatmas] . . . could prolong life but they could not destroy death"? Is death, then, an essential part of the process we call life? Is destruction as necessary to the scheme of things as creation? Why are the Mahatmas able to "palliate evil and relieve suffering" but not "destroy evil"? In later letters we will come upon further comments concerning the so-called problem of evil, but M's statements, as recorded by HPB in this letter, should prompt us to think deeply on such questions, particularly as related to current world events and the rise of terrorism as well as continued conflict.

The letter concludes with HPB's own concern for needing proof of her identity, since continued attacks on her are appearing in the *Civil and Military Gazette*, even accusing her of being a Russian spy. This is referred to again in Letter 31. As we know, accusations against HPB for all manner of things occurred not only during her years in India but continue even to the present day, resurrected in books, articles, news reports, and so forth, wherever her name is mentioned in a sensational way.

LETTER 31

A gain and again throughout the letters, the Mahatmas express concern not only about the welfare of the Society but also about the reputation of the Founders, HPB and Colonel Olcott, indicating that the two were so intertwined that the work of the Society itself could not progress unless the "position of the Founders," as stated at the outset of this Letter, was "perfectly and undeniably proved." This seems to be not only M and KH's concern but their superiors' as well. Regarding the individuals the Mahatma mentions in this letter as providing evidence to clear HPB's name of the accusations made against her: the "uncle" who wrote letters to both Sinnett and HPB was the Russian general, military writer, and renowned reformer Rostislav Andreyevich de Fadeyev (for a biographical sketch see *CW*, 3:506–7). The Prince Alexander Dondoukoff-Korsakov, also a military man of some renown, was a close family friend to whom HPB appealed for official assistance in clearing her name of the charges of being a Russian spy (for his biography see *CW*, 6:432).

The attack on Olcott as well as on Theosophy involved the publication in a pamphlet of two scurrilous articles that had originally appeared in a London and a New York newspaper. This occurred during the Colonel's visit to Ceylon in 1881; the entire story of the pamphlet's distribution and the Colonel's public response is recorded by Olcott in his *Old Diary Leaves* (2:310–11), and makes for most interesting reading. Concluding his account, Olcott writes: "This is the sort of warfare that we have had to encounter throughout the whole period of our Indian work; and almost invariably the offenders have been Protestant missionaries."

In reading the Mahatmas' concern that the good names of HPB and Olcott should be defended, we today may well marvel at each of the founders' loyalty and steadfastness in pursuing the work to which they were giving their total commitment. Lesser individuals might well have given up in despair, perhaps even doubting the sacredness of their mission and the support of those they considered their Teachers. We must surely ask ourselves what we would do in the face of continual ridicule, abusive attack in the press, and the questioning of our identity as well as our motives.

Continuing with Letter 31, M then comments on an individual named Suby Ram, a medium with a considerable following, who evidently had a "Society" established around a "guru" whom he and his followers considered the incarnation of "the one and only God of the Universe." It may be that Sinnett, who as we know was always interested in mediumship and mediumistic communications, had consulted this individual and even considered joining his Society. While M tells Sinnett there would be "no harm" in joining Suby Ram's Society, he gives Sinnett much to think about concerning the distinction between what he calls "mediums" and "sensitives." Especially significant is the Mahatma's comment on the "law of vision (physical and mental or spiritual)" and the "qualifying special law" that relates the nature of what is perceived to the individual's (whether a seer, a mystic, or a medium) own spiritual development. Particularly to be noted is M's statement: "Unless regularly initiated and trained . . . no self-tutored seer or clairaudient ever saw or heard quite correctly." True "spiritual insight" is the result of "training," and even more of "self-discipline," for which, as is stressed in all the Theosophical literature, a teacher is necessary.

M's statement "Go on [that is, receive instruction from Suby Ram] until he demands what you will be obliged to refuse" may puzzle us as to its meaning. What do self-proclaimed "gurus" always demand? Is it not absolute conformity to their statements, complete loyalty to themselves alone, the abandonment of one's free will to question or to judge what is said? Sinnett, being an independent thinker, would be unable to submit to such a demand. M cautions Sinnett further: "Remember your sacred promise to KH," reminding him that only two months remain of KH's "retreat." While we do not know the nature of Sinnett's "sacred promise to KH," we may assume from reading Sinnett's *Autobiography*, that he never joined Suby Ram's group.

For the student interested in knowing why there is a reference to Keshub Chunder Sen, the answer may be found in a statement by HPB concerning "the spurious Brahmo Samaj calling itself New Dispensation," a reform movement in Hinduism of which Keshub Chunder Sen was one of the leaders. HPB describes it as a movement "where all is to be taken on faith and the Universal Infallibility is claimed to have taken its Headquarters in the person of Babu Keshub Chunder Sen who has now come to comparing himself publicly . . . with Jesus Christ" (see *CW*, 6:12).

While it is a relatively short letter, Letter 31 does contain much of value, particularly in regard to what the Mahatma calls "the law of vision," whether that vision be psychic or spiritual.

LETTER 32

The quite brief Letter 32 is of interest for two reasons. First, it refers to the possibility of having applications and obligations for what is later called a women's Branch of the Society. Evidently Hume, who was in many ways much closer to the Indian population than was Sinnett, had at one time proposed such a Branch. I comment on this further in commentary on the next letter.

Second, it contains a remarkable statement by M: "I have a reason for everything of mine." We may well extrapolate from this that the Mahatmas do have reasons for everything they do, and while those reasons may not always be apparent to us, as they certainly were not to Sinnett, we may assume that with their greater wisdom and insight into the future they acted from quite a different perspective than we normally do.

M remarks that Sinnett "may learn some years hence" the reasons for the Mahatmas' present actions. Whether the Englishman ever did so learn, it is difficult to say, but as we study the letters and also acquaint ourselves with historical developments in the years following their receipt, we can speculate on some of those reasons.

LETTER 33

Frequently throughout the correspondence the Mahatmas quote from Sinnett's or Hume's letters, as M does here in Letter 33. It appears that Sinnett has addressed Morya as "Illustrious" or perhaps "Illustrious Highness." Both Sinnett and Hume occasionally spoke of the Mahatmas as "Their Highnesses" because they thought the Mahatmas deliberately made themselves unapproachable and withheld knowledge from them. Sinnett also accuses the Mahatma of being "satirical," which M denies, saying that what Sinnett has interpreted as satire is only "frankness in speech." Such frankness is particularly true of M's letters, perhaps a little less so in the letters from KH, who was often more gentle in his evaluation of Sinnett's character.

However, the important topic here is M's concern that his brother will be disappointed with the continued bickering, if we may call it that, between Hume and HPB. Evidently M enclosed with this letter to Sinnett an exchange of correspondence between those two individuals, the letter from Hume being "undignified, bitter, sarcastic," while the other from HPB was "undignified, foolish and childish." We do know that even though Hume often defended HPB against attacks in the newspapers, he frequently wrote her sarcastic and even cruel letters. She, with her fiery temperament, never failed to pick up the gauntlet. We can only keep in mind the psychological difficulties under which HPB labored, as KH explains in Letter 22. We know that both Mahatmas were endlessly patient with her, being aware of the complications of her nature.

M now takes up the question of establishing a women's Branch of the Society, a subject briefly referred to in Letter 32. He notes first that he is certain that HPB would not favor the idea, and second that neither he nor KH would involve themselves with it. KH, says M, "knows nothing" of women "with the exception of his sister," and yet he "always felt a need of enrolling" them in the Society. Regarding KH's sister, C. W. Leadbeater comments in *The Masters and the Path*:

> Of the Master's family I know but little. There is a lady, evidently a pupil, whom He calls "sister." Whether she is actually his sister or not I do not know; she might possibly be a cousin or a niece. She looks much older than He, but that would not make the relationship improbable, as He has appeared of about the same age for a long time. She resembles Him to a certain extent, and once or twice when there have been gatherings she has come and joined the party; though her principal work seems to be to look after the housekeeping and manage the servants. (page 33)

However, the issue of a women's Branch pales in comparison with the Mahatma's far greater concern over the welfare of the Society, which, as he says in Letter 31, involves the situation with the founders. He states frankly once again, "It is the vilification and abuse of the founders, the general misconception of the aims and objects . . . that paralyses" the work of the Society. Since M tells Sinnett that the objects are definite and need only be properly explained, it may be useful to note what were the Objects of the Society at that time. As revised earlier that year, specifically on February 17, 1881, at a meeting in Bombay, the Objects of the Society read:

1. To form the Nucleus of a Universal Brotherhood of Humanity.
2. To study Aryan literature, religion and science.
3. To vindicate the importance of this enquiry and correct misrepresentations with which it has been clouded.
4. To explore the hidden mysteries of Nature and the latent powers of Man, on which the Founders believe that Oriental Philosophy is in a position to throw light.

M follows this with a rather stern pronouncement regarding the motives for joining the Society. We may well compare what he says with motives that are apparent today. Do some still join "with the one selfish object of reaching power, making occult science their only or even chief aim"? Do any join "with the sole object of coming in contact" with the Mahatmas? What, we may well ask ourselves, has been our own motive in joining the Society, or even for not joining? Perhaps today no one finds there is "preach[ing] too much" about the Mahatmas—or is there "too little" emphasis on "Brotherhood"?

Certainly M's words, as applicable today as when they were written, can serve as a profound reminder of the real work of the Society: "It is he alone who has the love of humanity at heart, who is capable of grasping thoroughly the idea of a regenerating practical Brotherhood who is entitled to the possession of our secrets. He alone, such a man will never misuse his powers, as there will be no fear that he should turn them to selfish ends. A man who places not the good of mankind above his own good is not worthy of becoming our chela—he is not worthy of becoming higher in knowledge than his neighbour."

Much thought should be given to those words: "a regenerating practical Brotherhood." To what extent are we "seeking to know the truth yet not able to find it" because we seek it "only for [our] own private benefit . . . without giving one thought to others"? In the light of current events—the continuation of conflict and the seemingly insoluble problems of racial and religious hatreds, poverty, and ecological disaster—M's words are as meaningful today as in 1881: "The world has clouded the light of true knowledge, and *selfishness* will not allow its resurrection, for it excludes and will not recognize the whole fellowship of all those who were born under the same immutable natural law."

Yet in spite of the sternness and frankness expressed throughout this letter, the Mahatma concludes with reassurance that must have brought Sinnett some comfort and relief. He encourages the Englishman to use his "intellectual capacities for reasoning" even if he perceives matters "in a false light." And he tells him that "one superior quality" he possesses is that he does not "concentrate all the light" on himself. What is more, it is Sinnett's affection for KH that endears him to M—a reiteration of the beautiful bond between the two Mahatmas. It is because of that affection that "whatever happens," the two Adepts "will ever remain your friends"—a beautiful ending to a letter that in many ways reprimands Sinnett for his misunderstandings.

LETTERS 34 AND 35

Letters 34 and 35 can be considered together, as they both refer to the abusive attacks on HPB at this time and the Mahatma's hopes that Sinnett will act to ameliorate the situation. What is most moving is M's deep concern for HPB, knowing she is suffering "acutely" while he is "unable to help her," since his "Arhat vows" mean that he can neither "seek revenge nor help others to obtain it." He adds, "Revenge *is* unholy. But we have *defence* and she has a right to it. Defence and *full vindication she* must have." Thus he appeals to Sinnett to "write for her [HPB] a nice pungent letter signed with her name and Olcott's ... [to] be published first in the Pioneer [the paper of which Sinnett is editor]," and also to draft a "circular letter [to be sent] to every paper in the land."

Undoubtedly everyone would agree that we should never seek revenge even for what we know to be injustice or slander. But we need also to remember that one of the steps in HPB's "Golden Stairs" is "defense of those who are unjustly attacked." Since HPB is still the subject of slanderous attacks in books, newspaper and journal articles, and in the media generally, we may ask how we should respond today in defending her and whether we should "demand retraction" as the Mahatma advises Sinnett in Letter 34.

Concerning the Mahatma's "Arhat vows," it may be helpful to review HPB's statements on the "four grades of initiation" in the Buddhist tradition in *The Secret Doctrine* (1:206–7; see also the commentary on Letter 29). Other letters contain references to initiations, which we will examine as we come upon them. The fact that both M and KH often spoke of their "superiors" confirms what HPB states in the passage just quoted: the "Arhat vows" did not constitute the final step on the ladder of spiritual illumination.

In Letter 34, M speaks of the "Odessa Old Lady," who was, of course, HPB's favorite aunt, Madame Nadejda Fadeef (or Fadeyev), the recipient of the first letter from a Mahatma of which we have record. The "General" is HPB's uncle, General Rostislav Andreyvich de Fadeyev, whom HPB mentions in Letter 30 as sending an official letter of identification. The portrait of HPB known as "the lovely maiden" may be found in a number of places, perhaps most easily in Geoffrey Barborka's *H. P. Blavatsky, Tibet and Tulku.* Especially significant is M's comment that it is a portrait of HPB as he "first knew her," indicating that their association dated at least as far back as 1851, when she met her Master in London.

Later in Letter 34, M tells Sinnett he will send him an "explanatory appendix" in a few days. This is probably a reference to the document known as "Cosmological Notes," which Sinnett had received some two months earlier. It is included as an appendix in the chronological edition of the Mahatma Letters. I will comment at some length when we come to Letter 44. Perhaps because the Mahatma is more concerned at this time with HPB's "defence and vindication" such a supplement or "appendix" had to be deferred. In the meantime, Sinnett is advised to "develop your metaphysical intuitions"—which are certainly necessary for us as well if we are to fully understand the teachings conveyed in those "Notes." Incidentally, there is no evidence that such an appendix was ever received, so perhaps the Mahatma did not send it at all.

One significant and perhaps puzzling phrase in Letter 35 needs to be understood. In speaking of HPB's suffering from the attacks made on her, M says, "This is effect from causes which *cannot* be *undone*" and then adds "occultism in theosophy." We would probably say that the cause-effect connection is simply the workings of the law of karma, which of course it is, but it may be useful to read again the Mahatma's comments on the subject in Letter 29, page 86. In addition, the Mahatmas as well as HPB apparently made a clear distinction between occultism and Theosophy. In an article published in her journal, *Lucifer*, in April 1888, and since published in the small booklet *Practical Occultism*, HPB says there is an "essential difference between theoretical and practical Occultism; or what is generally known as Theosophy on the one hand, and Occult science on the other."

She continues: "It is easy to become a Theosophist. . . . But it is quite another matter to put oneself upon the path." The entire article as republished in *Practical Occultism* is worth studying. The student may also refer again to the commentary on Letter 2, where the subject of occultism and occult science is addressed. As HPB was certainly well advanced on "the Path" and is usually considered to have been a high Initiate, her phrase "occultism in theosophy" may have had a significance not easy for us to understand, but at least hinted at in KH's explanation of her psychological condition in Letter 22.

M makes an interesting side comment on the matter of karma when he tells Sinnett (page 104) that the Englishman is discharging some of his own karmic obligations by his defense of HPB. So, says M, "Courage"—a beautiful encouragement when Sinnett may have been feeling some despair.

LETTER 36

The very brief Letter 36 concerns the admission of some new members into the Society. The word "initiate" is used in connection with such an admission, as not only in the early days of the Society but for many years thereafter Lodges (or Branches) had "initiation ceremonies"—some more formal than others—to admit members. This practice seems to have decreased in recent years.

The reference to Hume's preoccupation with "his index," and the Mahatma's comment on what Hume may expect of him, are clarified by a remark of HPB's in a letter to Sinnett about this time (see *LBS*, 10): "Mr. Hume? Why Mr. Hume never said a word about the 'Brothers' . . . except to sneer at them once or twice. He said to me before leaving: 'In a week I will have done my work of "Stray Feathers" [the ornithological journal published by Hume] and I must receive a MS. from Morya if he wants me to go on.'"

From M's comment in Letter 36, there clearly will be no "MS." unless Hume asks questions of the Mahatma—a reminder that throughout the correspondence the two Englishmen were expected to pose questions before answers could be given.

This brief note ends with M's reiteration of the possibility (mentioned at the outset of Letter 33) that KH, on his return, will be disappointed that so little progress has been made in the work he has so much at heart. The final note about the "Prayag theosophists"—Prayag being the ancient name of Allahabad—takes us back to the letter HPB wrote from M's dictation (Letter 30).

LETTER 37

Letter 37 is perhaps the most interesting and in many ways the most moving letter in the correspondence. It is signed the "Disinherited," a frequent designation for Djual Khul (DK), a chela—undoubtedly of a high status—of the Mahatma KH. The letter is largely a message from KH to Sinnett, as given through DK, who states at the outset, "I am . . . commanded to be the hand to indite His message." DK also adds after the initial paragraph: "These are the Master's words, as with His help I am enabled to frame them in your language." From this, we may assume that DK was not familiar with English, and that KH, although still not in a position to communicate with Sinnett directly, could project not only the ideas but also the very language in which those ideas were to be clothed.

It is interesting to contrast this letter with Letter 30, in which a chela conveys a message from a Mahatma—in that case, HPB conveying a message from M, her teacher or guru. HPB served as the messenger for her teacher in other instances, most notably Letter 4 in *LBS*. Djual Khul certainly appears very faithful to KH's words, whereas we may feel that at times HPB, in communicating her teacher's ideas, may have interposed her own thoughts into the message.

Letter 37 opens with the significant statement "The Master has awaked and bids me write," indicating that KH's three-month retreat has concluded and that as his chela, Djual Khul may have been with his Master during that period, perhaps serving his physical needs or protecting him in some manner. While this is only conjecture, the fact that the chela was aware of KH's "awakening" from a "lifeless" condition, as M describes his Brother's state in Letter 29, suggests a special bond between pupil and master. While the whole subject of the chela-Master relationship has been explored earlier in our consideration of the letters, the student may find it useful to consider it again in connection with Letter 37.

One cannot help but be moved by the fact that on awakening from his retreat, KH's thoughts should turn to his friend and lay-chela Sinnett. Even though KH is still unable to correspond directly, he appears eager to inform Sinnett, through Djual Khul, that the retreat is concluded and that whatever further initiatory step he has taken, he is still "quite as friendly" as he had been before the long period of silence. His special feeling for Sinnett is evidenced by the assurance that the Englishman will hear from him "directly at the earliest, practicable opportunity."

We may recall that in Letter 33, and again in Letter 36, M has said that KH may be disappointed in Sinnett's lack of progress in his studies. How encouraging, then, are Djual Khul's words on behalf of

KH that Sinnett has proved his zeal in aiding "the Cause we love." The statement that Sinnett while "laboring for your neighbor" has "most effectually worked for yourself" echoes M's comment at the conclusion of Letter 35 that Sinnett should remember "you are working off by helping her [HPB] your own law of retribution." This aspect of the law of karma may be particularly important to consider in some depth. Certainly the law is far more complex in its operation than the simplistic interpretation often given to events and circumstances.

In Djual Khul's words that "a fixed period" of time must pass before KH can "expose Himself to the thought currents inflowing so strongly from beyond the Himavat" we may find a parallel to our own experiences. How often after a profound period of meditation do we feel the need to return to our normal activities slowly! The testimony of many mystics also indicates that after a genuine mystical experience time is required to assimilate it before resuming work in the world. Specifically in regard to KH, M wrote to Colonel Olcott about this same time [January 1882]: "KH's conditions are changed, you must remember, he is no more this 'Kashmiri' of old" (see *LMW*, Second Series, Letter 35). KH himself comments in a later letter (Letter 117), in regard to quite another situation, that since the communications began he "has been born into a new and higher light, and even that one, in no wise the most dazzling to be acquired on this earth."

We may pause to consider KH's injunction to Sinnett, as conveyed by DK, asking him to recognize the change that has taken place in himself: "The man of 1880 would scarcely recognise the man of 1881." Although we do not have Sinnett's letters to the Mahatmas during that first year of the correspondence, we may be able to judge in some measure, from the letters he received, the nature of this change. Of particular significance is KH's enjoining Sinnett to "meditate—alone, with the magic mirror of memory to gaze into" in order to compare and understand what has occurred. Perhaps should we all, from time to time, engage in such inner reflection if we would "see the Ego of aforetime in its naked reality" so that in viewing "the lights and shadows of the Past" we may also glimpse "the possible brightness of the Future, as well." Does the "magic mirror of memory," then, give us access to both past and future?

DK interrupts the message from KH, saying he is "permitted" to do so, in order to thank Sinnett "for the genuine sympathy which you felt for me at the time when a slight accident due to my forgetfulness laid me on my bed of sickness." M also refers to this incident in a postscript to Letter 34, and HPB describes it graphically in *LBS*, Letter 8. There she refers to Djual Khul as a "chela . . . of the 1st degree"—giving us the right to call him a chela of high degree, although he calls himself "but a humble chela." While expressing his gratitude to Sinnett, DK also comments on at least one aspect of "the training for adeptship," the conscious use of what the Mahatmas call "Will-Essence" and the capacity to "emit and feel this form of force." We may assume this to be what is generally known today as a healing energy or "long-distance healing," which has been studied in recent years. "Everyone is practically, albeit unconsciously demonstrating" the use of such healing power "every day and every moment," DK says. This is reminiscent of KH's statement in his first letter to Hume, that we are "continually peopling [our] current in space . . . a current which reacts upon any sensitive or . . . nervous organization which comes in contact with it in proportion to its dynamic intensity."

Although KH cannot communicate directly with Sinnett on his immediate return from his retreat and therefore is using DK to communicate his thoughts, he is evidently aware of events about to occur in Bombay. He has his chela inform Sinnett of the impending arrival (which actually occurred on January 10, 1882) of "a certain Mr. Bennett of America." An American Freethinker and editor of a journal called the *Truth Seeker*, De Robigne Mortimer Bennett is described by one biographer as "both the most revered and the most reviled publisher in America." Colonel Olcott devotes considerable space to him in volume 2 of *Old Diary Leaves* (327–31), calling him "a very interesting and sincere person, a Free-thinker who had suffered a year's imprisonment for his bitter—often coarse—attacks on Christian dogmatism." A sham case had been manufactured against him by an unscrupulous member of a Christian society in New York, and "he was prosecuted and sent to prison." Olcott continues, "He was made to serve out his whole term of one year, despite the fact that a petition, signed by 100,000 persons, was sent to President Hayes on his behalf. When he was discharged, a monster audience welcomed him enthusiastically at the most fashionable public hall in New York, and a fund was subscribed to pay his expenses on a world-round tour." It was in the course of that tour that Bennett called in at Bombay, spending some days with the founders. Extracts from a relatively new biography of Bennett appeared in an article, "The Theosophical Odyssey of D. M Bennett" in the September-October 2001 issue of *Quest*. The student can also consult *D. M. Bennett: The Truth Seeker*, by Roderick Bradford.

HPB, reviewing the first volume of Bennett's work, *A Truth-Seeker Around the World*, in the July 1882 issue of *The Theosophist*, describes Bennett's mission as "the unique one of studying and reporting upon the religious state of the world from the freethinker's point of view. It may be described," she adds, "as an anti-missionary or anti-religious pilgrimage." In Letter 37 we are informed that Bennett is "one of our [the Mahatmas'] agents (unknown to himself) to carry out the scheme for the enfranchisement of Western thoughts from superstitious creeds." So Sinnett is asked to give Bennett "a correct idea of the actual present and potential future state of Asiatic but more particularly of Indian thought."

More than a year later, in the March 1883 issue of *The Theosophist*, HPB reviewed the third volume of Bennett's around-the-world narrative and comments concerning the American's application for membership in the Theosophical Society: "This is not the first instance in which our Masters have looked into the heart of a candidate whom we might have rejected, because of his being under the world's frown, and bade us remember that we ourselves were not so blameless when they accepted us as to warrant our turning our backs upon any earnest yearner after truth."

There is a further comment about Bennett in a later letter (Letter 42, page 114) from M, which can be noted here. Sinnett was evidently not kindly disposed toward Bennett, so M writes: "You saw only that Bennett had unwashed hands, uncleaned nails and used coarse language and had—to you—a generally unsavoury aspect. But if *that* sort of thing is your criterion of moral excellence or potential power, how many adepts or wonder-producing *lamas* would pass your muster? . . . The unwashed Bennett is *morally* as far superior to the gentlemanly Hume as you are superior to your *Bearer*. . . . B—is an honest man and of a sincere heart, besides being one of tremendous moral courage and a martyr to boot. Such our KH loves. . . . There's a moral smell as well as a physical one, good friend." In the story of Bennett, there is much for us to take to heart and consider when we greet strangers who come to our doors.

DK again reports KH's words in his own voice: "He [the Master] desires me to let you know . . . that you should not feel such an exaggerated delicacy about taking out the work left undone from Mr. Hume's hands." This has reference to a series of articles Hume was writing for publication in *The Theosophist.* Crafted in response to questions put by one W. H. Terry of Melbourne, Australia, a Spiritualist and founder–editor of a journal called *Harbinger of Light,* the articles were titled "Fragments of Occult Truth." The first of the series appeared in *The Theosophist* in October 1881, but it seems that Hume soon grew tired of the undertaking and Sinnett took over the work. None of the series seems to have appeared after September 1882, and the teachings were later used in Sinnett's second book, *Esoteric Buddhism.*

DK concludes this letter, written on KH's behalf, by saying that the Mahatma "begs you to proceed for his sake with your metaphysical studies; and not to be giving up the task in despair whenever you meet with incomprehensible ideas in M Sahib's notes." This is yet another reference to the Cosmological Notes, which we will consider in connection with Letter 44.

Letter 37 ends with an interesting note: If Sinnett wishes to write to KH, the Mahatma is able to receive letters, although evidently not to respond until some time is passed. Any such letters should be sent through Damodar, which means that HPB was being spared for a time from her role as transmitter of the letters.

LETTER 38

The story behind Letter 38 is well summarized in the prefatory note. Addressed to Sinnett, the letter is from Stainton Moses, who is convinced that the Mahatmas cannot or do not exist since his guide, Imperator (+), knows nothing about them. The entire Moses story was discussed in the commentary on Letter 18; what is significant here is that when Moses' letter reached Sinnett it contained comments from KH.

One interesting remark concerns the Mahatma's possible use of the English medium William Eglinton. Here KH calls him an "honest medium." The extent to which he was called upon to acknowledge the Mahatmas' existence is told in Letter 55, so I defer further comment on him until we examine that letter.

In Letter 38 KH has underlined the statement that Moses records as communicated from Imperator: "We have been permanently your Guardian, and no other takes our place." Then follow KH's words: "No; the 6th principles cannot be shifted." These words call for some careful consideration. In Letter 18, KH says, regarding Imperator's identity: "Whenever under the influence of Imperator he is all alive to the realities of Occultism. . . . It is but when standing face to face with his inner Self that he realizes the truth that there is something higher and nobler than the prittle-prattle of pseudo Spirits." Could KH's comment inserted in the letter from Moses be suggesting that the "permanent . . . Guardian" is actually Moses' higher or inner Self? Certainly for each of us this must be the case, and, as suggested in a later letter as well as many of HPB's writings, the "6th principle" could stand for the entire immortal Self. However, each student should examine this idea for himself or herself.

KH's entire comment on Moses' assertion that Imperator "was clearly visible and audible" to him and that there were no such beings as "Brothers" since Imperator "knows nothing whatever" of them deserves deep study: "A Brother? Does *he* or even yourself know what is understood by the name of *Brother*? Does he know what we mean by Dhyan Chohans or Planetary Spirits, by the disembodied and embodied Lha?" Are we today so sure, even with all the explanations by HPB and her successors now available to us, that we really "know" what these terms mean?

As in Letter 18, the Mahatma takes great pains to point out to Sinnett not only how mistaken is Moses but also how easily the medium can be deceived. A passage from Colonel Olcott on this subject may be relevant here. In *Old Diary Leaves* (1:308) Olcott writes:

It is not widely understood that the developed psychical powers, covering the whole range of sublimated degrees of sight, hearing, touch, taste, smell, intuition (prophetic, retrospective, and contemporary), etc., bear to the awakened individuality a relation similar to that which the ordinary five senses do to the physical self, or personality. Just as one must learn to restrain one's perception of external things through the avenues of sense to concentrate one's thoughts on some deep problem of science or philosophy, so must the would-be sage control the activity of his developed clairvoyance, clairaudience, etc., if he would not have his object defeated by the wandering of his thoughts into bypaths they now open up. I have never seen this clearly stated before, yet it is most important to bear in mind. Through ignorance of this rule, Swedenborg, Davis, the Catholic saints, and religious visionaries of all other sects have, as it were, staggered, clairvoyantly drunk, through the picture galleries of the astral light, seeing some things that were and creating others that were not until they begot them; then giving out mangled prophecies, bad counsel, false science, and misleading theology.

In view of such a warning, we may find it useful to study the entire situation and all the further developments in the life and career of Stainton Moses.

LETTERS 39, 40, AND 41

These three very short letters need little comment. Letter 39 again refers to both Mahatmas' (KH and M) "desire" that Sinnett attend the Society's anniversary meeting, scheduled for January of 1882. This was mentioned in Letter 24 and in other letters, but, as we know, Sinnett did not accede to the Mahatmas' wishes. We should note particularly M's statement that the Mahatmas would never "force a cause of action," emphasizing again that individuals, whether chelas or not, have free will to make their own choices. We can contrast Sinnett's choice, however, with the way both HPB and Colonel Olcott almost always followed what they believed to be their Teachers' "orders."

Letters 40 and 41 are actually on the same sheet of paper, back to back. M writes, "As you see I am with you constantly." This indicates that the Mahatma is always aware of events both in the Society and in Sinnett's life, even if Sinnett himself was unconscious of that fact. As we know, Sinnett always hoped to be able to see the Mahatmas physically, but now, in Letter 41, M states that although he has appeared to two other individuals—Ramaswami and Scott—"it was an impossibility" to grant the same favor to Sinnett. Ramaswami ("Ramaswami" was his ordinary name, "Iyer" being the Brahmanical caste ending, so he is often referred to as Ramaswamier) was the recipient of several letters mainly containing personal instructions that tell us much about the guru-chela relationship. Those letters are published in *Letters from the Masters of the Wisdom*, Second Series, pages 94–10. The student may also want to see appendix A of the same book, which includes an article by Ramaswamier titled "How a 'Chela' Found His 'Guru.'"

LETTER 42

As we study the letters, we inevitably form ideas concerning the Mahatmas, perhaps even picturing them in our minds. Our conceptions may also be influenced by what others have told us or by what our leaders have written about them. In Letter 42, M tells Sinnett that he is not to judge the two Brothers—KH and himself—by his own worldly experience. This rather strong statement is reminiscent of KH's comment at the conclusion of Letter 38, where he asks Sinnett whether he knows "what is understood by the name of Brother." This is a good reminder to us, as we consider these letters, to examine our own views regarding what is a Mahatma.

Throughout the correspondence Sinnett is often chided for his impatience and impulsiveness, which so often seem to have brought about unfortunate consequences, one example being his sending copious extracts from one of KH's letters to Stainton Moses (see comments on Letter 18). Now it appears he has reported to Hume the Mahatma's criticism of a pamphlet Hume had written, again leading to some difficulty. Sinnett was impatient about receiving the teachings, and it certainly appears that the Englishman never did overcome that trait. There is reassurance, however, in M's comment: "You have done all you could, and that is as much as we ever intend asking of anyone."

Unlike M's usual letters, Letter 42 contains a certain ironic humor but also a certain playfulness. At the same time, there is great seriousness as he reminds Sinnett that he has a "life time" in which to learn the occult philosophy. There also seems to be some question as to the continuation of the correspondence due to Hume's behavior. Especially to be noted is Morya's statement that in writing he is using "the best English I find lying idle in my friend's brain," a reference to KH's more skilled usage of English. Perhaps the sympathetic rapport between the two Brothers was such that Morya could draw on KH's consciousness for whatever words he needed.

M gives Sinnett some extremely valuable advice: "You must thoroughly put aside the personal element if you would get on with occult study." This should cause us all to examine our own motives for attempting to understand the occult philosophy. To what extent do "the social affections" have control over us? As we progress in our studies, do we find "the fancies and antipathies of the [personal] self . . . weakened"? Do we "take all mankind into [our] heart and regard them in the mass"?

M makes a significant comment concerning Sinnett's request for instruction: "You have forced yourself" upon KH, "stormed the position, by the very violence and intensity of your feeling for him." We may be reminded of what KH writes in his first letter to C. W. Leadbeater: "Force any one of the 'Masters' you may happen to choose" [see The "K.H." Letters to C. W. Leadbeater, 12]. But in so forcing the Mahatma, the Mahatma becomes the one who must bear the "consequences in the future."

What concerns any Master is not the pupil's outer personality but rather his or her inner condition. As M says, "With the 'visible' one we have nothing to do. He is to us only a veil that hides from profane eyes that other ego with whose evolution we are concerned." This is reminiscent of HPB's statement in The Secret Doctrine (1:634): "It is the spiritual evolution of the inner immortal man that forms the fundamental tenet in the occult science."

In earlier letters (see Letters 24 and 39) the Mahatmas expressed their desire that Sinnett attend the Society's anniversary meeting. Sinnett did not do so, evidently using as his excuse the welfare of his wife and son, who had just returned from England. Now M indicates that while they did not "order" Sinnett to be present at that meeting, their suggestion was actually a kind of "trial" or "test." I propose that it is in the little things that we are often tested the most, for while we do rise to the great opportunities, it is in the seemingly insignificant mundane matters that we so often fail. M tells Sinnett that he "will have many such" small tests. We, too, may have numerous little "trials" of our "discretion and moral pluck."

M now turns to the influence Hume is having on Sinnett, pointing out Sinnett's concern with Hume's outer "official personality, his intellect and influences" and the consequent need to "tear away the 'cataracts' and see things as they are." One does wonder why Hume seems to have such a hold over Sinnett and why Sinnett felt so inferior to Hume and therefore continually sought his advice and even approval. Hume was, of course, some ten or eleven years Sinnett's senior and may have been better educated in the formal sense, having attended university. So we can ask ourselves: do we give greater credence to individuals who we feel are outwardly, from a personality point of view, superior to ourselves in some way?

Not only is Sinnett unduly influenced by Hume, but, as M reminds Sinnett, he is far too quick to judge others by their outer appearance: "Our greatest trouble is to teach pupils not to be fooled by appearances." M refers to Letter 5, where KH indicates that M even at that early stage of the correspondence knew what his Brother was writing to Sinnett. Now M tells Sinnett: "See how well KH read your character."

In that letter, KH reported that in his efforts to relieve HPB of the transmittal of the letters, he suggested she select one of KH's pupils to take a note to Sinnett. She chose Rattan Chan Bary, a member of the Arya Samaj, who was "pure as purity itself" but "not fit for a drawing room"—in fact, HPB had suggested to him "in guarded and very delicate terms" that he change his clothing, as he was "dirty and slovenly." The Mahatma comments with some chagrin: "Prejudice and dead letter again." Once again we are reminded that tests come as just such seemingly insignificant occurrences.

A second example is Bennett (see Letter 37), whose uncouth appearance and manners so repelled Sinnett. It is well to remind ourselves of the Mahatma's comment: "There's a moral smell as well as a physical one." How do we welcome into our groups individuals whose outer appearance does not meet our standards of dress or cleanliness? Are we quick to judge by visible appearance alone?

The letter continues with a renewed caution to Sinnett that he must "try to break thro' that great maya against which occult students, the world over, have always been warned by their teachers—the hankering after phenomena." To what extent are we desirous of phenomena? Or do we, "like your fabled Shloma"—by which M presumably meant Solomon—"choose wisdom" as our goal? As the Mahatma so rightly states, "If our philosophy is wrong a *wonder* will not set it right."

Near the closing is another reference to "your 'cosmogony,'" which Djual Khul, at the end of Letter 37, calls "M. Sahib's notes." This is the material that Sinnett titled "Cosmological Notes," which we will explore in connection with Letter 44. Indeed it is, as M tells Sinnett, "a life long task" that we have chosen, and perhaps we, like Sinnett, "instead of generalizing" have "manage[d] always to rest upon those details that prove the most difficult to a beginner."

Evidently KH was aware that M was writing to Sinnett, since M now says that his Brother has asked him to close with lines from a poem by Christina Rosetti. HPB quotes these same lines in *The Secret Doctrine* (1:268).

This thought-provoking letter concludes with a statement we should all ponder: "Knowledge for the mind, like food for the body, is intended to feed and help to growth, but it requires to be well digested and the more thoroughly and slowly the process is carried out the better both for body and mind." Ours, then, to study and assimilate the "eternal verities," as HPB called the great truths of the wisdom tradition we know as Theosophy.

LETTER 43

Letter 43 seems to be a continuation of the preceding letter, and like other early letters from M, it emphasizes the importance of clearing up the misconceptions then circulating about the founders, since apparently this issue was the "greatest impediment" to the continuation of the correspondence between the Mahatmas and the two Englishmen. Perhaps one essential reason was that if HPB continued to be under attack, misunderstood, and abused, she would not be in any condition to serve as the principal "astral postoffice" for the exchange of the letters.

This letter also emphasizes the importance of using one's knowledge for the benefit of others—a recurring theme from the very beginning of the correspondence: the teachings are not for the recipient's private use but are given for the benefit of humanity. M tells Sinnett that he should not "fail to make a profitable use of [his] newly acquired privileges," no doubt referring to the privilege of receiving instruction in occult philosophy. He has to "work for it, work for the shedding of light upon other minds" through his own. A beautiful passage in *The Voice of the Silence* tells us much the same thing in poetic language: "Know that the stream of superhuman knowledge and the Deva-Wisdom thou hast won, must, from thyself, the channel of Alaya, be poured forth into another bed" (fragment 3, verse 289).

M informs Sinnett that it will be three or four weeks before KH can resume the correspondence. Meanwhile, as we know, KH has sent word to his "lay-chela" through DK (see Letter 37) that he has returned from his "retreat." M also expresses concern, as he has in several previous letters, not only that Sinnett has assimilated well the teachings already given, but also that the "Chohan"—the Mahatmas' superior—"finds yourself and Mr. Hume more qualified than he did before to receive instructions through us." Thus in one of the most remarkable passages in the letters, M sets forth the requirement for receiving continued and additional teachings: "The pathway through earth-life leads through many conflicts and trials, but he who does naught to conquer them can expect no triumph. Let then the anticipation of a fuller introduction into our mysteries under more congenial circumstances, the creation of which depends *entirely upon yourself* [,] inspire you with patience to wait for, perseverance to press on to, and full preparation to receive the blissful consummation of all your desires."

To what extent are we willing to "conquer" the "conflicts and trials" that come to us? Have we the patience and the perseverance to work for greater understanding? How do we prepare ourselves to move forward on the spiritual path? A remarkable passage in one of HPB's Esoteric Section Instructions seems to parallel what the Mahatma is telling Sinnett in this letter: "Keep ever in mind the Consciousness that though you see no Master by your bedside, nor hear one audible whisper in the silence of the still night, yet the Holy Power is about you, the Holy Light is shining into your hour of Spiritual need and aspirations, and it will be no fault of the Masters, or of their humble mouthpiece and servant, if through perversity or moral feebleness some of you cut yourselves off from these higher Potencies (*CW*, 12:640–41).

Letter 43 concludes with a reminder to Sinnett to return certain portraits (see Letter 34) and to write to "the old *Generaless*"—HPB's aunt in Odessa. So the letter shifts, one might say, from the sublime to the mundane. Both Mahatmas could write of the deepest truths of occult philosophy while at the same time giving attention to practical concerns in the lives of their correspondents.

First Set of Cosmological Notes

As observed in the prefatory comments to Letter 44, there are two sets of Cosmological Notes. The first set was omitted from the first three editions of *The Mahatma Letters*. Fortunately they are included in the chronological edition as appendix 3 (page 508), although they are misdated. They were probably received in late October or early November 1881, not in January 1882. Their study naturally precedes the examination of Letter 44, which comprises the second set of Cosmological Notes.

The first set of Cosmological Notes was first published in abbreviated form in 1923 in *The Early Teachings of the Masters*, edited by C. Jinarajadasa. In that work, these Notes are preceded by the following comment of Sinnett's:

Notes from the Book of *Kiu-te*, the great repository of occult lore in the keeping of the Adepts in Tibet. I believe there are thirty or forty volumes, a great deal shown only to Initiates. What follows is merely some elementary catechism in the very beginning. We began to get these notes through Madame Blavatsky when Mr. Hume and I first set to work together. But we soon got off on to other lines of rail. The very first thing I ever had in the way of philosophical teaching I sent you [probably Jinarajadasa] a copy of last year; it was a sketch of the chain of worlds which I suppose you have somewhere still. Then we got in a fragmentary way the materials on which Hume wrote the first of the "Occult Fragments"—that relating to the seven principles in man. It is necessary to have an absolute comprehension of that division at starting. It runs through all nature in various shapes and ways. I now copy out of my MS. book. A.P.S. [Alfred Percy Sinnett]

One is immediately struck by Sinnett's reference to the "Book of *Kiu-te*," as there is no mention of that source in the Notes themselves. However, as students of *The Secret Doctrine* know, HPB refers to this work as the source of the Stanzas of Dzyan, on which she based her exposition. She may have told Sinnett and Hume that the "Book of *Kiu-te*" was the source of the Notes, and that some of the questions and answers were actually taken from it. In addition to the information about the "volumes of *Kiu-ti*" [*sic*] in *The Secret Doctrine* (1:xliii) and in the editor's note on page 679, HPB wrote an article on these texts, published posthumously, titled "The Secret Books of 'Lam-Rim' and Dzyan" (*CW*, 14:422–24).

Jinarajadasa's publication of the Notes was based on what Sinnett copied out of his "MS. book." The original document was probably sent to Hume, who then shared it with Sinnett. Copies of the material may have circulated among a number of early members. For example, Francesca Arundale, an early leader of the Society in London, wrote in *My Guest—H. P. Blavatsky* (page 14): "What did we study? There were no books, but we often received letters from Mr. Sinnett. . . .

There were also articles in *The Theosophist*, but the only books so far published were *Isis Unveiled* and *The Occult World*. . . . I have among my papers a copy of some early notes that were sent us, entitled *Notes from the Book of Kiu-Ti* [*sic*], a most metaphysical and philosophical discourse, strikingly different from the explanatory teaching of a later date." The notes to which Francesca Arundale refers may have been what we now call the first set of Cosmological Notes.

The Notes were next published in 1925 as appendix 2 in *The Letters of H. P. Blavatsky to A. P. Sinnett*. Two references aid us in identifying the author of the Notes as the Mahatma M and corroborating the date when they were received as late October 1881, not long after KH had entered upon his "retreat" and M had assumed the role of correspondent. First is the statement in HPB's letter of early November 1881 to Sinnett, already quoted in full following the commentary on Letter 29. She tells Sinnett that M has "ordered" her to see that Sinnett has "a true copy of the hitherto written sketches of *Cosmogony* with the Tibetan words, M's notes, etc. HPB is also ordered to have one, as she has to know thoroughly what Mr. Hume has noted and how much he has elaborated of the explanations."

Second is a reference to M as author of a set of notes in Letter 37 (page 106), written by Djual Khul on behalf of KH: "[Master] begs you to proceed . . . with your metaphysical studies, and not to be giving up the task in despair whenever you meet with incomprehensible ideas in M. Sahib's notes."

M's comment in Letter 34 (page 102) that he will send Sinnett an "explanatory appendix" may also be a reference to the Notes, which surely do need such an appendix. However, as I mention in the commentary on Letter 34, there is no evidence that Sinnett or Hume ever received such a work.

A valuable resource for comprehending the Tibetan terms used in the Notes is *Blavatsky's Secret Books* by David and Nancy Reigle, in particular the chapter titled "Notes on Cosmological Notes." As the Reigles point out, the original Notes were probably in M's handwriting, which is often difficult to read. Sinnett made his copy from the original, and his handwriting is also at times hard to decipher. As a consequence, there may well have been errors in the transcription, particularly of the Tibetan terms, which the Reigles have endeavored to correct with comments.

A comprehensive study of the Cosmological Notes carries the earnest student into some of the deepest realms of Theosophical metaphysics. Yet even a brief examination of the work may be helpful in understanding the underlying principles of the occult philosophy as conveyed by the Mahatmas in their letters. As I point out elsewhere, at the time the terminology used to express that philosophy was still in a somewhat fluid state. Furthermore, the teaching was being given not sequentially but in answer to specific questions. Both these Notes and the letters were written some six or seven years prior to the publication of *The Secret Doctrine*, and several Tibetan terms M uses in the Cosmological Notes appear again in HPB's major work.

Sinnett tells Jinarajadasa in the preliminary comment quoted above that the Notes contain "some elementary catechism." A careful reading of the Notes suggests just which questions and answers may have been taken directly from such an "Occult Catechism," to which HPB makes frequent reference in *The Secret Doctrine*, and which questions (with their answers) were probably asked by either Hume or Sinnett. I will comment further on this as we proceed with a study of the Notes.

The first four questions and answers of the first set of Cosmological Notes introduce us to the foundation on which occult, or esoteric, philosophy rests. That foundation is: the "real knowledge" of the essential nature of all things, how the universe came to be, the origin and destiny of humanity in the vast plan of manifested existence, and, above all, how we as self-conscious entities may come to possess that knowledge.

There are two kinds of knowledge: real and unreal—the one dealing with "eternal verities and primal causes," the other with "illusory effects." We might add alongside this statement the words from the little work *At the Feet of the Master*: "In all the world there are only two kinds of people—those who know, and those who do not know, and this knowledge is the thing which matters."

What is the real knowledge that matters? In number 2 of the series "Fragments of Occult Truth"—a series being written at the time by Hume, and later by Sinnett, that appeared in successive issues of *The Theosophist*—is the following statement, probably by Hume and clearly based on the Cosmological Notes:

> What constitutes real knowledge? The question lies at the very threshold of occult study. We say so, not merely because of the prominent way in which it crops up in this discussion, but, because as a fact . . . that query is, in actual practice, the first put before a regular student of occultism, who is taken in hand by the Professors of the Occult World. And the student is taught,—or is led to see,— that there are two kinds of knowledge, the real and the unreal; the real concerned with eternal verities and primal causes, the unreal with illusory effects. (*The Theosophist*, March 1882)

Hume continues: "The knowledge which appeals to the senses cannot but deal with illusory effects, for all the forms of this world and its material combinations are but pictures in the great dissolving view of evolution." Contrasting this unreal knowledge with the real, he adds: "The spirit of man which comes into direct and conscious relations with the world of spirit acquires the real knowledge." Later in the article he says: "There are those who know, of real personal knowledge, and they are living men who can communicate their knowledge to other living men. . . . Who possess the real knowledge as contradistinguished from the unreal?—the student of Occultism is asked, and he is taught to reply—that which we have shown to be the only possible reply—'the adepts alone possess the real knowledge, their minds alone *being en rapport* with the universal mind.'"

In a later letter from KH (Letter 69), we find the helpful statement: "Real Knowledge here spoken of is not a mental but a spiritual state, implying full union between the Knower and the Known." In the book

Damodar and Other Pioneers of the Theosophical Movement, by Sven Eek, is reproduced an article by Damodar titled "Real Knowledge." Written in early 1885, the article is prefaced by a statement by Laura C. Holloway: "Before Damodar left Adyar, he instructed those who asked his help, and one of his lessons, on 'Real Knowledge,' is of timely value." Damodar says:

> True perception is true knowledge. Perception is the capacity of the soul; it is the sight of the higher intelligence whose vision never errs. And that can be best exercised in true serenity of mind, as Mahatma KH observes: "It is upon the serene and placid surface of the unruffled mind that visions gathered from the invisible, find a representation in the visible world." In short—as the Hindu allegory has it—"It is in the dead of night that Krishna is born." . . . In the dead of night, that is, when there is complete physical and mental rest, when there is perfect quiet and peace of mind. It is only then that the individuality of man—his higher nature—becomes a fit vehicle for the manifestation of *The Word*.

The phrase, "Dgyu becomes Fohat," which we find in the response to the first question concerning the two kinds of knowledge, is repeated in sloka 2 of stanza 5 in *The Secret Doctrine*. As HPB points out in her commentary on that verse (1:108): "*Dgyu* is the one real (magical) knowledge, or Occult Wisdom; which, dealing with eternal truths and primal causes, becomes almost omnipotence when applied in the right direction. Its antithesis is *Dgyu-mi*, that which deals with illusions and false appearances only. . . . *Dgyu* is the expression of the collective Wisdom of the Dhyani-Buddhas."

Speaking of Fohat, whom she calls "one of the most, if not the most important character in esoteric Cosmogony," she says (*SD*, 1:109): "He is simply that potential creative power in virtue of whose action the Noumenon of all future phenomena divides, so to speak, but to reunite in a mystic supersensuous act, and emit the creative ray. . . . Fohat is transformed into that force which brings together the elemental atoms and makes them aggregate and combine." As M says in the answer to the fourth question in the Notes: "Everything in the occult universe . . . is based upon two principles—Kosmic [*sic*] energy (Fohat or breath of wisdom) and Kosmic ideation."

In *The Secret Doctrine*, HPB speaks of Fohat as the creative power that acts on the ideas inherent in Universal Mind to produce a manifested universe. She summarizes the process (1:16): "Fohat is . . . the dynamic energy of Cosmic Ideation; or, regarded from the other side, it is the intelligent medium, the guiding power of all manifestation. . . . Thus, from . . . Cosmic Ideation comes our consciousness; from Cosmic Substance, the several vehicles in which that consciousness is individualized and attains to self—or reflective—consciousness; while Fohat, in its various manifestations, is the mysterious link between Mind and Matter, the animating principle electrifying every atom into life."

The nature and function of Fohat is an almost endless study, but some basic grasp of its meaning should be obtained if the student would understand the cosmogonic processes. Note particularly that in the answer to the first question Fohat is said to be the "active agent of will." In Letter 44, we will find Fohat described as "the Universal *Sakti* . . . the Will-Force, or universal energy."

In a sense, then, Fohat has three aspects: First, it is a power, or *shakti*, the "active agent of will" by which "real knowledge," the "breath of wisdom," is transformed into activity. We may say that knowledge is power. Second, Fohat may be said to "light up" or bring into activity "Kosmic ideation" or Universal Mind (producing *chidakasha*, the "fabric of consciousness") as suggested in the answer to question 4. Finally, as HPB says in the statement cited earlier, Fohat energizes or awakens the collective Intelligences, the Dhyani Buddhas, who guide the process of manifestation, as detailed in HPB's commentary on stanza 5 (*SD*, 1:108–35). These three aspects are summarized at the conclusion of the answer to question 4: "In Fohat all that exists on earth as ultimates exists as primates."

Fohat, in other words, is the dynamism of the universe, the primary motive power without which nothing would or could come into manifested existence. Therefore, as HPB writes, Fohat is indeed "the most important character in esoteric Cosmogony." For a fuller explanation of that statement and the three aspects of Fohat, the student is referred to *The Secret Doctrine* (1:110–11). Another useful reference is the small book *This Dynamic Universe*, edited by Corona Trew and E. Lester Smith.

We need to be cautious at this point, for there may be a tendency to feel we now understand what is "real knowledge," when in actuality we have only touched the outermost fringe of its meaning. HPB states (*SD*, 1:108) that Dgyu or "real knowledge" is "the expression of the collective Wisdom of the Dhyani-Buddhas." Furthermore, it is "magical," which means that it is the power or energy that produces illusions. (All of manifestation is an illusion in one sense, hence it is frequently described as *maya*.)

The third question in the Notes asks who possesses such knowledge, and the answer is given: "The Lhas or adept alone possesses the real, his mind being *en rapport* with the Universal Mind." In *The Theosophical Glossary*, HPB defines the term *Lha* as "Spirits of the highest sphere," which equates the term with those Intelligences known as the Dhyani Buddhas, the highest planetaries (see Letter 18, page 63), and the Dhyan Chohans, who embody the "ideation" in the Universal Mind activated by Fohat. We may recall here KH's words in Letter 17 (page 55): "Believe me, there comes a moment in the life of an adept, when the hardships he has passed through are a thousandfold rewarded. In order to acquire further knowledge, he has no more to go through a minute and slow process of investigation and comparison of various objects, but is accorded an instantaneous, implicit insight into every first truth. . . . The adept sees and feels and lives in the very source of all fundamental truths—the Universal Spiritual Essence of Nature."

A number of the letters include statements indicating that there are several stages in adeptship. For example, at the conclusion of Letter 67, KH writes that the "degrees of an Adept's initiation . . . mark the seven stages at which he discovers the secret of the sevenfold principles in nature and man." As we shall see, in Letter 117 KH informs Sinnett:

"Verily the *Light of Omniscience* and infallible Prevision of this earth—that shines only for the highest Chohan alone—is yet far away from me!" How far, then, must we be from that state in which there is "the perfect junction of [the] soul with the Universal Mind in its fulness [*sic*]"—the state of consciousness in which the highest Dhyan Chohan lives "in the region of absolute intelligence" (to quote from the response to the third question)!

The promise of eventual achievement is implied throughout the letters and made explicit in HPB's beautiful words: "In the future manvantaras they [the Dhyan Chohans and Dhyani Buddhas] will have risen to higher systems than our planetary world; and it is the Elect of our Humanity, the Pioneers on the hard and difficult path of Progress, who will take the places of their predecessors" (*SD*, 1:267). So it is for us, in seeking to understand as best we can the magnificent teachings given to us by HPB and her Teachers, to set forth on that "hard and difficult path."

Turning to questions 5 and 6 and their answers, we are immediately reminded of many early statements in *The Secret Doctrine* that explain the ontological basis for the process of manifestation, whether of a universe or of any thing contained within it. The concept of space in occult metaphysics as "the one eternal thing in the universe" is not easy to grasp. Generally, we think of space in terms of dimensions and as containing objects but separate from the objects it contains. However, occultly speaking, space is the matrix out of which is born all that exists (literally, everything that stands forth) in the universe. As HPB comments on sloka 1, stanza 1, space "is the eternal, ever-present cause of all—the incomprehensible Deity . . . the *one eternal thing* . . . without dimension . . . and self-existent. . . . It is, as taught in the esoteric catechism, neither limitless void, nor conditioned fullness, but both" (*SD*, 1:35).

Earlier, in the Proem, she has quoted that "esoteric catechism":

"What is it that ever is?" "Space. . . ." "What is it that ever was?" "The Germ in the Root." "What is it that is ever coming and going?" "The

*Great Breath." "Then there are three Eternals?" "No, the three are one.
... That which ever is, is one, that which ever was, is one, that which is
ever being and becoming, is also one: and this is Space." (SD, 1:11)*

From the occult view, all *is* space and all is made of space, which is
both matter and spirit, both consciousness and the vehicles through
which consciousness expresses itself. We and all that exists are not so
much *in* space as *of* space, whether it be called *akasha, mulaprakriti,
svabhavat, alaya, chaos, pre-cosmic substance, pre-cosmic root-matter,*
or any of the other many names by which the one enduring "thing"
that is no "thing" but the essence of all things—may be known. Each
term, describing some feature of space, may aid us in understanding
this most mystical of concepts. Akasha, which is referred to frequently
in the letters, for example, is identified in answer 6 as co-existent with
space. Note especially Letter 65 (page 168), which says, "We recognize
but *one* element in Nature . . . which as the *Akasa* . . . pervades
throughout *space* and is *space* in fact." HPB, defining akasha in the
Theosophical Glossary, informs us: "[Akasha] is the Universal Space
in which lies inherent the eternal Ideation of the Universe in its ever-
changing aspects on the planes of matter and objectivity."

The student endeavoring to understand the occult view of space
may wish to explore these terms, each of which has a specific meaning
in relation to "the one eternal thing," as space is termed in question
5. Particularly interesting is the concept of chaos as related to the
occult view of space. Hume refers to this in question 23, to which the
Mahatma responds that people need to know "what real chaos is."

In the section on "Chaos—Theos—Kosmos" in volume 1, part 2
of *The Secret Doctrine* (342–49), HPB states that chaos and space are
synonymous, and she identifies chaos with akasha as well. She writes:
"*Space* . . . is, in reality, the container and *the body of the Universe* with
its seven principles. It is a body of limitless extent, whose Principles, in
Occult phraseology—each being in its turn a septenary—manifest in
our phenomenal world only the grossest fabric of *their subdivisions*"
(342). Perhaps to reassure us that we are not altogether stupid when

we fail to understand fully the occult meaning of space, since the subject is vast and not easily comprehended, she adds: "Chaos-Theos-Kosmos are but the three aspects of their synthesis—Space.... [They are] identified in all Eternity as the One Unknown space, the last word about which will, perhaps, never be known before our seventh Round" (344).

In a posthumously published article, "Eastern and Western Occultism" (*CW*, 14:232–45), HPB writes: "Chaos, as shown elsewhere, is Theos, which becomes Kosmos: it is Space, the container of everything in the Universe. As Occult Teachings assert ... [Space] is called ... Chaos, Confusion, because Space is the great storehouse of Creation, whence proceed, not forms alone, but also ideas, which could receive their expression only through the Logos, the Word, Verbum, or Sound" (243).

Although HPB says that "chaos" is "confusion," the usual meaning given to the term, notably the word also means an unorganized state of matter and therefore can signify what we may call pre-order, the condition out of which order arises. It is the action of Fohat that assembles, so to speak, cosmos out of chaos. From the "storehouse of Creation," which is space as just stated, Fohat, or "Kosmic energy," transforms "Kosmic Ideation" into the multiplicity of forms that comprise a manifested universe.

Fundamental to the process are the elements or aspects that are "co-existent with space," as stated in the answer to question 6. We have already commented on the fourth item, akasha, described as "the medium by which the Kosmic energy [Fohat] acts on its source [Space]." In calling it "Astral Light," attention is directed to that aspect of akasha that provides the model vehicle for the universe and all that it contains, analogous to the linga sharira, or etheric vehicle (called in the early literature the "astral body"), which provides the model body and the carrier of *prana*, or life energy, for the physical vehicle of every individual.

The first three of the "co-existents," duration, matter, and motion, are dealt with in detail in the early stanzas and the commentaries thereon in *The Secret Doctrine.* HPB says (1:43): "The appearance and disappearance of the Universe are pictured as an outbreathing and inbreathing of the 'Great Breath,' which is eternal, and which, being Motion, is one of the three aspects of the Absolute—Abstract Space and Duration being the other two."

Rather than "Abstract Space," HPB could have used the term "matter" as the second of the co-existents, meaning matter as pre-cosmic root substance or primordial matter. A term frequently used for that root nature is *mulaprakriti,* which the great Vedantist and colleague of HPB, T. Subba Row, defined as the "veil over Parabrahm" (see the first lecture in his *Philosophy of the Bhagavad Gita*). It is because of that veil that KH could write in Letter 18: "No adept has ever penetrated beyond the veil of primitive Kosmic [*sic*] matter. The highest, the most perfect vision is limited to the universe of *Form* and *Matter.*" We will find other significant statements on the subject in subsequent letters, for example, KH's words in Letter 88 (page 273): "We believe in MATTER alone, in matter as visible nature and matter in its invisibility as the invisible omnipresent omnipotent Proteus with its unceasing motion which is its life, and which nature draws from herself since she is the great whole outside of which nothing can exist." And in Letter 111 (page 379), KH writes: "The One reality is *Mulaprakriti* (undifferentiated Substance)—the 'Rootless root.'"

Much more could be explored concerning the nature and meaning of matter as "co-existent with space," and similar studies regarding duration and motion could engage the student. HPB's commentary on the second sloka of stanza 1 deals with the subject of duration (see *SD,* 1:37). Throughout the early stanzas in particular, considerable attention is given to the topic of motion, for as HPB writes (1:97): "It is a fundamental law in Occultism that there is no rest or cessation of motion in Nature."

Finally in the enumeration of the "co-existents with space" we find the term *Purush,* which the Mahatma calls the "7th principle of the universe." As Barborka points out in *The Divine Plan* (page 503), the term *purusha* has a number of meanings, the most common signifying "man." Its philosophical meaning, however, refers to the "animating principle . . . the spirit or soul" in the human being. In *The Theosophical Glossary*, HPB equates purusha with the "Heavenly Man," the archetypal model or divine paradigm (*SD*, 1:183): "Every form on earth and every atom in Space strives in its efforts towards self-formation to follow the model placed for it in the Heavenly Man."

The concept of "the primordial Archetypal Man" is truly a fascinating one, and there are many references to the subject in *The Secret Doctrine*. An excellent brief summary is found in *The Heavenly Man* by the English Theosophist E. L. Gardner.

In question 7 and its response we are told that purusha is not only co-extensive with but also identical to space. Here we are introduced to yet another term, *swayambu*, or as given by HPB in *The Secret Doctrine*, *svayambhu*, literally, the "self-existent" or "self-manifested." HPB defines it as "Universal Spirit . . . the Svabhavat in the highest aspect" (*SD*, 1:52), "Svabhavat" being the "mystic essence . . . the Universal plastic matter diffused through Space" (*SD*, 1:98).

In her discussion of the early "Races" of humanity, HPB writes: "Each Cosmic Monad is 'Svayambhuva,' the Self-Born" (*SD*, 2:311). As the answer to question 7 states, it is the "Self-existent"—or space as the cosmic womb of all existent things—that "becomes Purush when coming into contact with matter." In other words, the archetypal or paradigmatic "man" is present in ultimate Reality (space), to emerge ("Self-Born" or "Self-manifested") as the pattern for all manifested beings. We can understand, then, based on the answers to questions 8 and 9, that the "seed" or "germ" of individuality or even personhood is present in the very fabric of the universe, and that this seed, which is both spirit and matter, constitutes the "spiritual soul" in us.

Note that the Mahatma confirms with a simple "Yes" the suggestion in question 8 that the "spiritual soul" is produced by the action of spirit on matter, spirit in this case representing the dynamic force that animates matter. This is emphasized in the opening statement of question 14: "All matter . . . has inherent motion." Earlier, in response to question 4, that motion was referred to as "Kosmic energy," or

Fohat. In *The Secret Doctrine*, HPB refers to the spiritual soul as the individual monad (atma-buddhi) or the "Pilgrim." It is this monad, or "Pilgrim," impelled by the "motion" within its very nature, who takes on the evolutionary journey through all the cycles (planetary chains, rounds, and races) of manifestation.

HPB, in *The Secret Doctrine*, frequently refers to the law of analogy or correspondences, and Hume uses analogy in his question 8. Regarding the process discussed in questions 7 and 8 and their responses the following analogy may be helpful: that just as the One, the godhead, is "slain" (an image used in many creation myths), with each part becoming a feature of the manifested universe, so the Cosmic Monad or "Swayambu [which] occupies every part of space" is fragmented into the multitude of monads, each an entity subject to cyclic and karmic law. Within the soul of each is the memory of that archetype, the "Heavenly Man," an unconscious presence at the beginning of the journey but eventually a conscious ideal to be self-realized.

It may be helpful at this point to review the entire process of emanation, which is only hinted at in the Notes, as HPB presents it in *The Secret Doctrine*:

> It is from IT [Be-ness, Sat] that issues the great unseen Logos, who evolves all the other *Logoi*, the primeval Manu who gives being to the other Manus, who emanate the universe and all in it collectively and who represent in their aggregate the *manifested* Logos. Hence we learn in the "Commentaries" that while no Dhyan Chohan, not even the highest, can realize completely "the condition of the preceding Cosmic evolution . . . the Manus retain a knowledge of their experiences of all the Cosmic evolutions throughout Eternity." . . . The first Manu is called *Svayambhuva*, "the Self-manifested. . . ." [The] Monad emanates from the never-resting Principle in the beginning of every new Cosmic activity: that *Logos* or Universal Monad . . . that radiates *from within himself all* those Cosmic Monads that become the centres of activity—progenitors of the numberless Solar systems as well as of the yet undifferentiated *human* monads

of planetary chains as well as every being thereon. Each Cosmic Monad is "Svayambhuva," the Self-Born, *which becomes the Centre of Force, from within which emerges a planetary chain* (of which chains there are seven in our system), and whose radiations become again so many Manus Svayambhuva (a generic name, mysterious and meaning far more than appears), each of these becoming, as a *Host*, the Creator of his own Humanity. (*SD*, 2:310–11)

Barborka, commenting on this passage in *The Divine Plan* (page 512), proposes that "the term Manu, in this connection, is Dhyani Buddha," and adds that the passage provides a clue as to the origin of the human monads. He says further, "Just as the Cosmic Monad is the radiating center of its system, so is the human Monad the radiating center of its system. This means that the seven principles composing man's constitution are radiations or emanations from a central source, whilst the outermost sheath, the Sthula-sarira, is actually composed of tiny lives, each one of which is undergoing its transformations and cyclic evolution within the compass of the system as a whole."

These quotations from *The Secret Doctrine* and *The Divine Plan*, lengthy as they are, may be useful as we turn to questions 9 through 15 and their responses. With this series of questions and replies the topic shifts from the universal to the seven-principled human entity and the spirit-matter polarization that takes place within matter. Here we must keep in mind that matter, whatever its state or condition, is not only co-existent with space but also eternal. The latter point is stressed on several occasions in the letters, especially Letter 88 (pages 272–73). Further, throughout the letters we are told that spirit and matter are one. Note particularly the statement in Letter 65 (page 168): "Spirit and matter are *one*, being but a differentiation of states not *essences*."

Careful attention must be given to each of the Mahatma's several responses to Hume's questions on the nature, states, and conditions of matter, whether cosmic or organized, since we are so accustomed to think of matter as solid and visible, and spirit as immaterial and invisible. Matter is everywhere, and every thing is matter, but matter infused with life or spirit and therefore polarized, or, as we shall learn when considering Letter 44, self-polarized (page 118).

All of this—the everywhereness of matter and its polarization—is due to that dynamism inherent in the system known as Fohat. Consider the poetic words of stanza 3, sloka 12, (*SD*, 1:95): "Then Svabhavat sends Fohat to harden the atoms." That "hardening" process results in the various states of matter to which the term "planes" has been applied—states or conditions that actually form the vestures for the several principles of the human constitution. HPB comments on the sloka just cited, "'Fohat hardens the atoms,' *i.e.*, by infusing energy into them; he scatters the atoms of primordial matter," and she adds, "He scatters himself while scattering matter into atoms," a statement she attributes to "MSS. Commentaries." She goes on to say, "It is through Fohat that the ideas of the Universal Mind are impressed upon matter." This statement takes us back to the Mahatma's response to question 4 and underscores the basic thesis of the occult philosophy that consciousness (or intelligence) is primary.

Before taking up the table of human and universal principles (item 12), it is important to consider the Mahatma's response to question 10. While the seven principles of the human constitution may be called "states" or "conditions" and in much of Theosophical literature, "planes," M says he calls them "Kyen—cause; itself a result of a previous or some primary cause." We have seen this term in Letter 29 (page 89). M suggests that it is only in particular cases that results become primary causes, so the use of the term *Kyen* may involve more than the usual cause-effect relationship. It is for each student to determine what might be the more comprehensive meaning of the word. M responds to Hume's question (unnumbered) at the end of page 517, concerning design: "There is no finite or primordial design but in conjunction with organised matter. Design is Kyen, a cause arising from a primary one." Is, then, Kyen related to the archetypes that exist in the Divine Mind?

The listing of the human principles and their correlates among the universal principles, given in Tibetan, Sanskrit, and English, that constitutes item 12 is particularly valuable to students interested in the historical development of the delineation of the human constitution in esoteric philosophy. Just a brief glance at the table on page 510 reveals significant differences between the terminology presented here and in later presentations. In the Cosmological Notes as printed in Jinarajadasa's book, the listing is prefaced by the following parenthetical statement: "We were anxious to make out the correspondences between the seven principles of Man and of the Universe. M wrote out the following table."

Comments on and some corrections of the Tibetan terms are given by David and Nancy Reigle in *Blavatsky's Secret Books*. In *The Secret Doctrine* (1:23), HPB uses some of the same Tibetan terms, particularly those mentioned in question 13 and its response. The student may wonder at the omission of the term *buddhi* in the Sanskrit listing, but "Atman Mayava-rupa" is translated as "Spiritual Soul," which HPB identifies as buddhi in *The Key to Theosophy*. I suggest that buddhi, or spiritual soul, is in actuality a mayavic form or emanation of Atman, the highest Spirit given in the diagram as "Mahatma."

Keeping in mind Barborka's statement given above, that the principles are "radiations" or emanations from the central source, it may be that we are dealing here not with separate principles, at either the human or the universal level, but with characteristics at successive stages of differentiation of atman, itself an emanation of the Cosmic Monad or Ultimate Source, often referred to as the originating point of a system. Refer again to question 10 and its response, which emphasizes that what we call different states of matter (or different principles consonant with different states of matter), the Mahatma terms "Kyen—cause, itself a result of a previous or some primary cause." In terms of the human principles, then, atman may be the "primary cause" (equivalent to svayambhuva among the universal principles), while all the other principles are the results and as such are temporary or mayavic, illusory. This suggestion is based on HPB's comments in *The Secret Doctrine* (1:570–71): "*Atman* is the one real and eternal substratum of all—the essence and absolute knowledge—the *Kshetrajna*. . . . *Atman* (our seventh principle) being identical with the universal Spirit and man being one with it in his essence, what is then the Monad proper? It is that homogeneous spark which radiates in millions of rays. . . . It is *the emanating spark from the* Uncreated *Ray*—a mystery." (*Kshetra* means field or dwelling place, while *jna* refers to the knower; so *kshetrajna* indicates the knower in the field or body. Technically, this is buddhi-manas.)

For further elucidation of the nature of the principles, the student may find of particular interest an article by HPB published posthumously, entitled "The Seven Principles" (*CW*, 14:386–87). In that article, she elaborates on the concept that the principles are "the manifestation of one indivisible Spirit."

At some point in our studies, we may find it useful to make for ourselves a diagram of the various listings of principles, from the threefold Pauline division of spirit, soul, and body typical of most Christian writings, which HPB uses in *Isis Unveiled*, to the Vedantic classification and the Taraka Raja Yoga system. Especially helpful for such an undertaking is the chart in *The Secret Doctrine* (1:157). The student's chart might also include the terminology adopted by later writers, especially Besant, Leadbeater, and Taimni. The essential thing is to have a clear understanding of the human constitution, whatever system the student finds most meaningful. Familiarity with the various systems, however, gives the student a measure of flexibility in explaining the human constitution to inquirers and aids in distinguishing structure from function in considering the components of our own nature.

Questions 14, 15, and 16 concern Hume's curiosity about the nature of matter. M responds that even cosmic matter or *mulaprakriti*, "root matter," is both "molecular" (we may say "compound") and polarized. This is emphasized again in some of the early questions and answers in Letter 44, the second set of Cosmological Notes. However, here the important point is that only during the periods of *pralaya*, or nonmanifestation, which the Mahatma terms "the night of mind," does polarization into positive and negative cease and full equilibrium is reached. It is disequilibrium, then, that characterizes manifestation and makes possible the evolutionary advance of any system, whether planetary, solar, or human. In a "state of non-action or non-being," to quote the response to question 15, everything is at rest and no further development can take place.

M's response to question 16, particularly the long paragraph on page 512 that details the process of emanation, calls for careful attention. First, the Mahatma refers to the "panspermic and theospermic" theories prevalent at that time. Panspermia, the theory that reproductive bodies of living organisms exist throughout the universe and develop wherever conditions are favorable, was especially propounded in opposition to the theory of spontaneous generation, which the Mahatma states unequivocally the Adepts believe in. Theospermia would likely be termed creationism in today's scientific debates on the origin of life. In contrast to both, the Mahatma sets forth the occult view, which involves "the incessant work of . . . the *Central Point* in both its active and passive states." This leads us into a most fascinating study, which has been explained by Dr. I. K. Taimni in *Man, God, and the Universe*: "The eternal Ultimate Space which is referred to as the container" or vesture of "the Ultimate Reality is called *Mahakasa* in Hindu philosophy. . . . The eternal Point which serves as a centre round which manifestation takes place is called a *Mahabindu*. It is this Point which by its primary differentiation into polar opposites produces the focii of the dual *Siva-Sakti Tattva* and contains within its unfathomable depths the mental centres of all Solar Logoi and Monads" (page 21).

Dr. Taimni elaborates on the properties and significance of the Mahabindu, or Point, in chapters 23, 24, and 25. As he indicates,

The most wonderful property of a point is that it can serve as a meeting ground of any number of planes of different dimensions (page 287). . . . As a point can be the only meeting ground between the manifest and the unmanifest, manifestation always takes place through a point (page 289). . . . The projection of the worlds of manifestation from the Unmanifest, the expression of consciousness in the worlds of manifestation as mind, the functioning of mind . . . can be understood only when we have a clear grasp of the nature of the point (page 290). . . . The Occult conception of the relation existing between . . . different units of consciousness is based upon . . . different centres of spiritual consciousness being centred in one Common Centre . . . the *Mahabindu* (page 299).

M states in his response to Hume's question 16 that it is through or from that "Central Point," or "causative latent principle" that "during the day of activity . . . cyclic force [is] ejecting . . . cosmic matter." From the unmanifest state of pralaya, or rest, by the action of cyclic motion, manifestation appears and "begin[s] to acquire . . . the germs of polarity." M continues (page 512): "Then coming within the Universal mind Dyan Kam [the Dhyan Chohans] develops these germs, conceives, and giving the impulse communicates it to Fohat, who, vibrating along Akasa . . . (a state of cosmic matter, motion, force, etc.) runs along the lines of cosmic manifestations and frames all and every thing . . . in accordance with the prototypes as conceived in the eternal mind."

Questions 17, 18, and 19 with their responses need no comment, as they are brief and quite self-explanatory. Question 20 reads almost like a conversation between the argumentative Hume and the Mahatma. Evidently at some time, the Mahatma has used a simile of a "sugar refinery" to explain the origin of evil. This is the only reference to that simile in the letters. However, the question of evil is dealt with more extensively in later letters, particularly Letters 70C (page 212), 88 (pages 273–74), and 93B (page 313).

Question 21 is less a query than a restatement by Hume of the Mahatma's view concerning "an Absolute beyond the conditioned" and the unknowability by even the planetary spirits of whatever lies beyond the "limitless and eternal." Since M tells Hume, "That is just what we would say," we can read the Englishman's statement as an accurate summary of the occult thesis.

The answer to question 22 needs to be considered in some detail, since the term *Dhyan Chohan* is often used to refer to a number of different agencies or forces involved in manifestation. In the *Theosophical Glossary*, HPB states that the Dhyan Chohans are "the divine Intelligences charged with the supervision of Kosmos." In her commentary on sloka 3 of stanza 1 in *The Secret Doctrine*, HPB describes them as "the collective hosts of spiritual Beings—the Angelic Hosts of Christianity, the Elohim and 'Messengers' of the Jews—who are the vehicle for the manifestation of the divine or universal thought and will. They are the Intelligent Forces that give to and enact in Nature her 'laws.' . . . This hierarchy of spiritual Beings through which the Universal Mind comes into action, is like an army—a 'Host' truly" (*SD*, 1:38).

Later HPB indicates that there are "seven chief groups of . . . Dhyani-Chohans, which groups will be found and recognized in every religion, for they are the primeval seven Rays" (*SD*, 1:573). And in her commentary on slokas 2 and 4 of stanza 4, she discusses the "sacred Science of the Numerals," commenting, "It is on the Hierarchies and correct numbers of these Beings, invisible (to us) except upon very rare occasions, that the mystery of the whole Universe is built . . . the Hierarchies of the Dhyani-Chohans, called Devas (Gods) in India, or the conscious intelligent powers in Nature. To this Hierarchy correspond the actual types into which humanity may be divided; for humanity, as a whole, is in reality a materialized though as yet imperfect expression thereof" (*SD*, 1:89, 93).

There is much more to study about the Dhyan-Chohanic kingdom, of which the planetaries are one group. The student may find particularly helpful chapter 3, "Doctrine of Hierarchies," in Barborka's work, *The Divine Plan*. Two points need to be kept in mind: First, KH says about planetaries in Letter 18 (page 62): "There are many other grades and orders, but there is no *separate* and eternally constituted order of Planetary Spirits." Second, HPB comments (*SD*,

1:277): "Every 'Spirit' so-called is either a *disembodied or a future man.* As from the highest Archangel (Dhyan-Chohan) down to the last conscious 'Builder' . . . all such are *men,* having lived aeons ago, in other Manvantaras, on this or other Spheres, so the inferior, semi-intelligent and non-intelligent Elementals—are all *future* men. That fact alone—that a Spirit is endowed with intelligence—is a proof to the Occultist that that Being must have been a *man,* and acquired his knowledge and intelligence throughout the human cycle."

Moving toward the conclusion of this first set of Cosmological Notes, we have question 23 with its many sections interspersed with comments from the Mahatma. Hume is apparently attempting to clarify for himself the teaching he has been given concerning cosmogenesis, the differentiation of cosmic matter, the alternations of active and passive states, changes in polarity, and so on. At the beginning of his many-faceted question, Hume suggests that the "passive unmanifested state" may be regarded as chaos. I commented on this point earlier when discussing the occult concept of space.

Hume's conjectures about the cause of differentiation at the outset of manifestation prompt the Mahatma to make several significant points. He indicates (page 515) that "a primal atom is and will remain . . . a hypothetical abstraction" for science. Stating, "Science can know nothing of the nature of atoms outside the region of effects on her globe," M remarks on the divisibility of the atom, a fact well known today. Students familiar with current knowledge concerning the structure of the atom may wish to contrast contemporary views with those prevalent when the Mahatmas were writing to Hume and Sinnett.

The occult teaching regarding what M calls "the existence and properties of the universal solvent" introduces us to the concept of the "Panchamahabhutas," the five (*pancha*) gross or great (*maha*) elements or element-principles (*bhutas*). As Barborka points out (*The Divine Plan*, 174), some schools of Indian philosophy, particularly the Sankhya, regard the Mahabhutas as "the producers or primary essences which evolve the whole visible world." They are the products of the five primary elements—ether, air, fire, water, earth—and bring about the tangible world of sensory experience. A full study of the subject as developed in Sankhya philosophy may be found in any good book on the schools of Indian thought.

Referring to the "alternations of activity and passivity . . . the cyclic law of the universe," Hume asks if his summary is correct and then asks: "If . . . the entire universe goes into pralaya . . . how can anyone know anything about it?" Such a question is quite natural. Since pralaya, or the "night of the solar system," is a period of nonmanifestation, obviously there could be no witness to observe what, if anything, occurs in that state. But, responds the Mahatma, by the law of analogy the Adept can know the pre-cosmic state, the "Maha bardo," which is similar to the "period between death and regeneration [rebirth]" for the human being. The term *bardo* will be familiar to students who are acquainted with *The Tibetan Book of the Dead.* Probably the classic translation of that work is the one by W. Y. Evans-Wentz, which contains a psychological commentary by C. G. Jung and a foreword by Lama Anagarika Govinda. Robert Thurman, well-known scholar of Tibetan history and literature, states in his translation that the work is known in Tibet as "The Great Book of Natural Liberation through Understanding in the Between."

In the final paragraph on page 516, M again reminds Hume of some of the occult teaching. "Evolution," which M terms "an eternal protest," is the "unfolding of the evolute from the involute, a process of gradual growth." All operates according to law, and we live in a "self-governing universe," there being no "sign of . . . an intelligence" or "god" outside it. Again the Mahatma emphasizes that "matter is eternal," co-existent with space, and "not a *Kyen*—a cause, itself the result of some primary cause." I have already commented on the Tibetan term in connection with M's response to question 8 and noted also the Mahatma's identification of the term (page 517) as "design." Since the Mahatma tells Hume that he has correctly "seized the idea" concerning the cyclic alternation of periods of passivity and activity, we can read through Hume's statements as a summary of the occult teaching.

The statements with which the Mahatma concludes this set of Cosmological Notes are intriguing indeed, and we may only speculate as to their meaning. It does not appear that M ever gave either Hume or Sinnett "the six names of the principles of our solar system," although it has been conjectured that those names may have some relation to the seven sacred planets. The six names may also be related to what the Mahatma calls "the six primary forces in nature represented by the Astral light." In this connection, we can consider a statement by HPB (SD, 2:602): "Being under the rule of seven sacred planets, the doctrine of the Spheres shows from Lemuria to Pythagoras, the seven powers of terrestrial and sublunary nature, as well as the seven great Forces of the Universe, proceeding and evolving in seven tones, which are the seven notes of the musical scale." Barborka provides a useful commentary on HPB's words on pages 223–24 of The Divine Plan.

M may also have been referring to information contained in an article by T. Subba Row that appeared in The Theosophist in November 1881 (just a month after Hume received these Cosmological Notes). The article, titled "The Twelve Signs of the Zodiac," can be found in Subba Row's Esoteric Writings. HPB, after quoting extensively from that article in The Secret Doctrine (1:292–93), comments: "It [the enumeration of the "forces"] is all esoteric, though not covering the tenth part of what might be said. For one, the six names of the Six Forces mentioned are those of the six Hierarchies of Dhyani-Chohans synthesized by their Primary, the seventh, who personify the Fifth Principle of Cosmic Nature, or of the 'Mother' in its Mystical Sense. The enumeration alone of the yoga Powers would require ten volumes. Each of these Forces has a living Conscious Entity at its head, of which entity it is an emanation."

Since the Mahatma says these "six primary forces" are "represented by the Astral Light," we should take note of Subba Row's definition of that term in this same article: "The visible universe is the Sthula Sariram [physical sheath]. . . . The ancient philosophers held that as a substratum for this visible universe, there is another universe—

perhaps we may call it the universe of Astral Light—the real universe of Noumena, the soul as it were of this visible universe."

So we conclude this consideration of one of the most remarkable documents received from the Mahatmas during the early years of the Society. We have only touched on some of the concepts contained in it, but even to have opened the door to its wonderful teachings may encourage serious students to explore further and in greater detail its magnificent depths. We turn now to Letter 44, the second set of Cosmological Notes.

LETTER 44
(SECOND SET OF COSMOLOGICAL NOTES)

From reading the first quoted statement of Sinnett's, with which Morya begins Letter 44, it is evident that the first set of Cosmological Notes elicited further questions from both Hume and Sinnett. Letter 44 in fact constitutes a second set of Cosmological Notes—a continuation of the instruction concerning the process of manifestation discussed in the first set of Cosmological Notes, as well as additional valuable information relating to both the occult view of cosmogony and the esoteric teaching regarding the human constitution. Notably, most of the numbered items in Letter 44 are not so much questions as summary statements by Sinnett (perhaps in collaboration with Hume) to which the Mahatma responds either with the words "correctly conceived" or with further explanation.

However, there is a difference in tone between the two sets of Notes, evidenced in the terminology as well as the length of the responses. In the first set, a number of Tibetan terms are used, including the Tibetan terms (along with Sanskrit and English equivalents) for the principles of the human constitution as well as for the universe. In Letter 44 there is no Tibetan terminology, and the responses are more detailed, even when direct questions are not asked. One student has pointed out that this second set of Notes is less abrupt, and a kindlier tone pervades the answers, as though more time was given to each response. That student has also suggested that while Letter 44 is signed by M, perhaps KH helped M (who confessed to knowing little English and to using on at least one occasion "words left lying in my brother's [KH's] brain") to phrase the answers. We do know that although KH has not yet resumed the correspondence, he had "awakened" from his retreat and is concerned about Sinnett (see Letter 37), so such a suggestion may not be out of order. Moreover, M notes that he is at the time "in our KH's home." The two Mahatmas may well have been discussing the questions as well as jointly composing the answers.

In his response to an unnumbered question in the first set of Notes (page 516), M says, "Evolution means unfolding of the evolute from the involute, a process of gradual growth." In Letter 44, he further emphasizes this point as he comments (page 118) on Sinnett's statement: "Nothing in nature springs into existence suddenly, all being subjected to the same law of gradual evolution."

In addition, M once more advises Sinnett to understand the universal law of analogy or correspondences: "In studying esoteric cosmogony, keep a spiritual eye upon the physiological processes of human birth." Here the student may consider HPB's explication of this topic in her E.S. Instruction No. 1 (*CW*, 12:522–24), where she relates what she calls "the seven correspondential contents of the wombs of Nature and of Woman," showing the analogy between the cosmic and the human processes. M informs Sinnett: "Cosmology is the physiology of the universe spiritualized, for there is but one law."

The Mahatmas' emphasis throughout the teachings on the law of analogy is again and again underscored by HPB not only in her esoteric writings but also in *The Secret Doctrine*. Analogy is the basis for what M, in his comment 1 to Sinnett's opening statement, calls "the synthetic method," which he defines as the "blend[ing] [of] the macrocosm and microcosm." We need to keep in mind throughout our studies the well-known Hermetic axiom: "As it is above, so it is below; as it is below, so it is above." The Mahatma refers to this principle again in his comment on Sinnett's lengthy statement 4 on page 119: "The evolution of worlds cannot be considered apart from the evolution of everything created or having being on these worlds." The total system must be understood, the whole system perceived, before one can take up a study of its parts.

Certainly here is a crucial distinction between the method of occultism and that of modern science, in which the movement is from the particular to the general. The one follows deductive reasoning, the other, inductive reasoning. When one grasps, however slightly, the essential principle or law underlying the occult system, then one begins to see how everything emerges or emanates in accordance with that principle. As M states in this letter, "All is one Law" (page 120), or as he says in the first response, "Nature follows the same groove from the 'creation' of a universe down to that of a mosquito."

The responses to the Englishmen's questions 2 and 4 give us further insight into the evolutionary, or what HPB later termed emanational, processes, including the concept that those processes require the presence of an "irresistible Force at work"—the primary dynamic that HPB termed *Fohat*. The result of this "process of motion" is the self-polarization of "primitive cosmic matter," which is akasha or mulaprakriti, as discussed in the first set of Cosmological Notes (see page 512). Since the atomic structure of matter is referred to repeatedly in both sets of Notes, it is important to remember that here "atom" refers not to a little bit of separate something but more probably to a dimensionless point in abstract space. Consequently, there is nothing "outside" this atom, or point (see the commentary on M's response to question 16 in the first set of Notes), to polarize it. All is contained within it potentially, so it is in accordance with cyclic law that it polarizes itself.

This polarization results in what we consider to be the opposites: positive and negative, active and passive, spirit and matter, and so on. Recall that in Letter 18 (page 65) KH states: "All movement is, so to say, polar." However, as the Mahatmas emphasize in a number of the letters and as HPB states in *The Secret Doctrine* (see particularly 1:15–16), while spirit and matter appear as a duality in the continuum of manifestation, they are basically one and the same. In his comment 2 on Sinnett's second question, M amplifies our understanding of their apparently dual nature when he says: "the one and chief attribute of the universal spiritual principle" is the capacity "to expand and shed," while the essential attribute of "the universal material principle is to gather in and fecundate." Yet he also refers to their fundamental oneness on page 120: "You will easily understand what is meant by the 'one and only' element or principle in the universe and that androgynous." As KH says in Letter 90 (page 282), "The conception of matter and spirit as entirely distinct . . . could certainly never have entered my head, however little I may know of them, for it is one of the elementary and fundamental doctrines of Occultism that the two are one, and are distinct but in their respective manifestations, and only in the limited perceptions of the world of senses."

The Mahatma stresses an important occult concept in his response to question 4: the term "creation" is totally inaccurate. "Both planet and man are—states for a given time. . . . Their present appearance is transitory and but a condition concomitant of that stage of evolution at which they have arrived in the descending cycle." All has emerged from "one principle" or "one element." Letter 67 (page 182) refers to this one principle or element as the "one sub-stratum or permanent cause of all manifestations in the phenomenal universe" and then adds: "Call it Purush Sakti." This reminds us of an answer in the first set of Cosmological Notes where "the Purush" is named as the fifth among the "things co-existent with space." All else—returning now to Letter 44—is called *maya*, a term often translated as "illusion" yet really meaning transitory, nonpermanent, subject to continual change.

It is helpful, as the above remarks imply, to follow the response to Sinnett's statement 2 with a consideration of the reply to question 4, since in the latter the Mahatma elaborates upon the entire cyclic process, now in terms of the correspondence between the human and planetary principles. In the long paragraph on page 120, M states,

"Man has his seven principles, the germs of which he brings with him at his birth. So has a planet or a world." What a beautiful example he then uses! Finding the appropriate words "printed in one of the musick [*sic*] pieces in KH's old portmanteau," he likens the notes of an octave to the spheres in the cycle. The student may want to review the concept of the planetary chains, as well as the basic principle of cyclicity, which was introduced in Letter 18 (see page 64).

The musical analogy that Morya uses has a number of implications that should not be overlooked. The seven notes of an octave represent the seven globes of our planetary chain: three descending and three ascending (each note struck twice), while the seventh is our Globe D. The significance of playing the notes louder on the descending scale and more softly ascending suggests the descent into and the ascent out of dense materiality. The Mahatma's choice of piano notes (i.e., vibrations) was probably not casual, although it could be taken for that, since sound has great occult significance and is said to be the first manifestation of akasha. The seven vibrations also relate to the seven vowels chanted by the Egyptians as well as the seven vowels of the mystic word "Oeaohoo," which we find in the Stanzas of Dzyan, stanza 3, slokas 5 and 7 (*SD*, 1:68–71), on which HPB comments.

Continuing with response 4, M comments further on the "cycle of evolution" (page 120): "The one *Life-principle* when in action runs in *circuits*. . . . It runs the round in human body . . . and is to the Microcosmos (the physical world of matter) what . . . the cycle is to the Macrocosmos (the world of universal spiritual Forces); and so with the formation of worlds and the great descending and ascending 'circle of necessity.'" Then follows a general description of how each successive "sphere," or "planet" (of a planetary chain), is "born," together with the particular "kingdom"—mineral, plant, animal, and so on—for which that sphere provides habitation. Here M resorts to yet another helpful and graphic analogy. When a globe or world "is born, there comes with it clinging like barnacles of a ship in motion . . . the living beings of its atmosphere," and so with each succeeding globe in the evolutionary descent of life. "On the downward course 'life' becomes with every state coarser, more material; on its upward more shadowy." And the Mahatma adds a most significant point: "Nor can there be any responsibility until the time when matter and spirit are properly equilibrized. Up to *man* 'life' has no responsibility in whatever form."

Before we leave M's long concluding paragraph on Sinnett's question 4 (page 120), a final comment on the Mahatma's analogy between a planetary chain and our physical bodies may be useful. He compares the blood, which carries the "life" on its journey round the physical body, with the life wave making its journey round the globes of a chain. Some students may want to consider the correspondence between the organs (lungs, heart, brain, and so on) and the globes, particularly since the organs have an occult significance in relation to the seven principles. For such a study, the student is referred to HPB's posthumously published article "Psychic and Noetic Action" (*CW*, 12:350–74).

At this point we need to return to question 3, as M's response amplifies a statement he makes in his commentary on 4. In the middle of the long paragraph on page 120, M writes: "From first to last every sphere has its world of effects, the passing through which will afford a place of final rest to each of the human principles—the seventh principle excepted." The concept of "worlds of Causes and worlds of Effects" was explained by KH in Letter 18 (page 65). Now in question 3, Sinnett is asking whether in the process of descent through the globes or spheres of a planetary chain there is an alternation between worlds of causes and worlds of effects.

The Mahatma responds: "The worlds of effects are not lokas or localities. They are the shadow of the world of causes, their *souls*— worlds having, like men, their seven principles." From this statement, we may infer that the worlds or spheres of effects are subjective; that is, they do not exist as objects of perception. Keeping in mind M's earlier statement that we are to "blend the *macrocosm* and microcosm together," I suggest that just as the globes of a planetary chain embody universal principles and are the "effects" of previous worlds of "causes" (previous manvantaras), so the various vehicles that embody the principles of the human constitution (the microcosm) are the "effects"—the karmic consequences or "shadows"—of previous incarnations (the worlds of causes). By calling the worlds of effects the "souls" of the world of causes, the Mahatma is referring to the fact that, for the human entity, the "soul" is the mediator or agent (as the reincarnating entity) between the causes created in the past and the effects to be experienced in the present. It is also the mediator between the universal and the particular; it is the traveler and therefore the experiencer by which the ultimates become particularized. Moreover, it is through the "soul" that the journey is taken from ignorance to enlightenment.

The remainder of the answer to question 3 gives a deep insight into the human constitution, identifying the derivation of each principle and so giving the source to which it returns after the death of the physical. Note the sequence of the principles: physical (the body), the jivatma (the "life-principle"), the etheric (*linga sharira*), emotional vehicle (*kama-rupa*), the mind ("animal soul"), while the sixth and seventh remain unnamed. This sequence will be elaborated upon in Letter 68 (pages 192–93). However, the student may wish to compare the names given to the principles here, in question 3, with the designations the Mahatma used in the table in the first set of Cosmological Notes (page 510).

Before examining in detail each of the principles and its source as outlined by the Mahatma, it may be useful to consider some of HPB's comments concerning the human constitution. These not only elaborate and clarify M's instruction but also help to explain his statement in reply to question 5 that "all the seven principles as a germ" are present in the human entity "from the very instant he appears in the first world of causes" (page 121).

In *The Secret Doctrine* she writes: "Each principle in man [has] its direct source in the nature of those great Beings [the higher order of Dhyan Chohans], who furnish us with the respective invisible elements in us" (*SD*, 1:123). She also says, "Mankind in its first prototypal, shadowy form, is the offspring of the Elohim of Life (or Pitris); in its qualitative and physical aspect it is the direct progeny of the "Ancestors," the lowest Dhyanis, or Spirits of the Earth; for its moral, psychic, and spiritual nature, it is indebted to a group of divine Beings, the name and characteristics of which will be given [later]. . . . Collectively, men are the handiwork of hosts of various spirits; distributively, the tabernacle of those hosts; and occasionally and singly, the vehicles of some of them" (*SD*, 2:224).

In E.S. Instruction No. 2 (*CW*, 12:549), HPB refers to the Dhyan Chohans while discussing what she terms the "Seven Hierarchies of Being": "Each of which has a direct bearing upon and relation to one of the human principles, since each of these Hierarchies is, in fact, the creator and source of the corresponding human principle."

Further on in the same paper (*CW*, 12:561) she adds: "Those who have read the second volume of *The Secret Doctrine* will remember that these seven principles are derived from the seven great Hierarchies of Angels or Dhyani-Chohans, which . . . form collectively the Manifested Logos."

While the entire subject of the development of the human principles, including their relation to the "Celestial Beings" or the Dhyan Chohans who contribute to the human constitution, is the focus of volume 2 of *The Secret Doctrine*, a study of her commentary on stanza 7 in the first volume will provide the earnest student with what she calls an overview of this "Anthropo-Cosmogenesis," that is, the origin of the principles. This information about the Dhyan-Chohanic kingdom is an aid in understanding some of M's statements regarding the return of the "animal soul" to one or another of the seven "Hierarchies" of the "Dhyani-Chohans."

Other quotations from HPB are helpful as we examine the "fate" of the principles after the death of the physical vehicle. Again from her E.S. Instructions, this time No. 3 (*CW*, 12:607–8): "Speaking metaphysically and philosophically, on strict esoteric lines, man as a complete unit is composed of Four basic Principles [these are later designated atman, auric envelope, buddhi, and manas or the higher ego] and Three Aspects [given as "Transitory Aspects Produced by the Principles" and called prana, linga sharira, and lower manas or the animal soul] produced by them on this earth. In the semi-esoteric teachings, these Four and Three have been called Seven Principles, to facilitate the comprehension of the masses."

As we have become so accustomed to numbering the principles, two additional statements by HPB are significant for our study of Letter 44. In E.S. Instruction No. 2 (*CW*, 12:543), HPB states: "The old and familiar mode of reckoning the principles, given in *The Theosophist* and *Esoteric Buddhism*, leads to another apparently perplexing contradiction, though it is really none at all. . . . Prana, the life principle, can . . . have no number, as it pervades every other principle, or the human total."

In speaking of the principles in response 3, the Mahatma does not name prana nor indeed the auric egg, or auric envelope, which HPB introduces as a principle in her esoteric writings, which came much later. Of prana, she states (*CW*, 12:707) that it is the "Breath of Life," adding: "Every Principle is a differentiation of Jiva, and *the life-motion in each* is Prana." Of the auric egg (which she substitutes for atman), HPB says (page 608): "In its essence . . . it is eternal; in its constant correlations, it is a kind of perpetual motion machine during the reincarnating progress of the Ego on this earth." In her commentary on plate 1 (*CW*, 12:526–28), she says: "We see that Atman is no 'principle' but stands separate from the Man, whose seven 'principles' are expressed as follows," and she then gives the auric egg as the seventh. We need to remember this point when we take up M's brief comment on the seventh principle. A full study of this subject would take us far afield, but there is much to be learned about it from HPB's esoteric papers as published in volume 12 of the *Collected Writings*. Another useful reference on the subject is *The Inner Group Teachings of H. P. Blavatsky*, compiled and annotated by Henk J. Spierenburg, pages 6–7.

Another significant comment concerning the principles in the same section of HPB's E.S. Instruction No. 2 is: "The human principles elude enumeration, because each man differs from every other. . . .

Numbering is here a question of spiritual progress and the natural predominance of one principle over another" (*CW*, 12:547).

Boris de Zirkoff, the compiler of the *Collected Writings*, comments on HPB's teachings and diagrams concerning the principles (12:530–31): "While man is built of 'materials' and 'stuffs' drawn from the Cosmic reservoir [to which the principles return, as M indicates in response 3 of Letter 44]; yet he is not a mere bundle of substances and energies merely gathered together. Man is an intimately correlated *series of consciousness-centers*, and these are termed Monads. The essential or supreme Spiritual-Divine Monad is our ultimate source or root. It is continuously pouring forth streams of intelligence and life-substance which produce by their interacting energies the various 'knots' or foci of consciousness."

One more passage relevant to our current study is found in the extremely significant article "Tibetan Teachings" (*CW*, 6:94 *et seq.*). HPB states that she is quoting from a correspondent whom she identifies only as "a Gelung of the Inner Temple—a disciple of Bas-pa Dharma, the Secret Doctrine." The pertinent part reads as follows:

> From the dead body the other principles ooze out together. A few hours later the second principle—that of life [or prana]—is totally extinct, and separates from both the human and ethereal envelopes. The third—the vital double [linga sharira] finally dissipates when the last particles of the body disintegrate. There now remain the fourth, fifth, sixth and seventh principles: the body of will; the human soul; the spiritual soul; and pure spirit, which is a facet of the Eternal. The last two joined to, or separated from, the personal self, form the everlasting individuality and cannot perish. The remainder proceeds to the state of gestation—the astral self and whatever survived in it of the will, previous to the dissolution of the physical body.

Commenting on the letter she has quoted, HPB speaks of the "awful sacredness of the mystery of physical translation," and indeed, as we return to the information given by the Mahatma in Letter 44, we realize there is much of mystery in understanding not only the processes of death but the nature of the after-death states. Much more on this subject is presented in Letter 68, and many of the quotations just cited are relevant to our study of that letter. The "sacredness" of which HPB speaks is no doubt due to the nature of the source from which the various principles have arisen and into which they return.

Turning directly now to the Mahatma's statements in his response 3 to Sinnett's question, it seems fairly easy to understand what happens to the physical vehicle at death: "The *body* of man is wedded to and remains for ever within the body of his planet." Relevant here is the teaching given in volume 2 of *The Secret Doctrine* that as the human "body" became increasingly stable and solid through the succession of the "Root Races," so the planet occupied by the body also became more solid. In other words, there is a direct correlation between the outermost vehicle of the human being and the planet on which the human takes birth. M emphasizes this in his answer to question 6 when he states that the human "appears in the first world of causes as a shadowy breath, which coagulates with, and is hardened together with the parent sphere." We may take the "first world of causes" as either Globe A of the planetary chain or as the first root race. In either case, the first human appearance would be similar to a "shadowy breath," and the "globe" inhabited would be equally transparent.

We are next told that the "individual *jivatma* life principle, that which is called . . . *animal spirits*[,] returns after death to its source—Fohat." Now what is meant by the "jivatman"? The verbal root *jiv*, meaning "to live," when combined with *atman* may be said to refer to a living spirit, especially when associated with a vehicle or vehicles in incarnation. HPB identifies the term with the monad (see *SD*, 1:147) and also speaks of jivatman, or jiva, as a form of force, stating that "in man alone the Jiva is complete" (*SD*, 1:222). As the "individual . . . life principle" or monad, the jiva constitutes the true individuality, and as a force its root would naturally be in that fundamental dynamism, Fohat, to which the Mahatma states it returns after the death of the physical.

What is the individuality with which jivatman is identified? The answer is found in the Mahatma's response to question 7: "The whole individuality is centred in the three middle or 3rd, 4th and 5th principles. During earthly life it is all in the fourth, the centre of energy, volition—will."

The three aspects of the jivatman, the monad in incarnation, are the next principles named by the Mahatma: the "*linga shariram*," which derives from akasha and to which it therefore returns; the "*Kamarupa*," or body of desire, which "recommingle[s] with the Universal Sakti—the Will-Force, or universal energy," another aspect of Fohat; and the animal soul "borrowed from the breath of *Universal Mind*," which therefore returns to that class of the Dhyan Chohans known as the *manasaputras* (and by many other names as well).

Several points should be noted concerning these aspects. First, in regard to the third principle, linga sharira, generally called the etheric, we need to keep in mind that akasha is sevenfold, since it is the substratum of all manifestation, from the most subtle to the densest. We are not told into which level or state of akasha the model or etheric vehicle is drawn. One suggestion is that the etheric exists at the level often referred to as the astral light, so, on the death of the physical, the linga sharira withdraws into that state. Students may wish to explore this question further, particularly as the astral light is seldom mentioned in later literature but is frequently referred to by HPB in her writings as well as in the letters.

For those who think of kama only as desire in its grossest and most selfish manifestation, the statement that kama-rupa "recommingles" with "universal energy" presents an expanded view of its nature. Identifying its source as the "Universal Will-Force" indicates that this principle is related to a much larger force field than we usually consider. An exploration of Fohat as the binding or cohesive force in the universe, as the root of all relationship as well as of the powers of attraction and repulsion, will lead the student to some fascinating discoveries. This should be of particular interest since we are now in the "fourth round" of earth's planetary chain and therefore the focus of our development is on all the aspects of the fourth principle, kama. As we well know, desire or kama in its lower aspects is not always easy to deal with, but what is it in its higher ranges?

"Animal soul" is generally synonymous with the lower aspect of the mind principle, manas. Therefore it has the added connotation of kama-manas, the desire-mind. However, it is described as "borrowed from the breath of Universal Mind." Since anything associated with "Universal Mind" can scarcely be considered "animalistic," why is this principle called the "animal soul"? Is the "soul" in an animalistic condition only when it is unawakened, responding to external stimuli in a reactive and self-centered state? Humanity in general is said to be in the fifth stage or "race" of the fourth round; consequently, we are dealing with the development of the manasic aspect of kama. It is helpful here to turn to question 5 and the Mahatma's reply (page 121), noting that our "*fifth* principle is evolved from *within*" ourselves. To evolve the manasic principle from "within" surely means that we are responsible for its further development, a point made quite clear by HPB in *The Key to Theosophy* (my *Abridgement*, page 56): "The future state and the Karmic destiny of man depend on whether Manas gravitates more downward to Kama rupa, the seat of the animal passions, or upwards to *Buddhi*, the spiritual *Ego*."

Relevant to the mind or fifth principle HPB comments: "Occult philosophy teaches us that the human mind (or lower *Manas*) is a direct ray or reflection of the Higher Principles, the *Noetic* Mind. The latter is the reincarnating Ego which old Aryan philosophers call *Manasaputra*, the "Sons of Mind" or of *Mahat*, the Universal Cosmic Mind" (*CW*, 12:411).

There is much more to be understood about manas and why it is "evolved from within." Among HPB's many statements concerning the work we are to do in evolving the "animal soul," or kama-manas, through the stages of the human soul into its status as the "spiritual soul," we may note particularly her comments in the article "Mahatmas and Chelas" (*CW*, 6:239–41). Writing of the "process of self-evolution" in becoming a Mahatma, HPB first refers to the "lower portions of the fifth in which reside the animal propensities" and then to "the higher *Manas, the pure man,* which is associated with the sixth and the seventh principles." She adds: "An entity that is passing through the occult training . . . gradually has less and less (in each incarnation) of that lower *Manas* until there arrives a time when its *whole Manas,* being of an entirely elevated character, is centered in the higher individuality, when such a person may be said to have become a Mahatma."

Therefore, when M states that the "'animal soul' borrowed from the breath of *Universal Mind* will return to the Dhyan Chohans" (or that group of Dhyan Chohans who first activated manas in the human entity) it is we in our present human state who must ensure this development. To assist us with evolving the fifth principle from within, we have been given so many beautiful guides, including such Theosophical classics as *The Voice of the Silence, Light on the Path,* and texts on meditation and yogic disciplines.

Next in the Mahatma's response 3 is the "sixth principle—whether drawn into or ejected from the matrix of the Great Passive Principle." The "Great Passive Principle" is similar to alaya (literally, the nondissolvable), often called the storehouse-consciousness (alaya-vijnana) in which are stored all the "seeds" that become the direct cause for manifestation. It is often equated with akasha.

We are accustomed to naming this sixth principle buddhi and thinking of it as the "spiritual soul," which indeed is the way HPB usually designates it. But in *The Secret Doctrine* (1:17), HPB speaks of the "Universal Sixth principle" as "the Over-Soul," another term that could be identified with or at least similar to both alaya and akasha. As the "Over-Soul," the sixth principle is the means by which we realize our unity with all life, a realization akin to buddhic consciousness in which compassion and wisdom are united. The Mahatma comments that the sixth principle is said "to remain in its own sphere" but in two conditions: "either as part of the crude material" of an unevolved Ego or "as individualized entity to be reborn in a higher world of causes," and therefore as a fully evolved Ego. He also says that the sixth principle is either "drawn into or ejected from" the "Great Passive Principle." This may refer to the end and beginning of a manvantara, respectively.

Alongside M's statements here about the sixth principle, we need to consider also what KH says at the conclusion of Letter 67 (page 189): "Fathom the nature and essence of the sixth principle of the universe and man and you will have fathomed the greatest mystery in this our world—and why not—are you not surrounded by it? What are its familiar manifestations, Od force, etc.—all different aspects of one force capable of good and evil applications."

If there is a mystery concerning the nature of the sixth principle, the same can certainly be said about the seventh principle, which the Mahatma states will carry the entity "from the *Devachan* and follow the new *Ego* to its place of re-birth." Since atman, which is usually considered the seventh principle, is "no individual principle" according to HPB (as quoted earlier), it is difficult to see how it can "follow" anything. Perhaps, however, it is not atman that is referred to here but rather the auric egg, which HPB speaks of as the seventh principle esoterically, as already noted in a citation given earlier. Eight years later, in her E.S. Instruction No. 3, HPB states that the auric egg is "the preserver of every Karmic record. The storehouse of all the good and bad powers of man, receiving and giving out at his will— nay, at his very thought—every potentiality, which becomes, then and there, an acting potency" (*CW*, 12:608).

This description suggests that what follows "the new *Ego*" into rebirth can only be the auric egg or envelope, for it is the "karmic record" that influences and even determines the new incarnation. In *The Inner Group Teachings of H. P. Blavatsky*, HPB is reported to have said that the auric egg is "karmic" and that it is the "receptacle of all Karmic causes," "the transmitter from the individual lives to the eternal, from the periodical lives . . . to the eternal life" (Spierenburg, *Inner Group Teachings*, 6–7). In her E.S. Instruction No. 1, HPB says: "The reason why public mention of the Auric Body is not permitted is on account of its being so sacred. It is this Body which at death assimilates the essence of Buddhi and Manas and becomes the vehicle of these spiritual principles, *which are not objective,* and then with the full radiation of Atman upon it, ascends . . . into the Devachanic state" (*CW,* 12:526–27).

Further, in E.S. Instruction No. 3, HPB emphasizes: "The Auric Egg, on account of its nature and manifold functions, has to be well studied. . . . The Auric Egg contains, and is directly related to, both the divine and the physical man. In its essence . . . it is eternal; in its constant correlations, it is a kind of perpetual motion machine during the reincarnating progress of the Ego on this earth" (*CW,* 12:608). There is much more in HPB's esoteric writings concerning the auric egg, and a full exploration of this little-studied aspect of the human constitution can be most rewarding.

The Mahatma makes two additional comments in Letter 44 concerning the seventh principle. In the second paragraph of response 5 (page 121), he writes: "When we speak of the seventh principle it is neither quality nor quantity nor yet form that are meant, but rather the *space* occupied in that *ocean* of spirit by the results or effects . . . impressed thereon." "The *space* occupied in that *ocean* of spirit" may refer to akasha, an idea supported by HPB's statement that the "Auric Envelope . . . is the universally diffused primordial and pure Akasha, the first film on the boundless and shoreless expanse of Jiva" (*CW,* 12:607). The "film" might well be the "auric envelope" on which are "impressed" the karmic results of previous incarnations, which "follow" the reincarnating Ego to its next rebirth.

Again following question 6 (page 121), he says: "Seventh principle always there as a latent force in every one of the principles—even body. As the macrocosmic *Whole* it is present even in the *lower* sphere, but there is nothing there to assimilate it to itself."

Having already considered M's responses to Sinnett's statements and questions 4 and 5, we can now turn to question 6 and its very long response that continues the story of the cycles of descent and ascent that constitute our evolutionary journey. First we are told that "Man (physically) is a compound of all the kingdoms," presumably because the physical vehicle embodies all the kingdoms through which the Ego has passed on the downward cycle. At the same time, "It is not the *outward* or physical shape that . . . pollutes the five principles—but the *mental* perversity."

The meaning of the term "mental perversity," and the peculiar nature of the mental principle that permits or exhibits such a condition, calls for some consideration. A clue to understanding the subject may lie in M's next statement: "It is but at his fourth round, when arrived at the full possession of his *Kama*-energy and fully matured, that man becomes *fully responsible.*" In other words, during this present round, the fourth as the Mahatma states, the emphasis is on kama, or desire. However, we are only in the fifth developmental stage (root race) of the round, as M notes (page 123): "The individual entities" in this round "are unconsciously to themselves performing their *local* earthly sevenfold cycles," the local cycles being those of the root races, sub-races, and so on. And so the kamic energy is "tinged," or "polluted" to use the Mahatma's term, by lower manas.

We are dealing with the energy of kama-manas, as has so often been stressed, and until kama is purified—freed of the egoistic and selfish pull of the animal soul, the lowest energy of manas—the desire nature will not be fully "matured." This is not a matter of killing off the emotional nature but rather attuning or purifying it as a matured instrument for the soul's expression in the personality. Kama is to become a reflector of buddhi, which is possible only as we assume full responsibility for our emotions alongside our thoughts and actions. As M says in his response to question 7, at our present developmental stage, the center of energy is in kama, "volition—will."

In general, the human entity is to develop one principle in each of the seven rounds. Only in the present fourth round can we arrive at full possession of the kamic energy. Similarly, in the fifth round manas is destined for full development, as the Mahatma writes: "On their [the human] fifth round . . . they will have to appear on this earth as a still more perfect and intellectual race." In the sixth round, having developed the sixth principle, buddhi, the human entity may become a Buddha. In

Letter 66, Plato and Confucius are identified as "fifth round men" and the Buddha as a "sixth round man" (page 176).

Although I am not commenting in detail on all the information given here regarding the downward and upward cycles through the rounds of earth's planetary chain, I must mention the Mahatma's emphasis on our becoming *"fully responsible."* as a consequence of which "every individuality will be followed on its ascending arc by the Law of retribution—Karma and death accordingly" (page 123). The fourth, in any cycle, is always the turning point of the cycle; hence we may be said to be on the ascending arc in general (at the fifth developmental stage of the fourth round), although since within each cycle there are subcycles, we have yet to traverse a "downward course" in several of those subcycles that may be ever more difficult. So M states: "This downward course has not yet begun but will soon. Only how many— oh, how many will be destroyed on their way." This is reminiscent of KH's statement in Letter 18 (page 65) regarding the evolutionary cycle: that at the turning point there is the "annihilation of those unfit," the "laggard *Egos* perish by the millions"—not a very happy picture! So we must remember that immortality in this planetary chain is conditional on our successful evolution. It is not automatic.

Continuing with his response to question 6, M states that his description of the downward and upward progress is *"the rule"* and that "the Buddhas and *Avatars* form the exception." What then is an avatar, and who may be those who are "left to us on earth"? In the *Theosophical Glossary*, HPB defines an avatar as a "divine incarnation. The descent of a god or some exalted Being, who has progressed beyond the necessity of Rebirths into the body of a simple mortal." Then she gives some examples: "Krishna was an avatar of Vishnu. The Dalai Lama is regarded as an avatar of Avalokitesvara, and the Teshu Lama as one of Tsong-kha-pa or Amitabha." G. de Purucker in his *Occult Glossary* states that an avatar "signifies the passing down of a celestial energy or of an individualized complex of celestial energies . . . to overshadow and illuminate some human being." The entire subject is worth fuller study.

Finally in the process of "reforming [Sinnett's] conceptions," the Mahatma presents us with a truly grand picture of our human destiny. The individuality (consisting of the third, fourth, and fifth principles) that has "run successfully its seven-fold downward and upward course" has now "to assimilate to itself the eternal life-power residing but in the seventh and then blend the three (fourth, fifth, and seventh) into one—the sixth." We must be very careful in how we identify the "seventh" here, remembering that "Atman is no individual principle" and could not be "assimilated" by the individuality, although the "Auric Body," which HPB describes as assimilating the essence of buddhi and manas and "with the full radiation of Atman upon it," may achieve the status of full Adept (read again *CW*, 12:526–27).

The letter concludes on a truly beautiful and optimistic note: the possibility of blending the higher and purified principles into the love and compassion that characterize buddhic consciousness, the wisdom and spiritual perception that flow from buddhic awareness. Here is the goal for humanity. The achievement of such a state is "the chief object of our struggles and *initiations*" here on earth while yet incarnated. And if we are successful in attaining such a consciousness during the final cycles of this fourth round, we have "nothing to fear" in the succeeding three rounds of this planetary chain. To know that "our beloved KH is on his way to the goal" should give us all encouragement as we seek to follow in the way the Great Ones have gone.

LETTER 45

Evidently the Mahatma's responses to Sinnett's and Hume's questions that comprise Letter 44 called forth further questions from Sinnett, which, Morya says in concluding Letter 45, "will be attended to when I am not harassed with mightier business." Actually, those answers are provided by the Mahatma in Letter 46, which we will come to in due time. Meanwhile, it appears that Sinnett had another subject on his mind, the answer to which is given in the first paragraph of Letter 45.

Morya opens Letter 45 by saying that since Sinnett has addressed a letter to him, he is willing to reply. As we know, Sinnett had long been interested in the phenomena of Spiritualism and had evidently learned that one of the leading English mediums, William Eglinton, has arrived in India. When Sinnett was in England the year previous (1881, when his first book, *The Occult World*, was published), he may even have met Eglinton and so was now resuming an acquaintance. We do not know what Sinnett asked Morya regarding the English medium, but it seems fair to conjecture that Sinnett wanted Eglinton to exhibit his mediumistic powers before HPB and perhaps a number of other Theosophists. I suggest this on the basis of M's statement: "It does seem cruel to allow the poor sensitive lad to risk himself inside the lion's den," for HPB could certainly become a "lion" should the demonstration prove a failure!

The Mahatmas seem to be already familiar with Eglinton, as KH mentions him in a note inserted into a letter from Stainton Moses to Sinnett (see Letter 38). In that insertion, KH refers to Eglinton as an "honest medium" and evidently had intended training him in some way to become useful in the work of the Brotherhood. Little information is available about Eglinton beyond the fact that he was involved in Spiritualism as a medium; even the dates of his life have not been recorded. However, two events revolving around him are of special interest. The first concerns the "spirit" whom Morya refers to here as Eglinton's "mighty and far-seeing 'Ernest.'"

For the consequences of Eglinton's reliance on "Ernest," we can turn to a story told by C. W. Leadbeater that C. Jinarajadasa uses as the introduction to *The "K.H." Letters to C. W. Leadbeater*. This encounter with "Ernest" occurred at least two years after Eglinton's visit to India in 1882, and even after Sinnett had returned to England permanently in 1884. Here is Leadbeater's story, in his own words:

In the course of my inquiries into Spiritualism I had come into contact with most of the prominent mediums of that day, and had seen every one of the ordinary phenomena about which one reads in books upon that subject. One medium with whom I had much to do was Mr. Eglinton; and although I have heard stories told against him, I must bear witness that in all my own dealings with him I found him most straightforward, reasonable and courteous. He had various so-called controls—one a Red Indian girl who called herself Daisy. . . . Another was a tall Arab, named Abdallah. . . . A third control who frequently put in an appearance was Ernest; he comparatively rarely materialized, but frequently spoke with direct voice, and wrote a characteristic and well-educated hand. One day in conversation with him something was said in reference to the Masters of the Wisdom; Ernest spoke of Them with the most profound reverence, and said that he had on various occasions had the privilege of seeing Them. I at once enquired whether he was prepared to take charge of any message or letter for Them, and he said that he would willingly do so, and would deliver it when opportunity offered, but he could not say exactly when that would be.

. . . I at once provisionally accepted Ernest's offer. I said that I would write a letter to one of these Great Masters, and would confide it to him if my friend and teacher, Mr. Sinnett, approved. . . . When Mr. Eglinton came out of his trance, I asked him how I could send a letter to Ernest, and he said at once that if I would let him have the letter he would put it in a certain box which hung against the wall, from which Ernest would take it when he wished. I then posted off to Mr. Sinnett, and asked his opinion of all this. He was at once eagerly interested, and advised me promptly to accept the offer and see what happened.

Leadbeater wrote a letter to KH on March 3, 1884, sealing it inside a letter to Eglinton and asking the medium to put it in the box for Ernest. Eglinton responded, saying he had placed the letter into his box, that it had already vanished, and that if any reply were forthcoming he would forward it immediately. A number of months passed with no communication, though during that time HPB came to London, where Leadbeater, who had joined the Society in late November 1883, met her. In late October of 1884, Leadbeater came to London to say good-bye to HPB, who was to sail for India on November first. On his return home, some fifty miles or so outside London, Leadbeater found a letter awaiting him, the first of the KH letters that he was to receive. The letter began: "Last spring—March the 3rd—you wrote a letter to me and entrusted it to 'Ernest.' Tho' the paper itself never reached me—nor was it ever likely to, considering the nature of the messenger—its contents have."

The second event concerning Eglinton is the very dramatic one related in Letter 55, when, disappointed over his stay in India, he returned to England on a ship called the *Vega*. During that voyage, KH informs Sinnett, the Mahatma will appear to Eglinton, but he adds "He will see somebody quite different from the real KH though it will still be KH." It was this appearance of the Mahatma on board the *Vega* that brought about a "conversion" of Eglinton to Theosophy, resulting as he himself wrote to Sinnett, in his "complete belief" in the "Brothers." This may indicate why both KH and M took an interest in Eglinton and even attempted to shield him from anything that might hurt him during his stay in India.

Continuing with Letter 45, M communicates to Sinnett information truly significant concerning the conditions under which the Society was founded. In Letter 24 and again in Letter 39, Morya expressed the hope that Sinnett would attend the Anniversary meeting of the Society to be held in Bombay in January 1882, approximately the beginning of the Society's seventh year. Now writing in February and knowing that Sinnett did not attend that meeting, M must feel the importance of telling the Englishman just what had been in the Mahatmas' minds at the time the Theosophical Society was brought into existence. Evidently both Mahatmas had been given permission for an "experiment" that would bring to the attention of the world, in a discreet manner, the existence of the Brotherhood and open the way for a public presentation of "the Occult doctrine" under the name of Theosophy. The first seven years, a "term of trial," is coming to a close: "In a few more months the term of probation will end." The hope had been that "the world had so far advanced intellectually, if not intuitionally," that the esoteric doctrine "might gain an intellectual acceptance" at least. While permission had been given to the two Brothers to undertake such a "trial" or "experiment" as the founding of a Society, there was the clear condition that it would be independent of their "personal management" and "no abnormal interference by ourselves [i.e., the Mahatmas]." KH has already told Sinnett (Letter 5) of their regard for Olcott as leader of the movement; now M echoes that view. And in Letter 29, KH explained HPB's unique position, and M repeats the fact that despite "strong personal defects . . . there was no second to her living fit for this work." Evidently both Olcott and HPB were given a choice, for M says "both offered themselves for the trial for certain remuneration in the far distant future." Notably, M repeats here a phrase KH used in an earlier letter, speaking of the two founders as volunteering for a work "as soldiers volunteer for a Forlorn Hope."

Referring again to the conclusion of the Society's septenary term of "probation," the Mahatma warns Sinnett that unless the Brothers' status vis-à-vis the Society is clearly understood and accepted, they "will subside out of public view like a vapour into the ocean." He tells Sinnett: "Only those who have proved faithful to themselves and to Truth through everything will be allowed further intercourse with us." And about such intercourse there must be the pledge of silence. Did this mean there was to be no further talk about the Masters? One is reminded of a sentence in the famous 1900 letter from KH to Annie Besant: "The cant about 'Masters' must be silently but firmly put down." This statement, as well as M's in Letter 45, call for reflection, especially since so many groups and individuals alike claim to be under the tutelage of and in direct contact with various Mahatmas. How do we tell the genuine from the spurious, the authentic from the credulous? And when we do speak of the Masters and quote their writings, do we use them as authorities not to be questioned or as elder brothers whom we respect and revere but who encourage us to discover truth for ourselves? This letter certainly contains much to be taken to heart. We can also be grateful that while M seemed to give a dire warning to Sinnett, the correspondence with so much more of the teachings continued for another two years.

The letter closes with a comment about Hume and a small pamphlet, *Hints on Esoteric Theosophy*, published in Benares in that year, 1882. Undoubtedly one reason why the Masters put up with Hume as long as they did was the very fact that he did have strong "personal intuitions," although he seldom trusted them. It appears the pamphlet was not altered in any way, and it probably had an important influence in furthering the Society's work at that time.

Throughout the letters, both M and KH refer often to work in which they are engaged. Here Morya speaks of being "harassed with mightier business." The nature of that work is never really made explicit, but we may presume it concerned something other than the Society. At the same time, in another letter KH states that the Society "cannot be neglected." And to aid the Society, both Mahatmas give attention to the teachings, the occult doctrine, that may be conveyed through it. Hence in the next letter, number 46, M gives attention to Sinnett's further "cosmological questions."

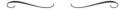

LETTER 46

In Letter 46 the Mahatma continues his explanation (from Letter 44) of the rather difficult subject of planetary chains, rounds or cycles, and what were originally called "races." While examining Morya's comments, which are certainly replies to Sinnett's further questions on the esoteric cosmological system, we should take notice of his statement at the close of the letter: "You ought to come to some agreement as to the terms used when discussing cyclic evolutions." At this early period in the communication of the esoteric doctrine, whether through HPB or in these letters directly from the Masters, the terminology was not firmly established. We can only speculate that the terms used by Sinnett and later adopted by HPB when writing *The Secret Doctrine* may have been only crude approximations of the actual ones, which Morya says here are "untranslatable." The Mahatma also stresses that a "good knowledge of our complete system" cannot be given to the Englishman, so it is certainly no wonder that many misconceptions may have arisen through the years.

These comments suggest that we should focus our attention on the pattern described for cyclic evolution, the development of a "planetary chain," and not confuse it with the planets of our solar system or with human racial evolution, which again must not be misinterpreted as applying to ethnic groups or skin pigmentation. At the outset of the letter, M emphasizes two factors significant in any study of evolutionary development: first, there appears to be "a fixed period" in the cycle to which the term *manvantara* is applied; and, second, the "rate of development" is "adjusted" to that time period. The key to both these factors may be said to lie in the basic concept that the system is a sevenfold one.

Students wishing to know more about the first factor, the "fixed period," may find interest in an unfinished essay by HPB, published posthumously (*CW*, 13:301–6) under the title "On Cosmic Cycles, Manvantaras, and Rounds." There HPB gives numerous figures, mainly from what she refers to as "exoteric Brahmanical works." The following quotations from that essay clarify that what we have been given is more about a pattern than of specific time periods:

> If we have the period of the Day of Brahma and if we know that there are seven rounds, that each round covers seven planets, that the period of rest of a planet in every round equals that of its activity, and if to all this knowledge we apply the key of the septenary arithmetical progression series . . . there is a gradual rise of, from

one to seven. The duration of the existence of humanity during the Seven Rounds is 1:2:3:4:5:6:7. In each Round, the duration of the existence of humanity, on the seven planets of our chain is 1:2:3:4:5:6:7. The period of human existence in seven races, on one planet, is again 1:2:3:4:5:6:7.

She concludes (though in fact the essay is unfinished):

> We have already stated that the above figures are exact, if the exoteric calculations of the Brahmins about the day of Brahma be correct. But we may again state here that that figure is not correctly given out in exoteric numbers. We may . . . add that the explanations given by us about the progressions . . . are facts. . . . And these processes we have explained because we know that not one of the exact numbers will ever be given out, as they pertain to the Mysteries of Initiations and to the Secrets of the occult influence of Numbers.

Internal evidence suggests that HPB wrote this essay in 1884. She turned again to this subject in a section titled "The Chronology of the Brahmans," in volume 2 of *The Secret Doctrine*, the content of which Geoffrey Barborka summarizes in *The Peopling of the Earth* (chapter 16, "Chronology for the Peopling of the Earth"). What we have been given, then, is the septenary pattern as it unfolds guided by "the life impulse," in strict accordance with what M calls in Letter 46, "the law of perfect justice and equilibrium which pervades nature." So it is that "periods of action and rest follow each other in everything in nature from the macrocosm with its Solar Systems down to man and its parent-earth." And when we consider our own humanity, "the spiritual individuality, the Monad . . . on its downward and upward cyclic rotation," M states: "The deviation of each one's course, and his rate of progress from Nirvana to Nirvana is governed by causes which he himself creates out of the exigencies in which he finds himself entangled."

The Mahatma informs Sinnett: "Motion is the eternal order of things and affinity or attraction its handmaid of all works," and "as planetary development is as progressive as human or race evolution," so "there are among the stellar galaxies births and deaths of worlds ever following each other in the orderly procession of natural Law." Yet the goal for our human life wave is to achieve the state of unitary consciousness called "Buddhahood." There is much to contemplate in M's words: "When the last cycle of man-bearing has been completed by that last fecund earth; and humanity has reached in a mass the stage of Buddhahood and passed out of the objective existence into the mystery of Nirvana—then "strikes the hour"; the seen becomes the unseen, the concrete resumes its pre-cyclic state of atomic distribution."

We learn later that there are also the "laggards," as HPB terms them, those who do not make the grade or achieve the goal set for a particular stage on the evolutionary ladder. They return to the same point where they left off to become, in their turn, the leaders and guides of the next life wave.

A few further comments on Letter 46 may be useful. First, in regard to the metaphor customarily used in speaking of planetary chains, that of "a chain of beads, and each bead a world," as M says. Because each bead on a chain is distinct, we are inclined to think of these domains of existence as quite separate from one another, each on its own level of materiality. This representation is very useful, and the explanations and diagrams in Barborka's work are extremely helpful in understanding the development of planetary chains, particularly the lunar and earth chains with which humanity is especially concerned. Yet it is important to remember that we are really speaking not of discrete objects but of different rates of vibration analogous to the seven grades of consciousness within the human being.

Further, we do well to keep in mind two sections in volume 1 of *The Secret Doctrine*, "A Few Early Theosophical Misconceptions Concerning Planets, Rounds, and Man" (pages 152–70), and "Additional Facts and Explanations Concerning the Globes and the Monads" (pages 170–98), in particular a quotation HPB attributes to her Teachers, which says in part: "As Globes, they are in coadunation but not in consubstantiality with our earth and thus pertain to quite another state of consciousness" (page 166). This can only mean that the "Globes" are united although made of dissimilar substances, and like the petals of a flower, unfold from a single center (or laya center), overlaying one another, each one perceived as a "privation" emerging from the subjective, to adopt M's words.

The Mahatma continues with comments on the then current scientific findings about the appearance of human beings on the planet, roughly correlated with the geological periods. There are at least two ways to approach this topic, often referred to as the doctrine of "racial evolution." One is to examine contemporary scientific knowledge concerning human development, attempting to correlate what M says with what science now knows. This will inevitably lead us into puzzling anomalies, especially regarding time periods. The other is to consider the subject from the perspective of overall esoteric doctrine. The subject is treated in its entirety in volume 2 of *The Secret Doctrine*, under the title "Anthropogenesis." There, HPB gives the student further excerpts from the Stanzas of Dzyan, the mystical work on which she based her first volume, and in her commentary includes not only the scientific understandings of her day but more importantly the occult tradition regarding our origins and development. Personally, I am inclined to agree with the statement of Sri Madhava Ashish in his introduction to *Man, Son of Man*: "The importance of the stanzas lies in their being a guide to man's true nature and not in their being a history of evolution on the surface of this planet." He notes further: "The real significance and purpose of these stanzas . . . lies in their being a symbolic account of psychic movements within us. . . . The stanzas are concerned with Man; and all the stones, waters, Mothers, and Fathers, are glyphs of the patterns of our inner and outer being woven by the powers of life" (pages 8 and 19).

In the letter we are presently considering, M comments: "There were not *four* but *five* races; and we are that fifth with remnants of the fourth." While the subject of "race" is taken up again in later letters, particularly Letters 61, 62, 66, and 67, as well as at some length in Letter 93B, all from KH, it is well to pause here to consider this much-abused term that is used by both the Mahatmas and HPB and just what it means from the point of view of occult philosophy. Particularly helpful in this regard is the chapter "The Doctrine of the Races" in Barborka's *The Divine Plan*. Barborka makes the important comment that in esoteric philosophy the term "indicates a specific type of evolutionary development, not only as regards physical development and outer characteristics, but also includes a specific intellectual as well as spiritual developmental status." This statement bears upon the unique doctrine, expounded by HPB in *The Secret Doctrine*, of a triple evolutionary scheme: the "Spiritual or Monadic, the Intellectual, and the Physical-Etheric" (see *SD*, 1:181).

The occult or esoteric meaning of the term "race" involves the hyphenated term "Root-Race," which as Barborka points out, is used "figuratively" and "conveys the meaning of a basis from which a race derives its origin as well as its growth, life and vigor." He adds further, "Although the individuals or personalities inhabiting a root-race may be new, these personalities are but the outer vehicular manifestations of the very same Monads, which had used the old personalities as vehicles for a period of manifestation." I would stress this point to suggest that when M speaks of "remnants of the fourth," he is speaking not of groups of people on the planet other than ourselves whose physical characteristics may incline us to think of them as inferior and therefore as "remnants," leftovers who have not achieved some desired state of development, but rather of all humanity within whom traces of the fourth developmental stage are still present to a greater or less extent. At all costs, we want to avoid assuming, even unconsciously, an attitude of superiority based solely on physical appearance. We may recognize that in our human life wave, individual monads may be experiencing different stages of evolutionary development, just as in a school students in different grades are learning the lessons appropriate to their grade. Furthermore, just as students in the upper grades carry within themselves the learnings and even attitudes of the lower grades, so in our evolutionary development—physically, intellectually, and spiritually—we have within us characteristics of all the previous evolutionary stages through which we have passed. We will return to this view when we consider some of the later letters regarding our evolution through those developmental stages known as the races and the root-races.

M's comment concerning Subba Row in the last paragraph of Letter 46 is interesting because as we know the Mahatmas had hoped this great Indian Vedantin, a chela of M's, would assist in teaching Sinnett and Hume at least the rudiments of the esoteric philosophy, but Subba Row was averse to teaching any "foreigner" (and Westerners were by definition foreigners) what he regarded as the most sacred knowledge. M clearly knows just what Subba Row is doing, since he tells Sinnett that the chela "is now at his *tapas*," which means his devotions or perhaps even on a retreat where he would not or could not be disturbed.

Although this sequence in the correspondence includes one more letter, Letter 48, from Morya, and there are an additional one or two much later, with Letter 46 we come to the end of the letters in which he communicates so much of the teachings. We turn now to a consideration of Letter 47, the first letter Sinnett received from KH after the latter's return from his retreat.

LETTER 47

One of the most beautiful as well as deeply significant letters in the correspondence between the Mahatmas and the two Englishmen, Letter 47 contains teachings that speak to us so directly and so intimately, and with such timeless relevance, that nearly every sentence calls for deep reflection. We know a little about what has transpired for KH during the months he was unable to communicate directly with Sinnett, as M has told Sinnett (see Letter 29) something of the nature and circumstances of KH's retreat. The careful student may note a decided change in the tone of KH's correspondence from this letter onwards. The Mahatma has no doubt undergone a momentous experience of tremendous impact, advancing him another stage in his evolution. Later Sinnett will learn that "the degrees of an Adept's initiation mark the seven stages at which he discovers the secret of the sevenfold principles in nature and man and awakens his dormant powers" (see conclusion to Letter 67). We may speculate, then, that KH's retreat had indeed been for the purpose of taking one or another of those "seven stages," and that the change in tone in Letter 47 is a direct result of taking that further step.

"My Brother," the simple salutation with which Letter 47 begins, carries within it such a feeling of genuine friendship, a relationship of caring and compassion, that one is inclined to pause here at the very beginning to let those words resonate in the heart. At the very outset of the correspondence, KH addressed Sinnett as "Esteemed Brother and Friend," and again as "Much Esteemed Sir and Brother." Now, as the correspondence between KH and Sinnett resumes, there is a quality of even deeper affection in the words "My Brother." One's sense of the Mahatma's concern and caring for Sinnett is heightened as one reads further that KH offers the Englishman his "first moment of leisure." With what genuine happiness Sinnett must have read this letter, realizing he was once again hearing directly from the Mahatma with whom he had such a close bond.

At the same time, one wonders if Sinnett felt some sadness in reading that "it is more difficult than before to exchange letters" because the distance between them in terms of consciousness, of inner realization, had appreciably increased. Perhaps he recalled the several times that M, in his letters during the long interval of KH's silence, had advised him to "get on with his occult study" (Letter 42) in order that he "should be ready . . . when KH shall say to you, Come up hither" (Letter 43). Sinnett may well have considered how he had used those months during which he received so many occult teachings from M (no fewer than nineteen letters in addition to the two sets of Cosmological Notes). Had he used that time for study, for persevering in understanding the teachings, for trying to follow his Teacher's advice? Now it is KH who is asking him directly, "Will you not try—for the sake of shortening the distance between us— to disentangle yourself from the net of life and death" in which the majority of humanity is caught?

After the opening salutation Letter 47 continues with the words "I have been on a long journey after supreme knowledge." Already, it seems, we sense a difference in KH. We can recall M's comment at the conclusion of Letter 44 that KH was "on his way to the goal—the highest of all beyond as on this sphere," which has been defined as Bodhisattvahood. Much later in the correspondence, in Letter 117, KH tells Sinnett that he had "been born into a *new* and *higher* light, and even that one, in no wise the most dazzling to be acquired on this earth," and he adds, "Verily the *Light of Omniscience* and infallible Prevision on this earth—that shines only for the highest Chohan alone—is yet far away from me!" So whatever he attained during the three months of retreat, KH knows there are yet further steps to be taken.

KH calls the journey a "long" one—a journey in consciousness, certainly, as we know that KH's physical vehicle lay nearly "lifeless," to quote the Mahatma M in Letter 29. Yet such an inner journey must have taken its toll on the physical body, since KH tells Sinnett he "took a long time to rest" after the conclusion of the retreat. The journey must have demanded complete inner concentration, perhaps inner alertness, inner focus of attention, and must have had its effect on the physical brain. Indeed, HPB in her E.S. Instructions (see *CW*, vol. 12) and in comments published as *The Inner Group Teachings of H. P. Blavatsky* provides valuable information about molecular changes in the physical brain brought about by meditation and concentration, as well as information about the nature of the brain generally that should be of interest to the serious student. Studying HPB's statements closely may lead us toward some slight understanding of KH's "long journey" during his three months of seclusion.

The inner journey, KH tells Sinnett, was in pursuit of "supreme knowledge." What, we may ask, is meant by "supreme knowledge"?

Surely it is not factual knowledge, information of the ordinary kind or even additional information about the world of occultism, although we may assume that the Mahatmas are continuing to learn more of the vast realm of the hidden side of things. Rather, the knowledge KH was after must have had to do with the experience of what we can only call a "totality of knowing," the result of blending higher and lower manas, and also with assimilating into manas what M calls (at the conclusion of Letter 44) "the eternal life-power" of the seventh principle. Again, a careful study of M's description of KH's journey "to the goal," along with a study of HPB's esoteric teachings, helps us to understand at least something of the journey that we all must eventually take if we, too, would seek "supreme knowledge" and become, in our turn, masters of the wisdom, Bodhisattvas, and, yes, future Buddhas.

KH tells Sinnett that on his return not only was rest required—no doubt to enable the physical vehicle to adjust to the Mahatma's new inner condition of expanded consciousness—but he was again involved with duty, his particular work within the Brotherhood and evidently participation in the New Year's "festivities." But his thoughts, he says, were concentrated on the "Great Problem." There has been much speculation as to the meaning of those words. The fact that KH goes on in the next paragraph to describe the human condition suggests that the problem to which the Mahatma was giving thought was how to bring about a total transformation of human consciousness and by so doing to ensure that our present human life wave will continue its evolutionary journey, rather than destroy itself as have other humanities in ages long past.

Whatever the "Great Problem" may have been, KH now tells Sinnett that he is "'Self once more"—and then asks, "What is *Self*?" Although the word is capitalized in the letter, we may assume that KH is referring to the human personality, which is indeed only a "passing guest." Yet it is through the personality that the lessons must be learned, and it was the human aspect of KH that needed to rest and that was obliged to take up duty again.

That question—"What is Self?"—is one we all ask at some time or other in our efforts to understand the various aspects of ourselves. It is not an easy question to answer, especially when the self—whether personal and human or impersonal and higher—seeks to define itself! It is well to remember that the concerns of the personal self "are all like a mirage of the great desert."

And as the letter continues, we find KH's beautiful statement of how he regards Sinnett: it is Sinnett's "inner Self [that] reconciles" the Mahatma to the weaknesses or flaws of his outer personality. Could we but perceive the inner Self of each person with whom we work, every person we meet, we too might discover that a "great man is he who is strongest in the exercise of patience" and so cultivate the virtue of forbearance for what we judge to be others' defects. Undoubtedly patience was the hardest lesson for Sinnett, for again and again through the letters he is reminded that he wants too much too fast. There is a certain amazing synchronicity in the fact that Sinnett's wife, whom he obviously adored, was named Patience!

Not for the first time does KH now call Sinnett's attention to the human condition. "Look around you, my friend," he urges the Englishman, "see the 'three poisons' raging within the heart of men— anger, greed, delusion." We may certainly be reminded, as probably Sinnett was, of KH's comments in his very first letter: human nature in general "is the same now as it was a million years ago. Prejudice based on selfishness; . . . pride and stubborn resistance to Truth . . . the characteristics of your age." Here, in Letter 47, the Mahatma details those "characteristics" as the five-fold "obscurities . . . ever preventing" humanity from "seeing truth: envy, passion, vacillation, sloth, and unbelief." In some Buddhist texts, the three "poisons" are referred to as three "fires," which ever burn in the heart, the smoke from which pollutes and obscures right perception. The Abhidharma (*Abhidhamma* in Pali) texts of the Buddhist tradition, to which KH refers Sinnett later (in Letter 68), trace all human suffering to "our tainted attitudes," defined as a "mental orientation rooted in greed, hatred and delusion," which can only be overcome by an ethical development that culminates "in the perfection of purity attained with the mind's irreversible emancipation from all defilements" (Bhikku U Rewata Dhamma, introduction to *A Comprehensive Manual of Abhidhamma*, 4–5). We will return to the Abhidharma teachings when we consider the relevant reference in Letter 68. For the present, in considering KH's statements in Letter 47, it is useful to look more closely at the three "poisons" or "fires," as well as the five "obscurities," to see to what extent humankind in general is still subject to these "defilements" of the mind. Can we not trace all our current world problems, all human suffering, to these causes—anger, greed, and delusion? And is not envy the result of greed, while passion arises from anger, and vacillation and sloth are grounded in delusion? As to "unbelief," perhaps KH is referring to ignorance, or what is called in so many texts avidya, which certainly leads to delusion and is indeed the cause of so much misery. But, as KH says, "Man, after all, is the victim of his surroundings while he lives in the atmosphere of society," so it is not easy to rid ourselves of these "poisons" and "obscurities" or to put out the "fires" of personal self-interest and egotism. Yet this is the work to which we, as students of Theosophy, have been called if we are serious in our aspirations and intentions.

The reference to "young Portman" has not been identified, although we can assume from the name that he may have been an English acquaintance of Sinnett's, perhaps a member of the Society in either Allahabad or Simla. What is interesting in the reference to him, however, is KH's differentiation between the qualifications for becoming a "monk or Lama" and those required for becoming a "living 'Lha' or *Brother*." It is comparatively easy to become a monk or Lama, while the training required for entering the Brotherhood, which is of course the path on which the Mahatmas are journeying, is a different and far more arduous path.

Whatever Sinnett may have been thinking as he read the letter—perhaps wondering why it should be "more difficult than before to exchange letters"—it must have come as something of a surprise to have KH tell him "I see your thought . . . but you are wrong." The next sentence may be a simple aphorism: "Blame not the holy man for strictly doing his duty by humanity," but there is the implication that the Chohan had in some way protected Sinnett and so the correspondence with KH could continue. Notably, once again KH refers to himself as "your trans-Himalayan correspondent," a designation he used in Letter 5 and will use again in Letter 55 that points less to his geographical location than to the occult system about which he is communicating.

In the next several sentences Sinnett is reminded of his "unconscious indiscretions," particularly his quoting to the English medium Stainton Moses what KH had said about Moses in an earlier letter (Letter 18), for which the Mahatma had reprimanded him (see Letter 21). In Letter 21, KH told Sinnett that he "saw the danger" that would be the consequence of his action. Now he tells Sinnett that "the cause generated at that time has now developed its results," with Moses not only leaving the Theosophical Society but determining "in his heart the utter annihilation of the British Branch." The saddest result, of course, was the formation that year, 1882, of the Society for Psychical Research, with Moses and several other prominent Theosophical Society members among its founders. Clearly, KH can foresee the future results that would take place, particularly the infamous Hodgson Report that condemned HPB as a fraud and charlatan.

We can only imagine Sinnett's feelings as he read KH's words: "It is you alone, the simple action of your swift pen which will have produced the *nidana* and the ten-del, the 'cause' and its 'effect.'" The word *nidana* is derived from the verbal root *da*, "to bind," and the prefix *ni*, "down," and in Buddhism refers to the bonds or fetters forming the causes of existence in the world as well as the causes for rebirth. The nidanas are usually listed as twelve in all Buddhist texts, where they are said to constitute the chain of dependent or interdependent causation. In *The Secret Doctrine*, HPB writes that the causes of existence are not only physical but "metaphysical . . . the chief of which is the desire to exist, an outcome of Nidana and Maya." And she adds, "This desire for a sentient life shows itself in everything, from an atom to a sun, and is a reflection of the Divine Thought propelled into objective existence, into a law that the Universe should exist" (1:44; see also her commentary on stanza 1, slokas 4 and 7). In *Transactions of the Blavatsky Lodge*, HPB points out that the nidanas constitute the "moral agents in the universe," and that they are awakened by maya, or ignorance. In the section of her E.S. Instructions called "Some Notes on Some Oral Teachings," HPB is quoted as saying, "We produce Nidanas in ignorance. Each cause started on the Physical Plane sets up action on every plane to all eternity. They are eternal effects reflected from plane to plane on to the 'screen of eternity'" (Spierenburg, *The Inner Group Teachings of H. P. Blavatsky*).

The Mahatma then gives Sinnett some advice concerning how to rectify the situation, even though that "simple act on your part is silently digging out a chasm between" the Master and himself. It is evident that in considering the total chain of cause and effect there can be "counteracting" forces, something to keep in mind as we seek to understand the law of karma. In the present case, KH informs Sinnett that while it is "the hand of the Chohan alone [that] can bridge" the chasm between them, "it must be yours [that is, Sinnett's] that places the first stone for the work." This is a reminder to us that there is work to be done from our side if we would approach the Mahatmas and seek their wisdom. KH refers Sinnett to an article in the February 1882 issue of *The Theosophist*, and he succinctly and beautifully expresses the nature of the work that must be accomplished: "I can come nearer to you, but you must draw me by a purified heart and a gradually developing will." He compares this process to "the law of the disembodied Principles," which M explained to Sinnett in Letter 44 (see response to question 3)—an indication that KH was aware of his Brother's teachings during his own absence from the correspondence. This law, which concerns the human principles after the death of the physical, is discussed again in Letter 68. For the present, we can think of it as the law of resonance or attraction based on what KH terms "a mutual affinity."

We need to pause to consider as deeply as we can the meaning of the phrases "a purified heart" and "a gradually developing will." Recalling that a "pure heart" is the third step of the "Golden Stairs" that HPB gave to her students, we can understand a "purified heart" to mean at the very least an emotional nature cleansed of all selfish concerns and filled with ever-expanding love for all humanity. As KH tells Sinnett, "M. spoke well and truthfully when saying that a love of collective humanity is his increasing inspiration." We, too, need to broaden our sympathies, to move steadily and surely from the personal to the impersonal, awakening the fullness of compassion for all beings within ourselves.

"A gradually developing will" may refer to one-pointedness of purpose, or *virya*, which HPB calls "the dauntless energy that fights its way to the supernal Truth" (*The Voice of the Silence*, fragment 3, verse 211). Such a "will" is characterized by perseverance despite all obstacles, by steady attention to the goal we are seeking without any sense of a separate self. All this and much more, no doubt, is implied in KH's words. The Master may be drawn to us as a magnet draws scattered iron filings, but it is up to us to prepare ourselves by purifying our hearts, developing a will that never deviates from its intent, and as KH says at the end of that paragraph, "overpowering the diffusive tendency [of the mind] by a stronger force [the 'gradually developing will']."

Once more KH reminds Sinnett that while he is still his friend, friendship alone is not sufficient to maintain the link between them and continue the correspondence; for the Mahatma has taken another step in his journey while Sinnett has not taken a corresponding step forward, hence the distance between them has widened. But with what patience and kindness KH goes on to encourage Sinnett, admonishing him to "keep a cheerful frame of mind"! And now the Mahatma informs the Englishman, in some of the most beautiful words in all the letters, of the nature of the relationship between the guru, or teacher, and the individual who steps "within the circle of our work." What a lesson is here for anyone who aspires to join the ranks of the Brotherhood through service to humanity! "Your strivings, perplexities and forebodings are equally noticed, good and faithful friend. In the imperishable RECORD of the Masters *you have written them all.* There are registered your every deed and thought." Whether entered in the "Record of the Masters" or in the "akashic records," our own karmic accounts consisting of our actions, desires, and thoughts, are undoubtedly and indelibly imprinted for both good and ill, with each incarnation providing an opportunity for balancing and adjusting the scales of justice.

In Sinnett's case, however, he was what was termed a "lay-chela," which HPB defines in her article, "Chelas and Lay Chelas" (*CW*, 4:611) as "a man of the world who affirms his desire to become wise in spiritual things," adding: "Virtually, every member of the Theosophical Society who subscribes to the second of our three 'Declared Objects' is such." (The second Object at that time—1882—read: "To study Aryan literature, religion and science.") HPB writes further in the same article:

> In joining the Society and binding himself to help along its work, he [i.e., the member] has pledged himself to act in some degree in concert with those Mahatmas, at whose behest the Society was organized, and under whose conditional protection it remains. . . . Lay Chelaship confers no privilege upon anyone except that of working for merit under the observation of a Master. And whether that Master be or be not seen by the Chela makes no difference whatever as to the result: his good thought, words and deeds will bear their fruit, his evil one, theirs.

Sinnett will learn much more concerning his status as a "lay-chela" in Letters 111 and 131 and will be reminded in Letter 134: "If you would learn and acquire Occult Knowledge, you have . . . to remember that such tuition opens in the stream of chelaship many an unforeseen channel to whose current even a "lay chela must perforce yield."

As Letter 47 continues KH tells Sinnett that he has "crossed the mystic line which separates your world from ours," and now whether he perseveres in acquiring further knowledge, or even in acknowledging the Mahatmas' existence, is for him alone to determine. The bond between the two of them, KH and Sinnett, however, cannot be broken because, says KH, Sinnett is now "virtually OURS." His "hidden *Self*," which must refer to the inner or immortal Self, "has mirrored itself in our Akasha; your nature is—yours, your essence is—ours."

Once again we come upon the term *akasha*. In the first letter Sinnett received, KH advised him of the importance of understanding thoroughly the nature of akasha, which HPB defines in *Isis Unveiled* as "the imponderable and intangible life-principle" (1:125), and which has also been described as the primordial substance or space in its occult sense, as original matter in its living, vibrating, pulsating essence, and as the root from which all things emerge and in which all things exist (see commentary on Letter 1). The Mahatmas are apparently fully familiar with the nature and functions of akasha, so that in at least one of its aspects it can constitute a protective shield, as it were, against the onslaught of thoughts and emotions from outside their domain. So it is that, a bit later in the letter, KH speaks of "the current of your [i.e., Sinnett's] thought . . . beating against my protecting barrier of Akas."

It is this substance, with its characteristic of what we may term impressionability, on which all things are recorded. Now KH informs Sinnett, "your *Karma* is ours," especially since he has stepped inside the Mahatma's world. While Sinnett was never to see KH at the physical level or with his physical eyes, as much as he longed for such a visit, still KH tells him: "You cannot avoid meeting us in *Real Existence.*" This can only mean, I suggest, that as Sinnett has crossed that mystic line between the Mahatma's world and the mundane world in which the Englishman carried on his life, the meeting ground was at interior levels whether Sinnett was aware of the meeting or not. As KH has told him early on, "in dreams and *visions* . . . when rightly interpreted" there is a meeting (see Letters 3A and 3B).

We must certainly take note of KH's statement to Sinnett: "Your *Karma* is your only personality to be when you step beyond." This is certainly true for every individual who comes within the orbit of the Mahatmas' influence, for as KH continues, "In thought and deed, by day, in soul-struggles by nights, you have been writing the story of your desires and your spiritual development. This, every one does who approaches us with any earnestness of desire to become our co-worker." But we need to consider what may be meant by the words

"your *Karma* is your *only* personality to be when you step beyond."
All that endures of the personality with which all the experiences of
an incarnation are experienced is what we may call the fruits of that
existence, the karma or results of all the actions, emotions, thoughts
in which we as individual persons engaged. We will return to this
subject when we consider Letter 68.

We can also take to heart the Mahatma's statement to Sinnett:
"What that 'inner Self,' impatient, anxious—has longed to bind itself
to, the carnal man, the worldlings' master has not ratified." We can
conclude from this that our spiritual aspirations need to be, indeed
must be, confirmed by and even grounded in the life we live daily. So
we may well ask ourselves: To what extent am I living a life consonant
with those deeper aspirations of the soul? Do my actions and thoughts
reflect, however inadequately, my heart's longing to come closer to
the Masters? For it is in the heart, writes KH, that one may "contact
. . . the mysteriously effulgent, and pure heart of Tathagata"—a truly
beautiful phrase.

The Mahatma's next words summarize the law of correspondences,
or the law of magnetic sympathy: "Nature has linked all parts of her
Empire together by subtle threads of magnetic sympathy . . . and your
thought *will find me* if projected by a pure impulse, as mine will find,
has found, and often impressed your mind." Everything in the universe
is interlinked, interconnected, as contemporary science suggests. It
is, of course, for Sinnett to determine whether the correspondence
will continue or not (and we can be grateful that whatever Sinnett
may have done to disturb the smooth flow of intercourse with the
Mahatmas, at least the correspondence did continue for another two
years), just as it is up to us to determine to what extent we come closer
to realization of their presence and so aid them in their great work for
humanity. What wonderful reassurance lies in KH's words: "It is our
law to approach every . . . one if even there be but the feeblest glimmer
of the true 'Tathagata' light within him."

The letter concludes with another admonition to be of good
cheer, to refrain from doubt, which "unnerves and pushes back one's

progress." True confidence is necessary—not "blind optimism" but the kind of hope or trust that arises out of doing all one can to bring one's life in accord with one's spiritual aspirations. However, Sinnett at this particular time faces a serious problem. "A cloud does lower over your path," a situation caused by his lack of discretion in confiding so fully in his colleague Hume, who at that time was "under a baneful influence." The circumstances are not quite clear, but it has been suggested that two individuals—a Mr. Davison or Davidson and Edmund Fern, both of whom evidently served Hume as secretaries—were somewhat psychic and cast what KH here calls "a spell of fascination" on Hume that was leading him further away from the Mahatmas. But, KH says, "the intended catastrophe [probably some attempt to disrupt the work of the Society] can be averted by redoubled vigilance and increased fervour of pure will." He advises Sinnett to "work then, if you still will, to turn the blow aside," as otherwise even he could be injured by the actions of Hume and his cohorts. There is reassurance, however, in the words "The cause will never be ruined," which are reminiscent of HPB's words in her E.S. Instruction No. 3 that she attributed to Master M: "You have still to learn *that so long as there are three men worthy of our Lord's blessing in the Theosophical Society, it can never be destroyed*" (*CW*, 12:588).

So closes one of the most significant letters in all the correspondence. Much more could be said about it, and certainly the serious student will want to consider many of its statements in depth and ponder their application to our own situation today as spiritual aspirants on the path to wisdom.

LETTER 48

Letter 48 concludes the series of letters from Morya written while KH was on retreat and therefore out of communication with

Sinnett. The letter itself is headed, in Sinnett's handwriting, "Reply to my remonstrance against treatment of Europe (Through Damodar)." Whatever caused the Englishman to remonstrate against M, he evidently had written to M before he received KH's letter and M felt obligated to respond directly to him. Why the letter was transmitted through Damodar rather than through HPB is not explained, but the phrase "Of course she will be frantic" indicates M's concern that she not be further disturbed by either Sinnett's comments or M's response.

The reference to the Rev. Joseph Cook, who was visiting India at that time, is rather interesting as illustrating the way in which the Christian missionaries of that period were so often railing against the Society as well as Spiritualism. Damodar, then working with HPB and Colonel Olcott at the Bombay Headquarters, countered some of the reverend's accusations in the public press. These may be read in Sven Eek's work, *Damodar* (pages 178–80). A delightful account of the Rev. Cook's visit to Bombay is given by Colonel Olcott (*ODL*, 2:329). However, our real interest in this letter is with a number of M's other statements.

Based on M's comments at the beginning of the letter as well as what we know about Sinnett, we can assume that Sinnett was particularly concerned with how Westerners, especially Europeans and more specifically the English, could be convinced of the existence of the Mahatmas as well as the value of the teachings he was receiving from them. M counters that while Europe is important, the work in which he and his Brother KH are engaged is for the entire world: "The sun of Theosophy must shine for all, not for a part." Then he makes an intriguing comment: "There is more of this movement than you have yet had an inkling of, and the work of the T.S. is linked in with similar work that is secretly going on in all parts of the world." The words "similar work" prompt us to speculate that all movements that foster the ideal of brotherhood, that strive to enlighten human consciousness, eradicate prejudice and selfishness, and work toward the betterment of humanity, must have not only the blessing of the Brotherhood but their active albeit secret influence at inner levels.

Then follows a reference to a "Greek Brother" evidently known to Olcott, although there is no indication in Olcott's writings, at least to my knowledge, of the "orders" that M asked him to transmit. This "Greek Brother" is referred to again in Letter 65, where KH speaks of him as a "semi-European" with whom KH has conversed. Perhaps this "Greek Brother" is the one later identified as Hilarion. This Adept may have had some role in the work for Europe, although we may puzzle, as no doubt Sinnett did, over the statement that it was not possible to "anticipate *how* the light will be shed there." M refers, with a touch of humor, to his Brother KH as "your Seraph," a designation that KH does not accept, as he indicates in Letter 49: "That I am not a 'Seraph' yet, is shown by the fact of my writing to you this endless letter." The letters do not specify whether KH did inform Sinnett of any of the "details" concerning either the work of the Greek Brother or how the work in Europe was going forward.

M next comments on several English members, all of whom were Spiritualists whom Sinnett probably met during his stay in England at the time of the publication of *The Occult World*. Sinnett may have proposed to Morya that these individuals would be useful in conveying the occult teachings to the Western world, but the Mahatma now indicates that while the Adepts "*do* influence individuals," they "*advise*—and never order," so Sinnett is told to search through "the Spiritualistic literature" for the years before 1877, when *Isis Unveiled* was published, to find any reference to the "occult philosophy or esotericism." Although Sinnett may not have recognized the mahatmic influence on Spiritualism and on scientific research after the appearance of HPB's first work, Morya suggests that there was such an influence, although it can never be proven. At the least, says M, the word "occultism," as well as concepts such as "elementary spirits" and "'astral' light," were unknown in America prior to the appearance of *Isis*.

The Mahatmas evidently endeavor to influence and therefore use people of note in their respective fields in order to introduce ideas that may be beneficial to humanity. This was particularly true, M says, with regard to Edison, Crookes, and Massey. The American inventor Thomas Alva Edison joined the Theosophical Society in 1878, before the founders left New York for England and India. Among his inventions were the first commercially practical incandescent lamp and the first successful phonograph. Charles Carlton Massey was an English lawyer who came to Chittenden, Vermont, in 1875 to verify for himself Colonel Olcott's published accounts of the Eddy phenomena. He was one of the first members of the Theosophical Society and later a founder and the first president of the Society in England. He was also a founding member of the Society for Psychical Research, but after the Hodgson Report was issued he resigned from the Theosophical Society. Sir William Crookes was a noted English physicist and scientist of considerable note who became a member of the Society and was one of its five counsellors for a time. HPB writes of him (*LBS*, 224–25) that he "preaches and teaches a very old occult Doctrine. . . . It appears (as I have thought from the first) that he is on the *orthodox occult* path, in his general method," adding that the Masters intended to help him.

Morya also mentions Dr. George Wyld, a homeopathic doctor in London who became the first president of the London Lodge, but whose very severe criticism of Sinnett's second book, *Esoteric Buddhism*, created quite a storm of protest and he was later expelled from the London Lodge. Here in Letter 48 the Mahatma speaks of him as "that old grim idol of the Jewish Sinai," while HPB in one of her letters called him "a bigoted ass" (*LBS*, 22) for his strong orthodox leanings. In another of her letters, HPB refers to Wyld as "an ugly, bigoted, jealous and indelicate brute," and says, "If he had not been kicked out of the London Lodge there would have been a revolution in our Branches against the Lodge itself" (*LBS*, 60). Later in the letter, M mentions Prof. Arthur Russell Wallace, the prominent British naturalist much interested in spiritualistic phenomena who was among the group that met HPB and Olcott when they stopped in London en route to India. He, too, was one of the renowned English scientists who attracted the Mahatmas' attention and are referred to in the letters. These men are some of the cast of characters that moved in and out of, or around, the Theosophical Society during its early years, each one given an opportunity to advance the Society's cause, each one perhaps influenced by the Mahatmas in their efforts to bring the teachings of occult philosophy to bear on human thought.

We return, then, to Letter 48, where a number of statements deserve our attention. We should certainly take note of M's somewhat puzzling comments about HPB, according to which she is sometimes forced to lie or at least to mislead people. Note the Mahatma's words: "*She is forbidden* to say what she knows. . . . She is ordered *in cases of need to mislead people*; and were she more of a natural born *liar*—she might be happier and won her day long since. . . . She is *too truthful, too outspoken, too incapable* of *dissimulation.*" Certainly as both the Mahatmas tell Sinnett on several occasions, their ways are not always our ways, and it is for us to understand—insofar as we can—the rules of the occult world!

The comment about the several kinds of cycles is also of great interest and could be pursued by the earnest student. Evidently, there are cycles within cycles, and all we can say for certain is that all of evolution—including life and form, the unfoldment of civilizations, the growth of humanity as of nature itself, indeed, all the processes we can name—is cyclic or subject to the law of cycles. This is a fundamental principle, enunciated by HPB in the Second Fundamental Proposition of *The Secret Doctrine* (*SD*, 1:16–17). To examine the law fully is surely a lifetime study, but, M suggests, to acknowledge the law means to wait patiently for the right time and therefore to "let evolution take its course naturally—lest we make it deviate and produce monsters by presuming to guide it." This is no doubt a cautionary note to Sinnett, who was not known for the virtue of patience! Part of every cycle, we may extrapolate from M's comments, involves the struggle between the forces for good and evil, here characterized by the "*Dugpas* and the *Gelukpas.*" The term *Dugpa* at that time referred to sorcerers and black magicians, while the *Gelukpas*, or *Gelugpas*, were, according to HPB (see *Theosophical Glossary*) "the highest and most orthodox

Buddhist sect in Tibet." It was the great Tsong-ka-pa who reformed the Gelugpa Order, to which His Holiness the Dalai Lama belongs.

M concludes his letter with another admonition to Sinnett, this one regarding the Englishman's attitude toward Olcott. As we know, Sinnett was always very critical of the American president–founder of the Society, feeling he lacked the refinement of English customs. Indeed, from Sinnett's point of view, anything American was inferior to the English way of life. But the Mahatma tells Sinnett that he knows Olcott very well; whatever is true in the Englishman's eyes the Adepts recognize, yet much of what Sinnett thinks is pure prejudice to which he is quite blind. M makes an interesting comment—that the Mahatmas might one day take Sinnett at his word and install him as president of the Society in place of Olcott, who would be granted his earnest desire to join the Brotherhood. Sinnett would then know that "martyrdom is pleasant to look at and criticize, but harder to suffer." This is a good lesson for all of us when we are wont to criticize those put in leadership positions in the Society. It is one thing to propose better ways of working or suggest constructive changes within the organization, but criticism based on even unconscious prejudice or only partial understanding of a situation achieves very little.

M nevertheless values Sinnett's views, given that he then asks the Englishman's opinion of what he wrote in the "Answers to Correspondents" section of the *Supplement* to the March 1882 issue of *The Theosophist*. Whether Sinnett ever responded to that request we do not know, or at least we have no record of any such response. With this, the correspondence between Sinnett and Morya effectively ends for several months. Except for a brief postscript to a letter from KH (Letter 75) in late August of 1882, M's next letter, number 89 chronologically, is not written until September of 1882. After that M writes only three more rather short letters: Letters 118, 125, and 137. However, as those letters reveal, M continues to be aware of the developments within the Society, especially in the Simla Branch, as well as of the actions of both Sinnett and Hume.

LETTER 49

The background of Letter 49, the second one Sinnett received from KH after the Mahatma's retreat ended, is explained in some detail in the prefatory note in the chronological edition of the letters. A fairly long letter that would have been even longer had not one page of the original been missing, Letter 49 is mainly concerned with several of the so-called "seers" or spiritualistic mediums Sinnett would have met during his time in England in 1881. KH uses the occasion to remind Sinnett of many matters about which he has already been instructed, at the conclusion emphasizing that the letter is "strictly *private*." Evidently the Mahatma put that restriction on the letter because of Sinnett's indiscretion in copying portions of a previous letter (Letter 18) concerning Stainton Moses and sending them to Moses.

Letter 49 begins rather abruptly, the Mahatma putting quotation marks around several passages, presumably quoting Sinnett himself. Sinnett must have written, in effect, "Perhaps someday I shall know as you know," apparently accepting the fact that whether or not the Mahatma would ever share his knowledge with him was not for him to say. So KH tells Sinnett, as he has on previous occasions, "*you alone*, have to weave your destiny." This is perhaps a lesson we all have to accept: whether or not we gain more knowledge or walk farther on the spiritual path is for each of us to say, for we are responsible for our own growth in understanding, wisdom, and the unfoldment of inner powers. But the occult rules cannot be violated, and KH cautions Sinnett, who was still very much attracted by spiritualistic phenomena, that walking along the "crowded thoroughfare" on which the "modern seers and prophetesses" are traveling will never lead him to the perception of Truth.

From the very beginning of the correspondence, the Mahatmas have emphasized that in the study of occultism, particularly if one seeks to come closer to the Mahatmas, even to be in communication with them, there are rules to follow that the Mahatmas themselves must follow. In the second letter, KH informs Sinnett: "The door is always opened to the right man who knocks. . . . Only, instead of going over to him he has to come to us" (page 8). And in Letter 20 (page 73), KH writes: "Let those who really desire to learn *abandon all* and come to us, instead of asking or expecting us to go to them."

Yet here in Letter 49, as in many of the letters, the Mahatma offers encouragement: "Believe me, we may yet walk along the arduous path together," but of course "it has to be along and on—those 'adamantine rocks with which our occult rules surround us'—never *outside* them." These words are reminiscent of KH's statement in Letter 18 (page 68): "For countless generations hath the adept built a fane of imperishable rocks, a giant's Tower of Infinite Thought." Sinnett may have referred to this statement, using the word "adamantine," which KH now adopts in this letter, signifying imperishable or impregnable. The same term is used again toward the end of the correspondence, in Letter 126, when KH once more reminds Sinnett of all that is required if the aspirant would approach the "adamantine gates and entrance" to the path of occultism.

Again, here in Letter 49, KH uses graphic, almost poetic, language as he describes the "motley crowd of candidates" who clamor for the gates to occult knowledge to open before them. There are rules, even though Sinnett has "failed to discover or even so much as suspect the reason and the operation of those laws," which therefore "appear so cold and merciless and selfish in your sight."

Once again, Sinnett is advised to have patience: "Remember: too anxious expectation is not only tedious, but dangerous too. Each warmer and quicker throb of the heart wears so much of life away. . . . [The one who strives to gain the heights] must not even desire too earnestly or too passionately the object he would reach: else, the very wish will prevent the possibility of its fulfilment." Yet with patience and in accordance with the law, one can reach the goal, for as KH says, "It is but from the very top of those 'adamantine rocks' of ours, not at their foot, that one is ever enabled to perceive the whole Truth, by embracing the whole limitless horizon."

KH asks Sinnett to read two articles appearing in the March 1882 issue of *The Theosophist*—incidental evidence that the two Mahatmas were much concerned with that publication and, as we know, often contributed to it themselves. The first article to which Sinnett is directed is "The Elixir of Life," published in two parts in the March and April issues. There are indications that the Mahatmas may have inspired the essay, and KH says it "contains references and explanations" that Sinnett may find useful.

In the magazine itself the title is followed by the words "From a Chela's Diary" within parentheses and then "By G...M...F.T.S." It was written by someone known as Mirza Moorad Ali Beg, whose real name was Godolphin Mitford, a member of a prominent English family that produced several noted writers. Born in India, Ali Beg, among other eccentricities, took up Eastern ways of dress and became a Muslim. At one time Colonel Olcott tried to help him with mesmeric healing, but in the end he could not be helped and died insane. Colonel Olcott relates much about him in *Old Diary Leaves* (2:289–91). HPB quotes from "The Elixir of Life" and comments on it at length in her article, "Is the Desire to 'Live' Selfish?" (*CW*, 6:241–48), and in a later article, "Re-Classification of the Principles" (*CW*, 7:350) she states: "'The Elixir of Life' was written by its author under direct dictation, or inspection." KH tells Sinnett in a later letter (Letter 74) to "Please read over the 'Elixir of Life' No. 2 (April, p. 169 col. 1, paras 2, 3, 4, 5, and 6)." Evidently a great deal of attention was given to this particular work, written by the strange individual who used the name Mirza Moorad Ali Beg and for a time was perhaps a conduit for the Mahatmas' teachings.

The second article to which KH directs Sinnett's attention was actually a reply by a man named William Oxley to a review of Oxley's book, *Philosophy of the Spirit*. The review, written by Djual Khul and published in a previous issue of *The Theosophist*, was in some respects quite scathing, to which naturally Oxley took exception. Oxley, another one of the British Spiritualists of that day, used the pseudonym "Busiris." KH calls him the "Manchester Seer," and says he "is *the only one* who has an inkling of truth."

As a brief background, Oxley had written a long letter to KH during the previous summer. That letter, dated June 24, 1881, is included with the Mahatma letters in the British Museum Library. The Mahatma sent it on to Sinnett with some marginal notes in a rather light vein. In the letter, Oxley described some of his spiritualistic experiences. However, as he indicates here in Letter 49, KH did not reply: "Having received no reply to his summons to K.H., he criticizes—mildly so far—the utterances of that 'Internal Power'—for which new title I feel rather obliged to him." This undoubtedly refers to a statement in Oxley's reply to Djual Khul's review: "Koot Hoomi Lal Singh, whether mortal man or an Internal Power, matters not for the present purposes." At one time Oxley had wanted to join the Simla Eclectic Theosophical Society, but the Mahatma refused him. Later, it appears, KH must have reconsidered, as he says at the close of Letter 86: "If he [Oxley] joins the Society I may help and even correspond with him" (see further Letter 83).

As might be expected, HPB could not stand Oxley's rather slighting reference to KH, and KH in his reply to the review of Oxley's book speaks of HPB's reaction: "Our blunderbuss Editor failed not to explode" (note *CW*, 4:190). KH continues: "Nor would she be soothed until Djual Khul, with whom the famous review was concocted . . . was authorized, under the safe *nom-de-plume* of 'Reviewer' to answer . . . the Seer, in a few innocent foot-notes." It would appear that KH had read Oxley's work rather carefully, since in addition to pointing out what is "ridiculous nonsense" and "mostly wrong," the Mahatma adds: "Yet he is positively and absolutely the only one whose general comprehension of *Spirit*, and its capabilities and functions after the first separation, we call *death*, are on the whole if not quite correct, at least approximating very nearly Truth."

Undoubtedly Sinnett was still much interested in and even fascinated by phenomena as well as by the messages being conveyed by the best-known "seers," "*mediums* and *clairvoyants*" of that time, many of whom he had met in England. So a great part of Letter 49 is devoted to the subject of mediumship and what the various mediums profess to know or not know. KH finally exclaims in almost a tone of despair, "Poor, poor Humanity, when shalt thou have the whole and unadulterated Truth!" Each of these seers, he says, seems to read but one page out of the whole volume of spiritual wisdom, and so he asks, "Why such stubborn oblivion of the important fact that there are other and innumerable pages before and after that one solitary page that each of those 'Seers' has so far hardly learned to decipher? Why is it, that every one of those 'Seers' believes himself the Alpha and Omega of Truth?"

He calls Sinnett's attention to the various individuals involved with Spiritualism: Stainton Moses, whom we have already met and commented on; Anna Kingsford, who later became president of the London Lodge and about whom there will be much to say regarding the affairs of that Lodge; Mrs. Kingsford's close associate, Edward Maitland; and the American medium, Mrs. M. Hollis-Billing (or Billings) who was active in the formation of the London Lodge, although she did not join it but remained a member of the Parent Society. As a footnote in the chronological edition of the letters indicates, Dr. and Mrs. Billing hosted the founders during their stay in England en route to India in 1879. As we will see in Letter 92, KH later has some rather severe things to say about Dr. Billing while at the same time describing Mrs. Hollis-Billing as "that good, honest woman, the only really and thoroughly reliable and honest medium I know of" (page 291).

Particularly interesting is KH's comment here in Letter 49 regarding Anna Kingsford and her "circle": he apparently attributes the authenticity of her statements to the fact that she and her associates "are *strict vegetarians.*" He goes on to remark on the atmosphere at the Headquarters, still at this time in Bombay, as needing to be "cleansed with various disinfecting drugs" since he was now even more sensitive to such vibrations than before his retreat. I am sure most of us who are vegetarians and refrain from tobacco, alcohol, and similar substances become keenly conscious of the distasteful atmospheres that surround individuals and places that do not observe these restrictions and so sympathize with KH's situation.

KH comments regarding Mrs. Kingsford that when she is "made to reveal that 'immortality is by no means a matter of course for all,'" she is "delivering herself of *actual*, incontrovertible *facts*." Later KH adds, "Immortality is *conditional*." This subject is taken up later, particularly in Letters 68, 70B, and 70C, where I discuss it in some detail. However, the earnest student might find helpful the pamphlet titled *The Imperishable Body* written by the distinguished Theosophist Edward L. Gardner.

The Mahatma now puts a question to Sinnett: These several mediums and many others you have heard or read of are all of them "thoroughly *honest*, *sincere*, and as intelligent, as well educated . . . even learned," and each one has his or her own guide or "*Revelator*"; so now "tell me, my friend, do you know of two that agree?" KH continues: "Why, since truth is one, and that putting entirely the question of discrepancies in details aside—we do not find them agreeing even upon the most vital problems—those that have either 'to be, or *not* to be'—and of which there can be no two solutions?" This important question must have caused Sinnett, as it should provoke any student, to do some serious thinking about Spiritualism and mediumship. KH returns to this point on a number of occasions throughout the correspondence as he strives to turn Sinnett away from a fascination with the phenomenal and awaken his intuitive perceptions. Particularly important is KH's statement that the Mahatmas "do not 'require a *passive* mind' but on the contrary are seeking for those most active, which can put two and two together once that they are on the right scent."

KH goes on to encourage Sinnett, who seems to have written an article that has pleased the Mahatma, telling him: "Little by little, the now incomprehensible will become the self-evident; and many a sentence of mystic meaning will shine yet out before your Soul-eye, like a transparency, illuminating the darkness of your mind. Such is the course of gradual progress." Perhaps this final phrase is just one more reminder to Sinnett to curb his impatience for occult knowledge, that the teaching cannot be given all at once, and much depends on

Sinnett himself. And KH gives Sinnett an example by referring to a work by the great occultist Eliphas Levi.

Levi, whose real name was Louis Constant, was a French abbé to whose writings M and KH as well as HPB often referred, indicating that they contained much value if one had the right key. Levi's article "The Secret of Time and Satan" was published under the heading "Death and Satan" in the October 1881 issue of *The Theosophist,* and would therefore have been read by Sinnett, who, according to KH in the letter we are studying, "failed to find the key" to understand it. (The article has been republished in the appendices of the chronological edition of the letters.) To underline the value of "gradual progress" in the study of the occult wisdom, KH writes toward the end of Letter 49: "You will find that it was never the intention of the Occultists really to conceal what they had been writing from the earnest determined students, but rather to lock up their information for safety-sake, in a secure safe-box, the key to which is—intuition. The degree of diligence and zeal with which the hidden meaning is sought by the student, is generally the test—how far he is entitled to the possession of the so buried treasure."

This advice to Sinnett reiterates what he was told in Letter 20: that the communication of occult knowledge is dependent on the individual's own awakening, for "the illumination must come from within." Surely this advice is as valid for us today as it was for Sinnett so many years ago.

KH deals with two or three other matters in the closing paragraphs of Letter 49. First, he comments on HPB's journal *The Theosophist,* in which the Mahatmas took such active interest, suggesting that in spite of "its numerous blemishes and literary defects" from some of its sentences a "bright light" may shine forth that could illuminate "some old puzzling problems." Anyone who has taken the time and patience to browse through the yellowed pages of those early issues of the magazine will indeed find much that is fascinating beyond description!

KH also refers briefly and casually to the "conditions" under which the Mahatmas work. We have met with this concept before and will do so again, although the specific nature of those conditions is never fully defined. But KH tells us here that they "can hardly work without them." What we do know is that, as KH tells Sinnett and in previous letters, "our ways" are not "your" ways. In the present context, the conditions to which KH refers seem to concern the transmittal of the letters, a task usually assigned to HPB, although Damodar was used for the transmission of Letter 48. Now perhaps another chela, Bhavani Shanker, sometimes called Bhavani Rao, might be used, as KH says "he is stronger and fitter in many a way more than Damodar or even our mutual 'female' friend"—a reference to HPB. Bhavani Rao lived for a time at the Bombay Headquarters and was present there with HPB and others at the time of the "Vega incident." He occasionally traveled with Olcott in India, and as we shall see in Letter 50, he was with the president–founder in Allahabad when another unusual phenomenon occurred. In later years, he left the Adyar Society to join the United Lodge of Theosophists.

Finally, KH comments on the difference in approach between the two Mahatmas in regard to presenting the teachings. He tells Sinnett: "What I blame him [M] for, is that he allowed you to begin from the wrong end—the most difficult unless one had thoroughly mastered the preparatory ground." Without a doubt, KH is referring to the two sets of Cosmological Notes. KH's remarks about Sinnett's bewilderment over much that was presented in those "notes" and his consequent longing "for more notes and information" carry a touch of humor, particularly as he chides his Brother, saying, "If his laziness overcomes his good intentions much longer," he, meaning KH, will have to address Sinnett's quandaries himself. Since the bulk of the correspondence from this point onwards comes from KH, we can imagine M saying to him, "All right, you carry on; I've done my stint while you were on retreat."

So ends a remarkable letter that contains a great deal of teaching on a number of subjects. It reveals once again KH's concerns both for the cause the Mahatmas have at heart and for Sinnett as an individual who could be extremely useful in furthering that cause.

LETTERS 50, 51, AND 52

It is necessary to consider the three brief Letters 50, 51, and 52 together for reasons that become apparent as one reviews the circumstances under which they were received. Sinnett's own note on Letter 50 says it was "received at Allahabad during the stay of Olcott and Bhavani Rao." As he indicated in Letter 49, KH intended to use one of his chelas, Bhavani Rao (sometimes called Bhavani Shanker) for the transmission of the letters rather than Damodar or HPB. To understand these three letters, the student may refer either to the long note preceding Letter 50 or read the full account given by Sinnett in *The Occult World* (pages 163–68).

Toward the conclusion of Letter 49 KH commented that the Mahatmas require certain "conditions" for the production of phenomena, and now in Letter 50, KH expands on this fact: "It is very easy for us to give phenomenal proofs"—something Sinnett constantly wanted, as we know—"when we have necessary conditions." He indicates that Olcott, Damodar, and Bhavani Rao meet the requisite requirements to be used for "phenomenal experiments," adding that Sinnett might also be so used but, as he has stated before, that depends on Sinnett himself. He then states an important warning to all who would attempt to produce such phenomena: "To force phenomena in the presence of difficulties magnetic and other is forbidden"—and, we could add, would surely border on "black magic." Evidently Hume had endeavored to have the Mahatmas produce phenomena of his own devising, but always surrounding them "with an aura . . . of mistrust, anger, and anticipated mockery."

Also from the time of Olcott's visit with the Sinnetts, we have the brief Letter 51 from KH addressed to Mrs. Sinnett, sending her a lock of his hair to wear as an amulet. Patience Sinnett was quite frail, and she had stayed in England for some months after her husband returned to India in July of 1881. The reason Sinnett did not attend the anniversary meetings of the Society in Bombay in January 1882, despite requests from both M and KH to do so, was because his wife and son arrived from England just about that time, and he felt he must accompany them home to Allahabad, no doubt because of concern for their health. Some time after sending Mrs. Sinnett a lock of his hair, KH sent a similar gift for the Sinnetts' son, Denny (see Letter 80). Sinnett evidently also had a lock of the Mahatma's hair, which he wore (see Letter 111). KH advises in Letter 51: "Harbour not ill-feelings, even against an enemy . . . for hatred acts like an antidote and may damage the effect of even *this hair.*" We have no clue as to who may have been the "enemy" who wronged Patience Sinnett. In fact, from all that we know about her, it is difficult to imagine anyone filling such a role!

Letter 52 only indicates that whatever magnetic power had been available for transmission through either Bhavani Rao or Olcott, who were then staying with the Sinnetts in Allahabad, that power had been exhausted. Hence this is a very short note. We can only speculate whether the "power" referred to was the Mahatma's own or that afforded by the presence of chelas who were in sympathetic accord with the Mahatma. The phrase, "Will write thro' Bombay" might certainly indicate that KH needed to utilize HPB for transmissions, since she was in Bombay at that time. KH did write through Bombay (Letter 54).

LETTER 53

Before considering the letter transmitted "through Bombay," we take up Letter 53, from HPB responding to an invitation from the Sinnetts to visit them in Allahabad. In many ways, it is a rather typical letter, reflecting HPB's changing moods, for rather than simply declining the invitation she takes the opportunity to reflect upon her own condition.

While recognizing that the Sinnetts continue to be among her best friends in India—and we know from her other correspondence that there was a genuine affection between HPB and Patience Sinnett particularly—HPB indicates she has reached the end of her endurance in serving as the "medium of communication" between KH (and M) and Sinnett. Then she launches into some tantalizing statements—at least they may have puzzled Sinnett—about her own nature, perhaps because she, as well as her Teachers, were concerned about the situation in the Society as its first seven years approached conclusion. Just what she means by her "*hour of triumph*," which she feels as near, is not clear, particularly as some of the cruelest attacks on her were still some years away. (Incidentally, the reference to the "Ripons" is to the Marquess of Ripon, who served as Governor-general and Viceroy of India from 1880 to 1884; he had become a Roman Catholic, and his appointment was the first time a member of the Roman church held that office, setting off a storm of opposition in England.)

Despite HPB's several biographies, including numerous accounts by those who knew her in one way or another, and many articles, booklets, and commentaries on her life, it is doubtful that we shall ever know the full story of that incarnation. One Theosophist called her "the Sphinx of the Nineteenth Century." We have "KH's Confidential Memo about the Old Lady," as Sinnett labeled the communication from the Mahatma received in late 1881 (Letter 22). Whether Sinnett was wholly satisfied by that explanation we do not know, but in now writing to her British friend HPB may have wanted him to understand that he really did not know, perhaps could never know, her "*Real Self*," whatever he might think. Perhaps on some occasion—and here we can only speculate—he had accused her of being "untruthful," for she tells him that to call her that is "the greatest mistake in the world" since "you *do not know* me; for whatever there is *inside* . . . , is *not what you think* it is." We may recall M's statement in Letter 48 that HPB was so often "*forbidden* to say what she knows . . . ordered *in cases of need* to *mislead people.*" Had HPB perhaps at some time misled Sinnett, so that he thought she was not telling him the truth?

In declining Sinnett's invitation to visit, was she correct in prophesying that one day he would even accuse KH of deception? True, Sinnett did always hope that the Mahatmas would make an exception for him in communicating all that he longed to know, but he never really accused them of any falsehoods. Her comment may refer to the fact that, in later years, Sinnett did prefer to believe the statements of mediums he consulted rather than those of KH that had come through the letters. At the close of the letter we are now considering, HPB repeats a fact that Sinnett should know well by this time: there would be and could be no exception so long as he had not changed his "mode of living."

Still reflecting upon her own nature, HPB continues: "No; you *do not hate me*; you only feel a friendly, indulgent, a kind of *benevolent contempt for HPB*." Was she perhaps reading Sinnett's very thoughts as he read her letter? Did he ever "find out [his] mistake concerning . . . the well hidden party," the real HPB beneath the "mud-plastered . . . crust"? He continued as her friend, but the extent to which he fully understood her is a question that remains unanswered.

Then HPB speaks of "Deb," whose real name was Gwala K. Deb, but his mystical name was apparently Dharbagiri Nath. The story, which concerned the relationship between Deb and a younger chela known as Babaji or Bawaji is well summarized in the prefatory note to Letter 53. Biographical information concerning Babaji is available in Sven Eek's book, *Damodar* (pages 537 *et seq.*), and is most interesting for the student endeavoring to understand the unique relationships among the various chelas. The nature of the work HPB had to do with Deb is not made clear, but—again to speculate—it may have had to do with training him in transmission of the letters or communication of the occult teachings.

A letter that reveals something of HPB and her relationship with the Sinnetts, yet leaves us much to ponder regarding who she really was in that incredible outer vehicle through which came a wisdom teaching that we are still endeavoring to understand—such is Letter 53 in this series.

LETTER 54

Letter 54 is one promised by KH in his short note (Letter 52) that would be sent "thro' Bombay," presumably meaning that HPB would serve as "postman." One interesting matter is KH's statement repeating almost verbatim the words he used in Letter 52, to which he adds now the word "here," making the original short note contain eight words. Does "here" refer to the Mahatma's location when he sent the note or to Allahabad, where Sinnett was at the time and where Olcott and Bhavani Rao were visiting? As we speculated in considering Letter 52, whatever was the nature of the phenomena that Sinnett wished to have produced, the combined "force" or energy provided by the presence of Olcott and Bhavani Rao, now spoken of in terms of his home place ("Mallapura"), was insufficient. Evidently, the necessary "conditions" were not present at that time.

Wherever "here" may have been, the most amazing statement KH makes is that to produce those eight words "cost" him "eight days recuperative work." What, Sinnett must have wondered—as we wonder also—was KH's "state" at this time? Had he not fully recovered from the retreat, during which his physical vehicle had lain "lifeless," as M said? Was this a state of consciousness so concentrated on other matters, his own work perhaps, that the vehicle or vehicles were depleted of energy? What kind of effort did the production of these letters require—not only framing the thoughts they contained but perhaps also transmitting them to the minds of chelas who would serve as "writers"? And what of the effort in producing the paper, the ink, and whatever else was needed at the physical level such that we have them still in visible, touchable form? There is much to consider here, even though we may never understand all that is involved.

Again, KH reminds Sinnett that merely witnessing phenomena does not convince anyone of their occurrence. "Conviction," he says, "must be reached by individual experience." Notably, KH indicates he might even wish that Sinnett would have the exhibition of phenomena, "for your personal gratification," but as we know from numerous other statements by the Mahatma, such exhibition is strongly discouraged. Sinnett has described several phenomena to which he was witness in *The Occult World,* and KH assumes that if further phenomena were produced, Sinnett would no doubt report them in the "second edition" of that book, but only the "credulous (or rather nonsceptical) mind" would be satisfied, and furthermore both Sinnett and his wife would be accused of mediumship. So he advises Sinnett to "bide [his] time," while continuing to put together the various aspects of the occult philosophy he is being given and which constitutes the "real dgiu [*sic*]," or wisdom.

This is reminiscent of the first question and M's answer in the first set of Cosmological Notes: "What are the different kinds of knowledge? The real (Dgyu) and the unreal (Dgyu-mi). Dgyu becomes Fohat when in its activity." And then: "Real knowledge deals with eternal verities and primal causes. . . . Dgyu stands independent of the belief or unbelief of man."

Of course Sinnett did continue to ask questions, which brought him more knowledge of the esoteric philosophy that he subsequently presented to the world in his second book, *Esoteric Buddhism.* KH states clearly why the Mahatmas were endeavoring to aid Sinnett in gaining as much knowledge of true occultism as could be given out: "Were it not for your exceptional intellect and the help to be derived therefrom," the correspondence would have been terminated. Sinnett is to use his own mind, to apply logic and philosophy, to "read and study," because the Adept Brothers have a definite object in view: the dissemination of the occult philosophy to aid humanity.

Apparently Sinnett was working on some scheme of "degrees," whether for the Simla Eclectic Theosophical Society or for the Parent Society is not stated. This idea seemed to have KH's approval and also to involve some "preparation for practical experiments to unfold psychic power in themselves." KH tells him: "You might hit upon something that would be good" for either the Asians or the Europeans, while "another hand might supply the lacking portion," that "hand" presumably the Mahatma's own.

Then after pointing up certain facts—the lack of books available to the Asians, the basic need for a guru or guide who would impart "oral teaching"—KH asks the basic question: "What test do you apply to decide" the "mental states" of those—Asian or European—who would be passing from degree to degree? As mentioned in comments on earlier letters, the Society at this time was comprised of three sections: the Mahatmas, the chelas or those who were in communication with the Brothers, and ordinary members. Perhaps Sinnett's scheme was a further elaboration of these three, or perhaps it had to do with some training that also involved study, since KH refers to the possibility of passing from one degree to the next by "mere 'cramming, copying, and substitute writing.'" The Mahatma makes a most interesting statement here concerning the necessity (or lack of it) of a formal education in acquiring occult faculties. What is required is a "psychic idiosyncracy," or what we might call a psychic disposition for the kind of "practical school" that Sinnett is proposing. The Mahatma's advice is no doubt still valid today: "All you can do is to prepare the intellect: the impulse toward 'soulculture' must be furnished by the individual." Therefore, as he says, "We have one word for all aspirants: TRY."

Evidently, before KH went on his retreat, Sinnett had made light of the dangers—"imaginary dangers" he must have termed them—to an individual who produces phenomena. Obviously he was referring not to the danger to the person who arouses unmanageable psychic faculties, but rather to the attitude of the public toward such a person. KH speaks of "the proposed test of the *Times*," which, it will be recalled, was the test Sinnett proposed at the outset of the correspondence. Now KH refers to what he calls the "trifling phenomena" produced by Eglinton, which evidently "provoked . . . bitter hatred" and nearly caused that medium's imprisonment. We do not know the nature of the phenomena produced by Eglinton (whom we met in Letter 38 and will hear more of in Letter 55); all we know, from the Mahatma's statement here, is that the public who witnessed whatever he did reacted severely, which contributed to or perhaps hastened his decision to return to England. KH implies that if HPB were to attempt to perform phenomena at this time, the result would be even worse for her. No doubt this was because at this period she was still under some suspicion by the authorities.

Eglinton had not believed in the Mahatmas' existence, mainly because his guide, "Ernest," claimed to know nothing about them and had said they did not exist. Apparently, M took some drastic action in this connection—"M., stalking in, into the motley crowd took the spooks by the skin of their throats"—resulting in the "unexpected admission of the Brothers." Sinnett is advised that the "lesson" here "may be useful" to him in the future—"events having to grow and to develop." Quite amazing events did indeed "grow and develop," as the next letter reveals. Meanwhile, the student may wish to read Sinnett's account of Eglinton's visit in Calcutta (see *Occult World*, 169–74).

LETTERS 55, 56, AND 57

It seems well to consider Letters 55, 56, and 57 together, as they relate to what is known as the "Vega incident," when Eglinton is visited by KH on board the SS *Vega* en route from India to England. There are several accounts of this incident. The story is well summarized in the prefatory notes to these three letters in the chronological edition, and Sinnett's account is available in *The Occult World*. Students may also wish to read the story as told by Virginia Hanson in *Masters and Men* (chapter 11) and by Sven Eek in his work, *Damodar and the Pioneers of the Theosophical Movement* (page 185 *et seq.*). While the entire incident may seem rather complicated, our basic concern here is with the lessons that may be derived from the occurrence.

Throughout the letters the Mahatmas are eager to set before the world the truths regarding what in Letter 55 is again called "the Occult

Science," and what we today consider the fundamental principles of the Theosophical philosophy or metaphysics. So, as KH states at the outset of Letter 55, he is simply reiterating the objections he and his Brother have "against Spiritual phenomena and its mediums." At the same time, a medium (in this case, Eglinton) is being used to convince, first, the medium himself and, second, through that channel the Spiritualist movement, of the existence of the Brotherhood and therefore of the knowledge the Mahatmas possess, which could be of benefit to the world at large. Up to this time, as KH points out, "the voice of truth came thro' a channel which few liked," a clear reference to HPB, so now the Mahatma intends to try another means to achieve the purpose he has at heart. (Recall that in the note KH inserted in Letter 38 from Stainton Moses to Sinnett, the Mahatma said that he "will try one more honest medium—Eglinton.")

The means chosen by KH is in fact a rather mysterious one. A great deal of concentrated energy must have been required to produce the phenomenon of a *mayavi rupa,* or an "illusory body," which was then infilled, if I can use such a term, with KH's life energy. Notably, the conscious creation of such a vehicle must be one of the "powers latent" in every human being, referred to in the Third Object of the Society. KH states that he has never before engaged in this particular phenomenal production, but he is determined to do it this one time, his motive being not only to convince Eglinton of the Mahatmas' existence but possibly to train him as a voice for the occult philosophy.

There is much to study, particularly in HPB's esoteric teachings as well as in the teachings she gave to her inner group, concerning the *mayavi rupa.* The student will find a number of references in the *Collected Writings,* all of which point to the fact that the production of such a "form" (*rupa*) is brought about by *kriyashakti,* or the power of thought. For the ordinary individual, the production is usually unconscious, while for the Adept it is conscious. Excerpts from HPB's E.S. Instruction No. 5 may be useful in understanding the nature of KH's appearance to Eglinton:

The Mayavi Rupa, or illusionary Body ... is of different degrees. All have the Chhaya [i.e., shadow] as upadhi [basis], but they may be unconscious or conscious. If a man thinks intensely of another at a distance, his Mayavi-Rupa may appear to that person, without the projector knowing anything about it. This Mayavi-Rupa is formed by the unconscious use of Kriyasakti, when the thought is at work with intensity and concentration. It is formed without the idea of conscious projection, and it is itself unconscious, a thought body, but not a vehicle of Consciousness. But when a man consciously projects a Mayavi-Rupa and uses it as a vehicle of Consciousness, he is an Adept. . . . When an Adept projects his Mayavi-Rupa, the guiding intelligence that informs it comes from the Heart, the essence of Manas entering it; the attributes and qualities are drawn from the Auric Envelope. . . . The Mayavi-Rupa is a Manasic Body . . . ; its projection is always a Manasic act, since it cannot be formed without the activity of Kriyasakti. The Mayavi-Rupa may be so strongly vitalized that it can go on to another plane, and can there unite with the beings of that plane, and so ensoul them. But this can only be done by an Adept. (*CW*, 12:706–7)

In a very interesting article, "Dialogue between the Two Editors," which first appeared in HPB's journal *Lucifer* in December 1888 (see *CW*, 10:224), HPB writes of the power of thought to create a shape or form. When asked, "Is that shape absolutely unconscious?" she responds:

Perfectly unconscious unless it is the creation of an adept, who has a pre-conceived object in giving it consciousness, or rather in sending along with it enough of his will and intelligence to cause it to appear conscious. . . . The wide distinction that obtains between the adept in this matter and the ordinary man must be borne in mind. The adept may at his will use his *Mayavi-rupa*, but the ordinary man does not. . . . It is called *Mayavi-rupa* because it is a form of illusion created for use in the particular instance, and it has quite enough of the adept's mind in it to accomplish its purpose.

As already said, the earnest student will find much to study regarding this subject, and in particular to try to fathom the meaning of KH's statement that Eglinton "will see somebody quite different from the real KH, though it *will still be KH.*"

In Letter 55, KH indicates his intent to appear to Eglinton in such a unique manner that there could be no question of fraud, which might well have been the accusation had KH visited the medium during his stay in Calcutta, particularly if HPB had been present. We know that Eglinton did not even meet HPB during the time he was in India and, in fact, did not meet her until two years later when she was in England. It is also evident that KH was endeavoring to protect HPB, while at the same time both KH and M (evidenced by statements in Letters 38 and 45) were testing Eglinton to determine whether indeed he could be utilized in the work.

So, as KH writes, "The time for the *experiment* has come," a reference to the fact that it was in the nature of an experiment to appear to Eglinton while at sea. That from one point of view the "experiment" was successful or at least partially so is evident from a letter to Sinnett from Eglinton, written after his arrival in England and in which Eglinton speaks of his "conversion to Theosophy and ... having seen the Bros" (see particularly *LBS*, 3–4 and 361). Another aspect of the partial success of the "experiment" to utilize Eglinton to aid in their work may lie in the fact that Letter 57 was sent from London and may well have been transmitted therefore through Eglinton as a further test of his abilities. However, as we will see in later letters (particularly Letters 62 and 63), Eglinton remained as he had been, an excellent medium, "gaining his living by his gifts," as he wrote, but never to return to India and never to become active in furthering the work that the Mahatmas had at heart.

Letters 55, 56, and 57 then turn to comments regarding Hume, first asking Sinnett to inform his friend of the Mahatma's then-anticipated visit to Eglinton and next to dissuade Hume from attempting to go to Tibet in order to find the Brothers. There are still those who think that by traveling to Tibet, they will encounter one or more of the Mahatmas, and many ask today, in view of the tragic take-over of Tibet by the Chinese, whether the Masters are still in that country. Perhaps KH's words are therefore as valid now as when written in 1882: "Those whom we desire to know us will find us at the very frontiers. Those who have set against themselves the Chohans . . . would not find us were they to go [to] L'hasa with an army."

Opportunities offered to promising individuals; the desire to relieve HPB of the burden she carried, including the calumny she was suffering and the strain upon her; the effort to help both Sinnett and Hume to understand the deeper truths of the wisdom in order that they might in their turn aid in the enlightenment of humanity— these are but a few of the messages to be found in these three letters that comprise the story of the "Vega incident." And, of course, the Mahatma's appearance to the English medium on shipboard far from land introduces us to one of the amazing faculties of the true Adept, a faculty that we all possess and must eventually learn to exercise in full consciousness.

∼ ∽

LETTERS 58, 59, AND 60

Once again, three letters, in this case Letters 58, 59, and 60, are best considered together, since all three involve correspondence from the brilliant Advaita Vedantin, T. Subba Row, and also because Letter 60 is actually the completion of Letter 59, the two together comprising KH's comments appended to a letter to HPB. The life and writings of Subba Row (or Rao, as it is sometimes spelled) are well documented, and there are now two volumes of his *Collected Writings*, compiled and annotated by Henk J. Spierenburg.

As background to Letter 58, we know that for some time HPB has been urging Subba Row to aid in instructing Sinnett in the occult philosophy, and it seems that Morya, the guru of both HPB and

Subba Row, has acquiesced in that request. At the conclusion of Letter 46, M wrote Sinnett: "You must have patience with Subba Row. Give him time. He is now at his tapas and will not be disturbed. I will tell him not to neglect you but he is very jealous and regards teaching an Englishman as a sacrilege."

Letter 58, then, is Subba Row's response to HPB's repeated requests, perhaps now stated specifically since he writes that he is "now ordered by——," the blank presumably standing for his Master, M. It is interesting that the Indian Vedantin scholar tells Sinnett that the Mahatmas "can hardly be expected to undertake the work of personal instruction," when, as we know, they did just that in answering numerous questions about Theosophical philosophy. But Subba Row, even though ordered by his Master, promises to give such instruction only under certain conditions, which he proceeds to set forth. First is a pledge of secrecy, which HPB also exacted when she established her esoteric school. Second is the matter of living a life "consistent," says Subba Row, "with the Spirit of the rules" to be given. We can contrast this condition with KH's recognition that Sinnett, under his present circumstances, could not be expected to change his mode of life (see Letter 20 for KH's explanation of the life required for chelaship and Letter 126 for KH's statement that Sinnett was neither "born for" nor "fitted for" the life of a chela; even when Sinnett had offered to give up "meat and drink" the Master "refused.") The third and fourth conditions would require Sinnett to promote the work of the Society, which indeed he was doing, and to act in accordance with the discipline he would be given. From the final paragraph of Subba Row's letter, we can assume that one aspect of the required "practice" would involve chanting certain Sanskrit invocations whose power is dependent on their correct and distinct pronunciation.

We know that Sinnett answered Subba Row's letter, although we do not know precisely how he replied. Subba Row sent the reply on to M, perhaps with a cover letter similar to the one addressed to HPB, extracts of which KH sent to Sinnett. It is clear that KH also read Sinnett's response to Subba Row. Sinnett, who from the very beginning of the correspondence with the Mahatmas has been chiefly interested in phenomena and its production, seems to have asked particularly about the "siddhis" or psychic powers, that Subba Row could help him acquire. But KH, having warned Sinnett on a number of previous occasions, again cautions the Englishman: "Occultism is not to be trifled with. It demands *all* or nothing." And it is evident that while the Mahatma appreciates M's intention in urging Subba Row to aid Sinnett in realizing his desire, KH does not agree, terming the "project *wild*."

There are comments in other letters indicating that the two Mahatmas do not always agree concerning methods, although certainly they were united in ultimate aims. Recall that in Letter 29, M, implying that the Brothers may not always be in full agreement, tells Sinnett: "We of the Indo-Tibetan hovels never quarrel" but "concern ourselves with the main facts." In a later letter, KH tells Sinnett: "I will never interfere in [M's] ways of training, however distasteful they may be to me personally" (see Letter 74, page 228). And in Letter 101 (page 341), KH says of his Brother: "We are not—as you know—always of the same way of thinking," and again, in Letter A (page 463), "Know my friend that in our world though we may differ in methods we can never be opposed in *principles of action*."

In Letters 59 and 60, KH, recognizing Sinnett's impatience to know what M thinks of his response to Subba Row's letter and whether the training for which he longs can proceed, attempts to dissuade him from undertaking what the Mahatma knows to be a "task beyond your strength and means." The Mahatma's cautionary note should be a warning for all who would undertake the disciplines leading to the acquirement of psychic faculties: "*For once pledged* were you to break your promise it would cut you off for years, if not for ever from any further progress."

KH undoubtedly is more familiar with Sinnett than M, even though M corresponded with Sinnett during KH's retreat. KH may be more aware of Sinnett's situation as a family man needing to earn a living and move in circles not conducive to changing his mode of life.

At the same time, KH realizes the difficulty faced by Subba Row, who is being urged by both HPB and his own guru to train Sinnett in at least the preliminaries to developing psychic abilities. Yet despite Sinnett's desire and HPB's and M's urging, there remains, as KH has told Sinnett on previous occasions, "the unpassable Chinese wall of rules and Law." Throughout the letters, in fact, there are references to the "Rules" to which members of the Brotherhood are pledged: note statements in Letters 2 (page 8), 15 (page 45), 21 (page 78), and 49 (page 136).

Presumably the conditions Subba Row sets forth in his letter to Sinnett are what KH terms "the first principles of . . . *Chela* training," and however Sinnett answered Subba Row, perhaps countering those conditions or even setting forth conditions of his own, the Englishman does not understand those "first principles." There is much in the letters, particularly the later ones, describing chelaship, and in Letter 68 (page 203), KH tells Sinnett that he may call himself a "Lay-Chela." While we will examine this subject in connection with various later letters, for a preliminary understanding of the terms "Chela" and "Lay-Chela" the student can read HPB's article "Chelas and Lay Chelas" (*CW*, 4:607–14). To quote briefly from that article: "A 'Chela' . . . is one who has offered himself or herself as a pupil to learn practically the 'hidden mysteries of Nature and the psychical powers latent in man.' . . . A Lay Chela is but a man of the world who affirms his desire to become wise in spiritual things."

We can assume, then, that because Sinnett did not really understand all that is involved in chelaship (though some aspects of it were explained in Letter 20) and also because KH knew quite well that Sinnett could not and should not desert his family, give up meat and alcohol, and abide by the other conditions required, KH considered him simply a "lay-chela." As such, "to become wise in spiritual things," he advises Sinnett to learn "the philosophy of the phenomena and our doctrines on Cosmogony." This is precisely what Sinnett did learn, on the basis of which he was able to write a textbook on that philosophy, *Esoteric Buddhism.*

KH touches on the question of terminology, recalling M's statement in Letter 46 that the terms are "untranslatable" and advising Sinnett to come to some agreement on the terms to be used "when discussing cyclic evolution." This matter of terminology is mentioned again in Letters 65 and 66. Now KH refers to the fact that Subba Row's terms derive from "the *Brahmanical* esoteric teaching," while the Mahatmas, being Buddhists, utilize the "'Arhat Buddhist' terminology." As we know, this question of terms used for describing the human constitution became a point of disagreement between HPB and Subba Row, and perhaps on occasion still leads to confusion, especially when speaking of the cycles known as the rounds and races.

One of KH's comments to Sinnett may seem puzzling. He writes: "In five or six years I hope to become my own 'guide' and things will have somewhat to change then." We can only conjecture that while KH took a further step on the initiatory path during his retreat, he is still accountable to someone on a higher rung of the ladder and acted, though willingly, as we know from other statements, under certain restraints. The meaning of his words "things will have somewhat to change" once he is completely free of those restraints and acting as his own "guide," we can only guess at, and even then, given how little we really know about the Occult Brotherhood's functioning, we would probably be quite wrong.

In order to complete the story concerning the possibility of Subba Row's instructing Sinnett, the student may want to turn next to Letter 64, before taking up the three intervening letters, numbers 61, 62, and 63. Therefore, I have inserted the commentary on Letter 64 here.

LETTER 64*

As noted, Letter 64 is Subba Row's response to Sinnett's "qualified assent . . . to the conditions" that the Vedanta scholar had laid

---

* Intentionally out of sequence.

down (Letter 58). Subba Row naturally reiterates much that KH told Sinnett in his first letter, as well as all that KH implied in his comments (Letters 59 and 60). There are certain rules that govern the transmission of the knowledge Sinnett is seeking, as we have seen in the comments made concerning earlier letters. Above all, there is a certain way of life, and Subba Row says that if Sinnett "find[s] it impracticable to change the present mode" of his life, then he must "wait for practical instruction" until he can fulfill those requirements. As we know from Letter 59, KH recognizes that at that time it was not possible, nor would he even recommend, for Sinnett to abandon his career and responsibility for wife and child, or any other aspect of his way of living.

One particular statement in Subba Row's letter should receive our attention, for so many individuals still seek to develop psychic powers without studying the philosophy underlying their development. Occult training, states Subba Row, involves "instruction" that would "in the course of time necessarily develop such powers." In other words, the training and the instruction accompanying it come first and involve what Subba Row here calls "the means of shifting gradually [the student's] sense of individuality from [the] corruptible material body to the incorruptible and eternal Non-Being represented by [the] seventh principle." He adds: "Please consider this as the real aim of Occult Science." What is called for, in other words, is a genuine "shift" from an ego-centered consciousness to a transpersonal awareness of the underlying source of all existence—not at all an easy task if we undertake all that is implied in walking the way of the Great Ones, the Buddhas and the Bodhisattvas.

Meanwhile, we can certainly follow KH's advice to Sinnett to learn as much as we can of the doctrine. So far as Sinnett was concerned, Subba Row states clearly that he was "fully prepared to give [both Hume and Sinnett] such practical instruction as I may be able to give in the Philosophy of the Ancient Brahminical religion and Esoteric Buddhism." We do not know the extent to which either Sinnett or Hume accepted Subba Row's offer; we do know they both continued to ask questions of the Mahatmas and to receive replies. And Sinnett used that knowledge to write his second book, which he titled *Esoteric Buddhism.*

LETTERS 61, 62, AND 63

Having concluded the exchange of correspondence with Subba Row, we can return to the chronological sequence and take up the three intervening letters. Letters 61, 62, and 63 should be considered as a unit, since the answers given to Sinnett's questions in Letter 61 are supplemented in what was termed an "Appendix," comprising Letters 62 and 63. The prefatory notes to Letters 61 and 63 explain the situation clearly. The only further comment is that since Sinnett kept the letters in a locked box, occasionally (so we have been told) extracting pages to reread either for his personal interest or for writing some article, the pages would inevitably get mixed up, especially when the Mahatmas, particularly KH, used different kinds of writing paper, as was the case with what we now know as Letters 62 and 63.

The numbered questions in Letter 61, together with their brief answers and information provided in the "Appendix," which is most of Letter 62, relate mainly to the doctrine concerning the rounds, races, and planetary chains. We have already noted that at the time of these letters much of the terminology was not clearly defined; moreover, the Mahatmas described the occult terms as "untranslatable." Certainly today we need to take great care in using words such as "races" and "planetary chains." In Letter 85B, KH warns Sinnett of "mistakes arising from occasional confusion of terms that I had to learn from you—since it is you who are the author of 'rounds'—'rings'—'earthly rings'—etc., etc."

The subject of planetary chains was introduced in Letter 18, which the student may wish to review. There KH stated that "the congeries of the star-worlds (including our own planet) inhabited by intelligent beings may be likened to an orb or rather an epicycloid formed of rings like a chain—worlds inter-linked together." Further information is found in Letters 66 and 67. While Sinnett provided the first public explanation of the subject in his second book, *Esoteric Buddhism*, additional descriptive references in the literature are fragmentary and, as E. L. Gardner has said, "symbolic." Gardner, certainly one of the ablest students of the early literature, particularly the writings of HPB, has pointed out that the references we do have "in their totality reveal a glimpse of little more than a frame outlining certain principles of creative manifestation" (see "The Earth Chain: The Planetary Chain Problem" in Gardner, *Whence Come the Gods?*).

Before leaving the topic of planetary chains, it may be useful to quote HPB, who devotes a section of *The Secret Doctrine* volume 1 to "A Few Early Misconceptions concerning Planets, Rounds, and Man," where she quotes from one of the Master's letters: "Our Globe [i.e., the earth] as taught from the first, is at the bottom of the arc of descent, where the matter of our perceptions exhibits itself in its grossest form. . . . Hence it only stands to reason that the globes which overshadow our Earth must be on different and superior planes. In short, as Globes, they are in coadunation but not in consubstantiality with our Earth and thus pertain to quite another state of consciousness" (page 166).

However, while endeavoring to understand the term "planetary chain", we may keep in mind HPB's statement at the beginning of the section just quoted: "Among the eleven Stanzas omitted, there is one which gives a full description of the formation of the Planetary Chains, one after another" (page 152). Presumably, then, the material we have on this topic is not only fragmentary and incomplete but belongs to some of the more esoteric teachings. Basic to the doctrine of planetary chains is the occult teaching that, as HPB points out, "Everything in the metaphysical as in the physical Universe is septenary." She continues, "Hence every sidereal body, every planet, whether visible or invisible, is credited with six companion globes.

The evolution of life proceeds on these seven globes or bodies from the 1st to the 7th in Seven Rounds or Seven Cycles" (*SD*, 1:158–59).

One further point needs to be understood. Writing of planetary chains in *Esoteric Buddhism,* Sinnett states that not only is there a "spiral progress" (the cyclic progression through the chain, each cycle called a "round"), but "the process which goes on does not involve the preexistence of a chain of globes which Nature proceeds to stock with life; but it is one in which the evolution of each globe is the result of previous evolutions, and the consequence of certain impulses thrown off from its predecessor in the superabundance of their development" (page 34).

Returning to Letter 61, we may note that Sinnett's early questions concern "fifth round" individuals. Here again HPB is helpful, writing in the same section of volume 1 of *The Secret Doctrine* just quoted from: "Our Earth, as the visible representative of its invisible superior fellow-globes . . . has to live . . . through seven Rounds. Its Humanity develops fully only in the Fourth—our present Round. . . . During the three Rounds to come, Humanity, like the globe on which it lives, will be ever tending to reassume its primeval form, that of a Dhyani-Chohanic Host. Man tends to become a God and then—God, like every other atom in the Universe" (page 159).

This is accomplished, she says, by the fact that "every life-cycle on Globe D (our Earth) is composed of seven Root-Races" (page 160). Notably, each "root race" is comprised of seven sub-races, each of which has innumerable branchlets. The term "race" has been tragically misunderstood. While in the early days of the Society the word seemed convenient and it has persisted in much of our literature, it has also caused problems. Geoffrey Barborka, in his works *The Divine Plan* and *The Peopling of the Earth,* speaks of a root race as "an evolutionary developmental stage," a much more accurate definition. It is particularly useful to keep this in mind as we read KH's elaboration in Letter 62 to his response to Sinnett's first query.

With all this as background, we can perhaps better understand Sinnett's first two queries in Letter 61, concerning "fifth round men."

KH states that even with the "fifth rounders" (more on this in Letter 66), there is "no great physical distinction yet." Presumably this is because the physical vehicles belong to the fourth round, in which the mass of humanity is still working.

To understand the whole subject more fully, it may be helpful to introduce here the concept of a "triple evolutionary scheme," which HPB explores in detail in *The Secret Doctrine*: "There exists in Nature a triple evolutionary scheme, for the formation of the three periodical Upadhis; or rather three separate schemes of evolution, which in our system are inextricably interwoven and interblended at every point. These are the Monadic (or spiritual), the intellectual, and the physical evolutions" (page 181). The entire passage on this subject needs to be read and studied, especially since Letter 62 begins with a reference to the "gigantic evolutionary journey" that "every Spiritual Individuality has . . . to perform." This is reminiscent of a statement that HPB makes later in *The Secret Doctrine*, volume 1: "It is the Spiritual evolution of the inner, immortal man that forms the fundamental tenet in the Occult Sciences" (page 634).

While answering Sinnett's second question, KH speaks of the Buddha as differing "as much in his physical appearance as in spirituality and knowledge," suggesting that his physical body was still that of a fourth rounder but his spiritual and intellectual evolutionary development would have an effect upon the physical, undoubtedly yielding greater sensitivity and a more refined appearance. The spiritual evolutionary scheme is referred to again in KH's further answer to Sinnett's second question (in Letter 62): "It is the *inner* man, the spirituality, the illumination of the physical brain by the light of the spiritual or divine intelligence that is *the* test."

In Letter 62, KH elaborates on his response to Sinnett's first question. "When I say 'man,' I mean a human being of our type. There are other and innumerable manvantaric chains of globes bearing intelligent beings—both in and out of our solar system—the crowns or apexes of evolutionary being in their respective chains, some—physically and intellectually—lower, others immeasurably higher than the man of our chain." We should take note of this statement in light of today's space probes searching for intelligent life elsewhere in the universe.

Sinnett's last question in Letter 61, which is unnumbered, returns us to the situation with Eglinton and the distinction between elementals and elementaries discussed in Letter 18. Here KH gives Sinnett additional information regarding the nature of the "guides" that mediums claim to have. To understand such "guides," KH tells Sinnett, he needs to understand "the evolution of the *corruptions* of elemental dross, and those of the seven principles" in human beings. This suggests that we are constantly shedding material from the various vehicles and that such material is taken up, or "ensouled," by mischievous elementals and elementaries.

KH further comments on Eglinton at the end of Letter 62 and continues his comments in Letter 63. Having called the English medium an "honest" person in an earlier letter (Letter 38), he now says that he is a "good fellow" and "naturally truthful," but evidently leading a "life of infamy" and unable to "resist the tide that threatens to submerge him." How many mediums and psychics follow a similar path! But as KH reminds Sinnett, "Occult Science is a jealous mistress and allows not a shadow of self-indulgence." Eglinton was given his opportunity, the Brothers doing all they could to aid him, but in the end he continued as a spiritualistic medium, content to earn his living by doing séances for the gullible.

Letter 63 ends on what must have been an encouraging note for Sinnett, as KH praises Sinnett's review of Anna Kingsford and Edward Maitland's *The Perfect Way*. He adds that the Englishman has begun to "attract the Chohan's attention." One wonders if Sinnett understood the significance of such a statement, but we do know that he benefited from the instruction he received by writing *Esoteric Buddhism* as a compendium of the occult teachings conveyed in the letters.

So many aspects of the doctrines are touched upon in these three letters that the earnest student needs to spend a great deal of time exploring them, especially since later letters elaborate on these doctrines.

LETTER 65

We turn now to the first of a series of three letters directed to Sinnett's colleague A. O. Hume. Parenthetically, it should be mentioned that the originals of these letters are not extant and what we have is in Sinnett's handwriting. Presumably, Sinnett and Hume compiled the questions in the three letters jointly.

The opening of Letter 65 suggests that the two men had become dissatisfied with M's responses to their queries and so now are addressing their queries to KH. However, KH says he is not certain that he will be able to satisfy them. At the end of the letter, KH tells Hume that he harbors "an unjust feeling towards my Brother," and that M "is better and more powerful than I—at least he is not as bound and restricted as I am." KH then reiterates what he has said in other letters: that much simply cannot be explained and much he cannot talk about because of his vow of silence, but because Hume appears to want to serve the Society, he will do what he can to help him understand the philosophy. Later in the letter, KH specifies two matters on which he must "remain silent": information concerning the Dhyan Chohans (we do not know what information Hume had requested, for certainly we have been given much on that hierarchy) and "the secrets concerning the men of the seventh round."

Once again, KH brings up the topic of terminology and "the tremendous difficulty of finding appropriate terms in English which would convey to the educated European mind even an approximately correct notion about the various subjects we will have to treat upon." For us today, the many statements made throughout the letters concerning the inadequacy of language to express occult concepts constitute a reminder of the danger of falling into what I call the pit of literalism. The essential thing is to understand the inner meaning of the terms, and this calls for the development of intuition.

KH now focuses on a basic tenet of the occult philosophy: the concept of "the one element for which the English has no name." This concept was mentioned at the very beginning of the correspondence (Letter 1) when the term *akasha* was used. Now, in Letter 65, the Mahatma uses the term *swabhavat*, so we need to pause to examine this word. Usually spelled *svabhavat*, the word is a Sanskrit term in the Northern Buddhistic tradition, derived from the prefix *sva*, meaning one's own or self, and the verbal root *bhu*, meaning to become as well as to be in the sense of growth. In a mystical sense, the terms *akasha* and *svabhavat*, as well as *alaya*—also a Sanskrit term and one that we find in *The Voice of the Silence*—all refer to the One Primal Substance or Source, each word connoting an aspect or quality of what HPB calls Absoluteness or Space. It is a condition of primordial consciousness in which spirit and matter are one, and so, as KH says, "It is both passive and active," while inherent within it is "Force," or perhaps better, motion.

The term *svabhavat* appears seven times in the Stanzas of Dzyan, on which *The Secret Doctrine* is based. Stanza 2, sloka 5, reads, in part, "Darkness alone was Father-Mother, Svabhavat; and Svabhavat was in darkness." HPB then defines svabhavat as "the 'Plastic Essence' that fills the Universe, is the root of all things." We next meet the word in stanza 3, sloka 10, regarding the awakening of the cosmos: "Father-Mother spin a web . . . and this web is the Universe spun out of the two substances made in one, which is Svabhavat." The subsequent stage is graphically described in sloka 12: "Then Svabhavat sends Fohat to harden the atoms," on which HPB comments that the process is accomplished "by infusing energy into" primordial matter. Later in *The Secret Doctrine* HPB quotes from Colonel Olcott's *Buddhist Catechism* and adds a parenthetical phrase: "Everything has come out of Akasa [or Svabhavat on our Earth] in obedience to a law of motion inherent in it" (*SD*, 1:635–36). For more on this concept, I refer the interested student to additional statements in *The Secret Doctrine* and also to an excellent essay, "The Doctrine of Svabhava or Svabhavat," in *Blavatsky's Secret Books* by David and Nancy Reigle.

The fundamental principle of the occult philosophy, which HPB gives as the First Fundamental Proposition of *The Secret Doctrine*, is the concept of a unitary source, whether termed the Absolute or the "one element," as here in Letter 65. It is referred to again and again throughout the letters. In Letter 67, as we shall see, this principle is called "Adi-Buddhi" and later in that letter, KH says: "The one element not only fills space and *is* space, but interpenetrates every atom of cosmic matter." In Letter 93B, he writes: "Since motion is all-pervading and absolute rest inconceivable . . . under whatever form or *mask* motion may appear . . . all . . . must be but phases of One and the same universal omnipotent Force [Fohat] . . . [which] we simply call the 'One Life,' the 'One Law' and the 'One Element.'" As HPB emphasizes and the Mahatma now reminds Hume, this basic principle is to be understood as the unitary or, more properly, nondual, source from which all manifestation and therefore differentiation proceeds.

KH then points out other fundamental principles. One is that motion is eternal, there is no immutability in the universe. Even in the periods between the cycles of manifestation known as *pralayas*, there is constant motion. We may well be reminded of HPB's excerpt from what she calls "The Occult Catechism": "'What is it that ever is?' 'Space. . . .' 'What is it that ever was?' 'The Germ in the Root.' 'What is it that is ever coming and going?' 'The Great Breath.' 'Then there are three Eternals?' 'No, the three are one. That which ever is, is one, that which ever was, is one, that which is ever being and becoming, is also one'" (*SD*, 1:11).

KH proceeds to castigate the scientific theories of that time, pointing up their fallacies from an occult perspective, after which he makes the incredible statement: "Modern science is our best ally." One student has suggested that KH was, in some way, forecasting the science of the twentieth (and, we would add, the twenty-first) century, as there are reputable scientists today working at the frontiers of science who would willingly entertain the views expressed in this letter. And so KH returns again to the one fundamental principle: "We recognize but *one* element in Nature (whether spiritual or physical)," calling it "the *Akasa*" that "pervades our solar system, every atom being part of itself, pervades throughout *space* and *is* space . . . which pulsates as in profound sleep during the pralayas . . . the ever active Nature during the Manvantaras." So "spirit and matter are *one,* being but a differentiation of states not *essences.*" Here again we meet the question of terminology, for in their philosophy the Mahatmas seem to have a single word for our rather awkward hyphenation "spirit-matter," which could give a dualistic tone to what is essentially one, or nondualistic.

The student interested in science will certainly wish to explore in depth KH's statements regarding energy and matter to compare them with contemporary ideas on these subjects. Particular attention should be given to KH's assertion: "Neither motion nor energy is indestructible and . . . the physical forces are in no way or manner convertible one into another. . . . It is neither *conversion* nor *creation,* but something for which science has yet no name."

Throughout the letters, hints are occasionally given concerning the guru-chela relationship. In Letter 20, for example, we learned: "The instructor [the guru] has to adapt his conditions to those of the pupil. . . . We have to bring ourselves into a *full* rapport with the subject under training [the chela]." Now in Letter 65, writing of electricity and magnetism, KH comments on an apparently physical mechanism by means of which "chelas are magnetized," adding "but their magnetism or rather that of *their rods* is not *that* electricity." Perhaps a kind of attunement is taking place between the consciousness of the guru and that of the chela, and since we know the Mahatmas had many chelas in India who would write and/or deliver their letters—chelas who could not possibly have been going in and out of KH's home in Tibet—perhaps that process of "re-magnetization" was not totally dependent on some physical instrument. Further, since the process was "to recuperate their nascent powers," presumably powers of a psychic and spiritual nature, "*their rods*" might be a reference to the spinal column, up which flows the *kundalini,* an energy basic to the production of psychic and spiritual phenomena.

The Mahatma then mentions the importance of personal experience in acquiring knowledge and urges Hume to turn his knowledge into "a permanent teaching in the form of articles and pamphlets." Hume did indeed write a number of books on Theosophical subjects, perhaps the best known being *Hints on Esoteric Theosophy*. While KH devotes much of the letter to information concerning matter, energy, force, and so on, he notes that such information "cannot reveal to man life in the higher regions. One has to get a knowledge of spiritual facts by personal experience and from actual observation."

This is undoubtedly as true today as when KH wrote those words to Hume. And, we may add, not only is personal experience necessary, but there is apparently a law in the occult life that as the aspirant uses the knowledge and spiritual understanding gained, sharing it with others, he or she receives further teaching. Because the two Englishmen did "put into practice" what they had "acquired in the way of useful information," KH was permitted to devote some of his time to their instruction.

The Mahatma makes reference to another member of the Occult Fraternity, the "semi-European Greek Brother" who was mentioned in Letter 48 (page 133) and is assumed to be the Master known as Hilarion. Evidently he followed the ancient Greek skeptic school of philosophy known as the Zetetics, meaning to seek or inquire. Interestingly enough, a Zetetical Society was formed in England in 1881 (the year before Letter 65 was written), and among its members were George Bernard Shaw and the socialist Sidney Webb, both of whom Annie Besant was associated with at one time. Perhaps the Greek Brother was, in some way, associated with that Society.

KH next comments on Hume's request, very like Sinnett's, to gain certain psychic powers and to be instructed personally in the occult doctrine. KH responds with one of the most meaningful and truly profound principles for gaining wisdom found anywhere in the letters: "For a clearer comprehension of the extremely abstruse and at first incomprehensible theories of our occult doctrine, never allow the serenity of your mind to be disturbed during your hours of literary labour, nor before you set to work. It is upon the serene and placid surface of the unruffled mind that the visions gathered from the invisible find a representation in the visible world. . . . It is with jealous care that we have to guard our mind-plane from all the adverse influences which daily arise in our passage through earth-life."

One is inevitably reminded of the famous words of the Buddhist teacher Nagarjuna: "What else is there but to keep watch over one's mind both day and night?" The discipline and control of the mind is paramount for coming to spiritual enlightenment.

Hume has apparently asked the Mahatma to teach him orally through the "astral light," a term used in the early days, and frequently by HPB, for what is now called the etheric. However, KH says that acquiring "the Siddhi [psychic power] of hearing occult sounds" would not be as easy as Hume seems to think, adding, "It was never done to any one of us, for the iron rule is that what powers one gets *he must himself acquire.*" As we know from the Mahatmas' other letters, both Sinnett and Hume were interested in obtaining psychic faculties, but without making the necessary effort. At the same time, KH is still encouraging: "Every earnestly disposed man *may* acquire such powers practically. . . . There are the powers of all nature before you, *take what you can.*" Presumably the same advice would apply today.

While not specifically stated, Hume may have become a vegetarian, for the Mahatma says he has more chance of acquiring powers than Sinnett, who even if he were to give up eating meat would still crave such food, "a craving over which he would have no control and the impediment would be the same in that case." In fact, we do know that Hume in his later years was both a vegetarian and an antivivisectionist. KH's love for words is apparent in referring to Sinnett as Hume's "zoophagous friend," a rarely used word that literally means feeding on animals, and thus a synonym for "carnivore." The earlier reference to Hume's wife, who was known as "Moggy," is interesting; we know that she was, or at least became, an alcoholic. Hume had hoped the Mahatmas might do something to cure her, but evidently that could not be accomplished.

Hume was always eager to find some means by which the correspondence could be carried on without the aid of HPB. Apparently, at this time he had some idea of constructing some kind of psychically charged box for exchanging the letters. KH says that he will consider Hume's idea, but comments that "the idea [of such psychic "toys"] is utterly repugnant to us as everything else smacking of spirits and mediumship. We would prefer by far using natural means." For us, who are entirely unfamiliar with all that was involved in the production and delivery of the Mahatmas' letters, the process can seem almost supernatural or phenomenalistic. We do know that a box such as Hume had proposed was never sanctioned or at least never used, and HPB continued to be the principal agent for the letters' transmission.

Letter 65 concludes with a reference to the work of the German philosopher Arthur Schopenhauer. KH comments that some aspects of his philosophy are "most in affinity with our *Arhat* doctrines." Schopenhauer, whose principal work, *The World as Will and Idea*, appeared in late 1818, acknowledged three sources for his philosophy: Kant, Plato, and the Upanishads. Certainly he was much indebted to both Hinduism and Buddhism, writing that Buddhism is more profound than Christianity and that the Hindus were deeper thinkers than the philosophers of Europe.

For Schopenhauer, known as a pessimist, the world and all its phenomena are maya and are only the objectification of will, which is the source of suffering. The ultimate wisdom is nirvana, achieved only by reducing to a minimum one's desire and will. KH encourages Hume to "utilize" Schopenhauer's philosophy by undertaking "a comparison or connotation of his [Schopenhauer's] teachings upon will, etc." Whether Hume ever engaged in such a comparative study we do not know, though this would certainly be an interesting project for today's student of Western philosophical thought.

So concludes an important letter that touches on a number of subjects, in particular, the occult doctrine of oneness underlying all existence.

LETTER 66

L etter 66 is the second of the three letters responding to Hume's (and presumably Sinnett's) many questions, with the hope that the responses would be used in articles the two Englishmen would write for *The Theosophist.* We are fortunate that this letter includes both the questions asked by Hume and Sinnett and the answers supplied by KH. Apparently Hume in particular was determined to gain as specific information as possible concerning human origins and development. However, the Mahatmas could reveal only so much of the occult doctrine, such that while KH's answers give us considerable information, not that much is revealed and much is left to our own intuitive understanding.

A passage in *The Secret Doctrine* has a bearing on this matter. In part 2 of volume 1 (pages 306–7), HPB writes:

> An adept must refuse to impart the conditions and means that lead to a correlation of elements, whether psychic or physical, that may produce a hurtful result as well as a beneficent one. But he is ever ready to impart to the earnest student the secret of the ancient thought in anything that regards history concealed under mythological symbolism. . . . Why do not the adepts reveal that which they know? One might answer: Why should they, since one knows beforehand that no man of science will accept, even as an hypothesis, let alone as a theory or axiom, the facts imparted. . . . An historical, real event was deduced—by those versed in the hieratic sciences—from certain emblems and symbols recorded in the ancient archives. . . . The religious and esoteric history . . . was embedded in symbols. . . . Such events were narrated only during the Initiation, and every student had to record them in corresponding symbols, drawn out of his own mind and examined later by his master, before they were finally accepted.

Both Hume and Sinnett were encouraged again and again to use their own intuitive faculties to seek the knowledge they desired. Recall KH's words to Sinnett in Letter 49 (page 141): "The degree of diligence and zeal with which the hidden meaning is sought by the student, is generally the test—how far he is entitled to the possession of the so buried treasure." Now, in Letter 66, KH states: "Though I am obliged to withhold information about many points yet if you should work out any of the problems by yourself it will be my duty to tell you so." Such statements should also encourage us in our efforts to gain an ever deeper understanding of the teachings the two Adepts were imparting.

In studying Letter 66—and there is much to be studied in depth in this letter—the student should keep two essential points in mind. The first is the septenary principle. The first sentence in the supplementary notes to the letter reads: "Whenever any question of evolution or development in any Kingdom presents itself to you bear constantly in mind that everything comes under the Septenary rule of series in their correspondences and mutual relation throughout nature." Keeping in mind, then, the "Septenary rule," we must always follow the law of analogy, which HPB calls "the only true Ariadne's thread that can lead us through the inextricable paths of Nature's domain toward her primal and final mysteries" (*SD*, 2:153). At the beginning of Letter 66, KH speaks of "the infinite ramifications of the number seven," the number being "one of our greatest mysteries," and "so closely allied and interdependent with the seven principles of Nature and man." One student of the letters has suggested that seven, as a mystical number, is the "root number" of our system, and while it is indeed a "mystery," it is also the number from which all other numbers derive. As HPB states, "Everything in the metaphysical as in the physical Universe is septenary" (*SD*, 1:158).

The second point is the question of terminology, which has come up repeatedly, most recently in Letter 65. In the present letter KH says, "M. advised Mr. Sinnett strongly to agree upon a nomenclature" and that "we have our arbitrary classifications and our nomenclature."

He adds: "It is possible that my nomenclature is faulty," pointing out: "Our mystic terms in their clumsy re-translation . . . are as confusing to us as they are to you." Sinnett comments on this issue in his preface to the original edition of *Esoteric Buddhism:*

> I have had to coin phrases and suggest English words as equivalents for the ideals which were presented to my mind. I am by no means convinced that in all cases I have coined the best possible phrases and hit on the most neatly expressive words. For example, at the threshhold of the subject, we come upon the necessity of giving some name to the various elements or attributes of which the complete human creature is made up. "Element" would be an impossible word to use, on account of the confusion that would arise from its use in other significations; and the least objectionable on the whole seemed to me "principle," though to an ear trained in the niceties of metaphysical expression this word will have a very unsatisfactory sound in some of its present applications. Quite possibly, therefore, in the process of time the Western nomenclature of the esoteric doctrine may be greatly developed in advance of that I have provisionally constructed.

Words, as any student of language knows well, can change in meaning and often carry connotations in social usage never intended when they were first used. For example, today the word "race" when applied to groups of people is easily taken in a pejorative sense, just as the ancient symbol of the whirling cross, the svastika, which for millennia has had an auspicious meaning, can all too easily arouse fear and anger. So also, the term "planetary chain," can be mistaken as referring to the physical planets of our solar system. Therefore, in reading both Hume's and Sinnett's questions as well as KH's answers, we must search out the inner meaning of the occult doctrine being presented.

Turning, then, to the first question in Letter 66, we have KH's response that there are "seven objective and seven subjective globes," with "our earth occupying the lower turning point" in the planetary chain in which we are now evolving. We may recall M's statement in Letter 44 (page 119): "The worlds of effects are not lokas or localities. They are the shadow of the world of causes, their *souls*." Perhaps the "seven subjective globes" that constitute the "worlds of effects" are the "shadow," not only of the causative spheres but also of the nature of consciousness, since they are not "localities." Support for this suggestion is found in HPB's section "On Chains of Planets and their Plurality" in *The Secret Doctrine* (2:699–709). Note particularly her statement on page 701 about speculating "on the nature of globes which, in the economy of nature, must needs belong to states of consciousness other and quite different from *any* which man experiences here." A full study of that section may help unlock the mystery concerning our system's objective and subjective globes. Yet further questions inevitably arise. For example, following the law of analogy, if the globes on which our evolutionary development is taking place have shadow or subjective counterparts, do the principles of the human constitution also have a shadow side, and does that shadow, or subjective aspect, comprise the elements or *skandhas* (referred to in Letter 68) that lead to rebirth?

KH's response to the second question seems to lead into yet deeper mysteries. He speaks of three elemental kingdoms that precede the mineral, vegetable, and animal domains, although he says little about the nature of these states, which may be related to the lokas and talas often referred to in *The Secret Doctrine* and commented upon briefly in connection with Letter 29. As Geoffrey Barborka explains (*The Divine Plan*, 169–72): "In so far as the esoteric philosophy is concerned, the lokas and talas have far greater significance than mere localities or abodes of . . . celestial beings. They may be compared to states of consciousness, into which a man may enter, the *lokas* representing the spiritual aspect, the *talas*, the material aspect." Or, using KH's own language, we could say the lokas are in the subjective region while the talas, popularly called "hells," are in the objective region.

KH says: "Two of the three former [i.e., kingdoms below the mineral] none but an initiate can conceive of; the third is the Inner kingdom—below the crust of the earth—which we could name but would feel embarrassed to describe," which suggests that he has experienced the nature of that domain. Again I refer the student to my comments on Letter 29; perhaps KH's three-month "retreat" included his meeting, in consciousness, with the inhabitants (elemental in nature) of the domain beneath the earth. An in-depth study of HPB's discussion of the subject, "Lokas and Talas, in Connection with the States of Consciousness," certainly indicates this as a possibility (*CW*, 12:663–73). In that section, she associates each loka-tala pair with a plane, the seven pairs being "planes from without within, and states of consciousness through which man can pass and *must* pass, once he is determined to go through the seven *paths* and *portals* of Dhyani. . . . All this is reached on earth in one or many incarnations." She continues: "See the order: the four lower ones . . . are *rupa; i.e.,* they are performed by the inner man with the full concurrence of the diviner portion or elements of the Lower Manas, and consciously by the *personal man.* The three higher states cannot be reached and remembered by the latter, unless he is a fully initiated Adept. . . . One thing must be remembered: . . . the "infernal" or terrestrial states are also the seven divisions of the earth."

This interpretation of KH's response, while speculative, may be useful in understanding his further comment: "These seven kingdoms are preceded by other and numerous septenary stages and combinations." From the esoteric point of view, as HPB indicates in the essay just quoted from, the kingdom "below the crust of the earth" is composed of matter more dense than any physical matter we know of. Furthermore, the span of an Adept's consciousness reaches into fields both "higher" and "lower" than the normal range of human consciousness. This brief response to Hume's question in this letter may unfold into a most interesting study concerning the many domains of the cosmos!

One final thought before leaving the response to the third question: This teaching, that three kingdoms occupy regions beneath the earth and are themselves composed of elementals, may be the basis for the many conceptualizations of hell found in cultural and mythological traditions throughout the world. A cross-cultural study of the subject might reveal why KH would not or could not describe "the third" or "Inner Kingdom—below the crust of the earth." Such a study might include an analysis of the nine levels of hell described by Dante in *The Inferno*, the first of the three books comprising *The Divine Comedy*.

At the heart of Hume's third question is a topic that concerns many students: How does the monad transit from one kingdom of nature to the next? Especially puzzling is the transition from mineral to plant, since, while we can see plants die, minerals (other than gases) seem to decompose so slowly that a transition state seems almost nonexistent. In fact, perhaps it is the consciousness and not the form that transits from one kingdom to the next, just as it is the consciousness that is involved in moving from one "race" to the next (in the human stage) and one "class" to the next (in the kingdoms below the human). KH defines the transition as "occult osmosis," although this definition leaves us not much wiser regarding how it actually happens. We might speculate here that since the mineral form outlasts the presence of the consciousness within it, perhaps the form is maintained as a vehicle for oncoming, or incoming, life from the elemental kingdom.

In replying to Hume's third question, KH first corrects the number of globes or spheres through which the monad passes, the Mahatma seeming to take special delight in Hume's word "inmetalliation." (As an aside, one of KH's endearing traits is his fondness for language, a quality that adds so much beauty to his writing.) Notice again the emphasis he gives not simply to the number seven but also to the numerous "ramifications" of the septenary principle in the almost endless series of multiples of seven, sub-sevens, sub-sub-sevens, and so at every stage of the monad's progress through the kingdoms. This helps us to realize that what is essential is the fundamental principle, rather than the specific numbers.

KH makes an important point when he says that in the three kingdoms—mineral, plant, and animal—classification is "according to their occult properties, *i.e.,* according to the relative proportion of the seven universal principles which they contain." We may presume, on the law of analogy, that something similar applies to the human kingdom, which is classified in terms of "Root Races, sub-Races," and so on. As KH advises Hume and Sinnett to "exercise" their own intuitions on this, we can do the same, looking for correspondences between the seven great classes of minerals and the seven principles as exhibited in the other kingdoms on up to the human.

It may be appropriate here to comment on the "monad," particularly as the final part of the third question concerns whether "every separate molecule of the mineral" constitutes a monad. In "About the Mineral Monad," part of a series of responses to questions asked by an English Theosophist, originally published in *The Theosophist* in September 1883, HPB states: "The term 'monad' applies to the latent life in the mineral as much as it does to the life in the vegetable and the animal" (*CW*, 5:171–75). Then she gives a lengthy explanation, part of which is repeated in *The Secret Doctrine* (1:178–79):

The "monad" is the combination of the last two Principles in man, the 6th and the 7th, and, properly speaking, the term "human monad" applies only to [the dual soul (atma-buddhi)], not to its highest spiritual vivifying Principle [Atman alone]. . . . It would be very misleading to imagine a monad as a separate entity trailing its slow way in a distinct path through the lower kingdoms, and after an incalculable series of transformations flowering into a human being. . . . Instead of saying a mineral monad, the correcter phraseology in physical science which differentiates every atom— would of course had been [*sic*] to call it *the* Monad manifesting in that form of Prakriti called the mineral kingdom. . . . The tendency towards segregation into individual monads is gradual, and in the higher animals comes almost to the point. . . . The Occultists . . . distinguish the progressive stages of the evolution of the Concrete from the Abstract by terms of which the "Mineral [Vegetable, Animal, etc.] Monad" is *one*. The term merely means that the tidal wave of spiritual evolution is passing through that arc of its circuit.

The "Monadic Essence" begins to imperceptibly differentiate [towards individual consciousness] in the vegetable kingdom.

The student can turn to *The Secret Doctrine*, especially the section titled "Gods, Monads and Atoms" (1:610), for more on this subject.

Responding to the final part of Hume's third question, KH says, notably: "Every molecule [and we could substitute "atom"] is part of the Universal Life." Hence, we can say that the "soul"—which KH defines here as the "fourth and fifth principle," or kama-manas—is composed of that "One Life" as it has evolved through the "progressed entities of the lower kingdom[s]." In other words, just as the physical body is made up of innumerable "life atoms," as HPB calls them, every cell constituting a "life," so our soul is a composite of "lives" proceeding through their own evolution while also contributing to our further development.

The fourth question plus KH's response constitute a further clarification of the terms used to define a cycle through the seven Globes A through G and the cycles within each globe. Once again, terms like "planetary chains," "rounds," "root races," and "sub-races" are only approximations of the occult terminology. It is obvious from KH's comment that volumes of knowledge remain of which we are ignorant and that even KH and M, as well as others of the Fraternity, are still learning, since KH states that only the "highest adepts" have the "keys" to the "most abstruse mathematical calculations" concerning these subjects. To appreciate the extent of the material still unavailable to us, the student should read the section in volume 14 of HPB's *Collected Writings* titled "The Secret Books of 'Lam Rin' and Dzyan." Meanwhile, we are fortunate in having been given what KH calls the "unitary or root idea," and certainly we are encouraged to use the law of analogy and to speculate, on the basis of that law, on the many aspects of the monadic evolutionary cycle.

Question 5 and its response again concern the three kingdoms below the mineral in which the "evolution of the elementals" is taking place. The answer to question 6 is only partial, as KH indicates that the figures Hume is seeking cannot be given out. He adds the intriguing comment that they are "interwoven with the profoundest psychological mysteries," knowledge of which would "put the rod of power" in the hands of those who would undoubtedly misuse it. Recall the equally intriguing statement in Letter 65 concerning the visits of chelas to KH's home for the purpose of magnetizing "their rods." We can only say that however much of the occult doctrine is revealed to us, a vast reservoir remains unknown, such that every answer leads to further questions. Two significant statements in KH's reply should be noted: first, that for the period of a "Solar Manvantara," the "number of existences of vital activities of the monad is fixed," although within that fixed number there are numerous variations; second, that "human *personalities* are often *blotted out.*"

That second point may be puzzling, especially since KH adds that "the entities" composing such personalities "complete" their evolutionary cycle. Presumably, the personalities that are "blotted out" are those that accomplish nothing, and the "lives" that constituted their vehicles are taken up by other entities moving onward in their own development. Statements made elsewhere in the letters throw some light on this matter. For instance, Letter 70C (page 212) says that the personality that achieves nothing leaves nothing on the record, as it were, yet "the Monad never perishes whatever happens." By the law of analogy, perhaps a correspondence exists between a day in a single lifetime of an individual and a single personality in the aeonic evolution through which the monad passes, and just as our wasted days account for nothing in the record of one life, so one personality, completely wasted, is removed from the record of our achievements.

The series of questions and answers 7, 7a, and 7b continue on the subject of rounds, races, incarnations, and so on, as Hume endeavors to gain a clearer understanding of these difficult topics. As both KH and M stress again and again, they withhold information not by choice but because they are bound by the Brotherhood's occult rules, one of which is "Thus far and no further." At the same time, the Englishmen are encouraged to use their intuition. As pointed out earlier, KH tells

Hume in his response to question 7b, "Though I am obliged to withhold information about many points yet if you should work out any of the problems by yourself it will be my duty to tell you so."

Undoubtedly the most puzzling of all the passages in the letters is KH's response to Hume's question 7b. Certainly every serious student of the letters has, at some time or other, endeavored to "solve the problem of the 777 incarnations" and understand what is meant by the "principle of acceleration and retardation" said to apply to the evolutionary cycle "in such a way, as to . . . leave but a single superior [race] to make the last ring [round]." Perhaps the "principle of acceleration and retardation" is related to the law of karma and involves the decision of an individual soul far enough advanced on the spiritual path either to speed up his or her monadic growth or to delay progress in order to assist others struggling along the way. We are told, in fact, that KH delayed his own progress toward full "Adeptship by undertaking the correspondence with the two Englishmen." However, the meaning of the statement that only one "superior" race of Egos will remain to complete the seventh round remains a matter for conjecture.

Students have proposed various solutions to the "problem of the 777 incarnations." Some have suggested that the number is mystical rather than factual. Others have worked out schemes based on the divisibility of 777 by the number 7, assigning series of incarnations to the several root races, sub-races, sub-sub-races, and so on. The ultimate question concerns the precise meaning of "incarnation" as well as the length of time between incarnations. Regarding the meaning of the term, we can keep two factors in mind: first, KH's reference in his response to question 6 to "human *personalities*," which we may call incarnations, and second, his comment in 7b that "only full average lives of consciousness and responsibility" are "computed." This could well eliminate all embodiments during at least the first three and a half rounds, before the achievement of full self-consciousness, and perhaps even the earliest races of the fourth round, before the manasic principle is fully awakened.

We have been told, furthermore, that some time during the fifth round all those monads who are not going to win full adeptship by the end of the seventh round will "drop out" and await the next life wave at the appropriate point in its evolutionary development. These monads, sometimes referred to as the "laggards," will be in an "advanced" status relative to the next cycle, as they will have already passed through the earlier stages. (See *SD*, 1:174–75, "Additional Facts and Explanations concerning the Globes and the Monads," in which HPB writes of the three classes of the "Monadic Host.")

Probably any solution proposed to the puzzles that KH's response to question 7 raises will not be wholly satisfactory to all students. What is certain is the fact, stressed in an earlier letter (Letter 62, page 159), that "no one of us can miss one single rung of the ladder," and therefore, having now gained self-consciousness, we must fulfill the obligations relating to the "rung" on which we currently stand. In other words, our present incarnation—whatever its number in the total sum of incarnations to be experienced—is the one demanding our full attention.

Question 8 and its response are mainly concerned with which round in the cycle of manifestation humanity is passing through at the present time. The two Englishmen felt confused, particularly by a statement of M's in his correspondence with them. KH's answer is quite clear and extremely interesting. Elsewhere in Theosophical literature it is pointed out that humanity has passed the middle of the fourth round and at that middle point "the door was closed" to the human kingdom and no further souls, or Egos, could enter, since there were no more vehicles sufficiently primitive for entities just making the transition from animal to human. While the wait until the next life wave may seem to us, with our human time-consciousness, so aeonic as to be unbearable, this is evidently not the case for those entities, since their consciousness is dull and unfocused. Again, this topic bears on a study of the entire second volume of *The Secret Doctrine*, which is devoted to the subject of anthropogenesis.

There appears to be a contradiction concerning the evolution of individuals relative to the evolution of rounds. On the one hand,

KH stresses that "the races and sub-races of one round must not be confounded with those of another round," and that the next round is said to have "commenced" only when there are no individuals left on earth belonging to the preceding round. On the other hand, he states that "the fifth round has not commenced on our earth" even though fifth round individuals "have been coming in for the last few thousand years," which suggests that the rounds, races, and sub-races overlap considerably. Moreover, he speaks of Plato and Confucius as "fifth rounders" and Gautama Buddha as a "sixth rounder," suggesting that a certain prefiguring of future types occurs. One key to resolving this dilemma may be the triple evolutionary scheme of which HPB wrote, from which we may infer that the fifth and sixth rounders appearing now must still occupy fourth-round bodies. Therefore, the development that marks, say, Plato as a fifth rounder has to do with the intellectual and/or spiritual "schemes" of evolution rather than the physio-etheric. As for the Buddha, said to be a sixth round man, students may wish to review HPB's essay "The Mystery of Buddha," published posthumously and found in volume 14 of the *Collected Writings.*

The chart that concludes KH's letter, prepared by his chela Djual Khul, provides a number of interesting points for study. First, it depicts the globes of our planetary chain in a different arrangement from the usual and seems to indicate that they are all on the same plane of manifestation or of the same nature as our earth. At the same time, as we saw in connection with Letters 61, 62, and 63, while the globes said to "overshadow" the earth are of different substances, they are also in close association (the term "coadunition" is used) as depicted in Djual Khul's diagram. A study of the chart and the accompanying notes, which Sinnett indicates were in DK's handwriting, provides a helpful overview of our present position relative to the work yet to be accomplished.

KH adds some "Supplementary Notes" to the letter in which he discusses mainly the development of humanity through the first three rounds to the point we have reached today, just past the midpoint of the fourth round. Several statements made in these "Notes" are worth our consideration. In Letter 65, KH emphasized the unitary nature of spirit and matter, and here he comments that "it is 'Spirit' which transforms itself into 'matter' and . . . matter *which resolves once more into spirit*," indicating the identical essence of what we tend to differentiate into two distinct substances.

KH also remarks that "*physical intelligence is the masked manifestation of spiritual intelligence*"—a point that may have some bearing on the earlier comment concerning the second of the three streams of evolution, which HPB called "intellectual," and that may apply particularly to the "Fifth Rounders." We might expect of such people what KH calls "a more refined form of mentality commingled with spiritual intuitiveness" because the fifth in any cycle has to do with the unfolding of manas, the fifth principle. Another, more familiar term for the mental faculty "commingled" with intuition is *buddhi-manas*, which might be well developed during the fifth round and even more fully awakened in the sixth round.

Rather puzzling is the statement that "there *must* be 'failures' in the etherial races of the many classes of Dhyan Chohans or Devas as well as among men." Failure, then, is evidently a necessity in the evolutionary process; we might surmise that it even fulfills a purpose, since those who fail in one cycle become the advance guard, we could call them, in the next. We have already touched on this point in connection with KH's reply to question 7b, but undoubtedly more remains to be explored. In the additional comment, for example, KH indicates that those who are "failures" are permitted to undergo a "series of rebirths" while they await the next cycle in order to "prepare themselves" for a future role in which they will transform themselves from "a latent or inactive spiritual force in the aura of the nascent world" to "an *active* Force."

These comments undoubtedly raise questions in the mind of the serious student. Must a certain level of achievement be attained at each stage of the evolutionary process, such that an entity is a failure if that level is not reached? Or just what constitutes "failure"? One is reminded of HPB's words in *The Voice of the Silence*: "Each failure is success, and each sincere attempt wins its reward in time."

KH's comments on the gradual development of "the full type of humanity" through the rounds is almost a preview of the more elaborate discussion on this subject in volume 2 of *The Secret Doctrine*. By the law of analogy or correspondences, the events of the first three rounds summarized by KH are reflected in the occurrences of the first three root races of this fourth round.

We may note especially the statement in connection with the second round that "mind is a slower and more difficult evolution than the physical frame," and that now, in the fourth round, "Intellect has an enormous development." Certainly we can see the effects of that development, particularly since we have passed what KH calls "the *axial point of the minor manwantaric cycle*" and crossed "the equator of [our] course" on earth. The focus on the intellectual stream of evolution, to use HPB's terms, during this fourth round, especially during the current involvement in the fifth root race and its sub-races, has led to the situation so graphically described by KH: "At this point then the world teems with the results of intellectual activity and *spiritual decrease.*" It does not take much imagination to see that we are in that period when "the spiritual Ego will begin its real struggle with body and mind to manifest its transcendental powers." So it is for us to heed the call of KH: "Who will help in the forthcoming gigantic struggle? Who? Happy the man who helps a helping hand."

My own conviction is that it was to give such help that the Theosophical Society was founded and that the teachings we have the privilege to study were given through HPB and, via these letters, directly from the Mahatmas themselves. As KH indicates, the "struggle" continues through the fifth round, so we have a long journey before us. It is an almost incomprehensible period of time in which to accomplish so much, and yet a most glorious opportunity for which we can only be profoundly grateful.

One final comment: While reading this letter, we need to remember that the Mahatma is speaking not so much of exoteric calculations of historical events but rather of the occult history of human evolution. In the conclusion of volume 2, part 1, of *The Secret Doctrine*, HPB writes of her "own personal conviction" that the Mahatmas or, "Masters of Wisdom have a consecutive and full history of our race from its incipient stage down to the present times . . . the uninterrupted record of man since he became the complete physical being" (page 437), to which she adds, "This knowledge is only for the *highest* Initiates." Inevitably, a multitude of questions are left unanswered, so that while we have been given enough material to occupy our attention for a lifetime, there is much more to be known. One day, in the fullness of time and with persistent work, perhaps we will be privileged to read further in the pages of the occult doctrine. I am convinced the possibility exists, but much depends on our willingness to understand the truths that have been given us and to use what we know, as both Hume and Sinnett were advised, in the service of humankind.

LETTER 67

Letter 67 is the last in the series of three letters addressed to Hume and dealing with the topic of the evolutionary development through the rounds and races. Like Letter 66, Letter 67 contains both the questions and KH's responses, although in this instance there are only two questions with very lengthy answers, such that one senses KH's determination to make the doctrine as clear as possible to the Englishmen.

Hume now asks whether the potentiality for development is present in every entity in every form in each of the kingdoms—mineral, vegetable, and animal—as evolution proceeds toward the state of a planetary spirit. The term "planetary spirit" was discussed in the comments on Letter 12, which the student may wish to review in order to understand the heart of Hume's question. In *Transactions of the Blavatsky Lodge*, comprising questions addressed to HPB during sessions with her students, HPB is asked about the distinction between

Dhyan Chohans, planetary spirits, builders, and Dhyani Buddhas. The following is her response:

> Dhyan-Chohan is a generic term for all Devas, or celestial beings. A Planetary Spirit is a Ruler of a planet, a kind of finite or personal god. There is marked difference, however, between the Rulers of the Sacred Planets and the Rulers of a small "chain" of worlds like our own. . . . It must be remembered that the planetary spirit has nothing to do with the spiritual man, but with things of matter and cosmic beings. The gods and rulers of our Earth are cosmic Rulers; that is to say, they form into shape and fashion cosmic matter, for which they are called *Cosmocratores*. . . . The Dhyani-Buddhas are concerned with the human higher triad in a mysterious way.

Further information is available in Geoffrey Barborka's *The Divine Plan*, especially the chapter "The Doctrine of Hierarchies." The student can also refer to *The Theosophical Glossary* for brief definitions of the terms KH uses.

Hume is specifically asking about the "development into a planetary spirit," which is a stage or rung of the ladder that we ourselves are ascending. It is said that when the seventh round of our planetary chain is completed, present humanity will have become Dhyan Chohans of various grades, including that of planetary spirit. Just as the entities now occupying that stage on the evolutionary ladder were once human, or equivalent, beings, so in aeons to come we will serve in that role for some future planetary chain. Hence HPB's clear statement in defining the Third Fundamental Proposition set forth in *The Secret Doctrine*: "No purely spiritual Buddhi (divine Soul) can have an independent (conscious) existence before the spark which issued from the pure Essence . . . has (a) passed through every elemental form . . . and (b) acquired individuality . . . thus ascending through all the degrees of intelligence, from the lowest to the highest Manas, from mineral and plant, up to the holiest Archangel (Dhyani-Buddha)" (1:17).

In "Summing Up" (*SD*, 1:275), HPB states more explicitly: "The whole Kosmos is guided, controlled, and animated by almost endless series of Hierarchies of sentient Beings.... Each of these Beings either *was*, or prepares to become, a man, if not in the present then in a past or a coming cycle (Manvantara)."

In responding to Hume's first question in Letter 67, KH is very clear about the entire evolutionary cycle undertaken during the course of that enormous span of time called a *manvantara*, known in the Brahmanical tradition as a "Day of Brahma" and calculated as 4,320,000,000 years. He tells Hume, "You must take each entity at its starting point in the manwantaric course as the primordial cosmic atom already differentiated by the first flutter of the manwantaric life breath."

Where, we may ask, did you and I begin? Certainly aeons more distant in time and space than the savannahs of Africa where human physicality began, particularly if we are to understand KH's statement: "The potentiality which develops finally in a perfected planetary spirit lurks in, *is* in fact that primordial cosmic atom."

KH identifies the problem facing both Hume and Sinnett, one that still confronts many students today: "The great difficulty in grasping the idea in the . . . process lies in the liability to form more or less incomplete mental conceptions of the working of the *one* element, of its inevitable presence in every imponderable atom, and its subsequent ceaseless and almost illimitable multiplication of new centres of activity without affecting in the least its own original quantity." It is not easy to grasp the fundamental concept of oneness—one element, one substance, which is at the same time one "force," one power, one "form of existence." This basic doctrine of the occult philosophy is stressed in earlier letters and will be stressed again, especially in *The Secret Doctrine*. KH again states unequivocally, "There is but one element and it is impossible to comprehend our system before a correct conception of it is firmly fixed in one's mind."

This "one element" is given a number of different names, including *akasha* and *svabhavat*. Each term gives us a slightly different understanding and aids us in our efforts to comprehend as fully as possible the fundamental principle. As akasha, it is, to quote HPB, "the undifferentiated noumenal and abstract Space" (*Transactions of the Blavatsky Lodge*, page 12). As svabhavat, it is the self-becoming and self-existing from which, and of which, all derives in obedience to Fohat, the law of motion inherent in it. Similar in meaning are such terms as *mulaprakriti*, root substance; *alaya*, or the indissoluble universal soul, the basis of all beings and things; and *pradhana* in the Brahmanical scheme, indicating the producing element out of which all material manifestations are evolved. It is also space in the occult meaning of that word and the "waters of space" in the Hebraic system.

Here KH introduces Northern Buddhist terminology, speaking of this "one element" as "Adi-Buddhi or Dharmakaya, the mystic, universally diffused essence," stressing the intelligence aspect of the one element, the term *Adi-Buddhi* meaning original wisdom and the word *Dharmakaya* pointing to its truthfulness or lawfulness. When it is seen as substance, or what I often call the "fabric of the universe," terms such as *akasha* and *svabhavat* seem particularly applicable, but when seen from the point of view of motion, force, and power, then terms like *Fohat*, the dynamic energy of divine creativity, or *shakti*, power, are used. KH tells Hume, "We will perhaps be near correct to call it *infinite life* and the source of all life visible and invisible, an essence inexhaustible, ever present."

KH takes great care to help Hume understand the distinction between the one element in its premanifestation condition and "when manifesting in the phenomenal world." For this, he uses two other terms: *pravritti*, meaning to roll forward or to come forth as a universe into manifestation and so designating the descending arc of evolution, and *nivritti*, meaning rolling back, equivalent to the ascending arc or the (involutionary) return journey. When the one element, which KH now calls "Parabrahma," is rolled outward into manifestation, it "breathes forth" a new cosmos, that very movement producing the mist or veil known as maya. Maya is also a mystical power or aspect of Fohat, and it is those two combined—Parabrahma plus maya—that, as KH points out, "becomes *Iswar* the creative principle." This is said again in Letter 88 in connection with the term "God". Here in Letter 67 the "creative principle," or *Ishvara* (which the Vedantins call "the highest consciousness in nature," and HPB terms "the sum-total of Dhyan-Chohanic *consciousness*"—see *SD*, 1:573) is also called *Avalokiteshvara*, often translated as the "Lord who looks down" and also as "the Lord who is seen or recognized," equivalent, occultly speaking, to the Third Logos.

We are accustomed to thinking of maya as illusion, but it is much more than that. As KH indicates in this letter, it is the energy or force that produces illusion. The well-known Indologist Heinrich Zimmer writes that maya "differentiates all the forms in the microcosm and macrocosm and unfolds them as divine forces made manifest. Thus the gods are not only in the body of man, they not only are his whole body, this aggregate of manifold forces and functions, they are also in all other life; this is an aspect of the world's unity, for all its multiplicity is formed out of *one* fluid, living substance, the *shakti* of God" (Zimmer, "The Significance of Tantric Yoga," 29).

Much more could be said about the long paragraph with which KH begins his response to Hume's first question, but leaving it, we will move on to the second paragraph. Here KH elaborates on the "differentiated aspects of the one . . . sub-stratum or permanent cause of all manifestations in the phenomenal universe," naming the "five cognizable elements . . . and . . . the one incognizable element," meaning the five elements known to the ancients as "ether, air, water, fire, earth" with the sixth given by KH as "Purush Sakti" and the seventh unnamed.

In *The Secret Doctrine*, HPB enunciates the basic concept concerning the elements:

> "Occult Science recognizes *Seven* Cosmical Elements—four entirely physical, and the fifth (Ether) semi-material, as it will become visible in the air towards the end of our Fourth Round, to reign supreme over the others during the whole of the Fifth. The remaining two

are as yet absolutely beyond the range of human perception. These latter will, however, appear as presentments during the 6th and 7th Races of this Round, and will become known in the 6th and 7th Rounds respectively. These seven elements with their numberless Sub-Elements (far more numerous than those known to Science) are simply *conditional* modifications and aspects of the One and only Element. (*SD*, 1:12–13)

Contemporary science, of course, does not recognize any of these "aspects of the One" as fundamental to the composition of the universe. We should also be careful not to confuse the use of the term "element" in occult science with the chemical elements of physical science. KH makes this clear in stating that not only are earth, water, fire, air, and ether "but the differentiated aspects of the one," but the term "element" indicates "their productive potentialities for numberless form changes or evolution of being."

The Mahatma then proposes an algebraic equation to illustrate his thesis: that fundamentally "there is but one element." Two points must be kept in mind: first, the endless permutations of the "one eternal immutable principle," and second, that "there is under all the activities of the phenomenal universe an energizing impulse inherent in that "one principle." An interesting exercise is to attempt to put the equation into some graphic form that illustrates the nearly infinite combinations (resulting in a manifested system), in all of which there is the same "informing, impelling, evolving *cause*, behind the countless phenomenal manifestations" that constitutes the cosmos.

To aid Hume further in understanding the key occult concept of the "one element," KH—like all excellent teachers!—proposes to "work out the idea with a single example" using the element "Fire," which he terms "the primal igneous principle" resident in the one. The Mahatma's choice of element is interesting, and the student may wish to consider the mystic, occult, and material nature of that element, including its unique importance in the esoteric and hermetic traditions. According to the occult doctrine, one element is developed in each round in an emanational progression. However, in *The Secret Doctrine* it is said that while fire is the fourth element (and so associated with our fourth round), it was the first to evolve and therefore appeared in the first round. HPB writes, quoting from a commentary:

"The worlds, to the profane," says a Commentary, "are built up of the known Elements." To the conception of an "Arhat, these Elements are themselves collectively a divine Life; distributively, on the plane of manifestations, the numberless and countless crores of lives. Fire alone is ONE, on the plane of the One Reality: on that of manifested, hence illusive, being, its particles are fiery lives which live and have their being at the expense of every other life that they consume. . . . Every visible thing in this Universe was built by such Lives, from conscious and divine primordial man down to the unconscious agents that construct matter." . . . "From the One Life formless and Uncreate, proceeds the Universe of lives. First was manifested from the Deep (Chaos) cold luminous fire . . . which formed the curds in Space. . . . These fought, and a great heat was developed. . . . Then came the first manifested Material, Fire, the hot flames . . . ; heat generates moist vapor; that forms solid water . . . ; then dry mist, then liquid mist, watery, that puts out the luminous brightness of the pilgrims (comets?) and forms solid watery wheels (Matter globes) . . . (the Earth) appears with six sisters. These produce by their continuous motion the inferior fire, heat, and an aqueous mist, which yields the third World-Element—Water; and from the breath of all (atmospheric) Air is born. These four are the four lives of the first four periods (Rounds) of Manvantara." (*SD*, 1:249–50)

The serious student who wishes to pursue the topic of the elements will find extremely helpful Geoffrey Barborka's explication in the section "The Seven Element-Principles" in *The Divine Plan*.

A discussion of the Mahatma's response to Hume's first question is not complete without some reference to the frequently mentioned sixth principle, which seems to be consonant with the sixth "element."

After enumerating the "five cognizable elements," KH adds to these "the one incognizable element . . . the 6th principle of the universe—call it Purush Sakti." Later he says, "There is a sixth principle answering to the sixth principle *Buddhi*, in man . . . but we are not permitted to name it except among the initiates. I may however hint that it is connected with the process of the highest intellection." The term *Purush Sakti*, can be literally translated as "spirit-force," although the Sanskrit word *purush* or *purusha* also refers to personhood or individual. Bearing in mind "the universal system of correspondences" and trying "to understand by analogy," as KH advises later in the letter, we can propose that just as the individual monad is constituted of atman (a universal principle) associated with buddhi (by which atman becomes particularized), so at the universal level there is a seed or germ of "personhood" of every atom of matter, an energy or power (shakti) that veils the Absolute, which is perhaps the seventh principle whose name is not given to us. The "process of intellection" may be related to the concept that the universe is through and through a fabric of consciousness and therefore of intelligibility. It is this sixth principle that embodies both wisdom and compassion, relatedness and relationship, through the dynamic known as Fohat, at the same time giving to everything in the manifested system its unique and distinctive nature. Thus a rock is a rock, a tree is a tree, a deer is a deer, and so on. "Purush Sakti" is the inherent power of the one element holding within it the germ of manifold uniqueness: "Every grain of sand, every boulder or crag of granite, *is* that spirit crystallized or petrified."

While this is speculation, of course, we may begin to recognize that the term *buddhi*—so often translated as intuition but really meaning to be awake, awake to what *is*, as well as containing such ideas as wisdom, compassion, discernment—is both a state of consciousness and a power or energy, and that its operation in the human constitution is a reflection (as KH indicates) of its activity in the cosmos. The sixth principle is referred to a number of times throughout the letters, one of the most interesting occurring in Letter 44 in connection with the disposition of the human principles following death (see page 119).

And certainly one of the most provocative statements concerning that principle occurs at the conclusion of the letter we are now studying, where Hume is advised: "Fathom the nature and essence of the sixth principle of the universe and man and you will have fathomed the greatest mystery in this our world—and why not—are you not surrounded by it? What are its familiar manifestations, mesmerism, Od force, etc.—all different aspects of one force capable of good and evil applications." Again, just as Hume and Sinnett were encouraged to speculate and use their intuitive capacities to understand the occult philosophy, so we, having access to much more of that philosophy, particularly in *The Secret Doctrine*, can use the key of analogy to explore some of the still unanswered mysteries of occultism.

We turn then to Hume's second question and KH's very long response, which contains so much that deserves comment and calls for careful study. As the question concerns the development of consciousness at the outset of a pralaya, or rest period, following the activities of a manvantara, the reply might seem more extensive than necessary. But KH takes the time to outline in considerable detail the entire process of the re-formation of a universe, the emergence of the several globes of a planetary chain, and the parallel appearance of the successive kingdoms of nature, from the three elemental kingdoms through the mineral, vegetable, and animal up to the human.

The term *pralaya* simply means dissolution and refers to a state of latency or rest between any two cycles; thus many kinds of pralayas can exist. KH states that there are "three kinds of pralayas and manwantara," to which, it may be noted, HPB adds a fourth. That "fourth kind of pralaya," is one of "constant dissolution . . . the change which takes place imperceptibly in everything in this Universe from the globe down to the atom—without cessation" (*SD*, 1:371). The student wishing to understand more concerning the various pralayas is referred to section 7, "The Days and Nights of Brahma," in *The Secret Doctrine* (1:368–78).

KH details the processes that follow a solar pralaya. However, as the Mahatma points out, "Law in Nature is uniform," so by analogy, the same processes occur after each minor pralaya. It would not be possible to answer Hume's question concerning "what becomes of the Spirit [or, we may say, the consciousness] that has not worked its way up to a man," the human stage, when a pralaya—whether universal, solar, or minor—begins without understanding the evolutionary process that takes place during a manvantara. Therefore, an in-depth study of the entire process as outlined by the Mahatma is required, perhaps attempting to delineate it by means of a diagram if the student is so inclined.

Certain key statements provide us with clues to the way evolution proceeds. (We should also note that the globe designated Z in the letter was later named G, since there are but seven globes in each planetary cycle.) In contrast with his later statement regarding a minor pralaya, in which "there is no starting *de novo*—only resumption of arrested activity," the Mahatma says that a solar pralaya brings about "a *complete* destruction of our system," necessitating "the absolute reformation of our system," but "each time everything is more perfect than before." Consequently, after a solar pralaya the globes of a chain must be re-formed, and this is the work of the elemental kingdoms. Further, each globe as each kingdom (elemental, mineral, vegetable, animal, etc.) occupying the globe has seven principles. Note especially that "from the first man has all the seven principles included in him in germ but none are developed," so "in each of the rounds he makes one of the principles develop fully." At the same time, the development of the principles "keeps pace with the globe" on which humanity dwells. KH states later, "Like every other orb of space our Earth has . . . to pass through a gamut of seven stages of density." So it appears that because the kingdoms and the globe[s] develop in parallel, the law of acceleration and retardation, referred to in Letter 66, comes into operation. The result is "that all kingdoms finish their work simultaneously" on the final globe (Z or G) of the chain.

As KH refers again to the Buddha as a "sixth round man" and to the influx of some "fifth round men," the student may want to review both the comments on this subject in Letter 66 and HPB's posthumously published essay "The Mystery of the Buddha" (*CW*, 14:388–99). Here, in Letter 67, after his remark regarding fifth and sixth round individuals, the Mahatma asks: "How can there be men of the 1st, 2nd, 3rd, 6th and 7th rounds" on our present globe D (the earth)? His answer, "We represent the first three . . . " is extremely significant. It implies that as fourth round people we contain within us the "fruitage" of the first three rounds. So when we speak of a first round humanity or a second or even third round humanity, we must recognize that we are they! We have within us all that was developed in those first three rounds, and we also have within us the foreshadowing of the qualities, represented by the principles, to be developed in the later rounds. The statement that Gautama was the first of *our* humanity to achieve the status known as Buddhahood can only mean that he was able to achieve the goal achievable by all of us, our human life wave, at the end of the present manvantara. Similarly, at the conclusion of Letter 44, the Mahatma M indicated that not only was "our beloved KH . . . on his way to the goal," but "the chief object of our struggles and *initiations* is to achieve" that status "while yet on this earth"—an awesome vision and at the same time a great promise as we cope with the challenges confronting us during this fifth race period on the fourth round!

In his final, intriguing comment, which points to the goal before us and to the results of its achievement, KH informs Hume: "The degrees of an Adept's initiation mark the seven stages at which he discovers the secret of the sevenfold principles in nature and in man and awakens his dormant powers." Here again we find a correspondence between the principles represented in the globe we are occupying ("in nature") and the principles to be awakened within our own constitution. Each principle carries its own "power" or faculty. Geoffrey Barborka, in *The Masters and Their Letters* (pages 3–4), suggests that these "powers" to be awakened are the various siddhis, capacities appropriate to each of the principles. The siddhis, which HPB defines in the *Theosophical Glossary* as "attributes of perfection," are detailed in section 4 of the *Yoga Sutras of Patanjali*. The student may wish to work out their correspondences with the seven principles.

The subject of rounds and races is given further attention in later letters, particularly Letter 93B. For the present, as we turn to Letter 68, we take up quite a different topic that came to absorb the attention of the two Englishmen.

LETTER 68

We come now to one of the most profound as well as important letters concerning the topic of after-death conditions, particularly that state known as *devachan*. A very long letter, consisting of more than fourteen pages in the published text, Letter 68 contains KH's responses to questions Sinnett posed after reading two items that appeared in the June 1882 issue of *The Theosophist*. Those items consisted, first, of a letter to the editor headed "seeming Discrepancies" and signed "Caledonian Theosophist," probably an individual named Davidson or Davison, an ornithologist who worked at one time with Hume as his private secretary. The letter points to what seem to be differences between statements in articles then being published in the journal under the general title "Fragments of Occult Truth" and statements made by HPB in *Isis Unveiled*. The letter to the editor is followed by a lengthy essay by HPB attempting to reconcile the apparent discrepancies. Her explanations inevitably led to further questions. Fortunately Letter 68 contains both Sinnett's questions and KH's responses. Those responses provoked further questions on the subject of devachan, which are dealt with in later letters, especially Letters 70C, 85B, and 104.

Rather than giving a direct reply to Sinnett's first question regarding the Ego's retention of the memory of its just-closed earth life, KH responds by quoting the Buddha's graphic depiction of the Buddhist heaven known as "Sukhavati." The description is somewhat materialistic, perhaps comparable to statements about a Christian heaven where streets are paved with gold and angels sit about playing their harps. However, KH indicates that the description is allegorical, and later he flatly denies that devachan has any resemblance to the "heaven of any religion." We can speculate on the inner meaning of the allegory: just what do the "*seven* rows of railings, *seven* rows of vast curtains, *seven* rows of waving trees," and so on, symbolize? Is there a relation between these "sevens" and the seven human principles in their after-death condition? We can consider, too, the meaning of the phrase "Its divine Udumbara flower casts a root *in the shadow of every earth.*" The *udumbara*, or "blue lotus," is said to be sacred to the Buddha and its blossoming is regarded as supernatural (see *Theosophical Glossary*). Perhaps its casting a root in the earth refers to the fact that it is out of earthly incarnations that ultimately a Buddha arises, although the occurrence is as rare as the blossoming of the blue lotus.

Sinnett's first question is actually answered in KH's second reply: the "new *Ego*" does retain "complete recollection" of its earth life once it is "reborn" into devachan. The meaning of the term "new Ego" is clarified further on in the letter. In a later letter on the subject (Letter 85B, page 263), KH qualifies what he means by saying that it is the "Spiritual life on earth" that is remembered. However, in stating that the "new Ego" can "*never* return on earth," the Mahatma is not denying reincarnation, as his answer to the third question clarifies. Turning to the third question, "Who goes to devachan?" we are told that it is the "personal Ego," but now purified, or retaining only the higher spiritual qualities. Understanding the terms "new Ego" and "personal Ego" calls for some care; it will be clearer after considering KH's response to Sinnett's fifth question.

Responding to Sinnett's third question, KH refers to the Ego as "the combination of the sixth and seventh principles." This combination is usually referred to as the monad, but the Mahatma may be using the term "Ego" to indicate that center of consciousness that becomes the "new Ego" when it is "reborn into the Devachan." This becomes more apparent as we continue through the letter. The entity "born" or "reborn" into the devachanic state can justifiably be called the "new Ego," since the "karma of evil" resulting from actions in the life just ended must be left behind. While such karma cannot follow the individual into devachan (or that condition would not be one of bliss), we are reminded that it will "follow [the entity] in his future earth-reincarnation." Such indeed, as KH reminds Sinnett, is the infallible "Law of Retribution." Similarly, HPB says, "Karma, with its army of skandhas, waits at the threshold of Devachan" (*CW*, 12:609) for the returning Ego, who, as a consequence of its karma, is attracted earthward once again.

KH's description of the devachanic state deserves our close consideration. He calls that state one of "intense selfishness" and "perpetual 'Maya,'" comparing it to an "evanescent dream." Two questions naturally arise: Why is the reward for unselfishness "intense selfishness"? What is the difference between *maya* in devachan and *maya* during physical incarnation? Other questions may occur to the serious student, leading to further exploration of the nature and purpose of the devachanic state of consciousness. While much of the third reply deals with mediumship, "spiritual communication," and such phenomena as psychography or automatic writing, a number of significant statements should be noted. For example, KH reminds Sinnett of the importance of an ethical life when he says that a "medium's moral state" is what determines the legitimacy of the phenomena produced.

KH's reply to Sinnett's fourth question extends the description of devachan, calling it an "ideated paradise" and "a sphere of compensative bliss." Since it is of the Ego's own making, devachan must necessarily be a state of many varieties of blissful experience. The Mahatma again emphasizes the "harmonious adjustment" of cause to effect and the fact that there are intelligences—Dhyan Chohans—who unfailingly "guide" the "impulses," or energies, that create the appropriate conditions for both the devachanic experience and rebirth into "the next world of causes."

The Mahatma's response to Sinnett's fifth question gives us further valuable information regarding the circumstances immediately following physical death. KH's initial statement that devachan is a "spiritual condition" only in contrast to the materiality of physical existence deserves careful attention. Remember that, from the Mahatmas' point of view, and as emphasized frequently in *The Secret Doctrine*, the entire manifested system is composed of matter of various grades or levels, since spirit and matter are essentially the same and there is only one substance, whether called matter, akasha, mulaprakriti, spirit, or consciousness.

Next KH refers to the "planet of Death," so we need to pause to consider the meaning of that phrase along with two related terms, "the eighth sphere" and *Avitchi*, or, more properly, *Avichi*, as often these concepts are confused. G. de Purucker offers excellent definitions of all three terms in his *Occult Glossary*, while HPB in her *Theosophical Glossary* deals only with the term *avitchi*. In the "planet of Death," or "eighth sphere," there is no possibility of return to incarnation, while such a return is possible from the state of avitchi. The Sanskrit word *avitchi* means "waveless," suggesting stagnation or immobility, and HPB speaks of it as "a state, not necessarily after death only or between two births, for it can take place on earth as well." Similarly, in Letter 70C Sinnett is told: "We *create* ourselves our *devachan* as our *avitchi* while yet on earth." In contrast, in Letter 104 KH describes the eighth sphere, or planet of death, as the condition into which fall "absolute *nonentities*," or those "whose divine monad separated itself from the five principles during their lifetime." Fortunately, as KH states later in Letter 68, such "utter obliteration of an existence" is extremely rare.

To fully understand KH's description of the after-death "struggle" between "Upper and Lower dualities," we need to have clearly in mind the classification of the human principles as then known by Sinnett, which he presented in *Esoteric Buddhism*. The student may also refer to Letter 44, which indicates the source of each of the principles, where they return following physical death (page 119). It may even be useful to draw a diagram for oneself correlating the information in Letters 44 and 68.

KH states that at the death of the physical, the second and third principles "die with him," that is, the lower triad—the physical, the linga sharira, and prana—disappear. This leaves a four-principled entity, which results in a struggle between the dualities (atman and buddhi on the one hand, and manas and kama on the other). We should note that this differs from most Theosophical literature, which identifies a higher triad and a lower quaternary. Presumably, the "struggle" between the two duads occurs in kama-loka—defined as "the world of Desire" by KH and as "the intermediate sphere between our earth and the *Devachan*" by HPB. As is made clear in Letter 70C, the Ego is unconscious during the struggle between the two polarities.

A further very important point is to be noted in connection with the "struggle" that takes place after death. KH points out, referring to a statement HPB made to Hume, that the sixth principle, or buddhi, cannot have conscious existence in devachan "unless it assimilated some of the more abstract and pure of the mental attributes of the fifth principle . . . its *manas* (mind) and memory." Evidently, what has often been called the "higher manas" must be associated with buddhi for the latter to be conscious—a point made in a number of places both in the letters and in HPB's writings. To cite one such statement: "The supreme energy resides in the *Buddhi*; latent—when wedded to *Atman* alone, active and irresistible when galvanized by the *essence* of 'Manas' and when none of the dross of the latter commingles with that pure essence to weigh it down by its finite nature" (Letter 111, page 375). Consequently we need to take care when considering the struggle between the two polarities as pitting atman and buddhi on one side with kama and manas on the other, since the dual nature of manas makes it, as it were, a party to the fight on both sides!

Little is said regarding the next stage in the after-death life, the "Gestation" state. The question naturally arises: just what is being gestated? Presumably, it is the "new Ego," or new center of consciousness, comprised of the highest portion of manas along with buddhi and atman, a three-principled being that is then "reborn" into devachan. This is the thrust of KH's reply to Sinnett's sixth question, and it again necessitates some portion of manas being assimilated to buddhi for "*personal* individuality" to exist. KH's response 6 gives the rationale of human reincarnation and reminds us of that infallible "Law of Retribution" by which devachanic existence is blissful, whereas the karma of our "evil deeds and thoughts" awaits us when we are drawn into incarnation once more.

HPB's comments made in connection with a controversy concerning occultism and appearing in both the original French and in translation as "Theosophy and Spiritism" (*CW*, 5:36) may be useful here. The relevant portion begins on page 42 of that document:

> Four principles or constituent elements can never be found together *in the gestation state* which preceded the *Devachan* (the paradise of the Buddhist Occultists). They are separated at the entrance into *gestation*. The seventh and the sixth, that is to say the immortal *spirit* and its vehicle, the immortal or spiritual soul, enter therein *alone* . . . or, which nearly always takes place, the soul carries in the case of very good people (and even the indifferent and sometimes the very wicked), the essence, so to speak, of the fifth principle which has been withdrawn from the *personal* EGO (the material soul). It is the latter *only*, in the case of the *irredeemably wicked* and when the spiritual and impersonal soul has nothing to withdraw from its individuality (terrestrial personality) because the latter had nothing to offer but the purely material and sensual—that becomes *annihilated*. Only the individuality, which possesses the most spiritual feelings, can *survive* by uniting with the immortal principle. The "Kama-rupa," the vehicle, and the *manas*, the soul in which the personal *and animal* intelligence inheres, after having been denuded of their essence, as described, remain alone in *Kama-loka*, the intermediate sphere between our earth and the *Devachan* (the Kama-loka being the *hades* of the Greeks, the region of the shades) to be extinguished and to disappear from it after a while. This unfortunate duad forms the cast-off "tatters" of the "spiritual ego" and of the personal EGO, superior

principles which, purified of all terrestrial uncleanliness, united henceforth with the divine monad in eternity, pass into regions where the mire of the purely terrestrial *ego* cannot follow, to glean therein their reward—the effects of the causes generated—and from which they do not emerge until the next incarnation. If we maintain that the *shell*, the reflexion of the person who was, survives in the land of shades for a certain time proportionate to its constitution and then disappears, we offer nothing but the logical and philosophical. Is that annihilation? Are we *annihilationists* without knowing it because we keep insisting that the human shadow disappears from the wall when the person to whom it belongs leaves the room? And even in the case of the most depraved, when dissociated from its divine and immortal double principle, and unable to give anything to the *spiritual* EGO, the material soul is annihilated without leaving anything behind of its personal individuality, is that annihilation for the *spiritual* EGO?

There is much more to HPB's reply to the "Spiritists," and the student may wish to read the entire article as it appears in the *Collected Writings*.

KH's response 7 opens with a truly delightful description of HPB's often confused statements when she attempts to explain some aspect of the teaching. The substance of this response summarizes the stages of the after-death life and the time associated with each. There are three sub-periods, as KH terms them, the first being the time in "*Kama-Loka* (the abode of Elementaries)," later called the lower regions of the astral. Not much is said about kama-loka in this or other letters, nor, indeed, by HPB. As to its duration, KH states it "may last from a few minutes to a *number* of years," when the personal ego "enters into its 'Gestation State,'" said to be "proportionate to the *Ego's* spiritual stamina." This could be a period still in kama-loka but in its higher, or more refined, regions. Later in the letter the Mahatma mentions seven lokas, or regions, of kama-loka, not always easily defined or distinguished one from the other. As Barborka points out (see *The Divine Plan*, 398), "The upper reaches of the Kama-lokic plane and the lower levels of Devachan blend one into the other with scarcely a dividing line."

The third sub-period is the experience of devachan, which "lasts in proportion to the good Karma." This is the state of consciousness most discussed not only in this letter but in several later ones. All three of these sub-periods KH terms as "*Rupa-Lokas*," or regions of form. Note also that there is a condition of unconsciousness as the entity "dies" to "the world of bliss to be reborn in a world of causes," or, as usually expressed, takes on a new incarnation, and that KH says it is "the *monad*" that is reincarnated.

A most helpful summary of the three after-death states is found in Barborka's *Divine Plan* (pages 393–409). The student may also want to see the useful compendium compiled by Geoffrey Farthing, *After Death Consciousness and Processes*. To see how Sinnett utilized the teachings given him not only in this letter but subsequently, see the chapters "Devachan" and "Kama-Loka" in *Esoteric Buddhism*. Many students will also want to compare the teachings of the Mahatmas and HPB, as brought together in the works just named, with the later descriptions of the after-death states, including kama-loka and devachan.

Other helpful references include two significant articles that bear on after-death conditions. The first, by HPB and titled "Tibetan Teachings," was written probably in 1882 but not published until 1894, when it appeared in the journal *Lucifer* (*CW*, 6:94). The second, by the French occultist Eliphas Levi, appeared in *The Theosophist* in October 1881. Titled "Death," it includes marginal comments by KH. The article together with the marginal notes was published as an appendix in *The Letters of H. P. Blavatsky to A. P. Sinnett* and is reprinted as an appendix in the chronological edition of the letters (page 501).

In his response to Sinnett's eighth and ninth questions, KH again emphasizes that the devachanee is unable to observe the life transpiring on earth, this time saying it is because "of the Law of Bliss plus *Maya*"—a most interesting description of the devachanic state that deserves to be explored as to all that it may mean. The Mahatma points out that while "every effect must be proportionate to its cause," the working out of effects takes far more time than did the production of causes. The question of time as it refers to nonphysical existence has always been a matter for speculation. Letter 93B makes the significant statement: "The individual units of mankind remain 100 times longer in the transitory spheres of *effects* than on the globes." The student may wish to read HPB's statements on this topic in *The Key to Theosophy*. Ultimately we must reconcile for ourselves the differences among the numerous statements by various individuals as regards the length of time spent in kama-loka and in devachan.

In considering the time factor, we must not overlook the phrase, "the duration of various *Karmas*," indicating that while the law itself is universal, karma operates at many levels and therefore in multiple modes. KH stresses this point later in the letter, saying, "We have several sorts of Karma," a phrase needing further examination. For the present, we can assume that as causes are constantly being produced in all regions of our being—physical, emotional, mental, and so on— their effects must have, as it were, their own timelines, resulting in a kind of accumulative "account" of effects to be experienced in the after-death states.

The seven-fold classification of entities within what may be considered the astro-ethereal sphere surrounding our planet is most interesting as indicating the nature of the inhabitants of the kama-loka region. These entities, states KH, are in "the subjective world around us," suggesting that we are all the time surrounded by such "beings," including those who are "the *intelligent* Rulers of this world of Matter." Not only Dhyan Chohans (notably, "Ex-men," reminding us that every being in the universe was, is, or will be human) are present around us, "obedient instruments of the One" and "active agents" of that "Passive Principle" elsewhere called buddhi, but also hosts of "demons," ghosts, elementals, and so on. These include "Pisachas," the "two-principled" entities (linga-sharira, or etheric, plus prana) that HPB defines as "fading remnants of human beings . . . shells" in kama-loka (see the *Theosophical Glossary*), as well as "three-principled" beings (linga-sharira, prana, plus lower kama) whose form (rupa) is of death (mara). Indeed the entities in the subjective realms around us are legion! There are worlds within worlds, each populated by a characteristic type of entity.

KH summarizes in one statement the vastness of the system: "From 'Sukhavati' [devachan] down to the 'Territory of Doubt' [apparently the lowest region of kama-loka, about which little information is given] there is a variety of Spiritual States," or, we might say, states of consciousness in nonphysical matter. Besides these states surrounding our "globe," or planet, similar states exist elsewhere throughout the universe, as KH indicates as he refers to "the Sakwalas." The term *Sakwala* HPB defines in the *Theosophical Glossary* as "a solar system of which there is an indefinite number in the universe." Then she adds, "Each Sakwala contains earths, hells and heavens (meaning good and bad spheres . . .); attains its prime, then falls into decay and is finally destroyed at regularly recurring periods, in virtue of one immutable law." The student may wish to read HPB's full description as well as consult Buddhist texts in which this term is found.

Responding to the unnumbered question at the bottom of page 196, the Mahatma turns next in his explanation of the kama-lokic state to the fate of those who commit suicide and those whose death is the result of accident. The use of the word "accident" may seem strange, since it is generally assumed that nothing can occur outside the law of karma. Care needs to be taken, therefore, in considering what is meant by the phrase "victim of accident." Further information concerning suicides and those who meet with accidental death is given in Letters 71 and 76 (pages 216 and 239). Meanwhile, KH's statements on the subject call for careful attention, particularly regarding mediumistic communications, since that was a topic of special interest to Sinnett.

Undoubtedly, the key to the philosophical, metaphysical, and psychological system propounded by the Mahatmas lies in KH's reference to "the metaphysics of Abhidharma." As Sinnett is invited to become "thoroughly well acquainted" with the concepts of karma and nirvana, which the Mahatma tells him are "but two of the seven great Mysteries of Buddhist metaphysics," so we need to explore at least the basic principles of Buddhism. The Abhidharma (or *Abhidhamma* in Pali) is generally accounted the third of the "Pitakas," or "baskets," of Buddhist teachings. Collectively known as the Tipitaka, or "three baskets," these comprise the Vinaya Pitaka, or book of discipline, containing the rules of conduct for monks and nuns and the regulations governing the Sangha (community); the Sutra Pitaka, a compendium of the Buddha's discourses delivered during his active teaching years; and the Abhidharma, the "basket" containing the metaphysical, psychological, and ethical foundations of Buddhism. The word *Abhidharma* derives from *abhi*, meaning high or special, and *dharma*, which has many translations including "truth," "law," "duty," and "religious teaching," and has also been rendered in plural form as "factors of existence." One scholar, Bhikku U Rewata Dhamma (in the introduction to *A Comprehensive Manual of Abhidhamma*, page 3), says that the Abhidharma "articulates a comprehensive vision of the totality of experienced reality," disclosing the true nature of existence as apprehended by a mind that has penetrated to the heart of things. It is said to be the most perfect expression of the Buddha's "unimpeded omniscient knowledge," that is, a statement of the way existence appears to the mind of the fully Enlightened One. Thus simultaneously a philosophy, a psychology, and an ethic, the Abhidharma is an integrated framework of a program for liberation.

The Abhidharma consists of seven books, each containing several chapters. Bhikku U Rewata Dhamma says that to be master of Abhidharma all the seven books, together with commentaries and sub-commentaries, have to be read and re-read patiently and critically (see the introduction to *A Comprehensive Manual*). Perhaps the most accessible to be read and studied is Lama Anagarika Govinda's book *The Psychological Attitude of Early Buddhist Philosophy*. Subtitled "And Its Systematic Representation According to Abhidhamma Tradition," this work presents the fundamentals of Buddhist thought, including an excellent discussion of the Four Noble Truths. A number of texts by Buddhist scholars deal extensively with the various subjects treated in the Abhidharma. One in particular is *A Manual of Abhidhamma*, translated by Narada Maha Thera, which presents both the Pali text and English translation of "Abhidhammattha Sangaha of Acariya Anuruddha."

We may ask why KH has singled out karma and nirvana as two "doctrines" important enough to call for in-depth study and how they might be related. The statement: "We have several sorts of Karma and Nirvana in their various applications" needs to be explored by the earnest student. One question that inevitably arises concerns how the law of karma may operate differently in the human kingdom from its operation in the animal realm. Another is what aspect or aspects of karma link its operations in the various fields of application that the Mahatma mentions. In addition to numerous references not only in HPB's writings and the writings of Theosophical authors generally, an interesting work worth consulting is *The Conception of Buddhist Nirvana*, by the Indic scholar Dr. Th. Stcherbatsky. Although Stcherbatsky bases his work on a text by the Mahayana Buddhist Nagarjuna, he does compare many of Nagarjuna's teachings concerning the doctrines of causality and nirvana with those of the Theravada (and therefore Abhidhamma) teachings. Further, the work has a superb introduction with a comprehensive analysis of the subject by the late Professor Jaideva Singh, who was an active member of the Theosophical Society.

What KH calls "the question of identity between the *old* man and the *new* 'Ego'" is one that still frequently arises in connection with reincarnation and karma. The Mahatma tells Sinnett, "It is a cardinal tenet ... that, as soon as any conscious or sentient being, whether man, deva, or animal dies, a new being is produced and he or it reappears in another birth." As this statement suggests that rebirth is immediate, we need to consider other, earlier statements regarding the time spent in the three after-death states (kama-loka, the gestation period, and devachan) before an entity returns to physical incarnation. KH states that "the guiding power" is karma, combined with "*Trishna* . . . the thirst or desire to sentiently live." Similarly, HPB states: "Karma, with its army of Skandhas, waits at the threshold of Devachan," and adds later: "the Devachanic entity, even previous to birth, can be affected by the Skandhas . . . by the desire for reincarnation" (see *Key to Theosophy: An Abridgement*, 86–87).

The link, then, between the old entity and the new one lies in the skandhas, literally, "bundles" or groups of attributes, to use HPB's definition. They are the entire set of material as well as mental, emotional, and moral tendencies that together form the finite parts of any being. Therefore, it is the skandhas that create those causal vibrations that attract the reincarnating Ego back to earth existence. We should note the Mahatma's teaching: "They are ever and ceaselessly at work in preparing the abstract mould, the 'privation' of the future being." A careful study of the skandhas seems essential for understanding the twin concepts of karma and reincarnation. There are many references in the letters themselves, as well as in HPB's writings. The student may wish to consult Buddhist texts, especially those based on the Abhidharma, for additional information.

An especially helpful summary of the teaching about the skandhas is available in *The Divine Plan*, including an important point that should not be overlooked. Referring to the statement that the skandhas are "left behind" when an entity enters the devachanic period, Barborka points out: "Every Skandha has become imbedded in the imperishable part of man's constitution" (page 421). HPB says similarly (*The Secret Doctrine*, Adyar Edition, 5:560) that the "Esoteric [Skandhas have to do] with the internal and subjective man." This "imperishable" aspect of our nature that contains the skandhas is known as the "Hiranyagarbha" or "Golden Egg" and constitutes what HPB called the "auric envelope."

Certainly one reason why the Mahatma has given so much attention to karma and the skandhas is to stress the undesirability, even danger, of resorting to mediumship. After explaining to Sinnett that "disembodied entities" who seek to satisfy their thirst for life are drawn to mediums, "And now, you may understand why we oppose so strongly Spiritualism and mediumship." We may well ask today whether the same strictures apply to the phenomenon of channeling about which much has been written.

KH's digression, as he calls it, in explaining to Sinnett that he got himself into a "scrape" with his superior (presumably the Mahachohan), gives us further insight into the nature of the Adept. While the Mahatma was evidently free enough to attempt the experiment of appearing to the English medium Eglinton on board the *Vega* (impersonating himself, as he wrote at the time; see Letter 55), his freedom was nevertheless circumscribed, such that he was reprimanded, we might say, for the consequences. We should note, too, the statement in the postscript: "But for the Rule that forbids our using one minim of power until every ordinary means has been tried and failed." KH might have used the power of precipitation to produce his letters—and we know this power was utilized for many of the earlier letters, although it was also apparently prohibited at one time. However, that is a story we have already touched upon.

Regarding the nature of the Adept, we can note that each of the Mahatmas is quite individual in what we may term their human side. KH refers to this in the postscript to Letter 68, when commenting on the "miserable appearance" of his letters, which, Mrs. Sinnett remarked, "make us as human beings, more thinkable entities." We may note, too, the reference toward the end of the letter to Sinnett's piano playing, an interesting reference because we know from other sources that KH himself was an accomplished musician; indeed, in other letters he refers to music and such composers as Mozart.

In the final paragraph on page 201, KH enters into a discussion of "individuality" and "personality." We can recall, in this connection, M's answer to Sinnett's question number 7 in Letter 44 on this subject. All of this material needs to be read very carefully so that it is quite clear in the student's mind "the difference that exists between individuality and personality" and the comparison between those two terms and the "doctrine," as KH calls it, of the "*Pacceka-Yana* and of *Amata-Yana*." Clarifying the distinction between the two "paths," or *yanas*, may even aid us in understanding the perplexing question as to the number of "incarnations" referred to in Letter 67. At least we must clarify for ourselves why KH refers to these two paths in order to stress the distinction between the "personal Ego" and "the Spiritual Soul."

Sinnett's final question concerning the "divisions of the seven principles" was never answered. While the Mahatma promised to send a "fly-sheet" indicating the "roots and Branches" of the fourth and fifth principles, kama and manas, there is no record that this was ever received. Perhaps we are intended to work out for ourselves how the various principles are divided and subdivided. Regarding the root of each principle, we can see again the answer to question 3 in Letter 44.

Significant certainly is KH's statement in the postscript concerning the reason so much "information about the A.E. Philosophy" ["A.E." refers to Aryan-Esoteric; T. Subba Row uses the same term when writing about the classification of the principles] is being shared with Hume and Sinnett. They seemed the "most likely to utilise [*sic*] for the general good the facts given you. You must regard them received in trust for the benefit of the whole Society; to be turned over, and employed and re-employed in many ways and in all ways that are good."

Undoubtedly this statement is as valid for us today as it was for the two Englishmen then. Are we utilizing the teachings that we have "received in trust" from our predecessors for the benefit of all humanity?

The postscript is also interesting for its revealing the extent to which KH is aware of what is occurring not only in Sinnett's life, but also with HPB, Olcott, and Damodar. The reference to "your *Pioneer* connection" suggests that the Mahatma knows of Sinnett's difficulties with the proprietors of the newspaper of which he was editor; indeed, he was given his termination notice less than six months after receiving this letter. HPB, who was ill and depressed, was denied permission to visit the Masters because of the unsettled conditions resulting from hostilities between England and Egypt (see *LBS*, 28; she received permission later—see Letters 85 and 92). Here, too, is the first intimation that Damodar may be removed from the outer scene of affairs (see *LBS*, 28). As for Olcott, he records in *Old Diary Leaves*, (2:368) that he sailed from Bombay for Sri Lanka on July 15, 1882, that date aiding us in dating this very long letter.

And so concludes one of the most remarkable letters in the entire series, replete with teaching concerning after-death states as well as so many other aspects of the philosophy. Indeed, one could spend a lifetime exploring all that KH has given of the esoteric doctrine in this one letter. The postscript ends with an exceptionally beautiful passage in which KH expresses his longing for rest and indicates that he at some stage in his progress had himself realized the nature of nirvana.

LETTER 69

A t the conclusion of Letter 68, just prior to the lengthy postscript, KH asks Sinnett, "How long do you propose to abstain from interrogation marks?" It is evident from Letter 69 that the Englishman did not "abstain" for long from asking at least two further questions, to which KH gives only brief replies. The opening paragraph implies that Sinnett's way of life is what prevents him from physically remembering any spiritual experience, and that psychic development has little to do with spiritual progress. The Mahatma's words: "The sense of magnetic refreshment is no true measure of spiritual benefit, and you may even attain greater spiritual progress whilst your psychic development appears to stand still" give us much to contemplate.

The response to Sinnett's first question seems amply clear as to require no comment. While the Sanskrit term *loka* actually means "place" or "locality," or even "world" or "plane," the Mahatmas again and again stress that in the esoteric teachings it refers to states of consciousness. KH comments that those states "belong to the various ethereal hierarchies or classes of Dhyanis and Pitris . . . some— among the Deva classes." Each state of consciousness, or loka, may be embodied in or by a particular class of dhyani or deva, that is, just as we in the human state "create" our world, so at subtler levels, it is the dhyanis or devas who "create" their world or loka in accordance with their state of consciousness.

The answer to whatever was Sinnett's second question is reminiscent of what the Mahatma M said concerning "Real Knowledge" in the first set of Cosmological Notes (page 508). Although the "verse quoted," to which KH refers, remains unidentified, it may have been something Sinnett was planning to use in one of the series called "Fragments of Occult Truth." KH's definition of the phrase "Real Knowledge" is most helpful and accords perfectly with M's statement that it "deals with eternal verities and primal causes" and is a condition when the Adept's mind is "*en rapport* with the Universal Mind." How to bring about that "spiritual state" is among the tasks that confront us on the spiritual path.

LETTERS 70A, 70B, AND 70C

The prefatory note to Letters 70A, 70B, and 70C provides an excellent summary of the background for these letters and need not be repeated here. From time to time, correspondence in HPB's journal *The Theosophist* or her editorial comments appended to such correspondence would call forth questions from Hume and Sinnett, which one of the Mahatmas answered, usually KH. Such is the situation with these letters, and we are fortunate to have both Hume's letter to the Master (Letter 70A) and Sinnett's letter to HPB (Letter 70B) after KH requested him to respond to the member whose letter to *The Theosophist* precipitated the entire exchange. Notably, this member, N. D. Khandalawala, was a provincial judge, a member of the General Council of the Society, and a loyal supporter of both HPB and Olcott, particularly during the Coulomb affair, which developed some years later. Khandalawala's letter, in turn, was prompted by an article by the French occultist and Kabbalist Eliphas Levi (*The Theosophist*, October 1881), referred to in the discussion of Letter 68, reprinted as an appendix in the chronological edition.

Letter 70C consists of KH's responses to questions Hume and Sinnett raised in their letters (70A and 70B). It begins rather abruptly with a denial that Levi is "in any *direct* conflict with our teachings." The Mahatma's comments here regarding what is "remembered" in the first after-death state, kama-loka can be compared with his response to the second question in Letter 68.

One of the most significant statements concerning what endures after death is in this letter: "*Love* and *Hatred* are the only *immortal* feelings, the only survivals from the wreck of . . . the phenomenal world." Notably, this statement is related and therefore limited to "feelings," that part of the kamic principle that is immortal. KH returns to this theme at the conclusion of his letter: "Unless a man *loves* well or *hates* as well, he will be neither in Devachan nor in Avitchi. 'Nature spews the luke-warm out of her mouth' means only that she annihilates their *personal* Egos . . . in the Kama Loka and the Devachan." The words KH places within quote marks are based on the New Testament text *The Revelation*, 3:16: "So then because thou art lukewarm, and neither cold nor hot, I will spue thee out of my mouth."

There is certainly much to ponder in KH's statement regarding love and hatred, especially in light of his later statements in this letter concerning immortality: "We call 'immortal' but the one *Life* in its universal collectivity and entire or Absolute Abstraction; that which has neither beginning nor end, nor any break in its continuity. . . . Immortal then is he, in the *panaeonic* Immortality whose distinct consciousness and perception of *Self under whatever form* undergoes no disjunction at any time, not for one second, during the period of his *Egoship*. . . . An *Ego* like yours or mine, may be immortal from one to the other Round."

Perhaps it is only such distinct feelings as love and hatred that insure the continuity of a center of consciousness, which KH calls

"Egoship," through the various cycles of races or rounds. I base this conjecture on KH's statement: "I remain as Koothoomi in my *Ego* throughout the whole series of births and lives across the seven worlds and *arupa*-lokas until finally I land again on this earth among the fifth race men of the full fifth Round beings." KH's definition of immortality is also noteworthy: "Complete or true immortality,—which means an unlimited *sentient* existence, can have no breaks and stoppages, no arrest of *Self*-consciousness."

Some care is called for regarding the distinction between the terms "personal Ego" and "Spiritual Ego." KH speaks of "the highest Chohans" as "the Planetary *conscious* 'Ego-Spirits,' which may be another designation for "Planetary Spirits," about which much was written in Letter 18. KH also says, "The Monad 'never perishes whatever happens'"—a statement that requires us to clarify the terms "Ego," "Egoship," and so on, especially in relation to the monad.

KH's several statements about immortality need to be studied in depth. I am reminded of HPB's statements in *The Secret Doctrine* to the effect that we must win our immortality. Recall that in Letter 49 (page 139), KH tells Sinnett: " . . . and immortality is *conditional*." Other useful references are the chapter "Personal Immortality" in E. L. Gardner's book *The Wider View* and HPB's Esoteric Section Instructions (*CW*, vol. 12).

Especially noteworthy is KH's statement regarding the "immortal feeling of love and sympathetic attraction," informing Sinnett that the "seeds" of that feeling "are planted in the fifth . . . blossom . . . in and around the fourth, but whose roots have to penetrate deep into the sixth principle." Here manas is the "soil" in which are planted the "seeds" of love, in order that they may "blossom" in kama (the fourth principle), while the "roots" are in buddhi (the sixth principle)—a beautiful description of how the principles intertwine or, we may say, are interdependent. Further, since KH points out that we create our own devachan as well as our own avitchi (see the discussion of Letter 68), we could say that in the creation of devachan, it is the immortal feeling of love that is essential, while avitchi is "created" by feelings of hatred.

KH then points out that the strongest feeling within us at the moment of death (and note especially that the brain is "the last organ that dies") may be what determines our future life. The Mahatma returns to this point in Letter 93B (page 326), where he writes: "At the last moment, the whole life is reflected in our memory and emerges from all the forgotten nooks and corners picture after picture, one event after the other. The dying brain dislodges memory with a strong supreme impulse. . . . That impression and thought which was the strongest naturally becomes the most vivid and survives so to say all the rest which now vanish and disappear for ever, to reappear but in Devachan."

We may well wonder at KH's assertion: "The potency for *evil* is as great in man—aye—greater—than the potentiality for *good*." This follows on the statement that not all "the evil co-workers . . . are annihilated," leading one to speculate on the uses of evil in the world. Two useful essays on the subject are the chapter "The Use of Evil" in Annie Besant's *The Spiritual Life* and the chapter "Theosophical Interpretations of Evil" in *Theosophy* by Dr. Robert Ellwood. As Dr. Ellwood so rightly states: "All disharmonies can be understood as conditions logically inherent in a manifested consciousness-matter universe, or inseparable from the struggles and dangers embedded in the developmental path sentient beings in such a universe must follow." After examining a number of explanations for the existence of evil, Dr. Ellwood concludes: "We can realize there is that in each of us which never has been, and can never be, wholly under the power of any evil. For its nature comes from realms higher than evil's reach, and to them it will return." As with so many questions that arise from studying the Mahatmas' teachings, students must determine for themselves how best to interpret those teachings, particularly as they relate to our own lives.

KH next refers Sinnett to one of HPB's statements in *Isis Unveiled* that the English Theosophist Charles Carlton Massey had evidently referred to and mistakenly interpreted. The question turns on the nature of the immortality experienced by those who engage in what the Mahatma terms a "co-partnership with nature for evil." The passage reads:

> The occult doctrine recognizes another possibility; albeit so rare and so vague that it is really useless to mention it. Even the modern Occidental occultists deny it, though it is universally accepted in Eastern countries. When, through vice, fearful crimes and animal passions, a disembodied spirit has fallen to the eighth sphere—the allegorical Hades, and the *Gehenna* of the Bible—the nearest to our earth—he can, with the help of that glimpse of reason and consciousness left to him, repent; that is to say, he can, by exercising the remnants of his will power, strive upward, and like a drowning man, struggle once more to the surface. . . . A strong aspiration to retrieve his calamities, a pronounced desire, will draw him once more into the earth's atmosphere. (*Isis*, 1:352–53)

Clearly, such a disembodied spirit will have a difficult time but *can*—perhaps in the higher regions of kama-loka—make the grade, as it were. HPB, later in her comment, calls attention to the fact that "Jesus, full of justice and divine love to humanity, *healed*" such spirits.

The Mahatma turns next to statements in Hume's letter regarding "the spirits of suicides and the victims of accident or violence." The question of whether, given the law of karma, any event can be called an accident remains a puzzle for many. KH's answer here solves that problem: accidental death can mean either that the "victim . . . is *irresponsible* for his death" or the death was caused by "some action in a previous life or an antecedent birth." In the latter case, "It was not the *direct* result of an act deliberately committed by the *personal* Ego of that life" in which the so-called accident occurred.

A study of KH's comments at this point could lead the student to believe there are separate Egos for each incarnation. When considered from the standpoint that each incarnation is accompanied by a new set of skandhas, or a new center of consciousness created by the skandhas, then we can understand the sense in which this could be true. KH's explanation may remind us of the biblical story of the man born blind who is brought to Jesus for healing, and the question that is asked: "Who did sin, this man, or his parents, that he was born blind?" To which Jesus responds: "Neither hath this man sinned, nor his parents: but that the works of God should be made manifest in him." We could interpret "the works of God," as some students have, to mean the fulfillment of the Law.

Especially significant are KH's words: "We tell you what we know, *for we are made to learn it through personal experience.*" What for us is usually theory, hypothesis, often speculation, is, for the Adept, knowledge gained not only from books and spiritual teachers but in some manner directly via experience—a clue for us, surely, as we attempt to ascend the ladder of spiritual awakening. Reading on, we can pause to consider the meaning of "Akasic Samadhi," a phrase that does not seem to be identical with the condition known as devachan.

Regarding the question of what occurs to the suicide, KH says, "It is the *cause* not the *effect* that will be punished, especially an unforeseen though probable effect." He says further, "*Motive* is everything and man is punished in a case of *direct* responsibility, never otherwise." In this connection, the student may wish to read the very interesting chapter "After-Death Experiences of Suicides" by Annie Besant in *Talks with a Class.* In the course of that chapter, Dr. Besant comments upon

> the case of the suicide which has been committed from a noble motive. I remember HPB mentioning that the suicide of the Czar Nicholas of Russia, just before the end of the Crimean War, was such a case. It was not known publicly that he had committed suicide, but as a matter of fact he had killed himself. His motive in killing himself was to put an end to the war. His life was an obstacle to that. His people were greatly devoted to him, for there was in the past a great devotion on the part of the mass of the Russian people to their

Czar: they looked upon him as their father. They would not consent to stop the war at the cost of his humiliation; they wanted to go on fighting on the vague chance that they might win in time, and thus save the Czar from the humiliation of defeat. He saw, as I suppose most of the people with more knowledge saw, that the defeat was inevitable because they were overmatched. He determined, therefore, to kill himself, so as to remove from his people the motive for continuing the war. . . . There you have a distinct act of self-sacrifice. He did not kill himself to escape something for himself, but to save the suffering which his people were enduring. It was an act of love and self-sacrifice. (pages 79–80)

As we know, both Englishmen were much interested in the phenomena of Spiritualism and continually questioned the Mahatmas regarding the possibility of communication with the "spirits" of the dead. Hume again raises this issue, asking why "the spirits of very fair average good people dying *natural* deaths" could not communicate—to which KH now replies: "Why should they?" However, his main point is that if there is such communication, the entity on the other side is already a "shell." He also makes a significant statement that we should not overlook: what is met with on the other side, at least in kama-loka, is the "*creature* not [the] creator," which is to say, we meet with that which we ourselves have produced during the lifetime just closed.

Hume, pressing the issue of communication with the "spirits" of the deceased, proposes that there are "pure circles" in which "the highest morality" is taught. KH naturally denies all of this, adding: "Preaching and teaching morality with an end in view proves very little." He cites the case of a "Dugpa-Shammar," a shaman-sorcerer or what HPB calls an "Adept of Black Magic," who was quite an orator, almost mesmerizing people with his preaching, but whose moral character left much to be desired. One fact seems very clear: no one becomes a saint simply by passing through the gateway of death and then appearing among the spirits in the séance room!

In concluding his letter, KH comments on a statement in Sinnett's letter (70B) concerning the "obscuration," or pralaya, of a planet or globe at the conclusion of a round. What both Sinnett and KH write on this subject deserve careful attention, for apparently some "fifth Round men" are evolving on a globe other than our present Globe D (the earth). KH's words can be interpreted variously, particularly in view of his indication that "the races of the fifth Round men . . . will 'be behind'" those who are "now here," which seems to mean on earth in our present fourth round.

At this point the student may find it helpful to review the information so far given us in the letters (particularly Letters 18, 44, 66, and 67) regarding the subject of the rounds, including the periods of "obscuration." While further information is given in later letters, it is useful to have as firm an understanding as possible as we progress. In addition to reading Sinnett's exposition in *Esoteric Buddhism,* the student will find especially valuable chapter 9, "The Doctrine of the Rounds" in Barborka's *The Divine Plan,* especially his explanation of the inner and outer rounds.

KH makes the significant assertion: "Nature is too well, too mathematically adjusted to cause mistakes to happen in the exercise of her functions," recalling to mind the statement in Letter 66 regarding the "principle of acceleration and retardation," which seems to provide the time necessary for each of the "kingdoms" (mineral, plant, animal, etc.) to complete its work before a universal pralaya occurs. The student may wish to reread KH's statements in Letter 67 responding to Sinnett's question regarding the kinds of pralaya (see pages 184–87).

Letter 70C concludes with KH's request to Sinnett to "reconcile" the teachings given by HPB in *Isis* with those presented by Eliphas Levi—teachings that appeared contradictory and therefore led to these three letters. Although KH tells Sinnett that he is sending him some of Levi's unpublished manuscripts, no record is available as to whether this was ever done. However, volume 4 of HPB's *Collected Writings* includes two sets of "Footnotes to 'Gleanings from Eliphas Levi,'" both sets preceded by HPB's editorial comments.

LETTER 71

Rather than a full letter, Letter 71 consists of two brief notes in KH's handwriting attached to proofs of a "Letter on Theosophy," which was to be sent to Stainton Moses in London for publication in the Spiritualist journal *Light*. The "Letter on Theosophy" was written by Sinnett and then sent to KH for review; hence the attached notes with the Mahatma's comments.

The first note concludes with a poem, which KH indicates is "Not for publication." Since the Mahatma gives no source for the very short verse, perhaps he himself authored those lines.

The second note is a further comment on the fate of people who commit suicide, distinguishing between those who were "good," those who were "neither good nor bad," and the ones who were markedly evil. Incidentally, HPB wrote two comments on the subject of suicide about the same time as this note from KH. The first is in an editorial footnote to "Letters on Esoteric Theosophy" published in *The Theosophist* in September 1882 (see *CW*, 4:189). The second is an article, "Is Suicide a Crime?" which appeared in *The Theosophist* two months later (see *CW*, 4:257–61).

LETTER 72

The opening statement in Letter 72 refers to a comment KH made in a footnote in Letter 68 concerning the skandhas. In that footnote (see page 199), the Mahatma quotes from the Abhidharma and other Northern Buddhist texts, "all of which show Gautama Buddha saying that none of these Skandhas is the soul; since the body is constantly changing." KH then quotes directly: "Mendicants!

remember that there is within man *no abiding principle* whatever, and that only the *learned* disciple who acquires wisdom, in saying '*I am*'— knows what he is saying." Sinnett asked whether the sixth and seventh principles were not "abiding" ones, to which KH now responds that "neither Atma nor Buddhi ever were *within* man," a response that needs considerable reflection.

Perhaps again indicating KH's European education, the Mahatma refers Sinnett to two Greek classical philosophers, Plutarch and Anaxagoras. Plutarch, the Greek biographer and philosopher of the Neoplatonic school, is chiefly known for his major work, *Parallel Lives,* in which he uses both factual and mythical anecdotes to portray character and its moral implications. Anaxagoras is accounted the first Western philosopher to hold that an all-pervading mind is the primary cause of physical change. Socrates, one of his pupils, professed to have learned the pre-eminence of mind or intelligence, the *nous,* in creation from Anaxagoras. In the *Theosophical Glossary* HPB defines *nous* as "a Platonic term for the Higher Mind or Soul," adding: "It means Spirit as distinct from animal Soul—*psyche*; divine consciousness or mind in man; *Nous* was the designation given to the Supreme deity (third *logos*) by Anaxagoras. Taken from Egypt where it was called *Nout,* it was adopted by the Gnostics for their first conscious Aeon which, with the Occultists, is the third *logos,* cosmically, and the third "principle" (from above) or *manas,* in man."

KH concludes his explication of the well-known statement that there is "within man no abiding principle" with another quotation from one of the sutra texts attributed to the Buddha. It is a beautiful statement equating the "one principle of life" with "the fire that burns in the eternal light," the ultimate reality that is "above, beneath, and everywhere."

The remainder of what Sinnett has called "extracts from letters" that he and Hume received from KH deals with Sinnett's desire to become clairvoyant. The Mahatma refers to such a faculty as the development of "lucidity," or, we might say, complete clarity of inner vision, clarity of thought, or spiritual perception. Although KH indicates that such "lucidity" may be developed by anyone—that it is based not on the faculty of reason but rather on "natural instinctive perceptions"— and even gives Sinnett the method used by their chelas for developing it, Sinnett does not seem to have ever undertaken the work required, nor is there any record that he was or became clairvoyant. Whether he adhered to the dietary advice the Mahatma gave we do not know. Altogether, Letter 72 contains some interesting information, not only helpful in explaining the philosophy but practical as well, and revealing the attention that KH gave to Sinnett's inquiries.

LETTERS 73 AND 74

Letters 73 and 74 must be considered together for the simple reason that Letter 74, while addressed to Hume, was enclosed in Letter 73, which was to Sinnett. The circumstances that called forth the rather long letter to Hume are well explained in the prefatory notes and need no comment. However, two points in Letter 73 seem unusual—first, that KH is "*forced* by the Chohan," to reply to Hume's letter complaining about the young psychic Edmund Fern, who had been placed on probation by the Mahatma M; second, that KH is asking Sinnett whether the letter he has written should be "sent or destroyed."

In regard to the first point, evidently every effort is being made to keep Hume satisfied or at least within the fold, although eventually he did resign from the Society. As to the second point, it offers a further glimpse into the close association between the Mahatma and Sinnett and the great regard the former had for the latter, addressing the Englishman as "My dearest Friend" and trusting his judgment as to the suitability of what he has written to Hume. However, as the prefatory note to Letter 74 indicates, in a postscript to Letter 75, the Mahatma M asks Sinnett not to send the letter to Hume but "to lock the foolish letter . . . into your trunk and leave it there to roost until in demand." Evidently Sinnett did just that, for we have the letter in its original form, and we can be most grateful for that since it contains valuable comments regarding chelaship.

The opening paragraph of Letter 74 sets forth so very clearly once again the Mahatmas' position in taking on and maintaining the correspondence with the two Englishmen. In effect, if Sinnett and Hume wish to receive their instruction, they must accept the Mahatmas' conditions and not attempt to impose their own. While the letter is written to Hume, we need to consider to what extent KH's words apply to our own attitude toward the Mahatmas. Certainly KH writes frankly, and the entire letter, relating as it does to the Master-pupil relationship, deserves the most careful study.

The two Englishmen felt that the very concept of probation, with what they saw as humiliating tests involving methods that seemed to include fraud and deception, was reprehensible. Yet now KH states unequivocally that probation is "something every chela who does not want to remain simply ornamental has *nolens volens* to undergo for a more or less prolonged period." And while warned beforehand of temptations and possible deceptions, a chela "under probation is allowed to think and do whatever he likes." Therefore, states KH, "the chela is at perfect liberty, *and often quite justified from the standpoint of appearances*—to suspect his Guru of being 'a fraud' as the elegant word stands." It appears that everything is done to see if the pupil will "deviate from the path of truth and honesty."

KH reminds Hume that he had earlier accused the Mahatmas of resorting to jesuitical methods. This was Hume's comment (see Letter 8) regarding the Mahatma's attitude toward Olcott: "I cannot but take exception to the terms in which you praise him, the whole burthen of which is that he never questions but always obeys. This is the Jesuit organization over again—and this renunciation of private judgment, this abnegation of one's own personal responsibility, this accepting the dictates of outside voices as a substitute for one's own conscience, is to my mind a *sin* of no ordinary magnitude." KH points out in no uncertain terms what he sees as the differences between the motivations of the Jesuits and the Brotherhood. As the Mahatma writes, "*apparently* our systems of training do not differ much" from an external point of view, but obviously they differ in the one thing that matters: the conveyance of truth. For, the Mahatma adds, "*we* know that what we impart is truth, the only truth and nothing but the truth." The entire passage here should be examined closely, as KH contrasts the essential basis of the training given by the Jesuits with that of the Brotherhood, pointing out: "We seek to bring men to sacrifice their personality—a passing flash—for the welfare of the whole humanity, hence for their own *immortal* Egos."

Now we come on what may be a rather puzzling statement and again one that needs to be examined thoughtfully. It appears that the Mahatmas utilize the dugpas, which HPB defines as sorcerers and "adepts of black magic," to draw "out the whole *inner* nature of the chela, most of the nooks and corners of which would remain dark and concealed for ever, were not an opportunity afforded to test each of these corners in turn." I suggest that in this instance the term *dugpas* may refer not so much to those entities that have been called the Brothers of the Shadow as to rather mischievous entities who can obviously be employed by the Mahatmas.

KH continues to discuss the difference between Eastern and Western ideas of motives, truthfulness, honesty, and so on: "We both [the Mahatmas and the Englishmen] believe that it is moral to tell the truth and immoral to lie; but here every analogy stops and our notions diverge in a very remarkable degree." Today we may well ask ourselves to what extent we accept what KH regards as a divergence of views. Especially interesting, in the light of KH's analysis of the distinction between Eastern and Western attitudes, are his remarks regarding the tendency to pretend to a feeling and the actual exhibition of that feeling, including his observation that "in the ideas of the West, everything is brought down to *appearances*."

KH next tells Hume: "Were M one to ever descend to an explanation, he could have told you," and so KH proceeds to give his idea of what his Brother might have written, a long passage showing the close rapport between the two Brothers and KH's comprehension of M's sense of humor as well as his somewhat disconcerting bluntness. This includes delineating many of Hume's good points; perhaps KH is speaking as much for himself as for his Brother when he writes: "While openly expressing my dislike for your haughtiness and selfishness . . . I frankly recognize and express my admiration for your many other admirable qualities, for your sterling merits. . . . Not only do I not bear you malice, and like you none the less . . . what I say is a strict reality, the expression of my genuine feelings, not merely words written to satisfy a sense of assumed duty." Indeed, later in the letter, KH expresses similar views as his own: "I wish you to believe me, my dearest Brother, when I say that my regard and respect for you . . . is great and very sincere. Nor am I likely to forget, whatever happens, that for many months past, without expecting or asking for any reward or advantage for yourself you have worked and toiled, day after day, for the good of the Society and of humanity at large in the only hope of doing good." We may certainly recall KH's statement in Letter 2: "Ingratitude is not among our vices."

Remembering that KH has told Sinnett in Letter 73 that he was "*forced* by the Chohan" to reply to Hume's letter, one might think that the Mahatma would be content with having conveyed what he feels would have been Morya's response. Now, however, KH proceeds to add his own views, thus lengthening his proposed letter to Hume. As elsewhere, one senses that KH not only enjoys writing but also wants to make very clear the Mahatmas' position on any issue that the Englishmen raise. In this case, the issue is that of chelaship, which KH has already touched on earlier in the letter and now takes up again. He reminds Hume that at different times the Englishman has offered himself as a chela, "but the first duty of one is to hear without anger or malice anything the guru may say." KH also reiterates a condition for chelaship set forth in Letter 2: "If you really want to be a *chela i.e.* to become the recipient of our mysteries, *you* have to adapt yourself to *our* ways, not we to *yours*." The student may wish to review that statement in conjunction with reading this passage.

The long paragraph covering more than two pages in the text calls for careful study, as several important points are made. We can note, once again, that KH is evidently junior to M in the statement that if M allows it, KH will see that Hume understands clearly the one thing that could "either make us friends and brothers" or would bring about the break that ultimately did occur. What that "one thing" is we can only surmise, but it undoubtedly concerned the "rules" governing chelaship. KH also refers to the upcoming anniversary of the Society (November 1882), marking the conclusion of the first seven-year cycle, when there could well be some crisis. That anniversary is referred to in several letters and appears to have been a particularly critical time that the Society nevertheless passed through safely.

KH returns to the question of honesty, touched on earlier in the letter, making a puzzling reference to the "ruffian Mussulman menial." This is none other than the individual who used the pseudonym "Moorad Ali Beg," also known as "Mirza Murad Ali Beg"—the Englishman Godolphin Mitford, author of the article "Elixir of Life," which Hume has been told to read. Evidently this person was intent on spreading falsehoods about Hume, the Society, and also two members, General and Mrs. Watson, about whom we know nothing other than this brief reference. However, the student may find of special interest a letter written by HPB at about the same time as this Mahatma letter. HPB's letter may be found in her letters to Sinnett (*LBS*, 29–34).

In regard to this recital of lies and appearances, KH then writes: "Apart from this I concede to you the right of feeling angry with M; for he has done something that though it is in strict accordance with our rules and methods, will, when known be deeply resented by a Western mind, and, had I known it in time to stop it, I would have certainly prevented it from being done." Further on, of course, KH says: "Even I will never interfere in his [M's] ways of training, however distasteful they may be to me personally." What M did we never learn, although undoubtedly it was in some way connected with Hume. In a later letter, undated and designated only as Letter A (page 463), we find the interesting statement: "Know my friend that in our world though we may differ in methods we can never be opposed in *principles of action.*"

KH points out that a chela is to be "tested, tempted and examined by all and every means, so as to have his real nature drawn out." Some may agree with Hume and Sinnett that such "testing" does not seem in accord with our normal standards of honesty and integrity, that it appears too drastic and borders on underhanded methods. But KH continues: "It is not enough to know thoroughly what the chela is capable of doing or not doing at the time and under the circumstances during the period of probation. We have to know of what he *may* become capable under different and every kind of opportunities." Even if such testing seems quite legitimate, we may question the methods used, in light of KH's remark that the chela (in this case, Edmund Fern) "was, is, and will be *tempted* to do all manner of wrong things." We can only acknowledge that whatever may be the tests and the temptations to which a chela or pupil is subjected, they are all in accordance with the rules of the occult Brotherhood.

Concerning Fern and his eventual expulsion from the Society, a most interesting letter to Fern from the Mahatma M, with a foreword by C. Jinarajadasa, is included in *Letters from the Masters of the Wisdom*, Second Series. There are also references to Fern in the work by Sven Eek, *Damodar*.

Apparently, now and again Sinnett and Hume thought the teachings they were given contained inconsistencies and even contradictions. KH refers to their questions and suggests that the two men "take notes of . . . the inconsistencies . . . and . . . the supposed contradictions" and send them to the Mahatma, who will "prove to you that there is not one for him who knows well the whole doctrine." KH adds that if Hume (as well as Sinnett) "had but patience, you would have received all that you would like to get out of our *speculative* philosophy," pointing out that it was necessarily speculative for "all but adepts." This is a very good reminder for all students while endeavoring to understand the teachings given in both the Mahatmas' letters and the writings of HPB. The teachings must remain speculative until we can prove them for ourselves.

So KH concludes a long letter to Hume, occasioned by Hume's complaints about his young secretary, Fern. It is a letter that contains much useful and valuable information about chelaship, what is demanded of any individual who desires to undertake the rigors of that kind of relationship with an Adept teacher, and what it means to be placed on probation.

LETTER 75

Letter 75 is quite a fascinating letter, showing both KH's delightful sense of humor and his deep regard for Sinnett as a friend in whom he can confide what he terms, perhaps with tongue in cheek, a "dreadful secret." It is, says KH, "a doleful story of a discomfiture," the tale of his own inadvertent involvement in the relationship among Morya, Hume, and Fern. Incidentally, we learn at the outset that the Mahatma's brief note (Letter 73) in which was enclosed the long letter to Hume (Letter 74) was mailed by regular post from the town of Bussawala in the Central Province by a friend characterized as "*free,*" which could mean someone who is not a chela on probation or who has not taken the vows of the Brotherhood.

KH's characterization of M as "that bulky Brother of mine" and then speaking of the "disreputable conduct of my wicked, more than ever laughing Brother" must bring a smile to the reader. Later in the letter he speaks of M as "that *alter ego* of mine, the wicked and 'imperious' chap, your 'Illustrious,' who took undue advantage of my confidence in him." (Later KH writes of M as "the *Illustrious*—who is a *pukka* [genuine] orthodox Occultist.") There is also wry humor in his comment that he has "come to regret . . . tasting in Europe of the fruit of the Tree of the Knowledge of Good and Evil," a reference to his student days in the West. Evidently, he studied in three universities: the University of Dublin, Trinity

College, in Ireland; Oxford University in England; and Heidelberg University in Germany. Be that as it may, he says, even if he had stayed in Asia, ignorant of Western ways, he would be laughing. As the story unfolds in this rather long letter, no doubt Sinnett was inclined to laugh—as we reading it today are as well—for it is an amusing tale despite all.

Another aspect of the letter that should not be overlooked are the several allusions to historic events and individuals that seem to come from KH's European education. For example, he compares himself to Warren Hastings, first Governor-General of British India, who took on himself responsibility for the misdeeds of the East India Company: "I am the W.H. for the sins of the Brotherhood." He also mentions Jean Paul Richter, pseudonym for Johann Paul Friedrick Richter, a German author of the late eighteenth and early nineteenth centuries who came into vogue when some of his writings were translated into English. And we must not omit KH's characterization of Fern as a "tavern Pericles," an allusion to the philandering Athenian statesman who lived about 400 BC.

We may note also the various epithets KH uses for both Hume and Fern, as they reveal his outspoken nature. For example, writing that Hume's "chief and only motive power . . . is really *bona fide* Selfishness, egotism," KH adds, "'Egotistic philanthropist' is a word which paints his portrait at full length." And there is a certain satire in the Mahatma's comment that "Hume's pride and self-opinion" make him wish "that all mankind had only two bent knees to make *puja* [worship] to him." As for Fern, who seems to have quite fooled Hume ("*bamboozled* him" is the phrase KH uses), KH calls him "that little double-dealing monkey." Of particular interest to us is the fact that since Morya had placed Fern under probation, he was not of concern to KH ("He did not interest me, I knew nothing of him, beyond his remarkable faculties"); at the same time, as we know from Letter 73, KH was "*forced* by the Chohan" to respond to Hume's complaints about Fern. Indeed, *their* ways are not always easy to understand!

Alongside KH's "doleful story," Letter 75 contains information concerning chelaship that adds to our understanding of that state in the training of an individual who aspires toward adeptship. So while reading the letter we can give particular attention to those statements that give us further insight into the Brothers' ways. Early on in the letter, KH states, "When we take *candidates* for chelas, they take the vow of secrecy and silence respecting every order they may receive." He adds, "One has to prove himself fit for *chelaship*, before he can find out whether he is fit for *adeptship*." Clearly, there are definite steps to take and rules to follow if one seeks to tread the spiritual path.

One aspect of chelaship frequently referred to in the letters is the period of probation, which we know was resented and strenuously objected to particularly by Hume. On several occasions both Sinnett and Hume expressed their disapproval of the "tests" given to all would-be chelas. As KH writes toward the end of Letter 75: "M. was training and testing Fern," and we know that ultimately Fern did fail as a chela. So we may ponder KH's words: "Do not allow your self to misconceive the real position of our Great Brotherhood. Dark and tortuous as may seem to your Western mind the paths trodden, and the ways by which our candidates are brought to the great Light— you will be the first to approve of them when you know *all*. Do not judge on appearances—for you may thereby do a great wrong, and lose your own personal chances to learn more. Only be vigilant— and watch."

KH also remarks on the method employed in writing the letters: "Very often our very letters—unless something very important and secret—are written in our handwritings by our chelas. Thus, last year, some of my letters to you were *precipitated*, and when sweet and easy precipitation was stopped—well I had but to compose my mind, assume an easy position, and—think, and my faithful 'Disinherited' had but to copy my thoughts, making only occasionally a blunder." (The "Disinherited" is KH's chela, Djual Khul, who, as indicated in this letter, was preparing for initiation.) This statement can be compared with KH's words at the opening of Letter 12, where he writes of the process of precipitation. As we know, it was the final part of Letter 12 that prompted the accusation of plagiarism against the Mahatma, which he explains in full in Letter 117. There appears to be some inconsistency among KH's statements regarding the production of the letters, so the student does need to consider the subject carefully, trying to understand the entire subject as much as possible.

Letter 75 concludes with a reference to a Colonel Chesney, evidently a friend of Sinnett's and an author whom Sinnett was trying to interest in Theosophy. Sinnett had shown him two portraits of the Mahatma that had come into his possession in rather unusual circumstances, which Sinnett recounts in *The Occult World* (pages 176–78). (HPB corrected a portion of Sinnett's account in a letter she wrote to him; see *LBS*, page 27.) One may wonder why Fern is so involved in the production of letters and with the Mahatma's portrait when he simply fades out of the picture, a failure from the occult point of view. Perhaps his story's importance is in once more illustrating what a razor-edged path we walk when we take up the spiritual or occult life.

Letter 75 has an addendum, the first two paragraphs of which are in KH's handwriting, while the final paragraph is in M's. Here KH again urges Sinnett to make note of what the two Englishmen perceive as "contradictions and inconsistencies." The reference to Sinnett's writing on "The Evolution of Man" suggests that he may have submitted the article to KH for suggestions or approval. The article appeared in three parts in the series "Fragments of Occult Truth" in *The Theosophist* for October 1882 (page 2), November 1882 (page 46), and April 1883 (page 161). The series is attributed to "A Lay Chela," the designation KH told Sinnett to use when writing the "Fragments." The articles are interesting for their showing how Sinnett was able to summarize the teachings given in the letters concerning planetary chains, rounds, root races, and the periods known as the obscurations.

The final paragraph, signed by M, refers to the Mahatma's letter to Hume (Letter 74), which he now calls a "foolish letter." Letters 73, 74, and 75, when read closely, tell us a great deal about the close relationship between the two Mahatmas while at the same time showing the differences in their methods of working with chelas. The letters also point up the fact that they made every effort to work with Hume; as KH says (in Letter 75), "notwithstanding his faults" he was "*absolutely necessary . . .* to the T.S." One can only speculate on the reason for all the help given to Hume and the Mahatmas' almost unlimited patience in dealing with him.

LETTER 76

The circumstances surrounding Letter 76, which is really two letters (one from Sinnett to the Mahatma and then a response to Sinnett from KH) are well explained in the introductory note and need not be summarized again. Once more, we can be grateful to have both sides of an interchange of correspondence and thus know what questions Sinnett asked in order to better understand the Mahatma's response.

Of particular interest is the brief note from KH that can be found in *The Letters of H. P. Blavatsky to A. P. Sinnett* (though the correct citation should be to letter no. 201, rather than 101) and has been reprinted in the chronological edition (page 499). In that brief note, KH comments on Sinnett's tendency to reduce abstract ideas to "concrete and false images." This, KH adds, poses a "danger," which I suggest is simply that by so reducing the abstract into the concrete, misunderstandings could easily arise. At the same time, KH appears to say that it is better to present "relative" truths to the public than none at all. This is certainly a view that needs careful consideration on the part of the student.

In Letter 76, Sinnett refers to the Mahatma's remarks in Letters 68 and 70C, and the student can review the relevant parts of those letters dealing with the after-death situation of victims of accident or those who have committed suicide. Here in Letter 76, KH comments on those who have been murdered, although he does not give definite information on this subject. The main point to be remembered seems to be that there are exceptions to every rule, and even exceptions to exceptions—a fact that makes it difficult for us, as it certainly did for Sinnett, to understand precisely the situation in kama-loka for those who die accidentally or by suicide or are murdered. We can only propose that wide differences exist and it is unwise to rush to judgment about any particular case. As the Mahatma tells Sinnett, we should "be always prepared to learn something new."

There are, in general, three conditions: first, those who "sleep in the Akasa" ("Akasa" is used here as a general term for the matter of all densities, so it can also include kama-loka); second, those who "become *Nature pisachas*" (called in Letter 68 "two-principled ghosts" or shells); and third, "a small minority" who are drawn to mediums and "derive a new set of skandhas from the medium who attracts them." However, knowing there are exceptions to every rule, we should hold such a classification tentatively until we have further information and certainly refrain from becoming dogmatic on such a subject.

KH's further comments are particularly interesting: in giving the teachings, he is "doing the work generally entrusted to . . . chelas" who, having been taught by the Mahatmas, "know enough to find themselves beyond the necessity of '*if's*' and '*but's*' during the lessons." How greatly privileged we are to have so much of the teaching given directly, through these letters, by the Mahatmas to Sinnett and Hume, even though, as KH and M have both stated, many of the letters were written by their chelas!

Finally KH turns again to Colonel Chesney, telling Sinnett that "*he is not a Theosophist*," a condition that seems to have special meaning if Sinnett is to work with him. The reference at the end of the letter to "Djual Khool's *idea* and *art*" concerns the portrait this chela drew of KH, which is mentioned near the end of Letter 75 as well as described by Sinnett in *The Occult World*.

LETTERS 77, 78, 79, AND 80

We can consider Letters 77, 78, 79, and 80 together, as they are short and little in them needs comment. The prefatory note to Letter 77 gives an excellent summary of the situation at the time, and in reading the letter itself one recognizes KH's quite human feelings of frustration and despair in having to deal with Hume. That frustration is repeated in the very brief note that is Letter 79. There is quite a lesson in this for us when we may be tempted to react similarly to individuals in the Society who we find difficult to tolerate. In spite of Hume's "*insatiable pride*," KH says in Letter 77, "For the sake of the Society, I would not lose him. . . . I will do *all* I can." And in the following letter (78), he speaks of Hume's "genuine, sterling, qualities." To what extent are we able to see in someone who seems intolerable to us their good qualities and possible usefulness to the Society?

In Letter 78, KH again mentions the Mahatma M's methods of dealing with chelas, which KH has said he found "distasteful," although he now adds that in view of all that is occurring, M "may be after all right." In several letters, KH has called attention to the importance of the seventh anniversary of the Society's founding, which may also have been the time for choosing those who had passed the test of probation as chelas. There is also almost a wistful longing in KH's words: "When will any of you know and understand what we *really* are, instead of indulging in a world of fiction!" This can be a call for us also to examine carefully our view of what constitutes a Mahatma or an Adept.

Letter 80 reveals again the close relationship between KH and the Sinnett family. The reference to the "Disinherited" (Djual Khul) being "on the watch" is one of several indications in the letters of attention being given to those about whom the Mahatmas are particularly concerned. Occasionally the Mahatmas themselves seem to do this, but usually, it appears, a chela is assigned to this duty. This procedure among the Adepts and their pupils is never fully explained; perhaps it provides a protection for individuals who are karmically connected, in one way or another, with the Mahatmas.

LETTERS 81 AND 82

Since Letter 82 continues the subject discussed at such length in Letter 81, the two can be considered together. However, to understand both letters, it is necessary to read the lengthy introduction that so ably summarizes the circumstances that gave rise to the letters. The events themselves are "extremely complicated," the introduction says, and since they occurred so many years ago, we may think these letters have little relevance to our work today. However, beyond these letters' value from a historical perspective—the Society's early years in India, the Mahatmas' relationship to those most intimately involved with the Society's work at that time, the character and motives of those receiving the Mahatmas' communications—Letters 81 and 82 do contain many lessons for us today.

One of the first things to strike us as we read Letter 81 is the tone of the letter as the Mahatma endeavors to explain to Sinnett the Brothers' view regarding Hume. They are clearly frustrated by the continued effort to work with an individual who, as KH says, "has neither delicacy of perception and feelings, nor any real, genuine kindness of heart." At the same time, KH is eager for Sinnett to understand that HPB was only obeying "orders" in writing *Isis Unveiled*, even though the later teachings from the Mahatmas themselves seemed to contradict some of the statements made in *Isis*.

(In connection with HPB's obeying "orders," we learn of a member of the Brotherhood we do not meet with elsewhere in the letters. Geoffrey Barborka mentions him in *H. P. Blavatsky, Tibet and Tulku* [page 32] in a listing of events in HPB's life. On May 27, 1875,

Barborka recounts, a notice was published in the Spiritualist paper *Spiritual Science* that two or more great "Oriental Spiritualists" had passed through New York and Boston, heading for California and Japan. HPB identifies them as the Mahatmas Hilarion and Atrya. So it has been proposed that HPB was instructed to write her first major work during the Mahatma Atrya's visit to New York.)

The Mahatma writes in Letter 81, "In *reality*, there is no contradiction between that passage in *Isis* and our later teaching; to anyone who never heard of the *seven* principles—constantly referred to in *Isis* as a trinity, without any more explanation—there certainly appeared to be as good a contradiction as could be." The fact that, as KH goes on to say, the Mahatmas "thought it was premature to give the public more than they could possibly assimilate" encourages us to consider two essential points in our work today: first, to what extent do we speak in terms easily understood by a contemporary audience, and second, are we always aware that what could be taken as contradictory teaching is, in reality, only incomplete knowledge or understanding. The latter point is emphasized in Letter 82, where KH tells Sinnett that "your knowledge is as yet so limited" such that "you yourself deduce but too readily from *incompleteness* 'contradiction.'" As HPB told her students, only a "corner of the veil" has been lifted. Despite the advances in science since the time these letters were written, KH's statement may still be true: "Only while the Western Sciences make confusion still more confused our Science explains all the seeming discrepancies and reconciles the wildest theories."

In many of KH's comments in Letter 81, we learn much about the two Mahatmas and the burden they willingly assumed in order to communicate as much of the occult wisdom as they could. We are also made aware of their human aspects alongside their mahatmic characteristics. In this, we are perhaps anticipating the statement in Letter 85B: "An adept—the highest as the lowest—is one *only during the exercise of his occult powers*"; otherwise, they are "ordinary mortals at all moments of [their] daily life." Consider KH's often scathing criticism of Hume in Letter 81, as well as his comments concerning the "potential selfishness there is in him," indicating a knowledge of elements in Hume's character possibly revealed in the future. He also indicates knowledge of the basis for Hume's present overweening pride, saying that Hume's "cruel, remorseless egotism" was "brought back with him from his last incarnation." Yet, in spite of all, KH says he is "personally ordered not to break" with Hume "until the day of the crisis comes." He also says, regarding M's feelings about Hume: "He [Morya] despises H. thoroughly; yet in a case of any real danger would be the first to protect him for the pains and labour given by him for the T.S." One can scarcely imagine an Adept feeling hatred toward any individual, so one is left to question whether such is possible. Such an attitude on the part of the Mahatma indicates his very human aspect.

KH says about himself and M, "We never were *Adwaitees*," a comment reiterated and enlarged upon in Letter 88, where KH states, "We are not Adwaitees, but our teaching respecting the one life is identical with that of the Adwaitee with regard to Parabrahm." KH and M, of course, were Buddhists and always referred to the Buddha with the greatest respect. The student may want to study the basis of Advaita Vedanta and contrast the premises of that philosophy with those of Buddhism.

Then there is the publication of the abusive letter written by Hume, the letter signed "H.X." that called forth a "Protest" from a number of chelas—"the result," states KH, "of a positive order emanating from the Chohan." We also learn that it was the Chohan who "*ordained*" the publication of the "offensive" article because the Mahatmas had "allowed our name to be connected with the T.S. and ourselves dragged into publicity," which apparently required them to permit "the expression of every opinion whether benevolent or malevolent." When Hume's letter—known as the H.X. letter—was published, HPB prefaced it with an editor's note in which she commented: "Had it not been for the express orders received from the Brothers we should have never consented to publish such a—to say the least—ungenerous document. Perchance it may do good in one direction; it gives the key, we think, to the true reason why our Brothers feel so reluctant to show favors even to the most intellectual among the European 'would-be' mystics."

Two lessons emerge as we review Letters 81 and 82. The first concerns accepting the consequences of our actions, which is what the Mahatmas had to do once they had opened the door to a knowledge of their existence; the second pertains to how we manage controversy and opposition. The Society's basic policy required that freedom of expression be permitted. As KH states in Letter 82: "Since we have mixed ourselves with the outside world, we have no right to suppress the personal opinion of its individual members, nor eschew their criticism . . . hence the positive order to HPB to publish Mr. Hume's article." However, continues KH, the world also has the "right" to see "both sides of the question"; hence the "protest" by a number of chelas was also published. Such a view may well cause us to consider: Do we give equal time to all sides of any issue that arises?

While these two letters seem so filled, perhaps overfilled, with criticism of Hume, they contain valuable lessons that apply to our current work within the Society. Besides those already suggested, a further lesson may be noted. The Mahatma re-emphasizes a point he has made in several earlier letters: the teaching will continue, "provided you [Sinnett] really profit by the tuition, and share from time to time your knowledge with the world." The instruction is not for Sinnett alone; he is to share it as widely as possible through his writings. So also, the time the Mahatmas spent and the patience they exhibited in dealing with this "Egotistic philanthropist," as Hume is called in Letter 75, were due to their hope that he would be a "useful tool" in furthering their work for humanity. While Hume eventually resigned as president of the Simla Eclectic Branch and later left the Society entirely, he did not altogether fail their hopes, for his work for India, as well as other acts of kindness to which the Mahatmas refer and for which they express their gratitude, may have balanced his karmic accounts. The message for us is simply that every individual is given an opportunity to be of service in the greater cause, and even those for whom we feel less than total affection may be valuable to the Society's work.

In concluding our consideration of Letters 81 and 82, I quote the words of Virginia Hanson, who commented on Letter 82 particularly (unpublished notes):

> There is a heavy note of sadness in this letter. The Mahatmas had hoped for so much when they undertook the correspondence with the Englishmen—or, at least, the Mahatma KH had. Out of love for humanity and a deep desire to enlighten those who were seeking, KH risked the Chohan's displeasure and undertook a very difficult and uncertain task. This made him vulnerable to attacks from the world outside as well as disfavor from among others of the Brotherhood, and his disappointment must have been very great at the havoc wrought by one egotistical and overproud man.

We can ponder what might have been our own reaction to the famous, or infamous, H.X. letter.

LETTER 83

Reading Letter 83, which is a really a footnote by Djual Khul to an article by the British Spiritualist William Oxley, submitted for publication in *The Theosophist*, one may indeed wonder why HPB was ordered to publish Oxley's rather strange and confusing article. I suggest two reasons, both of which point to the significance of Djual Khul's "declaration and statement" that was appended to Oxley's rambling discourse.

First, the publication of such an article indicates again the importance of permitting all views to be expressed, even though HPB as editor of *The Theosophist* really intended "to reject the MSS," as she said in her letter to Sinnett (see prefatory note to Letter 83). But, as KH wrote in Letter 81, "We must permit the expression of every opinion whether benevolent or malevolent." Also noteworthy is the extent to which both Mahatmas were involved in either writing articles for or "ordering" articles to be published in *The Theosophist* during that journal's early years. Notably, HPB, on leaving India for Europe, turned the journal over to Colonel Olcott, and since that time it has been the president's journal. Some have assumed that it is the journal of the Society, but such is not the case, although all the succeeding presidents have used the journal as a medium for official notices of the Society.

The second reason for "ordering" HPB to publish Oxley's article is undoubtedly the fact that it offered KH an opportunity to set the record straight about his alleged appearances to different individuals. There is some evidence in letters and other records that a number of members, particularly in India, were making claims that one or another of the Masters had appeared to them in physical form. DK refers to such claims when he writes: "To his regret my Master is forced to adopt this step [the use of "secret words" to verify authentic communications] as unfortunately of late such self-deceptions have become quite frequent." In the case of Oxley, in England, he had apparently written a rather pompous letter to KH, which the Mahatma did not answer but sent on to Sinnett (the letter has not been published but is with all the other letters in the British Museum Library). Presumably, Oxley, dissatisfied both with Djual Khul's review of his book and the Mahatma's failure to answer his letter, was determined to claim that he had been visited by KH. KH, then, took the opportunity to deny that allegation.

As the published correspondence contains only two letters from Djual Khul—the one we are now considering and Letter 37 written at the conclusion of KH's "retreat"—it is interesting to note how the tone of his writing is distinct from that of his Master. In both cases, Djual Khul indicates he has been "commanded" to write as well as instructed in what to say. We may note the chela's complete obedience to his Master's order and also his complete rapport with his Master in the transmittal of the Mahatma's thoughts.

One final note: after all Hume has been guilty of and the critical assessment of Hume's character, the Mahatma was apparently willing for him to have the passwords used to verify communications from the Brothers. As indicated in the prefatory note, however, those passwords were given not at this time but some months later, after Hume had resigned as president of the Simla Eclectic Theosophical Society. At the same time, it seems those three passwords were never actually used, as they are not apparent on subsequent letters.

LETTER 84

Although, the introductory note indicates, Letter 84 was simply a "cover letter," in which were enclosed the two-part letter numbered, for convenience, Letters 85A and B, it reveals yet another aspect of the chela-guru relationship, very likely a much earlier stage on the probationary path than we have seen with Djual Khul.

Djual Khul was apparently an advanced chela, soon to become a full initiate in the Brotherhood. The rapport between neophyte and Adept, spoken of in Letter 20 (see particularly page 73), is so complete in the case of Djual Khul and KH that the former is able to execute the latter's "command" in writing letters for him. Now, with Letter 84, we are introduced to two "young" chelas who are entrusted with the delivery of letters and instructed on how they are to behave in fulfilling that duty. So Sinnett is informed that the chelas "are forbidden to enter anyone's house without being invited to do so . . . to speak with any lady . . . [and] to shake hands with any man or woman." They are given "their mission and beyond that they must not go." Evidently, the chela on probation is expected from the beginning to be completely obedient to the "rules" of the Brotherhood—"our religious laws," as KH calls them in Letter 84. We may well remember that such obedience was the cause for Hume's denigrating statement that the Brothers used "Jesuitical methods."

There is another interesting aspect involved in the delivery of the letters that could indicate an aspect of the occult training a young chela would undergo. This concerns the utilization of the physical vehicle by another, whether a chela or a Master. As we know, HPB frequently vacated her body or at least set aside the consciousness using it in favor of one of the Adepts. Colonel Olcott refers to this phenomenon, which he witnessed on a number of occasions. He writes in *Old Diary Leaves* (1:212): "She would leave the room one person and anon return to it another. Not another as to visible change of physical body, but another as to tricks of motion, speech, and manners; with different mental brightness, different views of things, different command of English orthography, idiom, and grammar."

As background information for Letter 84, we learn that one chela, Gwala K. Deb (whose mystical name was Dharbagiri Nath), uses the physical vehicle of another probationary chela known as Babaji (also spelled Babajee, Bawaji, or Bowaji) to accompany "his brother Chela, Chandra Cusho" (whose real name was Keshava Pillai) to Simla to deliver the letters (85A and 85B) to Sinnett. However, in this instance, serious problems arose later, suggesting how a probationary chela may fall victim to a sense of egoism and undoubtedly fail. For the full story, see "Babaji" in the alphabetical notes in the *Readers' Guide to The Mahatma Letters* as well as the letters of the Countess Wachtmeister to Sinnett in *Letters of H. P. Blavatsky to A. P. Sinnett* (pages 277–86). As the Countess writes: "All chelas have terrible trials to go through and so we must have more patience with them than with common every day people."

A further reference, which the student may find of interest, is on page 341 of *Letters of H. P. Blavatsky to A. P. Sinnett*, in a letter from Dharbagiri Nath to Sinnett. The postscript to the letter reads: "Dharbagiri Nath is the mystic name given to an exoteric Sannyasi or Brahman which I became long before I knew of the Theosophical Society or became known to you. . . . As the name D.N. is purely Sanscrit and has been given to me by the exoteric Ascetics of a particular order of Adwaitees and followers of Sankaracharya while by 'birth' I belonged to what you call in your 'Esoteric Buddhism' as Vishishthadwaitees, who are apparently opposed to the teachings of Sankaracharya."

Three letters to HPB, signed "Babajee," are also of special interest (see *LBS*, 335–38) in attempting to understand just who this chela was, undoubtedly at times authentic while at other times masquerading under false pretenses. In a postscript to the first of the three letters, HPB comments: "I will produce the *true* Dharb. Nath—and show this one a little pretender," adding further, "The Countess *knows all*, I am not permitted to tell you the *whole truth*." So this simple "cover letter" leaves us with many questions regarding the identity of the two individuals who were fulfilling their probationary tasks in making the delivery at KH's request.

LETTERS 85A AND 85B

In several of the recent letters, KH has been requesting Sinnett and Hume to make a list of what they perceived to be contradictions between the teachings being given by M and himself and those presented by HPB in her first book, *Isis Unveiled*. Others also, including particularly Charles Carlton Massey, the British Theosophist who had been among the founders of the Society, were questioning statements in articles or editorial notes published in *The Theosophist*, believing them to be inconsistent with *Isis Unveiled*. We must remember that at the time of the letters (1880–1885), *Isis* was the only published book available to those seeking to know something of the occult doctrine. With the founding of her journal, *The Theosophist*, in October 1879, HPB began publishing articles by individuals versed in Eastern or occult philosophy, including pieces by the two Mahatmas. The French Kabbalist and occultist Eliphas Levi also had articles published in *The Theosophist*, and his article titled "Death" (pages 501–5), accompanied by KH's marginal notes and a lengthy editorial comment by HPB, raised a number of questions for the magazine's readers. The letters to the editor were also frequently controversial, as we see in Letter 81, referring to Hume's famous H.X. letter. Even a cursory glance through the early issues of *The Theosophist*, particularly between 1879 and 1883, when Sinnett published his second book, *Esoteric Buddhism*, gives the curious student a sense of the wide diversity of articles and their subsequent discussion in letters to the editor and HPB's editorial comments.

With that background, we can turn to Letter 85A, which consists of what Sinnett called "Famous Contradictions," indicating that he (no doubt in consultation with Hume) finally did prepare a list of the requested discrepancies. Virtually the entire list consists of quotations from three sources: from the first "Devachan Letter" (Letter 68), from what KH identifies as *"Notes on back of mine* to Old Lady" (Letter 70C), and from KH's notes on the proof of articles or "letters" Sinnett had written for publication in the London Spiritualist journal *Light* (see the prefatory note to Letter 76). We may assume, from the second paragraph headed (1), on which KH comments in his response, that Hume was far more critical in pointing up contradictory statements in the teachings than was Sinnett, who says at the outset that while he is obeying KH's request, he has prepared such a list "against my inclination" mainly *"because they do not fret me."* KH responds, "Nor do they fret me," but because the controversial statements could be used by Hume "in that nasty way, so pre-eminently his own," he will try to explain them.

However, before responding to the specific points Sinnett has identified, KH gives the Englishman a detailed analysis of "very important facts" relating to adeptship. This passage, written nearly two years after the correspondence with Sinnett began, is one of the clearest expositions of the use and function of occult powers by the Adept that we find anywhere in the literature. Up to this point in the letters, we have learned only that there are rules governing the Brotherhood of Adepts, that KH has taken a further step on the path of initiation, on the nature of which we can only speculate (see comments on Letter 29), and finally, that "the degrees of an Adept's initiation mark the seven stages at which he discovers the secret of the sevenfold principles in nature and man and awakens his dormant powers" (see conclusion to Letter 67). In addition, KH has said that he is not "a *full adept*" (Letter 70C, page 211), although the state of full adeptship is not defined. Throughout the early letters are other indications of what it means to be an Adept, and the student may wish to search out such hints, even make note of them, and then determine to what extent we really understand the subject. The initial chapter in Sinnett's *The Occult World*, published in 1881, scarcely a year after he began receiving the letters, shows us Sinnett's own understanding of adeptship at this stage. Today we have access to numerous later expositions concerning what it means to be an Adept, and the views we have formed may or may not correspond to the reality of their nature.

An individual, KH explains, may be said to be an Adept "*only during the exercise of his occult powers.*" From KH's description in this letter as well as his statements in earlier letters, we can assume that not only is such a person fully cognizant of the distinction between the "*inner* man" and the "ordinary," or outer, one, but he or she uses the occult faculties always from the highest, most selfless motive and never for personal gain or power. The "*inner* man" is the Adept, not the outer personality. Such an individual knows how to awaken that "sovereign will" that "unlocks the door to the *inner* man," who then can employ his (or her) occult faculties for the benefit of whatever work needs to be accomplished. KH tells Sinnett, and therefore us, the four means by which the outer vesture is "either completely or partially paralyzed" so the Adept can access occult power; however, he in fact tells us very little, simply because the modus operandi is still a secret and surely must remain so until, as we are told in Letter 20, "the neophyte attains to the condition necessary for that degree of Illumination to which, and for which, he is entitled and fitted."

So, we may ask, can KH make mistakes? Not when he is acting as an Adept, but perhaps or even certainly yes when he is no longer in that condition. We should note particularly, here, that there may indeed be "confusion of terms . . . mistakes of punctuation [that may alter meaning]," demanding that we always seek to understand the meaning within whatever has been written and to avoid both literalism and dogmatism. As frequently suggested, it was Sinnett who to a large extent provided the vocabulary for occult philosophy—terms such as "rounds," "root races," etc.—and KH now confirms this fact: "terms that *I had to learn from you*," for, as the Mahatma M wrote at the conclusion of Letter 46, "our terms are untranslatable."

A number of KH's comments in his rather lengthy introduction before taking up the numbered items in Sinnett's listing of discrepancies are noteworthy. He emphasizes the attitude of the chela, particularly the lay-chela (both Sinnett and Hume were considered such), saying, "The lay chelas ought to be forced to give the benefit of the doubt to their gurus." This attitude, as we know, was almost anathema to Hume, who seems to have resented anything that smacked of unquestioned obedience. No doubt Hume would also have found quite unpalatable KH's statement: "Even HPB was not allowed to become thoroughly acquainted with [many] of the subjects treated upon in *Isis*," which meant that while her statements were not contradictory, they might have been "misleading." Many still today are critical of HPB's first book because it does not mention the septenary nature of the human constitution, the question of reincarnation, and other topics she later discussed in *The Secret Doctrine*. Readers have asked the reason for these omissions, as well as whether HPB knew these doctrines at the time. Here, in Letter 85B, KH provides an answer to such queries. The thoughtful student needs to ponder the Mahatma's statements carefully.

A number of terms KH uses need to be clarified, again recalling that in these early years of the Society's existence, the terminology was still in a state of flux. For example, the use of the term "astral" could well have been confusing even to Sinnett. HPB in her *Theosophical Glossary*, which was compiled many years after these letters were written, defines "astral body" as the linga sharira and "astral soul" as kama-manas. Here in Letter 85B, KH makes a clear distinction

between the "astral monad"—identifying it with the "personal Ego"—
and the "immortal monad," or "spiritual Ego." If such a phrase as "the
exercise of ingenuity," used by KH, could bring about such a critical
interpretation as Sinnett evidently engaged in, it is no wonder that
there was confusion and even criticism (note the H.X. letter, pages
243–44) about such terms as "personal monad" and "immortal Ego."

Incidentally, KH first uses the phrase "I had to exercise my
ingenuity" in Letter 70C, and evidently Sinnett took exception to those
words, to which KH responded in Letter 81 (page 245) and refers to
it again in Letter 85B. We do not know what Sinnett wrote about that
phrase, but evidently KH considered his view a "terrible definition."

The final paragraph before KH begins responding to Sinnett's
list of "contradictions" deals with the portrait that Djual Khul (often
referred to as GK, as well as DK, and with various spellings of "Khul")
had painted. This was mentioned for the first time in Letter 75 (page
235) and again in Letter 78 (page 241). It seems to have been a subject
of considerable discussion, and even HPB refers to DK's work (see
LBS, 27).

So we come to the several statements that Sinnett cites as "alleged
contradictions." KH's "2" actually refers to Sinnett's comment in his
"1" concerning the rounds and the races. The Mahatma's comment
again reveals his delightful sense of humor, here bordering on
sarcasm. While all else in their system might be invented, what could
not be invented is Hume, for "to invent his like transcends the highest
Siddhi powers we know of." However, he says, to "know us *as we are*"
he has appended the information contained in Letter 85A concerning
adeptship. He also promises to give Sinnett an explanation on the
work by the well-known Buddhist scholar Rhys David, although it
does not seem to be included as part of this letter.

KH's comment 3, in response to the accusation of "contradictions
and inconsistencies," reminds us how easily words can be misinterpreted,
particularly when used by individuals with different backgrounds. If the
two Englishmen frequently misunderstood or misinterpreted what the
Mahatmas were trying to tell them, today more than one hundred years

later, we also need to be alert to their meaning, since the terminology has shifted through the years as successive teachers in the Society have endeavored to clarify the concepts. KH makes the important point that as "Occultists," the Mahatmas "have [their] own ways of expressing thought," ways quite different from those of Westerners.

In previous letters KH indicates that he has many duties to fulfill; here he again offers insight into his life, saying that he is often interrupted in writing his letters, so that there could well be gaps in the presentation of the teachings, providing opportunities for the Englishmen, especially Hume, to trip him up. KH's delightful humor is in evidence again as he tells Sinnett that his "colleagues" in the Brotherhood think he has a "proclivity to martyrdom," so that he has become "a kind of Indo-Tibetan Simeon Stylites." The Stylites were medieval ascetics who lived on top of pillars from which they never descended; they took their name from Simon Stylite of Syria, who spent sixty-eight years on different pillars, each loftier and narrower than the preceding one, the last being sixty-six feet high. He died in 596 AD. Tennyson, of whom Sinnett was particularly fond and whom KH sometimes quoted (see closing of Letter 18), wrote a very long poem in 1842 titled "St. Simon Stylite." This is another instance of KH's referring to something with which Sinnett would likely be familiar.

In fact, the entire paragraph, which is really KH's comment on points 3 and 4 in Sinnett's listing of presumed inconsistencies, is an excellent example of the Mahatma's sense of humor. C. Jinarajadasa comments that of the two, KH's sense of humor is "more akin of the French notion of wit," while that of Morya is "far more allied to what the Greek tragedians meant by 'irony,'" adding that it excludes "ridicule completely" and contrasts "with great dispassion facts as they are with what they are supposed to be."

Sinnett's note 5 is a quotation from Letter 70C (page 209) and concerns the question of remembrance in the after-death state. KH's elaboration on this in the long paragraph headed 5 needs careful study. The reference to the "disembodied *four-fold* entity" is to the statement in Letter 68 (pages 192–93) that with the death of the lower triad "the fourth, fifth, sixth and seventh principles form the surviving *Quaternary.*" The interesting comment that this entity sleeps "its akasic sleep in the Kama-loka" may simply refer to the fact that akasha, as the "fabric of the universe," is also the substance in which all is recorded and from which, therefore, remembrance returns when the entity awakens. Paragraph 6 continues the subject of remembrance, and KH indicates that the omission of the word "spiritual" when writing about what is remembered is what produced the misunderstanding.

KH's comment on Sinnett's item 7 simply reinforces the statement that everyone goes to devachan, with the sole exception of "that ego which, attracted by its gross magnetism, falls into the current that will draw it into the 'planet of Death,'" to quote Letter 68 (page 192). The Mahatma's elaboration on the devachanic state in his comment 8 is helpful in further understanding that condition. Especially significant is the point that just as every individual experiences happiness or misery in their own way so there must be a vast number of different states (a little later KH calls such states "inexhaustible") comprising the experience of devachan or avitchi. In other words we each have our own heaven and our own hell, much as we create our own heaven or hell here in incarnation. Therefore, no final description of devachan is possible, for the gradations therein are nearly infinite, the lowest level, if we may call it a "level," fading into "*Avitchi's* faintest state."

We should not overlook the Mahatma's statement regarding what he calls "a remorse of conscience," pointing out that such an emotion proceeds "*always from the Sixth Principle,*" and that even if felt only momentarily and even if "polluted" by desire, "this remorse *must* survive and *will accompany incessantly the scenes of pure love.*" Remorse is sometimes said to do little to compensate for an injury or injustice, so KH's words help us to a deeper understanding of the value of such an emotion. Perhaps the karma for some harmful action is in some manner allayed by a feeling of deep remorse, especially if it is a matter of conscience and has its source in the sixth principle, or buddhi. As KH invites Sinnett to "search in the depths of your conscience and memory" for the scenes or events that have become so engraved that he finds them replayed, so we might look into our own store of memories to see which occasions stand out and thus might be the basis for our own devachan. KH then reiterates a statement made in Letter 70C: "Yes; *Love* and *Hatred* are the only immortal feelings," now calling those feelings the "two poles of man's 'Soul' which is a unity." These feelings "mould the future state of man," the conditions of a person's post-mortem existence.

Responding to Sinnett's "complaint or charge" embodied in quotation 9, KH refers to "the Ratigans and Reeds," the proprietors of the newspaper of which Sinnett was editor, the Allahabad *Pioneer.* Particularly notable is the Mahatma's statement that Sinnett has never "transcended beyond the boundaries of the lower portion of [his] fifth principle with its vehicle—the *kama.*" We might ask ourselves to what extent we have moved beyond the kama-manasic aspect of our own nature; evidently, when that aspect is dominant throughout an incarnation, there is only "partial remembrance" of the life just past.

The comments 12A and 12B, with which KH concludes his letter, again reveal his sense of humor and almost tongue-in-cheek delight in reprimanding Sinnett for adopting Hume's attitude of splitting hairs over almost inconsequential matters. The "four lines of poetry" to which the Mahatma refers near the end of the first paragraph are found in Letter 71 (page 216), which KH there marked as not for publication. Many students find it rather incomprehensible that a Mahatma could feel such irritation as KH indicates he has felt toward Hume or that an Adept would be capable of making so many derogatory remarks. However, we need to accept the Mahatmas as they are as we seek to understand not only their nature but the teachings they so generously gave to us through their letters.

I remark on a few other references as this lengthy letter draws to a close. The "Hudibrasian couplet" refers to a long satirical poem in three parts titled "Hudibras," written by Samuel Butler between

1663 and 1678. Written in jingling, doggerel couplets, the poem was directed against the hypocrisy and intolerance of the Puritans, and its hero, Hudibras, is a caricature of various Presbyterian worthies of the Commonwealth. The reference to "Nobin's boy" is to the son of Babu Nobin Bannerjee, one of the signers of the protest to the H.X. letter; because of his joining in the protest, Bannerjee's fourteen-year-old son was accepted as a pupil in one of the lamaseries (see Letter 81, page 248). The designation "my little man" is a reference to Babaji or Bowaji, whose actual name was S. Krishnamachari (see introductory comments to Letter 84, pages 253–54); evidently he was of very short stature.

KH also refers to HPB, who had been ill for some time and, as on several other occasions, was not expected to live. KH says that he will have to stay at the lamasery near Darjeeling to interview her "if M brings her" there or she will be "lost for ever—at least, as far as the physical triad is concerned." That "triad" consists of the three lower principles: physical, etheric, and pranic. In a letter she wrote to Sinnett at this time (see *LBS*, 37), she describes her illness in rather lurid detail, and in another letter (*LBS*, 34), she tells him that she has received a note from KH in which he says: "I will remain about 23 miles from Darjeeling till Sept. 26th—and if you come you will find me in the old place." Her meeting with the Mahatma is described in Letter 92 (page 297).

In connection with this journey of HPB's to meet with the two Mahatmas, the student may want to read the article, "How a Chela Found His Guru," by S. Ramaswamier, another signer of the protest to the "H.X. Letter." Originally published in *The Theosophist* for December 1882, it is found in Barborka's *The Mahatmas and Their Letters*, beginning on page 321, and in *Letters from the Masters of the Wisdom*, Second Series.

The Mahatma's clarifications in this letter of what Sinnett and Hume considered inconsistencies are certainly valuable, although there is still much that we do not know. Further information on devachan is given in a few later letters, particularly in Letter 104.

LETTER 86

The circumstances surrounding Letter 86 are well set forth in the introductory comments. The particular individuals whom the Mahatma discusses—Colonel Chesney and Edmund Fern as well as William Oxley, referred to in the addendum—we have met with in earlier letters. There is a hint in a later letter (Letter 92) that Chesney abandoned the study of Theosophy, having determined that it was anti-Christian. As for Fern, we know that in spite of his proclivity for lying and practicing deceit, he was accepted as a chela by Morya (see Letter 75), and we know also that he eventually failed. Of some interest in this regard is KH's comment in Letter 101 that Fern and Hume (for whom Fern served as a kind of secretary, as noted earlier) were purposely brought together by "our chiefs." Oxley seems to fade out of the picture completely, as he is not referred to again in the letters.

What is truly significant as we look at this letter is the manner in which the Mahatma writes about these individuals. As we study their letters we may note the insight both the Mahatmas have into the character of the people who came, however closely or distantly, within the orbit of the Theosophical Society, which was developing in India at that time. They seem to perceive with keen accuracy the weaknesses and virtues of each individual and, as a consequence, give to every person an opportunity to develop the best in them without prejudgment as to success or failure. In the end, it is not the Mahatmas who abandoned them but they who abandoned the Mahatmas. Failure, which occurred with so many who were placed on probation, was never preordained. Rather, the door was always open, as they said, for the right one who knocks. There is surely much here for us to learn as people come to our doors, seeking to learn the truths of Theosophy or to work for the Society.

LETTER 87

Brief as Letter 87 is, and mainly concerning Hume, it contains much for our consideration. One such topic is the impatience that so characterized both the Englishmen, and particularly Hume, a fault that may be among our own weaknesses. Are we also guilty of misunderstanding the Mahatmas' mode of instruction and intentions because we want to hurry on? KH points out yet again that the occult doctrine "has to be cautiously given out, and bit by bit like a too powerful tonic. . . . Everything will be explained and given out, in good time if [they] are allowed [their] own ways." Recall what is said in Letter 20: "Knowledge can only be communicated gradually; and some of the highest secrets . . . might sound to you as insane gibberish. . . . Let those who really desire to learn *abandon all* and come to us, instead of asking or expecting us to go to them."

It seems fair to ask: Is this still true today, in terms of how we communicate the truths of Theosophy to the general public? How do we frame the teachings we have been given? Are there parallels between the manner in which the Mahatmas presented the teachings to Hume and Sinnett and the way in which we should present Theosophy to those who are seeking today?

This very short letter also contains the remarkable statement: "The Society will never perish as an institution, although branches and individuals in it may." HPB used similar words in her response to a letter written by two very critical members of the Society in 1886, a response since published as *The Original Programme of The Theosophical Society*: "The T.S. *cannot be destroyed as a body*. It is not in the power of either Founders or their critics; and neither friend nor enemy can ruin that which is *doomed to exist*, all the blunders of its leaders notwithstanding. That which was generated through and founded by the 'High Masters' and under their authority if not their instruction—MUST AND WILL LIVE. Each of us will receive his or her

Karma in it, but the *vehicle* of Theosophy will stand indestructible and undestroyed by the hand of whether man or fiend."

Even well-meaning members have voiced the view that while Theosophy can never be "destroyed" the fate of the Society as an institution may be another matter. Yet both in KH's and HPB's words we have the assertion that the Society will endure. Every earnest Theosophist might well ponder HPB's entire reply to the severe criticism leveled against the Society's organization in general and its president, Colonel Olcott, especially at that time. As the basic organization remains as it was since its founding, despite inevitable changes in the Society's structure through the years, students may ask themselves whether they feel equally certain as to its future.

Letter 88

Certainly one of the most challenging letters in the entire series, Letter 88 actually comprises "Notes" sent to Hume, who was then writing an "abridged" version of the occult philosophy as he understood the teachings thus far. While unfortunately the original is no longer in existence, we may assume that Sinnett was completely accurate in copying these Notes into his journal—although a few individuals have thought that the letter (and we can continue to call it that) is not wholly authentic. A few ellipses appear in the text as we have it, so presumably Sinnett omitted an occasional word or phrase during the process of transcription. Even so, it is doubtful that any such omission would alter the ideas the Mahatma sought to convey to Hume.

In approaching the letter, I suggest keeping in mind three key points. First, and quite obvious, we do not have the text of Hume's "Preliminary Chapter," which he had headed "God." We may assume that he had written something, perhaps a rough draft, on that subject, and sent it to KH, for the two Englishmen, whenever writing anything concerning the occult philosophy, would submit their writings to the Mahatmas for their review. And knowing of Hume's proclivity for feeling that he knew better than the Mahatmas how to present that philosophy to the public, we can even speculate that he was rather determined to use the term "God," ascribing to "Him" the characteristics that now KH so emphatically denies.

The second point to be kept in mind concerns the late-nineteenth-century context in which the letter was written, in India a period of great Christian missionary activity. Undoubtedly the concept of God then prevalent was less an abstract principle and closer to an anthropomorphic deity, a superhuman person, masculine, often wrathful, with power over nature and the fortunes of mankind. We know the Mahatmas felt a great sadness over the tendency of "their countrymen" to forget their own scriptures and traditions. Many statements in the letter reflect what may have been attitudes expressed by the missionaries, particularly as KH points to a "theological absurdity" in his discussion of the "God of the Theologians."

Finally, and most important, we must recognize that the Mahatmas were Buddhists, as indeed KH emphasizes: "We deny God both as philosophers and as Buddhists." Buddhism is a nondeistic religion. And the Buddhism of the Mahatmas is Buddhism in its original and all-embracing sense, free of sectarianism and grounded in the fundamental principles enunciated by the Enlightened One, principles to which KH refers at the end of Letter 88. Further, as the Mahatmas say elsewhere in the letters, "we teach but what we know," an indication that the doctrine presented can be known or experienced by the individual willing to undertake the necessary discipline.

With those three points in mind, we can turn to the letter itself, which deals with three important ideas: the concept of God, the concept of matter, and the concept of evil. The Mahatma is unequivocal in presenting the occult doctrine with respect to each of these, and therefore it is for us to study carefully and deeply, without prejudgment or bias, what he says.

The letter opens with the direct assertion: "Neither our philosophy nor ourselves believe in a God." Then we are told: "Our philosophy falls under the definition of Hobbes." The English philosopher Thomas Hobbes (1588–1679) set forth a philosophy of rationalist materialism, offending the religious views of his time. His major work, *Leviathan*, is said to have made him the first of the great English political theorists. Although his philosophy is usually considered mechanistic, KH evidently considered Hobbes' teachings to be in accord with their own: "the science of effects by their causes and of causes by their effects . . . the science of things deduced from first principle."

The Mahatma reminds Hume that he has been told their "knowledge was limited to this our solar system," a reference to a statement in Letter 18: "No adept has ever penetrated beyond the veil of primitive Kosmic [*sic*] matter. The highest, the most perfect vision is limited to the universe of *Form* and *Matter*" (page 65). At the same time, KH denies any charge of agnosticism; later he calls pantheism a "gigantic misnomer" for their philosophy. One student has suggested that the occult doctrine may be termed "panentheism," based on KH's statement: "When we speak of our One Life we also say that it penetrates, nay is the essence of every atom of matter." HPB, in *The Key to Theosophy*, discusses the question whether Theosophists are to be called atheists or pantheists (see the section "The Fundamental Teachings of Theosophy: On God and Prayer"). Students unfamiliar with the various terms used to characterize the Theosophical doctrine—"atheism," "agnosticism," "pantheism," "panentheism"—will find an ordinary dictionary helpful, in addition to KH's statements in Letter 88 and HPB's statements in *The Key to Theosophy*.

Many of the arguments KH now advances concerning the occult teaching, particularly the statement that "Parabrahm is not a God, but absolute immutable law, and Iswar . . . the effect of Avidya and Maya," are reiterations of teachings already given to Hume (see particularly Letter 67, page 181). A review of those statements may be useful in further understanding the Mahatmas' position on this sensitive subject. For now, KH affirms that the "word 'God' was invented to designate the unknown cause of those effects" that humankind has either "admired or dreaded" and adds that "the idea of God is not an innate but an acquired notion" (please note the typographical error in the completion of that sentence, which should read "we have but one thing in common with theologies").

The Mahatma further states, "We are not Adwaitees [because they are Buddhists], but our teaching respecting the one life is identical with that of the Adwaitee [because the Adwaitees are nondualists] with regard to Parabrahm," which echoes the teacher's words in Letter 67. It may be helpful at this point to quote T. Subba Row, who *was* an Adwaitee, as he provides an excellent summary of that tradition:

> The first principle . . . is the existence of what is called Parabrahman . . . the one essence of everything in the cosmos. . . . Now this Parabrahman which exists before all things in the cosmos is the one essence from which starts into existence a center of energy, which I shall for the present call the Logos. This Logos may be called in the language of old writers either Iswara or Pratyagatma or Sabda Brahman. It is called the Verbum or the Word by the Christians, and it is the divine Christos who is eternally in the bosom of his father. It is called *Avalokiteswara* by the Buddhists. . . . From its objective standpoint [Logos], *Parabrahman* appears to it as *Mulaprakriti*. This *Mulaprakriti* is no more *Parabrahman* than the bundle of attributes is the pillar itself; *Parabrahman* is an unconditioned and absolute reality, and *Mulaprakriti* is a sort of veil thrown over it. *Parabrahman* by itself cannot be seen as it is. It is seen by the *Logos* with a veil thrown over it, and that veil is the mighty expanse of cosmic matter. It is the basis of material manifestation in the cosmos. . . . Creation or evolution is commenced by the intellectual energy of the *Logos*. . . . This light of the Logos is the link, so to speak, between objective matter and the subjective thought of *Iswara*. It is called in several Buddhist books *Fohat*. (Row, *Philosophy of the Bhagavad-Gita*, pages 8–19)

In Letter 88, the Mahatma speaks further of Parabrahman as "the infinite and limitless space, duration and motion," the three aspects of the one Ultimate Reality, the Absolute, as HPB was to write of the "first principle" in *The Secret Doctrine*. A review of her exposition of the First Fundamental Proposition (see *SD*, 1:14 *et seq.*) may be helpful in clarifying what KH is teaching. She also writes (*SD*, 1:43): "The appearance and disappearance of the Universe are pictured as an outbreathing and inbreathing of the 'Great Breath,' which is eternal, and which being Motion, is one of the three aspects of the Absolute— Abstract Space and Duration being the other two."

In reading the Mahatma's analysis of the occult position in denying the "God of the Theologians," we cannot help but feel amazement once more at KH's citing of European philosophers who support or oppose the doctrine the Mahatmas are presenting. As I have commented earlier, tradition holds that KH was educated in Europe, so his familiarity with Western philosophy may not be unusual, yet he seems to remember all that he has studied or read (or does he have a library containing books from which he quotes?). Here in Letter 88 he turns not only to Hobbes, but to d'Holbach, Spinoza, and Clarke, the latter being extensively quoted and analyzed by d'Holbach. So it may be of some interest to identify these individuals.

Paul Henri Thiry, Baron d'Holbach (1723–1789), though born in Germany, is known as a French philosopher, a friend of Diderot and Rousseau, and is remembered chiefly as a stalwart opponent of positive religion. In Letter 93B (page 313), KH calls him "the greatest materialist of his times" and says further that his "views coincide entirely with the views of our philosophy. When reading his *Systeme de la Nature*, I might have imagined I had our book of Kiu-te before me." In the two-volume work KH refers to, translated by H. D. Robinson and titled *The System of Nature*, d'Holbach devotes a lengthy chapter (chapter 4 of volume 2) to "Examination of the Proofs of the Existence of the Divinity as given by Clarke." And as KH remarks, d'Holbach terms God "*un loup garou* . . . an imaginary power" or what we might call a "werewolf."

Dr. Samuel Clarke (1675–1729) was the author of *A Demonstration of the Being and Attributes of God,* published in 1705. It is probably from this work that d'Holbach quoted extensively and that KH now quotes from twice on page 271, the first beginning "God who hath made the eye, shall he not see" and the second beginning with the words "God, the self-existing being." Those quotations from Clarke are actually from the Robinson translation, page 215.

The well-known Dutch philosopher Baruch Spinoza (1632–1677) maintained that all existence is embraced in one substance—God or Nature. KH quotes his fourteenth proposition in the original Latin, although one word is misspelled; it should properly read: *praeter Deum nulla dari neque concipi potest substantia,* "Except God, no substance can exist or be conceived." Spinoza held that mind, matter, time—everything that appears is only a manifestation of the One, a view that is in accord with Theosophical doctrine.

Having considered the Advaitin's position, as well as the Western philosophers KH refers to, in order to correct Hume's use of the term "God," we can turn to the Buddhist perspective on that subject. *The Universal Flame,* published in commemoration of the centenary of the Theosophical Society (1975), contains an excellent article by William J. Ross, "The Concept of God," that succinctly sets forth the Buddhist doctrine. Ross writes:

> In Buddhism there is no mention of God. One finds in it no mythological vision, no tangible creed. It is as it were a therapy, a treatment for those who recognize the pain of the human condition and are strong enough to follow the cure which is prescribed. It is not so much a religious philosophy as the advice of a spiritual physician. The Buddha diagnoses the human problem. All is sorrow, he says. . . . Then he gives the cause—ignorant craving. Man suffers because he constantly wants, and when he gets what he wants he finds it does not satisfy his craving. . . . What is the cure? The cure as laid down by the Buddha is an operational one, a way of life, living in accordance with the noble eightfold path. It involves a

commitment to doing things, to living in a certain way, to having certain attitudes. . . . This frees us from our ignorant cravings and helps us to find that sense of identity, that feeling of wholeness, which is the mark of a healthy human being, a being who is at once aware of his own individual uniqueness and of his oneness with the whole of nature. None of this implies any idea of God. It is a way of life involving a feeling of responsibility, a recognition of man as the agent of his own destiny. It is in the context of this philosophical, Buddhistic point of view that we must see the words "we deny God."

Ross continues with comments on the use of the word "God" in *The Secret Doctrine*, particularly in reference to the three Fundamental Propositions. A useful way to examine more thoroughly Blavatsky's views on the concept of God is through the index of her major work, exploring each of the references listed under the term "God." Another interesting source is HPB's article "What is God?" which consists principally of lengthy editorial footnotes to a letter from a correspondent (see *CW*, 10:42), some of which sound very similar to KH's statements in Letter 88. Ross, in summarizing HPB's position, quotes her own words as found in *The Secret Doctrine* (1:280):

Man ought to be ever striving to help the divine evolution by becoming to the best of his ability a *co-worker with nature* in the cyclic task. The ever-unknowable and incognizable *Karana* alone, the *Causeless* Cause of all causes, should have its shrine and altar on the holy and ever untrodden ground of our heart—invisible, intangible, unmentioned, save through "the still small voice" of our spiritual consciousness. Those who worship before it ought to do so in the silence and the sanctified solitude of their Souls; making their spirit the sole mediator between them and the *Universal Spirit,* their good actions the only priests, and their sinful intentions the only visible and objective sacrificial victims to the *Presence.*

After quoting this passage, Ross concludes: "This, I think,
key to the understanding of the concept of God. It helps to fr
from the dichotomy of the religious and the secular, of God and man.
It brings us to a sense of wholeness, of unity, to the understanding that
the fundamental law of our system is the one homogeneous divine
substance-principle. This is the 'omnipresent Reality; impersonal,
because it contains all and everything.'"

Finally, students may find of interest Letter 56 in *Letters from the
Masters of the Wisdom*, First Series, which is a letter from the Mahatma
M, evidently written about the same time as KH's "Notes" to Hume,
and addressed simply "To a Member." C. Jinarajadasa, compiler
of those letters, notes that the letter was published in a Calcutta
newspaper of which Norendro Nath Sen, a devoted member of the
Society and later mentioned in *The Mahatma Letters*, was the editor.
The letter reads:

> A constant sense of abject dependence upon a Deity which he
> regards as the sole source of power makes a man lose all self-reliance
> and the spurs to activity and initiative. Having begun by creating a
> father and guide unto himself, he becomes like a boy and remains
> so to his old age, expecting to be led by the hand on the smallest as
> well as the greatest events of life. The saying, "Help thyself, and God
> will help thee," he so interprets that when an undertaking results to
> his own advantage, he credits it to himself only; when a failure, he
> charges it to the will of his God. The Founders prayed to no Deity in
> beginning the Theosophical Society, nor asked his help since. Are we
> expected to become the nursing mothers of the Bengal Theosophical
> Society? Did we help the Founders? No; they were helped by the
> inspiration of self-reliance, and sustained by their reverence for the
> rights of man, and their love for a country whose national honour
> has long been trampled into mud, under the feet of her meek and
> lazy sons, indifferent to her woes, unmindful to her dying glory. . . .
> Your sins? The greatest of them is your fathering upon your God
> the task of purging you of them. This is no creditable piety, but an

indolent and selfish weakness. Though vanity would whisper to the contrary, heed only your common sense. M

To return to reviewing Letter 88, we come now to the Mahatma's comments on the concept of matter. He asserts, "Matter we know to be eternal," and adds a bit later in the letter, "We believe in MATTER alone, in matter as visible nature and matter in its invisibility as the invisible omnipresent omnipotent Proteus with its unceasing motion which is its life, and which nature draws from herself since she is the great whole outside of which nothing can exist." Such statements may have come as a surprise to the scientific mind of Hume's day, but today with many concepts of classical Newtonian physics revised in the light of quantum theory, this view is not totally alien to the scientific mind. There is scarcely a school child who is not familiar with the Einsteinian equation $E=mc^2$, even without understanding it. The eternality of matter was already expounded to Hume, in the first set of Cosmological Notes, where it is identified as coexistent with space. HPB repeats the statement, "Matter is *Eternal*," in her summary of what she calls "proven facts" that conclude volume 1 of *The Secret Doctrine* (page 280). She adds: "It [matter] is the *Upadhi* (the physical basis) for the One infinite Universal Mind to build thereon its Ideations."

Notably, the Mahatmas never deny the reality of spirit, only spirit as a distinct principle apart from matter. This point is repeated in Letter 90: "The conception of matter and spirit as entirely distinct and both eternal, could certainly never have entered my head . . . for it is one of the elementary and fundamental doctrines of Occultism that the two are one, and are distinct but in their respective manifestations." Further on in that letter, noting that "matter *per se* is indestructible, and . . . coeval with spirit," KH adds, "Bereaved of Prakriti, Purusha (Spirit) is unable to manifest itself." Whether it is called prakriti or mulaprakriti, akasha, svabhavat, or simply space occultly defined, the Mahatma is speaking of that "*one* element in Nature (whether spiritual or physical) outside which there can be no Nature since it is *Nature* itself, and which as the *Akasa* pervades our solar system, every atom being part of itself, pervades throughout *space* and *is* space in fact" to quote from Letter 65 (page 168).

KH poses a rhetorical question, "Then what do we believe in?" to which he responds, "The much laughed at *phlogiston*." The Mahatma has rejected both the "theistic theory" and the "automaton theory." So we must endeavor to understand just what he means by "phlogiston." At first glance, it may have something to do with electromagnetism, since KH uses the term again in Letter 93B when he writes of the "magneto-electro aura—the *phlogiston* of the Sun." However, to better understand the term, we may turn to the article to which the Mahatma directs Sinnett's attention, "What Is Force and What Is Matter?" The article originally appeared in *The Theosophist* for September 1882, and in republishing it in the *Collected Writings* (4:208–26), Boris de Zirkoff, as compiler of HPB's writings, added a footnote concerning the term "phlogiston":

> This term is derived from the Greek *phlogistos*, burnt, inflammable, and *phlogizein*, to set on fire, to burn. It is a term used for the hypothetical principle of fire, or inflammability, regarded as a material substance. The term was proposed by Stahl, who, with J. J. Becher, advanced the *phlogiston theory*. According to them, every combustible substance is a compound of phlogiston, and the phenomena of combustion are due to the phlogiston leaving the other constituent behind. Similarly, metals are produced from their calces by the union of the latter with phlogiston. While abandoned now, the theory is not altogether without worth, and has occult implications.

Matter and fire are discussed extensively in the article just referred to. Actually it was written by KH, as we know from a letter of HPB's to Sinnett (see *LBS*, 8), in which she enumerates the items to be published in the September 1882 issue of *The Theosophist*. She writes, "And finally a criticism upon Col. O.'s lecture 'Is electricity Force or Matter' and an answer by Ma. KH—who is becoming a *true penny-a-liner,* a *proof reader* through astral light and what not." The story behind KH's writing the article is an interesting one: Colonel Olcott, in a lecture given in Madras (now Chennai) on April 26, 1882, stated that electricity, like air and water, is matter. A member of the Society in his audience took issue with that statement and challenged it in a letter to *The Theosophist*. HPB must have referred the letter to KH, who then penned the article that he now, in Letter 88, asks Sinnett to read.

In the article, which is quite long, the Mahatma mentions that three states of matter have been known for ages: solid, liquid, and gas. Then along came Sir William Crookes, English physicist and a member of the Theosophical Society, with his discovery of and experiments in what he called "radiant matter." The Mahatma calls this "one of the grandest [discoveries] in science," commenting: "If a *fourth* state of matter was discovered by Professor Crookes . . . there is nothing impossible that in time there will be discovered a fifth, sixth, and even *seventh* condition of matter, as well as seven senses in man, and that all nature will finally be found septenary." The Mahatma concludes:

> Therefore do the Occultists maintain that the philosophical conception of spirit, like the conception of matter, must rest on one and the same basis of phenomena, adding that Force and Matter, Spirit and Matter, or Deity and Nature, though they may be viewed as opposite poles in their respective manifestations, yet are in essence and in truth but one. . . . [Life] is as infinite and as indestructible as matter itself, since neither can exist without the other, and that electricity is the very essence and origin of— *Life itself.* "Purush" is non-existent without "Prakriti"; nor can Prakriti, or plastic matter have being or exist without Purush, or spirit. . . . Purush and Prakriti are in short the two poles of the one eternal element, and are synonymous and convertible terms. . . . Therefore, whether it is called Force or Matter, it will ever remain the Omnipresent Proteus of the Universe, the one element—Life— Spirit or Force at its *negative,* Matter at its *positive* pole; the former the Materio-Spiritual, the latter, the Materio-Physical Universe— Nature, Svabhavat, or Indestructible Matter.

The entire article is well worth reading for its outstanding explanation of the occult view of force and matter. Students may wish to compare the ideas KH presents with contemporary views in physics, particularly quantum theory, as expounded by reputable scientists who are writing nontechnical works for the lay person. The works of Amit Goswami, Paul Davies, David Bohm, and Brian Greene may be noted especially, along with the excellent work of the journalist Lynn McTaggart. It is no wonder that KH could write, in Letter 65: "Modern science is our best ally."

The portion of Letter 88 on the topic of evil contains much that calls for consideration. KH indicates that both good and evil proceed "from two causes," which then we need to examine thoroughly. In stating that "humanity . . . alone is the true source of evil," the result of "human selfishness and greediness," the Mahatma is defining the psychological nature of evil. Similarly, in Letter 70C he speaks of the human "potency for *evil*" being greater than "the potentiality for *good*." In commenting on that passage, I refer the student to articles by Annie Besant as well as to the writings of Dr. Robert Ellwood. It may be useful to review that material in considering KH's statements in Letter 88, particularly as the Mahatma identifies religion as "the chief cause of nearly two thirds of the evils that pursue humanity."

Some students may wish to examine the concept of evil in contemporary psychology, particularly regarding the writings of C. G. Jung. In his essay "Good and Evil in Analytical Psychology" (*Civilization in Transition*), he says: "Good and evil are in themselves *principles*." He then adds: "We must bear in mind that principles are known qualities of morality that exist on a collective level. Yet, when we speak of good and evil we are speaking concretely of something whose deepest qualities are unknown to us." In his most controversial work, *Answer to Job*, Jung addresses the religious question: how can a good God countenance the appalling evil apparent in the world at large? His concern is with "how a modern person with a Christian background comes to terms with the divine darkness which is unveiled in the Book of Job," at the same time pointing out that his own "psychological experience shows that whatever we call 'good' is balanced by an equally substantial 'bad' or 'evil.'"

An equally fruitful area of study in confronting the problem of evil is the many myths, found in nearly every culture of the world, that speak of a dichotomy in creation. Such a study could focus on the experience of opposition and conflict as represented in the pairings of inimical brothers: Cain and Abel, Set and Osiris, Satanael and Christ, Azazel and Yahweh, and Balder and Hoder in Norse mythology. In all these pairings, one of the brothers is light or good or heavenly, while the other is dark, earthly, or evil. In the Adam and Eve story, in which divine will places the Tree of Knowledge in front of humankind as a temptation, we cannot help feeling that the "fall" occurs by providential arrangement. In terms of human development, we may well ask whether the impulse to know, to become conscious, means also to become individual, separate; however, when ego-separateness exceeds its bounds, does evil become possible?

Undoubtedly many other questions may occur to the student while considering the problem of evil and seeking to resolve it from a moral point of view. In concluding his discussion, the Mahatma states that the origin of evil as well as "the problem of the origin and destruction of suffering" has been solved in the Four Noble Truths expounded by the Buddha and in the doctrine of "the chain of causation." Students unfamiliar with the basic tenets of the Buddhist philosophy would do well to consult an introductory text on Buddhism. (I can recommend *Buddhism: An Outline of its Teachings and Schools* by Hans Wolfgang Schumann, or *Exploring Buddhism* by Christmas Humphreys.) Useful also, and a work with which every Theosophist should be familiar, is the little work by Colonel Olcott, *The Buddhist Catechism*.

KH tells Hume to read "the Mahavagga," which is part of the Buddhist canon, more specifically, the "Vinaya basket," the first of the Tipitika, the three "baskets" or collections that comprise the Buddha's teachings. Since volume 13 of the *Sacred Books of the East*, which contains a translation of the *Mahavagga*, was published in 1881, Hume very possibly had access to that work. Happily, however, KH beautifully translates the passage that sets forth "the chain of causation," often referred to as the doctrine of dependent origination, or sometimes simply as the wheel of causation. This chain or wheel is composed of the twelve *nidanas*, the fetters forming the causes of existence in the world including the causes for rebirth. This theory is closely bound up with the theory of the instantaneousness and impermanency of all phenomena, a central teaching of Buddhism.

An excellent analysis of the teaching concerning the twelve nidanas is found in Lama Anagarika Govinda's work *The Psychological Attitude of Early Buddhist Philosophy.* In the book *Transactions of the Blavatsky Lodge,* which consists of answers to questions asked of her, HPB states that the nidanas are "moral agents in the universe" awakened by maya, or ignorance. HPB tells her students that "the nidanas are produced by Devas and Dhyan Chohans .... We produce Nidanas in ignorance. Each cause started on the physical plane sets up action on every plane to all eternity. They are eternal effects reflected from plane to plane on to the 'screen of eternity.'" She points out: "Nidanas are the detailed expression of the law of Karma under twelve aspects; or we might say the law of Karma under twelve Nidanic aspects" (Spierenburg, *The Inner Group Teachings of H. P. Blavatsky,* 16–82).

There is indeed much to study concerning the wheel of causation, which the Mahatma regards as the origin of evil in the world. The chain of dependent or interdependent origination is said to evolve in our own minds, turning back on itself with three factors: ignorance, desire, and action, which lead from one to the next respectively, thereby supporting one another. As KH translates the words of the Buddha: "From knowledge comes the cessation of this mass of misery." It is for each of us to become the "meditating Bhikshu," contemplating "the real nature of things." Such meditation means, as KH tells us, "the superhuman ... qualities or arhatship in its highest of spiritual powers." This no doubt seems a distant goal at this stage in our own development, but it is a goal nonetheless attainable, as the Mahatmas have shown. While Letter 88 is truly a challenge for the earnest student, it concludes on a note of hope and promise even as it encourages us to probe more deeply into the teachings that the Mahatmas and their agent, HPB, gave to us.

LETTER 89

Sinnett may have been somewhat surprised to receive a letter from Morya, who, as we know, disliked writing. However, as we read Letter 89, M's reason for addressing Sinnett becomes quite clear. Not only does M request Sinnett's assistance, he is also trying to aid his brother KH, a fact that once again reveals the close relationship between the two Mahatmas. M is evidently aware of KH's efforts to keep Hume within bounds, we might say, but feels that his brother "is too much of a *perfect* Yogi-Arhat" to bring Hume to some kind of realization of what he is doing. We may recall, in this regard, M's comment in the postscript to Letter 75: "KH is too sensitive by far." Now M takes a hand in the effort to prevent Hume from further destructive action, asking for Sinnett's assistance in impressing "upon his [Hume's] mind" the need to "take care of his *Eclectic* [the Branch in Simla] and to leave the Parent Society to take care of itself."

M's comments regarding Hume are quite scathing. He accuses him of acting "like a wild ass" and comments: "Let him remember, that we are not Indian Rajahs in need of and compelled to accept political *Ayahs*, and nurses to lead us on by the string." Hume, as we know, was fond of posing as a great benefactor of the Theosophical Society, presuming to know better than the Mahatmas or anyone else, including Blavatsky and Olcott, how the Society should be organized and how the teachings should be presented. M's remarks throughout this letter puncture that bubble of pride, giving an "*ultimatum*" that Sinnett is to convey to Hume: "I will not suffer him to interfere with his wisdom between our ignorance and the Parent Society," a wonderfully satirical statement.

M is concerned for KH's own welfare, which is undoubtedly the reason he has taken a hand in the situation. Pointing out that "the whole situation and future of the *Eclectic* hangs on Koothumi if you will not help him," the Mahatma indicates that his brother has even earned "the

Chohan's displeasure" by "sacrificing himself for a man [Hume] who is the evil genius of the Society." The extent to which Sinnett did or even could influence Hume we can only surmise, and in any case, the situation played itself out in due time with Hume's resignation both as president of the Eclectic Branch and as a member of the Society.

Beyond its historical context, this letter also contains statements that deserve our attention. M's comments imply that the Mahatmas desire neither reverence nor gratitude but simply acknowledgment that "either we are what we claim, or we are not. . . . If our knowledge and foresight do not transcend [that of an ordinary person] then we are no better than *shams and imposters.*" Whatever may be thought of them, says the Mahatma, "we claim the right to know our own business best." We may well keep M's words in mind as we study the teachings, particularly if we find on occasion that the Mahatmas' actions or words do not accord with our own conceptions of what Mahatmas should be like!

Before leaving Letter 89, we should take note of a letter from KH to Hume apparently written at about the same time as Letter 89 (see appendix 2, pages 481–84) and originally published in *Letters from the Masters of the Wisdom,* First Series (Letter 43, page 96). The length of the letter, much of it an attempt to persuade Hume to give attention to the Eclectic Branch of which he was president and dissociate himself from a member by name of S. K. Chatterjee who was doing considerable harm to the cause, indicates the amount of time KH was giving to Hume and so lends credence to Morya's remark that KH was courting the Chohan's displeasure. A few portions of the letter are worth noting:

> You notify me of your intention of studying Advaita philosophy with a "good old Swami" [the "Swami from Almora" with whom Hume had taken up (see Letter 81), the association that presaged Hume's eventual break with the Society]. The man, no doubt, is very good, but from what I gather in your letter, if he teaches you anything you say to me, *i.e.,* anything save an impersonal, *non*-thinking and non-intelligent Principle they call Parabrahm, then he will not be teaching

you the *true spirit* of that philosophy, not from its esoteric aspect, at any rate. . . . You are, of course, at liberty to try and learn *something*, since it seems that we could teach you *nothing*. Only since two professors of two different schools—like the two proverbial cooks in matter of sauce—can succeed but in making confusion still worse confounded, I believe I better retire from the field of competition altogether; at any rate, until you think yourself in a better position to understand and appreciate our teachings as you express it. (page 481)

In the next paragraph the Mahatma comments on the accusation by some people that the Mahatmas are "tantrikas": "The 'tantrikas'— at least the modern sect, for over 400 years—observe rites and ceremonies, the fitting description of which will never be attempted by the pen of one of *our* Brotherhood." He also says: "I cannot leave unnoticed the remark that your want of progress has been due to the fact that you were not allowed to come to us and be taught personally. No more than yourself was Mr. Sinnett accorded any such privilege. Yet he seems to understand perfectly well whatever he is taught. . . . Nor have we ever had one word of unpleasantness between us—not even between him and M whose bluntness in speaking out his mind is often very great" (page 481).

The Mahatma goes on to answer Hume's accusation that he often sounds like HPB and so is suspected of taking his impressions of Hume from "Olcott's and the O.L.'s heads." KH's response adds to our understanding of the relationship between Master and chela:

Kindly give thought to the following law, when alluding to my taking my ideas of you 'out of the O. Lady's head or Olcott's, or any one else's.' It is a familiar saying that a well matched couple 'grow together,' so as to come to a close resemblance in features as well as in mind. But do you know that between adept and chela—master and pupil—there gradually forms a closer tie; for the psychic interchange is regulated scientifically. . . . As the water in a full tank runs into an empty one which it is connected with; and as the common level will be sooner or later reached according to the capacity of the feedpipe, so does the knowledge of the adept flow to the chela; and the chela attains the adept level according to his receptive capacities. At the same time the chela being an individual, a separate evolution, unconsciously imparts to the master the quality of his accumulated mentality. The master absorbs *his* knowledge; and if it is a question of language he does not know, the master will get the chela's linguistic accumulations just as they are—idioms and all—unless he takes the trouble to sift and remodel the phrases. . . . Proof M who does not know English and has to use Olcott's or the O.L.'s language. So you see it is quite possible for me to catch HPB's or any other chela's ideas about you without meaning to do you any injustice; for whenever we find such ideas—unless trifling—we never proceed to judge and render our sentences merely on the testimony of such borrowed light; but always ascertain independently and for ourselves whether the ideas so reflected in us are right or wrong. (page 482)

The remainder of the long letter mainly concerns Hume's association with Chatterjee, whom KH characterizes as "the greatest enemy of the Founders, their traducer and slanderer and the open opponent of the Society." The letter then concludes on a friendly note: "Whenever you need me, and when you have done your study with the 'Swami'—then I will be again at your service." The time and trouble that KH must have given to writing such a letter surely verifies M's remark to Sinnett in Letter 89, "KH is too much of a *perfect* Yogi-Arhat."

LETTER 90

Although we have Letter 90 only in Sinnett's handwriting and have no access to the original, which was addressed to his colleague, Hume, we may assume the accuracy of the transcription and feel grateful to Sinnett for having copied it, thus preserving KH's teachings for our study. However, Sinnett headed his copy "Extract," indicating that there may be some portion, whether much or little we do not know, that he left out. Certainly what we have gives us much to ponder. We may well imagine that after receiving KH's comments on the chapter he was writing on the subject of God (see Letter 88), Hume wrote the Mahatma in a very argumentative manner, continuing to expound the theistic position of a creator who is also a "moral governor" of the system. Hence KH's response, which is at once one of the most difficult as well as one of the clearest expositions of the occult philosophy. To grasp fully all that is being said leads the student to the very heart of the teaching that the Mahatmas sought to convey.

Many statements in this letter echo principles enunciated in earlier letters; at the same time, they anticipate much that would be explained in greater detail in *The Secret Doctrine*. In fact, while reading through Letter 90, one becomes aware that KH's statements bear a striking similarity to the three propositions set forth in HPB's major work: absoluteness, cyclicity, and progressive unfoldment of consciousness. It is left to the student to see these correlations and thereby discover the occult doctrine's beautiful symmetry.

Two significant points deserve highlighting before we examine the letter in detail. First, KH repeats what M says to Sinnett in Letter 89 regarding the Mahatmas' knowledge. Writing of the "infinite mind," KH emphasizes "so far—we know" and comments that their knowledge is "owing to personal experience." Again, toward the end of the letter, KH uses words similar to those M uses in Letter 89: "Either we know something or we do not know anything." Throughout the letters, in fact, there is an underlying current of firsthand experiential knowledge from which the Mahatmas are sharing as much of the doctrine as they can communicate. Hence KH states, "There are a thousand questions I will never be permitted to answer," primarily, we may suggest, because the questioner is not prepared to understand the answer.

The second point concerns the nature of the Mahatmas' knowledge, which in the letters is referred to as occultism. The fact that it is an exact science has been said throughout the letters and is emphasized again at the end of Letter 90: "To show you how exact a science is occultism let me tell you that the means we avail ourselves of are all laid down for us in a code as old as humanity to the minutest detail, but everyone of us has to begin from the beginning, not from the end. Our laws are as immutable as those of Nature, and they were known to man an eternity before this strutting game-cock, modern science, was hatched."

In the body of the letter, KH indicates just how to undertake the study of occult science. Commenting that "the world of force is the world of Occultism," he then states: "Guided by his Guru the chela first discovers this world [the world of occultism], then its laws, then their centrifugal evolutions into the world of matter. To become a perfect adept takes him long years, but at last he becomes the master. The hidden things have become patent, and mystery and miracle have fled from his sight forever."

To get a sense of the "long years" required, we may note KH's statement: "Only I had to study for fifteen years before I came to the doctrines of cycles and had to learn simpler things first." Do we think that understanding the doctrine of cycles is a matter of one easy lesson in an introductory course on Theosophy? We can all take heed of the Mahatma's advice: "Learn first our laws and educate your perceptions."

Before leaving this subject, I want to mention two references that the earnest student may find of value. One is an article by HPB on "Occult or Exact Science?" (*CW*, 7:55–90). The other is a recent and excellent comparative analysis of contemporary science and Theosophical principles by one of the Society's finest students, Dr. Edi D. Bilimoria: *The Snake and the Rope: Problems in Western Science Resolved by Occult Science*, the Theosophical Publishing House, Adyar, 2006.

At the beginning of Letter 90, we should note that KH invokes the Hermetic or Kabbalistic axiom: "As it is above, so it is below; as it is below, so it is above." Hence the correlation of the universal with the human mind, based on the law of analogy or correspondences. The entire question of the brain-mind connection is still debated by today's scientists, and the student may wish to compare KH's statements with contemporary views. For example, the work of the Institute of Noetic Sciences in fostering research at the frontiers of consciousness, including brain-mind research, has attracted many leading scientists. The November 2007 issue of the IONS journal *Shift* is entirely devoted to current knowledge in the fields of the neurosciences and neurotechnology, including the emerging field of neuroethics. One writer notes: "For every change in consciousness, there is a corresponding change taking place in some area of the brain." On the other hand, as other current publications show, the mechanistic view is still very prevalent.

From KH's statements concerning the "infinite mind"—which he indicates should really be called "the infinite Force"—we may assume that while no physical brain, such as we have in our own heads, exists at higher levels or frequencies, something corresponding to the functions of the cerebrum and cerebellum evidently exists there. The discoveries of Freud, Jung, and their successors concerning the unconscious and, to use Jung's term, the collective unconscious, may aid us in understanding KH's comments on this point. Note particularly that KH refers first to what the Adepts know and then to what "the highest Planetary Spirits have ascertained" by "penetrating behind the primitive veil of cosmic matter," again suggesting a correspondence between the various levels "throughout the myriads of worlds." A review of the material concerning the planetary spirits in Letter 18 may be helpful at this point.

Just as an analogy exists between the functions of the cerebellum and cerebrum of the physical brain and the voluntary and involuntary actions of the "infinite Force" known as the Cosmic Mind, so an analogy may exist between what KH terms "the involuntary power of the infinite mind . . . to be eternally evolving subjective matter into objective atoms" and our own mental power to generate new ideas. We may remember the Mahatma's statement in his first letter to Hume that we are "continually peopling [our] current in space with a world of [our] own," the "offspring of [our] fancies, desires, impulses and passions." So it seems "the universal perpetual motion" of the Cosmic Intelligence "which never ceases, never slackens nor increases its speed" creates as well as dissolves forms and the worlds of form, from their "most spiritualized state" to their grossest and most physical. Pralaya, avers KH, is only "the temporary loss of every form, but by no means the destruction of cosmic matter which is eternal." As he states in Letter 88: "Matter we know to be eternal . . . we believe in Matter alone." Here in Letter 90 KH says again: "Matter *per se* is indestructible, and . . . coeval with spirit."

Thus, states KH unequivocally, there is no room in their system for "a most rascally God . . . a Being however gigantic, occupying space and having length, breadth and thickness . . . a Machiavellian schemer." Rather, it is the "motion that governs the laws of nature," the "plastic, invisible, eternal omnipresent and unconscious Swabhavat," that is the "Force or *Motion* ever generating . . . life." Here we may be reminded of KH's statement in Letter 1 regarding the need to acquire "a thorough knowledge of *Akas*, its combinations and properties," for akasha and svabhavat both refer to that primordial "self-becoming" substance, the fabric of the universe, of which all manifestation consists. As HPB states in *The Secret Doctrine* (1:635–36): "Everything has come out of Akasha (or Svabhavat on our Earth) in obedience to a law of motion inherent in it." That fabric of the universe is motion itself—a concept that is the root of the Buddhist doctrine of impermanence.

KH advises Sinnett to "study the laws and doctrines of the Nepaulese Swabhavikas." Several references to that school of Buddhism occur in *Isis Unveiled*, one relevant example being the statement that the "*Svabhavikas . . .* believed *in the eternity and the indestructibility of matter*, and hence in many prior creations and destructions of worlds, before our own" (*Isis*, 2:220). So also, in her article "What is Theosophy?" HPB writes of several schools of thought whose "conceptions can lead but to pure and absolute Theosophy," including "the Svabhavikas of Nepal," who "maintain that nothing exists but 'Svabhavat' (substance or nature) which exists by *itself* without any creator" (*CW*, 1:91). Undoubtedly Sinnett would have been familiar with these statements by HPB, while today's student may wish to explore further the relation between the doctrines of the Svabhavikas and Theosophy. Why the Mahatma refers to the Svabhavikas as "the principal Buddhist philosophical school in India" is somewhat puzzling, as the evidence does not seem to support the statement.

Next in Letter 90 we come upon a truly amazing statement: "There is a force as limitless as thought, as potent as boundless will, as subtle as the essence of life, so inconceivably awful in its rending force as to convulse the universe to its centre were it but used as a lever." Here, surely, is our good friend Fohat, that fundamental dynamic energy of cosmic ideation that assumes so many guises. Defined by HPB in the *Theosophical Glossary* as the "ceaseless destructive and formative power . . . the universal propelling Vital Force," she writes elsewhere: "Each world has its Fohat, who is omnipresent in his own sphere of action. But there are as many Fohats as there are worlds, each varying in power and degree of manifestations. The individual Fohats make one Universal collective Fohat—the aspect-Entity of the one absolute Non-Entity, which is absolute Be-ness, Sat" (*SD*, 1:143n.).

We have met with Fohat in earlier letters, particularly in the first set of Cosmological Notes (see comments on those Notes). The study of this protean force is nearly endless, and the earnest student must, at one time or another, engage in such a study if he or she wishes to grasp the occult doctrine in even slight measure.

Motion, force, Universal Mind, svabhavat, akasha—whatever name we give it, it is a singular substance that manifests in the infinite diversity of forms. As the Mahatma writes in nearly poetic language, all—including the vestures we wear whether in or out of incarnation—are "Children of Akasa, concrete evolutions from the ether," all due to the "varying action of Force. . . . It is *motion* with its resulting conflict, neutralization, equilibration, correlation, to which is due the infinite variety which prevails." Proteus-like, the one substance-force reveals itself in such a way that patterns exist yet no two snowflakes, no two persons, no two leaves on the same tree are precisely identical. The world "of ten thousand things" delights us in its variety, yet always we are called to realize its essential oneness of being.

On describing the circumstances under which he is writing, the Mahatma refers to his "nature-seeing, nature-influencing self," which he says he can awaken "to new perceptions and feelings." This seems to be a statement of another of the adeptic powers. Undoubtedly each of us is our "own Creator and ruler," but we are most likely unconscious of having such power, while the Adept is one who uses that power consciously. If we ask why the Mahatma did not use this power to warm the current of air so it would have unfrozen his fingers, perhaps the answer is that the Mahatmas—as they say on many occasions—never waste their powers on selfish purposes.

The Mahatma next turns to what must have been one of Hume's statements: that Nature's laws "arise." KH denies this: "Immutable laws cannot arise, since they are eternal and uncreated, propelled in the Eternity." So we may say that lawfulness, as order and purpose, is inherent in Absoluteness, the Ultimate Reality, or, in HPB's terms, "Be-ness," the First Fundamental Proposition of *The Secret Doctrine*. The Mahatma continues: " We recognize but one law in the Universe, the law of harmony, of *perfect* Equilibrium." This is the fundamental definition of the law of karma, which in *The Voice of the Silence* is called the law of compassion, the "Law of Laws." Since "motion is eternal," as KH writes a little later in this letter, and there is, further, "the eternal progression of cycles," the harmony that is the essence of the law is not a static condition; otherwise, there could be no manifestation, no evolutionary unfoldment of consciousness. HPB expresses this point so beautifully: "The Secret Doctrine teaches the progressive development of everything, worlds as well as atoms; and this stupendous development has neither conceivable beginning nor imaginable end" (*SD*, 1:43).

Indeed we could say that HPB's major work, *The Secret Doctrine*, is really a text of cycles, presenting the magnificent panorama of the "eternal progression" through all the cycles of nature, the manvantaras and pralayas and the cycles of the root races, or developmental stages of human consciousness, as well as the smaller cycles we experience in successive incarnations. The book presents a truly magnificent vision, to which the Mahatma directs our attention in just a few words here. How, it might be asked, can one *not* believe in the doctrine of cycles?

We are accustomed to speaking of spirit and matter as two distinct states, and to correct this misunderstanding KH wrote in Letter 65: "We recognize but *one* element in Nature (whether spiritual or physical) . . . consequently spirit and matter are *one*, being but a differentiation of states not *essences*." Now, in Letter 90, KH reiterates this point, which is "one of the elementary and fundamental doctrines of Occultism": "the two are one, . . . distinct but in their respective manifestations." This is not an easy concept to grasp, and evidently Hume found it impossible to understand, so the Mahatma resorts to an analogy: "the very simple phenomenon of ice, water, vapour and the final dispersion of the latter." In the beautiful language of the "book of Kiu-te," the work from which the stanzas of *The Secret Doctrine* are said to be excerpted, "Spirit is called the ultimate sublimation of matter, and matter the crystallization of spirit."

The very heart of Buddhist metaphysics, the Abhidharma, to which the Mahatma directed Sinnett's attention in Letter 68, is now magnificently summarized and deserves careful consideration: "There is a moment in the existence of every molecule and atom of matter when, for one cause or another, the last spark of spirit or motion of life (call it by whatever name) is withdrawn, and in the same instant, with the swiftness which surpasses that of the lightning glance of thought, the atom or molecule or an aggregation of molecules is annihilated to return to its pristine purity of intracosmic matter." Although a full study of the laya centers would take us too far afield at this time, some familiarity with the concept is useful in understanding this statement. In *The Secret Doctrine*, HPB refers to this instantaneous withdrawal of spirit accompanying the annihilation of matter as the laya center, the zero point, the mystical point where substance (akasha, svabhavat,

Mulaprakriti) becomes once more homogeneous and therefore unable to act or differentiate. She says further, "The 'imperishable Laya Centres' have a great importance, and their meaning must be fully understood if we would have a clear conception of the Archaic Cosmogony, whose theories have now passed into Occultism. . . . The worlds are built neither *upon*, nor *over*, nor *in* the *Laya* centres, the zero-point being a condition, not any mathematical point" (*SD*, 1:145).

Finally, almost as a summary of his refutation of Hume's arguments for belief in a "moral Governor of the Universe," the Mahatma again echoes the law of correspondence: "Matter, force, and motion are the trinity of physical, objective nature, as the trinitarian unity of spirit-matter is that of the spiritual or subjective nature. Motion is eternal because spirit is eternal. But no modes of motion can ever be conceived unless they be in connection with matter."

If Hume was, as KH declared, "unfit to learn" because his mind was already "too full" of his own preconceptions, we may hope that we at least have the necessary openness of mind to grapple with the stupendous truths that the Mahatma sets before us in this letter. Many of those truths are presented in earlier letters or repeated in subsequent ones, but if we had just this one letter, we would still have a remarkable entry point into the fundamental principles of the occult science. It is left to us to "learn first [the Mahatmas'] laws, and educate [our] perceptions."

~⁓ ⁓○

LETTER 91

The prefatory note to Letter 91 mentions two of the Mahatma's chelas whom we have met in earlier letters (Letters 53 and 84), Dharbagiri Nath and Babaji ("the little man"), and the confusion that sometimes existed between the two. KH's chief concern in this letter is the "imprudence and indiscretion" on the part of Babaji, an "*accepted* chela" who not only lost some money but then borrowed funds from a "probationary chela." Evidently, he also borrowed further funds from Sinnett "through Djual Khool," although it is not clear how that was accomplished. In any case, the Mahatma is sending Sinnett sums to cover both debts.

From his comments, we can infer something of the Mahatma's attitude toward the borrowing of money, particularly by a chela. Not only is KH disappointed by the chela's action, but he is concerned about its effect: "Money losses are nothing, but it is the results involved and the temptation that are terrible." We can speculate that such actions on the part of chelas, whether accepted or probationary, indicate moral transgressions that count against them. As we know, Babaji, even though at this time an accepted pupil, ultimately failed.

The brief reference to an individual named Padshah (Sorabji J. Padshah, editor of the *Indian Spectator*) recalls an incident recorded in Letter 21, when KH asks Sinnett's opinion of a poem written by Padshah. Padshah also received a letter directly from the Mahatma (see *LMW*, Second Series, 149). However, although KH says here that Padshah is "sincerely devoted to Theosophy and—*our* Cause," he later left the Society.

The Mahatma now expresses his concern for HPB (she had been in Sikkim and had been with the two Mahatmas, so KH writes, "We have left her near Darjeeling"), mentioning a letter that Hume has written to her. HPB refers to this letter in a letter she wrote to Sinnett while staying at Darjeeling (*LBS*, Letter 49): "I have received via Bombay a long article by Mr. Hume. The most impudent and insulting I ever read. If he thinks I will print it, he may whistle for it. I will send it to you tomorrow with my letter for him as Boss advises me to do. . . . I am very weak and must stop."

Another passage in HPB's same letter brings us close to the Mahatmas. Because she was very ill, she was permitted to travel to Sikkim, and had seen M and KH "in *their bodies* both," as she puts it. Then she writes: "Oh the blessed blessed two days! It was like the old times when the bear [referring to M] paid me a visit. The same kind of wooden hut, a box divided into three compartments for rooms, and standing in a jungle on four pelican's legs; the same yellow chelas gliding noiselessly; the same eternal "gul-gul-gul" sound of my Boss's inextinguishable chelum pipe; the old familiar sweet voice of your KH (whose voice is still sweeter and face still thinner and more transparent) the same *entourage* for furniture—skins, and yak-tail stuffed pillows and dishes for salt tea etc."

The cause of her illness as well as the method M employed to cure her came to light in a letter she wrote a year later to one M. Biliere in Paris: "Last year the doctors condemned me. I had Bright's disease in the last phase. . . . Well, I went to Sikkim, to the entrance of Tibet, and there my beloved Master repaired kidneys and liver, and in three days' time I was as healthy as ever. They say it was a miracle. He only gave me a potion to drink seven times a day, from a plant in the Himalayas."

As part of HPB's story at this particular time, I include here a curious paragraph from Colonel Olcott's account of the founders' move from Bombay to their new home at Adyar, an event that occurred not long after HPB returned from Darjeeling. First mentioning that she had been "away at Darjeeling with some of our members, having meetings in the flesh with two of our Masters," Olcott then says, "The Teacher (M.) came daily to see HPB, and I have it recorded that on 29th December, she 'made me promise that if she should die, no one but myself should be allowed to see her face. I am to sew her up in a cloth and have her cremated.' That, you see, was nine years before her corpse was carried to the Woking Crematory, near London; hence the possibility of her sudden death was even then kept in mind."

Olcott's report gives further meaning to KH's statement in Letter 91 that the Mahatmas were giving "the whole of our time to watching her . . . since she is now unable to take care of herself." It was undoubtedly one of those crisis times in her life, and we can only be grateful that she did recover, since during those final nine years she produced *The Secret Doctrine, The Key to Theosophy, The Voice of the Silence,* as well as numerous articles, in addition to founding the Esoteric Section (now known as the Esoteric School of Theosophy).

I conclude this commentary on Letter 91 by identifying the three references at the end of KH's short notes: first, the Mahatma refers to a long letter he was writing, which is Letter 92; second, KH states he will soon send a letter with answers to questions, which we have as Letters 93A and 93B; then, the Mahatma writes of a "ludicrous incident," which is the delightful story about the goat, related at the conclusion of Letter 92. KH ends with a warm welcome to Sinnett as the "new President" of the Simla Eclectic Branch, following Hume's resignation.

LETTER 92

Certainly one of the Mahatma KH's longest letters, Letter 92 is so focused on certain individuals that it seems to hold little interest for us today. However, as we give attention to the letter, several points emerge that are worth careful consideration. First, as remarked upon earlier, we should note the attention the Mahatma gives to each individual who comes within the orbit of the Theosophical Society, assessing not only that individual's strengths and weaknesses but also, and more important, his or her potential for either aiding or damaging the Society. Such is the bond of friendship between KH and Sinnett that the Mahatma feels at liberty to share his frank assessment of the current situation while at the same time encouraging the Englishman to understand more deeply the "rules" of the Fraternity. Furthermore, this letter contains beautiful statements concerning adeptship and chelaship, as well as a wonderful defense of HPB, and it concludes with an amusing incident that KH relates in a delightful way.

In order to fully appreciate KH's concern for the Society and its usefulness as a vehicle for conveying the teachings being given to Sinnett, it seems best to comment on the letter in a sequential manner, taking up each subject as it occurs. The letter opens with KH's evident pleasure over Hume's "abdication" of the presidency of the Simla Eclectic Theosophical Society and his acknowledgment of his own role in that event. And he sends Sinnett Hume's "last letter" (see appendix 3, pages 489–90). As mentioned earlier, Hume has taken up with a new teacher, "the good Vedantin Swami," known as the Swami from Almora. That individual wrote some articles on Advaita philosophy with which Subba Row had vigorously disagreed. In a letter to Sinnett (see *LBS*, 82), HPB mentions this Swami, saying he planned to "expose the Masters as Dugpas." She also wrote an article about him, titled "The Almora Swami" (*CW*, 4:560–69). The Swami is reported to have died shortly after Hume turned to him for the study he felt he was not receiving from the Mahatmas.

Notably, KH goes on to say that he would not like to see Hume sever his connection with the Society, since his literary contributions were valuable. Further, were he to leave the Society, he would undoubtedly become "an indefatigable though a *secret* enemy." It would be another two years before Hume did resign from the Society. We may also recall that at the conclusion of Letter 47, Sinnett was warned that Hume might "become your enemy."

The Mahatma next turns to Fern, whom the Mahatma M took some interest in because of his considerable psychic abilities. He warns Sinnett that the man is not to be trusted: "*beware of him*," he writes. Fern did indeed prove entirely untrustworthy and eventually was expelled from the Society, another sad story of a probationer who failed. Yet at the time of Letter 92, Sinnett was encouraged to "try to save him," since "it is a real pity" that Fern's gifts "should be drowned in a mire of vice." One senses, however, that it is not so much for Fern's sake that the Mahatma is asking Sinnett to help the man, but rather to prevent harm coming to the Society through that person's enmity.

"And now to C. C. Massey," KH goes on. Massey, an English lawyer more interested in Spiritualism than Theosophy, had been present at the founding meeting of the Society in New York on November 17, 1875, and became the first president of the British Theosophical Society. As the British Branch had lost some momentum, Massey and a few others, including Anna Kingsford and "her scribe," Edward

Maitland, were attempting to revive it. This group was hoping for direct instruction from the Mahatmas, but perhaps because of their treatment of HPB, or for other reasons not given, KH writes that "we would have no objection to teach them" but only "through" Sinnett. So the Mahatma states: "I will never refuse my help and co-operation to a group of men sincere and ardent to learn." Among those mentioned is Wyld, who is Dr. George Wyld, a homeopathic doctor who became the first president of the London Lodge, as we shall see later in the correspondence. One can only wonder why Wyld refused to admit Sir William Crookes into the Society, although we know Crookes was admitted later and even became one of the Society's counsellors.

KH states that a "great tidal wave of mysticism . . . is now sweeping over a portion of the intellectual classes of Europe." Concerning this growing European interest, HPB later wrote an article titled "The Tidal Wave," published in her journal *Lucifer* in November 1889 (*CW*, 12:1–8). At that time in history, England was the dominant power in the world, so the Mahatmas may have been particularly keen that the Society should have a firm base in that country so it could reach out from that base to influence all of Europe. This would also be the reason so much attention was given to individuals such as Massey and his colleagues in the Society. The prominent members in England were generally well-educated professionals—lawyers and doctors—as well as deeply involved in Spiritualism. Many were founding members of the Society for Psychical Research and left the Theosophical Society when HPB was so denigrated by the infamous Hodgson Report. The majority of the members of the British Theosophical Society at this early date were men, with the exception of such outstanding feminists as Anna Kingsford, Francesca Arundale, later Mabel Collins, and some years later, of course, Annie Besant.

Two significant statements concerning seeking knowledge of the occult wisdom must surely be as relevant today as when they were written. The first concerns the motive for seeking: "The quality of wisdom ever was, and will be yet for a long time—to the very close of the fifth race—denied to him who seeks the wealth of the mind for its own sake, and for its own enjoyment and result without the secondary purpose of turning it to account in the attainment of material benefits." The second concerns the student's absorption of the teachings: "I cannot undertake to furnish either them or even yourself with *new* facts until all I have already given is put into shape from the beginning . . . and taught to them systematically, and by them learned and digested. . . . I positively refuse to teach any further before you have understood and learned all that is already given."

We may well ask ourselves: Why do we seek more knowledge when we have not understood or applied the knowledge already given to us? What, then, is our purpose in seeking wisdom? Again and again, throughout the letters, the Mahatmas stress the importance of the motive with which we pursue the occult teachings. Equally important is the "use" to which we put them, discovering their practical applications and sharing the teachings with others.

KH goes on to state, "I am not prepared just now to afford the British Theosophists the proof of our existence in flesh and bones . . . all this is a question of time and—*Karma*." Anyone could easily impersonate an objective existence, but would that provide "the positive, moral certitude" that the appearance is not a bogus one? KH reminds Sinnett of the "fate" of such educated individuals as St. Germain and Cagliostro, both of whom continue to be regarded as imposters.

Now follows extensive comments on a number of individuals as the Mahatma paints a word picture of the deplorable tangle in human relations for which HPB suffers the most. He refers first to Swami Dayanand Sarasvati and Hurrychund Chintamon, the founder of the Arya Samaj and the president of the Arya Samaj's Bombay group, respectively. An excellent summary of the Theosophical Society's brief association with the Arya Samaj, a movement for the revival of the pure Vedic religion, after the founders arrived in India is given in appendix C of the *Readers' Guide*; a fuller account is included in *A Short History of the Theosophical Society*. Hurrychund, who had been expelled from the Society, had decamped to England, where, the Mahatma writes, he was "seeking and thirsting for his revenge." Living in Manchester at the time Letter 92 was written, Hurrychund founded an organization known as the Hermetic Brotherhood of Luxor (not to be confused with the Brotherhood of Luxor from whom Colonel Olcott had received communications in New York). He was forced to leave England and seems to have disappeared somewhere in the United States. Swami Dayanand, whom KH says "*was* an initiated Yogi" but had forfeited his powers, becoming a "moral wreck," later turned against Olcott and HPB, charging them with being converts to Buddhism and abandoning the Vedas.

The Mahatma next mentions another false friend, a Dr. Billing, "husband of that good, honest woman, the only *really* and thoroughly reliable and *honest* medium I know of," quite an unusual statement for KH to make. Mrs. M. Hollis-Billing (the name is sometimes given as Billings) was a prominent American medium who came to England, where she became active in the formation of the London Lodge, although she retained her membership in the Parent Society. (At that time, if a member of the Parent Society joined a Branch, membership in the former was usually forfeited.) When the founders went to England in 1879, en route to India, they stayed with Dr. and Mrs. Billing, and it was at their home that HPB produced phenomenally a china teapot, which is now in the archives at Adyar. About another individual KH mentions, C. Carter Blake, we know only that he was expelled from the Society for slander but was later permitted to rejoin. Certainly the letter contains severe indictments against Hurrychund, Billing, and Blake, as the Mahatma tries to help Sinnett understand all that was occurring in London.

We can speculate that Sinnett had asked not only about Massey but also about Stainton Moses, since the Mahatma's next comments seem to reflect whatever Sinnett had written about these two individuals. Having disposed of such "villains" as Hurrychund, Billing, and Blake, the Mahatma reminds Sinnett of what he had previously written about Moses. The question of Moses' "guide," known as Imperator or by the + sign, was explained fully in Letter 18. The student may want to review it at this point.

Turning next to "the *facts* and . . . the accusations against HPB," the Mahatma anticipates Sinnett's likely query: "But you will perhaps enquire, why *we* have not interfered?" Here again, as on so many previous occasions, Sinnett is told, "You are thoroughly unacquainted with our system," implying that were he so acquainted he would not ask such a question. As it is, KH does not believe he can make the Englishman understand why the Mahatmas do not interfere, since it involves the rules and disciplines under which they work. It is here that KH makes a key statement concerning chelaship:

> The fact is, that to the last and supreme initiation every chela—(and even some adepts)—is left to his own device and counsel. We have to fight our own battles, and the familiar adage—"the adept *becomes*, he is not *made*" is true to the letter. Since every one of us is the *creator* and producer of the *causes* that lead to such or some other *results*, we have to reap but what we have sown. *Our chelas are helped but when they are innocent of the causes that lead them into trouble*; when such causes are generated by foreign, outside influences.

KH follows this with a comment that we might keep in mind to be spared the karmic consequences of our own past actions: "Life and the struggle for adeptship would be too easy, had we all scavengers behind us to sweep away the *effects* we have generated through our own rashness and presumption." He could have added that this is true whether we have consciously or unconsciously produced the consequences we may now be experiencing. Karma is indeed an inexorable law, as both the Mahatmas and HPB point out, and we can only alter its action by our attitude toward the circumstances in which we find ourselves.

The Mahatma continues with further comments concerning chelaship to which we should give full attention:

> Before they are allowed to go into the world they—the chelas—are every one of them endowed with more or less clairvoyant powers;

and, with the exception of that faculty that, unless paralyzed and watched would lead them perchance to divulge certain secrets that must not be revealed—they are left in the full exercise of their powers—whatever these may be. . . . Thus, step by step, and after a series of punishments, is the chela taught by bitter experience to suppress and guide his impulses; he loses his rashness, his self-sufficiency and never falls into the same errors. . . . The first element of success in a candidate [is the] *unshaken faith* that his conviction rests upon, and has taken root in knowledge.

KH again repeats what has been said in other letters regarding the necessity of testing everyone who aspires to chelaship: "No one comes in contact with us, no one shows a desire to know more of us, but has to submit to being tested and put by us on probation." It was this "testing" that so irritated and even angered Hume and that also led so many probationary chelas to failure. Sinnett, when reading this letter, must have been encouraged, then, to learn that he had not only been "tested and tried" but had "not hitherto failed—at any rate not in one direction—that of discretion and silence."

Turning to HPB and the accusations being made against her, the Mahatma divulges a most unhappy fact: "All that now happens is brought on by HPB herself." He promises to reveal to Sinnett "her one great fault." That fault was apparently her overzealousness, which led to her proclivity to attribute to the Mahatmas the production of even the simplest of phenomena rather than acknowledging her own psychic gifts in such productions. In the letter's next pages, KH presents a magnificent defense of HPB. Stating that "*motive* is everything for us," the Mahatma then speaks of HPB's "motive—a sublime, self-denying, noble and meritorious . . . zeal," and adds: "She had to be allowed full and entire freedom of action, the liberty of *creating causes* that became in due course of time her scourge, her public pillory."

Reminding Sinnett that HPB suffers from "a psychological disease," KH admits that she is a "quaint, strange woman, a psychological riddle, impulsive and kindhearted, yet not free from the vice of untruth." Her condition, we may recall, was explained by the Mahatma in Letter 22, and the student may wish to review that letter at this point. It is because she is a "psychological cripple" as well as because of her particular nature, that KH now writes: "She is utterly unfit for a *true adept*: her nature is too passionately affectionate and we have no right to indulge in *personal* attachments and feelings. You can never know her as we do." Nevertheless, KH tells Sinnett, whatever may be her faults or however she may be judged by her associates, "we find a profounder wisdom in her *inner* Self than you will ever find yourselves able to perceive."

Later in the letter, KH speaks of "higher and *initiated* chelas such as HPB." And his description of her recent meeting with M and himself is truly a delightful word picture. So writes KH, "We cannot help feeling at times angry with, oftener—laughing at, her." (For HPB's own description of the meeting, see *LBS*, 38.)

KH tells Sinnett that he is now at liberty to share with Massey all that he has been told, since Massey is more likely to believe what Sinnett says "than what a dozen 'KH's' might tell him personally." Again, the Mahatma was evidently making every effort to help Sinnett not only understand the situation in England but also aid such individuals as Massey in order to stabilize the Society's work in that country. We can presume this from KH's next statements, as he returns to a subject that he knows "is very repulsive" to Sinnett, the subject of "testing" would-be chelas. So, in response to Sinnett's question, "Why should the Brothers refuse turning their attention to such worthy, sincere theosophists" as Massey, Hood (not otherwise identified), and Moses, KH says, "They were all tried and tested in various ways and not one of them came up [to] the mark." Such testing is carried out unbeknownst to the individuals under observation for the simple reason, says KH, that "a man's character, his true inner nature can never be thoroughly drawn out if he believes himself watched, or strives for an object." His Brother Morya, he says, "gave special attention" to Massey.

Mention is made next of Ross Scott, whom HPB was to have "furnished with a wife amply sufficient for his happiness." We met Scott in several earlier letters, a young Irishman and British civil servant whom the founders met on shipboard when sailing from England to Bombay in 1879. He received a letter from the Mahatma M, became first secretary of the Simla Eclectic Theosophical Society and—after HPB was told to find him a wife—married Minnie Hume, Hume's only daughter. In Letter 92, KH says that Scott had "a visit in astral shape from M." This may well have been in connection with Colonel Olcott's visit to the Branch in Lahore, when Olcott himself was visited by M. In *Old Diary Leaves* (3:434), Olcott records that on his visit to Lahore in 1887, "I found, as District Judge, our old friend Ross Scott . . . ever our brave colleague who had stood up for us through good report and evil report, despite the whole force of Anglo-Indian prejudice. On this occasion he most willingly took the chair at my lecture and spoke most kindly of the movement and of ourselves."

Olcott records meeting Ross Scott on a later tour, this time at Lucknow, where Scott was again serving as District Judge, and being invited to dinner at Scott's home (*ODL*, 6:298). No mention is made on these occasions of Minnie Hume Scott, and it is thought that the couple had separated. In a letter to Patience Sinnett, HPB wrote: "Poor Minnie Scott is getting blind, she is at the Jhut-Sing's [her father's] paternal residence." We know from other correspondence that Minnie Scott was quite antagonistic toward the Mahatmas and may have influenced her husband, but the cordial relationship that existed between Scott and Olcott seems unlikely had he harbored any enmity for HPB or the Society.

KH takes up again the case of Fern in this letter, pointing out that his story "affords . . . a useful study and a hint" concerning "methods adopted in individual cases to thoroughly *test* the latent moral qualities" of the person. The key point is that everyone is given a chance, for as the Mahatma writes: "Every human being contains within himself vast potentialities, and it is the duty of the adepts to surround the would-be chela with circumstances which shall enable him to take the 'right-hand path,'—if he have the ability in him. We are no more at liberty to withhold the chance from a postulant than we are to guide and direct him into the proper course."

And so he adds: "We were all so tested; and while a Moorad Ali—*failed*—I, succeeded." Moorad Ali Beg, the student may recall, was the pseudonym of Godolphin Mitford, whose article "The Elixir of Life," which appeared in *The Theosophist*, Sinnett was advised to read (see Letter 49). KH continues: "The victor's crown is only for him who proves himself worthy to wear it; for him who attacks *Mara* single handed and conquers the demon of lust and earthly passions; and not *we* but he himself puts it on his brow. It was not a meaningless phrase of the Tathagata that 'he who masters *Self* is greater than he who conquers thousands in battle'; there is no such other difficult struggle. If it were not so, adeptship would be but a cheap acquirement."

The lines KH quotes are verse 103 in the *Dhammapada*, which is said to contain the Buddha's true teachings as recorded by his disciples. The verse as translated by Dr. C. Kunhan Raja, longtime director of the Adyar Library, reads: "And he who may conquer in battle men in thousands and thousands, conquering his one self he indeed becomes the greatest of conquerors in battles."

The Mahatma now turns to other matters. "We have a reform in head," he writes and proceeds to propose a "remodelling [of] the present formation of Branches and their privileges." He advises ways that the membership may be urged toward more self-reliance rather than looking unnecessarily to the Parent Body for guidance. "Let them [the Branches] be all chartered and initiated as heretofore by the Parent Society, and depend on it nominally. At the same time, let every Branch before it is chartered, choose some one object to work for, an object, naturally, in sympathy with the general principle of the T.S.—yet a distinct and definite object of its own, whether in the religious, educational or philosophical line. This would allow the Society a broader margin for its general operations; more real, useful work would be done."

We should note the extent to which the Mahatmas took a keen interest in and offered advice to the Society in its early days. This "reform" proposed by KH is the basis for the current policy, which permits autonomy for each Branch, or Lodge, in its programs so long as its work is consonant with the Objects and principles of the Society. KH now proposes: "Each Branch has to choose its well-defined mission to work for; and the greatest care should be taken in the selection of Presidents"—advice that might well be taken today! He continues: "Solidarity of thought and action within the broad outline of the chief and general principles of the Society there must always be between the Parent and Branch bodies; yet the latter must be allowed each their own independent action in everything that does not clash with those principles."

The letter ends with the Mahatma's recounting of the famous "goat incident," which he calls "ludicrous" and which he had promised to tell Sinnett at the end of Letter 91. KH is indeed an accomplished storyteller, and the account is delightful to read. It is interesting to note also the lesson that the Mahatma learned from the incident, leading him "to hope for a relaxation of severity one of these days," referring no doubt to the "severity" of the rules by which the Fraternity is governed.

The reference in the final paragraph to "Nath" is to Dharbagiri Nath, the mystical name of one of the chelas (see page 144), probably Babaji, "the "little man" mentioned in connection with the goat incident. Of special interest in that final paragraph is KH's statement: "We all strive to become Dhyan-Chohans in *the end*." There is much for the student to consider in that statement, for which a full study of the Dhyan-Chohanic kingdom would be necessary.

No doubt it was with tongue in cheek that KH penned the words at the end of this very long letter: "I believe you will not complain of my letter being too short." He promises another "voluminous" epistle, answering Sinnett's several questions. That letter comprises the following pair: Letter 93A (containing the questions) and 93B (containing the Mahatma's replies).

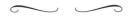

LETTERS 93A AND 93B

In the conclusions of Letters 91 and 92, the Mahatma KH has assured Sinnett that he will soon respond to his "many Questions," and that his answers will probably constitute a "voluminous correspondence." That the Mahatma has had these questions for some time is clear from Sinnett's reference in his first question to an "allusion in your last," which actually refers to a comment KH made regarding Hume in Letter 81: "You have no conception of the potential selfishness there is in him; of the cruel, remorseless egotism he brought back with him from his last incarnation." Sinnett very likely sent these questions to the Mahatma after receiving Letter 81, which concerns the "H.X. letter" and the protest signed by twelve of KH and M's chelas.

We are again fortunate in having in Letters 93A and 93B both Sinnett's questions and the Mahatma's responses. However, before asking any questions, Sinnett reminds KH that he has promised to send him "those unpublished notes of Eliphas Levi's with annotations." This is a reference to Letter 70C (especially page 215), at the end of which KH had written: "To reconcile you still more with Eliphas, I will send you a number of his mss. that have never been published, in a large clear, beautiful handwriting with my comments all through. Nothing better than that can give you a key to Kabalistic puzzles." KH signed the comments "E.O.," standing for "Eminent Occultist."

Sinnett, obviously interested in seeing the article or articles by Eliphas Levi, must have written to HPB complaining that it, or they, had not yet appeared in *The Theosophist*, for HPB wrote in a letter to Sinnett: "You speak to me of things for which I am not in the least responsible nor have I ever taken an interest in them. Except of the volume annotated on the margin by KH and sent to Hume and a MS. commented upon by Djwal Khool, I took no interest in Eliphas Levi's MSS." Evidently the material sent to Hume was in French, Eliphas Levi's native language, for HPB continues: "And who, pray, was there to *translate* them? Who, besides us two—broken down post horses is there to translate such things?" From reading further in HPB's letter, it appears the articles were sent to Mme. Gebhard, a prominent German Theosophist, who sent them on to Colonel Olcott, who spoke fluent French, as did both HPB and KH. (For the full text of HPB's letter, see *LBS*, particularly page 56.)

Now, in Letter 93A, Koot Humi tells Sinnett that the "unpublished notes" had been sent "long ago to our 'Jako' [*sic*] friend," referring to Hume, whose home in Simla, called Rothney Castle, was situated on Jakko Hill. Although not essential to our consideration of Letters 93A and 93B, the "fate" of these manuscripts is rather intriguing. Hume must have eventually translated part if not all of the material, as in the letter we are now considering KH states, "In the forthcoming *Theosophist* you will find a note or two appended to Hume's translation of Eliphas Levi's *Preface* in connection with the lost continent" (page 313). Incidentally, one of "E.O.'s" marginal notes concerns Jesus: " . . . but he preached a century before his birth." This intriguing situation leaves us with many unanswered questions, including how Levi's "mss." came into the Mahatma's possession in the first place.

The first three questions from Sinnett in Letter 93A are followed immediately by KH's answers. His curiosity piqued by KH's comment, already noted, concerning Hume's "last incarnation," Sinnett is naturally interested in his own past lives and whether the Mahatma possesses "the power of looking back to the former lives of persons now living." KH's response—"All of us . . . bring some characteristics from our previous incarnations"—should encourage us to consider what we ourselves may have brought with us into this incarnation from past ones. If as KH goes on to say, it is "more proper to study our own present personality before attempting to learn anything of its creator," we can ask ourselves if we are looking as objectively as possible at our present natural inclinations, habits of thought, and actions in an effort to understand ourselves as we are now and, from that understanding, to determine what may need changing.

The Mahatma tells Sinnett that while he does not like to use his ability to look back on previous incarnations, he may "some day . . . treat you to a little story," giving Sinnett only "a hint or two to test your intuitional powers." This "little story" may appear in part in folio 6 of the Mahatma Letters in the British Museum Library, although it was not included with the published letters. The story relates to Germanicus Caesar, born in 14 BC, who was sent to Germany in 13 AD to subdue the German tribes. He captured, among other prisoners, Thusnelda, the wife of a German chieftain who had been killed in one of the engagements. On his return to Rome, Germanicus was accorded a triumphal parade that included Thusnelda, along with other prisoners and spoils of war.

The item in Folio 6 of the letters consists of an envelope, a note signed by the Mahatma KH, and a photocopy of a painting titled in German, "Thusnelda in Triumphzuge des Germanicus." The painting depicts a Roman conqueror watching German prisoners being paraded before him. In the group is a young woman, obviously Thusnelda. The note signed by KH reads: "Left behind. It is from Mali's [or Mati's] dust basket and I save the fair Thusnelda—with whose beauty you were so struck—and Germanicus, for both of whom he [Mali] had already prepared a bed of infamy in a neighboring gutter." Mali [or Mati] is not identified but may have been a servant who cleaned house for KH. The phrase "with whose beauty you were so struck" and the picture seem to have some significance, else why would the Mahatma have retrieved the picture from a wastebasket and sent it to Sinnett? Another one of those intriguing incidents!

The first three questions and their answers are in what Sinnett has called section one. Section two of Letter 93A includes an additional twenty-nine questions, the responses to which comprise Letter 93B. Those questions may be roughly divided into three groups: questions 1 through 6 concern human evolution, the races, and their civilizations, including a query on the origin of evil; questions 7 through 14 relate to the physical sciences; and questions 15 through 29 are about devachan, the after-death states in general, and the process of reincarnation.

Before examining the Mahatma's answers to Sinnett's queries, it seems appropriate to note what he says in Letter 93B concerning the basis for his replies. On page 322 he writes that "all my [KH's] answers are based upon, and derived from, our Eastern occult doctrines," and that therefore he is giving the Englishman information "for your instruction as a student of occultism." He also reiterates a point made throughout the letters: on page 321 he notes that he is speaking from what "we *know*." A similar phrase occurs on page 317: "such is our knowledge and fruits of milleniums of observation and experience." Earlier, on page 311, the Mahatma says he is writing of knowledge that "is known and recorded in our books thousands of years ago." What is being conveyed to Sinnett, and consequently to us as we study not only Letter 93B but all the correspondence, is the occult wisdom handed down through the ages. At the same time, as we read the letter now before us, we see how familiar KH was with the scientific theories of the time, although many have since been discredited or at least questioned. It is therefore incumbent on us to separate the occult knowledge from statements of then-contemporary science.

The Mahatma's response to Sinnett's first question contains two distinct points to note. The first concerns what the Englishman has called the "curious rush into human progress" (which we, from the vantage point of the twenty-first century, can say has very much accelerated). We must remember that races and sub-races (using those unfortunate terms, which, as noted earlier, designate stages of evolutionary growth, not ethnic or national groupings) have a life cycle: they are born, grow through childhood and adolescence, mature, and fade into old age and death. KH writes of "the law of development, growth, maturity and decline [of] every race and sub-race," and says two impulses now at work to produce the effects we see: the first impulse comes from the fact that the fifth race, now more than half way through its life cycle, has begun "its downward course"; the second impulse derives from the stage at which the fifth sub-race is now moving, which is upward toward its halfway mark. The second noteworthy point is KH's sharp warning: do not judge the achievements of other civilizations and races merely by their extant historical records.

KH elaborates on that warning in his response to Sinnett's second question, giving it further attention in his lengthy reply to the third question. "Civilization," he says, "is an inheritance, a patrimony that passes from race to race along the ascending and descending paths of cycles." What, we may well ask, is meant by "civilization"? If cyclic evolution is essentially a growth in consciousness, we must consider the term more from the inner psychological viewpoint than from the materialistic one of technological achievements. Later in the letter (page 314), KH remarks, "Remember the difference we make between *material* and *spiritual* civilizations." By the way, the name "Cendrillon" undoubtedly refers to "Cinderella," based on the context in which it appears.

KH's answer to the second question contains an interesting allusion to the "second infancy" of the sub-races, strongly suggesting that each sub-race is "reincarnated" in each of the root races, preserving some of its earlier characteristics as it does so. This topic calls for further study, which is best pursued by reviewing HPB's exposition on the races and sub-races in volume 2 of *The Secret Doctrine*.

We in the modern era know something of the civilizations of ancient Egypt, Rome, Chaldea, Peru, and other long-ago cultures. These are all relatively recent, however, considering the chronology to which KH refers. As he tells Sinnett: "We affirm that *a series* of civilizations existed *before*, as well as after the Glacial Period, that they existed upon various points of the globe, reached the apex of glory and—died. . . . We speak of civilizations of the ante-glacial period." It is difficult to work out a chronology for even the root races on this globe, but those who wish to do so may refer to *The Secret Doctrine* (2:709 *et seq.*). Geoffrey Barborka, using the figures given by HPB, devotes a chapter to the chronology of the rounds, the root races, and the sub-races in his excellent work *The Peopling of the Earth*.

Before proceeding with a detailed study of KH's responses regarding the rounds and races, the student may want to review the discussion of those subjects in earlier letters, particularly Letters 46, 61, 62, 66, and 67, as well as the commentaries on those letters. Also helpful on this topic is the unfinished posthumously published essay by HPB, "On Cosmic Cycles, Manvantaras, and Rounds" (*CW*, 13:301–6), mentioned in the commentary on Letter 46.

The Mahatma indicates the antiquity of earlier civilizations when he speaks of "the 'Sons of Ad' or the children of the Fire Mist [who] preceded by hundreds of centuries the Age of Iron, which was an old age already when what you now call the Historical Period . . . had hardly begun" (page 311). The "Sons of Ad" were the "Elect" of the third root race who had learned the secret of immortality. This group, known also as the "Sons of Will and Yoga," and as the "Hierarchy of the Elect," was produced by *kriyashakti*, "the mysterious *power of thought* which enables it to produce external, perceptible, phenomenal results by its own inherent energy" (*SD*, 2:173). HPB says further about them:

> In the first or earlier portion of the existence of this third race . . . the "Sons of Wisdom," who . . . incarnated in this Third Race, produced by *Kriyasakti*, a progeny called the "Sons of Ad" or "of the Fire-Mist," the "Sons of Will and Yoga," etc. They were a conscious production, as a portion of the race was already animated with the divine spark of spiritual, superior intelligence. It was not a Race, this progeny. It was at first a wondrous Being, called the "Initiator," and after him a group of semi-divine and semi-human beings. "*Set apart*" in Archaic *genesis* for certain purposes, they are those in whom are said to have incarnated the highest Dhyanis . . . from previous Manvantaras—*to form the nursery for future human adepts*, on this earth and during the present cycle. (*SD*, 1:207)

In answering Sinnett's fourth question, the Mahatma again refers to the "Sons of the *Fire Mist*," this time adding, notably, the word "our" in referring to this group. He comments: "Everything comes in its appointed time and place in the evolution of the Rounds" and that "all an adept could do would be to predict an *approximate* time."

Perhaps, then, we should be cautious in assigning specific dates to the various time periods in the evolutionary cycles.

The answer to Sinnett's fourth question deals primarily with the so-called sinking of Atlantis, which in fact refers to two quite separate events: the sinking of the main continent about 850,000 years ago and the sinking of the final remnant some 11,000 years ago. Sometimes these two events are confused. KH refers Sinnett to "the incomplete and partially veiled tradition" concerning Atlantis that HPB recorded in *Isis Unveiled*, and indeed the student will most likely find her account of considerable interest. The subject of lost continents, both Atlantis and Lemuria, remains a topic of speculation for many people.

In his response to Sinnett's fifth question, concerning the origin of evil, the Mahatma refers his "lay-chela" to what is now Letter 88, another indication that the Englishman's questions had been with the Mahatma for a period of time. The student might want to review KH's comments on evil in that letter, which was actually sent to Hume, but of which Sinnett made a copy. The reason for KH's cryptic remarks concerning the fourth race being connected with evil can be found in stanza 7 of volume 2 of *The Secret Doctrine*. HPB's commentary on that stanza also explains the physical, intellectual, and spiritual inequalities now evident in humankind.

KH's remark: "M thinks that *for your purposes* I better give you a few more details upon Atlantis since it is greatly connected with *evil* if not with its origin" reveals how closely the two Mahatmas worked together. M must have been aware of what KH was communicating to Sinnett and might even have assisted KH in answering Sinnett's questions.

Regarding the science of that day, KH assures Sinnett that "your Science is right in many of her generalities," but "her premises are wrong, or at any rate—very faulty." While nineteenth-century scientific thought did conflict with the occult doctrine, KH is scrupulous in pointing out where it coincided with that doctrine.

Sinnett is reminded that "the law of cycles [is] one and immutable," a principle we also need to keep in mind when considering the topic of rounds and races. Furthermore, "No mother Race, any more than her sub-races and off-shoots, is allowed by the one Reigning Law to trespass upon the prerogatives of the Race or Sub-race that will follow it; least of all—to encroach upon the knowledge and powers in store for its successor." In accord with the law of cycles, then, only a portion of occult knowledge is available or given to each root race. Perhaps this is because we develop one principle as we pass through each root race and are fit to receive and ready to understand only the knowledge appropriate to that stage of our evolution. We can see a corollary to this in the fact that in our present fifth race stage, we have five physical senses, while two additional senses will be developed as we move into the sixth and seventh root races. It has been said that the Buddha could convey only Four Noble Truths, corresponding to our position on the fourth round, and that with each succeeding round an additional Truth will be expounded.

We are given a hint as to how the entire body of knowledge constituting the occult doctrine is preserved as KH speaks of the "tree" on which grows the fruit that is the "Knowledge of Good and Evil." "This tree is in our safe-keeping, entrusted to us by the Dhyan Chohans, the protectors of our Race and the Trustees for those that are coming." This rather mysterious concept may be related to the notion of the *shishta*, the seed-humanity who remain on the globe between rounds as the base on which returning humanity will build. Perhaps some, a class of Dhyan Chohans, are set apart to preserve the knowledge from round to round. This suggestion is based on statements the Mahatma makes elsewhere, particularly his advice in Letter 18 to Sinnett "to never lose sight of the hint given you in my letter upon the Planetaries." That letter could well be reviewed in the light of all that KH is now saying in response to Sinnett's fifth question.

Especially significant is KH's statement: "Every race had its adepts; and with every new race, we are allowed to give them out as much of our knowledge as the men of that race deserve." Two points we should not miss here: first, the "we" means the Brotherhood of Adepts to which KH belongs and whose "rules" he speaks of often; second, the word "deserve" implies that we must earn the right to the knowledge that the Adepts are permitted to divulge. Has our "race" truly deserved the esoteric wisdom that is now available to us?

Sinnett's sixth question is familiar to many Theosophists as one frequently asked by newcomers to the philosophy. It is really the ultimate question: what is the ultimate purpose, meaning, and value of the entire evolutionary journey? The rather glib answer sometimes given—that the journey is from unconscious imperfection through conscious imperfection to conscious perfection—is much too simplistic, as an in-depth study of the Mahatma's reply reveals. KH's explanation is undoubtedly one of the most important in the letters, providing as it does the foundation of the occult doctrine.

That explanation regarding the purpose for the cyclic journey is pitched, we may say, at two levels. The first is quite specific: the "good" of human evolution is considered in terms of manasic experience, existence as a Dhyan Chohan or the gaining of full Self-consciousness. The second takes the question further by asking what "good" can be seen when all is resolved into "spirit" in pralaya. This portion of the reply hinges on an understanding of spirit and matter as being not "distinct things" but two sides of one thing, as the Mahatma emphasizes in previous letters. (Recall particularly in Letter 68: "Spirit and matter are *one*, being but a differentiation of states not *essences*.") Therefore, the experience of manifestation (the cyclic or evolutionary journey) is not lost in pralaya any more than the experience of our last personality is lost in devachan. The evolution and the experience are absorbed, we may say, and thus change the essence of spirit-matter, producing thereby the conditions of the next manvantara.

KH asks rhetorically, "But what is 'Spirit' pure and impersonal *per se*?" and then gives the answer: "It becomes *something* only in union with matter—hence it is always *something* since matter is infinite and indestructible and *non-existent* without Spirit which, in matter is *Life*." Life, then, the interplay between spirit and matter in various differentiations of the one "essence," is the great container of experience in whatever form it manifests: "Life, after all, the greatest problem within the ken of human conception, is a mystery that the greatest of your men of Science will never solve. In order to be correctly comprehended, it has to be studied in the entire series of its manifestations, otherwise it can never be, not only fathomed, but even comprehended in its easiest form—life, as a state of *being* on this earth. It can never be grasped so long as it is studied separately and apart from universal life." The final sentence in this quotation is particularly significant, as it reinforces the Mahatmas' emphasis on the deductive or synthetic method as basic to occult study.

KH continues, "To solve the great problem one has to become an occultist," which means that we must accept the Mahatmas' doctrine, which he beautifully summarizes: "Since motion is all-pervading and absolute rest inconceivable, that under whatever form or *mask* motion may appear, whether as light, heat, magnetism, chemical affinity or electricity—all these must be but phases of One and the same universal omnipotent Force, a Proteus they [the scientists] bow to as the Great 'Unknown' . . . and we, simply call the 'One Life,' the "'One Law' and the 'One Element.'"

KH concludes his disquisition on the purpose of the evolutionary journey with the statement: "Spirit, life and matter, are not natural principles existing independently of each other, but the effects of combinations produced by eternal motion in Space." Therefore, purpose and meaning lie in experiencing spirit-matter or life "in all its phases" and absorbing that experience in terms of consciousness, then carrying the fruit of the experience into the next stage of manifestation. Just as we carry the fruit of the past into each new incarnation, so on the cosmic scale the "fruit" of past manvantaras provide the basis for future manvantaras with their cycles within cycles, all subject to the "One . . . universal omnipotent Force . . . the One Life . . . the One Law." The Mahatma thus presents a truly magnificent, completely coherent vision of a process that is —to use HPB's words in *The Secret Doctrine*— "without conceivable beginning or imaginable end."

Sinnett's questions and the Mahatma's replies 7 through 14 pertain to the physical sciences and the scientific theories current at the time of the letter, late 1882. Since then, of course, the "new" physics, based on the work of Einstein and his contemporaries and successors, has given us amazing insights into the workings of nature, and further discoveries in anthropology and paleontology have led to revisions in dating the appearance of Homo sapiens. There is scarcely a field of scientific thought that has not seen some new theory postulated, whether it remains accepted or was later displaced by yet further evidence. To attempt a correlation between current scientific thought and the Mahatma's statements is beyond my competence and, in any event, would serve little purpose, since science continues to rely on verifiable, observable evidence and repeatable tests, whereas the occult doctrine that KH is presenting to Sinnett (and us) is not always observable or verifiable or conforming to today's "gold standard" of scientific experimentation.

One can, of course, speculate as to what questions can be asked in light of contemporary thought and then suggest the answers an Adept might give, since those responses would still be founded on the principles—*facts*, as the Mahatma calls them—enunciated in the occult doctrine. It is precisely because KH's replies are from the standpoint of the occult sciences, which explain our visible nature largely by reference to the invisible, that he says to Sinnett (in answer to question 7): "But then comes the most important point: how far satisfactory will my answers appear to you?" That is, to what extent is Sinnett, and by extension are we today, prepared to understand and to accept the principles of the occult philosophy? As we consider KH's answers to Sinnett's questions on scientific matters, it seems essential to keep an open mind, seeking the broad general principles rather than becoming too concerned with details that may not accord with contemporary knowledge.

The lengthy response to Sinnett's eighth question deserves very careful study, with three main points to be especially noted. First is the statement that "we [the Adepts] know of no phenomenon in nature entirely unconnected with either magnetism or electricity." Today, physics speaks of the electromagnetic field, which, as Lynne

McTaggart explains, "is simply a convenient abstraction invented by scientists . . . to try to make sense of the seemingly remarkable actions of electricity and magnetism and their ability to influence objects at a distance." (McTaggart's book *The Field: The Quest for the Secret Force of the Universe* offers a very readable survey of the field theory.)

Remarking further on the primary nature of magnetism and electricity, KH speaks of "*akasic* magnetism incessantly generating electric currents." The term *akasha* is used frequently in the letters, as well as in *The Secret Doctrine*, so it should be familiar to students by this time. If each plane or region of nature has its own akasha, the root substance out of which all matter of that plane is produced, the akashic magnetism KH refers to may be a property of the akasha of our globe. While homogeneous, compared with the differentiated nature we see about us, this akasha may still have qualities relative to the progressively more homogeneous "akashas" (to pluralize the term even though akasha is essentially one, nondual, throughout the manifested universe) of the remaining six planes. This akasha would be the matrix, the "web," of our physical globe in which all tends to return to harmony; thus it also tends to restore distorted equilibrium. While we may never detect this root base physically, through a conceptual understanding of it much physical data at present appearing unrelated would be recognized as interrelated. Certainly, as KH points out in his first letter to Sinnett, "without a thorough knowledge of Akas" little else in the occult doctrine can be fully understood.

The second major point in the Mahatma's response to the eighth question is in the phrase: "the strongest connection between the magnetism of the earth, the changes of weather and *man*, who is the best barometer living." Science today is beginning to realize that the human being is a microcosm of the larger universe not only at a metaphysical level but at the physical level—the investigation of the effects of electromagnetic radiation from the planets of our solar system and from far distant objects (quasars, etc.) being one indication of the recognition of that "connection." KH's statement that we are "barometers" is reminiscent of folk wisdom, which has always said that human beings can predict weather through "intuition" as well as physical symptoms. Current studies of water are especially interesting in this regard.

The third major point is the statement: "High above our earth's surface the air is impregnated and space *filled* with magnetic or meteoric dust." Science now acknowledges the existence of meteoric dust belts surrounding our globe (the Van Allen belts, for example), as well as the effects of magnetic storms in our ionosphere. These magnetic storms correspond curiously to the relative positions of the planets in our solar system, suggesting that the various types of electromagnetic radiation (radio waves, ultraviolet, etc.) may stimulate magnetic activity on our globe. These factors may have more influence on our weather (and on ourselves) than the heat from the sun.

Sinnett's ninth question concerns the sun. The key to the Mahatma's response is his final sentence: "The Sun is neither a *solid* nor a *liquid*, nor yet a gaseous globe, but a gigantic ball of electromagnetic Forces, the store-house of universal *life* and *motion*, from which the latter pulsate in all directions, feeding the smallest atom as the greatest genius with the same material." This statement, made well before research into the nature of the atom had really begun, is one that no physicist would now dispute. The energy that the sun radiates is probably due to nuclear fusion (the combining of hydrogen nuclei to form helium being the first stage). This is indeed not a chemical process involving solids, liquids, or gases but a process involving changes in the very nature of the atoms themselves. The energy released is electromagnetic radiation.

The Mahatma's entire and quite lengthy response to Sinnett's ninth question rests on that final statement. For example, the sun's corona is currently explained in terms of electrical activity of the matter involved and is in no way related to fire or flames. The distortion that the atmosphere makes on all astronomical observations is well known today. Science also now fully accepts the view that force, or energy, is an equivalent of matter in a different state, as Einstein's famous equation, E=mc², precisely states. And physicists are aware that much remains to be understood regarding the law of gravitation, which KH speaks of here as "only attraction and repulsion." Finally, the Mahatma remarks on the effects of sun spot activity on our weather, a fact first discovered by the astronomer William Herschel in 1801 and shown to occur in eleven-year cycles.

In replying to Sinnett's tenth question, KH again speaks of "our very ancient theory that every phenomenon being but the effect of the diversified motions of what we call Akasa . . . the causative principle of all." We may notice particularly the statement that light "is not an independent principle."

KH's answer to Sinnett's eleventh question may seem among the most puzzling in the entire letter. We still know so little of Jupiter that we can neither accept nor dispute the information given. Regarding Jupiter's position in the solar system, it seems to have relatively recently moved nearer the sun. Also from current data we may assume that it is "warming up." But that it is mainly metallic in nature as KH asserts and that the metals are being transformed into gases does not seem to be an idea with which the physical sciences could at present agree. Even more strange is the statement concerning the "Raja Sun" or "king-star" behind Jupiter. The planets as viewed from the earth are moving across a background of fixed stars, so how Jupiter could permanently conceal a star is still a mystery. It has been suggested that "Raja Sun" may refer to quasars or quasi-stellar objects—"stars" that emit a fantastic amount of radiation in the form of radio and other waves. For students interested in pursuing the occult meaning of the Mahatma's statements, a lengthy commentary on "Raja-Stars" in available in *The Dialogues of G. de Purucker* (2:171–73).

The points made in KH's reply to Sinnett's twelfth question are easily understood. The sun needs no material to feed its flames, because it is a "nuclear reaction," which truly "gives *all* and takes back *nothing* from its system." In physical terms, it radiates the energy produced by nuclear fusion indiscriminately to the solar system. It needs no "extra fuel." Similarly, we now know that space is filled with both meteoric dust and hydrogen, the most fundamental atomic substance, and is not a vacuum at all. In calling the sun's energy "life," KH is reminding us that while we generally consider only its physical energy, the sun exists on many levels, serving functions on all. "Life" is a more universal term than energy.

The Mahatma's response to Sinnett's thirteenth question again emphasizes the magnetic nature of our globe. He advises the Englishman: "Study magnetism with the help of occult doctrines, and then that which now will appear incomprehensible, *absurd* in the light of physical science, will become all clear." Perhaps for us today, our study should be of not only magnetism but the several force fields known to physics, particularly the electromagnetic field.

KH's answer to the fourteenth and final question in the series concerning scientific matters contains several striking points. Regarding the reference to planets "in the orbit of Neptune": Pluto was discovered in 1930 and is indeed approximately in Neptune's orbit. Further, tradition has it that there is such a planet, Vulcan, within the orbit of Neptune. Concerning planets in formation and in obscuration, a planet passing through the early stages of formation would be not yet physical and therefore not visible. What we see of a planet is only its sthula sharira, its dense body, which forms at a later stage. The allusion to "Edison's tasimeter" may be considered prophetic. Edison was a member of the Theosophical Society, and KH's statement here that the inventor of the light bulb was "a good deal protected by M" is interesting indeed. Whatever may have been the fate of the tasimeter, we know that today the stars are studied not only in terms of visible light but also by means of infrared, X-rays, and so on. But surely KH's most dramatic statement, in light of the development of radio astronomy, is that "science will *hear* sounds from certain planets before she *sees* them." The word "planet" in this connection may be a substitute for star, yet even so, it is known that certain planets in our solar system are radio sources.

Sinnett's questions from this point on concern statements the Mahatma made in earlier letters dealing with devachan, the after-death states in general, and reincarnation. The majority of the references Sinnett cites are in Letter 70C, and Letter 85B contains further explanations, so the student may wish to review both letters before considering what the Mahatma says in Letter 93B. The after-death states, particularly devachan, are discussed again in later letters. A useful compilation and excellent reference for all the teachings on this subject in the Mahatmas' letters as well as HPB's many books is Geoffrey A. Farthing's *After Death Consciousness and Processes.* Students may also wish to compare these original teachings with those of later writers, such as Annie Besant, C. W. Leadbeater, and G. de Purucker.

The Mahatma's reply to Sinnett's fifteenth question is quite clear and needs no further comment. The responses to questions 16 and 17 may be taken together, as they are closely related and arise out of comments in Letter 70C. The initial remarks regarding 16 suggest that the process that determines an individual's "future pre-natal state and birth" is virtually automatic, involving the person's last thoughts as well as the predominant personal interests and desires that have shaped his or her entire physical incarnation. Reply 17 takes up this theme in more detail, emphasizing two points. The first concerns the mechanism that determines the nature of the next life. As KH states, "The dying brain dislodges memory with a strong supreme impulse, and memory restores faithfully every impression entrusted to it during the period of the brain's activity." It is left to us to ponder the immediate purpose and long-term purpose of reviewing one's past life at or just after the moment of death, as well as the ultimate fate of these memories.

The second point of interest concerns the actual moment of death. KH seems to be saying that the process of review continues to take place even after the heart has stopped, that the brain is still "active," even if not "alive" in the usual sense. He concludes his response with a beautiful admonition to those who may be present with a friend or loved one at the final moments of an incarnation: "Speak in whispers, ye, who assist at a death-bed and find yourselves in the solemn presence of Death. Especially have you to keep quiet just after Death has laid her clammy hand upon the body. Speak in whispers, I say, lest you disturb the quiet ripple of thought, and hinder the busy work of the Past casting its reflection upon the Veil of the Future."

While the response to Sinnett's question 18 is brief, it provides more detail on the topic at hand. The key word appears to be "full," in connection with remembering our lives. In devachan, the Ego remembers only the "spiritual" portions of its last earth life; similarly, at the end of each round it remembers the sum of its devachanic memories. However, at the end of "*all the seven Rounds*," which constitute a complete planetary chain, the Ego reviews the sum total of all its lives from the entire chain, even those portions that it did not remember in devachan. There appears to be a further difference between the remembrance following a particular earth life and the complete remembrance at the end of the planetary chain: in the former, the Ego remembers "the good, the true and the beautiful," however small a percentage of the past life they may represent, so that even a predominantly "bad" individual will have a devachanic period of rest. At the end of the chain, however, all "good" and "bad" are balanced one against the other, and the outcome of that balancing process becomes the basis for the individual's future manvantaric destiny. In this regard, "irretrievably bad must be that Ego that yields no mite from the fifth Principle [manas], and *has* to be annihilated." The "Eighth Sphere" or "Planet of Death" was discussed in the comments on Letter 70C. The phrase KH uses here, "*Avitchi Nirvana*," is indeed an awesome one.

As questions 19 and 20 are closely related, the Mahatma's responses to these two queries can be considered together. Sinnett is concerned about the "nature of the remembrance and self-consciousness of the shell" and "the extent of personal identity in elementaries" and suggests that Letter 70C contains contradiction on these points. The Mahatma's reply refers to the "dismemberment" of the discarnate entity, involving a "struggle between the higher and middle duad." The student may find it useful to review the explanations on this subject in Letter 68 (particularly pages 192–93). Setting aside for the moment the exception mentioned in the first sentence of answer 19, we find KH suggesting that consciousness and remembrance return to the shell (kama-rupa) only when the spiritual Ego has gone into devachan. However, it is "a kind of hazy consciousness of its own," perhaps something like a trace or "footprint" of the emotions experienced in the recent incarnation. What is missing in the shell, of course, which would not allow it any definite consciousness, is the higher aspect of the fifth principle along with the sixth and seventh principles.

Regarding the exception mentioned in the first sentence, we should take note of the phrase, "elemental parasites." The term "elementals" (discussed in connection with earlier letters; see especially Letter 18) refers to a class belonging to the kingdoms below the mineral; they are formless and have no notion of "good" or "bad" but merely respond to impulses they receive. Parasites are entities that rely on hosts for their nourishment and life. They may or may not be detrimental to their host. Putting these two ideas together, we arrive at a concept for these kamic or astral entities that we carry in our psychic aura. They live, we can say, on our emotions and desires and indeed thrive on them. They form an intimate part of the lower self and prompt many of our activities at that level.

Reply 20 provides more detail on the subject that so concerned Sinnett: "the nature of the remembrance and self-consciousness of the shell" and therefore the continuation of personal identity. KH makes three key points. The first concerns the material experiences, thoughts, sensations, emotions, and so on that result from the last incarnation. Everything related to the skandhas, the qualities and attributes of the personality, is lost, states KH, at the moment of death—although, notably, they are lost only in the sense that the Ego loses consciousness of them. These personal but earthly elements of the past life are seen once more before the spiritual Ego enters devachan and "for the *third* time *fully* at the end of the minor cycle," as discussed in reply 18. What remains is the personal though spiritually motivated experience that the monad retains for its devachanic life. This spiritual experience is apparently absorbed into the Ego, becoming an essential part of it. This, indicates the Mahatma, is "necessary . . . for the retention of a divine spiritualized notion of the 'I' in the *Monad*."

The second point of interest is the illustration concerning the candles. The analogy needs careful study, noting especially the statement that "the same matter, the same gaseous particles . . . will be called forth . . . to produce a new luminosity." Consider also what the flame and what the candle represent, and the distinction between a "reincarnation of the *personality*" and "the rebirth of Egos from *devachans* and *avitchis*."

The third point in response 20 concerns the distinction between memory and the perceptive faculty, which is crucial in understanding the nature of consciousness after death. During incarnation, our perceptive faculty is the mind, manas. We perceive through the senses, but it is manas that organizes sensation so we understand what we see. The same quality of self-consciousness, of "I am I," allows us to use our memories. An animal in which manas is not awakened and hence without self-consciousness cannot remember at will as a human can. Likewise a shell bereft of its higher mind and sense of "I" cannot will to remember. Neither can it, of itself, perceive very much because it has no senses through which to feel or see. It is only through a person serving as a medium, who supplies both manas, the "I," and a physical body that a shell can rebecome truly self-conscious. However, this lasts only while the medium allows such a state to continue. In this connection, the student may wish to reread the passages in Letter 18 concerning Stainton Moses, his "guide" Imperator, and C. C. Massey. KH's statements in reply 20 shed new light on the nature of Imperator.

KH's final statement in his reply to question 20 is on a topic that came up in Letter 85B; I point it out here because it is a matter that has caused some confusion: "Personal consciousness does leave everyone at death; and when even the centre of memory is re-established in the shell, it will remember and speak out its recollections but through the brain of some *living* being."

The first paragraph in KH's reply to Sinnett's lengthy question 21 carries on from the last paragraph of reply 20 and the subject of the shell. It is, in fact, a direct answer to Sinnett's question: "What is the nature of the remembrance and self-consciousness of the shell?"

Two points should be noted. First, the memory available to the shell must consist of those memories not taken by the spiritual Ego to devachan. Consequently, they must be trivial and very personal, consisting of the incidental events of physical life.

Second, KH says, "It is not even a portion of the fifth [principle] that is carried away." Rather, it is the "finest attributes" of manas that accompany the monad into devachan. In other words, it is not the mind *per se* that goes into devachan but only its spiritualized essence, which reflected the light of buddhi in manas. Thus devachan seems to be a monadic state strongly colored by the personal albeit spiritual experiences of the late physical life. KH's metaphor in describing the mind "shorn of its finest attributes" is quite beautiful: like "a rose crushed" from which its "aroma has suddenly departed."

Reply 21 continues with a number of points, each preceded by a letter corresponding to the same in Sinnett's long question. Answer *a* amplifies KH's earlier statements, confirming Sinnett's understanding that "the Spiritual *Ego* goes on evolving personalities, in which 'the sense of identity' is *very complete* while living." Here the student needs a clear understanding of the terms "spiritual Ego," "physical ego," and "shell." Referring to what was taught earlier, KH then says (*b*) that Sinnett is in error in suggesting that A. P. Sinnett is "an absolutely *new* invention," since he is "the child and creation of his antecedent personal self." It should be clear by this time that each incarnation is the "*Karmic* progeny," to use KH's phrase, of all our past embodiments.

One wonders if KH answers Sinnett's query *c* with tongue in cheek or at least a twinkling eye, since he assures the Englishman that at least "a few years of Theosophy" will provide "enough decent material" to give the spiritual Ego a reasonable time in devachan. While *d* needs no comment, the reply to *e* is interesting for its implication that the degree of consciousness that a shell experiences after the spiritual Ego has entered devachan is directly proportionate to the degree to which the person centered attention on the personality as opposed to the individuality during the incarnation just closed. In other words, the more one lives at a personal level in the present, the stronger and more coherent will be the shell in kama-loka and the greater the degree of consciousness (though still dim and hazy) it may have.

The Mahatma's replies to questions *f, g,* and *h* indicate that Sinnett had difficulty appreciating that devachan is a completely subjective existence. In that state, the spiritual Ego is not aware of anything external to itself and its memories and therefore cannot think of its shell; it is not even "conscious that the individuality is gone." KH reminds Sinnett of the Delphic oracle's famous utterance: "*Nosce te ipsum,*" generally translated as "Man, know thyself." And he says that the "'heresy of Individuality' [mentioned in Letter 68, page 199, as related to the sixth skandha] is a doctrine propounded . . . with an eye to the Shell." This can only mean that the sense of individuality refers to the personality; it is the personal "I" reveling in its separated existence (as it thinks) that creates this heresy. This illusion is the primary source of ignorance (avidya) and suffering, as taught by the Buddha.

The oracular injunction that we must know ourselves could be interpreted as follows: devachan is the sum total of all that was worthwhile in an incarnation, yet it is still *maya,* an illusion. (In Letter 68, especially pages 190–91, devachan is called "*a state . . . of intense selfishness . . . a state of perpetual 'Maya.'*") Ultimately, we will evolve beyond the necessity for such a state, but to achieve this means bringing the five lower principles completely under the control of the spiritual Ego, and to do this we must know ourselves.

The brief remark in response to Sinnett's question *g* suggests that the ultimate fate of the shell is to slowly disintegrate, losing as it does all trace of consciousness, until it can no longer be re-animated by a medium. Response *h* concerns the fate of "very material shells" who seek only to perpetuate a sense of self. "What happens," states KH, "is terrible for it becomes a case of *post mortem* lycanthropy." This is the delusion that one has become or assumed the characteristics of a wolf and relates to folkloric stories of werewolves, a truly frightening condition!

No comment is needed on the response to Sinnett's question 22, as KH says he has "no right to answer." We can assume that the answers touch on some of the deepest mysteries of the occult tradition. The

"Planet of Death" is first mentioned in Letter 68 (page 192), and what little we know about it indicates that the "Mara-rupas" disappear there (see page 196). As said earlier, this state is not avitchi, the antithesis of devachan, from which return to physical existence is possible.

The reply to question 23 was the basis of a controversy that raged through the Theosophical Society for many years and is all but dead now. The problem turns on the fact that Sinnett asked two questions and took the reply to the first as applying to the second. Mars, Mercury, the Earth, and four other planets constitute our "system of worlds," each in itself septenary, having seven globes. Thus as earth is Globe D of the earth chain, so the Mars we see is Globe D of the Mars chain, and so on. However, Sinnett's second question concerned the invisible companion globes of the earth chain. He assumed that the invisible companions of Mars and Mercury were the invisible globes of our earth chain and so concluded that Mars and Mercury were Globes C and E of our chain. This is not so, but many students continued to believe it. The subject is dealt with quite exhaustively in *The Secret Doctrine*, volume 1, in the section headed "A Few Early Theosophical Misconceptions," and every student should be familiar with HPB's analysis of the problem.

KH's response to question 24 seems quite clear. The sun we see is but the outward reflection of the "Central Spiritual Sun" at the center of the solar universe. In itself it is the apex, spiritually and materially, of our solar system. For further clarification, the student can refer to *The Secret Doctrine* (1:289–90). Incidentally, KH's reference to "septenary chains" is in sharp contrast to the ten-chain system mentioned by other writers.

The shell referred to in replies 25 and 26 is probably a "mara rupa" (compounded of fourth, fifth, and the dregs of the sixth principles), which is attracted to the "Eighth sphere," thought to be synonymous with the Planet of Death. KH also confirms here a previous statement concerning the length of time between incarnations. "No monad ever gets reincarnated before its appointed cycle," KH says. So exact is the law of karma that there is indeed a "right" time for every event!

No comment is required regarding the answer to question 27. In responding to question 28, KH repeats much that he has told Sinnett in earlier letters regarding the time intervals between lives (see especially Letter 66, page 175). The sphere of effects includes all the subjective after-death states—kama-loka, the gestation state, devachan, and so on. It is the aggregate of these states in which "the individual units of mankind remain 100 times longer . . . than on the globes." We need to remember that fifth round individuals are such by virtue of their psycho-spiritual evolution; physically they must incarnate in fourth round bodies (see again Letter 44). Finally, the "forms" to be used in the next round are dealt with briefly in *The Secret Doctrine*, where HPB mentions the *shishta* or seed-humanity who remain on the globe during the obscuration as the stock for the forthcoming fifth round humanity. But, as KH tells Sinnett in concluding his response to question 28, the Englishman is "putting . . . questions pertaining to the highest initiations," and therefore KH can respond with only "a *general* view."

To understand the reply to Sinnett's final question, we must be clear about the distinction between the monads or spiritual principles in their various kingdoms and the vehicles in which those monads are manifested. In the first round humankind appeared physically as a giant, though ethereal, ape, whereas in the last round the animal monads will occupy vehicles manifesting far more intelligence than they do now. KH explains: "At each Round there are less and less animals," while "during the seventh [round] men will have become *Gods*, and animals— intelligent beings." The principle is clear: "Everything is evolved and has but to proceed on its cyclic journey and get perfected."

To summarize, then, on each globe in the first round humanity has to incarnate in the vehicles of each kingdom—mineral, plant, animal—before it can evolve the first truly human forms of the round. Having produced human forms on Globe A, it has to re-evolve them on Globe B via the three lower kingdoms. However, in the second round, humanity merely continues the evolution of already existing human forms preserved by the shishta between rounds and so does not have to re-evolve through the lower kingdoms. As the Mahatma says, "The method changes entirely from the second Round." For example, in the fourth round on Globe D (earth) the Lunar Pitris (our shishta) produced ethereal bodies from themselves in which the human monads incarnated in the first root race. This entire subject is presented in further detail in volume 2 of *The Secret Doctrine.*

Thus concludes one of KH's longest letters, each reply to the many questions on several topics deserving more study and contemplation than we have been able to give it here. However, perhaps these comments have opened a few doors leading to deeper consideration.

LETTER 94

This letter 94, a brief note written on the front and back of a postcard, introduces to Sinnett, and so to us, one of the interesting early Theosophists, Mohini Mohun Chatterjee. While, as noted in the prefatory comment, Mohini's "mission" in contacting Sinnett is unknown, it may have been connected with the completion of the first seven years of the Society's existence.

Born in 1858, Mohini was by profession an attorney. He joined the Theosophical Society in April 1882 and became one of its most able exponents, later lecturing extensively in Europe and America. When Colonel Olcott opened the first Theosophical Sunday School in Calcutta in March of 1883, Mohini was appointed the teacher. Later, he traveled with the founders and, at the request of KH, accompanied them to Europe in 1884.

During the 1884–85 crisis in Europe, Mohini proved an able defender of HPB and her phenomena, testifying at several hearings before the Society for Psychical Research. The purpose of his trip, however, was apparently to give European members a deeper understanding of the occult doctrines. With Mrs. Laura C. Holloway, an American member and clairvoyant (whom we will meet in later letters) he collaborated in writing the work, first attributed to "Two Chelas," *Man, Fragments of Forgotten History.* (HPB later remarked on the presence of serious errors in the work; in any case, it has never been reprinted.) In 1886, while still in Europe, he co-authored with the German member Arthur Gebhard a scathing criticism of Colonel Olcott and the way the Society's work was being conducted. HPB replied to this highly critical diatribe with a lengthy pronouncement that was subsequently published (and continues in print) under the title *The Original Programme of the Theosophical Society,* a document that every earnest member should read and study.

One of Mohini's best-known literary works is in his English translation of Shankaracharya's *Viveka Chudamani,* or "The Crest Jewel of Wisdom." This appeared first in successive issues of *The Theosophist* from 1885 to 1888 and was later published by the Theosophical Publishing House, Adyar.

Mohini remained in Europe until 1887, when he returned to India to practice law. Unfortunately, during his last year in Europe, he seems to have become involved in some scandals in Paris—perhaps the adulation given him there and in London had become too much for him to withstand. In any event, he failed as a chela and resigned from the Society in 1887. He died in 1936.

As we will see, Mohini is mentioned on several occasions in later letters. He also received a number of letters from KH, which were published in *Letters from the Masters of the Wisdom,* First Series (see Letters 10, 11, 13, 14, 15, and 23) and Second Series (see Letters 57–62). The Second Series also contains an excellent article by Mohini, "The Himalayan Brothers: Do They Exist?" (see appendix B), which was first published in *The Theosophist* of December 1883.

LETTERS 95 AND 96

The reference to "the little Doctor" has never been identified, but the visit of that person along with Mohini may have had something to do with the forthcoming seventh anniversary of the Society. Certainly the Mahatmas, particularly KH, indicated that this was a critical moment in the Society's existence. KH repeats in Letter 95 a statement he made in Letter 92: "The fact is, that to the last and supreme initiation every chela . . . is left to his own device and counsel."

The reference to the "Prayag Fellows" takes us back to Letter 30, where the Mahatma M, dictating to HPB, said: "Because KH chose to correspond with two men who proved of the utmost importance and use to the Society, they all—whether wise or stupid, clever or dull, *possibly* useful or utterly useless—lay their claims to correspond with us directly." These were the Theosophists of Allahabad, who evidently continued to pester the Mahatmas about corresponding with them. Here, in Letter 95, KH clearly hopes Sinnett can put an end to this situation.

Letter 96, as indicated, is simply a postscript to Letter 95. Toward the conclusion of Letter 83, Djual Khul told Sinnett that messages from KH would be authenticated by "Three Secret Words," and in this postscript we are given those words. However, an examination of the originals of the letters suggests that those words were never used, so it is all something of a mystery.

LETTER 97

Despite its brevity, which suggests that it needs no comment, Letter 97 raises an interesting question for the student to consider. We know from earlier letters that Sinnett had long hoped for a personal visit from the Mahatma and that again and again it was denied him. Here he is told once more that the time is "not yet."

In fact, it appears that Sinnett never was granted a visit from the Mahatma in his physical form. Yet throughout the early years of the Society's existence in India, one or another of the Mahatmas appeared physically to various members on a number of occasions, and we have written testimony to that effect. Why, then, was the recipient of the majority of the Mahatmas' letters—certainly far more letters than any other individual—denied a personal visit? While our response can only be conjecture, consideration of the question itself could help us understand better the ways the Adepts work with individuals.

LETTER 98

The historical background for Letter 98 is very well set forth in the prefatory note, but certain portions of the letter deserve special attention. To begin with, in several letters KH refers to his superior, "our venerable Chohan," who he needs to consult from time to time. It was the Chohan (often called the Mahachohan) who permitted KH to undertake the correspondence with the two Englishmen (see Letter 65, page 168), and in a few early letters we find that some of Sinnett's questions could only be answered with the Chohan's approval. Since KH could evidently foresee possible future consequences if he were to acquiesce in Sinnett's plan for a new newspaper promoting India's political freedom, he feels that he must place the proposal before his superior. He expresses this intention in the present letter and reports on the Chohan's views in Letter 99. Several subsequent letters then concern what is known as "the Phoenix venture," KH himself becoming quite involved with Sinnett on the project.

However, the main thrust of Letter 98 concerns what KH acknowledges as a trivial incident that, because it hinges on a series of deliberate untruths, could become the "*cause* which will yield unpleasant effects." Hume, of course, is the culprit in the whole affair which has led to a "perversion of facts," and KH outlines why it is important now to set the record straight. To that end, he requests Sinnett to recall as accurately as possible a certain meeting of the Eclectic Society, including the words used.

While all of this may seem of no importance today, it may well hold a lesson for us. How often has some apparently trivial incident, especially if it involves misinterpretations and deliberate lies, had unforeseen consequences later on? How accurate do our recollections of key events need to be to avoid additional misunderstandings? It would be interesting to know how Sinnett answered the Mahatma, but the matter does not come up again in subsequent letters, so we may assume that whatever Sinnett reported satisfied the Mahatma.

LETTER 99

Letter 99 contains KH's report of his consultation with the Mahachohan concerning Sinnett's proposal to inaugurate the *Phoenix,* a newspaper devoted to India's political freedom. Reading through the several numbered items constituting the "memorandum" setting forth the Chohan's views, we can note the care given to the business details of the venture. While the Brothers, KH says, can "direct and guide . . . in general," the "effort must be made by your [Sinnett's] friends in the world." The next statement is as encouraging to us today as it must have been to Sinnett: "Tho' separated from your world of action we are not yet entirely severed from it so long as the Theosophical Society exists." Since the Society continues to exist, we may hope that the link with the Adept Brotherhood remains unbroken!

We usually think of the Mahatmas as unconcerned with financial matters and certainly not as "capitalists." Yet KH's advice, which he says is "agreeable with the Chohan's opinion," regarding how Sinnett should raise the capital, how it should be invested, what salary he should receive, and so on, indicates the Mahatma's familiarity with the world of finance. KH also foresees possible difficulties: "Deep-seated prejudices and suspicions would cause native capitalists . . . to hesitate" to invest in the enterprise because "the whole Anglo-Indian community now suffers . . . for the commercial sins of dishonest houses who have heretofore broken faith" with native investors. At the same time, cautions KH, Sinnett should see that his own interests are protected.

The Mahatma further advises that "the whole capital should be paid in before the journal is begun," that some inducement be offered to investors, that a "Sinking Fund" be created "to provide for any unforeseen exigency," and that "surplus capital as well as earnings . . . be distributed from time to time." Proper contracts and "co-partnership papers" should be drawn up at the outset. However, the Mahatma makes no mention of his or the Chohan's involvement in editorial matters or the content and policies of the paper other than its general purpose. Evidently the specifics regarding editorial policy were left to Sinnett's discretion. As KH states, "You should certainly have entire control over the journal," with any transfer of control based on "the consent of a majority of the capital represented in the ownership." Publication is to cease should it become "apparent that the journal was being used against the interests to promote which it was launched." It seems that the Chohan and KH have given attention to virtually every contingency.

However, KH is not finished with his comments on what he calls "our future journalistic operations"—his use of "our" surely indicating his intent to work with Sinnett on the project. KH has listened in on a conversation in which several members, including Colonel Olcott, were discussing the proposed newspaper. (The presence of one of his chelas, Norendro, in the group may have provided the occult link necessary to attract KH's attention to the conversation, thus permitting him to overhear what was being said.) All we know about the individual named Norendro is that he was a chela of KH as well as the editor of an Indian paper *The Indian Mirror*. The Mahatma evidently felt it would aid Sinnett in his efforts to raise capital for the *Phoenix* if he were aware of the crosscurrents of motivations, fears, prejudices, and so on likely to arise among those whom he would be approaching for support. Incidentally, the "5 lakhs" KH mentions as being necessary to launch the new paper would have amounted to about 500,000 rupees.

Sinnett must have written an additional letter asking KH's advice concerning notifying his present employers as to his intention to start a new paper. The Mahatma cautions him that it would be premature to speak of his plans at this time and might only cause the proprietors of *The Pioneer*, his employers, to do all possible to retain him in their employ. KH comments: "without forcing events—in violation of our Laws, save the Chohan's permission." We can extrapolate from this statement that, because it would violate their rules, the Mahatmas are constrained never to force events even when they might know—as they have said—the likely outcome of a course of action; however, their superior, the Mahachohan, may, if the situation warrants it, give permission to set the usual rules aside.

The letter's final paragraph focuses again on Hume, who has apparently been writing vitriolic letters about HPB, the Mahatmas, the Society, and so on, to C. C. Massey and Stainton Moses in London. Hume, says KH, has now "placed himself" under the influence of the "Dugpas," a word meaning sorcerers and adepts of black magic (see *Theosophical Glossary*).

LETTER 100

Letter 100 continues the saga of the "Phoenix venture." It seems that Sinnett had written with further ideas about the project. "Mr. Dare" has been identified as William John Dare (1853–1941), manager of the Allahabad *Pioneer*, and therefore a colleague of Sinnett's. He was apparently sympathetic to the "Phoenix proposal," and KH later anticipates his assistance (see pages 382, 392). Most significant in KH's response to Sinnett, however, is his saying that while the Brothers "will help the enterprise from first to last as fully as possible within our rules," the work must be done by Sinnett and his friends. The reason is simple: the law of karma, the "the strict law of justice," requires that the "merit" resulting from an undertaking accrues to the individual who makes "the dream a reality."

So also, were the Mahatmas to resolve the problems that confront us or the world in general, the karma of such action would be theirs; so it is we who must undertake the necessary action to resolve the problems we ourselves have created. We can have their guidance and assistance, if we are open to and aware of their presence. This, incidentally, is a basic lesson in the Bhagavad Gita; Krishna can aid Arjuna, advise him and instruct him, but ultimately it is Arjuna who must perform the needed action.

Evidently, Sinnett was considering leaving India and returning permanently to England, but he would remain in India if KH so wished. Here too, we may conclude, the law of karma is involved. The decision to stay or leave must be solely Sinnett's and not based on what he thinks KH wants him to do. Thus the karma of this decision is Sinnett's, too.

The final paragraph of Letter 100 concerns the anniversary celebration of the Society. In a number of previous letters, KH has urged Sinnett to attend that occasion, and now the Mahatma thanks him for intending to do so, as his presence will help "to neutralize the evil influences which the enemies of Theosophy" have focused on the organization. Colonel Olcott's report of the occasion is insightful in this regard. He had received from several members "the suggestion to make the anniversary meetings of the T.S. into representative conventions of all our Indian Branches. I recollect that I felt rather dubious about the practicability of the scheme, but I passed it on to HPB [who evidently agreed] . . . and when our Seventh Anniversary was celebrated . . . on 7th December, we had fifteen Delegates present and addresses from several of them. Mr. Sinnett had come from Allahabad and officiated as Chairman at my request. . . . Thus was inaugurated the system of Annual Branch Conventions which is now universal" (*ODL*, 2:390–91).

Another account of the occasion, including a list of the delegates present, is found in Josephine Ransom's *A Short History of the Theosophical Society* (pages 173–74). She notes, among other things, that 'Mme. Coulomb had made a fine new crimson banner of the Parent Society, and thirty-nine shields were inscribed with the names of Branches. There was a crowded audience, for apparently the public was admitted."

In the final sentence the Mahatma notes that "the dead-point of the revolving cycle" was November 17 of 1882, even though the anniversary celebration actually took place on December 7. KH states that the new cycle began on December 17, and that Sinnett should "watch and see." According to Olcott, on December 17 the two founders left Bombay to take up residence at the new Headquarters at Adyar, Madras—quite a beginning for the new cycle!

LETTER 101

From time to time in the letters, the Mahatma KH is concerned that Sinnett should really understand the nature of the Adepts. In Letter 101 KH states once again, at the outset, "The time has come for us to try to have you, at least, understand us better." Much of the letter is then devoted to telling Sinnett of the machinations Hume is up to by means of letters he has been writing to influential members in London. The Mahatma tells Sinnett near the letter's conclusion that assembling the evidence in order to make Sinnett aware of the situation's gravity has been "an unpleasant and distasteful task," and he has waited (he says at the letter's beginning) until he had such evidence as would prove conclusive to Sinnett.

As we read through this sometimes confusing letter, several significant points merit our consideration. First is the importance given to the welfare of the "British T.S.," which concerns particularly the work in London involving such individuals as C. C. Massey, Anna Kingsford, and their associates. Second is the confidence the Mahatma places in Sinnett as a friend and brother (terms he so often uses in addressing his lay-chela) and also as an exponent of the Theosophical philosophy. The first seven-year cycle of the Society's existence has apparently passed successfully, since KH writes: "No harm can come now to the Society." But, he adds, "There is great personal danger for the British T.S. as for yourself." This is the reason why the Mahatma now proposes to furnish Sinnett and C. C. Massey "with some facts and a key to the true situation," which means revealing "Mr. Hume in his true light."

We have met Massey in several earlier letters. In summary, he was a prominent member of the Society in London, a lawyer, and a Spiritualist, who had visited the United States to verify for himself Olcott's accounts of the Eddy phenomena in Vermont and was among the original founders of the Society. Later he was a founder and the first president of the Theosophical Society in England and also one of the founders of the Society for Psychical Research. Here in Letter 101, KH says that Massey was "third on the list of failures" and that "with all he is the noblest, purest, in short, one of the best men I know . . . but he lacks entirely—correct intuition." His principal weakness seems to have been that he accepted as absolute truth everything derogatory that anyone told him about the Society, HPB, and the Mahatmas.

We may wonder why the Mahatma is so concerned over the situation in London, to the point where he now writes to Sinnett "We demand neither allegiance, recognition (whether public or private) nor will we have anything to do with, or say to the British Branch— *except through you*. . . . We have no present intention of making any further experiments *with Europeans* and will use no other channel than yourself to impart our Asian philosophy."

To find the answer, we need to consider the larger context in which the Society's work was being carried forward. If a major reason for the Society's founding, if not the central purpose, was to introduce to the Western world the ageless wisdom of the occult philosophy, including the realization of true brotherhood, then, since England was at that time the dominant world power, it was only natural that the Adept Fraternity looked to prominent, educated, spiritually inclined individuals in that country to aid in furthering their aim. Although the Society was founded in the United States, it had become largely inactive there; at the same time, it was beginning to attract serious attention among influential individuals such as Massey, Stainton Moses, and Anna Kingsford in English Spiritualist circles. It was also British Spiritualists who formed the Society for Psychical Research in the year previous to this letter (1882). From its inception, that society had shown promise of giving legitimacy to at least some aspects of the occult philosophy; note KH's statement in Letter 111 regarding the Society for Psychical Research: "Its work is of a kind to tell upon public opinion by experimentally demonstrating the elementary phases of Occult Science." In 1885, following the publication of the infamous Hodgson Report, a number of its original founders who had been interested in Theosophy repudiated the Theosophical Society, and the organization became the vehicle through which the worst accusations against HPB were made.

We can understand, then, the Mahatma's endeavor to convince Sinnett of Hume's perfidy and to urge Sinnett to aid his friends in London in understanding correctly the nature of the Adepts and the work of the Society and the basic esoteric teachings correctly. KH comments first on Anna Kingsford (whom we met in earlier letters and will learn more about in later ones), who has "conditionally accept[ed] the presidentship of the British T.S." Here KH tells us she is "a *fifth rounder*" but "not exempt from quite a considerable dose of vanity and despotism." (For a review of what it means to be a "fifth rounder" see the commentary on Letter 66.) The Mahatma's concern relates to the doctrine of reincarnation and the differences between the views of Allan Kardec (see Letter 70C) and those of the occult philosophy as propounded by the Adepts, and he tells Sinnett to write to Massey with the truth on the subject. KH's request prompts us to ask: what is the "truth" about reincarnation? Since the letters were written many books have been published on the subject, so the student may find it useful to determine the Theosophical view of the doctrine.

About Hume's time as president of the Simla Eclectic Branch of the Society, KH makes an illuminating comment: "It was Mr. Hume's attitude when the *Eclectic* [the Society's Branch in Simla] was formed that caused our chiefs to bring Mr. Fern and Mr. Hume together. . . . The two were brought into the closest relationship in order to bring out their mutual virtues and defects—each to shine in his own true light." He follows this with a significant comment: "Such are the laws of Eastern *probation*."

This insight into the meaning of probation gives us much to consider. We know from statements in earlier letters that the individual on probation is subjected to a variety of "tests," some of which may seem strange to us. The Mahatma says further in Letter 101: "Nothing, my friend,—even apparently absurd and reprehensible actions—is done by us without a purpose." That purpose in this case is presumably to "test" the individual's character, including his or her motives, integrity, and determination, Hume and Fern being illustrative examples.

While so much of Letter 101 is devoted to what KH calls the "evidence of his [Hume's] untruthful, cunning nature" (and note that the Mahatma says he was "made to collect" that evidence), it also contains other statements that deserve deep consideration. One concerns the achievement of adeptship: "The victor in the struggle for adeptship was ever *Self* and Self alone." What "Self" does this refer to? What role does the personality play in the "struggle"? Other questions may arise in the mind of the earnest student as we seek to understand the Mahatma's words on this important topic.

A comment toward the conclusion of Letter 101 provides yet another clue as to how the Mahatmas work. Concerning what KH calls "queries arising at M.'s will in Olcott's mind," he comments that what Hume "did had my approval, since it was a necessary part of a preconceived plan to bring out—besides Mr. H's *true* nature . . . ultimate good." It is not always easy to see how "ultimate good" can come out of seemingly disastrous circumstances. We can only recall what has been said so often: *Their* (the Mahatmas') ways are not *our* ways, and until we can come out of our world into theirs, we cannot fully understand the ways in which they work.

Letter 101 then concludes with the surprising suggestion from KH that "unless you [Sinnett] go to London and with C.C.M's [Massey's] help explain the true situation and establish the Society *yourself*," Hume's letters will do irreparable harm to the cause. Here again is evidence of the trust the Mahatma has in the Englishman. KH obviously thinks of this journey as only a "temporary absence" from India. Sinnett did go back to England with his family, but never to return to the land he had come to love so much. Following KH's further suggestion, he used the "large store of materials" that he then possessed—the correspondence containing so much of the teaching—to write his second book, *Esoteric Buddhism,* published on June 10, 1883, six months after Sinnett received this letter.

LETTER 102

Having provided Sinnett with evidence of Hume's perfidy in Letter 101, KH in Letter 102 cautions his lay-chela to be lenient and prudent in his treatment of Hume. He says that Hume has been "pushed on and half maddened by evil powers, which he has attracted to himself and come under subjection to by his innate moral turbulence." This is certainly a warning to all to be morally alert and thus to avoid opening oneself to undesirable influences. Hume's condition, KH says, was caused "by the injudicious practice of *pranayam*," resulting in the development of some slight mediumship. Pranayama is the practice of regulating the breath, a discipline considered essential in the yogic life. According to HPB—presumably referring to the more extreme forms of pranayama—it can be a dangerous practice (*CW*, 12:615–22).

Dr. I. K. Taimni provides an excellent explanation of pranayama in his book *The Science of Yoga,* particularly in his commentary on sutras 49 through 53 in section 2 of Patanjali's Yoga Sutras. Dr. Taimni has ably summarized the essential features of the practice and comments: "While abstaining strictly from the ill-advised practice of *Pranayama* proper there is no harm in trying to understand its rationale and the limit to which one can go with safety in the manipulation of breathing for the sake of promoting physical and mental health" (page 260).

KH tells Sinnett again that Hume has "opened wide the door to influences from the wrong quarter," and he asks Sinnett to "avoid him, but do not madden him still more." The Mahatma refers to Hume as Sinnett's "chela, the captive of your spear and bow," since it was Sinnett who persuaded him to join the Society and to come into correspondence with the Mahatmas. At the same time, KH assumes "the *whole blame*" for Hume's present condition, particularly since, he tells Sinnett, "[You] acted under my own instructions" and so "I would not allow a single speck of the present disastrous results to taint *your* Karma." The Mahatma's statement here touches on an interesting aspect of the theory of karma: that of the possible transfer of merit or demerit from one person to another. One writer, Dr. Bruce Reichenbach, in *The Law of Karma: A Philosophic Study,* devotes an entire chapter to this subject. He points out that the concept of the transfer of merit (and demerit) is found in the ancient Vedic literature but with the emergence of Buddhism and particularly of Jainism, the emphasis changed, since those systems stress individualism and so maintain that no transfer of karmic consequences occurs. However, with the development of Mahayana Buddhism and its emphasis on the Bodhisattva ideal, the concept of a Bodhisattva assuming some of the karma of the chelas was introduced. The Mahatmas indicate in a number of places in the letters that they willingly assumed responsibility for their chelas, although the question remains whether that included taking on some of their pupils' karma. In any event, it appears that KH took responsibility for Hume's malicious and perfidious actions.

The reference to "another vain and ambitious malcontent—Dayanand S." reminds us of the early days of the Society, when it was temporarily associated with the Arya Samaj. Swami Dayanand is mentioned in Letter 92 (page 293) as one who "*was* an initiated Yogi" but became "a moral wreck" and ultimately antagonistic toward the Society. Here again, the emphasis, as with Hume, is on the moral character of the individual.

Letter 102 concludes with a reference to the occult novel *Mr. Isaacs* by F. Marion Crawford, at one time editor of the *Indian Herald*. Crawford was the nephew of Sam Ward, an American businessman and "one of our most enthusiastic members," according to Olcott. He was in London at the time Sinnett was receiving some of the letters. We meet with Ward again in later letters, where KH's comments show that the Mahatma held him in some regard. The Crawford novel was reviewed in the February 1883 issue of *The Theosophist*, probably by Sinnett. Colonel Olcott, to whom Ward had given a copy of the book, comments: "Ward . . . wrote certain interesting particulars about its [the book's] production. It was—he told us—inspired by the published accounts of Mahatma KH, and the idea so took possession of Mr. Crawford that, having once begun writing, he gave himself no rest, scarcely even food, until it was finished. He wrote it in less than four weeks, and Mr. Ward says that it almost seemed as if his nephew had been under the influence of an outside power" (*ODL*, Second Series, 394).

Olcott has some praise for the novel, but also considerable criticism, as he believes the behavior of Ram Lal, the Adept hero, is often depicted below the level of a true Adept. In closing Letter 102, KH makes a humorous comment concerning the depiction of himself as the principal character in the novel.

As a sidelight to the publication of the review of the Crawford novel, in the March 1883 issue of *The Theosophist* (the month following the publication of Sinnett's review), a correspondent who signed himself "A***8111" took issue with some favorable comments in the review, particularly regarding the author's attempt to depict KH as the novel's "adept hero." HPB added a footnote to the letter: "We are sorry to see Mr. A***8111 so underrating—though we may have, in his opinion, *over*rated Mr. Isaacs. There are two of the 'grandest occult truths' in it, though neither our critic, nor even the author himself, may be aware of them." Her comment certainly arouses one's curiosity, but as the book has long since been out of print and it is rather difficult to obtain a copy, one can only conjecture what those two "grand truths" may have been. Perhaps some enterprising student will search for a copy and discover those truths

LETTERS 103A AND 103B

There is really nothing to be said about Letter 103A beyond what is in the prefatory note. Much of the letter remains obscure, as no further description of the incidents the Mahatma refers to are available. They obviously involved, at least in part, the honesty of Mrs. Hollis-Billing. The letter's opening sentence indicates that a letter from C. C. Massey, first sent to Sinnett, had been sent on to KH, who then forwarded it to Olcott, who was instructed to "return it to Allahabad," which could only mean to Sinnett, since that was his place of residence. We can speculate that Massey's letter, since HPB did not see it, consisted largely of an attack on her as well as on Mrs. Billing and on the phenomena produced by one or both of these women.

The Mahatma attempts to set the record straight when he points out the error of so many in thinking that "the selection of members and the actions of the founders and Chelas are controlled by us." To some extent, this error still persists, as the question occasionally arises as to why the Mahatmas "permitted" certain individuals who later became antagonistic to the Society to join in the first place. Similarly, the question sometimes comes up: why didn't the Mahatmas prevent such and such an event from happening, since they are supposed to be relatively omniscient and able to see into the future?

In Letter 103B, KH reiterates what he has explained elsewhere in the letters—that the Mahatmas do not and cannot interfere with the karma of the individuals concerned nor with events brought about by human agency: "We have no concern with, nor, *do we guide the events generally.*" Then, referring to individuals cited in Massey's letter, KH proceeds to indicate each one's contribution to the Society's work. He makes the extremely interesting point that in every instance of a seemingly wrong action on someone's part, even to the point of apparent disaster, some good came out of it—a revealing insight into how the Mahatmas work. They do not interfere with karma or with the free action of human beings, but they seem to help on to fruition whatever seed of goodness is inherent in the action. Most significant for us to consider, he writes: "In each instance the individual traitor and enemy was given his chance, and but for his moral obliquity might have derived incalculable good from it to his personal Karma."

We have met some of the persons KH names here in previous letters: Hurrychund, the treasurer of the Arya Samaj through whom the founders made their first connections in India, who unfortunately later decamped with the Samaj's funds as well as with the fees paid to the Arya Samaj by the Theosophical Society before the founders moved to India; Dayanand, the head of the Arya Samaj who later, through outraged vanity, turned against Olcott and HPB; and Hume "who has aided it [the Society] greatly by his influence and will promote it more despite himself."

Two rather minor characters in the drama of the Society's early days are Edward Wimbridge and Rosa Bates. They were English, but both were living in New York at the time of the Society's founding. Wimbridge was an artist and architect; Rosa Bates was a teacher. Both accompanied Olcott and Blavatsky on the journey from New York to India. Olcott indicates (*ODL*, Second Series, 110) that Wimbridge was a "pretty decent sort of person" but that he had some reservations about Miss Bates. He begged HPB not to take these two with them to India, but "her invariable answer was that the two, being patriotic English in feeling, would afford by their company the best possible guarantee to the Anglo-Indian authorities of [their] innocence of any political designs." HPB said that she herself would take the consequences, so the two did accompany them on the journey. The subsequent story concerning Wimbridge and Rosa Bates and their involvement with Olcott and HPB during the time the Society's Headquarters were in Bombay may be read in *Old Diary Leaves*.

KH turns next to Mrs. Hollis-Billing, echoing what he said about her earlier, that "among mediums she is *the most honest* if not the best" (see Letter 92, page 291). (As mentioned earlier, HPB and Olcott stayed with Dr. and Mrs. Billing in London when they were on their way to India in 1879.) KH makes the interesting comment that "Ski," her spirit-guide, "has more than once served as carrier and even mouthpiece for several of us." The reference here to a "Scotch Brother" is intriguing, and we know no more than this about such a person. Evidently, HPB could also call on "Ski" to deliver a letter, if she so wished, particularly since at this time "M. [has] forbidden her to exercise her own occult means."

KH makes it very clear that he finds it repugnant to go "into particulars about this, that, and the other phenomenon that may have occurred," adding the significant statement: "They are the playthings of the tyro." While the Adepts have sometimes gratified a few individuals' craving for phenomena, their real concern is communication of the teachings: "For the present we offer our knowledge—some portions of it at least—to be either accepted or rejected on its own merits independently—entirely so—from the source from which it emanates." There is much to ponder in this statement, as well as in the comment that follows: "In return, we ask neither allegiance, loyalty, nor even simple courtesy." We may well ask ourselves whether we give credence to the teachings conveyed in the letters and in HPB's writings because we believe them to come from the Adepts or because of their inherent logic and meaningfulness.

The remainder of the letter is largely a defense of Mrs. Billing against a series of accusations apparently made by Massey, mostly on the authority of others. The events involved in these accusations are not at all clear, but the implication is that, in spite of Massey's sincerity, he has been deluded by others who seek to injure both Mrs. Billing and HPB. Perhaps the lesson in all this for us today is to consider to what extent we are influenced by the word of others on some matter without ourselves investigating the issue.

The letter concludes with the Mahatma's repeating what he said in an earlier letter: that he refuses to deal directly with the London Lodge, but promises to work through Sinnett in imparting something of the occult philosophy. Certainly both KH and M must have been pleased that the Englishman presented so much of the teachings in the books he produced, particularly his second work, *Esoteric Buddhism.*

LETTER 104

Sinnett headed Letter 104 "Devachan Notes Latest Additions, Answers to Queries." Therefore, before considering the subject matter as treated by KH here, the student may want to review the earlier letters that dealt with devachan. The first letter on the subject is Letter 68, which fortunately includes both the questions posed by Sinnett and Hume and the Mahatma's answers. Further questions that arose in the minds of the two Englishmen were addressed in Letter 70C. In Letter 85A, Sinnett pointed out a number of seeming contradictions in the teachings about devachan, which KH responded to in Letter 85B, particularly in sections 5 through 10 (pages 263–65). From statements in Letter 104, we learn that Sinnett was still not satisfied with, or perhaps failed to understand, the information he had been given, so he submitted further questions.

In responding to Sinnett's first question, which may have been rather long since the reply consumes nearly six pages, KH speaks of the reasons for Sinnett's problem. First, the Mahatma writes of his "inability to describe the—*indescribable*," which repeats a point he made in Letter 85B (see page 264). The source of Sinnett's misconception of the nature of devachan, KH says, may lie in "the shallowness and even fallacy of that 'system of pure (materialistic) reason,'" echoing a comment that the Mahatma has made many times in the course of the correspondence. As on those occasions, Sinnett is told that an awakened intuition is necessary: "Unless the intuitive perceptions of a trained chela come to the rescue, no amount of description [of devachan]—however graphic—will help. Indeed, no adequate words to express the difference between a state of mind on earth, and one outside of its sphere of action, no English terms in existence, equivalent to ours; *nothing*—but unavoidable (as due to early Western education) preconceptions, hence—lines of thought in a wrong direction in the learner's mind, to help us in this inoculation of entirely new thoughts!"

In view of the difficulties before him—the indescribability of the devachanic state and Sinnett's reliance on pure reason rather than intuitive perception—we can only feel grateful for the Mahatma's efforts in so patiently answering the Englishman's questions, seeking to correct misunderstandings and to explain at length that devachan is a "state, not a locality." As we ourselves strive to understand the teachings, we appreciate more fully KH's efforts to explain the nearly inexplicable, even as he writes of the "formidable difficulties" and asks, "Why should the West be so anxious . . . to learn anything from the East, since it is evidently unable to digest that which can never meet the requirements of the special tastes of its Esthetics." To what extent, we may ask ourselves, are we able today to "digest" the teachings given to us?

As the Mahatma seeks to disabuse Sinnett of the idea that devachan is a "monotonous condition," he asks him to "keep in mind that there are two fields of causal manifestation, to wit: the objective and subjective." It is "the grosser energies" that "manifest objectively in physical life," while it is "the moral and spiritual activities" that "find their sphere of effects" in devachan. Sinnett has evidently misunderstood an earlier statement (see Letter 70C) that the last thought of the dying individual will govern the devachanic period, taking this literally to mean that devachan consists of "one moment." It now becomes clear that the "keynote" in the dying brain's retrospective vision that predominated that life is what subsequently governs the devachanic life, becoming the central theme around which isolated "moral and spiritual" events will be grouped. There is change and progress and hence no monotony.

"That other misconception" that KH addresses in the first reply concerns the nature of time. Sinnett's query was: If we are unaware of the passage of time in devachan, what difference does it make (*a quoi bon*—what is the good of it) how long it lasts? "No," responds KH, "there are no clocks, no timepieces in Devachan," but, most significantly, he adds: "The whole Cosmos is a gigantic chronometer." The whole cycle of existence, with its many minor cycles, is an inevitable process. The outcome is up to us, but the cycles will proceed and will reach their respective conclusions.

Ultimately, time, as much as anything else in the conditioned universe, is finite and hence illusory. So to question the relative amounts of experience gathered in different scales of subjective time is to question the whole purpose of existence. If we do not yet know the answer to this problem, KH implies, we are wasting our time trying to understand details such as devachan. The Mahatma goes on to say that our conception of time alters depending on our condition, and he adds, "I may also remind you in this connection that *time is something created entirely by ourselves.*"

The Mahatma's entire discussion of the nature of time needs careful study, and the student may wish to compare the statements made here with the contemporary view of time as expounded by leading physicists, including Paul Davies and Amit Goswami. KH's statement that "*time* is not a predicate conception" is a fundamental comment on the nature of the cosmos. There is a relative time and an absolute 'time': relative time is created by our senses and exists only for that consciousness, while absolute time is intrinsic to the very essence of the cosmos. The student may wish as well to review the subject of time in *The Secret Doctrine*. In the proem to *The Secret Doctrine* volume

1, space, duration (or time), and motion are discussed as the three fundamentals of the cosmos. Each is necessary to the other. Motion implies change, and change implies time as the measure of that change. While studying this topic, it is helpful to keep in mind what KH says in this letter: "Finite similes are unfit to express the abstract and the infinite; nor can the objective ever mirror the subjective."

Consider also these two statements that are part of this discussion: "Western critical idealism . . . has still to learn the difference that exists between the *real being* of super-sensible objects and the shadowy subjectivity of the ideas it has reduced them to," and "Unless we learn to distinguish between the matter and the form of our knowledge of sensible objects, we can never arrive at correct, definite conclusions." Both statements point to the fact that the "archetypal" universe, the plan on which the physical world is based, is more real on its own level than physical objects are to us. The eternal ideas in the Universal Mind are infinitely more real than our subjective mental ideas concerning them. The crux of KH's criticism is that Western philosophy, following Kant, has taken the subjective image for the real thing and therefore has lost its way.

The Mahatma makes it clear that the process experienced in devachan is analogous to that on earth. KH says, "As physical existence has its cumulative intensity from infancy to prime, and its diminishing energy thenceforward to dotage and death, so the dream-life of Devachan is lived correspondentially." Said differently: "As in actual earth-life, so there is for the Ego in Devachan—the first flutter of psychic life, the attainment of prime, the gradual exhaustion of force passing into semi-unconsciousness, gradual oblivion and lethargy, total oblivion and—not death but birth: birth into another personality." In other words, the very nature of the cosmos is process, and devachan is no exception. We re-live our earth life in devachan and will progress or retrogress in much the same way. Accordingly, there can be no sense of unreality in devachan if the individual did not experience it on earth. Thus in no sense are we cheated or fooled by nature, as Sinnett appears to have thought, when in the subjective devachanic condition. As KH states: "What the lives in *Devachan* and upon Earth shall be respectively in each instance is determined by Karma." This creates the cycle, or as KH puts it: "And this weary round of birth upon birth must be ever and ever run through, until the being reaches the end of the seventh round, or—attains in the interim the wisdom of an Arhat, then that of a Buddha and thus gets relieved for a round or two."

KH follows this description of the process with comments on the types of individuals and the types of devachan they experience. The colorless personality will have a colorless devachan as contrasted with the "absolute *nonentities*... whose divine monad separated itself from the five principles during their life-time . . . and who have lived as *soulless* human beings . . . persons whose sixth principle has left them . . . their fifth or animal Soul of course goes down 'the bottomless pit.'" He returns to the topic of the eighth sphere and the state of Avitchi, which he discussed in Letters 70C and 85B. Noteworthy here is the distinction drawn between the "taper glimmer," easily puffed out, of the soulless entity and the fierce, powerful, maleficent energies of the one destined for Avitchi. The statement concerning the nonentities who are "entirely remodelled" may throw light on the statement in Letter 18 (page 65) that in the fifth round "the laggard *Egos* perish by the millions." Evidently, what annihilates them is their own psychic and moral feebleness and inertia.

The candidate for Avitchi, on the other hand, must be "punished," not merely annihilated, indicating the very different positions that the two types of entities occupy in relation to karma. The candidate for the eighth sphere has run out of karma just as much as he or she has run out of energy and purpose, and thus equilibrium can quite easily be restored. On the other hand, the "monster" has set many causes in motion, with many and varied results accruing at both the physical and the spiritual levels. Nothing short of repeated incarnations can restore the karmic balance in such a case. Hence, "he must not be simply *annihilated* but PUNISHED." Moreover, since Avitchi is the "complement" to devachan, the same laws apply to both states.

Only after more than five pages in the text does the Mahatma give what we may call the formal answer to Sinnett's "query No. 1." The reply seems simple in itself: "Yes . . . there is . . . a continual change in Devachan, just as much—and far more—as there is in the life of any man or woman . . . with that difference, that to the *Devachanee* his special occupation is always pleasant and fills *his* life with rapture. Change there must be." All the information that has preceded this simple a statement, however, aids greatly in our understanding of Devachan and so needs careful study. And KH responds to the Englishman's view that devachan must be rather monotonous with a beautiful, almost poetic description: "That one note, as I said, struck from the lyre of life, would form but the Key-note of the being's subjective state, and work out into numberless harmonic tones and semi-tones of psychic phantasmagoria. There—all unrealized hopes, aspirations, dreams, become fully realized, and the *dreams* of the objective become the *realities* of the subjective existence. And there behind the curtain of Maya its vapours and deceptive appearances are perceived by the adept, who has learnt the great secret how to penetrate thus deeply into the Arcana of being."

As we do not have question 2 in full, the intention of the answer is not very clear. Presumably, it concerned the point when the recollection of one's series of incarnations takes place. The subject of the rounds is familiar by now, having been discussed in several earlier letters. Here KH informs Sinnett "that at the end of each of the seven rounds" (and we are in the fourth round) there is only a partial remembrance, while "the *complete* recollection of all the lives—(earthly and devachanic) *omniscience* . . . comes but at the great end of the full seven Rounds." Note that at the end of each great cycle, having achieved the full evolution of that stage, we return to Parabrahm. We then reappear as separated objective entities at the dawn of the next great cycle as Dhyan Chohans. For further study, the student may wish to consult the references in *The Secret Doctrine* that bear upon the subject of the goal set for our humanity on the completion of "the full seven Rounds" which constitute a manvantara.

We need to be clear as to the meaning of the terms the Mahatma uses here, particularly the distinction between "nirvana" and "devachan." See also at the end of the reply to Sinnett's fourth query, where he states, "Nor is Nirvana itself comparable to Para-Nirvana." Particularly useful comparative definitions for "nirvana" and "para-nirvana" are found in *The Theosophical Glossary*.

The point made in reply 3 is quite clear. Apparently Sinnett had asked whether two Egos can be in communication in devachan, and KH replies that each will "work out its own devachanic sensations, making the other a sharer in its subjective bliss." So while we can be conscious of others in our devachanic life, they appear not as real objective people but only as the idealized memory of them. From all that has been told us of devachan, this seems the only logical possibility.

Query 4 and its reply deal with the structure of the after-death states. KH again emphasizes that "devachan is a state, not a locality," a point that seemed difficult for Sinnett to grasp and may be difficult for others to understand fully. The "three spheres of ascending spirituality"—kama-loka, rupa-loka, and arupa-loka—were discussed in Letter 68. Note that KH says, following a reference to arupa-loka, that this state is "the last of the seven states," without naming the four other states. Each sphere contains endless gradations of states, "differentiating *ad infinitum*," as KH writes, each corresponding to the states of the entities who inhabit them. The gradations of kama-loka correspond to psychic states, those of rupa-loka to mental states, and those of arupa-loka to states of mental spirituality. Similarly, Avitchi may also be divided into rupa and arupa states. The Mahatma concludes his response 4 with another summary of the entire process of evolution, a statement that merits our pondering: "Not even the most exalted experience of a monad in the highest devachanic state in *Arupa*-Loka . . . is comparable to that perfectly subjective condition of pure spirituality from which the monad emerged to 'descend into matter' and to which at the completion of the grand cycle it must return."

The reply to query 5 directs Sinnett to read again the Mahatma's responses in the "Famous contradictions," a reference to Letter 85B. While we do not know the text of Sinnett's question, in the answer KH emphasizes that one's stay in kama-loka is *un*conscious.

The point to grasp in reply 6 is simply that just as physical life must run to its inevitable conclusion, so the psychic or mental life, which is incomplete at physical death, must run to its conclusion in the after-death states. "The stay in Devachan is proportioned to the unfinished psychic impulses originating in earth life." The reason for the incompleteness of the psychic life at physical death lies in the frustrations and inequalities of physical existence, which inevitably draw the entity "by the force of *Tanha*," the thirst for sentient existence, back into incarnation.

Again stressing what is needed to understand the teachings about the after-death states, particularly the nature of devachan, KH writes: "One must see with his spiritual eye, hear with his Dharmakayic ear, feel with the sensations of his *Ashta-vijnana* (spiritual "I") before he can comprehend this doctrine fully; otherwise it may but increase one's 'discomfort,' and add to his knowledge but little." This statement offers a great deal for every student to ponder deeply, particularly if we are inclined to feel that we know all that is to be known about devachan—or indeed about any of the teachings that the Mahatmas or their pupils have presented.

The answer to query 7 contains detailed examples of the workings of the law of karma, linking a series of lives. The Mahatma stresses that "like attracts like." This fundamental occult principle is applied here to psychic, mental, and spiritual conditions in which it determines the necessary and logical outcome after death as well as in the next life. Therefore, there "could be no more flagrant misnomer" than the phrase "accidents of birth." As KH states, "Personality is the synonym for limitation," and the "*skandhas* are the elements of limited existence." While Sinnett seems to have felt the whole doctrine concerning devachan was "profoundly unsatisfactory," we may need to think deeply over it to come to our own conclusion as to its reasonableness in relation to the entire occult philosophy that has been given to us.

In the middle of response 7, KH refers to the fact that Sinnett plans to write another book for which he has already selected the title: *Esoteric Buddhism*. The book will be, as KH puts it "a sequel to or amplification of" the series of articles "Fragments of Occult Truth" currently being published in *The Theosophist*. The student may like to read the chapter "Devachan" in that book to see how Sinnett explains the doctrine in light of the information he was given in the several letters named at the beginning of this letter's commentary and in this letter itself.

Before the Mahatma closes the letter, he refers to a number of other matters that deserve at least a passing comment. First is the reference to Sinnett's "wild scheme." As we know, Sinnett always longed for a direct, personal visit with the Mahatma, and now it seems he has devised some plan to bring that about before his departure for England. Apparently he had the idea of going to Darjeeling, thinking this would facilitate a meeting, but KH tells him this is not "*wild*, but simply impracticable." Yet he is given some hope, as KH writes: "The drift of your energies [possibly referring to using his energy in writing his new book] is carrying you slowly yet steadily in the direction of personal intercourse."

Second is mention of the fact that the members of the London Lodge were refusing to contribute to the support of the Parent Society; the Mahatma asks who among them would think of trying to avoid payment of dues to any other society, club, or organization. Even today, some members feel that either the dues are too high or membership should be without any dues at all. KH mentions the sacrifices of the two Founders, HPB and Olcott, and relates how the Mahatma M had made a contribution to help Olcott's sister in America—a touching insight into the compassionate nature of M as well as HPB. KH's statement: "Our laws and restrictions with regard to money or any financial operations ... are extremely severe" offers another peek into the "rules" that govern the members of the Hierarchy.

In Letter 102 (page 350), the Mahatma asked Sinnett how he liked the book *Mr. Isaacs,* by F. Marion Crawford. We know that Sinnett reviewed the book for *The Theosophist*, but we do not know whether he did so for the *Pioneer*, the newspaper where he had been editor and which he was now leaving. The new owners were not sympathetic to his interest in Theosophy and so had terminated his employment.

The letter's closing sentence is interesting in view of the fact that some writers place Djual Khul's achievement of adeptship much earlier than the time of this letter, early 1883. KH's statement that his chela Djual Khul is "striving to reach 'the other shore'" may indicate that the chela became an initiated Adept at this time.

~ ~

LETTERS 105, 106, AND 107

The three brief Letters 105, 106, and 107 concern the "Phoenix venture," the attempt by Sinnett, with KH's encouragement, to establish a newspaper devoted to promoting political freedom for India. The idea for such a paper arose in Sinnett's mind when he was given notice of termination of his employment as editor of the Allahabad *Pioneer* and is first referred to in Letter 98. In that letter, KH said he would consult his superior regarding Sinnett's proposal, and the Mahachohan's response is reported in Letter 99. Capital for the new paper was to be raised from among Sinnett's friends "in the world, and every Hindu theosophist who has the good of his country at heart." This matter of securing funds for the *Phoenix* is the principal subject of these three letters.

In fact, there is little to comment on in these letters, and the references are generally clear. Hume, here referred to as "the Rothney Swedenborg," has been engaged in what KH calls "malevolent meddling," evidently making it difficult to obtain the necessary funding. Hume's home in Simla was known as Rothney Castle. Colonel Gordon, referred to in Letter 107 as "a loyal friend and trustworthy ally," is mentioned in earlier letters, particularly in Letter 55, when he and Mrs. Gordon hosted the English medium William Eglinton at their home in Howrah, a Calcutta suburb.

The allusion to dates—"The 30th is as good as any other day"—refers to the date on which the Sinnetts might sail for England. In Letter 108, the Mahatma suggests an April date, but Sinnett was becoming impatient to leave, having made all his plans, and the family sailed from Madras on March 30, 1883. They never returned to India, but the correspondence with the Mahatmas continued for some time after the Sinnetts' arrival in London.

Another example of KH's unique sense of humor is in his words: "Some are born for diplomacy and intrigue; I rather think that it is not my particular province." In reading these short letters, as indeed in reading so many of KH's communications to Sinnett, one is struck by the close attention the Mahatma gives to the attitudes and concerns of many of the people who play a part in the Society's activities, including the movements of both HPB and Olcott and the general situation as it affects Sinnett.

Letter 107 ends on a rather sad note, as KH says that he will not concern himself again with "worldly enterprises": "I have lost much of my optimism in the late affray." Here is yet another example of the Mahatma's use of language and metaphor: "No fish undertaking a ramble on the river's bank and outside its own element need complain of catching lumbago. . . . Once I take my leap back into the crystal wave—few will ever have a chance of seeing me peeping out again." However, the "death-knell" of the "Phoenix venture" is not sounded until Letter 114.

LETTER 108

Addressed to "My dear 'Ward,'" using a term that Sinnett must have signed himself on some occasion, perhaps because he had called the Mahatma his "guardian," this letter is the last one Sinnett received before leaving India. In this letter KH suggests "on or about April 7th" as a departure date, but as already noted, the Sinnett family sailed on March 30. It is not at all clear why the Mahatma took such interest in designating a date for their departure, even calling the April date "this desire of mine" and indicating that it would be a "personal favour" if Sinnett sailed on that date.

Many of KH's statements in this brief letter leave us with questions the answers to which we can only speculate, attempting to use our intuition. Sinnett must have asked the Mahatma for information "concerning 'stars' and *obscurations*," meaning perhaps not so much astronomy per se but the evolutionary cycles through the rounds. We do not know what HPB told Sinnett regarding why the question could not be answered at that time. *The Secret Doctrine* contains a number of references to "obscurations," a term used for periods of rest or pralayas, in relation to the rounds (see particularly vol. 1, pages 159–60 and the footnote on page 171). Sinnett may also have asked a question concerning the "obscuration" of planets, based on the Mahatma's statement in Letter 93B on this subject (see page 325, response 14), and that further information on the matter could not be divulged at that time.

Having declined to answer Sinnett's question, KH continues with a rather provocative statement: "My task becomes with every letter more dangerous. It becomes exceedingly difficult to teach you and hold at the same time strictly to the original programme." Why has writing the letters and conveying the teachings become not only "difficult" but "dangerous"? Was it dangerous for the Mahatma or for Sinnett? At the outset of the correspondence, KH said that he would answer Sinnett's questions in so far as he remained consonant with the "Rules" to which he was pledged. We can certainly understand that answering some of Sinnett's questions may not have been easy without in some way pushing the boundary, so to say, between what could be communicated and what should not because of its occult nature. As KH states at the close of the letter, "Let us hold at present to the simply intellectual aspect of our *intercourse* and busy ourselves but with philosophy . . . and leave the rest to *time* and its *unforeseen developments.*" Did Sinnett perhaps ask about occult practices that lead to the awakening of *siddhis*, occult "powers" for which special training and discipline are required along with a life of complete purity?

Such a conjecture is based on the information we have been given about the trials and tests of chelaship. But it does not clarify what constituted the "danger" in KH's continuing to write to Sinnett, so here again we can only speculate. Is it because, as the Mahatma M told Sinnett, that KH "had to bear the consequences" of having taken Sinnett as his "lay-chela" (see Letter 42, as well as some earlier letters from KH)? These comments arise out of the Mahatma's current reference to "further psychological experiments," indicating that KH may have attempted to aid Sinnett in gaining some psychic or occult faculty. There is, moreover, a reference to Djual Khul's making an attempt to open Sinnett's vision. Apparently Djual Khul was able to assist Sinnett but did not succeed in opening his inner vision, for reasons that Sinnett himself "correctly surmised." Perhaps Sinnett recognized his own inability to achieve his desired goal due to factors that surely included his dietary habits, his use of alcohol, and his smoking, personal habits on which KH comments a number of times in the earliest letters. Another obstacle for Sinnett may have been in his karmic relationship with Hume. To what extent was Sinnett still influenced by his Simla friend whose "incessant *underground* intrigues" had now brought him "entirely in the hands of the Brothers of the Shadow"?

To anticipate, we may note here the Mahatma's statements at the opening of Letter 126 that Sinnett is "entirely unfit for practical occultism" but he will nevertheless "make one more effort . . . to open [Sinnett's] inner vision." In the present letter, KH does give Sinnett some encouragement: "Ever bear in mind that *whenever* and *whatever* is possible will be always done for you unurged," but Sinnett is not to ask for special favors. The Mahatma reminds him: "I have pledged my word to you to teach them [the members of the British Theosophical

Society] through your kind agency our philosophy." This is a reiteration of KH's statement in Letter 93B (page 343) that he "will use no other channel than yourself to impart our Arhat philosophy." We need to remember these clear assertions when we come to the correspondence to and concerning the London Lodge. The letter concludes on the beautiful note of KH's continuing affectionate friendship for the Englishman.

LETTER 109

There is little to comment upon in the two brief notes that constitute Letter 109. They accompanied the transmittal of a newspaper clipping relevant to the "'obscuration' doctrine," as KH says. The clipping is presumably from a London newspaper, although we do not have any evidence for its source. It certainly indicates the Mahatma's familiarity with current events, particularly as they concern occult doctrines. The subject of "obscuration" was discussed in Letter 93B. Students may wish to consult a contemporary work on astronomy for the latest developments on the subject. Certainly, the several space probes have disclosed far more information than was known at the time of the letters not only about the planets in our solar system but far beyond.

LETTER 110

Although Letter 110, concerning the fate of the "Phoenix venture," was written to Colonel Olcott, it was evidently sent on by him to Sinnett. Since so much of the letter is a kind of warning to Sinnett about the machinations of Hume, now called "[Sinnett's] quondam friend of Simla," one wonders why the communication was not sent directly to Sinnett. Perhaps it was important for Olcott, who had been quite enthusiastic about the possibility of the new paper, to be informed about the "checks upon checks" that were causing "delays, disappointments, trials of patience" with regard to the project.

The story of Olcott's many healings is well known to all students familiar with the president–founder's life and activities. Olcott related much of his healing work in his record of the Society's founding and early days, published as *Old Diary Leaves*. At the time of this letter, he had been on a lengthy tour in Ceylon and had "been ordered home for a rest" and not to engage in further healing work until he heard from his own guru, M. Eventually the Mahatma told Olcott to cease doing any healings.

Among the noteworthy statements in this letter is a comment about chelaship, which, KH writes, "is yet almost a complete puzzle for" both Olcott and Sinnett. Without obedience to the rules, purity of life, and a selfless motive, the attempt to awaken psychic faculties, "the rapid scramble up the Himalayas as would-be chela[s]," insanity could ensue. "Few men know their inherent capacities—only the ordeal of crude chelaship develops them." There is much more about chelaship in subsequent letters, and the student may recall comments on the topic in earlier letters as well.

The full name of "Bishenlal," one of the chelas who became insane and failed, is Lalla Bishen Lall, who was president of the Rahilkhund Branch in Bareilly. Damodar K. Mavalankar, at the time joint recording secretary of the Society, wrote a fascinating letter to Bishenlal concerning what Damodar conceived "to be the chief duties of a Branch of the Parent Theosophical Society" (see Eek, *Damodar*, 175–77). The emphasis on brotherhood in Damodar's letter is of particular importance for students tracing the history of the Society's Objects.

The sentence in Letter 110: "The turn of the Kingsford-Maitland party has come" seems to foreshadow developments in the London Lodge, of which Anna Kingsford had become president. As the letter indicates, Hume wrote a letter to Olcott in which he attacked practically everyone, including Sinnett, whom he called a "credulous imbecile." The Mahatma had that letter duplicated by occult means and sent to Sinnett to prepare him for the mischief Hume was creating in the London Lodge, which led, in part, to problems discussed in later letters. The Mahatma begs Olcott's pardon for what he calls the "bad taste" that compelled him to so duplicate the letter.

In a letter to Patience Sinnett, then in London, and addressed to "Beloved She-Fellow and Sister," HPB expressed her thoughts about the London situation:

> Since your departure I am eternally in hot water for that blessed paper [referring to the *Phoenix*]. KH *used* me . . . like a post-horse. I stirred up all our 69 Societies in India and letters sent to your dear *Hub* [husband], will show to him and you that I have been kicking in this atmosphere like "un diable dans de l'eau benie" [a devil dancing in holy water]. . . . If the Boss does not come to India I will emigrate "armes et bagages" to Ceylon or Burma. . . . You ask me, dear, whether "the money will come at all." And how can I know! Goodness, what can I do when even KH seems to give it up in disgust and despair. There is some infernal power at work most assuredly, and one of these powers is our *Jhut-Sing* of Simla, the Seer of the mountains, the "pet chela" of Jacolet the Swami of Almora. Ah if the old Chohan only but permitted our Masters to exercise their powers for one day! . . . Well, very little hope, I am afraid for us. Better not to deceive ourselves. My Boss M says that Mr. Sinnett does "an immense good" in England.

A final comment on Letter 110 concerns KH's rather puzzling statement: "M sends you thro' me these vases as a home greetings." Vases may seem a strange gift for the Mahatma to be sending to Olcott. However, the matter came to light a few years latter, in 1886, after the infamous Hodgson Report of the Society for Psychical Research had been published. In a letter probably addressed to Sinnett, HPB says, "The German Theosophists cannot understand or justify the phenomenon with the Japanese vases received by Olcott," followed by a long, rather complicated account that seems to hinge on whether Mme. Coulomb tried to trick Olcott and HPB in order to prove to Hodgson that HPB was a fraud. The full story is too long to reprint here but may be found in *The Letters of H. P. Blavatsky to A. P. Sinnett* (pages 139–41). Interestingly enough, Letter 110 concludes with the assurance that the letter is indeed from KH, and that Olcott is to inform Sinnett of its validity.

LETTER 111

This letter, along with Letter 112—undoubtedly sent at the same time and perhaps with one enclosed within the other—is the first communication Sinnett received after his return to England. As Letter 112 indicates, the Mahatma informs Sinnett that he may, if he wishes, read Letter 111 to the members of the London Lodge. As he does so often in the correspondence, KH seems to delight in using metaphor and flowery language to express what could be said in relatively few words. Some phrases read almost like poetry. For example, KH reminds Sinnett of "olden time, when you threaded the streets of your metropolis," words that give quite a different feeling than "when you walked the streets of London." The comparison between "the circumambient ether" of the devachanic state and the "circummuded British Channel" is wonderfully graphic. The Mahatma's command of English is truly remarkable, and the contemporary reader may pause to enjoy the language of the letter as much as Sinnett must have on receiving it.

That aside, it is evident from the opening paragraph that Sinnett, having just seen his second book, *Esoteric Buddhism,* published almost immediately on his return to his homeland, has been actively meeting with the members in London and no doubt sharing with them what he has learned through the correspondence with the Mahatmas. He has thus, in KH's words, been "essentially aiding to build the bridge over which the British metaphysicians [perhaps a sly dig at some members such as Massey] may come within thinking distance" of the Adepts. As we have seen in relation to preceding letters, KH told Sinnett, before he left India, that he would only teach the British members through Sinnett. This letter seems to follow that promise.

The reference to "the great Vedanta Philosophy" is interesting in light of KH's statement (Letter 88, page 271) that "we are not Adwaitees." The phrase the Mahatma uses here is often translated. "The Atman may be known only by the Atman"; the source of the two-line poetic rendering has not been identified. The essence of the saying is found in the works of Sri Shankaracharya, particularly in *Atmabodha*, usually translated as "Self-Knowledge."

The subject of devachan is obviously still under discussion and, with Sinnett's *Esoteric Buddhism* now in print, we can assume that Massey and others were avidly reading his chapters on the topic yet still finding obscurities or contradictions in the teachings. In the August 1883 issue of *The Theosophist* there appeared a "Memorandum on Devachan," preceded by an editor's note (HPB was still the editor): "The Memorandum that follows emanates from a British Theosophist. It was sent to 'Lay Chela,' the author of *Esoteric Buddhism*, in response to whose desire that the objections should be explained away, the three Replies subjoined have been sent. They come from three different sources." The "British Theosophist" is obviously Massey. The identity of the "three different sources" is unexplained, but from the contents of Letter 111, KH was probably one of them. As indicated in the editor's note, the "Memorandum" was first sent to Sinnett, who sent it on to KH, who sent it to HPB for publication along with one of the replies.

Massey's question may be summarized briefly: could there be "actual companionship" between two "*subjective* entities" in devachan, such that each would know of the other's presence? The three replies are quite detailed and merit the earnest student's consideration.

(Many Theosophical libraries have bound volumes of the early issues of *The Theosophist,* so where these are available it is possible to study the replies to Massey's query.) The first reply discusses the word "subjective," commenting: "The Occultist postulates an ascending scale of subjectivity which grows continually more real as it gets farther and farther from illusionary earthly objectivity: its ultimate, *Reality*—Parabrahm." The author continues: "Death itself being powerless to sever psychic association there, where pure spiritual love links the two," the devachanic "dream" is the reality for the devachanee.

The second reply, which contains such phrases as "in the light of our doctrines," says, "A monad in Devachan has *but one state of consciousness* [which] cannot be compared with any other state," and that "the intercourse between the monads is real, mutual, and as *actual* in the world of subjectivity, as it is in this our world of deceptive reality." The third reply states: "Buddhistically speaking, there are states and states and degrees upon degrees in Devachan, in all of which, notwithstanding the (to us) objective isolation of the principal hero, he is surrounded by a host of actors in conjunction with whom he had during his last earth-life created and worked out the causes of those effects that are produced first on the field of *Devachanic* or *Avitchean* subjectivity." Whether the three lengthy replies satisfied Massey or were helpful in furthering Sinnett's understanding we do not know, but they do give us today additional information valuable in our own efforts to comprehend the nature of a state of consciousness so unlike our ordinary one.

As the letter continues, KH seems to enjoy weaving word pictures to describe Sinnett's work in conveying the teachings he has received as "building spans for a royal bridge." The Mahatma ends the first paragraph on page 373 with one of the most beautiful statements to be found in our literature concerning our work as Theosophists: "Still the theosophist's duty is like that of the husbandman; to turn his furrows and sow his grains as best he can; the issue is with nature, and she, the slave of Law." This is truly a reminder that we have the responsibility for sharing the wisdom, but never with any concern as to the fruit of our action.

Then follows a long paragraph discussing the dangers of chelaship and the tragic results that occur when an individual has forced the premature development of psychic powers or, as the Mahatma puts it, "snatches at forbidden power before his moral nature is developed to the point of fitness for its exercise." The description of one who has fallen into physical and moral wretchedness probably relates to the tragedy of Mirza Moorad Ali Beg, whose real name was Godolphin Mitford, author of the article "Elixir of Life," on which the Mahatma commented in Letter 49. This unfortunate individual is referred to elsewhere in the letters. Here, in Letter 111, KH gives only "a glimpse into the hell" into which a "lay-chela" may fall and advises Sinnett to "think well over the article 'Chelas and Lay Chelas,'" published in the July 1883 *Theosophist* (*CW*, 6:606 *et seq.*).

Every aspirant certainly must "think well over" the seven qualifications HPB lists in this article. She says they are from "Book IV of *Kiu-ti*," also the source for the Stanzas of Dzyan (given in *The Secret Doctrine*). HPB comments on the qualifications for chelaship: "With the sole exception of the first [perfect physical health], which in rare and exceptional cases might have been modified, each one of these points has been invariably insisted upon, and all must have been more or less developed in the inner nature by the Chela's UNHELPED EXERTIONS, before he could be actually put to the test."

Since in the light of the several qualifications so many of the chelas failed, presumably almost superhuman strength and stamina are required to achieve even the probationary stage on the path to adeptship. While much is said in the letters concerning chelaship, the statements in Letter 111 constitute the gravest warning on the subject and so deserve our careful consideration. One wonders, too, how this was received by those in the London Lodge who were eager for preferment, assuming Sinnett read the letter to the members as KH had asked him to do.

The Mahatma turns next to expressing his pleasure that Sir William Crookes has joined the Society. Crookes became one of the Society's five counsellors, appointed to that position by Olcott. The

Mahatma M commented in Letter 48 that Crookes had "brought science within our hail in his 'radiant matter' discovery." In two letters to Sinnett, HPB comments on Crookes, saying that he "preaches and teaches a very old occult Doctrine" (*LBS*, 224–26). Now, in Letter 111, KH suggests that the scientist should further his discoveries by endeavoring to "find the 'Kama-rupa' of matter—its *fifth* state." KH then adds, "but to find its *Manas* he would have to pledge himself stronger to secrecy than he seems inclined to." Later in the letter, the Mahatma mentions "the *sixth* condition of matter," presumably connected in some manner with buddhi. These are provocative ideas indeed, seeming to hint that there is mind in matter, a concept that must have surprised Sinnett and the London members with whom he shared the letter but would not be so surprising to anyone today. As the Mahatma said in Letter 88: "We believe in MATTER alone, in matter as visible nature and matter in its invisibility as the invisible omnipresent omnipotent Proteus with its unceasing motion which is its life, and which nature draws from herself since she is the great whole outside of which nothing can exist. . . . The existence of matter then is a fact; the existence of motion is another fact, their self existence and eternity or indestructibility is a third fact."

Continuing with his comments on the work of Crookes, the Mahatma emphasizes that it is not mental or intellectual but rather spiritual development that will "create irresistible *attractions* and compel [the Adepts'] attention." He then remarks: "The supreme energy resides in the *Buddhi*; latent—when wedded to *Atman* alone, active and irresistible when galvanized by the *essence* of 'Manas' and when none of the dross of the latter commingles with that pure essence to weigh it down by its finite nature." This seems to point to the importance of training and purifying the mind so it can reflect the buddhic principle. Such is the object of Yoga as detailed by Patanjali in the *Yoga Sutras*.

Apparently Sinnett had asked, at some time, whether he could attempt some mesmeric cures such as those Olcott was doing with considerable success. He must also have referred to possibly doing such cures with the aid of a lock of KH's hair, which he kept in a locket that he wore (see Letters 51 and 80 for indications that each of the Sinnetts possessed such a lock of the Mahatma's hair). KH responds that there is no reason why Sinnett should not attempt such cures "by the help not of your locket but the power of your own will." And he comments: "Set your will in motion." By that means he will utilize the "psychic current which ever runs between himself [KH] and his severed tress." There is much for the student of the healing arts to explore in the Mahatma's comments, particularly the statement: "To heal diseases it is not indispensable, however desirable, that the psychopathist should be absolutely pure."

KH discusses next some misunderstandings by several Buddhist scholars whose works were then being published, especially the well-known Thomas William Rhys-Davids, professor of Pali and Buddhist literature at University College in London, whose works on Buddhism are still often cited. The Mahatma seems disheartened over such commentators' failure to understand "the core of our abstruse doctrines." He cites particularly the definition of "Avalokitesvara," quoting Rhys-Davids, and then discussing the term in some detail. We may note especially that: "It is, when correctly interpreted, in one sense "the *divine Self* perceived or seen by *Self*, the *Atman* or seventh principle ridded of its *mayavic* distinction from its Universal Source— which becomes the object of perception for, and by the *individuality* centred in *Buddhi,* the sixth principle, something that happens only in the highest state of *Samadhi*. . . . Avalokitesvara implies the seventh *Universal* Principle, as the object perceived by the Universal *Buddhi,* "Mind" or Intelligence which is the synthetic aggregation of all the Dhyan Chohans."

The Mahatma continues with reference to a statement of St. Paul ("the Christian Adept, the Kabalistic Paul") and an elaboration of the meaning of *Avalokiteshvara* in both Christian and Chinese contexts. The entire exposition needs careful study, as it is not easily summarized. The student may also wish to explore the concept of Avalokiteshvara in recently published Buddhist texts, as so much more is available today, including translations of Tibetan and Sanskrit works unavailable at the time of these letters. Particularly useful is the work by Dr. Har Dayal, *The Bodhisattva Doctrine in Buddhist Sanskrit Literature*, which presents a detailed analysis of the name *Avalokiteshvara*. Also of special importance for the Theosophical student in understanding the Chinese forms of the name to which KH refers is HPB's commentary on stanza 6, sloka 1 in *The Secret Doctrine* (1:136–38). There HPB points up the esoteric meaning of the two names, which she gives as "Kuan-Shih-Yin" and "Kuan-yin," a slightly different spelling than KH uses. One cannot help but note KH's statement that "a too correct rendering of our *Avalokitesvara* and *Kwan-Shai-Yin* might have very disastrous effects" as it would "amount to showing Christendom the true and undeniable origin of the . . . mysteries of its Trinity" and other doctrines. HPB also comments on the correlative expressions of Avalokiteshvara in the Christian tradition.

Continuing his discussion of Avalokiteshvara, KH provides a superb and helpful interpretation of the Theosophical Seal, particularly the meaning of the double triangle. The sentence "the *chela* who can explain this sign from every one of its aspects—is *virtually an adept*" should cause every Theosophical student to consider carefully the significance of the Society's seal, endeavoring to discover deeper meaning in every aspect of its parts. The Mahatma's brief reference to "the only one among you who got none of her ideas from books" is undoubtedly to Anna Kingsford, spoken of later in the letter as "that remarkable seeress." Sinnett's review of her book, *The Perfect Way*, written in collaboration with Edward Maitland, has been mentioned in previous letters, most particularly in Letter 63. KH speaks of the two authors of that work as laying "their hands several times upon the keystone of Occultism."

The Mahatma emphasizes the number 6, saying that it is "mentioned more often than 7—this last figure, the central point, being implied, for it is the germ of the six and their matrix." The number 6 has been called the first "perfect number," and in works on sacred geometry the hexagonal figure appears more often than any other both in nature and in human artifacts. The Society's seal thus contains interlaced triangles, which KH speaks of as "the upper pointing one to Wisdom concealed, and the downward pointing one Wisdom *revealed* (in the phenomenal world)." He says further, "In symbology the central point is *Jivatma* (the 7th principle), and hence Avalokitesvara." So the seal depicts both the macrocosm and the our very selves, the microcosm.

Letter 111 concludes with a reference to a criticism probably written by Hume—whom KH this time calls "the Marcus Aurelius of Simla"—concerning the subject of evolution. We may be surprised at KH's statement that "neither you [Sinnett] nor any other man across the threshold has had or ever will have the 'complete theory' of Evolution taught him; or get it unless he guesses it for himself." Although he adds, "some—have come *very near* it." This can only make us wonder to what extent we understand the theory from the occult point of view. The cause for lack of understanding is simply "the shadow of *Manas* projecting across the field of *Buddhi*—to prove the eternal law that only the unshackled Spirit shall see the things of the Spirit without a veil."

Other factors include "incomplete explanations" and "the poor vehicles of language at our disposal," to which KH adds, "Our language must always be more or less that of parable and suggestion." There is also the fact that "you [Sinnett] cannot be given the real figures and difference in the Rounds." Similarly, in *The Secret Doctrine* HPB writes of "blinds" that hide the true numbers and obscure some of the subjects. Perhaps we need to take to heart KH's admonition: "You share with all beginners the tendency to draw too absolutely strong inferences from partly caught hints, and to dogmatize thereupon as though the last word had been spoken." How many times have we witnessed this tendency if not in ourselves then in other Theosophists!

A most wonderful letter is this one, containing much to study in further depth, opening as it does on vistas of knowledge and vast fields of wisdom to be explored. Even though the Adepts "have [their] own peculiar modes of expression and what lies behind the fence of words is even more important than what you read," the Mahatma is always encouraging, repeating the word he uses so often in his letters to Sinnett: "Try."

LETTER 112

Two matters seem to be of concern to KH as he writes this "*Private* but not *very* Confidential" letter to Sinnett, which undoubtedly accompanied Letter 111, and which *could* be shared with the London members. The first involves the prospects for the success (or failure) of the "Phoenix venture." The Mahatma, identifying himself as "we Aryan exiles in our snowy retreat," begins by expressing his distress over the sad condition into which India has fallen from a spiritual point of view. He speaks of the "moral and spiritual condition of my people" and "the selfish baseness of human nature," though he also comments that this situation is the "concomitant . . . of the passage of humanity through our stage of the evolutionary circuit."

Considering the world today, and recalling KH's statement in the very first letter to Sinnett that "human nature in general . . . is the same now as it was a million of years ago," we can ponder our own role in these times and the extent to which we can aid suffering humanity. What is "the task of the T.S." in which "we would so gladly assist"? How may we best aid humanity on its "passage" through what have been called the dark days of Kali Yuga?

KH tells Sinnett that he has "stepped outside our usual limits to aid your particular project" (the newspaper), but evidently Sinnett has published an unfortunate letter, probably in the *Times* of India, since that is where the disastrous affect was felt. So although we do not know the letter's contents, it must have reflected what the Mahatma here calls Sinnett's "English prejudices and the sinful antipathy towards *our race* and colour." Then he adds, "'Madame' will tell you more." This HPB proceeded to do in no uncertain terms in a very long letter to Sinnett, a portion of which reads as follows:

> First you blow me up and reproach me for feeling and *knowing* that this letter in *Times* would be made a pretext for upsetting the project. It is not that I blame or ever blamed you for the spirit of your letter or the views in it . . . but for its too early issue [and] for your writing it at all. Your letter was *noble, generous, well-meaning.* It was all that and yet it *was born* out of time—either too late or too early. Had you written it when at Madras [that is, before the Sinnetts left India]—it would have brought you thousands of friends. (*LBS*, 48–53)

HPB goes on to say that many wealthy Indians who had considered subscribing to the *Phoenix* were "the first to back out" when his letter appeared. Moreover, "all of us, we shall lose a thousand times more if the last and supreme attempt of KH fails: *for we are sure to lose Him* in such a case." The entire letter is well worth reading, for it is quite typical of HPB.

As we know, the *Phoenix* project did indeed fail, and despite HPB's warning, Sinnett did not "lose" KH, as the letters continued. As for KH's own intentions, he indicates in Letter 112 that if the paper does not succeed he will dedicate himself "to our prime duty of gaining knowledge and disseminating through all available channels such fragments as mankind in the mass may be ready to assimilate," a truly wonderful statement concerning the work of the Adepts.

The second matter to which KH gives attention in Letter 112 concerns the problems of two London mediums, Mrs. Hollis-Billing, whose spirit-guide was known as "Ski," and a Mrs. Simpson, referred to in Letter 103B as a "Boston medium" who evidently had a spirit-guide of the same name. The circumstances involving these two women are impossible to unravel; the one understandable feature is that HPB is blamed for at least part of the business. So the Mahatma defends her, ending the letter with words that we should always keep in mind: "We, my dear sirs, always judge men by their motives and the moral effects of their actions." Indeed as KH says in Letter 92, "*Motive is everything for us.*"

Letter 103B (page 352) includes a reference to "a 'Scotch' Brother"; Letter 112 mentions "our Brother H—then in Scotland," who may or may not be the European Mahatma known as Hilarion, perhaps on a visit to the Scotch Brother. This is conjecture, of course, but we do know that the Masters, particularly KH, traveled a great deal.

LETTER 113

The French phrase with which KH opens Letter 113 translates as "the quarter hour of Rabelais," a reference to an episode in the life of the Renaissance writer, monk, medical doctor, and humanist best known for his satirical romances. Generally meaning that the time has come when accounts must be settled or consequences faced, KH uses the phrase here to stir Sinnett into a decision regarding the "*Phoenix* venture." The proposition put before Sinnett, which KH tells the Englishman will shock him, is not only complicated in its own right but mixed up with the tangled political situation then existing in India. The background to the situation is well summarized in the letter's editorial introduction. Now KH indicates how Sinnett can use those circumstances to gain financial support for his new paper, particularly if he returns to India to serve as editor.

Incidentally, Letter 106 in *The Letters of H. P. Blavatsky to A. P. Sinnett* (page 230) contains some strong comments regarding the political situation that is the principal subject of Letter 113. Although published among her letters, that letter is almost certainly from KH, not HPB, for although it is not signed, it is in the Mahatma's style and was written about the same time as Letter 113. It contains a rather strong indictment of jesuitical machinations and asserts categorically that a Jesuit father was the real author of the "Ilbert Bill," which, "had it passed, would have been more disastrous for England than the Indian Mutiny, and for the Hindus—worse still."

The opening paragraphs of Letter 113 contain much that may puzzle us. The Mahatma makes a suggestion to Sinnett which, he says in advance, will be repugnant to him but would save both England and India from "a great evil that overhangs both." We may be startled by the interest the Brotherhood is taking in the politics of the two issues: the Bengal Rent Bill and the Ilbert Bill. The first was favored by the Brothers, while the second KH calls "idiotically *untimely*." It is puzzling to say the least that Sinnett is asked to oppose—even "*apparently*"—the work of the Brotherhood, who have a "plan of action of a purely Asiatic character." The Mahatma admits that this "may be found *too* Jesuitical" for Sinnett's taste. Indeed it is "a riddle, verily." The Mahatma seems to be saying that the end justifies the means, leaving us with a number of questions to ponder if we are to understand the ways in which the Adept Brothers work.

For several pages KH tries to explain the entire political situation from the Brotherhood's point of view and his own efforts "to defend the teeming millions of the poor and the oppressed in India," at the same time advising Sinnett to side with the zemindars, who are the landowners, having rights under the British government of private property by paying the government a fixed revenue raised from the *ryots*, the tenant farmers. KH tells Sinnett: "If the offer of the Zemindars [a substantial financial offer to aid the new publication] is rejected—the *Phoenix* will never come into existence." The decision must have been a difficult one for Sinnett, but as we shall see in the next letter, he did adopt the Mahatma's suggestion over a deep revolt in his own conscience, but then was relieved from his promise by the Mahatma. This was a very interesting turn of events, leaving us with the question: why, in view of KH's assertion that "we . . . are enabled to discern future events," did the Mahatma not foresee the outcome of the entire situation?

As we read through the pages of KH's explanation to Sinnett, who is in England, of all that was occurring in India we find several statements that deepen our understanding of how the Adepts work. Consider these words:

> You look *without,* I *see within.* . . . I am bound to devote the whole of my powers as far as the Chohan will permit me to help my country at this eleventh hour of her misery. I cannot work except with those *who will work with us.* . . . You do not know, you *cannot* know the extent of the limitations I am placed under. . . . Having pledged my solemn word of honour to Him to whom I am indebted for everything I am and know, I am simply helpless . . . prohibited as I am to use any but ordinary powers.

KH warns Sinnett that their "future intercourse" rests on his decision regarding the Mahatma's suggestion, after which KH encourages Sinnett: "With a few undetectable mistakes and omissions notwithstanding, your *Esoteric Buddhism* is the only right exposition— however incomplete—of our Occult doctrines. You have made no cardinal, fundamental mistakes." However, in a later letter (Letter 128), KH mentions some "real vital errors" in the book, although he says that "no one, so far, has noticed" them.

Letter 113 concludes (after greetings to Mrs. Sinnett and "Morsel," a pet name for Sinnett's son Denny, who was quite small for his age) with the assertion once again that "neither M. nor I have contradicted each other" in their statements. A number of comments in the final paragraph deserve further study, particularly those concerning the "inner" and the "outer" rounds. This subject is treated in *Esoteric Buddhism,* with further information available in *The Secret Doctrine.* Probably the clearest explanation is found in Geoffrey Barborka's *The Divine Plan* (page 379 *et seq.*). Briefly, the *inner* round is the passage of the monadic hosts from globe to globe *within* a chain of seven globes, while the *outer* round is their passage from one planetary chain to another and beyond.

In closing Letter 113, KH informs Sinnett: "Nor will you be able to ever comprehend the process of the *obscurations* until you have mastered the mathematical progress of the *inner* and the *outer* Rounds and learned more about the specific difference between the seven." Then he adds, "We . . . find each man his *God*—within himself in his own personal, and at the same time *impersonal* Avalokiteswara." Just what is meant by these final statements requires further study!

LETTER 114

As much of Letter 114 consists of comments on the ill-fated *Phoenix* project, including KH's review of the financial backing it received, the letter at first glance may seem to hold little of concern for us. Yet it turns out that we can learn much from it. Between Letters 113 and 114, KH evidently received a letter from Sinnett in which he raised objections to the Mahatma's proposals to accept financial support from the zemindars, or landowners. As a result, KH relieved Sinnett of the need to make a decision concerning the offers that were so repugnant to him. Note that later in the letter, the Mahatma informs Sinnett that he would have made his statement of permission to abandon the affair even stronger but he did not want to "assume the responsibility of blocking your [Sinnett's] free-will."

Two relevant references to the Mahatma's action may be mentioned here. First, Colonel Olcott's diary entries (not included in *Old Diary Leaves* but found in his original diary held in the Society's archives at Adyar) include this notation: "KH sent dispatch by cable to Sinnett today, releasing him from his promise and leaving him to act unbiased." The second reference is a letter from HPB to Sinnett (see *LBS*, 53 *et seq.*):

> For over two months I have been ordered by KH not to meddle any further in the paper business and—of course I obeyed. Some six weeks ago he came to send through me a letter to you, and there

were telegrams passed between Norendro Babu . . . and myself. I then felt very much surprised at Norendro's hope *that you would ever consent to serve the cause of the Zemindars*—one that KH himself had pronounced infamous. . . . Now Norendro telegraphs that *you consented* and accepted *the offer of the Zemindars*. . . . I understand this Zemindar business is a regular conspiracy to *defraud* and starve millions of poor cultivators. If so, KH must know it, how *can* you then accept such a terrible thing! I have left no stone unturned to raise the money. . . . M told me to write to you so much about this and—*to meddle no more*—the same words as said by KH.

According to what KH quotes from Sinnett's letter, Sinnett seems to have decided not to pursue the financial offer further. He did agree to the Mahatma's proposal concerning the Rent Bill solely because he thought KH wished it, even though it constituted a "somewhat repulsive pledge"; however, in so agreeing, he "cast the moral responsibility" on KH. The Mahatma writes back that this cannot be done, for "you have been given plainly the option." Since Sinnett was given the choice, he must accept full responsibility for his decision.

How much we can learn here on the issue of karmic responsibility and free will! We, too, when called upon to make a choice may consult someone wiser than ourselves and then follow the course that this individual advises us to choose. If the results are not to our liking, we may blame that person. Yet whose is the karma? KH is very definite: we must accept responsibility for decisions we make, even if we take advice from others. In the situation under discussion, the Mahatma tells Sinnett that the choice "must be entirely upon your own judgment and responsibility. . . . You were entirely and absolutely free in your choice." Hence the karma of the choice is Sinnett's. This explains why the Adepts do not interfere, even when they foresee unfortunate, even painful eventualities following upon certain courses of action.

KH does accept karmic responsibility in one respect, however, that of "having hinted at the probable consequence of your refusal."

Then, speaking of "the rule of our Order as regards Karma," the Mahatma tells Sinnett that in encouraging the establishing of the new paper "I was so confident . . . that I allowed you to grow equally and even more confident than myself. Others, whose intuition and foresight had not been blinded by their superiors, thought differently, and some would have dissuaded me. . . . I was permitted to watch the project and use natural external means to aid its consummation." This comment gives us further insight into the freedom granted KH in his work with Sinnett and the permission he received from the Chohan, his superior, since the work was for the benefit of India.

Another factor in the situation was the way Sinnett (and by extrapolation we today) usually looks at matters compared with the way the Adepts may view them. The contrast is pointed up in KH's words: "I had forgotten that *external* appearance is everything in your world. . . . I should be most unwilling, apart from the rule of our Order as regards Karma, to draw you into a position where I could not recompense you in any way for loss of social prestige or financial disappointments." Then he adds a most significant statement: "To all, whether Chohan or chela, who are obligated workers among us the first and last consideration is whether we can do good to our neighbour, no matter how humble he may be; and we do not permit ourselves to even think of the danger of any contumely, abuse or injustice visited upon ourselves."

He assures Sinnett: "You have your path to tread in the more 'practical' world and *your* standing in it must not be jeopardized," and offers these encouraging words: "Your decision to follow my lead into the Phoenix matter even with the, to you, certainty of social degradation and pecuniary loss, had the reward of its Karma already." Then, in case Sinnett was considering this a "test"—a term that both he and Hume disliked—KH says it was not, "yet you were as good as tested and you have not quailed." Hence, as the Mahatma continues, "the fiat of contingent non-intercourse between us has been partially revoked"—in other words, the communications will continue. At the same time, "this is not the last of your probations." Then KH makes a statement we should all take to heart: "It is not I who create them [that is, probationary tests] but *yourself*—by your struggle for light and truth against the world's topics."

The letter concludes with a reference to the "eighth sphere," which KH calls a "confidential mystery." The subject was discussed in Letters 93B and 104, and it was on the basis of what he had learned from the remarks in those letters that Sinnett rather indiscreetly mentioned the subject in *Esoteric Buddhism*, provoking considerable discussion as well as curiosity. F. W. H. Myers, an English scientist and member of the Society for Psychical Research, wrote to *The Theosophist* querying the rationale of the "eighth sphere," and a number of replies were published, most of them written, as KH indicates here, by M. HPB, whose health had again taken a turn for the worse, bitterly complained about having to use so much space in the magazine over the whole matter. In a letter to Sinnett (see *LBS*, 46), she writes in her inimitable style:

> Why bless you only the *half* of the Replies fill up a whole form of the September *Theosophist*! . . . It is *I* who had to copy most of the Replies written half by M, half by either chelas or handwritings that I see for the first time, and as no printer the world over could make out M's handwriting. It is more red and fierce than ever! and then I do not like them a bit the replies. Where's the necessity of writing three pages for every line of the question and explaining things that after all none of them except yourself, perhaps, will understand. . . . And who is Mr. Myers that my big Boss should waste a bucket full of his red ink to satisfy *him*? . . . For Mr. Myers will *not* be satisfied with negative proofs. . . . But does he really think that any of the "adepts" will give out their real *esoteric* teaching in the *Theosophist*?

So we can write *finis* to the entire "*Phoenix* venture," and to discussions of the political situation in India at the time. The Ilbert Bill, however, is mentioned in a later letter, as we shall see.

LETTERS 115 AND 116

As the introductory notes indicate, with Letters 115 and 116, which are actually telegrams sent by Colonel Olcott to HPB, we have a complete change of subject. For a firsthand account of the events that prompted the two telegrams, we have Colonel Olcott's report in the third volume of his *Old Diary Leaves*, chapters 2 through 5. The story is one of the most fascinating and amazing episodes in Theosophical history, and every student should be acquainted with the main features at least of the biography of Damodar K. Mavalankar, who is mentioned frequently in the course of the letters.

The third member accompanying Olcott and Damodar on their tour in Northern India was William Tournay Brown, a young Scotsman who had joined the Society in London and almost immediately thereafter came to India, arriving shortly before Olcott's tour was to begin. He was invited to join the journey and thus became one of the witnesses to the events that occurred during the party's stay at Lahore. Not only was he visited by the Mahatma KH at that time, but he also received at least two letters from KH, both of which are included in *Letters from the Masters of the Wisdom* (First Series, 57–60).

Using the pseudonym of Carwood Gerald Clark, Brown eventually wrote a series of articles for the Rochester (New York) *Post-Express*, titled "Scenes in My Life." One article in the series is devoted to "Lahore and Koot Hoomi," while another is titled "What Damodar Has to Say." The entire series, together with an excellent biographical sketch of Brown by Michael Gomes, has been republished as a monograph by *Theosophical History* under the editorship of Dr. James Santucci (*Theosophical History Occasional Papers*, volume 4).

Perhaps surprisingly—although Olcott wrote that it was no surprise to those who really knew him—Brown eventually left the Society and became a Roman Catholic. So another who had been a promising worker for the cause joined the ranks of those who chose another path.

LETTER 117

The editorial commentary introducing Letter 117 summarizes one of the most interesting and amazing incidents in the history of the communications between the Mahatmas and Sinnett. Briefly, the affair arose when an American Spiritualist, Henry Kiddle, read Sinnett's book *The Occult World* soon after its publication in 1881. He discovered in it several passages that he claimed had been taken verbatim from a lecture he, Kiddle, had given in the United States a year earlier, in 1880. The passages in question occurred in one of KH's letters (Letter 12), which Sinnett had quoted in his book with the Mahatma's consent. Kiddle first wrote a letter to Sinnett (who said he never received it) and later wrote a letter to the editor (who was Stainton Moses) of the British Spiritualist journal *Light*, asking for an explanation. Moses published Kiddle's letter, and the controversy followed. A more complete version of what came to be called "the Kiddle incident" is available in Mary K. Neff's book *The 'Brothers' of Madame Blavatsky* (see chapter 10), excerpts of which appear as appendix E of the *Readers' Guide to The Mahatma Letters to A. P. Sinnett*. As the editorial commentary mentions, the affair prompted a considerable correspondence, most of which was published in various Spiritualist journals.

As we look back on the issue from our own time, it seems incredible that so many people became involved, writing letters either supporting Kiddle's accusation of plagiarism or defending KH. In addition to letters from such Spiritualists as Stainton Moses and C. C. Massey (who signed themselves as two "Occidental Humourists"), letters were written by HPB, Olcott, and even T. Subba Row. As Kiddle's lecture, which he claimed was plagiarized by KH, was published in the American Spiritualist journal *Banner of Light*, William Q. Judge also entered into the correspondence. Sinnett, who had not received Kiddle's first letter and therefore became aware of the allegation only after Kiddle's letter was published in the British Spiritualist organ *Light*, responded directly to Kiddle:

> For the moment all I can say is that the passage is introduced by my revered friend with the expression, "Plato was right . . . ," which seems to point to some origin for the sentences immediately following that may have lain behind both the letter and the lecture. To obtain further explanation of the mystery from India [by this time Sinnett had returned to England, with no expectation of returning to India] will take time; but meanwhile I may point out that the path leading to acquaintanceship with the Adepts is always found strewn with provocation to distrust them, for reasons very fully detailed in my books; their policy at present is rather to ward off than to invite European confidence.

And what did HPB think of the whole affair? In a letter to Sinnett written from Adyar (see *LBS*, 66–67), she expresses herself in her usual explosive terms:

> KH *plagiarised* from Kiddle! Ye gods and little fishes. . . . If they knew what it was to *dictate mentally a precipitation* as D. Khool says—at 300 miles distance; and had seen as all of us . . . the original fragments on which the precipitation was photographed from which the young fool of a chela had copied, unable to understand half of the sentences and so skipping them, then they would not be idiotic enough to accuse not only an *Adept* but even the two "Occidental Humourists" of such an absurd action. Plagiarise from the *Banner of Light*!! that sweet spirits' slop-basin—the asses! KH blows me up for talking too much—says He needs no defence and that I need not trouble myself. But if He were to kill me I cannot hold my tongue. . . . Of course if He has said—nor explained this to you then he must have good reasons for it. But ever since Subba Row brought to us the original scrap of Kashmir paper (given to him by my Boss) on which appeared that whole page from the letter

you published—I understood what it meant. Why that letter is *but one third* of the letter dictated and was never published for you have not received it. There *is no connection* as it now reads between the first portion and that which begins with the words "Ideas rule the world" and it looks . . .

At this point in HPB's letter KH has inserted the following: "True proof of her discretion! I will tell you all myself as soon as I have an hour's leisure." Keeping to his promise, the Mahatma provided the explanation in Letter 117, to which we now turn our attention.

At the outset of the letter, KH requires from Sinnett (and from Sam Ward, whom we first met in Letter 102) a "*pledge never to explain without special permission from me the facts*" that he, the Mahatma, is now to divulge. As we will see, that restriction is later removed. In the early pages of Letter 117, KH goes to considerable trouble to recapitulate the charges and countercharges resulting from Kiddle's accusation that the Mahatma was an outright plagiarist. Especially noteworthy is KH's statement: "What constitutes plagiarism [is] a borrowing of *ideas* rather than of words and sentences." He goes on to say, "Having *distorted* the ideas 'appropriated,' and, as now published [that is, Kiddle's lecture published in the American journal]—diverted them from their original intention to suit my own 'very different purpose,' on such grounds my literary *larceny* does not appear very formidable." One wonders whether KH's argument would hold up in the face of today's plagiarism laws, since the use of actual words and sentences is usually the basis for a charge of plagiarism.

After speaking of his interest in the "intellectual progress" of Spiritualism, which had led him to direct his attention to the occasion of Kiddle's lecture, KH states that he remembered some of the ideas and "detached sentences" heard at that gathering. It is possible that these "remained impressed on [his] memory" such that in dictating his letter (Letter 12) to a chela, perhaps some exact words or even sentences appeared in the precipitated document. However, as he now reviews the "original impression," he finds that there was no copying of anything he had heard at that Spiritualist gathering.

Two points in KH's initial explanation are of interest for their revealing more about the powers of an Adept. First, the Mahatma could direct his attention to events or occasions of particular concern, but that attention is impersonal in nature. Second, he could call up before his inner vision the "original impression," evidently the original message before it was precipitated—in this case quite imperfectly—into physical manifestation. This must mean that the original, perhaps we could call it the original thought-form, still exists in what the early literature referred to as the "astral light," or akasha at the etheric level, prior to its precipitation into physical form. These two points alone offer us much to explore.

KH then says, "I must give you some explanation of this mode of *precipitation.*" From the very outset of the correspondence there have been allusions to the phenomenon of precipitation, which was often used for exchanging communications. The student may wish to review Letters 10, 12, and 15 and their commentaries as we consider KH's statements here. "Mental telegraphy," says the Mahatma, calls for two factors: "close concentration in the operator, and complete receptivity in the 'reader' subject." A careful study of the Mahatma's explanation is called for at this point.

In the case of Letter 12, which KH was "transmitting" to a young chela, who was to transcribe it into the physical document that Sinnett received, perhaps the "mental picture" sent by KH was too "feeble" (to use the Mahatma's word) for accurate reading or perhaps the chela to whom the letter was "dictated mentally" was inattentive and therefore failed to read the complete impression. KH himself says that the chela was "not yet expert at this branch of psychic chemistry," an interesting description of what may be one type of precipitation.

As a sidelight to KH's story, later Sinnett was apparently given a clue as to this chela's identity. Two years after the affair, the Countess Wachtmeister, in a letter to Sinnett (*LBS*, 273) in which she recorded various phenomenal events to which she had been a witness in order to refute the charges in the Hodgson Report, comments, "I will add one more incident to my story which I know will *interest you*, but this you must if you please keep private. While writing I came to the second chela who visited us at Elberfeld, and this you must know was the chela who had to do with the Kiddle affair. I was on the point of writing his name when the thought struck me that it possibly [would] be unpleasant to him to be brought again before the public notice."

This identifies the chela as Babaji (or Bowaji), mentioned in Letter 53. He visited Elberfeld, Germany, when HPB and the Countess were both staying there and created quite a bit of difficulty. Sometime later Olcott wrote a letter to the Countess in which he explains that Babaji was an epileptic and "went into furious rages" (*LBS*, 331). At the time of the Kiddle business, he was resident at the Society's Headquarters.

In Letter 117, KH compares the technique of thought transference and the mental concentration needed for "mental telegraphy" with the process involved in mesmeric or magnetic healing. In the light of the widespread use today of such alternative healing modalities as Therapeutic Touch, the interested student might explore whether the two factors KH names as required for thought transference are essential in these modern healing practices.

Before examining the reconstituted portion of the letter that was so disastrously mangled by the inexpert chela, we may note two points in KH's account. First, he says he will transcribe the original passages himself "this once," indicating that generally his letters (probably also those from M) were transcribed from the invisible thought "substance" (akasha or the astral light) by chelas skilled in the art of reading the Mahatma's thought or at least so attuned to the Mahatma's intent that a letter could be "precipitated" without error. It is worth rereading the opening paragraph of Letter 12, where KH describes how he "writes" or "precipitates" a letter. Relevant information is also found in the early part of Letter 85B, particularly on page 258, concerning mistakes that may be made in writing a letter. Nevertheless, we are still left with many questions regarding the specifics of producing the letters, and every student should examine the matter carefully.

Second, KH says that since "the palmy days of the 'impressions' and 'precipitations'" he has "been born into a *new* and *higher* light." This, of course, refers to the evidently initiatory experience he underwent on his retreat. Reviewing Letter 29 may be appropriate here.

A careful reading of the "copy *verbatim* from the restored fragments," comparing the passages in Letter 12 with the now-complete version of the letter, is called for. Certainly the Mahatma is unequivocal in his condemnation of Spiritualism, as he continues in Letter 117, writing of the Spiritualists' "pernicious intellectual tendency" and "their gross and unsavoury materialism." In my comments on the distorted passages in Letter 12, I suggested that here is a study assignment for all students of Theosophy: the origin and destiny of humankind, "the relation of the mortal to the immortal" and the nature of "Immutable Law." The importance of that study directive is even more evident as we read the "original document as now restored." Note especially the Mahatma's words: "It is not physical phenomena . . . but . . . universal ideas that we . . . study; *the noumenon not the phenomenon*." Here is the fundamental guideline for true Theosophical study!

The Mahatma turns to a few other matters before he closes Letter 117. His delightful sense of humor is once more in evidence as he describes the effort of Mrs. Kingsford when in a trance state to conjure up the Mahatma. He is at once semiserious and semihumorous when he says "There seems to be very little *affinity* between our two natures," and we cannot also help smiling when he writes of himself as just "insignificant me." Anna Kingsford, at this time the president of the London Lodge, has been referred to a number of times in the letters thus far, and there will be further correspondence regarding her role in the Society's work. The reference to "Mme. Gebhard" is to the Gebhard family, who played an important part in the development of the work in Europe. HPB, Olcott, Countess Wachtmeister, and other leading members were often guests in the Gebhard home. (For biographical data on the Gebhard family, see *CW*, 6:434, and Eek, *Damodar*, 592.)

KH briefly mentions places he is about to visit: Madras, Singapore, Ceylon, and Burma. The Mahatma traveled a good deal, not only from one monastery to another in Tibet but to other parts of the world. Mary K. Neff, in the book mentioned at the beginning of this commentary, devotes a carefully researched chapter to "The Travels of Koot Humi." He was educated in Europe, was fluent in both English and French, and from time to time apparently "listened in" to conversations or meetings in England and America (one example being the Spiritualist gathering at which Kiddle gave his talk).

In the light of later developments. it is interesting that KH concludes his letter by remarking that he would "see *you* [Sinnett] President, if possible," Presumably, the presidency of the London Lodge was coming up for a turnover, but as we shall see, the outcome, after considerable controversy, was quite different. In the addendum following his signature, KH refers to a plan for "a Society within *the* London Society." Indeed, he later recommended something along these lines.

Finally, KH expresses unqualified support for Subba Row, who was an authority on Advaitism and one of the leading participants in the early history of the Society in India. The General Cunningham mentioned is probably Sir Alexander Cunningham (1814–1893), an English archeologist and army engineer who headed some archeological surveys of India in 1861–1865 and again in 1870–1885. Thus concludes one of the most fascinating and informative letters in the series.

LETTER 118

Letter 118 may seem rather confusing, and we can only speculate why it should come from M, who had not been involved with the correspondence for some time, the last letter from him being Letter

89. Letter 118 was enclosed in a letter to Sinnett from HPB, who was at Adyar at the time, and since she was M's chela, the Mahatma could easily use her as the means for its transmittal. There were also other enclosures with HPB's letter, including a letter to Prince A. M. Dondoukoff-Korsakoff that Sinnett is to send on registered from London, but that is another story. For those who are curious, that story begins with HPB's letter to Sinnett (*LBS*, 211) and continues to its conclusion with two letters to the Prince published in Jinarajadasa's *H.P.B. Speaks*, (2:129–41).

M may have written at this time because KH was away on one of his extensive travels (as he announced in Letter 117). While this is only conjecture, we do know that the two Adepts were very close, so it would not be unusual for M to write when KH was engaged in other duties.

Letter 118 begins by reminding Sinnett of an "agreement made at Prayag"—a promise first mentioned in Letter 83, from Djual Khul on behalf of KH, and spelled out by KH later, in Letter 96. One can only presume that the "pass-words" referred to were somehow indicated, although they do not appear on the original document, which is in the British Museum Library. The original, as we learn from the letter itself, is on a sheet of Sam Ward's monogrammed note paper. The monogram, incidentally, is a rather curious one, consisting of a red compass face about three-quarters of an inch in diameter in the upper left-hand corner of the sheet. Outside the circle, in the southwest quadrant, are the letters "S.W.," which would normally mean "southwest" but in this instance obviously stand for Sam Ward.

As a bit of background to the letter, I should mention that Sinnett was still interested in spiritualistic phenomena in addition to his Theosophical activities with the members in London. He had never entirely let go of his fascination with Spiritualism, although he was sure that his interest was wholly scientific. William Eglinton, who had experienced such a remarkable visit from the Mahatma KH on board ship returning to England after his stay in India, had continued his mediumistic activities and, in fact, was earning his living in that manner. Letter 118 is concerned for the most part with a séance that Eglinton was holding in Sam Ward's quarters, located above the bookshop owned by Charles Sotheran in Piccadilly. (Sotheran had been one of the founding members of the Theosophical Society, at that time visiting in New York.) M's attention had been attracted to this séance, he says, as he became aware that HPB's handwriting was being forged and a false message purporting to come from him, Morya, was being produced. He immediately went there, in some way invisible of course, and so, though still physically in Lhasa, "put aside [his] pipe and watched." We can compare this with KH's attention being attracted to the gathering of Spiritualists at which Henry Kiddle was one of the speakers. Evidently whenever their attention is turned toward some event, the Adepts are able to "go" there in some manner, watch or listen to the proceedings, perhaps creating a *mayavi rupa* (an illusory form composed of astral-mental matter) for the purpose. This seems to be one of the siddhis, or powers, of an Adept.

After describing what occurred at the séance, the Mahatma turns to a defense of Eglinton, who, he says, "was utterly *irresponsible* on that night." He is a "poor epileptic . . . really honest in his way and to be pitied." So he asks Sinnett not to be "too hard upon the wretched young fellow," although any idea of his belonging to the London Lodge is "pure nonsense." Of particular interest is M's suggestion that Sinnett request KH "to beg a favour from Mr. Ward." This seems a rather roundabout way for the Mahatma to act; why would he not simply ask Sinnett to speak to Sam Ward directly rather than concerning KH with such a task? The aim, as indicated, was to secure "an appointment somewhere," which we may interpret as securing employment for Eglinton so he could earn a living other than by mediumship. Again, what is of interest to us is how the Adepts work.

On a number of occasions in their letters, the Mahatmas express strong views regarding Spiritualism, mediumship, and the production of phenomena, KH's strong language on the subject in his reconstituted letter (Letter 117) being a recent example. Here in Letter 118 Morya is saying: "Woe to the spiritualists! Their *Karma* is heavy with the ruin of men and women they entice into mediumship, and then throw off to starve like a toothless dog." Today, too, the hungering for phenomena and interest in developing mediumistic abilities continues, such that warnings about the dangers continue to be relevant. The Theosophical student has a responsibility to point out, whenever possible, the risks involved.

M advises Sinnett to ask Eglinton for the "card of *Upasika* [HPB] with her alleged writing." Apparently Sinnett did so, as it is in one of the folios of letters in the British Museum Library, although it has never been published. In her letter to Sinnett (mentioned at the beginning of these comments) with which Letter 118 was enclosed, HPB added a note that reads: "When did I write to Eglinton a visiting card? guess not. Either my 'handwriting or a very good imitation of it'? Some spookish fraud, I suppose. . . . Well, go ahead and believe it. I am tired to set all of you right. May you all become wiser when I am dead and gone."

M concludes this letter with a reference to the upcoming elections in the London Lodge, saying "I am the first to advise Mrs. K.'s [Kingsford's] re-election," even though he adds that he would trust Eglinton's clairvoyance more than hers. KH, as we have seen, has written that he would like to see Sinnett elected to the presidency. And HPB, expressing herself in no uncertain terms, concludes her note in the letter to Sinnett: "A nice mess between you and Kingsford. The hypocritical she-devil. Masters order us to send her letter to you and yet *They will* have her President!"

Apparently, two letters from HPB to Sinnett arrived together: the one already mentioned, to which she added the paragraph containing the comments about Eglinton and Kingsford just quoted. The other letter (see *LBS*, 21) reads:

> There's a love chit for you just received. I guess my Boss splits himself owing to Eglinton's *haut fait de magie* [great feat of magic] and explains as promised. Of course you would not believe me—if the card was such a "good imitation of my handwriting" and I am

sure Mr. C.C.M. [Massey] must have strengthened your belief that it was some new fraud.... Was it not he, and *he alone* who proposed and had her [Kingsford] elected as the only possible Saviour of the British Theos. Society? Well now thank him and keep her to turn all of you into a jelly. Of course she will wag you as her tail more than ever. I know it will end with a scandal. Well Olcott is coming and then you will have *nolens volens* to accept the decision of the "nominal" President. My boss gave him instructions and hurries him on. Yours—but not Mrs. Kingsford's HPB.

With that, we turn to the affairs of the London Lodge and the turmoil that ensued over the election of the president. The next four letters, all from KH, concern that subject, but they also contain some remarkable statements that deserve careful study.

LETTER 119

Toward the conclusion of Letter 117, KH told Sinnett that he would like to see Sinnett become president of the London Lodge. Now in Letter 119, KH asks Sinnett not only to forego any thought of candidacy but to support—as the Mahatma must, since it is the wish of his superior, the Chohan—the reelection of Mrs. Kingsford. Notably, what is being tested in all this is Sinnett's own statement of a "readiness to follow [the Mahatma's] advice in almost anything." This is not at all easy for Sinnett, who very much wanted to be president, nor is it easy for us when we have said that we are willing to do anything for the work of the Society and someone whom we consider our superior refuses our offer when the time comes. In any event, Sinnett did not withdraw his candidacy.

This seems an appropriate moment to briefly review the life of Mrs. Kingsford. Frail and in poor health from birth, Anna Bonus Kingsford seems to have been a talented and quite charismatic woman. Married to a cousin, Algernon Kingsford, who was a vicar, she made a pact with him that she would be allowed to pursue her own interests. While still in her teens, she became active in a movement to reform property right laws in England as they applied to married women. In her twenties, she edited her own magazine and enrolled in medical school, having decided that the only way she could become an effective voice for the two causes she most espoused, anti-vivisection and vegetarianism, was to become a medical doctor. By the age of thirty she was awarded the degree of Doctor of Medicine by the Faculté Médecine of the Sorbonne in Paris. While still a student, she began a correspondence with Edward Maitland, a noted writer on spiritual subjects, and their correspondence resulted in a lifetime partnership and collaboration. Probably the most significant of the works they authored together is *The Perfect Way, or the Finding of Christ,* which presents Hermetic Christianity as a form of the Ancient Mysteries. Mrs. Kingsford later organized the Hermetic Theosophical Society, first within the London Lodge and then as an independent body. Her short yet active life ended early; she died of tuberculosis at age forty-two. Maitland was her first biographer, writing the book *Anna Kingsford: Her Life, Letters, Diary and Work.* A brief biographical sketch together with a list of all her published works is found in volume 9 of HPB's *Collected Writings* (438–40).

A sidelight regarding Kingsford may be of interest to students of Theosophical history. Josephine Ransom writes in *A Short History of the Theosophical Society* that when Anna Kingsford first became president of the London group, the Society there, at her suggestion, adopted the name "London Lodge of The Theosophical Society." This was the first time the term "Lodge" was used; until then (1883) all the groups had been called "Branches." Ransom adds that this change was "no doubt because the Founders spoke of the Great Brotherhood as 'The Lodge.'"

Letter 119 provides at least one of the reasons why the Mahachohan approved of Anna Kingsford as president. "You should know that her anti-vivisection struggle and her strict vegetarian diet have won entirely over to her side our stern Master." (I might point out here that these two causes are still of great concern, and many Theosophists working under the aegis of the Theosophical Order of Service continue efforts to promote both anti-vivisection and vegetarianism.) Kingsford was extremely skeptical about the Mahatmas, possibly because she never had direct contact with or received messages from them. Letter 117 mentions that in one of her trances she tried to meet KH, but the Mahatma comments that there was "little affinity" between their natures.

HPB never really forgave Mrs. Kingsford for her attitude toward the Mahatmas, sometimes speaking of her as "the divine Anna" and on one occasion, in an excess of irreverence, calling her "the divine Whistle-breeches" (see *LBS*, 89). In another letter to Sinnett, HPB writes of receiving a "three yard long letter" from Mrs. Kingsford and adds, "She demands of KH to make her 'the Apostle in Europe of *Eastern* and *Western* Esoteric Philosophy'!!! . . . I am too sick to bother myself with her flapdoodle interpretations. . . . Why Mahatma KH should have inflicted upon your Society such a plaster as Mrs. K. seems to be, a haughty, imperious, vain, and self-opiniated [*sic*] creature, a bag of Western conceit—'God' knows, I do not. My belief is that the Chohan has interfered suddenly as he often does" (*LBS*, 63–64). That, of course, is precisely what KH's superior did, as just noted.

Enclosed with Letter 119 is a "paper" to be read "before a general meeting composed of as many theosophists as you can gather." That letter is Letter 120, truly one of the most significant letters concerning the Society to have come from an Adept. Especially interesting is KH's comment about the letter, that "it contains and carries within its folds and characters a *certain occult influence* that ought to reach as many theosophists as possible." Was this an "influence" from the entire Brotherhood or perhaps from its senior members represented by the Mahachohan who had taken such interest in the outcome of the London Lodge's election?

One curious detail concerning the enclosed Letter 120 is that not only was the letter to be given "*sealed*" as Sinnett received it, but the Mahatma suggests that C. C. Massey may be the "best fitted" to read it to the assembled members. Later in Letter 119, KH writes rather scathingly of Massey, calling him "a bit of a misanthrope," subject to doubt, and in "pitiable" psychological condition. He is, continues KH, "the prey of illusions of his own creation" and quite likely to leave the Society, which he did following the Hodgson Report. We can speculate, then, why KH recommends that Massey be the one to open the sealed letter and read it to the meeting of the London Lodge.

KH then responds to "a few" of Sinnett's philosophical questions. The first evidently asked for further clarification regarding devachan. Sinnett never really liked the concept of devachan and always seemed to misunderstand its nature. In this instance, he must have been attempting to correlate the several states of matter with the stages of subjectivity in the devachanic condition. KH's statement that an Ego that "belongs to the three-dimensional condition," continues in that state in devachan, while an Ego existing in the seventh state of matter would be in nirvana rather than in devachan, opens the door to further exploration of both devachanic life and the nature of matter.

Sinnett's first question, about the states of matter in devachan, and his second question, about the molecular composition of space, may have arisen from his further study of the first set of Cosmological Notes. A review now of the relevant portions of the Notes may prove useful. (As a reminder: the first set of Notes begins on page 508 of the chronological edition.) Particularly noteworthy is KH's statement that our tendency to "put an objective construction upon what is purely spiritual" leads to confusion and hence to misunderstanding the doctrine. The Mahatma's reference to "the book of Kiu-te" is to the work from which HPB derived the Stanzas of Dzyan on which *The Secret Doctrine* is based. The occult doctrine concerning space is, as is well known, dealt with comprehensively in HPB's work. Note KH's statement equating space with Universal Mind; manifestation is the projection of ideation into objectivity without in any way affecting Universal Mind or Consciousness. We may recall Krishna's statement to Arjuna, in the Bhagavad-Gita (chapter 10, verse 42), "Having pervaded this whole universe with one fragment of Myself, I remain."

The third of Sinnett's questions may have been prompted by KH's comments in Letter 66 (see page 175), particularly the injunction: "Try to solve the problem of the 777 incarnations." Perhaps Sinnett was attempting to arrive at that number by proposing that only incarnations that show intellectual acumen should be counted. But KH denies this idea, pointing rather to the "strong craving for physical existence" as a key factor in the working out of "the Law of Affinity act[ing] through the inherent *Karmic* impulse," so that an individual "may be attracted at the time of rebirth to a body born in a family which has the same propensities as those of the reincarnating Entity." There is much to be considered in that statement, and it does help us to understand more of the entire process of reincarnation.

KH concludes his letter with an interesting reference to Charles Bradlaugh and Annie Besant. This is the first mention of Annie Besant in the letters, and it certainly indicates that her work and career were already attracting the attention of the Adept Brotherhood. At the time, a few years before she met HPB and subsequently joined the Theosophical Society, Besant was active in the National Secular Society in England of which Bradlaugh was president. Together Besant and Bradlaugh had undertaken the publication of a small booklet, *The Fruits of Philosophy*, written and previously published by an American physician, Dr. Charles Knowlton, that advocated birth control based on the Malthusian philosophy of population control. Besant tells the full story of "The Knowlton Pamphlet," and the court case that followed its publication, in a chapter of that title in her *Autobiography*. Arthur H. Nethercot also gives a detailed account of the entire affair in his biography, *The First Five Lives of Annie Besant* (see chapter 7).

The Mahatma describes the pamphlet as "infamous and *highly pernicious*" and considers it to have an "unclean spirit" and "the advices offered . . . abominable." Besant records her own later rejection of the work as the result, in her words, of "the view of the problem set before me by H. P. Blavatsky when she unrolled the story of man, told of his origin and destiny, showed me the forces that went to the making of man, and the true relation between his past, his present, and his future."

After his strong denunciation of the Knowlton booklet, KH closes Letter 119 by saying, "The journey before me is long and tedious and the mission nearly hopeless." There is no further explanation of either the journey's destination or the nature of the mission, but we can assume that he was obliged to set forth on another of his many travels to various parts of the world, all in the interests of the Brotherhood and in service to the upliftment of humanity.

LETTER 120

The prefatory note introducing the quite remarkable Letter 120 explains the circumstances surrounding its transmittal. In Letter 119, Sinnett was told that the enclosed Letter 120 was to be delivered sealed to one of the "Councilors" of the London Lodge, and C. C. Massey was named as the recipient. Sinnett also learned why Anna Kingsford was to be re-elected as president of the London group: her work for anti-vivisection and vegetarianism had "won entirely over to her side our stern Master," the Mahachohan. But events, as we shall see, turned out quite differently, suggesting that while the Mahatmas may see further into the future than we do, freedom of action can alter the course of history as unforeseen occurrences create new patterns and bring about results that had not been contemplated.

To our knowledge, this is the only occasion when the Mahatmas and the Mahachohan intervened in the administration of a Lodge or Branch of the Society. And Letter 120 is one of the clearest and most beautiful expositions of the work before us. Therefore, it deserves our careful consideration.

KH writes that "the *Chohan* Himself" desires Mrs. Kingsford's reelection not only for the reasons indicated in the previous letter but because she is "fitted for the purpose we have all at heart, namely the dissemination of Truth through Esoteric doctrines, conveyed by whatever religious channel, and the effacement of crass materialism and blind prejudices and skepticism." No statement of purpose could be more eloquent, and we may well consider whether that purpose is still central to our work today. As KH suggests, the public at the end of the nineteenth century was better prepared to accept the teachings of esoteric Christianity than the doctrines of esoteric Tibetan Buddhism. As Mrs. Kingsford was an exponent of the Hermetic philosophy, which, states KH, "suits every creed and philosophy and clashes with none," it is advisable for her to head the London Lodge. Neither the Mahatmas' personal preference nor whether Mrs. Kingsford accepts or rejects their existence is the matter of concern, but rather the presentation of the teachings that best accords with the times. So we may ask: what is the best presentation for today, when so many Tibetan Buddhist texts have been translated and Buddhism is far more widespread in the Western world?

The Theosophical student will want to become familiar with the Hermetic philosophy, which KH calls "the boundless ocean of Truth"—acknowledging that it is Theosophy under another name. HPB, in the preface to volume 1 of *Isis Unveiled* (vii), writes, "Our work . . . is a plea for the recognition of the Hermetic philosophy, the anciently Wisdom-Religion, as the only possible key to the Absolute in science and theology." She also writes, in a footnote to an article by a Dr. Fortin, president of the Theosophical Society of Paris, "Hermetic Philosophy, or rather so much as can be found now of it in traditions, differs in no wise from the Arhat-Tibetan or Aryan secret doctrines, except in its externals, names and later religio-theological additions and interpolations" (*CW*, 5:279). Students unfamiliar with Hermeticism may wish to consult the excellent article on the subject in the *Theosophical Encyclopedia*. Another resource is the translation of the well-known *Corpus Hermeticum* by the scholar and Theosophist G. R. S. Mead.

At this point in Letter 120, KH informs the members of the London Lodge that there are "three centres of the Occult Brotherhood in existence, widely separated geographically, and as widely *exoterically*—the true esoteric doctrine being identical in substance though differing in terms; all aiming at the same grand object, but no two agreeing *seemingly* in the details of procedure." Students will recall that while the Society's founders were still in New York, and actually before the Society was inaugurated, Colonel Olcott received letters from members of the Brotherhood of Luxor, also known as the Egyptian Brotherhood. Later Colonel Olcott is said to have been transferred to the Himalayan Brotherhood, where HPB had trained and of which the Mahatmas M and KH were members. I suggest that the third "center" comprises the group known as the Yucatan Brotherhood. Little has been written about this section, but a chapter titled "The Yucatan Brotherhood" is included in Annie Besant's book *Talks with a Class.*

The comment that one frequently finds "students belonging to different schools of occult thought sitting side by side at the feet of the same Guru" underscores the fact that understanding the fundamental principles is the primary purpose of our studies. We can become caught up in arguments over terminology or methods of approach, forgetting, as KH says, that "the only object to be striven for is the amelioration of the condition of MAN by the spread of truth suited to the various stages of his development and that of the country he inhabits and belongs to. TRUTH has no ear-mark and does not suffer from the name under which it is promulgated—if the said object be attained." As examples, the Advaitin Subba Row and the esoteric Buddhist HPB were chelas of the same Master, M, and the Buddhist Mahachohan is desirous of a Hermeticist being re-elected as president of the London Lodge. What then is the common thread running through the philosophies of Hermeticism, Advaita, and Buddhism? A model for considering this question is the diagram in *The Secret Doctrine* (1:157) in which HPB gives "in a tabular form the classifications, adopted by the Buddhist and Vedantic teachers, of the principles of man."

At the same time, the methods used for presenting these basic principles of the occult philosophy should also be considered, keeping in mind KH's statement: "It is plain that the methods of Occultism, though in the main unchangeable, have yet to conform to altered times and circumstances." How do we interpret the Mahatma's words in this electronic age? This question every serious student should ponder as we seek, first, to comprehend the teachings presented to us by the Mahatmas and HPB, and, second, to convey those teachings in a manner suited to the times in which we are living.

At the conclusion of Letter 117, mention was made of "a plan of a Society within the London Society." Now in Letter 120, the Mahatma makes a specific suggestion: those who wish to follow Mrs. Kingsford may do so, while, to use his words, "it seems necessary for a proper study and correct understanding of our Philosophy and the benefit of those whose inclination leads them to seek esoteric knowledge from the Northern Buddhist Source, and in order that such teaching should not be even virtually imposed or offered to those Theosophists who may differ from our views, that an exclusive group composed of those members who desire to follow absolutely the teachings of the School to which we, of the Tibetan Brotherhood, belong should be formed under Mr. Sinnett's direction." However, the Mahatma adds, both groups must be "*within*" the London Lodge—this is "the desire of the Maha Chohan."

The Mahatma's optimism shines through as he says that such an arrangement is "calculated to lead to a harmonious progress" of the Lodge. Undoubtedly having two study groups meeting under the umbrella of the chartered group could have worked if all the members had held—as KH said—to the Society's fundamental "principle of wise and respectful toleration of each other's opinions and beliefs." This principle is explicitly stated in the Society's Rules, to which KH refers. Article 6 of the 1883 Rules reads, in part: "No officer of the Society, in his capacity of an officer, nor any member, has the right to preach his own sectarian views and beliefs, or deprecate the religion or religions of other members to other Fellows assembled, except when the meeting consists solely of his co-religionists."

However, it is the Mahatma's further suggestion, regarding administration of the Lodge's affairs, that was scarcely conducive to harmony in the long run. The idea that there should be "at least *fourteen* Councillors—one half openly inclining towards the Christian

Esotericism as represented by Mrs. K., and the other half following Buddhist Esotericism as represented by Mr. S." may have been an ideal arrangement in KH's mind. But anyone who has worked in a group in which there are two divergent, even irreconcilable, points of view as well as two very strong personalities knows the problems in attempting to bring about harmony as the Mahatma envisioned it. We are all at times prone to forget what KH tells Sinnett:

> Every Western Theosophist should learn and remember, especially those of them who would be our followers—that in our Brotherhood all personalities sink into one idea—abstract right and absolute practical justice for all. And especially to be remembered are those remarkable words: ... discord is the harmony of the Universe. Thus in the Theos. Society, each part, as in the glorious fugues of the immortal Mozart, ceaselessly chases the other in harmonious discord on the paths of Eternal progress to meet and finally blend at the threshold of the pursued goal into one harmonious whole, the keynote in nature ... OM [the Sanskrit word-symbol for the Whole].

These words call for deep meditation leading to the realization that only out of harmonious disagreement can progress ensue. For harmony is not a matter of everyone singing the same note; that is monotony, which has no forward movement. Harmony is the beautiful blending of all notes, a discord that then resolves itself into a new and even more beautiful chord. An excellent article addressing this subject, "Discord is the Harmony of the Universe" by Dr. John Algeo, appeared in the July 2005 issue of *The Theosophist* and was reprinted in *Quest* for November-December 2005.

The Mahatma's proposed plan, although a fragile arrangement, might have worked and all might have gone well for the affairs of the London Lodge, had it not been for an unfortunate complication. About a month before Sinnett received Letter 120, Mrs. Kingsford and her colleague, Edward Maitland, vice president of the London Lodge, had issued a circular titled "A Letter Addressed to the Fellows of the

London Lodge of the Theosophical Society by the President and a Vice-President of the Lodge" that expressed severe criticism of the teachings in Sinnett's book *Esoteric Buddhism.* This hardly improved the already strained relations between Kingsford and Sinnett.

Some time after Letter 120 would have been read to the London members, T. Subba Row, having learned of the Kingsford-Maitland letter, collaborated with, he says, "another still greater scholar" (believed to be M) to issue in pamphlet form a reply to the circular titled "Observations on 'A Letter Addressed to the Fellows of the London Lodge of The Theosophical Society by the President and a Vice-President of the Lodge" (T. Subba Row, *Esoteric Writings*). Subba Row sent this to HPB, who was at Adyar, requesting her to forward it to the London Lodge. She did so, writing to Sinnett:

> By order of my Boss I send you the Kingsford letters to fondly read and preserve for Olcott when he comes. . . . Subba Row's answer (by order) to the President and the Vice-President of the London Lodge T.S. is ready and I hurry on the printer to finish it this week. It was impossible to finish it as the Boss wanted the same week, for it is three times as long as the attack and wanted careful revision, Subba Row having lavished such *uncultured* words as "*stupid,*" "*absurd,*" "*misrepresentation*" etc. that would never do in a pamphlet destined for the refined ears of the members of the L.L. But I do believe he has settled them both the *Vice*-President and *vicious* President—whose shadow be trampled upon! It shows what fools they are with all their culture and genius and conceited idea of themselves. As Boss says she is the most foolish woman to open at once all her weakest points, and thus the fittest to be the President of most of the western would be members. . . . Yesterday Subba Row showed me a letter to him in Telugu from our *mutual* Boss M. with instructions to say some more things in the *answer* to K. and M. Among other things there was a funny news. It appears that you go against my Boss's advice that there should be 14 councillors in your Lodge—7 for you and 7 for Kingsford. . . . He writes the particulars

now for Subba Row's information in writing the pamphlet and his words are: "I thought my Peling friend, Sinnett Sahib more perspicacious—tell him I have advised only 7 councillors on the side of the yellow haired woman because I knew that it was *four too many.* She is needed in the Society, but not as the head of it if it can be helped." Now what does all this mean? Do *they* or do they not want Mrs. K. for je suis au bout de mon Latin. . . . They tell me nothing and—I ask nothing.

HPB then tells Sinnett that she has been "mortally ill" and that M has ordered Olcott to take her to Southern France "to some secluded village or to the Alps for a long and entire rest of three months at least." She has consented to go to Europe for the rest cure, but "with the following condition . . . *I must not, shall not, and will not, go to London.* . . . With the exception of you two [Mr. and Mrs. Sinnett] whom I sincerely love, the very idea of London and your groups (Theosophical and Spiritualistic)—is loathsome to me! As soon as I think of MA. Oxon, of C.C.M, of Wilde, Kingsford, Maitland and some others I feel a feeling of horror, of inexpressible *magnetic disgust* creep over me." We will have cause to remember this declaration of HPB's when we consider the events surrounding Letter 122.

Subba Row's response to the Kingsford-Maitland circular can be found in *Esoteric Writings of T. Subba Row.* Footnotes that HPB appended to Subba Row's pamphlet, which are of some significance, appear in her *Collected Writings* (6:131–35). Subba Row's "Observations" was followed by a "Reply to 'Observations'" by Kingsford and Maitland. Then C. C. Massey issued a pamphlet, "The Metaphysical Basis of 'Esoteric Buddhism,'" to which Damodar responded with an article published in *The Theosophist* for May 1884, which may be read in Sven Eek's book, *Damodar and the Pioneers of the Theosophical Movement* (428–41). While we have neither the Kingsford-Maitland circular that initiated the debate concerning Sinnett's book nor Massey's pamphlet, nevertheless, reading Subba Row's lengthy and detailed defence of Sinnett's work and Damodar's comments is an exercise of great value for the serious student of esoteric philosophy.

After this summary of the events and circumstances influencing the election as well as the program of study in the London Lodge, we can turn to the next letter.

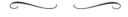

LETTER 121

The purpose of Letter 121 is clearly to transmit a separate letter, Letter 122, to the London Lodge; however, this time Sinnett is to act in his "capacity as Vice–President of the Parent Society," rather than as a Lodge member. One may speculate as to the Mahatma's reason for such an instruction. Perhaps it was to prepare the members for the president–founder's visit by reminding them that Sinnett was officially his representative. Perhaps the Mahatma felt that if Sinnett presented the letter in his official role, the Mahatma's words would take on greater authority. Or perhaps, by asking Sinnett to act in— and therefore remember—his official duty in the Society, KH was suggesting that Sinnett needed to take a more impersonal view of the situation within the Lodge.

Whatever the reason for KH's request regarding the letter's transmittal, what is significant is the Mahatma's statement that the current turmoil within the London group is better than "the old paralytic calm" that had prevailed previously. The Mahatma compares the situation to a fever attacking the physical body, calling it "nature's evidence that she is trying to expel the seeds of disease."

So often when controversies erupt in the Society at whatever level, national or international, we feel only dismay at the lack of harmony, saying that such difficulties would not arise if we all acted in a brotherly manner. But here the Mahatma is indicating the possible benefit that discord may have (remember it is the "harmony of the Universe"!). If we can learn how to handle controversy without becoming personally embroiled in it, a new level of activity or understanding may be achieved. And, of course, karma is always involved, as it was in the case of the London Lodge. As the Mahatma indicates, "Karma . . . required that the repose should be broken by the agency of the one most responsible" for the problem, that individual being Massey, who initially caused Anna Kingsford to become president of the London Lodge. Further, writes KH, while Mrs. Kingsford "*has not accomplished her object*"—and we do not really know what that object was, although it may have been using the Lodge to teach Hermetic philosophy—yet "*Karma has its own.*" Though not fully explained, that phrase may mean that the karma of the entire situation, involving several individuals as well as the Lodge's collective membership, has been satisfied. In other words, the consequences of the past have been completed and the London Lodge, as well as Mrs. Kingsford, Sinnett, and possibly others such as Massey, will now move in a new direction.

The Mahatma's further comments to Sinnett are both encouraging for his future work in the Society and cautionary regarding his mode of action during the immediate situation. He is told that his karma "destines" him to take a "more conspicuous part in European theosophical affairs" than he has previously. Reading through Sinnett's *Autobiography*, we may find it difficult to determine to what extent KH's prophecy was fulfilled. However, KH's advice must surely have caused the Englishman to examine his mode of conduct: "My desire is that you should be gathering together all the reserved forces of your being so that you may rise to the dignity and importance of the crisis." KH then makes a significant statement that surely applies to everyone who is awake to the spiritual life: "Remember that your interior growth proceeds every instant." Our attitudes, actions, and reactions in every moment affect our spiritual development as well as the "accumulated merit" (and demerit) we bring into succeeding lives.

The final paragraph of Letter 121 concerns Olcott's impending visit; he is to be accompanied by Mohini, the chela who was "introduced" to Sinnett in Letter 94. No mention is made about HPB coming also, but we know that she did travel with the two men to Europe, staying in Paris and then, quite unexpectedly and dramatically, arriving in the middle of the London Lodge election meeting. However, that story takes us on to the next letter.

In concluding Letter 121, KH, fully aware of Sinnett's somewhat disdainful attitude toward Olcott as a rather unpolished American, asks that he "dignify" the office of the president, since in that capacity "he represents the entire Society." He adds that it is by virtue of that office, if for no other reason, that Olcott "stands with Upasika [HPB], closest to ourselves in the chain of Theosophical work."

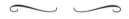

LETTER 122

The lengthy introduction to Letter 122 summarizes the events that led up to, culminated in, and followed upon the election meeting of the London Lodge. It was at that meeting that HPB, who had some time earlier written to Sinnett that she absolutely would not come to London (see my comments on Letter 120), most unexpectedly appeared. Letter 122 is the letter referred to as enclosed in Letter 121, which Sinnett is to present to the Lodge in his capacity as vice president of the Parent Society.

The letter's opening sentence refers to the two telegrams mentioned in the introductory summary as well as to Letter 120, the Mahatma's first letter to the London Lodge. The Mahachohan is still very much engaged in the Lodge's affairs, having now "ordered" KH to "advise the postponement of the annual election." It is not often that the Mahatmas use the term "ordered" other than when dealing with their chelas, and even in that relationship, as has been pointed out, the Adept is more likely to suggest, advise, or recommend than to order a certain course of action. So the importance of the future governance of the London Lodge was evidently of great concern not only to KH but to his superior. We can only speculate why this was the case, as well as why "the postponement [of the election] *was found absolutely necessary.*"

It may seem contradictory that the Mahatma, having conveyed the Mahachohan's wish regarding the election and saying that the postponement was necessary, should now dwell on the matter of authority or the use of names to lend support to one's own agenda. KH quotes Mrs. Kingsford's own words from her inaugural address as president of the Lodge, in which she had asserted the need to dissociate "the authority of names . . . from abstract principles." At the same time, KH reminds the members that the lady nevertheless wanted the Mahatma's approval of her views, asking that he name her the "Apostle of Eastern and Western Esotericism."

As we read the very long paragraph on this subject, we may consider how often we too are inconsistent in our words or actions. Do we make the Mahatma, as he suggests would be the case if he acceded to Mrs. Kingsford's desires, the "quasi-Pope," while at the same time demanding our freedom of thought?

KH makes a number of important statements concerning the Adepts' views on individual freedom: "Far from our thoughts may it ever be to erect a new hierarchy for the future oppression of a priest-ridden world. . . . One [can] be both an active and useful member of the Society without inscribing himself our follower or co-religionist. . . . We have no right to influence the free will of the members in this or any other matter. Such interference would be in flagrant contradiction to the basic law of esotericism that personal psychic growth accompanies *pari passu* the development of individual effort, and is the evidence of acquired personal merit."

One senses KH's distaste for even the idea that he could violate the principle of freedom and then be classed with such individuals as Joseph Smith, founder and leader of the Church of Latter-Day Saints, and Thomas Lake Harris, an American mystic born in England who founded the Brotherhood of the New Life in 1861. We are again made aware, as KH cites these individuals, of the Mahatma's knowledge of events and people in various parts of the world.

Particularly significant for us today is "another consideration" in the matter of the election debate in the London Lodge: "However little we might care for personal subservience to us, the accepted leaders of the Founders of the Parent Theosophical Society, we can never approve or tolerate disloyalty in any member of whatsoever Branch *to the fundamental principles represented by the Parent Organization.* The rules of the mother-body must be lived up to by those composing the Branches; provided of course, that they do not transcend the three declared objects of the organization."

This policy is still in effect, so that the Rules or By-Laws of a Branch (Lodge) must be in conformity with those of the National Society (Section) of which it is a part and the By-Laws or Rules of the Section must be in conformity with the International Rules. A resolution of the General Council on "Freedom of Thought" appears regularly in the president's journal, *The Theosophist,* and in many Section journals as well.

The two short notes following the signature concluding Letter 122 are the only parts of the letter in the Mahatma's handwriting, as the letter itself was written by a chela, Bhola Deva Sarma, under KH's direction. The first note gives advice that we may all take to heart whenever controversies arise: "Let meaner natures wrangle if they will; the wise compound their differences in a mutually forbearing spirit." The second refers to Subba Row's response to the Kingsford-Maitland circular, which was already mentioned in the comments on Letter 120.

While no further comments on Letter 122 are necessary, the student may want to pursue references that complete the saga of the London Lodge election story. Colonel Olcott, who had come to London because of the difficulties that had arisen and who presided at the meeting when the issue between the Kingsford and Sinnett parties was resolved by G. B. Finch's election as president, records his summary of the occasion in *Old Diary Leaves,* Third Series, chapter 8.

Of particular interest is his character sketch of Mrs. Kingsford, this occasion of his visit to the London Lodge being the first time he had met the woman:

> In the London struggle in our Branch I had to deal with a learned, clever, self-confident woman, ambitious and eccentric; a unique personality, who believed herself the angel of a new religious epoch, the reincarnation of Hermes, Joan of Arc, and other historic characters. . . . I cannot say I altogether liked her, although it did not take many minutes for me to gauge her intellectual power and the breadth of her culture. There was something uncanny to me in her views about human affection. She said she had never felt love for a human being. . . . Yet she lavished excessive love on a guinea-pig and [according to her colleague, Edward Maitland] carrying the little beast around with her in her travels, lavishing on it her caresses.

As we know, it was at the election meeting that HPB unexpectedly arrived, and we have three accounts of that occurrence. Olcott comments only that "things were proceeding smoothly, in the usual manner, when they were interrupted by the sensational appearance of HPB, whom I had left in Paris, but who took a flying trip so as to be present at this meeting."

Sinnett, in his *Autobiography*, records the proceedings of the meeting including HPB's appearance in his usual reportorial style:

> On the 7th of April [1884] a very sensational meeting of the Society was held for the purpose of electing the new President, at Mr. Finch's Chambers in Lincoln's Inn. By this time I had become convinced that Mrs. Kingsford's re-election was not desirable and though some members wished to propose myself it seemed to me better under the circumstances to appoint someone else. I therefore proposed Mr. Finch, a barrister, who in his time had been senior wrangler at Cambridge. . . . When the voting was

taken Mrs. Kingsford's candidature was found to have no support whatever and Mr. Finch was elected. . . . But this was not the only sensation of the evening. Quite unexpectedly in the middle of proceedings Madame Blavatsky made her appearance, the whole meeting being of course thrilled with excitement.

A third account of the meeting is found in C. W. Leadbeater's book *How Theosophy Came to Me.* Leadbeater, who by now had joined the Society, attended the weekly meetings and on this occasion, arriving a little late, slipped into a bench just opposite the door to the room. Olcott and Mohini, who had accompanied the president–founder to London, were on the platform, when, as Leadbeater records:

suddenly and sharply the door opposite me opened and a stout lady in black came quickly in and seated herself at the other end of the bench. . . . She sat listening to the wrangling . . . for a few minutes, and then began to exhibit distinct signs of impatience. As there seemed to be no improvement in sight, she then jumped up from her seat, shouted in a tone of military command the one word "Mohini!" and then walked straight out of the door into the passage. The stately and dignified Mohini came rushing down that long room at the highest speed, and as soon as he reached the passage threw himself incontinently flat on his face on the floor at the feet of the lady in black. Many people arose in confusion, not knowing what was happening, but a moment later Mr. Sinnett himself also came running to the door, went out and exchanged a few words, and then, re-entering the room, he stood up on the end of our bench and spoke in a ringing voice the fateful words: "Let me introduce to the London Lodge as a whole—Madame Blavatsky!" The scene was indescribable, the members wildly delighted and yet half awed at the same time, clustering round our great Founder, some kissing her hand, several kneeling before her, and two or three weeping hysterically. After a few minutes . . . she was led up to the platform by Col. Olcott.

Thus concludes the saga of the London Lodge and the turmoil that accompanied the 1884 election of officers, apparently the only occasion when the Mahatmas and the Mahachohan engaged themselves in the affairs of any of the Society's Branches. All in all, it was a most significant event historically and one from which we today may learn a number of lessons as we read about those events.

LETTER 123

Now that the affairs of the London Lodge had been resolved with the election of a set of new officers, Sinnett may have felt frustration, even depression, with the necessity to devote attention to his "family duties." As is evident from earlier letters, he had looked forward to taking a leading role in the work of the London group, conveying at least to the members if not to the public the teachings he had received from the Adepts. But he also had to give time to meeting his family's immediate needs as he reestablished himself in England. The following are some notes concerning the background for this short letter.

In late 1882, Sinnett received notice of the termination of his employment as editor of the Allahabad *Pioneer*. He had been granted a year's grace period before final dismissal, so he, with his wife and child, did not leave India until early 1883. The reference in Letter 123 to the "past year" during which he had been caught up in "family duties" is to the period between mid 1883 and the spring of 1884, when the London Lodge election took place. We can assume that from the time of his arrival back in England, he was not only involved in meetings with the members, renewing acquaintances, and so on, but also concerned about finding a suitable home in or near London, some kind of employment particularly in light of the failure of the *Phoenix* venture and therefore the unlikelihood of any return to

India, and generally becoming reestablished in his native land. He had used the long voyage homeward to write *Esoteric Buddhism*, which was published, as we have already noted, in June of 1883, putting into that work the basic teachings he had received from the Mahatmas. However, we know that from early 1883 on, he received no further teachings, perhaps because he was too preoccupied to ask further questions of a philosophical or metaphysical nature.

A few other details may be noted: Sinnett, at the time of his return to England, was forty-three years of age; he and Patience, his wife, whom he had married in 1870, had lived in India since the end of 1872, a period of eleven years. Their only child, a son named Denny, was born in 1877, but was always sickly and indeed died from tuberculosis in 1908, the same year that Patience died. As Sven Eek wrote in an article about Sinnett (*The American Theosophist*, July 1966), the years in India "were probably the happiest in his life; a good income, social position, and professional recognition combined to make life agreeable for the Sinnetts." Now, at the time of Letter 123, although vice president of the London Lodge and still vice president of the Parent Society, Sinnett is necessarily concerned for his own and his family's future.

It is against this background that we can consider KH's wonderful statement: "What better cause for reward, what better discipline, than the daily and hourly performance of duty?" On numerous occasions in letters to both Sinnett and other recipients of correspondence, the Mahatmas emphasize duty. Similarly, in *The Key to Theosophy*, HPB writes of "Theosophy as the quintessence of duty" and comments that "the first of the Theosophical duties is to do one's duty by *all* men, and especially by those to whom one's *specific* responsibilities are due," particularly family and friends. So also, Annie Besant, in a lecture titled "The Law of Duty," one of a series of lectures published as *The Laws of the Higher Life*, says that "the Law of Duty" is "the first great step towards the attainment" of realizing the Self as One and "the first truth which a man must obey." Annie Besant emphasizes that it is by being faithful to the responsibilities before us that we climb the

ladder of spiritual evolution, or as KH states in his letter to S͏
through the performance of "small plain duties" we eventually "ris͏
the larger measure of Duty, Sacrifice and Charity to all Humanity."

The question naturally arises: Just what is our duty? More specifically, what is *my* duty? This is never an easy question to answer, especially when one is confronted with seemingly opposing duties. Does my responsibility lie first to my family, to friends, to associates, or to the work I have taken on, to some cause to which I have given myself? In a letter to Francesca Arundale (*LMW*, First Series, Letter 20), the Mahatma KH advises: "See to it that the continual performance of duty under the guidance of a well-developed Intuition" is undertaken. Only as we develop the intuitive faculty can we really know what is our duty, but that development may well be brought about or strengthened by fulfilling the "small plain duties."

I am reminded of the story of the Zen master whose pupil approached him asking, "What should I do?" The Roshi responded with a question, "Have you eaten your breakfast?" to which the pupil replied, "Of course." "Then," said his master, "go and wash your dishes." To recognize one's responsibility in the immediate present does not always seem that simple, yet it may well become that simple if we are willing to do what is right before us, in the spirit that KH indicates in the words: "the daily conquest of Self, the perseverance in spite of want of visible . . . progress."

Dr. Besant provides some beautiful guidelines in "The Law of Duty": "To all and each one that we meet, we owe a duty. . . . Duties are obligations we owe to those around us; and everyone within our circle is one to whom we owe a duty . . . the duty of reverencing and obeying those who are superior to us . . . the duty of being gentle and affectionate and helpful to those around us . . . the duty of protection, kindness, helpfulness, and compassion to those below us."

She suggests that we discover the full import of the law of duty "by studying our own place on the ladder of evolution, by studying the circumstances around us that show our karma, by studying our own powers and capacities, and ascertaining our weaknesses." No doubt the key to discovering our true duty lies ultimately in forgetfulness of self, in performing whatever action is required in the moment, and in adhering to KH's advice in the letter "To a Chela" (*LMW*, First Series, Letter 24): "Try to fill each day's measure with pure thoughts, wise words, kindly deeds."

Above all, as KH advises Sinnett in Letter 123, we are not to be discouraged, nor are we to give way, as evidently Sinnett was inclined to do, to a "mental and moral indolence . . . inclining to drift with the currents of life." All of us no doubt fall short of our aspirations, but we must be willing to "steer a direct course" as we see it and on our own, maintaining, as KH says, "a calm and brave spirit toward outward events in the present, and a hopeful spirit for the future."

Truly, this letter says as much to us today as it did to Sinnett in 1884.

LETTER 124

The reader will remember that KH had been charged with plagiarism as a result of Sinnett's publishing some portions of Letter 12 in *The Occult World*. The Mahatma ultimately explained in full, in Letter 117, how Letter 12 had been written or precipitated. That explanation came with the restriction that Sinnett was not to publish or even share these "facts" with others.

Now, in Letter 124, we learn the reason for the restriction. The Mahatma knows that if Sinnett were to reveal the full explanation, it would be used against both of them, Sinnett and the Mahatma. Sinnett would be charged with "credulity," while the Spiritualists, who were inclined to consider the Mahatmas mere figments of HPB's imagination, would use it as a "pretext for poking fun at occult sciences." The "golden-haired nymph of the Vicarage" is a reference to Anna Kingsford with whom Sinnett has just had some unhappy dealings in the London Lodge election; her husband was a vicar.

In this letter KH removes the restriction he placed on Sinnett in Letter 117. However, KH tells the Englishman that he must be "prepared to stand the fire of furious denial and adverse criticism." Regarding himself, the Mahatma adds: "I would not have 'the propagation of Theosophy' impeded on my account and to save my name from a few extra blows."

The Mahatmas' attitude is always impersonal, for the cause of Theosophy was, for them, far more important than any personal consideration. In this particular case, however, the Mahatma is concerned about the affect that publicizing of the mode by which they work might have on Sinnett. A wonderful lesson is offered here, as we may ask ourselves to what extent we are courageous enough to withstand the scorn and ridicule that often comes when we speak of occult matters.

LETTER 125

Letter 125, which is from M, reminds us again of the close relation-ship between the two Brothers. M indicates that he is writing because KH, Sinnett's "guardian," is "occupied upon official business" and unable to attend to matters in London. An interesting point to note is M's reference to precipitation as now "the more difficult, not to say costly method" of producing the letters. We can appreciate the word "difficult" because of the energy involved in producing a precipitation, remembering KH's comments on the subject in connection with the Kiddle affair. As to "costly," perhaps the clue is in the final words of the sentence: "to our reputations in the West." We know there was considerable skepticism regarding the existence of the Mahatmas and that HPB was being charged with fraud and forgery. The idea of a precipitated letter would only fan the fires of doubt, bringing the names of the Mahatmas into further disrepute.

As a matter of interest, the last letter from M was Letter 118, and since he so disliked writing, we can conjecture that he wrote that one also because KH was otherwise occupied, although this is not explicitly said. M writes only one further letter after this one. That is Letter 137, a brief note written a year or so after the letter we are now studying and not long before the correspondence between Sinnett and the Mahatmas ceased.

Much of Letter 125 is devoted to the welfare of Mohini, who accompanied Olcott and HPB to Europe and went on with Olcott to London for the election meeting of the Lodge. Mohini was introduced to Sinnett in Letter 94, and in Letter 121, KH refers to him as one "whom I have chosen as my chela and with whom I sometimes communicate directly." KH may have proposed that Mohini travel to Europe so he could assist the members there in understanding the Eastern doctrines made public in Sinnett's *Esoteric Buddhism.* This idea is substantiated by M's comments in Letter 125 that Mohini is needed to aid the members in Paris and on the Continent generally, where Theosophical work was just beginning in earnest. It was during his time in London that Mohini collaborated with Laura Holloway in writing *Man: Fragments of Forgotten History,* published as written by "Two Chelas" in 1885.

M makes two points in this letter that add to what we have already learned about chelaship. First, as a chela, Mohini is "not a free man—in the ordinary acceptation of the term." Earlier statements regarding chelaship may shed light on what M means here: in Letter 95, "We never *guide* our chelas . . . nor do we forewarn them," and in Letter 92, "*Our chelas are helped but when they are innocent of the causes that lead them into trouble.*" We thus understand that when Mohini is accommodated in a very cold room, KH surrounded him "with a double shell against a death cold that threatened him" because the chela was obviously "innocent" of the cause of his problem. Mohini, or any chela, is "free" to make his own mistakes and must suffer the consequences—"the effects produced by causes of their own creation" (Letter 95)—but whenever the causes are "generated by . . . outside influences" (Letter 92), because of the connection between chela and master, help is given to ameliorate the effect.

Second, since Mohini was in close rapport with his Master, the Mahatma could use him to achieve the purpose he had in mind, which was conveying "occult education" to the members in London and Europe. Therefore, the physical vehicle needed to be protected from a "death cold." Just what this "double shell" consisted of we are not told, but we can speculate that it was a kind of etheric or akashic protection. How this was done is another mystery.

As Letter 125 concludes, we find M taking Sinnett to task over his attitude toward both Olcott and Mrs. Kingsford. Sinnett, as pointed out before, wasn't ever completely comfortable with the president–founder, considering him lacking a certain refinement both in language and in dress. M speaks of Olcott's "extravagant Asiatic undress," because Olcott was inclined to wear an Indian dhoti even in London. This obviously bothered Sinnett, who, it is said, always wore evening dress at the Society's meetings and probably expected other members to do the same. To relieve Sinnett of having to provide hospitality for Olcott, M directed Olcott to stay with Francesca Arundale and her mother, with whom HPB had stayed during her visit to London. Regarding Mrs. Kingsford, the letter implies that Sinnett harbored a sense of spite toward her and, quite pleased that she had been defeated in the election, even wanting to "mortify" her in some way. M makes it clear, in his usual direct way, that unless Sinnett changes his attitude, he risks severing his tie with KH—a reminder, actually, of so much that he has been told throughout the correspondence. KH reiterates the same advice in the next letter, as we shall see.

The basic lesson in Letter 125 is clear: "Learn to dissociate your consciousness from your external self." This lesson, as valid today as it was when M wrote this letter, is one we all need to learn at some time or other. If we seek to tread the occult path, to come closer to the Mahatmas and live the kind of life that ensures our usefulness to them, it is we who must change. We cannot expect the rules of the spiritual life to accommodate our feelings and prejudices. This is the lesson of learning to act from the higher or inner Self, of responding from an impersonal point of view rather than from the personal self, with its likes and dislikes, emotional entanglements, and judgments of others.

Taking as examples the three individuals referred to in this letter, we can consider how the Mahatma's rebuke might apply to us. First, Sinnett was probably quite unaware of Mohini's discomfort; similarly, we can ask ourselves how often we are oblivious of another's suffering that we might have alleviated if we had paid attention. Second, Sinnett's judging Olcott by external appearances can remind us to notice how frequently we judge others by their dress or speech or some other outer characteristic that does not accord with our own sensibilities. Finally, Sinnett's attitude toward Mrs. Kingsford is a reminder to consider whether we take some delight in the downfall or humiliation of someone whom we would like to see defeated. While this brief letter may be thought to have only historical relevance, in fact—as indeed is the case with virtually all of the Mahatmas' letters—it contains invaluable life lessons for today.

Students of Theosophical history may appreciate the fact that it was during this period, when the founders were away from Adyar, that the seeds of the Coulomb conspiracy were planted. The full story is told in Josephine Ransom's *Short History of the Theosophical Society*, in the chapter headed "The Founders Visit Europe." In brief, when Olcott and HPB, with Mohini, left Adyar for Europe, the president–founder designated certain members of the General Council (the Society's governing body) to act as a "Board of Control" during his absence. This committee consisted of Dr. Franz Hartmann, a member from Germany who loyally supported HPB through the Coulomb difficulty; St. George Lane-Fox, a newcomer to Adyar from England who later became somewhat hostile to the Society; W. T. Brown, a member of Olcott's party on a tour in North India who received a note from KH during their stay in Lahore and subsequently other letters from the Mahatma; and Alexis Coulomb, Emma Coulomb's husband left in charge of maintenance at Headquarters. Of particular interest, because it seems to have been a warning to Olcott, is a letter that the president–founder received in an unusual manner. As Olcott wrote in his diary:

> Dropped in railway carriage, April 5ᵗʰ, 1884, as I was reading a lot of letters from L.[ondon] L.[odge] . . . the particulars about the Kingsford-Sinnett quarrel. This letter fell just as I was noting a paragraph in B.[ertram] K.[eightley]'s letter about the Mahatmas. Present in the railway carriage only Mohini and myself. The letter from KH said in part: Do not be surprised at anything you may hear from Adyar. Nor discouraged. It is possible—tho' we try to prevent it within the limits of karma—that you may have great domestic annoyance to pass thro'. You have harboured a traitor and an enemy under your roof for years, and the missionary party are more than ready to avail of any help she may be induced to give. A regular conspiracy is on foot. She is maddened by the appearance of Mr. Lane-Fox and the powers you have given to the Board of Control. We have been doing some phenomena at Adyar since HPB left India to protect Upasika [HPB] from the conspiracy.

The nature of the phenomena the Mahatmas were doing is not known, but this warning from KH undoubtedly disturbed Olcott as he faced the turmoil in London. It certainly indicates the Mahatmas' prescience and their endeavor to prevent a most tragic occurrence in the history of the Society. But as KH writes in Letter 121, *"Karma has its own."*

LETTER 126

Letter 126 is, in my opinion, one of the most significant letters concerning the occult path in all the correspondence and one from which we can learn a great many lessons about living the spiritual life. We are quite aware at the letter's outset that Sinnett has reacted to M's reprimand in Letter 125. Judging from the words KH places in quotation marks, we presume that Sinnett has complained of M's "unfriendliness" and of being "unjustly treated" by M. In writing to his "Guardian," as M called KH, no doubt Sinnett has attempted to defend himself, perhaps trying to justify his feelings about Olcott and Anna Kingsford and, in regard to Mohini, perhaps protesting, "Why didn't he tell me he was cold?" All of this would have been a natural reaction to what KH calls "M's natural *brusqueness*." Indeed, how often do we not feel hurt when someone critiques an attitude or action that we think is fully justified and then seek to defend ourselves? Of course, at this stage in the correspondence, Sinnett should be quite familiar with the terse manner in which M expresses himself, except in the longer letters where he is conveying the teachings. In general, M's letters are more impersonal than those from KH, who often addressed Sinnett as a good friend.

In Letter 126, however, KH is no less severe than M has been, although as usual he couches his rebuke in a fuller, more detailed explanation. He notes that Sinnett's attitude indicates that he is "entirely unfit for practical occultism"—certainly hard words for Sinnett to come upon—even while he acknowledges Sinnett's "better aspirations," which have been nourished by a "real devotion" to KH. The words that open the letter, "My poor, blind friend," strike such a note of sadness that we marvel at the teacher's patience up to this point in helping Sinnett understand the nature of the occult life. The depth of KH's friendship for Sinnett is at once apparent as he tells Sinnett that he is permitted to make one last effort "to open [Sinnett's] inner intuition" and help him move beyond "every protest and doubt of [his] purely intellectual nature."

The first page of the letter reveals an interesting contrast between the conflict KH is facing and the one that is before Sinnett. For KH, the choice is between the friendship he feels for Sinnett and his duty, and for him there is really no choice. He expresses in beautiful words his absolute dedication and unfailing commitment to the duty owed to *his* Master. For KH, duty is an "abiding principle . . . the indestructible cement" that has held the Brotherhood of Adepts together throughout the ages. This surely is the "larger measure of Duty" spoken of in Letter 123—what Annie Besant has called the "Supreme Duty"—the exercise of which begins with the observance of small daily and hourly duties.

The conflict within Sinnett, on the other hand, is at a personal level and perhaps therefore more familiar to us. It is also less easily resolved. This is the choice between his "purely worldly intellect" and his "better aspirations"—between head and heart, we might say, or between his everyday family life and the life demanded of one who would walk "the path to the Occult Sciences." Here we find the sharp contrast between "cold, *spiritually blind* reason" and the whisperings of the heart that need to become loud and clear.

Regarding the statement that KH places in quotation marks, "Patience, patience. . . . A great design has never been snatched at once, " it may be of interest to know that folio 6 of the letters in the British Museum Library includes a verse written in the Mahatma KH's familiar blue pencil, presumably to Sinnett. This, it would seem, is the original of the line now quoted in Letter 126; it has been placed at the very beginning of the published volume of HPB's letters to Sinnett where it reads :

> . . . It was thy patience that in the waste
> Attended still thy step, and saved MY friend
> For better days. What cannot patience do.
> . . . A great design is seldom snatched at once,
> 'Tis PATIENCE heaves it on . . . KH

Here in Letter 126, we find the clearest, most succinct and powerful statement concerning all that is needed for treading the spiritual path. This is a statement to be read and reread, meditated upon, and certainly taken to heart:

The path to Occult Sciences has to be trodden laboriously and crossed at the danger of life; . . . every new step in it leading to the final goal is surrounded by pit-falls and cruel thorns; . . . the pilgrim who ventures upon it is made first to confront and *conquer* the thousand and one furies who keep watch over its adamantine gates and entrance—furies called Doubt, Skepticism, Scorn, Ridicule, Envy and finally Temptation—especially the latter; and . . . he who would see *beyond* had to first destroy this living wall; . . . he must be possessed of a heart and soul clad in steel, and of an iron, never failing determination and yet be meek and gentle, humble and have shut out from his heart every human passion, that leads to evil.

We may well be reminded of HPB's stirring words, so often quoted:

There *is* a road, steep and thorny, beset with perils of every kind, but yet a road, and it leads to the very heart of the Universe: I can tell you how to find those who will show you the secret gateway that opens inward only, and closes fast behind the neophyte for evermore. There is no danger that dauntless courage cannot conquer; there is no trial that spotless purity cannot pass through; there is no difficulty that strong intellect cannot surmount. For those who win onwards there is reward past all telling—the power to bless and save humanity; for those who fail, there are other lives in which success may come. (*CW*, 13:219)

Pondering KH's statement, we may well ask ourselves, as the Adept asks Sinnett, "Are you all this? Have you ever begun a course of training which would lead to it?" Consider for a moment what KH calls the "furies" that guard the entrance to the path: "Doubt, Skepticism, Scorn, Ridicule, Envy and finally Temptation," with a special emphasis on the last. How subtle is the temptation not so much to undertake some act that deflects us from our aim but to engage a feeling or thought of unkindness, envy, pride, selfishness, self-centeredness, egoism, or desire in its many forms! The Christian prayer asks: "Lead us not into temptation" precisely because of the subtle nature of that "fury" that arises within us almost without our knowing it.

KH cites two reasons why Sinnett is not "fitted for the life" of a "regular *chela*"—although he is a "lay-chela." First, he tells Sinnett, "you were not born for it," referring to the fact that each of our incarnations is the karmic consequence of our own past. I am reminded here of much that HPB wrote, both in her letters and in the little work published as *Practical Occultism*, concerning the need to give attention to all the events and circumstances in our lives so we may learn from them and awaken our spiritual intuition. Somewhere in one of her letters, she says in effect that if we cannot attain our goal in this lifetime, we can at least prepare our emotional and mental "baggage" for the next. Second, Sinnett is "a family man with wife and child to support, with work to do"—a statement reminding us of the importance the Mahatma gives to the performance of even the most mundane duties (see Letter 123). Undoubtedly, KH hoped that Sinnett, even as a lay-chela and constrained by the two factors KH mentions, was preparing himself for an eventual fully committed life of chelaship. Here we find the first mention of the fact that Sinnett had actually offered to give up meat and drink, an offer KH refused because, again, the Englishman could not in this incarnation "become a regular *chela*."

KH speaks of his own lack of "personal freedom," a provocative phrase that causes us to consider once again the nature of adeptship. Two ways in which an Adept loses personal freedom come to mind. The first refers to a statement KH makes to Hume at the conclusion of Letter 67: "The degrees of an Adept's initiation mark the seven stages at which he discovers the secret of the sevenfold principles in nature and man and awakens his dormant powers." (One of those "stages" may relate to the further step that KH took during his retreat.) Speculating on the matter, I suggest that "personal freedom" becomes less and less as an individual advances through the various stages that comprise "an Adept's initiation." That is, the call of the personality becomes fainter, while the call of the soul becomes stronger. At the same time, KH indicates that at some point he will have "personal freedom," which may mean that at some stage on the path the initiate is working through such a purified personality that he or she has freedom at the personal level. Yet that individual would never be swayed by personal desire or use that freedom for personal aims.

The second aspect of his lack of "personal freedom" KH himself has already mentioned in the opening remarks of this letter: the fact that his "first duty is to [*his*] Master." Just who he is referring to is left to speculation. Later in the same paragraph he mentions "our Supreme Chief"—which could mean the Mahachohan, the head of the Brotherhood; the Buddha, who is spoken of in the letters with the greatest reverence; or a superior Adept not yet named. Certainly while much is said throughout these letters about both adeptship and chelaship, much still remains obscure. Even the extensive information in HPB's writings is in fact only general hints and suggestions, while many matters remain veiled. What is clear is that KH is bound by pledges of obedience to the Brotherhood in general and specifically, we may assume, to his own teacher.

In the very first paragraph of Letter 126, KH says that he was the "only one" of the Brotherhood to seek some slight relaxation of the stern rules governing chelaship. KH was educated in at least one European university and, as has been suggested, was also "younger" on the path to full adeptship than his Brother M; therefore, he was perhaps more familiar with Western ways and thought, as well as closer to our ordinary level of humanity, and so was eager to give an opportunity to those who showed any promise of walking the "path to Occult Sciences." In her article on "Chelas and Lay Chelas" (*CW*, 4:607–14), HPB states that "since the advent of the Theosophical Society . . . the rules of Chela selection have become slightly relaxed in one respect," although the results of even that small relaxation "have been far from encouraging." Here in Letter 126, KH states that he "failed" in his attempt to have even a "small reform." Fortunately for us, KH was permitted to enter into this amazing correspondence with

Sinnett, as well as with Hume and others, for as he says, "All I could obtain was to be allowed to communicate with a few."

KH reminds Sinnett that he had been "chosen" to serve "as the exponent of our doctrine," an interesting statement that prompts us to ask: "Why was Sinnett so chosen?" There may be at least three reasons: First, undoubtedly a karmic tie existed between the Mahatma and Sinnett, a bond perhaps from some distant past. That bond may well have led to the whole chain of circumstances—the arrival of the founders in India, the initial contact between HPB and Olcott and the Sinnetts, HPB's producing phenomena while a guest of the Sinnetts, HPB's attribution of such phenomena to her Teacher—all leading to Sinnett's desire to contact the "Brothers." Second, Sinnett's interest made him available. He had a questioning mind and seemed willing to probe ever further into the entire field of occult studies. It is just such a mind, given to inquiry, that seems to be essential on the spiritual path.

The third reason for choosing Sinnett may have been the dual factors that he was a man and also a journalist. Regarding his gender, at the end of the nineteenth century, women did not command the respect they do now. The only substantial work of a Theosophical nature available to the English-speaking public at the time was *Isis Unveiled*, written by a woman—H. P. Blavatsky. It was a groundbreaking work and introduced the world at large to many ideas of the occult philosophy. But something else was needed at that time —a coherent basic textbook of the occult doctrine—and while HPB did eventually write such a book containing the occult philosophy, Sinnett as a well-educated Englishman was able to supply what was needed as a result of his correspondence with the Mahatmas. With the publication of *Esoteric Buddhism*, in spite of its flaws and inadequacies, the world was presented with an easily readable text. (KH says of the work in Letter 113: "with a few undetectable mistakes and omissions notwithstanding your *Esoteric Buddhism* is the only right exposition—however incomplete—of our Occult doctrines.") The fact that Sinnett was a journalist and therefore accustomed to reportorial writing must surely have been a factor in the Mahatma's choosing him.

KH then offers us a glimpse into further aspects of his life and work. The precise nature of that work is difficult to define, but throughout the letters we are told that the Mahatmas have their own occupations, and we can only guess what they might be. Clearly, however, they are not permitted to use "any psychical powers" to bring about even desirable results that might benefit people or causes. At the same time, KH refers to "small means of action," which may well consist of influencing the minds or actions of their chelas or other individuals open to such influence. The "attempt" referred to is, of course, the Phoenix venture, the topic of previous letters. The reference to the "Ilbert Bill excitement" takes us back to Letter 114.

The comments about karma take on particular significance as KH reviews for Sinnett his early attitude toward Indians, the failure of the Phoenix proposal, and the "quarrel between the L[ondon] L[odge] and Kingsford," all of which seem related in some way. To help Sinnett understand the relationship between his attitude and its karmic consequences, the Mahatma tells him, "If you have any intuition, you will work out *cause* and *effect* and realize *whence* the failure." This is certainly advice that we might all take to heart, especially in light of KH's further statement that all the events and circumstances he has just named were brought on by Sinnett himself. There is much to ponder in KH's statement: "You know nothing of the *ins* and *outs* of the work of karma—of the 'sideblows' of this terrible Law." Later KH asks Sinnett to "have another look at *Karma* . . . and remember that it ever works in the most unexpected ways." Evidently, the many threads of action, thought, and attitude, including the failure of the Phoenix venture, have combined in such a way that KH tells Sinnett he is now granted permission only "to write to you occasionally . . . as a special favour." This could well be a hint that the correspondence is drawing to a close; certainly no actual teachings are given in the succeeding letters, although they contain much of value concerning the spiritual life.

With wonderful patience, and at the same time with a directness that may have surprised and undoubtedly hurt Sinnett, KH now explains how Sinnett has "treated both H.S.O. and H.P.B. in a very *cruel* way." As we know, from the time the two men first met, Sinnett considered Olcott inferior both "socially and intellectually" and was critical of the president–founder's management of the Society's affairs. When the founding of an Anglo-Indian Branch of the Society, later called the Simla Eclectic Society, was proposed, both Sinnett and Hume had asked that Olcott have nothing to do with it, a request the Mahatmas refused. On many occasions Sinnett was equally critical and even suspicious of HPB. Even with regard to Mohini's suffering from the cold, Sinnett evidently suspected HPB of complaining to the Mahatma about the situation and accusing the Englishman of some intentional wrong.

The Mahatma defends HPB and even quotes her, whether from a letter she wrote to her Master or from her thoughts we do not know. She must have said that Sinnett never really intended to do anything wrong. But KH is clear that the wrong was Sinnett's own "*carelessness.*" By way of defending HPB as well as Olcott, KH tells Sinnett that it was Mme. Mary Gebhard, who was apparently on one of her visits to London and staying with the Sinnetts at the time, who conveyed the thought of Mohini's suffering to the Mahatma. KH, however, already knew and was doing his best to remedy the matter and, because he knew it was not intentional on Sinnett's part, felt no "unfriendliness" toward him. Most interesting in all of this is the fact that KH was alerted in thought to the reproach that a number of people felt.

Mme. Gebhard was a member of a German family quite prominent in the early days of the Society in Europe. The Germania Theosophical Society was organized at the Gebhard home in Elberfeld on July 17, 1884. It is said that Mme. Gebhard "combined refinement and culture with rare capacities for occult studies." She remained a faithful worker for the Adept Brothers and on more than one occasion received letters from them (see *CW*, 6:434–36 for her biography). An interesting sidelight, perhaps again one of the "sideblows" of karma, concerns Mme. Gebhard's third son, Arthur (she had six sons and one daughter, all the sons becoming members of the Society), who fell under the influence of Mohini and with him drew up what HPB called a "Manifesto" titled "A Few Words on The Theosophical Organization," which severely criticized Colonel Olcott for alleged despotism. HPB wrote a lengthy defense of Olcott, later published and still available as *The Original Programme of the Theosophical Society*. Arthur Gebhard later became an American citizen and with William Q. Judge published the journal *The Path*. He lectured and wrote on the occult significance of Richard Wagner's musical dramas. In 1940, he published a little book, *The Tradition in Silence*, in which he paid tribute to HPB and her work. This is perhaps a long digression, but it traces some of the karmic threads linking people and events, thus illustrating the Mahatma's statement that indeed the law of karma "ever works in the most unexpected ways."

KH suggests that Sinnett should ask himself how far he is justified in entertaining suspicions against Olcott and HPB, neither of whom knew anything about Mohini's situation. This is an occasion for all of us to learn how easily "mere suspicion" can degenerate "into *conviction* and become objectivised in written reproaches and very ungenerous expressions" that in fact are "*undeserved.*"

Drawn into the whirlpool of suspicion is Francesca Arundale, to whom Sinnett is said to have "complained bitterly" about a letter from HPB. This seems to be a letter that HPB wrote to Sinnett some months previously at M's direction, adding, in her usual way, some colorful comments of her own without bothering to tell Sinnett that these were her thoughts. The subject was mainly Mrs. Kingsford, and Sinnett, perhaps still smarting over the whole affair in the London Lodge, replied quite sharply to HPB, who then wrote another letter apologizing and saying, "I find I am a fool. . . . I trusted too much in your intuition as to imagine that without a dash or something to indicate where the Boss's suggestions ended and my own flapdoodle began, I went on speculating and advising and thus led you into the natural error of taking my own words for those of Master! . . . Master had come, and he went away. And I, having delivered myself of his chief message—made a mess of the rest" (see *LBS*, page 89).

Referring to this entanglement of suspicions, misunderstandings, and allegations against innocent parties, KH tells Sinnett frankly: "You have brought suffering upon yourself, upon your lady and many others—which was quite useless and might have been avoided had you only abstained from creating yourself most of its causes." Sinnett's perception has apparently become so clouded that KH reminds him: "He who will not find our truths in his soul and within himself—has poor chances of success in Occultism." And because "you are yourself ruining that which you have so laboriously erected . . . unless you shake off yourself the ghastly influence that is upon you I can do very little."

Before closing the letter, KH clarifies one more situation: the role of the American widow Mrs. Laura Holloway, a clairvoyant who came to England and worked for a time with Sinnett and Mohini. In fact, HPB states in a letter to Sinnett (*LBS*, 91): "I must tell you plainly that Mrs. H. having been sent from America here [London] by the Master's wish who had a purpose in view—*if you make her go astray* and force her unwittingly into a path that does not run in the direction of the Master's desire—then all communication *between you and Master KH* will stop." HPB had been hoping, we might add, that Mrs. Holloway could be trained to take over the work of intermediary that HPB had carried on for so long for the Mahatmas. More is said about Mrs. Holloway in Letter 134.

Apparently, Sinnett had asked if he could tell Francesca Arundale what the Mahatma had told him through this clairvoyant. At this point, KH disclaims any communication through her, saying, "I have never bound you to anything thro' Mrs. H.; never communicated with you or any one else thro' her—nor have any of my, or M's chelas, to my knowledge, except in America, once at Paris and another time at Mrs. A[rundale]'s house. She is an excellent but quite undeveloped clairvoyante." Unfortunately, Sinnett was still convinced that the Mahatma *had* communicated through her, and KH strongly rebukes him: "You have proudly claimed the privilege of exercising your own, uncontrolled judgment in occult matters you could know nothing about—and the occult laws you believe you can defy and play with impunity have turned round upon you and have badly hurt you." However, KH does say that Mrs. Holloway *did* see correctly when she was being helped, but "when left alone to herself, never has she left one single statement undisfigured."

A light is thrown on the alleged communication through Mrs. Holloway in Sinnett's book *The Early Days of Theosophy in Europe* (page 61): "On the evening of 6th July we had an interview with the Master KH through Mrs. Holloway. On this occasion he actually took possession of her and spoke to us in the first person." Sinnett therefore chose to believe that the Mahatma's denial of that communication was a "fabrication of the O.L. [Old Lady]." This is clearly in a letter from HPB written about July 18 or 19, which is Letter 127. One student of the letters suggests that *The Early Days of Theosophy in Europe* shows why the correspondence between the Mahatma and Sinnett had to end. Sinnett had become almost childish in his jealousy and suspicion, until he was making trouble for everyone, including himself—as Letter 126 clearly shows.

However, KH seems to give Sinnett yet another chance to continue on the path toward further understanding of the occult science. He tells him, "If, throwing aside every preconceived idea, you could TRY and impress yourself with this profound truth that intellect is not all powerful by itself; that to become a 'mover of mountains' it has first to receive life and light from its higher principle—Spirit, and then would fix your eyes upon everything occult, spiritually trying to develop the faculty according to the rules, then you would soon read the mystery right."

Finally, he reminds Sinnett: "You have two roads lying before you; one leading thro' a very dreary path toward knowledge and truth—the other . . . but really I must not influence your mind." Above all, KH adds later, do not stop "*midway.*" He asks Sinnett to be present and speak at a meeting, which was probably the farewell meeting for the founders held a few days after this letter was received. It seems, though, that while he did attend and gave a talk, Sinnett suspected HPB of inserting the request to attend the affair into KH's letter (we have evidence for such as insertion in Sinnett's *Autobiography*).

So ends a long letter covering many aspects of Sinnett's relationships with other workers, his attitude, his unwarranted suspicions, his efforts at justifying his actions, and more, all pointing to the fact that his temper or mood and his blindness to his own failings made him "entirely unfit," as KH says, "for practical occultism." Thus this letter tells us much that we can take to heart in our own efforts to live the life that leads to wisdom. "Two roads" lay before Sinnett, and perhaps the same two roads are before us: the spiritual path leading to knowledge, wisdom, enlightenment, and the path of the world—the path of phenomena, temporary pleasures, and illusory goals. Which road do we take?

Yet even in closing this letter of rebuke, KH is, as always, kind and gentle; he is still Sinnett's friend, and he is grateful for all Sinnett has done for the cause so dear to the Mahatma's heart. As he said on an earlier occasion, "Ingratitude is not one of our vices." One feels this is a letter of a friend speaking very honestly to a friend, one whom he hopes will understand and open his intuition to the greater realities of existence.

LETTER 127

The background and references in Letter 127, which is from HPB, are well covered in the prefatory note. It seems that she was aware of the reprimands the two Mahatmas were delivering to Sinnett and now adds her effort to theirs to encourage a change of attitude in him. We can only surmise that Sinnett found it difficult, and certainly wounding to his ego, to receive three such communications in fairly quick succession: first, from M (Letter 125), then from his own "Guardian" (Letter 126), and now from HPB. All three of his correspondents are warning him that he is "blind" (to use KH's term) to his own weaknesses and that if he cannot "learn to dissociate [his] external self," to use M's words, from his true Self, he is in danger of losing KH.

Perhaps HPB's letter encouraged Sinnett to give thought once again to the words of his own teacher, KH, and reflect on the extent to which they rang true. Whatever Sinnett may have thought after receiving HPB's letter, we can ask ourselves how the message conveyed in all three letters may apply to our own attitudes and behavior.

Two essential lessons emerge from HPB's letter. First there is the matter of self-deception, to which HPB refers in the opening sentence, telling Sinnett that he is so "ready to *deceive* [*himself*] so willingly." Is it possible that we, too, convinced that our suspicions are correct, weave about ourselves a cloud of self-deception that no amount of explaining by another will disperse? In this case, Sinnett has evidently questioned the validity of Letter 126, simply because it did not agree with his preconceived views and his conviction that Laura Holloway had spoken through and even been possessed by the Mahatma. So, HPB writes, having "*bamboozl[ed]*" himself, Sinnett has become the subject of his own self-deception. The "warning" she then gives only repeats what M has told him—that he may "lose" KH and so terminate the correspondence. We likewise need to consider whether we—like Sinnett—accept ideas only when they "dovetail with [our] own feelings, and reject all that contradicts [our] own notion of the fitness of things."

The second lesson, which concerns Sinnett's attitude toward Olcott, is simply that we must not judge by appearances. HPB acknowledges that the president–founder has on occasion shocked her "susceptibilities" (perhaps a better word would have been "sensibilities"), but like KH, she defends Olcott because he is willing to "confess" his errors and "to say *mea culpa* before all the Theosophists." KH says regarding Olcott in Letter 126: "What we want is *good results*, and you will find that we have them" from the work Olcott has accomplished—yet another valuable lesson for us!

Before we leave HPB's letter, it seems appropriate to introduce here references to several accounts of the further events that transpired concerning the investigation undertaken by the Society for Psychical Research. The founding of that society by a number of friends and even members of the Theosophical Society, including Stainton Moses, C. C. Massey, and Dr. George Wyld, was first mentioned in Letter 47 (page 130). In that letter, KH makes a rather dire prediction as to its future impact on Theosophical work, and now in Letter 128, HPB comments, "Things are getting dark and hazy." As the introduction to Letter 127 indicates, the Society for Psychical Research had decided, following meetings with Olcott and Blavatsky, to send an investigator to India to determine the validity of the phenomena the founders had reported. This action was spurred on by the publication in India, in the *Christian College Magazine*, of articles by Mme. Emma Coulomb, then housekeeper at the Adyar Headquarters, along with fraudulent letters that she claimed had come from HPB.

The investigator that the Society for Psychical Research sent to Adyar was Richard Hodgson, a young man who was a graduate of two universities, keen, intelligent, but completely ignorant of India. He was also somewhat brash and totally inexperienced, quite unaware of the responsibility for unbiased investigation that rested on his shoulders. Further, available funds being limited, the investigation had to be made in one very short visit to Adyar. The result was the infamous and totally biased Hodgson Report, issued in December 1885, which had such a devastating effect on both HPB and the Society and whose conclusions were to linger as a shadow over the Society for many years.

The full story of the Coulomb affair and Hodgson's report of his so-called investigation can be read in the following sources: H. S. Olcott, *Old Diary Leaves* (vol. 3, chapters 9 and 14); Josephine Ransom, *A Short History of the Theosophical Society*, the chapter "The Coulomb Conspiracy"; Howard Murphet, *When Daylight Comes*, chapters 19 and 20; Michael Gomes, *The Coulomb Case*; and Vernon Harrison, *H. P. Blavatsky and the SPR: An Examination of the Hodgson Report of 1895*.

LETTER 128

L etter 128, received sometime during the eventful summer of 1884, is evidently KH's response to a request Sinnett made for permission to publish the correspondence. We can conjecture that the request was prompted by the reprimands Sinnett has received in the last three letters, so that by publishing in full all the letters, he would justify himself before the world as having been accorded the singular privilege of corresponding with the Adepts. However, we do not really know why, at this stage of the correspondence, even with the hints that the correspondence might come to a close, Sinnett is eager to have all the letters published.

The Mahatma's answer is unequivocal: "The letters . . . were not written for publication or public comment upon them, but for private use, and neither M nor I will ever give our consent to see them thus handled." Clearly, both Mahatmas felt that the teachings as given were necessarily sketchy, incomplete, and even imperfect—a comment that throws light on the seeming discrepancies that often puzzle and confuse the student. We know that much could not be told, and still more could hardly be put into words with the vocabulary available, even if the laws of the Brotherhood had permitted it. In fact, this letter seems tinged with regret that the "experiment," as KH called it, was ever attempted—a regret that surely few students share.

It is true that in several letters technical doctrines are presented, doctrines that we are still struggling to understand today. However, even these teachings were always in response to questions rather than intended as a systematic presentation of metaphysical concepts. Events and individuals are discussed, yet taken as a whole the letters constitute a commentary and guide for a way of life that must be lived if one would tread the long and difficult path to enlightened Selfhood, to total awareness of the Oneness of Life, and to full capacity to help and serve in the human struggle. The approach is more Platonic than

Aristotelian, although the latter has been the dominant influence in Western thought through the centuries. Ultimately, the letters cannot be categorized; more than anything else they may be said to stand alone, intrinsically authentic, unique in literature, an exhaustless fount of the wisdom.

As to whether the letters should ever have been published (a point still sometimes debated), it seems obvious that they should not have been published at or near the time they were written, when so many of the characters who cross the stage of the correspondence were still living. As it was, almost fifty years passed before they were published. H. P. Blavatsky's major work, *The Secret Doctrine*, written with the help of the authors of these letters and expounding in more detail the concepts little more than hinted at in the letters, had been published. Most of the individuals mentioned in the letters were no longer living, and there was little risk of unfortunate consequences. At any rate, the letters *have* been published (so far, in three editions plus the chronological edition), much to the benefit of the members of the Theosophical Society as well as the world at large, even though that world has yet to appreciate their full value. Written not for public comment but for private use, the letters' greatest influence remains in that sphere, the domain of individual lives, so we can endeavor to live in accordance with the Mahatmas' rules, to move from our world into theirs as much as our karma and our understanding permit.

KH's reference to the "*Secret Doctrine*" in Letter 128 does not mean HPB's major work, which was written later and not published until 1888. At the time of this letter, 1884, the Mahatmas had decided to form a committee of high chelas centered around the Adyar Headquarters; this committee, which was more or less secret, was to receive letters and teachings from the Mahatmas and then to compile them in a systematic way. The work would then be issued as a "secret doctrine." HPB was "purposely excluded" from this group, known as the Library Committee, "to avoid new suspicions and calumnies." This committee is not mentioned again in the letters, and we can only assume that it did not fulfill its purpose or perhaps was never formed, so that the essential work of presenting the teachings in a more systematic manner awaited HPB's indefatigable efforts to produce her two volumes titled *The Secret Doctrine*.

Mention is made of Laura Holloway, who was apparently in danger of losing her sanity at that time, and of a number of "other wrecks" on the path of occultism. KH poses the question: "Why will 'would-be' *chelas* with such intense self personalities, force themselves within the enchanted and dangerous circle of probation!" We should take serious note of the fact the failure of some chelas was simply due to "self-personality," an obstacle that afflicts so many today as well.

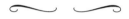

LETTER 129

The introductory note gives us the necessary background for the brief note that is Letter 129. Sinnett is apparently still harboring doubts about the authenticity of Letter 126. He remains convinced that KH did take possession of Laura Holloway and speak through her, in spite of the Mahatma's denial. Now KH asks, "When shall you trust *implicitly*, in my heart if not in my wisdom for which I claim no recognition on your part?" This is truly the plea of a friend, especially when KH goes on to say how much it pains him to see Sinnett "wandering about in a dark labyrinth created by your own doubts." How often do we create our own dark rooms of doubt and depression, closing ourselves off from our higher selves as well as from the beneficent forces all around us?

The letter also gives us a further hint regarding chelaship: "Know . . . that even the chelas of the same guru are often made to separate and keep apart for long months" because the "process of development" may require "mutual and INDIVIDUALIZED development in some one direction." There is much to speculate on in this statement, which suggests that the Mahatmas are aware of the need to carefully balance energies in those they accept as pupils in order to bring about a two-fold development. The first is a "mutual" one, a kind of "group" growth, which may mean the ability of the chela to work in harmony with others and, as spiritual growth continues, with the Brotherhood of Adepts. The second must be an "individualized" development, a uniquely personal growth perhaps along some particular line in consonance with the dharma or destiny of the chela. We too can reflect on these two dimensions of growth as we undertake the spiritual path: the ability to work with others and the development of our own potential.

LETTER 130

It is somewhat of a relief to come to a letter indicating that Sinnett has gotten better control of himself and improved both physically and mentally. No doubt his changed perspective was a result of traveling in Europe, getting away from home, and freeing himself from the doubt and despair that surrounded him in London. A little later in Letter 130, KH tells Sinnett that his "house . . . has a colony of Elementaries [phantoms or shadows of disembodied souls] quartering in it," a condition perhaps caused by the depression Sinnett must have been suffering, so the "flight from London and from yourself was necessary." The miasma in which he had been immersed may also have been a product of his reaction to the letters of admonition he had received (Letters 125, 126, and 127).

In any event, the change of scene and its consequent dispelling of the "influences of [the] . . . 'social season' and of [his] own house" seem to have restored Sinnett. KH can now tell him that he has come through "one of [his] minor cycles" and enduring the suffering and struggles has given him added strength and a "better comprehension" of the ordeals that every aspirant on the spiritual path must experience. This implies that Sinnett has taken to heart KH's words in Letter 126 regarding the "path to Occult Sciences." Notably, the Mahatma has somehow prevented him from arriving at Elberfeld (although he and his wife did go later), where HPB and others, among them Mrs. Holloway, had been visiting the Gebhard family, until he has gained sufficient strength "to bear the strain of the present situation"—a reference to the rapidly developing Coulomb conspiracy (see the commentary on Letter 127).

While HPB and the Society would suffer the most devastating effects of the Coulomb affair and the Society for Psychical Research investigation, Sinnett would not be exempt. KH warns him that not only is he one of the "'shining marks' at which the conspirators aim" but "tenfold greater pains than heretofore will be taken to cover you with ridicule for your *credulity*, your belief in me . . . and to refute your arguments in support of the esoteric teaching." It is clear that this warning strikes directly at Sinnett's weakest point when we remember how he doubted the validity of the Mahatma's statement regarding a visit to Sinnett through Laura Holloway (see Letter 126) and how on other occasions he felt that HPB may have been tricking him. KH knows Sinnett so well, both his good qualities and his weaknesses, that he realizes Sinnett's confidence could well be shaken by all that will soon occur. At the same time, KH emphasizes that what is about to transpire is but another instance in the long history of the "death struggle between Truth and Error" as seen by the Brotherhood of Adepts, "who have watched mankind through the centuries of this cycle." He reminds Sinnett that while some Theosophists, undoubtedly Sinnett included, may be "wounded in [their] 'honour' or [their] purses . . . those who held the lamp in preceding generations paid the penalty of their lives for their knowledge." Indeed, how many martyrs have there been in the cause of Truth!

The tone of the letter now changes rather dramatically, as though KH is speaking to the entire London Lodge if not the entire membership of the Society: "Courage, then, you all, who would be warriors of the one divine Verity; keep on boldly and confidently;

husband your moral strength. . . . All will come right in time—only you, the great and prominent heads of the movement be steadfast, wary and united." The tone is suddenly oratorical, as though KH has taken sentences out of Cicero, and then immediately returns to the familiar intimate tone as KH discusses Laura Holloway once more. It appears that Mrs. Holloway is still being trained or used in some way as an "occult instrument," probably to replace HPB as "astral postoffice" for the transmission of letters and teachings.

The Mahatma's advice to maintain a certain atmosphere in the home in order to counteract "morbific physical influences" should be of value to all of us. The importance of fire and incense in cleansing rooms and houses of influences potentially harmful to the occupants is well known. We are all familiar with entering a room and sensing an atmosphere of peace or a feeling that something dreadful has taken place there. Most essential, as KH now points out to Sinnett, is "to live purely in deed and thought." Certainly atmospheres can be changed by sending out thoughts of peace, harmony, goodwill, and happiness.

The "step HPB was permitted to take" refers to her resignation as Corresponding Secretary of the Society in order to dissociate herself from the administration at Adyar, a direct result of the Coulomb conspiracy. She was in London at this time, having returned from Elberfeld. Several friends in London persuaded HPB to withdraw her resignation, but this only postponed her action for a few months, since in March of 1885, she made the resignation official and it was accepted. It is not made clear why this action on her part had a *direct relation with*" and came "as a direct result of the appearance" of Sinnett's two books, *The Occult World* and *Esoteric Buddhism*, except that those two works had drawn public attention specifically to the Masters' existence as well as to their teachings. While much good came of the publication of those books in terms of strengthening the Theosophical movement and spreading the occult philosophy, certainly they brought a heavy karmic responsibility borne mainly by HPB and bringing about a parting of the ways between her and

Sinnett—an example of how fortune and misfortune, in karmic terms, may result from the same event.

KH gives another type of warning to Sinnett, this time not that the correspondence may end but rather that the Mahatmas' aid could be withdrawn if Sinnett (and others) fail "to remain true and stand faithfully by the T.S." Not only are the teachings that have been conveyed important; so is the instrument for their dissemination. Beyond the teachings is the "original policy" of the Society, and that must be vindicated. From the very beginning of the correspondence, that "original policy" concerned the emphasis on brotherhood. As KH says in Letter 5, "The term 'Universal Brotherhood' is no idle phrase. Humanity in the mass has a paramount claim upon us. . . . It is the only secure foundation for universal morality. If it be a dream, it is at least a noble one for mankind and it is the aspiration of the *true adept.*" Again in Letter 12, KH writes, "The *Chiefs* want a 'Brotherhood of Humanity,' a real Universal Fraternity started; an institution which would make itself known throughout the world and arrest the attention of the highest minds." These are but two of the numerous references to the principle of brotherhood as the "original policy" for which the Society was formed, and it remains today the First Object of the organization.

We must remember that Sinnett's initial interest in the Society and so in Theosophy was not a response to such an ideal or policy but rather to the phenomena produced by HPB. It was out of his desire to understand the modus operandi of such phenomena that he initiated contact with the Mahatmas, who again and again, through the letters, remind him that the information and teachings they are offering in response to his questions are not "so much to gratify individual aspirations as to serve our fellow men" (Letter 2). The remarkable document known as the "View of the Chohan on the T.S.," (see pages 477–80), comprised of "notes" from KH to Sinnett for the benefit of the "Simla Eclectic T.S.," responds directly to Sinnett's continuing desire for training in the production of phenomena: "Perish rather the Theosophical Society with both its hapless founders than that we should permit it to become no better than an academy of magic and a hall of occultism."

Now, in Letter 130, Sinnett is told in no uncertain terms that the "Soc. will be unable to stand, when based upon 'Tibetan Brothers' and phenomena alone." KH's next statement carries overtones of regret: "All this ought to have been limited to an *inner* and very SECRET circle." Many students have similarly suggested that giving Sinnett permission to publish some of the letters, as he did in *The Occult World*, and thus bringing the existence of the Masters into public view, was considered a mistake for which KH would have to pay a price. In fact, elsewhere KH does say that a price is always exacted for sharing esoteric knowledge, and in this instance he was willing to pay.

Sinnett is admonished once again, this time for a "hero-worshipping tendency," which may have developed along with the petty jealousy and rather childish display of antagonism toward a number of people, including HPB, that characterized his attitude during this period. KH tells him firmly, "If you would go on with your occult studies and literary work—then learn to be loyal to the Idea, rather than to my poor self." This is valuable advice for all of us, for I would propose that more people leave the Theosophical Society because of disillusionment with the members, leaders, and speakers than with the "Idea," the fundamental principles. Is our loyalty based on personal predilections, so that when we see weaknesses in the Society's leaders and proponents, we feel the Society itself is no longer of any value, or is our loyalty to the great ideas for which the Society serves as an instrument for conveying them to a world hungry for spiritual nourishment?

KH offers yet another hint regarding the nature of adeptship as he tells Sinnett that while he knows of but "*one* KH," and indeed he can know of only one, "there are two distinct personages answering to that name *in him* you know." He reminds Sinnett that the solution of this "riddle" lies in understanding "what a real *Mahatma* is." This should cause us to review again HPB's excellent article, "Mahatmas and Chelas" (*CW*, 4:239–41), as well as the many references throughout the letters to the nature of adeptship, particularly in Letter 85B.

KH now makes an amazing comment concerning the way an event or circumstance that appears disastrous at the time may have beneficial results. He suggests that perhaps the whole Kiddle affair was "allowed to develop to its bitter end for a purpose" to emphasize that "even an 'adept' when acting in his body is not beyond mistakes due to human carelessness." Earlier KH chided Sinnett for his carelessness in regard to Mohini's comfort, and now he admits that even an Adept can be careless when acting as an ordinary human being. KH is speaking only as an ordinary person when he says that he is "far from being perfect, hence infallible in all I do," yet he may also be speaking as an Adept still aspiring to full adeptship and consequently still learning from his superiors.

KH offers here another reason for the Mahatmas' reluctance to see their letters published at that time. He explains his habit of quoting whatever he sees lying around in the "Akasic libraries, so to say," an intriguing allusion to the fact that all that has ever been said or written endures on that impermeable record of substance, akasha, the very fabric of the universe. One of the truly psychic powers of an Adept is the ability to read that record, and evidently KH had a remarkable memory for whatever he read there. While the ordinary world sees the use of such words and sentences read from the "akasic" as plagiarism, from KH's point of view it is a natural occurrence. I know myself that words and phrases I have read often stay in my memory and I employ them without quotation marks only because I fail to remember where or when I read them and often consider them original with me! Perhaps there is nothing "original" in any writing or speaking, but only new combinations of words and phrases. So, as KH says, "which plagiarized from the other?" This whole passage in Letter 130 is quite delightful and typical of the Mahatma's occasional light touch.

In the final paragraphs of Letter 130, KH is once again serious and asks Sinnett to give thought to the "Christian-mission-Coulomb" conspiracy that is rapidly developing. The Mahatma does not "urge" Sinnett to continue as his "mouthpiece and secretary" for the "Inner

Circle," particularly if Sinnett should feel he is not "equal to the situation," perhaps because he still harbors resentment toward HPB or still feels hurt by M's and KH's reprimands. Whatever Sinnett's choice, KH tells him that any further letters and "occasional instructions"—presumably for the inner circle—will come only through Damodar, as HPB has been "permitted to retire" as "our post-office" and must be saved the exertion required for that task.

KH gives three reasons for relieving HPB from this work: First, as the Coulomb affair progresses to its unhappy conclusion the Society can be "disconnected" from responsibility for the phenomena she produced—an indication that the Society must stand on its own in accordance with its "original policy" as the instrument through which the esoteric philosophy can be made known. Second, "the chief cause of the hatred against" the Society, which was HPB herself, would thus be removed. Third, HPB is kept alive so she can do the work she has yet to do, which was principally writing *The Secret Doctrine*.

Indeed the black clouds have gathered over the Society, but KH ends on a hopeful note, reminding Sinnett of the old axiom "*Post nubila Phoebus*"—after the darkness, the dawn. Letter 130, then, is altogether an encouraging letter for Sinnett, if he reads its message aright, even as it contains warnings along with helpful advice if he proves strong enough to meet the challenges that lie before him in the Society.

LETTER 131

Letter 131 is one of the last three that attempts to aid Sinnett in maintaining his overt connection with the Mahatmas, the other two being Letters 134 and 136. As we have seen, the actual conveying of the teachings has long since ceased. Certainly from the time of the London Lodge crisis, culminating in the election of new officers, the correspondence has been concerned with Sinnett's own spiritual welfare in a kind of final effort by KH to ensure that the link between Sinnett and the Brotherhood is not irreparably damaged.

The first paragraph of Letter 131 contains much to puzzle us. It opens with the sharpest warning yet that Sinnett's attitude has become a threat to further communication. Evidently the circumstances surrounding the Sinnetts' visit to the Gebhard family at Elberfeld, Germany, were such that KH could not write to him there, through either Laura Holloway or HPB, who were both guests of the Gebhards at the time.

This contrasts diametrically with Sinnett's own perception of the situation. In his *Autobiography*, Sinnett writes about his sojourn with the Gebhards: "I received some notes from KH through Mrs. Holloway of which Madame Blavatsky apparently knew nothing." He continues, "To this day [1914] I do not understand the true inwardness of the whole transaction, but something had gone wrong with Madame Blavatsky who was in a queer and unusual state of mind." We know from Letter 130, that HPB had been relieved of her function as "astral postman" and that Mrs. Holloway was proving unsatisfactory as a substitute, but Sinnett evidently still believed that she was being so used, in spite of KH's denial. He says that his "personal and mutual relations" with HPB were unusually strained and there had been numerous arguments between them, perhaps some of them over Sinnett's conviction that she was all too often using the "Master's name," as he put it, "to do violence" to his relationship with the Gebhards and others (see Sinnett, *Autobiography*, 28–29).

Since KH used what he calls the "common post" to send this letter and the envelope in the folio in the British Museum bears a postmark of October 9, 1884 at Bromley, Kent, we can only wonder who actually mailed the letter and who was the "friend" whose "expenditure of power" was required to transmit it. Certainly, putting a letter in the common post would be an easy and ordinary thing for someone in England to do. We can only say that KH's statement remains a mystery. My own conjecture is that the friend may well have been an

English chela of KH's who was producing and sending the letter even while being tested for the ability to use his psychic power for such a purpose. The reason for my conjecture would require too long a digression to include here.

KH is certainly endeavoring to do all he can to awaken Sinnett from his condemnatory attitude toward HPB as well as Olcott and apparently anyone who contradicted his convictions first, that Laura Holloway was serving as the mouthpiece of KH and, second, that HPB was the one responsible for all his problems. KH tells him, "Insensibly to yourself you are encouraging a tendency to dogmatism," perhaps as a consequence of the praise he had received for *Esoteric Buddhism* without recognizing that it might also contain errors and also because of an "unjust misconception of persons and motives," particularly of course his current view of HPB.

As the Coulomb affair was gathering more momentum and the situation in London was far from satisfactory with Sinnett engaging in endless "squabbles with the O.L.," to quote from his *Autobiography*, it is little wonder that KH says a "crisis is here." The Mahatma gives the very stern advice: "Beware . . . of an uncharitable spirit, for it will rise up like a hungry wolf in your path, and devour the better qualities of your nature that have been springing into life. Broaden instead of narrowing your sympathies; try to identify yourself with your fellows, rather than to contract your circle of affinity." Or as he says elsewhere in the letter: "Stop justifying yourself and keeping alive your doubts, giving way to depression, and suspecting HPB as the cause of your current situation, constantly arguing with her, it really doesn't matter who 'has sown the seeds of the present tempest,' it is time for a 'united struggle.'" And again: "It is a time for the utmost practicable expansion of your moral power." However, Sinnett is caught so securely in a psychological web of his own weaving that he cannot extricate himself long enough to see the need for a complete change of heart and attitude. How often, as we reflect on our own attitudes and efforts at self-justification, do we become caught up in the immediacy of some misunderstanding or petty squabble and lose sight of the larger perspective as well as the greater good to which our energies should be directed?

Sinnett seems to have lost direction and certainly seems to have forgotten the earlier lessons concerning "probation" and "chelaship," which applied to him even as a "lay-chela." KH reminds him: "You forget that he who approaches our precincts even in thought, is drawn into the vortex of probation." This is an apt reminder for us all as we turn in thought to the Masters, to not ignore the implications of our desire to approach them.

The entire paragraph deserves our careful study and invites us to take to heart its lessons. We may feel free of the "pride" and "'dignified contempt'" to which Sinnett obviously was prey, but we may forget that to the extent we have awakened our desire for occult knowledge and shared, in however small a measure, our understanding of the knowledge given to us, we have also stirred to life the "faithful guardians"—whether "gnomes or fiends"—of that treasure house that we call Theosophy. Sinnett had requested access to that knowledge and so was given an incredible amount of information, which, to his credit, he did utilize in his two books, *The Occult World* and *Esoteric Buddhism*. This, we are told, did "not pass unnoticed under the eyes of those faithful guardians." However, his present attitude must change if the correspondence is to continue. We might say that it is not more knowledge that he needs. Indeed, he is apparently no longer asking questions about the philosophy except perhaps in clarification (see Letter 132, from HPB) but rather is focused on personal affairs (see Letter 123) and his continuing antagonism toward HPB.

KH is clearly attempting once more to break through the hard shell of Sinnett's obstinacy, self-justification, and "tendency to dogmatism" mentioned at the letter's beginning. There is the reminder that "it is absolutely necessary that those who would have that knowledge," meaning knowledge of the occult sciences, "should be *thoroughly* tried and tested." One can only wonder what Sinnett did "infer" from that statement, as the Mahatma tells him to understand his meaning however he interprets the words. And again, KH reminds him that he and M were the only ones "among the Brotherhood who have at heart the dissemination (to a certain limit) of our doctrines" and that HPB was, up to that point, "our sole machinery, our most docile agent." Sinnett must have been amazed, indeed, to hear HPB described as "docile," surely not an adjective one would ordinarily use in characterizing her. KH concedes that HPB may well be difficult, but whatever her weaknesses, her failings, including her volcanic temper, do not in any way excuse Sinnett for his attitude toward her. Again, a wonderfully clear lesson for all of us in realizing that whatever weaknesses we may see in another, our work is with ourselves! The entire defense of HPB, along with the comments about Laura Holloway, makes for important study, not so much for understanding these two individuals as for recognizing the efforts of the Mahatmas in utilizing each of them in the service of the work they hoped to accomplish. Indeed, as KH points out, "*our* ways are not *your* ways," with a note almost of despair that "there remains but little hope for us in the West."

Sinnett has quite obviously written to the Mahatma complaining about HPB and delivering an "ultimatum" that the Mahatma paraphrases as follows: "Either Mrs. H[olloway] passes a week or so at our house, or I leave the L[ondon] L[odge] to get on as best it can." In Letter 130, KH told Sinnett that his house "has a colony of Elementaries quartering in it"—certainly not an appropriate place for the training KH was hoping to give to Mrs. Holloway! Perhaps it was because of the atmosphere in the Sinnett house that she herself "did not really want to go" there.

KH is almost as blunt and candid in his analysis of Sinnett's situation as M has been: "You either trust in me, or do not." And, as we know, Sinnett had begun to doubt KH. Yet for all the stern reproach, KH still addresses Sinnett as "Friend," warning him of the "two worst snares" that entangle anyone who "aspires to climb the high paths of Knowledge and Spirituality": pride and egoism, the two "vices" most prominent in Sinnett. Yet even in attributing such vices to him, we should take care that we are not overlooking their hold on us.

There is some indication that HPB may have told someone in the London Lodge about the situation with Mrs. Holloway, and the whole affair was a blow to Sinnett's pride. This is speculation, of course, but obviously Sinnett was very displeased over something that HPB had done in regard to Laura Holloway.

KH states with regard to M that "my brother . . . has more authority than I," pointing here explicitly to the fact that M is senior in occult status. Perhaps it is because of KH's pushing the limits of his own authority in his desire to bring about a major change in Sinnett, so that the correspondence might continue and Sinnett continue as the major exponent of Theosophy in the West, that he refers to "the *fix* I am in" and comments that nevertheless "I, personally, can do very little." He will continue to do all he can for Sinnett, but it is for Sinnett to change, not HPB or Olcott or anyone else.

We can only guess at the meaning of the statement that the current crisis, involving the entire Society, "is rather fanned than weakened from Shigatse." Since Shigatse was the seat of the Himalayan Brotherhood, this statement indicates that something much more serious than a personal affront to Sinnett's pride is involved. The Coulomb-missionary plot in India had broken over the heads of the Society's leaders while the Sinnetts, HPB, Laura Holloway, and others were visiting at Elberfeld, and that plot was to be followed by the infamous Hodgson investigation. The fact that all of this was "fanned" rather than "weakened" at Shigatse prompts the speculation that the entire occasion was being used as a testing of different persons. The importance of the crisis from the Mahatmas' point of view is reflected in the final paragraph (before a lengthy postscript) of Letter 136.

Some, of course, were inclined to blame Olcott and HPB entirely for the unfortunate developments. But the two founders have, the Mahatma insists, "that in them . . . which we have but too rarely found elsewhere—UNSELFISHNESS, and an eager readiness for self-sacrifice for the good of others," adding, "what a 'multitude of sins' does not this cover!" It is "real manhood when one boldly accepts one's share of the collective Karma of the group one works with, and does not permit oneself to be embittered, and to see others in blacker colours than reality, or to throw blame upon some one 'black sheep,' a victim, specially selected." Therefore, adds KH, "the present situation . . . has been gradually created by all of you as much as by the wretched 'Founders.'" We share in the karma of the group to which we belong, and as members of the Theosophical Society, we must be willing to acknowledge our part in its karma. There is also a national karma, as well as what we might call the karma of being human. The warning and urgency of the Mahatma's words while specifically for Sinnett at that time should echo in our own hearts.

To be "sublimely *unselfish*," willing to "sink [the] personality in [the] cause" and take "no heed of discomforts or personal obloquy unjustly fastened upon" us: this is the high standard to which we are called. The Mahatma concludes this letter: "One who would have higher instruction given to him has to be a *true* theosophist in heart and soul, not merely for appearance." For those who heed the soul's call, the way is clear, and though we stumble often and at times feel the standard is too high and difficult to achieve, we soon find there is indeed "no other way to go." As Sinnett was told at the conclusion of Letter 126: "You have two roads lying before you." Now, in Letter 131, the Mahatma implies what Sinnett must do if he is to continue on the road his heart truly desires. There is a sweet sadness in the closing: "Meanwhile, receive my poor blessings."

LETTER 132

Letter 132, which is from HPB, was written while she was still in London after she, the Sinnetts, Laura Holloway, and several other members returned from their visit with the Gebhard family in Elberfeld, Germany (see the comments on Letter 130). The letter needs to be read in conjunction with another letter written in October 1884, probably soon after this one: Letter 34 in *The Letters of H. P. Blavatsky to A. P. Sinnett* (pages 92–93). In both letters, HPB refers to Wilhelm Hubbe-Schleiden, one of the group visiting the Gebhard family in July (he later became the first president of the Theosophical Society in Germany) and Frank Gebhard, one of the Gebhards' sons. On the basis of these two letters, we can guess that the concept of planetary chains and the mystery of the "777 incarnations," mentioned in Letter 66, were among the subjects discussed during that visit.

Sinnett had devoted an entire chapter (chapter 3) to the subject of planetary chains in *Esoteric Buddhism*, based on the information given to him by the Mahatmas, particularly in Letters 66 and 67. (The student may wish to review those letters.) Perhaps at Elberfeld, HPB was pressed for further information on these topics and in Letter 132 she wants to clear up apparent confusion, for she denies having said that "the existence of our seven *objective* planets was an allegory." Though on the other hand, at the conclusion of Letter 132, HPB seems to contradict herself when she says that while Sinnett "gave the truth," although not the complete truth, "about rounds and rings," what he gave "was only at best *allegorical*."

In that letter in *The Letters of H. P. Blavatsky to A. P. Sinnett*, HPB enlarges on this topic and tells Sinnett that he "may copy this" and send it on to Hubbe-Schleiden and Frank Gebhard:

> Let me tell you once more about the planets, rings and rounds. . . .
> I said there were no such garlands of sausages [here she sketched a small depiction of the globes as usually depicted] as they thought of planets; that this representation was not even graphical but rather allegorical; that our seven planets were scattered about; that Rounds meant what you said, though the explanation was very incomplete, but that the *rings* what you call *i.e.* the seven root races and the evolution of man in his eternal septenary geration [*sic*] *was misunderstood*, not only by you but could not be understood clearly by any one *uninitiated*; and that, even that which *might* have been told by you, you had not told it for you have misunderstood one of

Master's letters. . . . It is a difficult subject, Mr. Sinnett, and one can give it out fully only under two conditions. *Either to hear Master's voice . . .* or to be an initiate oneself.

HPB says similarly here in Letter 132 that "outside of the *initiates* no one knew the *mot final* of this mystery" and that Sinnett could not be told "the *whole* doctrine." As a result, apparent inconsistencies are inevitable. Indeed, some have criticized the teachings and even abandoned the study of Theosophy altogether because of "inconsistencies" and "contradictions" among the various presentations of the more abstruse doctrines. Certainly many earnest and sincere students have "cudgeled their wits," to use a common expression, over the mystery of the "777 incarnations," and while many solutions have been offered, none seem entirely satisfactory. Yet as the Master tells Sinnett in Letter 66, we should "try to solve" it. Those who are truly in earnest to understand the fullness of the teachings should continue to work on the puzzle, convinced that as the intuitive faculty increases they may come to a "knowing" that opens the door to further enlightenment.

HPB was to deal with the subject of planetary chains and rounds in greater depth in *The Secret Doctrine*, a work not yet available to the group discussing the matter at Elberfeld. (See *SD*, 1:152–91, the sections headed "A Few Early Theosophical Misconceptions Concerning Planets, Rounds, and Man" and "Additional Facts and Explanations Concerning the Globes and the Monads.")

LETTER 133

Written on board ship as HPB was enroute from England to India, Letter 133, though brief, is significant for a number of reasons. One is HPB's delightful, almost ironic description of the circumstances and events surrounding her writing of the letter. Another is the fact that Djual Khul appeared in her cabin (or at least his hand appeared; whether or not his full form appeared we are not told), writing a letter dictated by his Master, KH. We know, from other letters and commentaries, that the Mahatmas frequently used chelas to write their letters, but this seems to be the only occasion when an advanced chela, whom we might term a "fledgling Adept," was visibly perceived taking "dictation." We can speculate as to the method chosen to produce the letter, which HPB was to send on to Sinnett after reading it herself, when precipitating the already-written letter directly into HPB's cabin might seem to us more expeditious.

Much of Letter 133 concerns Laura Holloway and her "probation," which apparently involves HPB in some way, since she complains that much has been done over her "long-suffering back." More is said about Laura Holloway in Letter 134, which is the letter dictated to Djual Khul, enclosed with Letter 133. HPB obviously has little use for Mrs. Holloway, but it seems that if the Master had not explained certain facts about her "probation," there could have been a serious misunderstanding between HPB and the Sinnetts, such that HPB would have departed from London leaving a very bad impression of herself. An especially interesting comment in HPB's letter should be noted: "I was also a chela and guilty of more than one flapdoodle." The use of the past tense, "was," inclines us to speculate—as many students have—on the exact nature of HPB's occult status and her unique relationship with the Adepts as their amanuensis in presenting the wisdom tradition. Her comment also reminds us of the many references throughout the letters to chelas on probation having a great deal of freedom; see, for instance, Letter 92 (page 294): "The fact is, that to the last and supreme initiation every chela . . . is left to his own device and counsel."

An interesting sidelight to Letter 133, although not mentioned in the letter, concerns C. W. Leadbeater, who had joined the London Lodge in November 1883 and by the following spring had begun receiving communications from KH (see *The "K. H." Letters to C. W.*

Leadbeater). In the second letter Leadbeater received, KH tells him, "It was *my desire* you should go to Adyar *immediately.* . . . Sail on the 5th if possible [the date when HPB and her party left London]. Join Upasika [HPB] at Alexandria." Because he received the directive only a few days beforehand, Leadbeater was unable to leave at the time of HPB's departure, but he joined her later at Port Said (where HPB tells Sinnett to "write a word . . . *poste restante*"). It was also at Port Said that HPB received instructions from her Master to go to Cairo immediately, along with the Cooper-Oakleys, who were traveling with her, and now Leadbeater, who had joined the party. It was in Cairo that HPB learned a number of damaging facts about the Coulombs and their duplicity.

LETTER 134

Although most of Letter 134 concerns Laura Holloway, who is first mentioned by KH toward the conclusion of Letter 126, it also contains much about chelaship that is important for us to note. We can also learn a lot by considering her life and character as they relate to the work that the Mahatmas hoped to achieve through her. So it is useful to review what we do know about her before examining Letter 134 itself.

Laura Holloway was an American widow, a natural clairvoyant, who came to London about the time of the London Lodge election controversy. KH had clearly been aware of her existence for some time, perhaps because the Mahatmas had been searching for someone to either aid or replace HPB as the channel for their communications. KH says in Letter 134 that she had been "aroused" a year and a half previously "to enthusiastic envy . . . to spasmodic, hysterical curiosity" by reading Sinnett's two books and then had determined "to find out the truth" and become a chela herself, mainly for the purpose of writing books that would either excel those of Sinnett or "upset the whole imposture." It was this determination that prompted her trip to London, where she met not only Sinnett but also Mohini as well as Colonel Olcott, HPB, and members of the London Lodge, including Francesca Arundale.

According to Sven Eek (*Damodar*, 626–28), Laura Holloway became a member of the Theosophical Society after meeting HPB in London. However, she may have joined earlier while still in New York, as Eek also quotes a letter to Olcott from W. Q. Judge, then General Secretary of the American Section, suggesting Mrs. Holloway as a possible "successor to HPB."

At the outset of Mrs. Holloway's visit to London, we may assume all went well, since KH tells Sinnett: "Her thoughts were for a certain period guided, her clairvoyance made to serve a purpose. . . . The poor woman is naturally good and moral; but that very purity is of so narrow a kind, of so *presbyterian* a character . . . as to be unable to see itself reflected in any other but her own *Self.* She alone is good and pure."

So it was that "the intense personality of her lower self" overshadowed "her sincere aspirations," and KH writes with what must have been some regret: "A great boon was offered her—her wayward spirit would allow her to accept of none that was not shaped in accordance with her own model." Thus she became, like so many other would-be disciples who have failed somewhere along the way, a "creature of Attavada," as KH calls her at the beginning of Letter 134. In Letter 68, writing of the skandhas, the Mahatma named "Attavada" as the seventh of the attributes that unite to form the personality and calls it "the doctrine of Self." HPB, in her *Theosophical Glossary*, defines it as the "sin of personality." We may call it self-conceit or simply egotism. Indeed, the "giant weed of self" is not easily extricated from the soil of our natures.

It was during her stay in London, much of the time in the home of Francesca Arundale and her mother, that Mrs. Holloway and Mohini wrote the book *Man: Fragments of Forgotten History*. KH refers to this work toward the conclusion of Letter 134, commenting that the book was excellent "in part" but marred by Mrs. Holloway's "alleged inspirations and dictation by 'Student,'" a character created by her imagination.

Laura Holloway received a number of letters from KH, all concerning the requirements for chelaship. These letters are included in the First Series of *Letters from the Masters of the Wisdom* and may be studied with great profit to understanding the initial steps on the way. Since Sinnett is told he may share Letter 134 with Mohini and Francesca Arundale, I note here that both of these individuals received letters from the Mahatmas that are also included in that volume.

Mrs. Holloway left England soon after the publication of *Man* and returned to the United States, later marrying a Colonel Langford. She did some writing for Theosophical journals, signing her initials variously LCL and LCH. She resigned from the Society after a few years but remained friends with many members, particularly with Mrs. Belle Mitchell, Colonel Olcott's sister. When Colonel Olcott toured the American Section in 1906, she met with him, no doubt reminiscing about her time in London as well as other matters.

To many sincere and earnest students it seems incredible that after all the correspondence Sinnett has received from the Mahatmas— letters containing occult teachings, letters of personal counsel, letters of warning concerning the dangers and difficulties encountered on the spiritual path—that Sinnett would now fall under the spell of a newly met friend, Laura Holloway, and come to doubt KH's word. KH recognizes the situation, stating frankly that Sinnett's last letter to the Mahatma, whatever it may have contained, was not the product of his own thought but the work of his self-absorbed American friend. How soon has Sinnett forgotten the words of his mahatmic teacher and "guardian," as he so often called him, cautioning him to be alert to those "furies called Doubt, Skepticism," etc., as KH called them in Letter 126.

How many would-be disciples through the years have been led astray by the glamour of some newfound teacher, by the charisma of an individual consumed by his or her own self-righteous nature. It is so easy to become a victim of self-deception, to become blind to truth and deaf to the true voice of wisdom.

KH's words to Sinnett are a stern warning, edged with sadness:

> Ah, how long shall the mysteries of chelaship overpower and lead astray from the path of truth the wise and perspicacious, as much as the foolish and the credulous! How few of the many pilgrims who have to start without chart or compass on that shoreless Ocean of Occultism reach the wished for land. Believe me, faithful friend, *nothing* short of full confidence in us, in our good motives if not in our wisdom, in our foresight, if not omniscience—which is not to be found on this earth—can help one to cross from one's land of dream and fiction to our Truth land, the region of stern reality and fact.

One can only wonder what Sinnett thought as he read those words. Whatever was his response, the words are as relevant to our attitude today, if we would tread the spiritual path, as it was when KH sent them to his English friend. They bring to mind HPB's enumeration of the steps to be taken, the "Golden Stairs" that lead to the "Temple of Divine Wisdom," for two of the steps are a "loyal sense of duty to the Teacher" and "a willing obedience to the behests of Truth, once we have placed our confidence in and believe that Teacher to be in possession of it" (*CW*, 12:503).

Sinnett is next advised "to study more seriously the laws that govern our 'Occult World.' . . . It is not so much that new facts should be revealed . . . as that old puzzles and mysteries should have been explained and made clear." And he comments that "passing evils . . . are as necessary to the growth" of such groups as the Theosophical Society as "cataclysms in nature" are to humanity as a whole. How is it possible, we may ponder, that an earthquake can be beneficial or "a tidal wave prove salvation to the many"? We may understand that such natural disasters are "necessary" according to karmic law, but viewing them as a benefit to those who suffer from them is not an easy task.

KH continues with comments regarding Laura Holloway and "those self-opinionated volunteers and candidates for chelaship who will rush under the dark shadow of karma's wheels." He speaks of her "great clairvoyance, her chelaship, [and] her selection," commenting that "her clairvoyance is a fact, her selection and chelaship, another." Then the Mahatma makes a point that every student needs to ponder:

> However well fitted psychically and physiologically to answer such *selection*, unless possessed of spiritual, as well as of physical unselfishness a chela whether selected or not, must perish, as a chela in the long run. Self personality, vanity and conceit harboured in the *higher* principles are enormously more dangerous than the same defects inherent only in the lower physical nature. . . . They are the breakers against which the cause of chelaship, in its probationary stages, is sure to be dashed to pieces unless the would-be disciple carries with him the white shield of perfect confidence and trust in those he would seek out through mount and vale to guide him safely toward the light of Knowledge.

The Mahatma stresses this occult law, that selfishness is more dangerous in the higher principles than in the lower nature, with the metaphor of the "deadly upas-tree of Evil." This large evergreen tree grows in the lowland areas of Southeast Asia west of the Philippines and was used as a poison for arrows and darts. It was formerly believed to be so poisonous as to destroy any living thing in its vicinity. Certainly we can say that the world still lives and moves under its shadow, a fitting metaphor for the present human condition.

Now KH explains a principle, often emphasized by genuine spiritual teachers, that karma that is normally "distributed" throughout the entire lifetime of a person "who is content to remain an average mortal" is concentrated in a relatively short but intense period in the life of a chela. "That which is generally accumulating to find its legitimate issue only in the next rebirth of an ordinary man, is quickened and fanned into existence in the chela." This must have been particularly true in the case of Mrs. Holloway, who "*forced* herself into the dangerous path." We can compare this statement concerning the use of force or will from a selfish motive with KH's advice in his first letter to C. W. Leadbeater: "*Force* any one of the 'Masters' you may happen to choose; do good works in his name and for the love of mankind; be pure and resolute in the path of righteousness (as laid out in *our* rules); be honest and unselfish; forget your *Self* but to remember the good of other people." But sadly, as the Mahatma continues in his letter to Sinnett, "there are persons, who, without ever showing any external sign of selfishness, are intensely selfish in their inner spiritual aspirations. These will follow the path once chosen by them with their eyes closed to the interests of all but themselves, and see nothing outside the narrow pathway filled with their own personalities. They are so intensely absorbed in the contemplation of their own supposed 'righteousness' that nothing can ever appear right to them outside the focus of their own vision distorted by their self-complacent contemplation."

Before we begin attributing unworthy motives and self-righteous airs to those we consider the present Mrs. Holloways in the Theosophical Society, we need to examine carefully and honestly our own motives and what we may harbor, even unknowingly, in our own inner nature. Indeed, as KH concludes his letter to Sinnett, "If you would learn and acquire Occult Knowledge, you have . . . to remember that such tuition opens in the stream of chelaship many an unforeseen channel to whose current even a 'lay' chela must perforce yield, or else strand upon the shoals; and knowing this to abstain forever judging on mere appearance."

Before leaving Letter 134, we must consider the book authored by the "Two Chelas," Mohini Chatterjee and Laura Holloway, *Man: Fragments of Forgotten History*, since it is so frequently mentioned not only in these letters but also by other early students. First published in 1885, the book appeared in a second edition in 1887, and today is no longer in print.

In Letter 134, KH tells Sinnett to "try to save 'Man' by looking it over with Mohini, and by erasing from it the alleged inspirations and dictation by 'Student.' . . . Upasika [HPB] was ordered to see

that Mohini should carefully expunge from it all the objection-
able passages." KH then adds, "I . . . will not permit it to remain
unpublished," so despite the book's many errors, there must have
been some purpose in its issuance.

The book is dedicated to "Helena Petrovna Blavatsky, the Brave
Disciple of the Mahatmas, and Faithful Servant of Humanity." The
brief introduction is followed by two prefaces, the first "By the Eastern
Chela," the second, much longer, "By the Western Chela." Chapter
titles include: "Supra-Mundane Man," "Primitive Man," "Evolution of
Sex," "Growth of Language and Religion," "Man and Other Orders
of Existence," and "The Occult Hierarchy." The introduction contains
the following significant statement:

> It will . . . be asked—What is the source of information, who are
> the Teachers? They are the sages of the East, the inheritors of
> the knowledge of the Magian, the Chaldean, the Egyptian, and
> the ancient Rishis of India, from one of whom, a beloved and
> revered Master, known to many in the West as well as in the East,
> the present writers have received the instruction, part of which is
> presented to the world in the following pages. With the accuracy of
> the information here afforded . . . the writers are satisfied.

About the time the book was published, and evidently following
her Master's request to "explain" to Sinnett much that is in the text,
HPB wrote a long letter to Sinnett (see *LBS*, 245–54) so that he may, as
she put it, "realise what led even Mohini *off* the right mechanical track
and made him write the unutterable flapdoodle he has in *Man*—from
the simply mechanical-*cosmos*-arrangement standpoint and tolerably
correct one, if understood as applying to the 'simultaneous evolution'
of the *six races*.'" Then follow more than five pages concerning the
rounds and lokas, with some useful diagrams, all of which the student
will find of great interest. HPB concludes, "I am not myself very steady
upon those things and liable to mix up things and produce mistakes.
But Master said to me that if 'nothing happened out of the way,' He

would help and the Mahatma [undoubtedly KH, as M was her Master] also, as They are often here now for the Secret Doctrine."

Either enclosed in her letter to Sinnett or sent directly to Mohini, who was still in London, were more than seven pages titled "All the private notes for Mohini . . ." and tabulated under two headings: "Mistakes in the First Edition" and "Corrections for the Second Edition" (*LBS*, 254–61). These "notes" Mohini was instructed "to read to Mr. Sinnett." Obviously HPB intended the corrections to be incorporated in the second edition, which was issued two years later, but this was not done.

About a year after the publication of *Man*, HPB wrote an article, actually a letter, that she evidently intended for publication in *The Theosophist*, although it never appeared there (see *CW*, 6:412–13). Headed "To the Theosophists," the letter reads as follows:

> Gentlemen and Brothers,
>
> Having received and still receiving a number of letters from Theosophists asking me for the meaning of the great discrepancy between the doctrine of *Rings* and *Rounds* in *Esoteric Buddhism* and *Man*,—and enquiring which of the doctrines I approve of and accept, I take this opportunity to declare the following:
> *There is a mystery* connected with the writing and publication of MAN which I am not at liberty to make public in all its details. But since my name is in it and that the book is inscribed to me—I become indirectly responsible for its contents. Therefore shall I try to explain as much as I am permitted to. MAN is the production of two "Chelas" of whom one the "Eastern Chela" was a pucka disciple, the other the "Western Chela"—a candidate who failed. I could *certainly* never recommend the book as a *standard work* on Theosophy as it *now stands*, but ask the Theosophists to have patience and bear with it until it comes out in its second corrected edition. [As stated above, the second edition did not contain the corrections.] The "Western Chela" left it in a chaotic half-finished condition and went away from London, leaving the "Eastern Chela"

in a very perplexed state. Those who had ordered the book to be written *to try the psychical developments* of *Chela* and *Candidate*— would have nothing more to say about it. Finding himself alone and left to his own resources, unwilling to meddle more than he could help with the MS. of his ex-colleague, the "Eastern Chela" did the best he could. It was found *impossible* to publish it as it stood: he finished those portions he had undertaken, rewrote many of the passages from the pen of the other *amanuensis* and left it to stand or fall upon its own merits. In justice, we must say that, with the exceptions of those portions that relate to the Rounds, Root-Races and *Sub-races* in which there is a most terrible confusion, there is much of very important information in it, but on account of the confusion above described, it cannot be recommended as a book of reference. In the *Secret Doctrine*, all the errors and misconceptions shall be explained away and corrected, I hope.

In volume 1 of *The Secret Doctrine*, page 184, HPB states:

"Man" which came later [than *Esoteric Buddhism*] was an attempt to present the archaic doctrine from a more ideal standpoint, to translate some visions in and from the Astral Light, to render some teachings partly gathered from a Master's thoughts, but unfortunately misunderstood. This work also speaks of the evolution of the early Races of men on Earth, and contains some excellent pages of a philosophical character. But so far it is only an interesting little mystical romance. It has failed in its mission because the conditions required for a correct translation of these visions were not present. Hence the reader must not wonder if our volumes [*The Secret Doctrine*] contradict some earlier descriptions in several particulars.

So we may write "finis" to the history of one of the early books to make its appearance on the Theosophical scene, a work by two would-be chelas, both of whom failed and both of whom ultimately left the Society.

Letter 135

Although Richard Hodgson, the young investigator sent to India by the British Society for Psychical Research, had completed his investigation (see Letter 128) by the time HPB wrote Letter 135, a long letter to Sinnett, the report had yet to be issued. However, it is evident from the opening paragraphs of the letter that HPB already knows that the report will brand her a fraud and that the names of her Teachers will be "dragged before the public and . . . desecrated." She is sorry, she writes, and one feels her sadness and inner as well as outer exhaustion, "that the Mahatma should have selected [her] to fight this new battle." And she says, in closing, "I am tired, tired, tired and so disgusted that Death herself with her first hours of horror is preferable to this." Yet as we read through the letter, we still sense HPB's indomitable fighting spirit, her determination to help Sinnett understand the situation, and her unwavering devotion to her Master.

At the letter's outset she accepts the blame for having yielded to her own "great zeal for the cause" and the pressure of those around her to introduce into the Society "the occult element" and make known the names of the Mahatmas. She reminds Sinnett that from its inception, as KH has informed him and she herself has emphasized, "the T.S. is first of all a universal Brotherhood, not a Society for phenomena and occultism." This, indeed, continues to be its primary object, the reason for its existence, and all else must subserve that principle.

The whole sorry tale of the Hodgson investigation is well known in Theosophical history. Hodgson found much of the evidence contradictory, as HPB states, largely because some of the Indian members whom Hodgson questioned were not at all helpful. They felt that occult truths are not proper subjects for this type of investigation, so they often took pleasure in trying to confuse him. Subba Row became a clam, refusing to say anything. Judge Khandalawala, one of the most loyal members, entirely distrusted Hodgson, considering him ignorant and clumsy in his methods. It is no wonder then that the young Britisher, lacking experience in the art or science of investigation, as well as totally unfamiliar with Indian customs and with the ideas being presented through the Society, on hearing contradictory stories from different witnesses should conclude that it was all a giant hoax perpetrated by HPB, who was not always her own best defender.

HPB's reference to Damodar introduces us to the final episode in the life of a young chela who succeeded in realizing his goal of joining his Master. She writes: "He went to the land of Bliss, to Tibet and must now be far away in the regions of our Masters." As we know, Damodar had come to the Bombay Headquarters in late 1879, later moving with the founders to Adyar, and had proved of invaluable assistance in the work. The full story of his "disappearance" to Tibet is related by Colonel Olcott in *Old Diary Leaves* (3:259–68), as well as by Sven Eek in *Damodar*.

The "brooch" incident that HPB mentions is quite a fascinating story, being the subject of Letter 3B and explained in its prefatory note. Sinnett records all the details concerning "Brooch 1" and "Brooch 2" in *Occult World* (68–79 and 96–102). The second brooch is related to what Sinnett called the "pillow incident." These occurrences were among the early exhibitions of HPB's production of objects by occult means. Now, in Letter 135, she terms them "the accursed phenomena."

Evidently Hume was at Adyar at this time, because HPB continues her letter with a recounting of Hume's proposal to "save" the Society. He had called a meeting of the Council at which he presented some most amazing demands, including forcing the resignation of HPB and Olcott, selling the Headquarters, and establishing a new organization. HPB writes, "Mr. Hume is a queer 'Saviour!'" adding later that he "is more liberal than the Padris."

As one reads the history of the Society, one wonders at the number of members who have, at one time or another, brought forward proposals designed to "save" the Society from the perceived "mistakes" of its leaders, including proposals to substantially alter the Objects, change the administration, or expel certain individuals. Yet through the years, constructive changes have occurred in all areas of the Society's functioning and succeeding administrations have introduced new policies and ways of working, all the while retaining the Society's name and its Objects, as well as its Headquarters.

HPB comments on her physical condition, prophesying "I will not see another year." She wrote this in early 1885, but she did not die until 1891. As on so many other occasions, she seemed to recover in this instance almost miraculously "thanks to Master's protecting hand." A survey of her life reveals the number of healings that occurred when she seemed at the point of death.

The "shrine" HPB mentions in the next paragraph figured prominently in Hodgson's investigation and led to considerable controversy, mainly because during HPB's absence in Europe, Alexis Coulomb had made some significant alterations in the cabinet in HPB's room where she had often deposited letters to the Mahatmas. The full story about the "shrine" is told in *The Coulomb Case* by Michael Gomes, as well as in a booklet titled *Obituary: The "Hodgson Report" on Madame Blavatsky* by Adlai E. Waterman (the pen name of Walter Carrithers).

Arthur Gebhard, mentioned next in HPB's long letter to Sinnett, was a member of the prominent family of Elberfeld, Germany, who had hosted HPB on numerous occasions. He had fallen under the influence of Mohini and had turned temporarily against HPB, accusing her of fraud. A review of his activities is included in the comments on Letter 126. Particularly of interest to us, here in Letter 135, while denying Gebhard's accusation, HPB provides Sinnett with additional information concerning the transmission of letters. The process of precipitation has been mentioned on a number of occasions (particularly see Letter 117), but now we learn of two other modes of transmission.

HPB begins this elucidation with the statement: "I have often facilitated phenomena of letter-transmission by easier but still occult means," adding that anyone not familiar with the laws of occultism would not "know anything of either difficult or easy means of occult transmission." This is certainly true for the majority of us, who at least are sympathetic with occult principles even though we may not understand them fully. The first method HPB mentions involves what she calls "transmission by *mechanical* thought transference (in contradistinction with the conscious)." The transmitter must first attract the attention of a chela or Mahatma; then the letter is opened and "every line of it passed over the forehead, holding the breath" until a bell is sounded indicating that the letter has been read by either the chela or the Mahatma. The second method HPB describes is "to impress every sentence of the letter (consciously of course) still mechanically on the brain, and then send it phrase by phrase" to the individual who is to receive it. Both methods, while involving "mechanical" processes, also seem to require an enormous amount of concentrated energy. Finally, she adds, "in both instances the letter must be open and then burnt with what we call *virgin fire.*" This is not explained, but as she describes rubbing the letter "with a resinous, transparent little stone," perhaps the application of friction with some substance causes the paper and the resultant ashes to "become immediately invisible." The entire paragraph describing letter transmission is intriguing and offers us much to ponder over.

Much of the rest of the letter reflects HPB's discouragement over the measures being taken to try to ruin the Society as well as to defame her. One senses a dispiritedness in her words, perhaps due to her ill health at the time and also a feeling of isolation, with the consequent need to pour out her heart to Sinnett and his wife as true friends. She writes that while the Society will live on in India, "it seems doomed in Europe, *because I am doomed.*" She has served as the link between the Mahatmas and the Europeans, and now her weariness leads her to think this may be her last letter. However, as we know, the Society did live on in Europe and continues to be strong and vital in many European countries. And, of course, she did recover and live to write *The Secret Doctrine*, *The Key to Theosophy*, and that priceless gem, *The Voice of the Silence*, in addition to much else. From the time of this letter, six fruitful years still lay ahead of her.

Mention should be made of the Oakleys, who came upon the scene at Adyar during the Hodgson investigation and about whom

HPB writes: "They have full confidence in the Masters; nothing, they say, will make them doubt their existence. . . . They are staunch theosophists and as they say my best friends." HPB had met them in London, and they traveled with her on her return to India in 1884. A. J. Cooper-Oakley became sub-editor of *The Theosophist*, served for a time as recording secretary of the Society, and was a lecturer at several international conventions. He became a disciple of T. Subba Row and left the Society when his teacher died in 1890. Isabel Cooper-Oakley performed many valuable services for the Society, principally as a lecturer and writer, and traveled through Europe, where she organized the work in Hungary and Italy. She spoke in Australasia and was a representative of that part of the world at the World Parliament of Religions in 1893. Later, Annie Besant, early in her presidency, appointed Mrs. Cooper-Oakley head of an International Committee for Research into Mystic Traditions, as the result of which Mrs. Cooper-Oakley wrote a biography of the Comte de St. Germain and also *Masonry and Medieval Mysticism: Traces of a Hidden Tradition*.

HPB concludes her long letter on a sad note, saying that all the accusations against her and the Society, all the turmoil caused by the Hodgson investigation and the Coulomb conspiracy, have happened because "we have profaned Truth by giving it out indiscriminately—and forgot the motto of the true Occultist—To know, to dare, and to KEEP SILENT." Perhaps there is a question for all of us today to consider in those final words: just what does that "motto" mean as we seek to share Theosophical wisdom with those who are hungry for spiritual understanding?

LETTER 136

As indicated in the prefatory note, Letter 136, which is from KH, was enclosed in a letter to Sinnett from HPB. Her letter opens with the words: "I am compelled to write to you once more. My own reputation and honour I have made a sacrifice of, and for the few months I have to live yet I care little what becomes of me. [In Letter 135, as we have seen, she says that letter may be her last and that she may not live another year.] But, I cannot leave the reputation of poor Olcott to be attacked as it is, by Hume and Mr. Hodgson who have become suddenly *mad* with their hypotheses of fraud more phenomenal than phenomena themselves" (*LBS*, 75–77).

It was evidently in an effort to clear Olcott's name that she wrote a letter to Richard Hodgson, which was also enclosed in her letter to Sinnett. She requests Sinnett to correct it and send it on to Olcott to forward to Hodgson. In her letter to Hodgson, HPB takes him to task, writing, "You may believe of me personally what you like, but you have no right to express your slanders publicly." She adds that she expects a written statement from him, over his signature, of all he has "heard from the Coulombs about me being a *spy*". (She never received such a statement.) "I will also beg of you," she continues, "the paper or papers she showed you, for this time I mean to sue her and put an end to such an infamy. This is a serious affair, Mr. Hodgson, and it is yourself who have forced me into this course of action." Obviously Sinnett never sent this letter on, as HPB requested, since we have the original letter among Sinnett's papers. Sinnett has stated elsewhere that he had considerable difficulty keeping HPB from becoming further embroiled in Hodgson's investigation. Olcott, following the legal counsel from members attending the Adyar convention in December 1884, finally dissuaded her from bringing suit against the Coulombs.

Turning now to Letter 136 itself and KH's remarks, the opening statement suggests that Sinnett, after receiving HPB's despairing letter (Letter 135) in which she mentioned Arthur Gebhard's "accusation," wrote to the Mahatma for an explanation. Undoubtedly aware of the impending release of the Hodgson Report and the attendant publicity that will declare HPB a "charlatan," KH tells Sinnett: "Dozens of events of a far more distressing character . . . are ripe and ready to burst over her head, wounding as badly the Society."

KH seems to note the irony of Sinnett's asking for his "personal opinion and explanations," since the Mahatma had failed to satisfy the doubters and skeptics, the "rigorous logicians," among whom Sinnett was one, in the "Billing-Massey" (Letter 92) and "Kiddle-Light" (Letter 117) affairs. One senses that Sinnett cannot believe that Gebhard, whom he knew from his stay in Elberfeld when HPB was also there as a guest, would so turn against HPB and that he perhaps doubts her word about Gebhard's accusation of fraud. Incidentally, Gebhard was influenced not only by Mohini, with whom he collaborated in writing the "Manifesto" about Olcott's "mismanagement" of the Society, but also Hume and was party to Hume's extraordinary paper calling on the founders to resign. All of this is of interest today less as a review of the history than as a reminder of how easily skepticism can be nourished when someone we have come to trust plants the seeds of doubt in our mind.

KH states he will leave any explanation to HPB, who has explained the situation as best she could in Letter 135. He adds that what she has told Sinnett is "only simple truth." In effect, the Mahatma is telling Sinnett: either believe what HPB has told you or accept what Gebhard, Hume, and others are saying. How often in such complicated situations do we fail to accept the simple truth of the matter and look elsewhere for lengthy explanations instead!

The Mahatma then turns to other topics. First, he asks Sinnett to understand that "the centennial attempt made by us [the Adepts] to open the eyes of the blind world—has nearly failed." This has reference to the well-known proposal that at the end of every century an effort is made by the Adept Hierarchy, either through an individual or through a group, to enlighten humanity. The birth of the Theosophical Society in the last quarter of the nineteenth century has long been seen by many as an integral part of that "program." Some have suggested that reading the cultural, social, and even political history of previous centuries one can identify similar movements that have come on the world scene or been given special impetus during the final years of each century. We today, however, noting the influence that the Society and its teachings have had in numerous areas from the arts to the sciences may recognize that the Theosophical movement did not and has not failed. And while not large in numbers, it continues to live on and undoubtedly will do so as long as even a few remain loyal to the great ideas it promulgates.

We should take note of KH's words: "There is but one chance of salvation for those who still believe: to rally together and face the storm bravely." Following the Hodgson Report the truth of those words was tested, as they have been on a number of occasions in the Society's history. One cannot help but remember words that HPB penned in response to the attack from Arthur Gebhard and Mohini Chatterjee: "The T.S. *cannot be destroyed as a body.* It is not in the power of either Founders or their critics; and neither friend nor enemy can ruin that which is *doomed to exist,* all the blunders of its leaders notwithstanding. That which was generated through and founded by the 'High Masters' and under their authority if not their instruction—MUST AND WILL LIVE" (*Original Programme of the Theosophical Society,* 36). And then there are the words of M that HPB quotes in her E.S. Instruction No. 3: "You have still to learn *that so long as there are three men worthy of our Lord's blessing, in the Theosophical Society, it can never be destroyed.*" (See also *LMW,* First Series, 116).

In Letter 136, the Mahatma refers to a "secret committee" that had been formed at the Headquarters for the purpose of receiving letters and teachings from the two Mahatmas in that critical year of 1884. The principal members of that committee were apparently some of the Westerners then at Adyar, among them Dr. Franz Hartmann, whom Olcott had appointed Chairman of the Board of Control during his absence; St. George Lane-Fox, a recent arrival; and Hume, who had not yet resigned from the Society. However, as KH tells Sinnett, because of the accusations then flying around, "there comes a forcible end to the projected occult instructions." It was these individuals, forming this "secret committee," who were unwilling to receive occult instructions through Subba Row and Damodar—a situation that probably seems almost inconceivable to students today! No wonder KH reminds

Sinnett of what he has said in several previous letters: "It is an old truism that none of you have ever formed an accurate ideas of either the 'Masters' or the laws of Occultism they are guided by." We can only wonder whether we today have an "accurate" understanding of the same. At the same time, we must take care not to ascribe infallibility to the Mahatmas, for as KH goes on to state: "*We are not infallible, all-foreseeing 'Mahatmas' at every hour of the day.*" As he explains in Letter 85B: "An adept—the highest as the lowest—is one *only during the exercise of his occult powers.*"

Next KH returns to the charge made against him, that of plagiarism in the case of the Kiddle incident. Perhaps Sinnett still felt there had been some truth to the charge and that the Mahatma did not really understand what plagiarism means. KH is now at pains to explain, first, that because he did have a Western education, he understands the Western point of view although he does not agree with it and, second, how an Adept goes about writing on a subject unfamiliar to him. The difference in the Western and the occult procedure is remarkable. "When you write upon some subject you surround yourself with books of references etc.; when we write upon something the Western opinion about which is unknown to us, we surround ourselves with hundreds of paras: upon this particular topic from dozens of different works—impressed upon the Akasa." As every writer knows, phrases, even sentences from other sources, can easily remain in the mind and then be used on some occasion, with the assumption that they are original to that author.

KH's phrase "And now for Occultism" announces that he is shifting topic yet again. He seems almost frustrated in having to remind Sinnett once more that a study of the occult tradition is a hard taskmistress, that without effort he cannot expect to know the hidden laws of nature when "generations of occultists" have engaged in research to "wrench her secrets from the heart of Nature." Sinnett, we know, has sometimes complained about the "incompleteness" of the presentation of a concept and in particular has "grumbled" about the nature of devachan, never fully understanding that after-death state. So the Mahatma emphasizes: "He who holds the keys to the secrets of *Death* is possessed of the keys of *Life*."

The last paragraph of the letter (prior to the lengthy postscript) contains one of the most significant statements concerning the Society's importance, a statement that every earnest member should ponder to understand it fully, applying it to the Lodge or Branch to which he or she belongs and to whatever "crisis" may appear on the horizon:

> Could but your L[ondon] L[odge] understand, or so much as suspect, that the present crisis that is shaking the T.S. to its foundations is a question of perdition or salvation to thousands; a question of the progress of the human race or its retrogression, of its glory or dishonour, and for the majority of this race—of *being or not being*, of annihilation, in fact—perchance many of you would look into the very root of evil, and instead of being guided by false appearances and scientific decisions, you would set to work and save the situation by disclosing the dishonourable doings of your missionary world.

What a clarion call to work this is for Theosophy and for its vehicle, the Theosophical Society!

However, KH has not finished with all that he wants to tell Sinnett, so Letter 136 has a long and very useful postscript, principally about chelaship. Perhaps sensing that Sinnett, a lay-chela, was beginning to be skeptical about many matters, the Mahatma asks, "Why is it that doubts and foul suspicions seem to beset every aspirant for chelaship?" He considers the ancient methods of testings and initiations and says that now "the aspirant is . . . assailed entirely on the psychological side of his nature." This is a statement we all need to keep in mind if we would tread the path to adeptship! Every germ of good and bad in our temperament has to be faced and studied, the good developed and the bad remedied or destroyed. "The rule is inflexible," continues KH, "and not one escapes whether he but writes to us a letter, or in the privacy of his own heart's thought formulates a strong desire for occult communication and knowledge." Reiterating what he has said in Letter 134 regarding the speeding up of karma for one entering the path, KH says that the teaching "brings into fierce action every unsuspected potentiality latent" in the individual aspirant. Few Europeans, he adds, have stood this test. For this reason, "henceforth, the policy of absolute neutrality of the T.S. in occult teachings and phenomena will be rigidly enforced," and "whatever is imparted will be to individual members" not to groups. Undoubtedly, it was this policy that led HPB to establish, just a few years after this letter, the Esoteric Section of the Society, known today as the Esoteric School of Theosophy, independent from the Society itself. Finally he reminds Sinnett: "Every step made by one in our direction will force us to make one toward him." Surely this must still be true for the sincere and earnest aspirant!

The postscript closes on a wistful note: "Accept my blessing and parting greeting, *if* they have to be my last." What a note is sounded in that little word, "if"! Indeed, this was the last major letter from KH to Sinnett.

LETTER 137

One can speculate why, after more than a year since he last wrote to Sinnett, the Mahatma M should now send him the brief note that constitutes Letter 137. It is the last Sinnett receives from that Mahatma, and in a way it seems to be a farewell. Sinnett had never felt comfortable with the Indian chelas, judging them lacking in the refinements of dress and manner that were so important to him. So the Mahatma asks him to bear "their defects" and recognize that they help in the work to which the Adepts are committed. He also reminds Sinnett that he has in him " concealed a power to help . . . for the poor Society will even yet need all it can get."

The Hodgson Report is about to be issued, and this will rock the Society. "We cannot alter Karma," writes M, "or we might lift the present cloud from your path." Whether that "cloud" consisted of the Society's problems for which the Mahatma asks Sinnett's help or the Englishman's personal financial problems that were causing Sinnett's depression is not made explicit. At any rate, Letter 137 concludes with a message of support: "Have hope and faith" and the Adepts may be able to "disperse" the cloud. Sinnett has been taught much, so while there may not be "many left true to the 'original program'" of the Society, M obviously expects Sinnett to be among those few who remain loyal.

LETTER 138

With six words, "Courage, patience and *hope*, my brother," the remarkable correspondence between Sinnett and the Mahatmas comes to a close. Whether Sinnett realized that Letter 138 would be the last direct communication we do not know, nor does he say in his *Autobiography*. Over a period of five years, from October 1880 to sometime late in 1885, there had been a nearly constant flow of letters between the world of the Adept Brothers and Sinnett's world of mundane activity, a world we all know so well. Sinnett, and his friend Hume, had asked numerous questions on a wide range of topics, seeking to know the secrets of what their Teachers called occultism. With great patience, those Teachers—Koot Hoomi and Morya— responded to the queries in so far as they could, within the bounds set by their own pledges to their superiors and in a language often ill-suited to convey the deeper truths concerning life, death, the cycles of existence, and the stages on the spiritual path to illumination. KH addressed Sinnett at the opening of the correspondence as "Esteemed Brother and Friend," and now in his last message he calls Sinnett "my brother." What a wealth of meaning lies in the simple word "brother," indicating a bond of common parentage, so that while one may be the elder and the other the younger, both are of one family.

From the correspondence with his Teachers, Sinnett managed to distill much of the occult doctrine into two books, *The Occult World* and *Esoteric Buddhism*. While those works are not widely read today, we must not underestimate their value at the time of their publication, when the Western world was largely unaware of the occult philosophy. Individuals interested in Spiritualism, as well as anyone questioning the religious and scientific dogmas of the day, might well have come upon HPB's two-volume work *Isis Unveiled* and read her opening sentence: "The work now submitted to public judgment is the fruit of a somewhat intimate acquaintance with Eastern adepts and study of their science." But who were these "adepts" and what was their "science"? Sinnett answered the first part of the question in *The Occult World* and provided an introductory response to the second in *Esoteric Buddhism*. As we look back over the letters, as Sinnett may have done after receiving this final message, would we have done as well in making known the Mahatmas' existence and presenting their teachings?

At the conclusion of the correspondence, a number of questions naturally arise in the student's mind: Why did the correspondence end at this time, just prior to the Hodgson Report's release? Was there a connection between the sorry events taking place at Adyar—the Coulomb affair, the Hodgson investigation, Hume's defection—and the cessation of the letters? Was it more difficult to transmit letters to Sinnett in London than it had been when he had been resident in India? Was HPB, who was now settled in Europe, never to return to India, and working steadily at writing *The Secret Doctrine*, no longer available as a channel for the transmission of letters? Were none of the chelas available for work in the Western world? Did the correspondence cease because Sinnett was no longer asking questions about the occult philosophy? Or did it cease because KH (and M as well) were requested, even ordered, by their superior to do so? Had as much of the occult philosophy as could be given at that time been said, and further elaboration was to be the work of HPB? Such questions are worth pondering over, even if no definitive answers are possible.

Some two and a half years after this final message from KH, Sinnett became convinced that communication with the Mahatma and himself had been reestablished through a medium whose identity he never revealed but whom he designated "Mary." In his *Autobiography*, he says that he "gathered a great deal of miscellaneous information" through this contact, but this activity was kept "profoundly secret from our Theosophical friends generally—in accordance with the Master's wishes." Many students have expressed considerable skepticism about this development, but reading Sinnett's *Autobiography* leads me to suggest that we need to withhold judgment.

"Courage, patience, and *hope*, my brother": these words stand not simply as an encouraging farewell to Sinnett but as a message to all true aspirants. Meanwhile, to complete our study, we need to look at three letters written by HPB to Sinnett, and also at a few mahatmic messages that are impossible to date.

LETTER 139

Letter 139, the first of three letters from HPB to Sinnett written soon after the Hodgson Report was issued, is significant for its explanation of her knowledge of English and how she produced *Isis Unveiled*. She opens the letter by saying that she has been "impressed" to give Sinnett certain information, presumably meaning that her Master has requested her to tell her friend about the "most extraordinary" vision she has had. Was the vision, which is a retrospective one, induced by the Mahatma so that she will record for Sinnett (and so for posterity) the experiences she relates here? Why did such a vivid dream come just when she was in such despair after reading

Hodgson's vilification of her? Was it to help Sinnett understand her better and so remain loyal to the cause when others were defecting? These questions may be worth our pondering as we read through this amazing letter.

The first scene in the vision takes place in KH's home in Tibet, where she is studying Senzar, which she defines in the *Theosophical Glossary* as " the secret sacerdotal language or the 'Mystery-speech' of the initiated Adepts." According to HPB, it is the original language of the Stanzas of Dzyan, on which *The Secret Doctrine* is based. Students unfamiliar with HPB's references to this mystery language may wish to read the excellent monograph "Senzar: The Mystery of the Mystery Language," by John Algeo. Her English at that time was apparently crude (we do know that as a child she had a Yorkshire governess, and apparently she spoke with that accent and used the Yorkshire idioms), but daily for two months KH would place his hand on her forehead "in the region of memory."

With the second scene in her retrospective dream, she is in New York, writing her first major book, *Isis Unveiled*, with the aid of both Mahatmas, KH and M, who dictated so much of it. Colonel Olcott comments, "Whence did HPB draw the materials which compose *Isis* and which cannot be traced to accessible literary sources of quotation? *From the Astral Light*, and by her soul-senses, from her Teachers. . . . How do I know it? By working two years with her on *Isis* and many more years on other literary work." For Olcott's reminiscences concerning the writing of *Isis*, the student should read chapter 13 of the first volume of *Old Diary Leaves*.

Now in writing to Sinnett, HPB affirms that she learned her English from KH, adding "What wonder then that *my* English and The Mahatma's show similarity!" She does not expect to be believed, yet since an explanation has been demanded of her, she is responding. If there are differences in handwriting, that too can be explained: "Has Master KH written himself all *His* letters? How many chelas have been precipitating and writing them—heaven only knows." (She then explains "precipitation" as "the *photographic* reproduction from one's head" to another person, who may then do the actual writing.) Resorting to logic, HPB states that either she has invented the Masters or she has not. If they do not exist, then neither does their handwriting; if she has invented them, then she has invented their writing, and hence how can she be called a "forger"?

At the time of this letter, HPB was in Wurzburg writing *The Secret Doctrine*, which she now states "will be 20 times as learned, philosophical and better than *Isis*." Her new work, she adds, will show "the extreme lucidity of *Esoteric Buddhism* and its doctrines proven correct mathematically, geometrically, logically and scientifically." This must surely have given pleasure to Sinnett.

Returning at the letter's end to the slanderous report issued by the Society for Psychical Research, with its "lies, false testimony, etc.," HPB seems in a less depressed mood than when she began writing. She says: "Hodgson is very clever, but he is not clever enough for *truth and it shall triumph*." Since the Society for Psychical Research released a statement in 1968 that the Hodgson Report of 1885 did not necessarily reflect the views of that entire society but only those of its author, we can say that truth has indeed been triumphant. Two valuable works on this topic are: "Madame Blavatsky Unveiled?" by Leslie Price, a monography published by the Theosophical Research Center in 1986, and *H. P. Blavatsky and the SPR* by Vernon Harrison.

LETTERS 140 AND 141

Letters 140 and 141, both from HPB to Sinnett, need to be studied together. During the time between them, Sinnett replied to the first; however, his letter is not available, so we do not know what he said. The opening paragraph of Letter 140 concerns HPB's association with Agardi Metrovitch. Students unfamiliar with this episode in her life may find several references to be of interest. One of these is another letter to Sinnett (*LBS*, 142 *et seq.*) detailing further information about Metrovitch and his wife that HPB wrote about a month after the two letters we are now studying. Sinnett has evidently requested a full account of the Metrovitch "incident," hoping to include it in the work he was writing, *Incidents in the Life of Madame Blavatsky.* To that request HPB responds: "I say *we must not.* These *Memoirs* will not bring *my vindication.* This I know as well as I knew that *The Times* would not notice my letter against Hodgson's Report. Not only will they fail to do so . . . simply because 'Metrovitch' is only one of the many incidents that the enemy throws at my head" (*LBS*, 143).

Further in the letter in *LBS* she remarks, "One thing in the whole world could do it [that is, vindicate her] if I ever could consent to it; and it is *the truth* and nothing but the truth—the Whole of it. . . . I do not want to lie, and I am not permitted to tell the truth." That letter continues: "I say at the same time to the world: 'Ladies and gentlemen, I am in your hands and subject and subordinate to the world's jury *only since I founded the T.S.* Between H. P. Blavatsky from 1875 and HPB from 1830 to that date, is a veil drawn and you are in no way concerned with what took place behind it. . . . Anything you like after 1875. My life was a public and an opened life since then, and except during my hours of sleep *I was never alone.*"

HPB adds, in this long letter (*LBS*, 146): "It is far more important what I myself think of me, than what the world does. It is that which I *know* of myself that will be my judge hereafter. . . . Three days after my death all the world save a few theosophists and friends will have forgotten my name—let all go, I say."

This last is one of her prophecies that has certainly not proved accurate, for far from forgotten, HPB is still the subject of biographies, false accusations, slander and misunderstanding on the part of many. At the same time, among Theosophists the world over, of whatever affiliation or none, her name is honored, her writings still studied, and her memory undimmed by the passage of time. Other useful references about the Metrovitch incident are: *When Daylight Comes* by Howard Murphet (pages 62–64); chapter 25, "The Metrovitch

Incident" in *Personal Memoirs of H. P. Blavatsky,* compiled by Mary K. Neff; and the extensive and well-researched information in Jean Overton-Fuller's biography, *Blavatsky and Her Teachers.*

Returning to Letter 140: Sinnett had apparently written to HPB that the work of the Branches in Europe as well as in London is at a low ebb, "paralyzed and helpless." In response to Sinnett's defeatism, HPB asks the bracing question: "How is this? *You* are not dead. The Countess lives. Two or three fellows around you breathe. . . . Blind are those who seek the destruction of the T.S. . . . The Society . . . can NEVER die."

These words look ahead to what HPB would write a few months afterward in *The Original Programme of The Theosophical Society:* "The T.S. cannot be destroyed. . . . That which was generated through and founded by the 'High Masters' and under their authority if not their instruction—must and will live." Stirring words indeed, as relevant today as when she wrote them to Sinnett in late 1886. Now in Letter 140, HPB is essentially saying to Sinnett: "Why don't *you* do something to remedy the situation?" This is certainly a question we can ask of ourselves if we begin to feel that the Branch or Section of the Society to which we belong is dying and that the work has been fruitless. What are *we,* each one of us, doing to revivify the work?

As Letter 140 continues we can sense a change in tone, perhaps more impersonal while at the same time conveying sympathetic encouragement. Is it only HPB who is reminding him to be "intuitional" or is someone else speaking through her? "Oh, do try and be intuitional—for pity's sake do not shut your eyes and because you cannot see *objectively* do not paralyze *subjective* help which *is* there living, breathing, evident." These are words that KH has often used with Sinnett, and they sound somehow familiar. Again and again, the Mahatma has told Sinnett he must use his intuition to understand the teachings or the situation in which he is involved. Again, Letter 140 closes with: "Do try to arouse for once your intuitions if you can."

HPB refers to this injunction at the outset of Letter 141, where she tells Sinnett that much of Letter 140 "had been dictated" to her by KH "in an unalloyed spirit of kindness, sympathy for and appreciation of yourself [Sinnett]." No wonder there is a marked change of tone in Letter 140 as KH writes, through HPB, about the choices before Sinnett and about the Society itself, whose welfare was so dear to him.

In Letter 140, as on several previous occasions and most explicitly at the conclusion of Letter 126, Sinnett is told there are two roads before him and also before the London Lodge of which Sinnett was a leading member. One is a path to the study of "*practical* occultism," while the other would make of the Lodge "an open and fashionable body." This may well be a choice before every Branch of the Society: should our programs cater to the fads and fancies of the day in order to attract as large an audience as possible, or should they focus on study of the Theosophical teachings? Or is there some compromise between the popular and the arcane? Is it possible to maintain "the strong element of *worldly* Society within the Occult body"? These are questions that deserve careful consideration, even as we keep in mind the clear statement in Letter 140: "It is not so much the quantity we are in need of, but the quality, to make the Society a success."

The Mahatma advises the Englishman through HPB, if indeed these words are part of the message dictated to her: "If the L.L. is composed only of six members—the President the *seventh*, and this 'vielle garde' faces the enemy cooly, not allowing him to know how many you are, and impressing him with outward signs of a multitude by the number of pamphlets, convocations and other distinct, material proofs . . . you will soon win the day." Some people may view this advice to falsify the facts almost unethical. Perhaps there are occasions when the end justifies the means even though the means may seem deceptive.

How, we may ask, should the Theosophical Society present itself to a still skeptical public? Rather than speak of our smallness, perhaps we need to emphasize our internationality and our global presence. If every small study center, utilizing all the information pamphlets and other materials available from its National Headquarters, spoke as it can of the worldwide nature of the Society, could it not accomplish apparent miracles in disseminating the Theosophical philosophy? Indeed, today, as when Letter 140 was written, the one thing that can or will "kill" the work is—"*Passivity.*" Perhaps the words "Make your activity commensurate with your opportunities and do not turn away from the latter, even from those that are created for you" should be engraved on the charter or certificate of every group, if not in the heart of every earnest member. Not the number of members, not the money in the treasury, nor any external resources but the opportunities before us are what determine our activity in the world. And the opportunities are manifold, calling each one to study, to meditate, to be of service.

Sinnett evidently recognized the style of the Mahatma in much of Letter 140 and took the remarks as a criticism, and he obviously conveyed this to HPB in his response. But HPB, in acknowledging that it was indeed "dictated" by KH, avers that "never was there so much kindness, genuine feeling for you [Sinnett], and an utter absence of 'criticism' or reproach" than in that dictation. She adds: "Open your *inner* heart and feeling entirely and do not judge through your world and cold reason spectacles."

Two of HPB's comments deserve our careful attention. The first is her remark concerning the dictation: "I watched the 'thoughts and feeling-lights' and aura" of the Mahatma. How such observations are then translated into words is not described, but it is intriguing to consider this statement of HPB's alongside KH's statement in Letter 20 (page 73) that "we [the Adepts] have to bring ourselves into a *full rapport*" with the chela.

The second is HPB's statement regarding the two chelas: that this is a "more serious question." The reference, of course, is to Mohini and Bowaji, both of whom were said to be failures. We know that both of them came to Europe, one at the Mahatma's request and the other accompanying HPB and Olcott. We know, too, that both fell victim to a sense of self-importance as a result of the adulation they received. In addition, both were able to influence others (we may note HPB's statement about Francesca Arundale "going to pot in their company"), and HPB was concerned that their influence would extend to American members. Their stories provide examples of the tragedy that comes from an unchecked growth of the "giant weed" of the personal self, which is indeed a serious matter because it can so infect others who are led astray by the maya of appearances.

HPB's final paragraph includes a reference to the ill-fated *Phoenix* attempt, for which she held William Gladstone, then Prime Minister of England, responsible. She was convinced (see Letter 140, page 458) that he was a Catholic convert and in league with the Catholic Church to ensure that the proposed newspaper would be a failure. The reference to the "Ilbert Bill" takes us back to Letter 113.

Scattered throughout the correspondence with the Mahatmas are nine letters from HPB, two of which we have just considered. We can only speculate as to why Sinnett placed these letters in his "strong box," as he called it, that contained the correspondence from the Mahatmas. One possible reason is that each of these letters has bearing on mahatmic letters he received at or near the same time. Generally, however, Sinnett placed HPB's letters in another "box"; those letters were published as *The Letters of H. P. Blavatsky to A. P. Sinnett,* to which I have referred throughout this commentary. Eventually, all of her known letters will appear in a multivolume series, *The Letters of H. P. Blavatsky,* edited by John Algeo. Volume 1 of that series, including her correspondence between 1861 and 1879, was published in 2003.

Letters A, B, C, and D

It is generally agreed that dates cannot be assigned to these four communications, so they are simply designated A, B, C, and D. All four, however, are in KH's familiar handwriting in blue ink. Of the four, only Letter A contains statements helpful in understanding further how the Mahatmas work and thus is relevant to our studies.

Since Sinnett indicates that he received Letter A through Mohini, this must have been sometime during the Indian chela's stay in England, which was in 1884. It seems to be a response to Sinnett's continued perplexity over the, to him, apparent contradictions between the teachings coming from the two Mahatmas KH and M. While KH agrees that they do indeed differ in their methods of teaching, they can never be "opposed in *principles of action.*"The difference between their teaching methods is perhaps most apparent in how they respond to philosophical and metaphysical questions. For M's style, the student may want to look again at the first set of Cosmological Notes (page 505 *et seq.*) as well as Letter 44, which constitutes the second set of Cosmological Notes. These can be compared with KH's style in Letters 65, 66, and 67.

We can remember also Djual Khul's advice, written on behalf of KH, at the end of Letter 37: "Proceed with your metaphysical studies. . . . [Do not give] up the task in despair whenever you meet with incomprehensible ideas in M. Sahib's notes." We can keep in mind as well M's important statement in Letter 44: "In our doctrine you will find necessary the synthetic method; you will have to embrace the whole . . . before you are enabled to study the parts separately or analyze them with profit to your understanding." So we can learn from each of the Mahatmas, although we may find ourselves more in accord with one method than the other.

From the letter's contents we can speculate that, following the Hodgson Report, Sinnett had proposed gathering together a group interested in the correlation between Theosophical teachings and the findings of science. The Mahatma, while fully in favor of such a pursuit, emphasizes once more that such study must support "the broadest and most practical application of the idea of the Brotherhood of Humanity." From the outset of the correspondence and underlying all the teachings, the two Mahatmas have emphasized Universal Brotherhood. This fundamental principle, the golden thread uniting all our endeavors, must underlie all our studies. Notably, the correlation of Theosophy with contemporary scientific thought continues to be a major area of research pursued by many members, either singly or in groups.

KH's request that Sinnett should show this note to Annie Besant suggests that Sinnett met Mrs. Besant some years before the latter joined the Theosophical Society in 1889, although he does not mention any such meeting in his *Autobiography*. We know from KH's statement at the end of Letter 119 that the Mahatma was very much aware of Mrs. Besant's work, and now we can only speculate as to why she should see this particular letter or note. Several students have remarked that KH's request to Sinnett to "use every effort to develop" a relationship with Mrs. Besant so their "work may run in parallel lines and in full sympathy," points to the Mahatma's foreknowledge of the role she would eventually play in the Society. The "parallel lines" may be, on the one hand, Sinnett's work in disseminating Theosophical ideas through his work with the London members and his writings, and on the other hand, Mrs. Besant's labors at that time for the cause of socialism and the welfare of the "down-trodden." Both "lines" help to further the object KH identifies so clearly in Letter 120: "the amelioration of the condition of Man."

Most encouraging, not only for Sinnett at the time but for all of us today who strive to serve the Society in the promotion of human solidarity, are the Mahatma's words, "Not one of those who have only tried to help on the work of the Society, however imperfect and faulty their ways and means, will have done so in vain." Equally encouraging in those moments when we may find the road rocky and perilous, is KH's message: "In travelling your own thorny path I say again *courage* and *hope*."

Although the three other letters need no comment, I will add that many have pondered over the Mahatma's unusual request in Letter C. What could be the significance of "three pebbles" of "three different colors" retrieved from "the shores of the Adriatic"? It is a puzzle not likely to be solved, but one that teases the mind!

CONCLUSION

Perhaps it is appropriate that this commentary on the letters concludes with a kind of riddle (KH's request for three pebbles in three colors in Letter C), for even a cursory reading of the letters gives rise to questions. With questions comes a longing for a response. Yet answers, even provisional ones, to be truly meaningful—and all answers at our stage of development should be considered provisional until we probe further—must arise from within. As KH so often counseled Sinnett, awaken your intuition, for intuition, he says in Letter 49, is the key to occult knowledge.

For the serious student, the study is never really concluded. One returns to the letters again and again as to an ever-flowing fountain of living water to quench an inner thirst. The letters are redolent with the atmosphere of another world, a domain of consciousness that calls us onward to deeper and more comprehensive knowing. As we read with growing inner perception, we may become aware of stepping even momentarily "out of our world into theirs," glimpsing however dimly a realm of truth and beauty unparalleled in our ordinary existence. For a little while, we seem to walk with them, Masters of wisdom and compassion, Mahatmas, great souls, Brothers, knowers of "every first truth," who are ever sending out upon the world blessings of light and love and the benediction of their presence.

The letters, while written over a century ago, remain a living, breathing, vital testament to the existence of a Brotherhood singularly devoted to the amelioration of humanity's present condition of pain and sorrow. Such a Fraternity of Adepts has existed, we are told, from time immemorial, and the letters invite us to share in some small measure the fruits of their experience, the wisdom of which they are custodians. Every rereading of the letters seems to open a little wider the door to their world. The letters speak of timeless truths. They tell of a road not easy to travel, a way of life at times uncomfortable in its demands upon time and energy, a commitment of mind and heart to the noblest ideal: the realization of human solidarity, Universal Brotherhood.

May these letters call you to undertake the journey, as they have called me to keep on exploring. For truly there is no other way to go!

BIBLIOGRAPHY

Algeo, John. *Senzar: The Mystery of the Mystery Language*. London: Theosophical History Centre, 1988.

Arundale, Francesca. *My Guest: H. P. Blavatsky*. Adyar, India: Theosophical Publishing House, 1922.

Barborka, Geoffrey A. *The Divine Plan*. Adyar, India: Theosophical Publishing House. 1961.

———. *H. P. Blavatsky, Tibet and Tulku*. Adyar, India: Theosophical Publishing House, 1966.

———. *The Mahatmas and Their Letters*. Adyar, India: Theosophical Publishing House, 1973.

———. *The Peopling of the Earth*. Wheaton, IL: Theosophical Publishing House, 1975.

———. *The Story of Human Evolution*. Adyar, India: Theosophical Publishing House, 1980.

Barker, A. T., comp. *The Letters of H. P. Blavatsky to A. P. Sinnett*. Pasadena: Theosophical University Press, 1973.

———. *The Mahatma Letters to A. P. Sinnett*. 3rd rev. ed. Edited by Christmas Humphreys and Elsie Benjamin. Adyar, India: Theosophical Publishing House, 1962.

Besant, Annie. *Autobiography*. Adyar, India: Theosophical Publishing House, 1939.

———. *The Laws of the Higher Life*. Adyar, India: Theosophical Publishing House, 1997.

———. *The Spiritual Life*. Wheaton, IL: Quest Books, 1991.

————. *Talks with a Class*. Chicago: Theosophical Press, 1922.

Bhikku U Rewata Dhamma. Introduction to *A Comprehensive Manual of Abhidhamma*, edited by Bhikku Bodhi. Kandy, Sri Lanka: Buddhist Publication Society, 1992.

Bilimoria, Edi D. *The Snake and the Rope: Problems in Western Science Resolved by Occult Science*. Adyar, India: Theosophical Publishing House, 2006.

Blavatsky, Helena P. *Collected Writings*. 14 vols. Wheaton, IL: Theosophical Publishing House, 1966.

————. *Isis Unveiled*. 2 vols. Wheaton, IL: Theosophical Publishing House, 1972.

————. *The Key to Theosophy: An Abridgement*. Edited by Joy Mills. Wheaton, IL.: Theosophical Publishing House, 1972.

————. *The Original Programme of the Theosophical Society*. Adyar, India: Theosophical Publishing House, 1931.

————. *Practical Occultism*. Adyar, India: Theosophical Publishing House, 1972.

————. *The Secret Doctrine*. 2 vols. Adyar, India: Theosophical Publishing House, 1978.

————. *The Secret Doctrine*. 6 vols. 5th Adyar Edition. Adyar, India: Theosophical Publishing House, 1962.

————. *Theosophical Glossary*. Los Angeles: Theosophical Publishing House, 1918.

————. *The Voice of the Silence*. Reprint, Adyar, India: Theosophical Publishing House, 1953.

Bradford, Roderick. *D. M. Bennett: The Truth Seeker*. New York: Prometheus Books, 2006.

Brown, W. T. *Scenes in My Life*. Fullerton, CA: Theosophical History Occasional Papers, vol. 4, 1995.

Chin, Vicente Haó, Jr., arr. and ed. *The Mahatma Letters to A. P. Sinnett, transcribed and compiled by A. T. Barker, in Chronological Sequence*. Adyar, India: Theosophical Publishing House, 1998.

Collins, Mabel. *Light on the Path*: Adyar, India: Theosophical Publishing House: 1966.

Conger, Arthur L., ed. *The Dialogues of G. dePurucker*. 3 vols. Covina, CA: Theosophical University Press, 1948.

Cranston, Sylvia. *HPB: The Extraordinary Life and Influence of Helena Blavatsky, Founder of the Modern Theosophical Movement*. Santa Barbara: Path Publishing House, 1993.

Dayal, Har. *The Bodhisattva Doctrine in Buddhist Sanskrit Literature*. Delhi: Motilal Banarsidass, 1999.

de Purucker, G. *The Dialogues of G. de Purucker.* Edited by Arthur L. Conger. 3 vols. Covina, CA: Theosophical University Press, 1948.

———. *H. P. Blavatsky: The Mystery.* San Diego, CA: Point Loma Publications, 1974.

———. *Occult Glossary.* Pasadena: Theosophical University Press, 1956.

Eek, Sven. *Damodar and the Pioneers of the Theosophical Movement.* Adyar, India: Theosophical Publishing House, 1965.

Ellwood, Robert. *Theosophy: A Modern Expression of the Wisdom of the Ages.* Wheaton, IL: Theosophical Publishing House, 1986.

Evans-Wentz, W. Y., trans. *The Tibetan Book of the Dead.* 2nd ed. London: Oxford University Press, 1949.

Faivre, Antoine. *Theosophy, Imagination, Tradition.* Albany: State University of New York Press, 2000.

Farthing, Geoffrey A. *After-Death Consciousness and Processes.* San Diego: Point Loma Publications, 1993.

Fuller, Jean Overton. *Blavatsky and Her Teachers.* London: East-West Publications and Theosophical Publishing House, 1988.

Gardner, Edward L. *The Heavenly Man.* London: Theosophical Publishing House, 1952.

———. *The Imperishable Body.* London: Theosophical Publishing House, 1948.

———. *Whence Come the Gods?* London: Theosophical Publishing House, 1959.

———. *The Wider View.* Adyar, India: Theosophical Publishing House, 1962.

Godwin, Joscelyn. *The Theosophical Enlightenment.* Albany: State University of New York Press, 1994.

Gomes, Michael. *The Coulomb Case.* Fullerton, CA: Theosophical History Occasional Papers, vol. 10, 2005.

Govinda, Lama Anagarika. *The Psychological Attitude of Early Buddhist Philosophy.* London: Rider and Company, 1961.

Hanson, Virginia. *Masters and Men.* Adyar, India and Wheaton, IL: Theosophical Publishing House, 1980.

Harris, Philip S., ed. *Theosophical Encyclopedia.* Quezon City, Philippines: Theosophical Publishing House, 2006.

Harrison, Vernon. *H. P. Blavatsky and the SPR: An Examination of the Hodgson Report of 1885.* Pasadena: Theosophical University Press, 1997.

Hoskins, Ianthe, arr. *Foundations of Esoteric Philosophy: From the Writings of H. P. Blavatsky.* (Includes the "Bowen Notes.") 2nd ed. London: Theosophical Publishing House, 1990.

Jinarajadasa, C., ed. *The Early Teachings of the Masters*. Chicago: Theosophical Press, 1923.

———, comp. *The "K.H." Letters to C. W. Leadbeater*. Adyar, India: Theosophical Publishing House, 1941.

———. *Letters from the Masters of the Wisdom*, First and Second Series. 6th ed. Adyar, India: Theosophical Publishing House, 1988.

———, ed. *H.P.B. Speaks*. 2 vols. Adyar, India: Theosophical Publishing House, 1950.

Jung, C. G. *Civilization in Transition*. Vol. 10 of *The Collected Writings of C. G. Jung*. Princeton: Princeton University Press, 1964.

Laszlo, Erwin. *Science and the Akashic Field*. Rochester, VT: Inner Traditions, 2004.

Leadbeater, C. W. *How Theosophy Came to Me*. Adyar, India: Theosophical Publishing House, 1930.

———. *The Masters and the Path*. Adyar, India: Theosophical Publishing House, 1940.

Linton, George E. and Victoria Hanson. *Readers' Guide to The Mahatma Letters to A. P. Sinnett*. Adyar, India: Theosophical Publishing House, 1988.

McTaggart, Lynne. *The Field*. New York: Harper Perennial, 2002.

Narada, Maha Thera. *A Manual of Abhidhamma*. Kandy, Sri Lanka: Buddhist Publication Society, 1968.

Neff, Mary K., comp. *Personal Memoirs of H. P. Blavatsky*. Wheaton, IL: Theosophical Publishing House, 1971.

———. *The "Brothers" of Madame Blavatsky*. Adyar, India: Theosophical Publishing House, 1932.

Nyanaponika, Thera. *Abhidhamma Studies: Research in Buddhist Psychology*. Kandy, Sri Lanka: Buddhist Publication Society, 1965.

Olcott, Henry S. *Old Diary Leaves*. 6 vols. 2nd. ed. Adyar, India: Theosophical Publishing House, 1941.

Parisen, Maria, comp. *Angels and Mortals: Their Co-Creative Power*. Wheaton, IL: Quest Books, 1990.

Payne, Phoebe D. and Laurence J. Bendit. *The Psychic Sense*. Wheaton, IL: Quest Books, 1967.

Pelletier, Ernest. *The Judge Case*. Edmonton, AB: Theosophical Society, 2004.

Raja, C. Kunhan, trans. *Dhammapada*. Adyar, India: Theosophical Publishing House, 1956.

Ransom, Josephine. *A Short History of the Theosophical Society*. Adyar, India: Theosophical Publishing House, 1938.

Reichenbach, Bruce R. *The Law of Karma.* Honolulu: University of Hawaii Press, 1990.

Reigle, David and Nancy Reigle. *Blavatsky's Secret Books.* San Diego: Wizards Bookshelf, 1999.

Row, T. Subba. *Collected Writings.* Compiled and annotated by Henk J. Spierenburg. San Diego: Point Loma Publications, 2001.

———. *Esoteric Writings.* 2nd ed. Adyar, India: Theosophical Publishing House, 1931.

———. *Philosophy of the Bhagavad-Gita.* Adyar, India: The Theosophist Office, 1912.

Sinnett, A. P. *Autobiography of Alfred Percy Sinnett.* London: Theosophical History Centre, 1986.

———. *Early Days of Theosophy in Europe.* London: Theosophical Publishing House, 1922.

———. *Esoteric Buddhism.* London: Theosophical Publishing House, 1972.

———. *Incidents in the Life of Madame Blavatsky.* London: Theosophical Publishing Society, 1913.

———. *The Occult World.* 9th ed. London: Theosophical Publishing House, 1969.

Spierenburg, Henk J., comp. *The Inner Group Teachings of H. P. Blavatsky.* 2nd ed. San Diego: Point Loma Publications, 1995.

Stcherbatsky, Th. *The Conception of Buddhist Nirvana.* Delhi: Motilal Banarsidass, 1977.

Suzuki, D. T. *On Indian Mahayana Buddhism.* New York: Harper & Row, 1968.

Taimni, I. K. *Man, God and the Universe.* Adyar, India: Theosophical Publishing House, 1969.

———. *The Science of Yoga.* Wheaton, IL: Theosophical Publishing House, 1961.

Transactions of the Blavatsky Lodge of the Theosophical Society. Los Angeles: The Theosophy Company, 1987.

Trew, Corona and Lester E. Smith, eds. *This Dynamic Universe.* Wheaton, IL: Theosophical Publishing House, 1983.

Warcup, Adam. *Cyclic Evolution.* London: Theosophical Publishing House, 1986.

Zimmer, Heinrich. "The Significance of Tantric Yoga." In *Spiritual Disciplines,* edited by Joseph Campbell. Papers from the Eranos Yearbooks, Bollingen Series 30, New York: Pantheon Books, 1960.

INDEX

chelas and chelaship
  communication in, 79
  consciousness and, 98–99
  dangers of, 419, 508
  development of, 488–89
  doubts of, 523
  duties of, 307
  failure of, 533–34
  lay, 191, 222, 312, 419, 475
  letters written by, 299
  Mahatmas' assistance to, 468–69
  of Olcott and Sinnett, 414
  probation in, 296
  psychic abilities and, 336–37, 353–54
  qualities needed in, 24, 419
  selection and, 296, 509
  testing of, 22, 354–55, 431–32
"Chelas and Lay Chelas" (Blavatsky), 191, 222, 476
Chesney, Colonel, 297, 299, 318
Chhaya (shadow), 217
chidakasha (fabric of consciousness), 135
Chin, Vicente Haó, Jr., xvii
Chinese religion, 421–22
Chohan. See Mahachohan
Christian College Magazine, 485
Christianity, 421–22, 445, 450
Church of Latter-Day Saints, 459
Cis Himalayan, 15
Civil and Military Gazette, 105
civilization, 28, 198, 363
Civilization in Transition (Jung), 331
clairvoyance, 45, 287–88
Clark, Carwood Gerald. See Brown, William Tournay
Clarke, Samuel, 325
coadunition, 248

Codd, Clara, 78
co-existent
  akasha and space as, 138–40
  duration, matter, and motion as, 139–40
  matter and space as, 143, 151
  purusha and space as, 156
Collected Writings (Blavatsky), 25, 244, 474
Collected Writings (Row), 219–20
collective unconscious, 340
Collins, Mabel, 350
color, 44–45
Combined Chronology for Use with The Mahatma Letters to A. P. Sinnett and The Letters of H. P. Blavatsky to A. P. Sinnett (Conger), 17, xvii
communication
  with deceased, 69, 73, 84, 284
  with Mahatmas, direct, 41–43
  with sound and color, 44–45
Comprehensive Manual of Abhidhamma, A (Bhikku), 187, 272
Conception of Buddhist Nirvana, The (Stcherbatsky), 273
"Concept of God, The" (Ross), 325–27
Confucius, 170, 248
Conger, Margaret, xvii, 17
conscience, 29
consciousness
  of adepts, 241
  after death, 377–78, 418
  buddhic, 171
  centers of, 162
  empty mind and, 91–92
  evolution of, 363

Quest Books

encourages open-minded inquiry into
world religions, philosophy, science, and the arts
in order to understand the wisdom of the ages,
respect the unity of all life, and help people explore
individual spiritual self-transformation.

Its publications are generously supported by
The Kern Foundation,
a trust committed to Theosophical education.

Quest Books is the imprint of
the Theosophical Publishing House,
a division of the Theosophical Society in America.
For information about programs, literature,
on-line study, membership benefits, and international centers,
see www.theosophical.org
or call 800-669-1571 or (outside the U.S.) 630-668-1571.

Related Quest Titles

To order books or a complete Quest catalog,
call 800-669-9425 or (outside the U.S.) 630-665-0130.